D1473832

ADAMS
BUSINESSES
YOU CAN START
ALMANAC

2nd Edition

Adams Media
Avon, Massachusetts

Published by Adams Media, an F+W Publications Company
57 Littlefield Street, Avon, MA 02322. U.S.A.
www.adamsmedia.com

ISBN 10: 1-59337-562-X
ISBN 13: 978-1-59337-562-1

Printed in the United States of America.

J I H G F E D C

Library of Congress Cataloging-in-Publication Data
available from the publisher.

This publication is designed to provide accurate and authoritative information with regard to the subject matter covered. It is sold with the understanding that the publisher is not engaged in rendering legal, accounting, or other professional advice. If legal advice or other expert assistance is required, the services of a competent professional person should be sought.
> —From a *Declaration of Principles* jointly adopted by a Committee of the American Bar Association and a Committee of Publishers and Associations

Many of the designations used by manufacturers and sellers to distinguish their product are claimed as trademarks. Where those designations appear in this book and Adams Media was aware of a trademark claim, the designations have been printed with initial capital letters.

This book is available at quantity discounts for bulk purchases.
For information, call 1-800-289-0963.

CONTENTS

Startups Between $1,000 and $5,000   /   117

Startups Between $5,000 and $15,000 / 285

Startups Over $40,000 / 561

Part Three: Business Tips   /   651

Part Four: Appendices   /   687

INTRODUCTION

There has never been a more exciting time to start your own business! New businesses are springing up every day all across the country. Whether these new ventures are inspired by women re-entering the job market, young people starting their careers in home-based businesses, previously employed middle managers seeking new opportunities and greater job satisfaction, or just regular folks looking to earn some extra cash on the side, more and more people are finding themselves caught up in the entrepreneurial spirit.

What has led to this entrepreneurial boom? First, there has been a sharp increase in downsizing at both large and medium-sized businesses. In recent years, many of the larger corporations in the United States, like IBM and General Motors, have been laying off workers in record numbers, and it appears the end is not yet in sight.

As companies are learning to be leaner and meaner, career-minded professionals cannot expect job security the way they could in the past. In today's economy, chances are good that the average individual entering the workforce today will not stay at one company throughout his or her professional career. And a growing number of people feel that the best way to prevent an almost inevitable layoff is to take the skills they have and open up shop for themselves.

Changes in government programs and tax benefits for minority-owned businesses provide still more clues why entrepreneurship is on the rise. Despite affirmative action programs, it is still a statistically proven fact that there is a lack of opportunity for women and minorities within medium- to large-sized companies. Thus, thousands of women and minorities are recognizing that their earning potential is much higher "on their own" than it would be in the corporate world, and that there is no glass ceiling to block your opportunities when you are your own boss. In addition, it is now easier for minorities and women to get financing to start new ventures, either through local banks or government programs.

The success rate is good for new minority and women-owned startups. According to the U.S. Census Bureau's 2002 Survey of Business Owners, more than one in four owners of U.S. businesses with paid employees are women, and nearly two-thirds of them are at least forty-five years old. And minority-owned businesses are doing particularly well, growing more than four times as fast as U.S. firms overall.

Other population groups are jumping on the entrepreneurial bandwagon as well. Burgeoning technological advances have opened up new opportunities for the physically challenged. In the past, persons with disabilities were limited in their professional choices by their physical handicaps. Affordable computers, the Internet, and greater public acceptance of home offices have opened up a wide range of opportunities for those with physical limitations, and many have launched successful ventures as a result.

The concept of the home office continues to rise in popularity. Many entrepreneurs have even been able to start new ventures while still employed at another firm, thus increasing their capital and minimizing their day-to-day financial risk. With an answering machine, a cell phone, a computer, some letterhead, and business cards, many home-based businesses can literally run themselves while you keep your day job, leaving you to fill orders or talk to clients on your off time. A few years ago, this type of business practice would not have been acceptable. But now, many new businesses are getting off the ground just this way. And if you do choose to quit your day job and work at home full-time, a fax machine and high-speed Internet connection can help you stay in touch with the outside world during business hours, too.

All of these cultural changes working together have created an atmosphere of opportunity in the entrepreneurial environment. The rest is up to you. Making the decision to become an entrepreneur is the hard part. All you have to do now is choose the type of business that best meets your financial, emotional, and intellectual requirements, and get going!

WHY THIS BOOK?

The *Adams Businesses You Can Start Almanac* is unique among the plethora of business ideas books. The majority of businesses highlighted here are based on the assumption that you already have some area of interest, or skill, that you would like to apply to your own business. Most of the businesses here are considered white collar, but there are also plenty of ideas for the person looking to work with his or her hands. All of the businesses are significant and realistic ventures; the majority of them can be started right in your own home.

This book emphasizes the potential for many businesses to become offshoots of others. Not every business can exist on its own as a full-time enterprise, although many can be used as opportunities for supplemental income. Check the index for "companion-type" businesses—two part-time opportunities that can be merged into one full-time profitable venture.

Most importantly, this book provides a view from the trenches. In researching this book, we spoke with business owners across the country about how they did it, why they did it, and what they would have done differently. And we were amazed by the frank and honest answers we received. Many business owners were quick to tell us about their mistakes, and even more willing to talk about what they would have done differently if they knew then what they know now. Many of their interviews, and all of their advice, are included in full detail.

Lastly, there's the emphasis on your bottom line. Aside from a brief description of five hundred businesses, there is a thorough analysis of what it will take in terms of money, equipment, and personal qualifications to get each new venture up and running, as well as the kinds of profits you can expect. We've made an attempt to consider the hidden costs for each business, too, so that you can make an educated decision as to which venture is truly the best match for your interest, abilities, and financial resources.

HOW TO USE THIS BOOK

There are three ways you can use this book to find a business that is compatible with your background and interest level. First, you can choose the kind of business you want to launch based on the amount of money it will take you to do so. The five hundred businesses profiled are categorized into five startup cost categories:

Under $1,000: These businesses can be started with very low out-of-pocket expenses. They require no more capital than you probably already have in savings or could raise using credit cards, if you had to. Generally, these are businesses that can turn a profit in a hurry, to keep funding the costs you'll be incurring.

$1,000–$5,000: These businesses require some preplanning. The necessary startup capital might come from your prior savings or through creative personal financing (for example, a home equity loan). The financing for these businesses would probably not require—or qualify for—a small business loan. Many of these are excellent part-time opportunities that can be turned into full-time careers once your business is established.

$5,000–$15,000: You might be able to call on relatives and friends to help raise the necessary capital for these businesses. Otherwise, you will definitely need a significant savings cushion before you embark on any of these opportunities as full-time endeavors.

$15,000–$40,000: You would probably qualify for a small business loan or second mortgage with any of these opportunities. At the very least, you will need to line up a few firm commitments from clients before quitting your day job. Putting together a thorough business plan is essential, so that your financiers can gauge your potential success level.

Above $40,000: At this startup level, you'll usually need to obtain a bank loan or look for investors just to get the business off the ground. The businesses in this category usually require the purchase of large machinery, specialized equipment, sizable inventories, or warehouse space. As with the previous category of businesses, you'll definitely need a thorough business plan.

Another way to use this book is to consult the category index to search for your area of interest. You might get some ideas for jobs in a field related to yours, or find a niche for something that you've always wanted to try.

Lastly, you can simply flip through the pages at your own pace to learn more about all of the different types of businesses out there. Who knows—you might just stumble onto something that addresses a lucrative skill or interest you didn't even know you had.

As you read each business description, you'll notice some specific statistical information at the beginning of every entry. It is organized as follows:

Startup costs: These costs are calculated by adding together all equipment, advertising, and operating capital costs. We tried to consider every possible cost, and then asked the question: "What's the least amount of money you would need to start this business?"

Potential earnings: This range is calculated by multiplying typical fees by the 2,080 billable hours in each year (40 hours a week for 52 weeks). This is a gross figure and does not account for costs and overhead.

Typical fees: We researched each field to determine the average hourly rate or per-project rate. For many entries, you will see a range instead of one flat fee. This is because your geographic location may dictate the demand for your goods or services, and demand is what drives prices up.

Advertising: Here, we rounded up all of the possible ways you could promote each type of business, from methods that cost nothing, such as networking, to long-term media contracts that cost several thousand dollars. The advertising costs are built into the startup costs.

Qualifications: This category contains everything you need to know about professional certifications, personality requirements, and other information pertinent to what it takes to run your business.

Equipment needed: We researched and surveyed the equipment purchases you'll likely need to make to run your business effectively. You may need anything from a basic home office setup to specific industry-related machinery.

Home business potential: Many of the businesses can be launched and run out of your own home. We've also identified those that really need more space (such as a manufacturing facility), and those that you can run from your home even if you are not actually doing a lot of the work there.

Staff required: A high percentage of the businesses profiled can be one-person operations, but those needing additional staff are identified, often with a suggested number of employees.

Hidden costs: This is probably the most important element of each entry. The costs that you don't think about are often the ones that can drive your business into the ground. We've tried to uncover costs you might not have thought of when developing your business plan or strategy. They include insurance coverage, workers' compensation, and even fluctuating materials costs. Many of these are costs you simply cannot predict—or might not have realized will be incurred as you work to abide by state and federal government requirements.

The balance of each entry, divided into three sections, provides a comprehensive guide to each individual business. With each, you'll get a total picture of what's involved in successfully running the business in question so that you can zero in on those which best match your background and expertise.

Lowdown: This section supplies the details of exactly what each type of business demands of its owner, what your day-to-day activities will be, and who your customers are. This section also includes information on specific marketing opportunities.

Startup: Here, you'll find an in-depth breakdown of your startup costs, including everything from office furniture and computer equipment to advertising costs. You'll also find valuable information on how to arrive at specific earnings goals for each business.

Bottom Line: This section points out the positive and negative aspects of each business, so you'll know exactly what you're in for. Remember, no business is perfect; there are pluses and minuses to every opportunity.

BUT WHAT IS RUNNING YOUR OWN BUSINESS REALLY LIKE?

One business owner answered that question pretty eloquently when he said that the best thing about owning your own business is that it's your own business, and the worst thing about owning your own business is, well . . . that it's your own business. While owning your own business is the opportunity of a lifetime, you may come to find out that the opportunity to work—or worry—24 hours a day is not one worth having. But you'll never know until you try. And what might be one person's burden is another person's ticket to financial independence and personal fulfillment.

The trick is to manage your entrepreneurial journey well enough to expect the good with the bad—and not pressure yourself to perform flawlessly every time. After all, this is new ground and no one expects you to be perfect. While this book certainly does not provide all of the answers, it does address several issues you'll need to think about to determine if owning your own business is really right for you.

As a potential new business owner, the most important place you can start is with a solid idea of what you want to do, and what it will take to achieve your goals. We wish you good luck as you embark on what will surely become the most interesting journey of your professional life!

PART ONE

PUTTING YOUR BUSINESS TOGETHER

LEGAL ISSUES FOR SMALL BUSINESSES

Many startup businesses do not have a lawyer, and some companies operate for years without ever needing legal advice. The owners have done their homework and understand the legal situations likely to arise in their areas of business. They know which of the government's rules and regulations affect them and have set up systems to insure that they dot their *i*s and cross their *t*s consistently, keeping accurate records to prove it.

DO YOU NEED A LAWYER?
It costs money to hire a lawyer, but, as a general rule, entrepreneurs find that working with an attorney who specializes in small business issues is worthwhile for the time, worry, and (possibly) large sums of money it can save them over the long run. If you are wavering in your decision, it may be helpful if you think of your attorney as one of many "business advisor" relationships that strengthen your organization rather than simply deplete its resources. You will definitely need to work with an attorney:

- If you decide to incorporate or form a partnership.
- When you need to sign a contract or agreement (an attorney can help you understand the legal language so you know exactly what you are committing your business to do).
- Whenever you prepare a contract or agreement for others to sign.
- If someone brings a lawsuit against you.

FINDING AN ATTORNEY
To find a good attorney, start by asking friends and business associates for recommendations. Then, before committing to anyone, check each lawyer's business experience and learn about his or her general approach to working with clients. You are looking for direct, no-frills service that provides substance at the least

possible cost. You will need to find an attorney who is willing to be part of a real relationship—someone who responds to your calls within a reasonable period of time, answers your questions in plain English, and takes an active interest in the success of your business. Most attorneys are willing to provide an initial consultation at no charge. Take advantage of this "free" time to get all your questions answered, especially the ones about fees. Once you have chosen a lawyer with whom you can be comfortable, develop a fee or retainer plan that fits your budget. Finding a compatible attorney can be a somewhat lengthy process, but it is time well spent. And don't wait until a crisis hits to begin your search. In fact, having an attorney you can call on before you take an action might just save you from tedious, expensive trouble later on. What are your chances of being sued? If you know the danger is high, in addition to keeping an attorney on retainer, you might want to also consider insuring your business against potential legal costs.

AVOIDING LEGAL TROUBLE

Most businesses never get sued, and clearly you want to do everything you can to be in that category. Establish and conduct your business with the aim of keeping legal troubles from arising. Get business agreements in writing, and maintain clear, organized records of each transaction. Add to the files your notes on what is said during any subsequent telephone calls or meetings in which expectations, promises, modifications, and other issues are discussed.

Know and follow the laws and regulations that apply generally to businesses, as well as those that apply specifically to your business type. Make sure your employees and customers know what your policies are, and set an example by following them yourself. This is an area where your leadership will have a more powerful effect than all the memos and employee handbooks in the world. When you do what you promise and follow through immediately to resolve complaints, you create an atmosphere of trust. That's the best legal protection your business can have.

AGREEMENTS

New business owners may not recognize that many situations are considered agreements or contracts, even though no official piece of paper has been written to label them as such. Do you get paid in advance for a service or product to be delivered later? Do you send payment to a supplier and receive delivery of the materials at a later date? These constitute agreements: Money is exchanged on the expectation that a desired result will occur.

As you become more experienced, you will no doubt discover the same painful truth many slightly more experienced business owners have come to appreciate: Agreements aren't always honored by the other party. Suppose you provide a service that requires you to lay out money, to buy the paper to produce a catalog, hire an associate, or accumulate travel costs, for example. You intend to send a bill when the job is complete, but the client keeps asking for one small change after another. You finally send the bill—but it never gets paid. Unless you have kept excellent records of what the client asked for, what you promised up front, and what you actually delivered, you may have no way of recovering this loss. One situation like this can destroy a fledgling business. For safety's sake, ask your attorney to set up a formal agreement procedure that you can follow before you do any business. That's the best way to make sure your fingers do not get burned.

CONTRACTS

If written contracts are part of your business, you will need to work with your attorney to draft the kind that will protect you. Getting all requests, plans, and promises down on paper is actually a good selling technique: Your customer knows exactly what to expect, and you have a checklist to make sure that you perform the work to expectations. When you put everything in writing, there will be no gray areas that could lead to discomfort, disagreements, and disappointment later. You protect your business, while at the same time, you guarantee customer satisfaction. It's a win-win situation.

Contracts tend to be more formal than agreements. If you prefer to write your own, have your attorney create the first one as a model, then ask him or her to check any major variations that you may make in later versions. If you are asked to sign a contract prepared by another organization, READ EVERY WORD OF IT. Have your attorney read it, too, and ask him or her to explain the murky parts. Again, you can't provide complete customer satisfaction if you don't have a clear understanding of what you're supposed to do. Renegotiate whatever provisions you do not wish to meet. The other party has the option of doing this as well. Carrying out this process in a positive manner can be a key to selling successfully. Think of it as the first step in simply building a satisfactory working relationship: providing your products or services to meet your client's needs in a mutually agreeable way.

PROTECTING YOUR GOOD NAME

Copyrights and trademarks are tools you can use to protect your rights to "intellectual property," that is, ideas, words, names, and so on. These two types of protection are very different in their ease of use, and they have different effects. Neither is a guarantee of anything. They simply give you the right to try to enforce your ownership. Major legal cases involving copyright infringement occasionally receive national attention in the news media, but the day-to-day application of copyright and trademark protection, regardless of the size of the case, is extremely complex.

Copyrights

The copyright symbol © is familiar to almost everyone. You can simply apply it yourself to the beginning of a literary, musical, dramatic, choreographic, or visual work you have created and the work is automatically protected. Typically, a copyright claim takes this form: Copyright © 2006 by Mary Smith. You can't copyright an idea or a title, but you can use a claim to protect an article, photograph, painting, record, or tape. The copyright gives the creator the sole right to copy or reproduce a work; anyone else who tries to do so is in violation of the copyright. Registering a copyright with the federal government costs $30. Registration is not a requirement; it merely establishes a public record of your copyright claim.

Copyrights, even those that are formally registered, do not guarantee that your work will never be used without your permission. Anyone who works with business material knows that copyrights are regularly infringed upon. Sadly, people steal or "borrow" the work of others all the time. It's a frustrating situation, and there is no squad of government enforcers riding out from Washington, D.C., in defense of the injured parties. By all means, claim any copyright you deserve, but be aware that you will have to shoulder the burden of proof if you suspect an infringement. It can be hard to distinguish what is original and therefore protected, from what is only a slight alteration of your work or simply "common knowledge" and therefore not considered original at all.

Trademarks

Trademarks apply specifically to business situations. You may trademark your business name, product name, symbol (logo), or combination of symbol and name so that no other organization is entitled to use it. A trademark helps protect the reputation for quality and service attached to your business name from use by unscrupulous persons who might seek to ride on your coattails.

In order to enjoy legal protection, it is essential that your trademark be registered, and the process is complex enough to require the assistance of an attorney who specializes in this area. The first step will be an extensive search to be sure that no one else has used the name you have decided on. Given the size and dynamics of the U.S. economy, it can be quite a challenge to come up with a business name that is not already in use. A national trademark search serves two purposes: to make sure, prior to launching your business, that you are not about to unintentionally infringe on the trademark of an established business, and, later, to make sure no one else has infringed on yours.

Again, there is no guarantee that a trademark will protect your business, but it will help prevent accidental use of your name by another organization. And it will at least discourage flagrant copycatting. To a great extent, your good name conveys the value and quality your customers have come to expect from your products and/or services. Your customers find you by your name, and they use your name to spread the good word to others. Your business or product name is far more than just a phrase you print on your business cards; it is a symbol of all that you stand for. Trademarking helps protect it.

PUTTING TOGETHER A SOLID BUSINESS PLAN

A business plan is a detailed document that describes the vital elements of your enterprise, outlines the basic assumptions you are making as you develop the organization, and details your financial projections. The plan establishes your goals: What are you trying to achieve? What specific steps will you take to achieve these goals?; What resources will be required? A well-thought-out, well-written plan is essential for gaining funding from banks and other investors. More importantly, however, putting together the plan forces you to think through your business concept in a systematic way.

Think of your business plan as a living document. Every six months, you should take the opportunity to reassess the effectiveness of the strategy you have laid out in the plan. How accurate were your assumptions? What do you now know that you can use to help your business grow and prosper?

Business plans may vary depending on the type of business, geographic area in which it is located, and the audience you wish to address. If you are submitting your plan to a bank in the hopes of securing a loan, obtain a model plan from the loan officer for guidance. Read as many other plans as you can, and work with your business advisors as you write. The Small Business Administration Web site (*www.sba .gov*) has some helpful tips, too. Keep your readers in mind, and be sure to address their concerns. Do not assume that your readers will be familiar with the jargon and technical terminology of your business. Above all, state the assumptions behind your financial projections. Offer evidence to support each claim you make. Why is your market attractive? What information supports your projected sales figures for each of the next five years? How have you calculated your materials costs?

While business plans differ in terms of specific goals, strategies, and financial projections, they all should include the same basic elements: an executive summary, a company profile, a product or service analysis, a market analysis, a marketing plan, a financial analysis, and a description of your management team.

EXECUTIVE SUMMARY

The executive summary is critical because most investors will read it first to gain a sense of your business as a whole. (Note: Even though the summary will be read first, you should write it last, only after you have worked out all the details of your plan.) Within a few pages, you should:

- Define your company and describe the management team—their expertise, management ability, and experience with startup businesses.
- Outline your products and/or services and highlight the benefits they offer to your target market.
- Show evidence that your product or service is accepted by your market.
- Describe your target market.
- Analyze your competition.
- Summarize your financial prospects.
- State the amount of money you need to launch the business.
- Show how the money will be used.
- Explain why your business will be successful.

COMPANY PROFILE

This is where you have the opportunity to describe your planned company in detail, to outline the products, markets, and history of your business. The goal of this section is to convince your readers that you will be able to achieve the results you are projecting. Here is where you establish your competitive edge—the factors that make you stand out from the competition and appeal to your target market. This section also contains your general, long-term business goals.

PRODUCT OR SERVICE ANALYSIS

In this section, you will establish exactly why and how your product or service is different from what other businesses already make available. What do you offer that your target market can obtain in no other way? The features of your product are important, but the benefits customers will derive from your product are what you must emphasize here.

- Outline the resources you will need to deliver the product or service: raw materials, skilled technicians, packaging, office space, etc. Discuss availability and cost.
- Describe your facility and delivery methods, equipment needed, utility costs, and other factors that influence the day-to-day operations of the business. Transportation, suppliers, and manufacturing issues must be outlined here.
- Explain why your product or service is unique. What value will it add to your customers' lives? Is your technology legally protected? How will you keep what you offer up to date?

MARKET ANALYSIS

A market analysis supports all successful businesses and requires a great deal of research. Consult the library, local trade associations, and business groups such as your local chamber of commerce to obtain the necessary data. The point of your market analysis is to illustrate the potential demand for your specific product or service. What needs are currently not being met, and why? How does your product address them? What trends affect your market area? What changes are occurring in the business climate that will affect your company in particular?

Describe your competitors: the products or services they offer, the market segment to which they appeal, and the reasons why their customers buy from them. Describe your likely customers: number, demographics, trends, location. Clarify the pluses and minuses of your products versus those of your competitors: price, quality, market appeal.

MARKETING PLAN

The marketing plan shows how you will reach your target market(s). How will those who need your product or service come to understand that it is available from your business? This plan covers pricing, and the relationship of your prices to those of similar products and your competitors. It also covers distribution, delivery, returns, and replacements.

Here is where you will outline your plans for the sales process and the methods of payment you will accept. You will describe your promotions and advertising approaches. Most importantly, you will project your sales, month by month for the first year and, more generally, for the four years after that.

FINANCIAL ANALYSIS

Investors with a serious interest in your business will read this section in detail. It's the heart of your business plan. The financial analysis describes where the money will come from and how it will be spent, with projections for cash flow, income, and debt. This section includes:

- A balance sheet, in order to provide a snapshot of your company's assets, liabilities, and net worth;
- An income statement, comparing your revenues and expenses over a specific period of time in order to demonstrate your net profit or loss;
- Projected income statement, which estimates income and expenses at a future period;
- Projected cash flow, which shows how you will manage the most difficult problem for many businesses (spending and collecting cash);
- A break-even point, the date at which your company will begin to make a profit!

MANAGEMENT AND ADVISORY TEAM

Potential investors will want to know how your company is organized and who fills each role within it. In this section, you will need to outline the responsibilities planned for each position. It is customary to also provide biographical information about each member of the management team, either in narrative form in this section, or by including detailed resumes in an appendix.

Include enough details on key people to allow for a formal background check. Describe their experience and highlight the strengths they bring to your specific business. Describe the amount each person has invested in the business and how much they will be compensated for their services and expertise. Include here the names of outside owners and such business advisors as your attorney, your accountant, and other people important to the enterprise.

WHY SOME STARTUPS FAIL
(AND WHAT YOU CAN DO TO SURVIVE)

Figures compiled at the Center for Economic Studies, U.S. Bureau of the Census, show that a third of new businesses fail within two years; half close their doors within four. It goes without saying that you don't want to be one of them. So how can you protect yourself when you think you're hitting hard times? Start by knowing what causes businesses to fail and some strategies you can use to address those challenges.

PRIMARY REASONS BUSINESSES FAIL
Here are some major reasons that businesses don't succeed:

- *Undercapitalization.* You don't have enough to pay the bills and keep the creditors off your back. The phone is ringing, but you hate to answer it because it's more likely a creditor than a customer. The problem is pretty basic: You're spending more than you're taking in.
- *Poor leadership/direction.* Your staff is running around in circles, and nothing seems to get accomplished. You spin your own wheels trying to assign blame rather than solve the problem. Maybe you just weren't trained to be a good manager; get training now.
- *Shaky business plan.* Remember that all-important document you were supposed to work on—the one that answered all the questions about where your money would come from and how you would keep it rolling in? Maybe it's time for a look back; rereading your business plan a few months down the road can often provide important clues to what's happening and what's not in your business. Come to think of it, you should have been looking back and updating your business plan every few months all along, or you might have avoided the mess you're in now altogether.

- *Miscalculated market potential.* Your marketing strategy should have pointed out all of your areas of opportunity, but what if you were flat wrong? What if your idea was a good one for New York City but not for Boise, Idaho? Let's face it: When first working on a marketing plan, we all tend to be a bit overly optimistic. That's why it's a good idea to have another (more cynical and objective) person look over your marketing data; that person can play the role of devil's advocate, and you'll thank him or her for it later.
- *Ineffective marketing.* You've spent tons of money on advertising and wonder why it isn't paying off. Could it be that you were advertising in the wrong place—or, worse yet, to the wrong people? Once you've committed advertising dollars to one or more media, it's hard to admit you might have been wrong and pull them out when you get no response. Test your markets, and don't commit to long-term contracts until you've gotten at least a 15 percent return on three consecutive ads.

PRIMARY STRATEGIES FOR SURVIVAL
To avoid that fate, follow these steps:

- Take a hard look at your debt. Too many of us shy away from what we fear most. Have the courage to get it all out into the open—and, if you don't have any courage left, call a professional bookkeeper who can help put everything in the right column again.
- Work out alternative payment plans wherever you can. Often, all you'll need to do is tell your creditors you're thinking of filing bankruptcy. The word alone makes them jump at accepting payments that are significantly less than they would have gotten otherwise (to them, some money will be better than no money).
- Sell whatever you can, if you can. If you have equipment that's worth something and you can do without it, put it on the market as soon as you can. If it's critical to your business, you obviously can't sell it; however, if it's a piece that you could just as easily lease, think of the money its sale might bring in.
- Don't think of expansion as the answer. Too many entrepreneurs think that if one aspect of their business isn't working, they should add another (rather than subtract the one that's not working). Don't make the mistake of growing bigger to avoid problems; you're only distracting yourself from the real issue at hand and possibly postponing the inevitable.
- Cut expenses across the board. Some entrepreneurs get narrow-minded about controlling expenses; you'll lose your business for sure if you're not flexible in where you can save money.
- Consider the worst thing that could happen. In your survival plan, you'll need to picture the most terrible thing that can happen in order to be

able to work back to the most positive. Know it, face up to it, and then work your plan accordingly.

- Maintain a positive attitude. It's hard to remain positive when you feel as though you're losing control of your business, but you need to remember that all businesses go through trying times. Moreover, you'll need to be positive for your employees and your customers, so that they don't lose faith in you during what might wind up being only a temporary problem. If you are to survive, you can't afford to lose their confidence.

PART TWO

500 Businesses You Can Start

Startups for under $1,000

AIRBRUSH ARTIST

Startup cost:	$500–$1,000
Potential earnings:	$25,000–$50,000
Typical fees:	Varies; could be as low as $125 and as high as several thousand per project; $100–$200 per hour is not unusual
Advertising:	Local art galleries, art studios, art supply houses, Web site
Qualifications:	Graphic design, art background or degree
Equipment needed:	Airbrush, paints, hose, canvas, cloth, masks
Home business potential:	Yes
Staff required:	No
Hidden costs:	Ventilation system, rising materials costs

LOWDOWN:

Airbrush art is found in many different places, such as on billboards, and T-shirts, even pickup trucks and motorcycles. An art background is a must for this job. It's essential that you can separate colors as well as mix them. The ability to think in fine detail and visualize is also essential. Build your reputation as an artist wherever you can find work. For broad exposure, try magazines, ad agencies, and public relations firms, but don't neglect local opportunities either. Restaurants and retail shops, for example, sometimes display the work of local artists free of charge. Galleries are another route, but keep in mind that you will have to give up a percentage of any money you make on the sale of your work at a gallery. You might also try entering a contest or displaying your work at an art fair or craft show. The icing on the cake, of course, would be to get your work commissioned for private or public display. Either way, this shows that someone (hopefully with big money) has noticed your work and is willing to pay for it. You're well on your way.

STARTUP:

Most of your initial investment will be entry fees for contests and art fairs or craft shows. And because you are working in a visual medium, you will probably, at some point, want to invest in a Web site and/or some type of promotional piece, such as a brochure or postcard for a direct mail campaign. This is not a field you can enter without a good deal of practice, which means you should already have the tools you need because of your background training (startup could be as little as $500). Be prepared to start out slowly until you build your reputation. If you hit some craft shows and are lucky enough to get into an exhibit, your monthly income could soon be approximately $1,000–$3,000. But don't quit your day job just yet, since your income is bound to be unpredictable. It's the nature of the creative beast to live paycheck to paycheck.

BOTTOM LINE ADVICE:

If you live for creativity, the sky is the limit. You can airbrush on all types of materials: wood, fabric, brick, film, metal, glass—you name it. Sure, it will take a while before you'll make really big money, but in the meantime you can console yourself with the fact that this is a growing industry and you will have repeat business once you've completed at least a few good projects and the word gets around.

APARTMENT PREPARATION SERVICE

Startup cost:	$500
Potential earnings:	$25,000–$35,000
Typical fees:	$75 and up per apartment
Advertising:	Yellow Pages, direct contact with apartment owners/landlords
Qualifications:	Knowledge of cleaning procedures and painting skills
Equipment needed:	Cleaning supplies, vacuum, carpet cleaner, mops, buckets, painting equipment
Home business potential:	Yes
Staff required:	No
Hidden costs:	Insurance, equipment maintenance and upgrades, vehicle large enough to accommodate your equipment

LOWDOWN:

You pick up where the vacating tenants leave off by adding the finishing touches to apartments before the next tenant moves in. To increase your marketability, offer several services, including carpet cleaning, wall washing, painting, and wallpaper repair, as well as overall cleaning services. Set fee schedules appropriately depending on individual services (or offer an all-inclusive package price). Advertise your services to many apartment complexes and landlords. To cut down on driving, try to get a contract with a multiunit apartment complex offering short-term lease options.

STARTUP:

Invest in good quality cleaning equipment, including a vacuum and carpet cleaner. Startup costs can be as low or as high as you want, depending on the services you offer and the quality of the equipment you purchase. This business can be started for a relatively low cost with high return on investment; you can always upgrade your equipment, even add staff, as your business grows.

BOTTOM LINE ADVICE:

This business is not for someone who is afraid of good old-fashioned elbow grease. Even the tidiest tenants often fail to clean adequately, so be prepared to encounter some messy situations. You may be spending quite a bit of time on your hands and knees cleaning baseboards and floors—consider the health of your back and always wear a back corset. In addition, invest in good pairs of knee pads and rubber gloves.

ARTS FESTIVAL PROMOTER

Startup cost:	$500–$1,000
Potential earnings:	$20,000–$45,000+
Typical fees:	40 percent of registration fees from artists; you may also make a commission from each ticket sold
Advertising:	Word of mouth, ads in artists' newsletters and publications, direct mail to artists, newspaper/billboard ads for the event itself
Qualifications:	Strong organizational skills
Equipment needed:	Computer with desktop publishing software and laser printer, cell phone
Home business potential:	Yes
Staff required:	No (but you will probably need to solicit volunteers to work at each festival)
Hidden costs:	Insurance and low attendance due to poor advertising or inclement weather

LOWDOWN:

Annual arts festivals abound in nearly every community, and you could cash in on the public's interest in the arts by sponsoring or promoting your own group of arts festivals. Give your events a flashy name so that you can win instant recognition with your buying public and among artists (many of whom get barraged with requests to appear in shows all over the country). You'll need to promote your festivals two ways: first, to artists who might like to participate; second, to folks who might like to attend. So, your advertising budget must be split in order to reach both sets of "customers." Find a way to set your festivals apart, perhaps by inviting only particular types of artists/craftspeople or by attaching your festivals to some sort of theme (such as an Oktoberfest or Independence Day arts festival). That way, you've set an approximate annual date for the show to recur so people can start looking forward to it. Build your mailing list for subsequent years by requiring attendees to sign in (or, better yet, by offering a drawing for an exquisite work of art).

STARTUP:

You'll need $500–$1,000 to launch this interesting and artistic enterprise; your seed money will primarily cover the cost of your desktop publishing software, plus out-of-pocket expenses for materials related to set-up, security, and advertising. Once you have a couple of shows under your belt, you can begin to use your profits to pay for subsequent events. Within a year or two of staging several successful events, you will have established a name for your arts festivals that will guarantee annual repeat business in certain areas and begin to make you $45,000 or more per year doing something you truly enjoy.

BOTTOM LINE ADVICE:

You love the arts. So what's the downside? It takes real effort and dedication to get this business off the ground; you can expect to work long hours to ensure the success of your first few events and to get your system down. And, of course, there are bound to be things over which you have no control, namely the weather. You're out of luck if it rains on your parade of artists. Of course, you can always avoid weather mishaps by holding all of your events indoors; that will raise your costs, but, in the end, the payoff may be worth it.

ATHLETIC RECRUITER/SCOUT

Startup cost:	$1,000
Potential earnings:	$15,000 or more
Typical fees:	$25–$50 per hour
Advertising:	Networking, referrals, participation in athletic boosters clubs, attendance at games
Qualifications:	Knowledge and love of sports, enthusiasm for young people, ability to spot talent, commitment to the team and/or school for which you want to recruit
Equipment needed:	Car, cell phone
Home business potential:	Yes
Staff required:	No
Hidden costs:	Transportation costs, telephone bills

LOWDOWN:

You do this anyway, right? Every game you go to, you notice the players who stand out, who make the great catches, who come through in the final minutes with the setup that leads to the winning score. You see the "unsung heroes" who support the stars, and you have a sense for the kids with commitment. You can turn these interests into a business by contracting with a college athletic team or teams as a scout. As a recruiter, you will establish the initial contact with the player and his or her family. You will acquaint them with the opportunities that may be available for scholarships and for participation in a sports program with spirit and great coaching.

STARTUP:

All you really need to do is get yourself to the games (not much more than $1,000 will be needed initially). You can use your home computer to write reports, or, if your spelling's not so great, dictate your thoughts into a tape recorder and hire a secretarial service to type them for you. Depending on how much time you put in and the budgets of the colleges you work with, $15,000 is an achievable annual figure for part-time work. If you're good at what you do and the players you recruit turn out to be stars, you might consider expanding your services to pro teams.

BOTTOM LINE ADVICE:

You'll need to be the kind of person in whom athletic directors, coaches, players, and parents feel confident. You'll need the patience to sit through the games that lack excitement and the games that are played in bad weather. Transforming yourself from an ordinary amateur sports fan to a professional scout means losing some of the spontaneity of just watching and enjoying the contest. Instead, you'll be analyzing all the time: How is this player progressing? Who was able to spark the team to greater effort in the second half? Will this player look so good at the next level of competition? But if you enjoy watching sports anyway, why not make a little money at it? This is not a way to get rich, but it gives you satisfaction in knowing that you're bringing out excellence and helping young people find opportunities.

Auctioneer

Startup cost:	$500–$1,500
Potential earnings:	$500–$10,000 per auction
Typical fees:	10 to 15 percent of total auction take
Advertising:	Yellow Pages, community newspapers, fliers, word of mouth
Qualifications:	Some states offer certification as an auctioneer
Equipment needed:	Car, gavel, telephone
Home business potential:	Yes (but your work will primarily be done at each auction site)
Staff required:	No
Hidden costs:	Insurance

LOWDOWN:

Auctioneers speak a language all their own . . . at such a rapid rate, it's a wonder that those bidding can even understand or hear themselves think. As an auctioneer, you'll auction off everything from fine china to farm animals; much of your work, however, will entail auctioning off the remains of estates. You'll need to work with the executors of wills, attorneys, and others when participating in an estate auction; often, you'll be paid a small fee ($35 to $75) in addition to a commission (usually 10 to 15 percent of total sales). Generally speaking, you'll get better pay when handling estates than when working with smaller auctions such as those involving animals. However, don't rule out auctions of individual items, especially those with big-ticket prices such as farm equipment or real estate; 10 percent of a used combine that goes for $28,000 is nothing to sneeze at . . . and it's just one piece of equipment you might sell that day! Sometimes, particularly when dealing with antiques or fine art, you may have to appraise each item for its value; if you aren't trained as an appraiser, you'll need to hook up with a good one (and maybe trade referrals with each other).

STARTUP:

Your startup will be relatively low ($500 to $1,500) and will mostly cover the cost of certification and/or training, plus business cards. Twenty-seven states currently have certification requirements for auctioneers, so you'll need to check whether your state is one of them. Since the only equipment you really need is a phone so potential clients can get in touch with you, your overhead will be extremely low. All you have to do is get out there and sell, sell, sell—and in a few hours of auctioning off big-ticket items on a Saturday afternoon, you could easily make $5,000 to $10,000.

BOTTOM LINE ADVICE:

This is a fun, fast-paced occupation, but to make a good, strong living at it, you'll need some training or an apprenticeship with an experienced auctioneer. Once you have a little experience under your belt, you'll want to position yourself in the more affluent neighborhoods. In other words, you'll need to be where the rich folks are, since their "toys" are the ones that will bring you the most in commissions. If you don't know how to smell money a mile away, you probably won't do very well as an auctioneer.

AUTO PAINT TOUCHUP PROFESSIONAL

Startup cost:	$500–$1,000
Potential earnings:	$15,000–$25,000
Typical fees:	$30–$50 per hour
Advertising:	Memberships in car clubs and active participation at car enthusiast events, direct mail, fliers, referrals from dealers and auto repair stores, radio spots, classified ads in auto sales section of newspaper
Qualifications:	Some experience with auto paint work, sales skills
Equipment needed:	Inventory of popular paint colors, sander, brush
Home business potential:	Yes
Staff required:	No
Hidden costs:	Inventory and disposal of used chemicals

LOWDOWN:

It's not the big things that drive us crazy, it's the little ones—the dings in our car doors and the chips off the hood. For an entirely new paint job, or the replacement of a crumpled fender, plenty of sources are available in most communities. But how can people keep those little scratches and chips from slowly widening and ultimately ruining the appearance and resale value of their cars? That's where your service comes in. You can fix the small stuff, which is important nowadays just to keep a car's body panel warranty in effect. Your business meets the need for a smaller, less expensive way to maintain the smooth surface that your customers' vehicles had when they were new.

STARTUP:

Costs are low (about $500 for materials); your skill in doing neat-looking paint touchups is both your product and your main selling point. On a part-time basis alone you could earn in excess of $15,000.

BOTTOM LINE ADVICE:

Your customers are everywhere; always be on the lookout for new opportunities. Could you fix the scratches on every car in the parking garage or lot of a huge company? Can you supplement the services provided by a local detailer, car wash, or used car lot? What about those MG owners who gather at the park once a month to swap parts and stories about their cars? You decide—and market yourself accordingly, perhaps offering group discounts.

AUTOMOTIVE LOAN BROKER

Startup cost:	$500–$1,000
Potential earnings:	$50,000–$70,000
Typical fees:	Percentage of loan amount, paid by the lender or borrower
Advertising:	Classified ads in local and national newspapers and magazines, networking, Web site
Qualifications:	Finance background would be helpful; established contacts with lenders essential
Equipment needed:	Office furniture, computer, printer, fax, cell phone
Home business potential:	Yes
Staff required:	No
Hidden costs:	None

LOWDOWN:

A loan broker brings together the people who need money with the institutions that are in the business of lending it. As an automotive loan broker you will be specializing in a type of loan applicable to almost every household in the country. There are roughly 1.8 vehicles per household in the United States., and most of the new vehicles sold are purchased with loans. That's a huge potential market. How can you become a part of this picture? You have a list of lenders, hopefully a long one. You have obtained their trust with a well-organized business plan. You advertise for borrowers, and maybe work with local auto dealerships to obtain referrals. And you don't have to restrict yourself to your own geographical area either; much of your business can be conducted by phone or online. Be sure to have a written agreement before you begin the loan search process; most of the clients who use your service instead of approaching a bank directly do so for credit reasons (i.e., they've been turned down for a loan in the past or have had trouble securing credit in a more traditional way).

STARTUP:

Essentially, you're a middleman. You bring borrowers and lenders together. Typically, the borrowers will visit the lenders, not your office. Your only startup costs are for advertising and the equipment to support your paperwork and communications, all of which you can have for under $1,000. Eventually, you'll probably want your own Web site in order to extend your reach. Weigh the minimal startup costs against earnings of as much as $70,000 (if you have marketing savvy), and it's pretty apparent that the potential for success in this business is high. All you need is drive and the ability to produce.

BOTTOM LINE ADVICE:

Clarity with regard to goals and expectations is vital to the professional, ethical conduct of a loan brokering business. Make it clear to the potential borrower up front which expenses are to be reimbursed; your fee is a commission on a completed loan. Skill at bringing the two sides of the automotive transaction together can enable you to earn a very high income once you are established. You'll have to work hard, of course, because as is so often true in the world of small business, persistence pays off.

BAND MANAGER

Startup cost:	$500–$1,000
Potential earnings:	$15,000–$100,000
Typical fees:	10 to 25 percent of a gig
Advertising:	Industry trades, local paper, direct mail, nightclubs, bulletin boards, musicians' associations, Web site
Qualifications:	An ear for what will sell, management and negotiation skills
Equipment needed:	Computer, laser printer, cell phone
Home business potential:	Yes
Staff required:	No
Hidden costs:	Band could fire you without notice; it's a good idea to represent several

LOWDOWN:

You're into the club scene; you know instinctively what's hot and what's not. You see a few up-and-coming bands who need representation (because, truthfully, most musicians lack business skills). If you've got the ability to convince musicians that you can really sell them and make their jobs easier by handling all of the business details they'd probably rather not think about anyway, you can make a decent—and if you go national or garner a recording contract, maybe even a darn good—living. You'll need to be well-connected in the club scene, and if you are clued in on where to plug your band(s), you could successfully book them for regular gigs and earn a steady flow of income for yourself in the process. Of course, you need to really believe in your bands, because if you don't, you won't be able to develop and promote them properly and it will show in your presentation. Good negotiation skills are a must.

STARTUP:

You'll need some initial capital ($500–$1,000) to help get your first band off the ground and to lay the groundwork for some publicity. The ability to negotiate good contracts is important not only to the band, but to you because you get roughly 10 to 25 percent of whatever the band makes. With percentages like that, you could make $15,000–$100,000 (depending on how many bands you represent and how popular they become).

BOTTOM LINE ADVICE:

Expect to spend long hours on the phone trying to get bookings. At the start, you'll probably still have a day job, so expect your evenings and weekends to be tied up. Start out at small clubs and work your way to bigger ones as your band(s) get more confident.

BARTENDING SERVICES

Startup cost:	Under $1,000
Potential earnings:	$10,000–$20,000
Typical fees:	$15–$30 per hour, or a flat per-event rate
Advertising:	Classified ads, bulletin boards, community newspapers
Qualifications:	Must be legal age; previous bartending experience and/or knowledge of how to make drinks without stopping to look them up
Equipment needed:	None
Home business potential:	Yes (but you'll be traveling to the party sites)
Staff required:	Possibly; a stable of other bartenders you can call on for assistance might be a good idea
Hidden costs:	Watch your mileage and be aware of potential liability issues if you "overserve" or inadvertently serve an underage drinker

LOWDOWN:

Being a traveling bartender, providing service for private parties, is a great way to meet people and make money at the same time. You'll mix libations for everyone from wealthy executives to guests at a family celebration, and the time will always pass quickly. You'll need to make sure that if you are expected to bring the beverages, you secure the necessary funds from your client ahead of time to avoid outlay of your own cash. Be sure to mark up the prices so that you cover the cost of delivering the goods as well. Check on those all-important garnishes, too. If you need to provide the olives, lemon and lime wedges, and maraschino cherries for your drinks, make sure you add in the purchase price and a little extra for the time it takes you to prepare them. To build your bartending business, invest in some professional-looking business cards and leave them prominently displayed on the bar at a few of your first jobs. In fact, you may want to do your first few jobs for tips only (if you feel you'll get a lot of attention)—that could be all it takes to start the highballs rolling!

STARTUP:

Given that you have virtually nothing to lose but your time, a bartending service can generate a respectable living. Invest in a couple of good mixology handbooks and keep up on the latest drink crazes, and you're off to a great start! You may want to make the rounds of the more progressive bars in your area from time to time to see if the bartenders are making any interesting new drinks—the more you can offer your clients, the happier they'll be.

BOTTOM LINE ADVICE:

Bartending work can be fun and full of variety, but it means standing on your feet in one place for a long period of time. And while you might be tempted to bring a bar stool for yourself, don't. Sitting down on the job can be bad for business. Invest in a good pair of shoes with soothing inserts instead!

BARTER SYSTEMS

Startup cost:	$500–$1,000
Potential earnings:	$15,000 and up
Typical fees:	$15 or more per transaction
Advertising:	Penny savers, community newspaper classifieds, bulletin boards, fliers, networking, participation in community activities related to recycling, cooperative grocery stores
Qualifications:	Friendliness, attention to detail, organizational skills
Equipment needed:	A computer to help you keep track of the information, or an easy-to-use paper system, cell phone
Home business potential:	Yes
Staff required:	No
Hidden costs:	Phone bills may be higher than expected

LOWDOWN:

You know lots of people. You never waste a penny. You love to solve problems, and to help other people solve theirs. That's why you'll derive great satisfaction from your barter system business. It's really just putting two and two together: what one person has with what another person needs, and vice versa. Making it all work as a profitable business can be a bit challenging, but then you've been doing this on an amateur basis most of your life, so making the switch to professional status shouldn't be too much of a stretch. Your barter system might be a case of trading service for service, or it could be a warehouse operation, in which you buy bulk odd lots, then try to trade them. In either case, you will need to become well known in the bartering community, so you can gather information about offerings and needs, and then work continually to make matches. Be aware that one of your biggest problems may be creating a valuation system for disparate objects and services. You'll be faced with dilemmas like: How does a carwash match up with a soccer ball? A straightforward transaction like trading small ski boots for larger ones will seem like a piece of cake.

STARTUP:

Startup costs will be minimal; expect to spend only about $500 to launch your bartering business. You'll need a way for your clients to reach you, and some way to track what is bartered. At the minimum, you'll want to have a computer and cell phone, plus an e-mail address; as you get up and running, you might also consider a Web site to promote the products and services you have available to a wider audience. Your resourcefulness and the ability to make good matches are the real assets you bring to this business. A part-time bartering service should net you around $15,000–$20,000.

BOTTOM LINE ADVICE:

Barter systems appeal to people who try to live inexpensively and not wastefully. You'll develop repeat customers if you can help people achieve their wants, and get rid of their don't-wants, without the exchange of much money—aside from the small fee they'll pay you for the privilege of easing the transaction. This business is a classic example of making something out of nothing. There's virtually no investment or training required, just hard work and persistence on your part.

BLADE-SHARPENING SERVICE

Startup cost:	$500–$1,000
Potential earnings:	$8,000–$15,000
Typical fees:	$10–$20 per blade
Advertising:	Yellow Pages, community newspapers, word of mouth, cold calls
Qualifications:	None
Equipment needed:	Blade sharpener
Home business potential:	Yes
Staff required:	No
Hidden costs:	Insurance, equipment maintenance

LOWDOWN:

Knives get dull, and most households and small businesses either don't have sharpeners or the time to deal with such an inconvenience. You can market your service through the Yellow Pages and through cold calls to restaurants and other venues where knives, cleavers, and scissors are used on a regular basis. And don't forget about lawn mower blades; they need sharpening too. You could offer package deals (i.e., six knives for $25) or special promotions—a spring special on yard tools perhaps. Network with kitchen and restaurant equipment suppliers to provide counter-referrals. Check with fabric and craft stores, too. Perhaps you can arrange to bring your sharpener in one afternoon so that seamstresses can have their scissors sharpened for a small fee. You won't make tons of money in this business, but the work is simple and the hours are few and flexible—you pick up the knives, put them through the sharpener, and return them in tip-top condition. It's an excellent retirement possibility or opportunity for supplemental income.

STARTUP:

You'll spend $500 or less on your blade sharpener and the rest on your Yellow Pages and other forms of minor advertising (such as business cards to leave at kitchen supply stores). This is a sporadic and highly specialized type of business, so your income potential is limited to $8,000–$15,000 per year (unless you live in an urban area and manage to work out regular contracts with large restaurants and restaurant supply houses).

BOTTOM LINE ADVICE:

A blade-sharpening service is simple and straightforward—what's not to like? Well, the low-income potential perhaps... but then it's unlikely you'd choose this type of specialized service if you were looking to make a full-time living at it.

BOARDINGHOUSE OPERATOR

Startup cost:	$500
Potential earnings:	$20,000–$60,000
Typical fees:	$100 per week, per room; more if you feed your boarders
Advertising:	Classified ads, community bulletin boards, penny savers
Qualifications:	Capacity for hard work
Equipment needed:	Furnished rooms
Home business potential:	Yes
Staff required:	No
Hidden costs:	Increased utilities, insurance, wear-and-tear replacements

LOWDOWN:

Through the centuries, people, particularly single women, have supported themselves by taking in boarders. Many people, especially students and transients, need an inexpensive, temporary place to live, and if you have a house with extra rooms, you can meet this need. The classic boardinghouse operator is a widow or divorcee whose children have fled the nest and who does not want to give up the old house that is now too big and expensive to maintain. By opening her home to boarders, she can fill up the rooms, avoid living alone, and bring in some income at the same time. Boardinghouse operators can make a business out of supplying rooms near universities and other organizations or institutions that attract a large group of transient people who need to save their pennies and have a decent place to live. You may or may not serve meals to your boarders; if you do, add another $35–$50 per week to cover the cost of providing breakfast and dinner. You don't need a college degree or any special training to start this type of business. You do need a willingness to work hard, a sense for who will be a suitable, safe renter, and a firmness about collecting rent when it's due.

STARTUP:

If you are using rooms and furniture you already have, your startup costs could be as little as $500. If you buy or rent a house specifically to start this business, you will, of course, require a lot more. Just one boarder can bring in between $5,000 and $7,500 per year. Ideally, you'll have two or three boarders at any given time.

BOTTOM LINE ADVICE:

Overall, most people are wonderful human beings who are a privilege to know. But then there are those bad apples. Finding good boarders is always a challenge in this business and references are a must. Hopefully, you will always rent to friends or friends of friends who cause no trouble and always pay their rent on time. But be aware that you may encounter difficult boarders from time to time and that you will need to have policies in place to deal with them.

BOOK INDEXER

Startup cost:	$500–$1,000
Potential earnings:	$15,000–$30,000
Typical fees:	$2.50–$4.00 per printed book page
Advertising:	Direct mail to book publishers, Yellow Pages, industry newsletters
Qualifications:	A strong eye for detail and subject matter; impeccable organizational skills
Equipment needed:	Computer with alphabetical sorting capability, printer
Home business potential:	Yes
Staff required:	No
Hidden costs:	Your time—indexes can be complex and time-consuming, and they must be accurate

LOWDOWN:

When you're reading a book and you want to find information on a specific topic, where do you look first? The index, of course. But it probably didn't occur to you that someone had to put together that index or that the job required painstaking accuracy and attention to detail. Those qualities are what set professional indexers apart from other editorial types. These folks are typically not writers (although they can be), and they are not really editors, either. Their expertise is sought after the book is written and edited, but prior to publication; they provide readers with a service that enables them to more efficiently conduct research or simply locate topics of interest, saving them from having to comb through an entire book. Obviously, indexers work with nonfiction books, but the subject matter can be extremely varied and could include everything from automotive manuals and medical textbooks to business or self-help guides, even cookbooks. A good place to start if you feel that your organizational skills are up to this kind of work is the American Society of Indexers (*www.asindexing.org*). Joining the organization could instantly raise your credibility level; simply checking its Web site might help you decide whether this is a business you even want to pursue.

STARTUP:

Startup costs are almost negligible for indexing. Begin with memberships in key organizations, then submit a letter of interest or resume to book publishers in and out of your area. Set aside at least $500–$1,000 for working capital; you may need it to furnish your office with a comfortable chair (a must). Charges are typically set by your client, but you can generally expect anywhere from $2.50–$4.00 per printed book page; for example, a 200-page book will net you $500 minimum for your indexing work.

BOTTOM LINE ADVICE:

Low initial investment makes this a win-win if you don't mind detail-oriented work. The hours are sometimes long and the turnaround time for a finished index is often quicker than you might prefer, but the ability to generate income is there for those with talent and the willingness to meet tight deadlines.

BOUNTY HUNTER

Startup cost:	$500–$1,500
Potential earnings:	$1 million+
Typical fees:	Extremely varied; could be as high as $500,000 per job (plus expenses)
Advertising:	Word of mouth, referral from federal/municipal law enforcement agencies
Qualifications:	Extensive training in fugitive tracking and self-defense
Equipment needed:	Computer with printer and Internet access, cell phone/pager
Home business potential:	Yes
Staff required:	No
Hidden costs:	Insurance, threats to your life

LOWDOWN:

Bounty hunter? Sounds like something out of the Old West, but while it might seem far-fetched in this day and age to consider quitting your cushy desk job to become a bounty hunter, it isn't all that unusual. In fact, many FBI retirees and ex-CIA investigators opt for careers as bounty hunters, and why not? They've already learned tracking techniques and know how to find criminals. Granted, every day won't mean a search for al Qaeda operatives, but it will be every bit as challenging to locate a deadbeat dad who's reneged on the child support payments. As long as there are felons on the run, bounty hunters will be a necessary component of our criminal justice system. Bounty hunters have a key role to play and they have the tenacity and resources to track relentlessly. Police and federal investigators simply don't have the time or funds to conduct the same kinds of thorough searches.

STARTUP:

You'll need minimal amounts of cash ($500–$1,500) to start this business, because, if you succeed in your initial assignment, your first clients will pay you enough to keep you financially solvent for a long time. If you don't already own a computer, you will definitely want to purchase one for online detective work. Otherwise, keep your office expenses as limited as possible; you'll be on the road most of the time. If you're good at what you do, and produce tangible results, you could easily earn a cool million or more your first year in business. Typically, the people who hire bounty hunters pay anywhere from $100,000–$500,000 (plus expenses) per assignment.

BOTTOM LINE ADVICE:

Not everyone who needs a bounty hunter can afford to pay you for your services, and you will have to do some work pro bono (free). In lieu of payment, ask these folks to offer testimonials that you can use to secure other clients. Network regularly with the law enforcement community to let them know of your availability; they may offer you contract work on a case they simply don't have the resources to handle in-house, particularly one that is high-profile or high-publicity. Remember, just as it was in the Old West, you have to bring 'em in alive to collect the highest bounty.

CAKE DECORATOR

Startup cost:	$100–$250
Potential earnings:	$5,000–$25,000
Typical fees:	$2–$10 per slice; $15–$1,000 per cake
Advertising:	Word of mouth, newspaper ads, neighborhood bulletins
Qualifications:	Cake baking and decorating knowledge
Equipment needed:	Baking pans and utensils, decorating supplies, ingredients, oven; a camera so you can build a scrapbook of samples to show to prospective customers; vehicle if you deliver
Home business potential:	Yes
Staff required:	None
Hidden costs:	Make sure you have enough kitchen space for finished cakes; you may need a second oven or other facilities as business grows; some local health departments require permits.

LOWDOWN:

People love home-baked goodies. All it takes to satisfy that need is an oven, some recipes, and a way (brochure, advertisement) to tell customers you're in business. Birthday cakes for children are especially popular; a home baker can customize and personalize them in countless ways to please the customer. Wedding cakes can be very lucrative but require more time and equipment than cakes for other occasions. You can be creative in what you offer, too. Nowadays people want to choose from more than chocolate, vanilla, and yellow cakes—the sky's the limit!

STARTUP:

Startup costs for a cake-baking business are minimal. Some great recipes, baking pans, decorating supplies, utensils, and an oven (your kitchen range will do just fine) are all that you need. If you can't easily learn to decorate cakes from a book or by trial-and-error, you may want to invest in an inexpensive cake decorating course. If you plan to deliver the cakes, you will need an appropriate vehicle.

BOTTOM LINE ADVICE:

The potential market out there is huge, especially since most working women and men don't have time to bake, but still want homemade cakes. There are so many special occasions to celebrate, and most of them feature great cakes: graduations, birthdays, anniversaries, retirement parties, baby and wedding showers, weddings . . . the list is endless! A cake that you can make for as little as a dollar can sell for as much as $25—a nice profit for your efforts! On the downside, it may take some practice to make beautiful cakes. You also need patience and good marketing skills to build your business.

CALLIGRAPHER

Startup cost:	$150–$500
Potential earnings:	$10,000–$15,000
Typical fees:	$75–$100 per original invitation, other items on a per-job basis
Advertising:	Classified ads, bridal fairs, bulletin boards, Web site
Qualifications:	A steady hand and a love for lettering
Equipment needed:	Calligraphy pens and ink, parchment or specialty paper
Home business potential:	Yes
Staff required:	No
Hidden costs:	Don't spend too much on advertising until you're sure of your market

LOWDOWN:
The fine art of calligraphy dates back to medieval times, when monks joyously and laboriously produced Biblical text using intricate, artistic lettering. This regal writing appears today in items such as wedding invitations, birth notices, and certificates of merit. You can also use calligraphy to create suitable-for-framing family trees (the customer would, of course, need to supply the data). Without a huge initial investment, you can offer your services to schools (for diplomas), brides-to-be (for invitations, addressing envelopes, place cards, etc.), new parents, athletic teams, and even corporations that are involved in recognition programs where certificates are in order. The market is large, diverse, and has become quite challenging—because there are many software programs on the market that can produce certificates having the same look as hand-lettered ones. Consider branching out and offering both hand-produced and computer-generated calligraphy, and you'll stand a good chance of continuing this fine and delicate tradition.

STARTUP:
Calligraphy pens and paper are all you need to start this business, although you will have to work hard to get the word out. Perhaps you can mail hand-lettered invitations to those who might need your service, inviting them in for a free consultation. Networking with bridal salons and attending bridal fairs may also help build business. Charge at least $50 for any service you provide, since what you do is specialized and time-consuming.

BOTTOM LINE ADVICE:
The freedom and creative nature of this age-old art form is in demand by those who still place value on the handmade; but, with the ability to quickly generate calligraphic style on a computer, you may find the market challenging, at best. Being a professional calligrapher isn't necessarily going to make you rich, but it's not a bad way to satisfy your creative urges while you earn some extra pocket money, either.

CANDLEMAKER

Startup cost:	$150–$500
Potential earnings:	$3,000–$10,000
Typical fees:	$5–$25 for simple candles, $40–$60 for more elaborate designs
Advertising:	Local craft shows, specialty retailers, festivals
Qualifications:	Creativity and the ability to learn a skilled trade
Equipment needed:	Wax, wicks, scented oils, dyes, molds, flowers
Home business potential:	Yes
Staff required:	No
Hidden costs:	Fire prevention and storage coolers

LOWDOWN:

The great thing about candlemaking is anyone can do it and it's not terribly expensive. You may not get rich, but you could earn a tidy little side income if you work the arts and craft shows throughout the year, or if you hook up with some retail outlets that are willing to stock your products. Your investment is low because nearly all of the equipment you need can be picked up at your local craft store or at grocery stores. There are different types of candles: hand-dipped, beeswax, honeycomb, confectionery, molded, and decorative. Decide early on what you'd like to specialize in, and try to set yourself apart by coming up with your own unique designs and style. If you want to make some serious money at this, try to market to a crafts distributor (if you can really set your candles apart enough from the others they represent). If you're looking to add variety, you might want to network with other candlemakers and form a cooperative (that way, you can all save money on booth rentals).

STARTUP:

Investment is so low that the first dozen or so candles you sell will more than double your profit (you may invest as little as $150 to start). Depending on the volume you want to produce, you could gross $3,000 for part-time work.

BOTTOM LINE ADVICE:

If you stick to basic candles, you can produce large quantities very quickly. If you want to specialize, say in confectionery candles (making wax look like a dessert, such as ice cream) or decorative styles (adding dried flowers), the process will take just a little longer, but you will be able to sell the items for more. The only drawback to candlemaking (and it's a potentially big one) is that wax is highly flammable. If you're going to do this inside your home, use caution and keep your insurance policy up to date.

CANING SPECIALIST

Startup cost:	$50–$150
Potential earnings:	$1,000–$2,000 per month
Typical fees:	$1.25–$2.50 per hole for repairs; $25–$75 for original designs
Advertising:	Country magazines, furniture manufacturers, local paper, craft publications, Web site
Qualifications:	Should be an apprentice first
Equipment needed:	Cane, splints, rush, razor blades, scissors, tack hammer/puller
Home business potential:	Yes
Staff required:	No
Hidden costs:	Vehicle (and gas) for deliveries

LOWDOWN:

Before venturing into this profession on your own, you should be an apprentice, since caning is a time-honored tradition. It takes patience and an eye for detail to reweave wicker that has worn with time, or to add wicker to a piece of furniture that didn't have it to begin with. It helps if you are dedicated to the task at hand, because if you're good at what you do, you'll get lots of referrals; there are so few caning specialists around these days. Still, caning is a slow process. Once you get an order, allow for soaking (about one day), drying (about two days), and the actual caning itself (approximately four to six hours per chair). You might want to partner with a chair maker to make your business more profitable; the two of you can co-promote one another and provide a constant flow of referrals both ways. Craft shows are a good place to pick up business; you'll attract more attention if you demonstrate your work. You might also consider picking up additional income by teaching classes, either at your own studio or as part of an adult education program.

STARTUP:

Cane is sold in hanks (1,000 feet)—enough to make four chairs. Plan to pay approximately $10–$15 per hank, depending on where you buy it. Total cost for materials is so low that, if you market yourself well, you could make a decent living of around $15,000–$24,000 per year.

BOTTOM LINE ADVICE:

This could be a high-risk venture if you haven't done your homework or let enough potential clients know about your services; expect to spend a great deal of time promoting yourself in the beginning. The best part is you are considered a craftsman and artist for the beautiful work you weave; your talent will be highly respected. You will, however, need to like working by yourself and have enormous amounts of patience.

Cartoonist

Startup cost:	$150–$500
Potential earnings:	$15,000–$60,000 (if regular at a daily newspaper)
Typical fees:	$15–$20 per hour, or $20–$500 per piece
Advertising:	Send work to art editors at newspapers and magazines
Qualifications:	Natural talent, ability to express ideas
Equipment needed:	Drawing media, access to a copier and fax machine
Home business potential:	Yes
Staff required:	No
Hidden costs:	Postage, drawing materials

LOWDOWN:

Do you have a burning need to present a particular viewpoint in pictures? Have you always turned to the comics page first in the newspaper, before reading the top story of the day? If so, you may be a cartoonist in the making. Of course, you'll need to have some artistic ability, as well as a unique way of expressing your viewpoints. Competition in this field is fierce, and only the truly innovative (or downright wacky) seem to survive. Assertiveness is the most important trait needed to start this business. Mailing out pieces of work is the only way to get noticed, so do it often and everywhere. Leave no stone unturned. Advertising businesses pay the best ($20/hr.+); you might also try to secure a regular column at a newspaper or for corporate newsletters. If you are into comic strips, consider syndicating, but keep in mind that in exchange for distributing your strip to dozens of newspapers, the syndicate will take a chunk out of your profits. Local and specialty publications use cartoonists too, but their pay is usually less ($20+ per piece). Best advice: Try to sell your cartoons to a computer software company; more and more programs featuring creative clip art are being produced and sold to companies that would prefer to keep their art production in-house (and inexpensive).

STARTUP:

This is an inexpensive business to launch, because the real product being sold is your innate ability to create (which can't be bought for any price, right?). Artistic materials can be purchased at local stores as needed for various prices ($5–$150), and copies to send out can be made for a dime or less each. Postage costs can really add up as large-scale mailing begins; stay on top of changes in postage, too.

BOTTOM LINE ADVICE:

As with any creative undertaking, frustration is inevitable. It can take many tries before your work is published. Although there is a lot of opportunity in this field, competition is tough. Art editors use only a small percentage of the thousands of submissions they receive each year. Believing in yourself and the uniqueness of your work is vital to surviving the numerous rejections you are bound to receive before ultimate success. If you really believe in what you're doing, don't give up—but don't quit your day job, either!

CHILD CARE REFERRAL SERVICE

Startup cost:	$500
Potential earnings:	$10,000–$35,000
Typical fees:	$25–$50 per client
Advertising:	Classified ads, bulletin boards
Qualifications:	Should be detail-oriented and good at multitasking
Equipment needed:	Answering machine, pager, or cell phone
Home business potential:	Yes
Staff required:	No
Hidden costs:	Liability issues could arise if a caregiver you suggest turns out to be unscrupulous

LOWDOWN:

This is a perfect match for those who like to work alone and are eager to serve as a valued resource person. As a child care referral agent, you provide names and phone numbers of reputable child care professionals in your area—at a cost of about $25–$50 per client. You would most likely get your start by placing a classified ad in your local newspaper: As the calls come in, you would schedule a meeting time with the prospective client to discuss his/her specific needs and preferences with regard to the type of professional sought. For instance, some career couples are in need of a caregiver to watch their kids from 8 A.M. to 6 P.M. daily throughout the work week, while others just need part-time or after-school care for their children. Some will want individualized care, others will be interested in child care centers.

STARTUP:

With a $500 minimal startup, which would cover your initial advertising and telephone costs, you could begin to pull in a profit almost immediately. You will need to build a vast network of child care professionals, which is easily accomplished by making calls, posting fliers in public places (such as Laundromats and grocery stores), and combing the ads in your local newspaper to find babysitters and nannies who are available for hire. You might also consider investing in professional-looking stationery and business cards so that you can convey the best-possible image to your clients and their potential babysitters or caregivers.

BOTTOM LINE ADVICE:

This low-overhead business lets you set your own hours and exercise complete control over your workload; you are free to work as much or as little as you like. Your biggest obstacle to success may be limitations with respect to the availability of child care providers or those who need them. If you live in a small town or rural area, this business could max out in a month—but if you are located in a thriving metropolitan area, you could make some decent cash for what is, essentially, part-time work.

CHILDBIRTH INSTRUCTOR

Startup cost:	$500–$1,000
Potential earnings:	$15,000–$35,000
Typical fees:	$175 per couple
Advertising:	Bulletin boards, parents' newsletters, OB/GYN offices
Qualifications:	A nursing degree or midwifery training is helpful and would lend credibility to your business; you will need good teaching skills, compassion, and patience
Equipment needed:	No
Home business potential:	Yes
Staff required:	No
Hidden costs:	You may want to invest in some educational materials such as models, books, and videos

LOWDOWN:

Giving birth is a natural experience that doesn't come so naturally—that's why we need childbirth instructors to show us the way. First-time parents are especially uneasy (even frightened) about the pending event, and their fears are best calmed with detailed and expert information from a reliable source. If you know your way around a delivery room, and have a nursing degree or midwifery training, you would be a terrific candidate for this type of work. A childbirth instructor is essentially a teacher, so you must develop (and stick to) a teaching plan much the same as any other teacher. You can offer your services in a classroom setting or counsel couples during individual sessions in the comfort of their homes. Childbirth classes typically meet once a week for four to six weeks, so you must learn to space out your materials and information accordingly. Begin with the basics and end with a strong visual, such as a childbirth video. Your "students" are bound to have a lot of questions. Be sure that you allot plenty of time to answer them all, even the ones that seem obvious or a shade ridiculous. Always demonstrate patience, courtesy, and compassion. Remember, most of your clients haven't a clue what they're in for, and it's your job to ease their fears and help ensure a calm, secure birthing experience.

STARTUP:

You will be competing against hospitals (unless you contract with them to provide their prenatal classes), so you will need to spend some advertising dollars to get your name out there. In addition to advertising in newsletters aimed at expectant parents, you may also want to consider posting fliers at a children's consignment store, which often have bulletin boards. You could offer to provide referrals in return. And while we're on the subject of referrals, get to know obstetricians and midwives in your community; they will undoubtedly become your strongest word-of-mouth source for new business.

BOTTOM LINE ADVICE:

The birth experience is a joyous occasion, and you will likely enjoy telling and retelling the story of the miracle of bringing a baby into the world. On the downside, the repetition can get on your nerves . . . you will have to be creative in finding new and exciting ways to describe how babies are born.

Children's Party Planner

Startup cost:	$500–$1,000
Potential earnings:	$20,000–$35,000
Typical fees:	Hourly rate of $50–$75 or per-party fee of $150–$200; add extra for party supplies, favors, food, and mileage
Advertising:	Yellow Pages, flyers, referrals/networking
Qualifications:	Creativity, resourcefulness, organizational skills; you must love children to do this job!
Equipment needed:	Planning system, computer, cell phone, pager, answering machine, fax, camera, or camcorder (to record parties so that other potential clients can see your work)
Home business potential:	Yes
Staff required:	No, but from time to time, you may need a helper or two
Hidden costs:	Travel expenses (mileage), out-of-pocket costs for props, prizes, and party supplies

LOWDOWN:

Remember the wonderful birthday parties you went to as a child? Today's parents would like to create those same kinds of memories for their kids, but when both are working, who has the time to plan and stage a memorable children's party? You do. If you're creative, energetic, and just plain love kids, you can make a respectable living as a children's party planner. You'll suggest a theme—circus, pirates, princesses, Harry Potter, Star Wars, whatever—then put together the decorations, food, favors, and entertainment to carry it off. You'll do the serving and clean-up, too, so all the parents have to do is sit back, watch, and enjoy the fun. Don't limit yourself to birthday parties either—you can organize and stage kids' parties to celebrate Valentine's Day, Halloween, Christmas, Hanukkah, the end of summer, graduation from kindergarten—just about any event kids and their parents are likely to get excited about.

STARTUP:

It'll take more creativity than cash to launch this business. You may want to invest in a few costumes or props, but otherwise, all you'll need are flyers to post in places where children and their parents are likely to hang out—the YMCA, dance and karate studios, kids' consignment shops, grocery stores, pediatricians' offices, and day care centers. By all means, spring for a Yellow Pages listing and work with your local newspaper to possibly secure a feature article on one of your parties. Since you'll need to lay out some cash for supplies and food in advance of the party, it's a good idea to ask the parents for a portion of your fee up front. That way, you're not footing the bill and waiting for reimbursement.

BOTTOM LINE ADVICE:

To get your business off the ground and start building that all-important word-of-mouth advertising, throw a few parties at first for your friends' children free of charge, or give a party away as a prize in a charity auction. Referrals can easily keep you busy throughout the year and you'll make good money. The only downside is that most of your work will be on weekends, and there's only so much of you to go around. Once you've booked a Saturday afternoon, that time and your expertise are unavailable to anyone else.

COLLEGE APPLICATION CONSULTANT

Startup cost:	$500–$1,000
Potential earnings:	$15,000–$30,000
Typical fees:	Extremely varied; some consultants charge as much as $1,000 per student for this service
Advertising:	School and local papers, direct mail, Yellow Pages
Qualifications:	Familiarity with various colleges and programs; research skills
Equipment needed:	Computer, Internet access, reference materials
Home business potential:	Yes
Staff required:	No
Hidden costs:	Long distance phone calls and online time

LOWDOWN:

The hardest part of getting into a college nowadays is choosing the right one; it's a vital decision for a young person's future, with far-reaching implications. A high school degree is no longer enough; now more than ever, a bachelor's degree is a requirement to secure a decent, well-paying job. And although some high schools have advisors who are qualified to counsel students about their higher education choices, many more do not invest the time and money they could and should in this important aspect of continuing education. That's where you come in. As an independent college application consultant your services are in high demand in a field where the competition is low. What more could a businessperson ask for? If you are amenable to long hours of research and documentation, this business could provide you with just the challenge and professional satisfaction you need. Your biggest hurdle will be problem-solving: You'll have to deal with emotional/sentimental issues (primarily of the parents) while you attempt to help high school juniors and seniors access the information they need to effectively narrow down their college choices. You will likely start by conducting a skills/needs assessment in order to match each student with an appropriate choice of universities. Once you have narrowed the choices, you'll assist your clients in obtaining and completing the financial aid and application forms properly (not to mention making sure they mail them in on time). You will also relay necessary facts about: the ACT/SAT exams, placement tests (such as those for assessing math, English, and foreign language skills), degree options and requirements for their completion, and extracurricular activities offered by the school that might be of interest to the student.

STARTUP:

Hopefully, you already have a computer; if not, you will need to purchase one. Expect to spend about $1,200 or so to get the speed and memory you will need. While you can obtain a lot of information about individual schools online, you will probably also want to secure copies of college catalogs which show listings of the courses offered along with detailed descriptions of each, as well as general information about application procedures, fees, deadlines, entrance requirements, and other miscellaneous facts about the school. The catalogs are generally free for the asking, but you may also wish to acquire a few of the specialized publications available in bookstores that rate universities or provide little-known information about them; some of these are rather expensive, but since they are the basis of your business, you will find them well worth the investment. Most of your clients will come through networking and word-of-mouth. However, you may wish to place a few small ads in student newspapers or the dailies and weeklies serving your market area. When purchasing ad space, keep in mind that frequency is more important than size; opt for a smaller ad and run it several times. It is likely that you will be making a lot of long-distance calls to colleges, which can add up quickly, so remember to monitor your phone time and be sure that you factor it into your fees. Your charges can be determined in a number of ways: hourly, per student, per task, or per package of tasks; just be sure that no matter which method you choose, all of your out-of-pocket expenses are covered.

BOTTOM LINE ADVICE:

Good listening skills and problem-solving abilities are your biggest assets in this business. Your clients—the students and their families—are trusting you with a very important aspect of their lives: their futures. High self-motivation and research skills will help keep you enthused and knowledgeable about colleges and what's new on campuses all across the country. If you enjoy being the "middleman" in an important quest for information, then college application consulting is for you.

COMEDY WRITER

Startup cost:	$500–$1,500
Potential earnings:	$10,000–$30,000+
Typical fees:	$35–$50 a joke; up to $1,000 for a stand-up routine
Advertising:	Industry trade publications, word of mouth, comedy clubs
Qualifications:	Sense of humor, ability to write clearly and for audiences
Equipment needed:	Computer, laser printer, video camera/tape recorder
Home business potential:	Yes
Staff required:	No
Hidden costs:	Travel, union dues

LOWDOWN:

Do you have a talent for making people laugh—at themselves, each other, and the world? If so, and if you have writing ability to boot, you could make a living as a professional comedy writer. But beware, this is an extremely competitive field, and you'll need to be decidedly different (albeit unusual, even a little wacky perhaps) to set yourself apart from the rest of the funny people out there. Your best bet in starting out is to write your own material and perform it at a local comedy club's open mike or amateur night. The laughter (or lack thereof) you get in response to your routine will provide a clear and immediate indication of whether this is the field for you. If you'd rather leave the performing to someone else, you can write the material and try peddling it to a local comic or to an on-air radio personality. It takes more than good writing to be successful in this business, however. Good comedy writers also need to be organized, concise, and dedicated. And it certainly doesn't hurt to be confident that your material is funny and to be persistent in shopping it around.

STARTUP:

The sky's the limit in terms of what you can make down the road if you end up in New York or Hollywood, but be prepared to shell out some savings in the meantime for hotels, travel, postage to mail your scripts, and union dues to protect your material. Expect to spend between $500–$1,500 just to get started. Your earnings may vary from year to year, but should grow exponentially as you make contacts and get noticed in bigger markets. Expect to earn $10,000–$30,000 after the first couple of years, much more if you land a writing gig for Jay Leno or David Letterman, of course.

BOTTOM LINE ADVICE:

Not everyone has the same funny bone, and what looks good on paper may bomb when delivered live. The trick will be to find someone—anyone—who likes your material well enough to pay for it. Expect to spend long hours shopping the studios, agencies, and other writers during the day and the comedy clubs and stand-up comedians at night. The competition is tough, especially considering that many stand-ups write their own material.

COUPON DISTRIBUTOR

Startup cost:	$500–$1,500
Potential earnings:	$10,000–$35,000
Typical fees:	$3–$5 per drop site or a bulk rate for mailings (usually $300 per thousand)
Advertising:	Word of mouth, cover letter with resume
Qualifications:	Knowledge of postal regulations; a clean driving record
Equipment needed:	Postage meter; dependable vehicle
Home business potential:	Yes
Staff required:	No
Hidden costs:	Insurance, mileage

LOWDOWN:

Coupon books are a quick, positive way for a company to get its message across to consumers; what better incentive to buy than a discounted price for doing so? Producers of coupon books often don't have the time or resources to distribute the books themselves, so they hire out services such as yours to make sure that potential buyers receive their "golden" opportunities. You'll either drive around your community distributing the books by hand, or you'll use direct mail to ensure delivery by a specific date. Because coupons are of a time-sensitive nature, you'll always need to stay on track—invest in a good time-management system (a PDA or even a simple planner) to make sure that you never miss a deadline. Familiarize yourself early on with postal regulations; post offices regularly hold classes that can teach you all the ins and outs of mass mailing. Keep in mind that bulk mail moves with less urgency than its first-class cousin, so you will need to plan ahead. Since you are simply a distributor, not the originator of the book, you'll find that networking with printers, advertising agencies, and coupon book producers will bring you the most business; advertising your services in a publication is probably a waste of money.

STARTUP:

If you already have a dependable vehicle, you'll spend between $500–$1,500 getting this business off the ground. Mostly, you'll spend it on postage equipment and your own self-promotion. You'll charge about $300 per thousand, or $3–$5 per drop site if you're using your own vehicle for distribution. You can expect your annual earnings to be between $10,000–$35,000 (depending on which method you choose to deliver the books).

BOTTOM LINE ADVICE:

This is a good part-time profession, but it isn't exactly dependable, as many coupon book producers are disreputable or go out of business in a short period of time. Align yourself with the tried and true, and all will go smoothly. Otherwise, you might consider becoming the coupon book producer yourself.

DOLL REPAIR SERVICE

Startup cost:	$500–$1,000
Potential earnings:	$20,000–$40,000
Typical fees:	Depends on what needs to be replaced and whether the doll is an antique (could be $50–$300 or more)
Advertising:	Yellow Pages, antique shows, specialty shops, hobby magazines
Qualifications:	Enjoying the art of doll-making and repair; special knowledge of antique dolls and repair techniques
Equipment needed:	Spare parts, precision tools
Home business potential:	Yes
Staff required:	No
Hidden costs:	Liability insurance, shipping

LOWDOWN:

This could be a fun little business, but beware—it will probably be more a labor of love than a huge moneymaker. As dolls get older, they do become more popular to collect—and if they're going to be worth anything later on, they will need to be in the best possible shape to command the highest dollars. For instance, one early Barbie doll can be worth as much as $500, but only if she's in mint condition. That's where you come in: You repair and restore dolls to their original state—and sometimes that means purchasing used dolls for spare parts. Keep all types of doll parts on hand and network with other repair services to locate spare parts. Pay attention to detail and have the hands of a surgeon. Dolls aren't just made from plastic, of course—there are many different types, such as bisque, china, wax, and mechanical. Know what is special about each doll and what precautions you should take when repairing them. Market your service especially hard at antique fairs and specialty shops, and get your business cards beside as many antique shop cash registers as possible. To boost your income, you may want to offer related services such as collectibles connections (matching buyers and sellers) and retail doll sales.

STARTUP:

Advertising will be the key to generating most of your business (expect to spend about $1,000); the rest of your costs will go to spare parts (about $500 to start). Some may be expensive, so you may want to hold off ordering until you actually have a need. You will be repairing high-end and antique dolls, so gauge your earnings between $20,000 and $40,000.

BOTTOM LINE ADVICE:

Some doll repair services in the past have given the business a bad name. You'll have to overcome this by knowing the ins and outs of doll-making. It is much easier to repair something if you know how it is put together. Take your time to learn your craft so that you know what you are doing; if you ruin a doll you may have to buy it. Be sure your packaging is secure when you deliver or ship to avoid any damage.

ETIQUETTE ADVISOR

Startup cost:	Under $1,000
Potential earnings:	$20,000–$50,000
Typical fees:	$15–$35 per student, per class
Advertising:	Newspapers, business publications, networking with community organizations
Qualifications:	Extremely good taste and a sense of "moral superiority"
Equipment needed:	Good resource materials
Home business potential:	Yes
Staff required:	No
Hidden costs:	Networking in high places could set you back considerably cashwise—be careful not to live too well until you're making enough money to cover your expenses and then some

LOWDOWN:

It's a sad fact but true: The people who know and practice good manners are few and far between these days. Yet you've always known the answers to those seemingly out-dated questions: Which fork do I start with?, and What's that spoon across the top of my plate really for? People rely on your expertise for coping with such sticky situations as who to invite to a wedding, where to place divorced parents in a room together, when not to send a thank-you card, and how long is too long to wait before responding to an RSVP. It's clear that your talents are needed, but by whom and how can you put a price on what you know? Easy—call yourself an etiquette advisor and offer your services in six simple courses. It's practically impossible to make serious money handling questions of etiquette individually, so develop a curriculum and offer your classes to the public or (better yet) to the "Corporate Confused" seeking to become the "Corporate Elite." You can offer tips on everything from conducting a proper conversation to handling a potentially embarrassing situation: Who hasn't wondered, "What should I do if my crou-ton shoots out from my plate and onto the boss's during lunch?

STARTUP:

Your startup costs are so minimal, you needn't worry about whether it is proper to launch this business. Just make sure you have good reference materials for the questions that stump you—and leave a little extra so that you can actually do some entertaining that will allow your students to practice what you've preached. There's nothing like facing up to a real place setting with three forks and five spoons to separate the socially savvy from the clods!

BOTTOM LINE ADVICE:

You'll love the authority and power of being a moral authority—but try not to let it go to your head. The last thing any one of your clients needs to encounter is a know-it-all. Be matter-of-fact, and try to inject some humor into your presentation. This is, after all, only etiquette, not a matter of life and death.

FENG SHUI CONSULTANT

Startup cost:	$500–$1,000
Potential earnings:	$30,000–$50,000
Typical fees:	$75–$125 per hour, or $250 per consultation
Advertising:	Direct mail, Yellow Pages, word of mouth/referrals, Web site
Qualifications:	Feng shui training (check the Internet for courses and schools); background in interior design, fine arts, environmental studies, city planning, health care, or psychology may be helpful
Equipment needed:	Some practitioners use a ba gua (octagonal compass), others rely only on a door or main entrance to analyze a room; computer, printer, fax, phone
Home business potential:	Yes
Staff required:	No
Hidden costs:	Travel expenses; most consultations are done on-site

LOWDOWN:

The constant pressure of living 24/7 connected to electronic calendars, computers, and cell phones, has lots of people looking for ways to slow down, smell the roses, and reconnect with their sense of well-being. Feng shui is one such approach. Literally translated, feng shui means wind and water. Imported from China, it's an ancient way of looking at the relationship between people and their surroundings. Advocates of this discipline believe that physical environment affects one's physical, mental, and emotional health. Create harmony in the physical environment through proper placement of objects and effective use of space, light, color, and sound, and the result is a happier, healthier, and more productive workplace or home. As a feng shui consultant, you will work with individuals and corporate clients to determine the best room layouts, including the most effective placement of desks, beds, computers, chairs, and couches. Most consultations are conducted on-site, although they can also be done off-site using a scale drawing of a floor plan or the entire property. Typically, you will provide a written report and a floor plan containing your recommendations for feng shui remedies at the close of your on-site consultation or within a few days. You may also make yourself available for follow-up phone consultation as needed.

STARTUP:

Startup costs and overhead are minimal; all you are selling is your time and expertise. You can expect to spend between $500 and $1,000 for business cards, a Yellow Pages ad, and a direct mail campaign. Since many people are still unfamiliar with the concept of feng shui, you will need some explanatory literature; a simple, tri-fold brochure and perhaps, eventually, a Web site, should do the trick. How much money you can make as a feng shui consultant is pretty dependent on the type of clients you pursue and how hard you want to work. The biggest money will come from the corporate sector; chief executives at companies like Coca-Cola, Ford, and Hewlett-Packard have already given the nod to feng shui. Consider approaching schools and municipal parks and recreation and city planning departments, too.

BOTTOM LINE ADVICE:

If feng shui sounds a little like pseudoscience to you, consider this: Feng shui consultants outnumber architects in America these days. And even the architects themselves, along with interior designers, decorators, and real estate agents use feng shui principles in their work. You may, in fact, find some of your best clients and steadiest workflow by networking in these areas. One of your biggest challenges will be getting the word out about feng shui in general. Many people still don't have any idea what it is. In the interest of education—and perhaps, indirectly, some business down the road—you may want to offer free talks at libraries or make yourself available as a speaker for community organizations and service clubs.

FIRST AID/CPR INSTRUCTOR

Startup cost:	$300–$500
Potential earnings:	$15,000–$20,000
Typical fees:	$10–$20 per participant
Advertising:	YMCA, hospitals, churches, associations, schools, health/swim clubs
Qualifications:	American Red Cross or American Heart Association certification required
Equipment needed:	"Resusci-Annie" dummy for practice
Home business potential:	Yes (but you will be traveling to various sites to teach)
Staff required:	No
Hidden costs:	Some educational materials could set you back a pretty penny; find out what you really need from your training instructor

LOWDOWN:

The blonde woman is stretched out on the floor, with a small crowd of people around her. "Annie, Annie—are you okay?" someone asks. She's not breathing, and one person gives mouth-to-mouth resuscitation while another thumps her chest in an effort to restart her heart. Does this scene ring a bell? Many of us have taken CPR training at schools, churches, or health clubs. If you've always been interested in being the one who teaches other people how to save lives, this could be your calling. Don't expect to make big money in this line of work; volunteers from many not-for-profit associations offer similar courses at no charge. The challenge for you is to set your course apart by taking your class directly into the workplace or by adding on a related service, such as a speakers bureau that offers tips on 'CPR in the Age of AIDS' or some other topic of current concern.

STARTUP:

It doesn't cost much to instruct others in lifesaving techniques; your biggest up-front cost will be for the practice dummy and related resource materials such as models, diagrams, and videos. Most CPR courses require the student to come to the instructor; turn it around and take your course to the student. For example, offer your services to restaurants; typically, they post diagrams of what to do in an emergency, but do their staffs really read them and have they ever actually practiced CPR? Not likely. Offer them a group discount!

BOTTOM LINE ADVICE:

The challenge of setting yourself apart from competing services that are offered free of charge might seem overwhelming at first—but get creative and you can build a small, yet profitable, business for yourself. Be positive and look to the big guys who can provide you with a steady flow of business (i.e., health clubs, restaurant associations, and human resource managers at large corporations).

GARAGE SALE COORDINATOR

Startup cost:	$500–$700
Potential earnings:	$15,000–$25,000
Typical fees:	Often a flat fee of $25–$50 per garage sale + reimbursement for out-of-pocket costs; you may also strike a deal whereby you earn a commission on total sales (10 to 15 percent is not unreasonable)
Advertising:	Classified ads, bulletin boards, community newspapers, condo/neighborhood associations
Qualifications:	Organizational skills, strong marketing ability
Equipment needed:	Phone, computer with letter-quality printer, fax, e-mail, hammer and nails for posting signs
Home business potential:	Yes
Staff required:	No
Hidden costs:	Gas and mileage may get out of hand; try to cover these costs in your fee

LOWDOWN:

Are you a garage sale goddess? Do you spend your entire weekend cavorting around town in search of great bargains? This could be a business made in heaven expressly for you. As a garage sale coordinator/marketer, you would first advertise your services stressing your skill at saving folks time and energy so that they can relax and make money from their old stuff. Then you would organize all of the details involved in putting together a successful garage sale, including marketing (posting signs and placing publicity in newspapers, etc.), and running the sale itself (tagging, bartering, and keeping a record of what's been sold). Don't wait for the individual, single-home customers to build your business; try to work with condo associations, churches, and apartment complexes to organize large-group garage sales—these will bring in your best dollars and provide you with the greatest marketing opportunity, since many bargain hunters like the idea of one-stop shopping.

STARTUP:

This business could be a real bargain for you, because it involves minimal startup cost and the ability to be paid for something you truly enjoy. Advertising your services as a garage sale coordinator in the newspaper classifieds will be your biggest cost, averaging $500–$700, depending on how often and in how many newspapers you run the ads. You can, however, earn a pretty good penny for yourself in all of this, especially when you work with large groups. Charge between $25–$50 per garage sale, and add on a percentage of the profits (10 to 15 percent is not unreasonable).

BOTTOM LINE ADVICE:

Be sure that your clients know up front that they will reimburse you for any out-of-pocket costs, such as classified ads for their sales. Many large newspapers offer free garage sale kits, complete with signs, records, and tips for making a garage sale a success. Call or write to request one of these kits—it could become the model for your business and would certainly make your job even easier.

GENEALOGICAL SERVICE
(FAMILY HISTORY WRITER)

Startup cost:	$500–$1,500 (depending on whether you have a computer and family tree software)
Potential earnings:	$15,000–$40,000
Typical fees:	$25–$125 per month (searches typically take four to six months); $200–$500 per written family history
Advertising:	Magazines with a historic slant, newspapers, Yellow Pages
Qualifications:	Interest in history, research abilities, good listening skills, attention to detail
Equipment needed:	Computer with family tree software program; inkjet or laser printer; Internet access
Home business potential:	Yes
Staff required:	No
Hidden costs:	If you're billing on a per-job basis, watch your time; it can add up quickly!

LOWDOWN:

Everyone would like to know their roots, and what better way to find out than through a genealogical service? A genealogical service can help a family learn about everyone in its past, from the first generation all the way down to the black sheep that every family seems to have. As a family history writer, you would meet with family members to obtain every known detail about a family—and then, using those details and whatever information you can gather from genealogical sources and online research, compile the details into a family tree diagram and/or written report. Mind you, not all may be known about every member of every family, but a good source of information is the Mormon church. From their headquarters in Salt Lake City, the Mormons operate an extensive genealogical service that you can use to find seemingly obscure bits and pieces of information, and it's available to everyone, not just Mormons. You might also check census reports at major metropolitan libraries and, of course, spend some time surfing the Web. If you aren't afraid of research and detail-oriented writing work, this could be a great business for you. Every family has a different, yet fascinating, story to tell.

STARTUP:

You'll need to have a good computer system, genealogical software, and Internet access to produce the kinds of detail-oriented reports necessary in the family history writing business. Expect to spend anywhere from $500–$1,500 on these items alone, then factor in your advertising costs at around another $350–$500 (depending on the circulation of the publications you advertise in).

BOTTOM LINE ADVICE:

Your work is much in demand in these nostalgic times, and while there is not a high up-front investment, keep in mind that your time is worth money—and, if you are not careful, you can easily spend more of it than you are being paid for. You're in business to make a profit so make sure you budget your time accordingly and that in the end, you come out ahead.

GERONTOLOGY CONSULTANT

Startup cost:	$500
Potential earnings:	$25,000–$40,000
Typical fees:	$20–$40 per hour
Advertising:	Direct mail, networking with psychologists and medical professionals, speaking engagements
Qualifications:	Background in psychology, social work, gerontology, or related field
Equipment needed:	Computer, Internet access, telephone
Home business potential:	Yes
Staff required:	No
Hidden costs:	None (but watch your mileage)

LOWDOWN:

As the baby boom generation nears retirement age, the population over the age of 60 is expected to comprise as much as 65 percent of the total U.S. population. The increase is due to a combination of factors—medical advances that have boosted life expectancy and the decision by many adults to practice healthier lifestyles. With more and more folks still in control of their lives and living alone well into their 80s, the need for skilled professionals who understand the process and effects of aging is becoming increasingly apparent. As a gerontology expert, you will work in conjunction with hospitals, physicians, psychologists, and social workers to help patients and, more specifically, their families adjust to the many changes and challenges of growing older. You will counsel families on issues ranging from health care to assisted living programs, and may be called on frequently as a resource person for hospitals and the community at large.

STARTUP:

Assuming that you already have the necessary credentials (i.e., a college education in psychology, social work, gerontology, or a related field), your startup costs will be minimal. You'll need to get the word out about your services, which will require professional-looking stationery and business cards for a direct mail campaign and possibly a few small ads in local newspapers; allow about $500 to cover these expenses. As a gerontology consultant, the bulk of your work will be performed on-site; that is, at a hospital, rehab center, or assisted living facility, or in individual homes. You can easily use your own home as your office, but you will need dependable transportation in order to meet with health care providers and families.

BOTTOM LINE ADVICE:

While you are performing a vital service for families, keep in mind that many of your clients—the sons and daughters of elderly parents–are under unbelievable stress, caught in the middle between their own careers and child care responsibilities and the growing needs of their aging relatives. They simply can't be in two places at once, and you may find it difficult to sometimes get the support you need as a result.

GRAPHOLOGIST

Startup cost:	$500–$1,000
Potential earnings:	$10,000–$50,000
Typical fees:	$30–$50 per hour; business clients, such as banks, may prefer a monthly retainer of $1,000
Advertising:	Classified ads, business publications, banking publications/ newsletters, networking
Qualifications:	Training in character details/nuances of handwriting; certification lends greater credibility
Equipment needed:	A good eye, magnifier; computer and scanner if you elect to analyze handwriting on the computer
Home business potential:	Yes
Staff required:	No
Hidden costs:	Travel expenses

LOWDOWN:

With inventions like computerized scanning and computer programs that can mimic a person's handwriting, forgery is easier than ever these days. Important items such as checks, credit card receipts, and insurance policies can slip right past store clerks, tellers, and others who are skilled in their work but not in detection of fake signatures. That's where the graphologist's, or handwriting expert's, special ability comes in. As a handwriting expert, you will work on a contractual basis with a variety of clients, including financial institutions, insurance companies, and even *Fortune* 500 firms, combing through suspect documents to look for the nuances that make each individual's written words different and distinct. You will identify and mark each curve of every letter in your search for similarity, and assist in prosecuting the guilty forgers once they are apprehended. As part of your work, you may even be asked to appear as an expert witness in court, which brings up another potential source of income as an expert witness for hire. Expert witnesses can earn up to $500 per day for their time and opinions in criminal matters.

STARTUP:

Some states require certification in order to work in the public sector; if your state is one of them, set aside another $500 or so for accreditation courses and/or testing. However, keep in mind that, even with certification costs, your startup expenses will be minimal for this business. You'll need some business cards, stationery, and related office materials (costing about $500–$700), of course; earmark another $300 or so for direct mail or advertising in a business publication. Expect to charge $30–$50 per hour, or $1,000 per month if you are on a retainer with a bank or other large business. Lectures and seminars can help boost your income, too.

BOTTOM LINE ADVICE:

If you aren't afraid of detailed work and are good at keeping confidences, graphology has a lot to offer you in terms of job security and financial reward. Still, you'll need to be aggressive in marketing your services to be able to attract enough business to stay afloat. And be aware that the service you offer isn't always welcomed, especially by those who are rightly—or wrongly—accused of forgery.

HANDBILL DISTRIBUTION

Startup cost:	$200–$500
Potential earnings:	$15,000–$20,000
Typical fees:	$5–$10 per drop-off
Advertising:	Fliers or classified ads
Qualifications:	Marketing sense, time-management skills
Equipment needed:	A method for tracking and processing payments due to your crewmembers
Home business potential:	Yes
Staff required:	Yes
Hidden costs:	Spot-checking your distribution crew, insurance

LOWDOWN:

Businesses are moving beyond the traditional marketing avenues (magazine and newspaper advertising, radio spots, etc.) to develop less expensive, more effective alternatives. In many areas of the country, there is a return to an old tried and true advertising method, handbill distribution. If you live in an area with a high concentration of people and plenty of retailers, restaurants, and services nearby, you can develop a handbill distribution service. Unless you are willing to log a lot of miles on foot yourself, you will need a crew of people to do the actual distribution, but you will have to carry out spot checks to make sure they are actually handing out each bill and not simply dumping them along the way. If you recruit and manage a good crew, handbill distribution can be an effective marketing approach for your clients and a profitable business for you.

STARTUP:

Aside from the fliers with which you promote your own business, your primary costs will be what you pay to your crews. You may need to carry insurance against work-related mishaps; check with your agent to be sure you are covered. You will derive your income from the clients whose handbills you distribute. Expect to bill between $5 and $10 per drop-off; add extra for jobs involving more time and effort.

BOTTOM LINE ADVICE:

The simplicity of this business has great appeal, especially for those who thrive on person-to-person, face-to-face interaction. You'll be building a business that is almost pure service, which can be quite satisfying. Expect, however, to expend a lot of your energy in marketing your operation and in hiring and managing your crew.

HANDYMAN NETWORK

Startup cost:	$500–$1,000
Potential earnings:	$20,000–$45,000
Typical fees:	$15–$60 per hour for the repairs; repairmen are paid 20 to 25 percent of the repair cost
Advertising:	Yellow Pages, community newspapers, coupon books
Qualifications:	Good communications skills
Equipment needed:	Cell phone, well-stocked van(s) with tools
Home business potential:	Yes
Staff required:	Yes (reliable stable of handymen willing to work on-call)
Hidden costs:	Workers' compensation, insurance, tool maintenance costs

LOWDOWN:

A handyman network is a perfect way for the retired tinkerer to pick up a little extra money. Although you might find yourself making a few repairs yourself; in most cases you'll function as a referral service, where you get the call and then match a fixer-upper to a customer in distress. You'll dispatch one of a dozen or so handymen in your stable, then sit back and let the work happen. When it's done, the handyman will bring you a completed work order and a check for the service rendered. At regular intervals (typically twice per month), you'll cut a check to each handyman for a percentage of each completed job. Most of your calls will be for repairs—dripping faucets, leaky roofs, and the like—but occasionally you may be called upon for bigger projects, such as building a deck or replacing shingles on the roof. The possibilities are pretty much limited only by your staff's capabilities. Make sure to hire a wide variety of specialists, so that you have plenty of workers with a variety of skills to cover any anticipated project.

STARTUP:

Ideally, your handymen will supply their own transportation and tools. If not, you will need to have a van available for carrying tools and equipment to house calls. If you have one already, that's a plus; you'll need only $500–$1,000 to get started in this business. Then, with some hard work and heavy promotion, you can easily turn a profit of $20,000–$45,000. One tip: Make sure you advertise on your van; it's surprising how many handyman networks get referrals this way.

BOTTOM LINE ADVICE:

This is a win-win situation . . . you're helping out retired and possibly displaced workers who need to do something to make ends meet, while at the same time, you're helping a customer solve a problem in his or her home. The income is not fantastic, but it's certainly respectable. One word of caution, however: Know your limitations. Even though you might be tempted to say, "we can fix anything," be realistic about the skills of your crew and recognize when a job is beyond them. Your customers will appreciate your honesty.

HEALTH INSURANCE CONSULTANT

Startup cost:	$500–$1,000
Potential earnings:	$20,000–$30,000
Typical fees:	$15–$25 per hour, or per-client fee
Advertising:	Yellow Pages, networking/referrals
Qualifications:	Knowledge of the insurance industry, sales background, research/Internet searching skills
Equipment needed:	Computer, printer, Internet access, phone, fax
Home business potential:	Yes
Staff required:	No
Hidden costs:	Mileage (you'll most likely be meeting with your clients in their homes), online access, long-distance phone charges

LOWDOWN:

America has a health care crisis. At last count, close to half of our population either had inadequate health insurance coverage or no health insurance at all. And with the costs of pharmaceuticals, outpatient care, and hospitalization continually on the rise, the people with little or no health insurance are surely headed for disaster. A single accident or serious illness is all it would take to send them into bankruptcy. In many cases, the problem is not that adequate health insurance isn't available; the problem is that much of what is, is financially out of reach. But suppose there were affordable options out there that individuals and families weren't aware of simply because they didn't know where or how to look for them. That's where a health insurance consultant comes into play. A health insurance consultant doesn't represent any insurance company, nor does he or she sell insurance policies. The consultant is merely a conduit, a person who understands the language of insurance, knows his or her way around the Internet, and is willing to search long and hard to find the policy/policies that most closely match the needs of a client in terms of both coverage and price. As a health insurance consultant, you have no vested interest in any one particular product. In this role, your primary concern is your client—the individual or family that needs and wants insurance but doesn't know where to turn. You'll collect information about your client's health history, insurance needs, and financial limitations; then search for policies that best match a set of criteria you determine.

STARTUP:

You can get started in this business easily for probably less than $750. Since most of your clients will come from referrals and networking, you'll need business cards and a Yellow Pages ad. A sales personality will be helpful. Even though you won't be selling a product, you will be selling yourself and the need for your services. Build a list of contacts by talking to everyone you know. Freelancers, sole proprietors, and other self-employed entrepreneurs are prime targets. So are persons who have recently lost their jobs. Watch your local paper for news about layoffs, mergers, and downsizing. You might also approach small businesses regarding group policies and align yourself with outsourcing firms that provide resources and career counseling to the newly unemployed. The members of service clubs, like Rotary and Kiwanis, are often small-business owners and entrepreneurs; make yourself available as a luncheon speaker.

BOTTOM LINE ADVICE:

This isn't a job you're likely to get rich at, but it's one you can be proud of because you're helping individuals and families connect to something they desperately need—affordable health insurance options. Everyone knows they need health insurance, but no one likes a hard sell. In fact, the very word *insurance* may cause some people to turn and run when they see you coming. Be sure that you let everyone know up front that you're selling a service, not a product. The sooner they learn that your goal is to simply find them an affordable health care plan, not pressure them into buying it, the more likely they'll be eager to talk with you.

HOMESCHOOLING CONSULTANT

Startup cost:	$300–$1,000
Potential earnings:	$15,000–$45,000
Typical fees:	$25–$45 per hour
Advertising:	School boards, Yellow Pages, local newspapers
Qualifications:	Degree in education, plus a teaching certificate
Equipment needed:	Books, teachers' guides, monthly planners
Home business potential:	Yes
Staff required:	No
Hidden costs:	Mileage

LOWDOWN:

Communication, organization, and the ability to juggle several tasks at once are the requirements for making it in this field. Your job will be to set up the school curriculum and schedule classes for parents who seek to teach their children at home instead of in public (or even private) schools. You might be working with a parent who doesn't want his or her child in the school system for religious or intellectual reasons, or one whose child has to be out of school for a long period of time due to illness or injury. If you are establishing a new curriculum, you will need the ability to evaluate the individual child's skill level. If you are helping a student who is away from his or her classroom for an extended period of time, you will need to communicate with the school and/or classroom teacher on a regular basis.

STARTUP:

Assuming you already have your degree and certification, startup costs are low. Be prepared to buy textbooks up front and to be reimbursed for them later. Charging $45 per hour on a regular basis can earn you up to $45,000 per year.

BOTTOM LINE ADVICE:

You may need to join a national, state, or local education association program in order to obtain referrals from your local school system. If you enjoy teaching, but hate the everyday hassle of a traditional classroom, you will thrive in this business. You are your own boss and if you find you don't care for the environment, you can quit at any time. Networking is a definite necessity, but with enough contacts, you should be able to stay busy with work year-round.

Horse Trainer

Startup cost:	$800–$1,000
Potential earnings:	$10,000–$20,000
Typical fees:	$25+ per hour
Advertising:	Referrals from vets, equestrian clubs, special interest groups
Qualifications:	Love for horses and skill in handling them; first aid training
Equipment needed:	Riding gear, stable, access to horse trails
Home business potential:	Yes
Staff required:	No
Hidden costs:	Insurance—horses are powerful animals, you can get hurt

LOWDOWN:

Riding is a popular recreational activity in many parts of the country, and, to be suitable for it, horses must be carefully trained. A skilled, sympathetic trainer can make a decent living breaking horses to the saddle and teaching them to respond to their riders' commands. If you have the skills and experience necessary to even consider training horses as a business, you probably have observed other trainers at work and can choose one as your mentor. Once you learn your trade and become known around the area, you can depend on referrals for new business. Your days will be spent working with the animals you love and teaching their owners to both respect these powerful creatures and avoid injury. In addition to perfecting your riding and horse handling skills you will need to be trained in first aid for both animals and people.

STARTUP:

Because you are selling only your time and talents, your startup costs are very low, unless, of course, you decide to offer boarding services as well, in which case you will need a barn or stables and paddocks. You can expect then to spend approximately $10,000–$50,000, depending on how elaborate you want to make your facilities. For your training expertise, charge an hourly rate of at least $25; your time is worth that much, and the clients who will pay it are certainly out there.

BOTTOM LINE ADVICE:

For people who love horses, just being around them is its own reward. All horses need training and skillful work can greatly increase their value. For outdoorsy, active people who love animals, horse training can be a wonderful business. You may find, however, that to make ends meet you will need to add boarding or breeding services and you will have to lay out some significant cash in order to do so. Horse owners can sometimes be difficult to please, and of course your work depends largely on something that is outside of your own control, the horses themselves. This is hard work, requiring strength, agility, and a tolerance for bad weather, but then you probably already know that. You wouldn't even be considering this business otherwise.

HOSPITALITY SERVICE

Startup costs:	$500–$1,000
Potential earnings:	$15,000–$25,000
Typical fees:	$10 to $15 per hour
Advertising:	Personal contacts with bus companies, chambers of commerce, hotels/motels, local restaurants
Qualifications:	Knowledge of the culture or area in which you are operating
Equipment needed:	Dependable transportation and a stack of local newspapers, city guides, and coupon books
Home business potential:	Yes (but you'll be on the road constantly)
Staff required:	No
Hidden costs:	Insurance, mileage

LOWDOWN:

Weary travelers entering a new city have literally no idea where the best of anything is (restaurants, shows, shopping, etc.). As a professional host or hostess, you can offer your "insider" knowledge through hotels or local travel bureaus and spend your days assisting those travelers with finding suitable entertainment or special places of interest in your hometown. You won't necessarily get rich doing this job, but if you enjoy meeting people from all over the world and like to show off your town, this is a business worth looking into. You can devise your own walking tours of historic neighborhoods, or contract with bus companies that need local tour guides. Familiarize yourself with everything that's happening in your town; study the history of your hometown and read every entertainment paper your city publishes.

STARTUP:

Startup costs are minimal; mostly, you'll spend your dollars on business cards that you'll spread all over town (at restaurants, hotels, travel agencies, and wherever else tourists are likely to congregate). Charge your customers $10–$15 per hour, or work out package deals with hotels; stress how you can augment their customer service efforts by providing individualized tour opportunities.

BOTTOM LINE ADVICE:

Cultivate contacts with hotel concierges and convention managers, as well as your local chamber of commerce and convention and visitors bureau. You don't have to live in a heavily populated urban center to succeed in this business; even small towns attract out-of-towners. Look around for ideas about what might bring visitors to your area, then cultivate your own clientele accordingly.

Housesitter/Caretaker

Startup cost:	$500 or less
Potential earnings:	$5,000–$10,000 for occasional house-sitting; $35,000 to $75,000 if you land a long-term caretaking gig
Typical fees:	$15–$20 a day per house for housesitting; caretakers typically receive a salary in exchange for specific services
Advertising:	Word-of-mouth and referrals; fliers are optional
Qualifications:	Reliability and a spotless background; caretakers may need to have home repair and landscaping skills
Equipment needed:	Reliable vehicle, phone, computer and Internet access for researching long-term availabilities
Home business potential:	Yes (but you'll be traveling to and from or staying in someone else's house)
Staff required:	No
Hidden costs:	Insurance and/or bonding; mileage

LOWDOWN:

Gone are the days when people, getting ready to leave on vacation or for a business trip, simply asked a relative or neighbor to keep an eye on things while they went away. These days, the relatives live in another state and the neighbors are complete strangers. Enter the professional housesitter/caretaker. For a fee, housesitters agree to pop in once or twice a day to collect the mail, pick up the newspaper, water the plants, adjust the heat or air-conditioning, and just generally take a look around to make sure everything's secure. Housesitters sometimes even walk the dog or play with the cat, but be aware that animal care can be whole business in and of itself (see Petsitting later in this section). If you decide to include animal care as part of your housesitting services, you can command a higher daily fee. There's another facet to this housesitting business that's especially appealing to retirees with no particular place to go and lots of time on their hands. They become full-time caretakers. Caretakers typically serve a wealthier clientele who have second—and sometimes even third or fourth—homes. They can't live in two places at once and because, since 9/11, insurance companies will no longer insure vacation properties that are vacant for many months at a time, they hire a live-in caretaker. Caretakers are typically compensated in one of two ways: they're either paid a small fee to simply occupy the property, or they're required to provide some services, in which case they receive a salary in the neighborhood of $35,000–$75,000, depending on the extent of their responsibilities.

STARTUP:

It costs virtually nothing to become an ordinary housesitter; you don't need business cards, brochures, or advertising. What you do need are references, referrals, and a reliable vehicle to get you from one place to another. Start by housesitting for neighbors and people you know, then branch out to people they know and so on and so forth. In the unlikely event that you exhaust your list of contacts, you can put together a simple flier and drop it on doorsteps, but don't expect to be overwhelmed with calls. People are a little leery these days about turning their house keys over to a complete stranger, even one with good references. For added credibility and your own protection, you will probably want to be bonded and to carry insurance. Long-term caretaking assignments require full-blown background checks and bonding, which are usually paid for by the homeowner. To keep tabs on long-term availabilities, you'll want to subscribe to *Caretaker Gazette*, or visit its Web site, *www.caretaker.org*.

BOTTOM LINE ADVICE:

Short-term housesitting is a relatively easy way to pick up a few extra bucks close to home. Long-term assignments are a little harder to come by; you'll have an easier time of it if you carry a minimum of baggage and don't have pets. On the upside, you get paid to live in a beautiful home and still have the freedom to pursue other interests; on the downside, you may have to do all the cleaning, maintenance, and yard work. But if you're energetic, flexible, and looking for a way to live rent-free while you paint landscapes or write the great American novel, caretaking can be a pretty good deal.

ICE SCULPTING

Startup cost:	$500–$1,000
Potential earnings:	$15,000–$25,000
Typical fees:	$125–$200 per sculpture is not uncommon
Advertising:	Yellow Pages, fliers, direct mail pieces to fundraising groups and caterers, networking
Qualifications:	Artistic ability
Equipment needed:	Chisel, hammer, and related sculpting equipment
Home business potential:	Probably not; ice sculpting is usually done on-site to avoid melting
Staff required:	No
Hidden costs:	Travel expenses; a portable freezer if you elect to sculpt small pieces at home

LOWDOWN:

The iceman cometh! Despite the short-lived nature of this art form, ice sculpting is popular—particularly among hoteliers, caterers, and special events planners. Why? There's just something so fascinating about watching an artist carve a figure out of a challenging medium, one that begins melting almost immediately. Ice sculptures can last a surprisingly long time in air-conditioned environments, and the aesthetic appeal can add sparkle to any buffet table. As an ice sculptor, you'll be contracted to perform specific, yet detailed work in a setting where others will likely be watching you. If you don't mind artistic voyeurism and are willing to work under pressure, ice sculpting can be an enjoyable, even educational, experience. If you prefer to work in private, you can, but you will need to invest in a portable freezer so you can move your work from your studio to the site of the party.

STARTUP:

Materials and equipment should cost you no more than $1,000 total. Charges for your services will vary according to the size and complexity of the project, but it's not atypical for a sculpture to run $125 or more.

BOTTOM LINE ADVICE:

Be sure to price your sculptures so that you are adequately compensated not only for the materials but also for your expertise and talent. Anything less is likely to cause a meltdown!

IDENTITY THEFT RECOVERY SPECIALIST

Startup cost:	$500–$1,000
Potential earnings:	$20,000–$45,000+
Typical fees:	$10–$15 per hour to start
Advertising:	Word of mouth, brochure, business cards, Yellow Pages and newspaper ads, networking
Qualifications:	Strong organizational skills, attention to detail, patience (you'll be spending a lot of time on hold!), dogged determination to set your client's record straight
Equipment needed:	Computer, printer, Internet access, copier, shredder, phone, fax
Home business potential:	Yes
Staff required:	No
Hidden costs:	Insurance, out-of-pocket expenses for long-distance phone calls and postage

LOWDOWN:

Computers were supposed to make our lives easier; instead, we're only just learning that they've played a significant role in severely complicating the lives of millions. In the blink of a keystroke, thieves can hack into databases that contain the most sensitive information—Social Security and driver's license numbers, bank accounts, health histories, credit reports, computer passwords—and, just as quickly, steal away with someone's identity. Before the victim is even aware his or her identity's been stolen, bank accounts can be emptied, credit destroyed, and the good name this hardworking person has labored an entire lifetime to establish forever tainted. Identity theft has reached epidemic proportions in our country, and if you fall prey to the disease, you'll quickly discover how difficult and time-consuming it can be to recover. Restoring your good name and reputation can take many months—sometimes even years—and who has time to write all the letters and make all the calls that are necessary to set the record straight? You, if you choose to become an identity recovery specialist. You'll meet with the victim of identity theft to learn the details of the crime that's been perpetrated against him or her, obtain copies of credit reports and other sensitive documents, including credit card and bank statements, Social Security cards, driver's licenses, insurance policies, etc. You'll be the one who assesses the mess, writes the letters and places the calls that will straighten it all out, then follows up to make sure all of the records are truly cleared and the documentation is corrected. You'll also want to provide your clients with tips and techniques for keeping their identity safe once the initial situation is resolved and you move on to other clients and their messes.

STARTUP:

You won't need a lot of money to get started. With less than $1,000, you can put together professional-looking business cards and a brochure describing your services. You will want to be listed in the Yellow Pages, of course; discuss the most appropriate category with your sales rep. Most of your business will come from networking and referrals; however, a few well-placed newspaper ads may be needed in the beginning. To get your name known, consider offering seminars on protecting against identity theft to individuals and businesses. Because this is such a new field, it's difficult to determine a fair pricing structure. However, once you have completed your work for three or four clients, you will probably have a pretty good idea of the time it takes to resolve an identity theft issue; you can adjust your hourly rates accordingly, or consider switching to a monthly retainer or per-case fee structure. How much you can expect to make is largely dependent on how hard you want to work. You won't lack for prospects, that's for sure. Statistics show that every 79 seconds in America, someone is a victim of identity theft.

BOTTOM LINE ADVICE:

It can take months to resolve just one case of identity theft, so be prepared to spend a lot of time on the phone and make sure that you are adequately compensated for both your hours and out-of-pocket expenses. Your clients are the victims of a crime and, as such, they may be alternately angry and tearful. Don't take it personally, but do react with understanding and compassion. Also, be aware that you are dealing with sensitive information about your clients; don't leave it lying around where someone else might see it. Keep scrupulous records of your time and activities and protect your own identity as well as that of your client; shred everything before discarding it! You should be prepared to offer references to prospective clients and you may want to carry insurance or be bonded, for added credibility and your own protection.

IN-HOME MAIL SERVICE

Startup cost:	Under $500
Potential earnings:	$10,000–$15,000
Typical fees:	50 to 75 cents per envelope
Advertising:	Fliers and mailings to companies that do not have in-house mailing services
Qualifications:	Knowledge of postal regulations
Equipment needed:	None required; postage meter and folding machine are options
Home business potential:	Yes
Staff required:	No
Hidden costs:	Watch out for clients who seek to pay a flat fee, then dump extra work on you

LOWDOWN:

Companies who use direct mail in their advertising or promotional campaigns need help stuffing the envelopes and getting them properly sorted, tagged, and bagged for bulk mailing. If you're skillful at the manual end of this business (folding/stuffing/sealing envelopes), you'll be amazed at how much you can earn with only a few hours' worth of work. You'll need to market your services aggressively. If you find that you have more business than you can handle on your own, this is a perfect opportunity to call in reinforcements—handicapped and retired folks who may be on the lookout for straightforward, low-pressure work opportunities. Make sure you schedule your jobs realistically to allow for quick turnaround, because that is what most of your clients will likely expect.

STARTUP:

You may spend a few hundred dollars or so on special equipment such as folding machines and envelope sealers, perhaps even a postage meter; otherwise, this business shouldn't cost more than $500 to launch. Get the word out by networking with small to medium-sized companies; they are the ones that often do not have in-house mailing services. Charge between 50 and 75 cents per envelope, depending on how many items need to be folded and stuffed, and try not to quote a flat rate for the entire job if you can help it; you may find your clients trying to slip in extra work after the ink on your agreement has dried.

BOTTOM LINE ADVICE:

Let's face it, stuffing envelopes can be downright boring work. If you don't mind the tedium—and you can manage to keep one eye on your work and the other on Oprah—this could be a perfect way to either supplement an existing income or build a modest little nest egg. Keep in mind that your success depends largely on your marketing ability; be aggressive in your efforts to snag a steady stream of assignments.

INCORPORATION SERVICE FOR BUSINESSES

Startup cost:	$500–$1,000
Potential earnings:	$25,000–$45,000
Typical fees:	$175–$300 per client (depending on area)
Advertising:	Yellow Pages, business publications, direct mail to entrepreneurial groups, classified postings online
Qualifications:	A good working knowledge of incorporation law, attention to detail
Equipment needed:	Computer, fax, phone, legal forms, business cards
Home business potential:	Yes
Staff required:	No
Hidden costs:	None

LOWDOWN:

With more business startups than ever before, there's a real need for quick, inexpensive help in forming a corporation. Many people who consider starting a business simply have no idea which form of business is the most advantageous for them. You can point out the benefits of incorporating, not the least of which is that the owner is personally protected from any lawsuits filed against the company (in other words, if the company is sued, the owner probably won't lose his or her house or car). As an incorporator, you'll be networking with entrepreneurial groups to find clients in need of your services and fielding the calls that result from your carefully placed advertisements in the Yellow Pages and business publications. You'll meet with client(s) to fill out the necessary, and usually straightforward, forms required by the government. You may also assist in setting up your client's Employer Identification Number, and you'll present him or her with a complete corporate package, including easy-to-fill-out forms for such necessary items as the Articles of Incorporation, minutes from board of directors meetings, stock certificates, etc. Essentially, you'll be helping a company get started on the road to greater growth or expansion potential.

STARTUP:

Advertising will be your largest out-of-pocket expense (between $500–$1,000). You'll also need to have business cards for networking (add another $100–$200). Your fees can range from $175 to $300, depending on the area you serve and the size and complexity of the client company.

BOTTOM LINE ADVICE:

If you don't mind working day in and day out filling out the same forms, this business could be just what you're looking for. If, on the other hand, you thrive on excitement and variety, you may want to look for additional ways you can help fledgling businesses, such as putting together business plans and designing comprehensive marketing programs.

Interim Executive

Startup cost:	$0 (unless you decide to build a personal Web site)
Potential earnings:	Significant, usually more than your previous salary
Typical fees:	Vary, usually on a per-project or daily/monthly basis
Advertising:	None; these positions usually find you
Qualifications:	Significant prior experience as a CEO, COO, CFO, or management executive
Equipment needed:	None
Home business potential:	Yes; this is a contract position; however, most of your work will probably be done on-site
Staff required:	None
Hidden costs:	None

LOWDOWN:

Do you have top-level corporate executive experience? You could be just what some company is looking for temporarily to realign strategies, bring the budget into balance, solve a specific problem, or teach its staff a technology they don't know. As a retired CEO, COO, CFO, or other top-of-the-line management professional, you have valuable experience and expertise to offer a company that's in trouble, in between executives, or just looking for innovation and fresh ideas. You may be hired for a few months or a couple of years, on a full- or part-time basis. Compensation is typically on a project-by-project basis or it may take the form of a daily or monthly rate. Since you'll be treated as an independent contractor and receive no employee benefits, you can usually expect to earn fees in excess of your previous salary.

STARTUP:

How much money do you need to launch this business? Not a penny. Yes, you read that right. You don't go looking for positions at this level, they typically find you. Yellow Pages ads, in fact any kind of ads or promotional pieces, are worthless. You can align yourself with one of the many employment agencies that specializes in placing former CEOs and technical experts, but you don't even have to do that. A little networking with executives and corporations in your area may be enough to land you an interim position. You might, however, want to invest some money in building a Web site that describes your particular accomplishments and areas of expertise . . . just in case someone might be searching the Internet for a person with your talents and background. You can also register with employment Web sites that specifically cater to former CEOs, COOs, and CFOs who are in the market for temporary assignments. One such Web site is *www.thephoenixlink.com*.

BOTTOM LINE ADVICE:

Even if you're serious about retirement—you wouldn't dream of going back to work full-time—interim assignments are a good way to keep your hand in the business world while you make new contacts and possibly even learn new skills. Although some executives use their interim experiences as stepping-stones to new full-time jobs, most are satisfied to just dabble in the corporate world for however long the position requires, then return to a life of leisure until another short-term management opportunity comes along. Or not.

JEWELRY DESIGNER

Startup cost:	$500–$1,000
Potential earnings:	$25,000–$75,000
Typical fees:	Some pieces sell for $50–$75; others for thousands
Advertising:	Jewelry trade shows, newspapers, jewelry retailers, craft shows
Qualifications:	Geological Institute of America (GIA) certificate may be helpful but is not required; some formal art training and knowledge of jewelry
Equipment needed:	Vises, pliers, jeweler's loupe, magnifying glass, molds, melting equipment
Home business potential:	Yes
Staff required:	No
Hidden costs:	Travel expenses

LOWDOWN:

For those who like to create intricate detail with their hands and have an artistic flair, this business could be ideal. Some people are able to just jump in, relying solely on their natural ability; others, especially those who really want to make it big, will need to have some form of formal art training and will want to align themselves with a major distributor. When you're just getting started, you'll want to hit the jewelry trade, craft, and antique shows with a vengeance. Take samples of your work and plenty of business cards with you. You'll find a GIA certificate helpful in terms of garnering respect within the industry; the certificate is a sign that you've studied different types of precious and semiprecious stones and that you know the value of your pieces and have priced them accordingly. And since the certificate also allows you to call yourself a licensed jewelry appraiser, you'll have additional income potential; you can buy back old jewelry and reset the stones in your own designs.

STARTUP:

Jewelry has one of the highest markups going (100 percent minimum). So with little investment (only around $500 if you're not buying raw materials like gold, silver, and precious stones), a lot of imagination, and some smart marketing, you could be well on your way to a first-year income of $25,000. Try to get noticed by the press; a feature article on your work will boost your visibility and soon you'll have more business than you can handle because people really appreciate having unusual, one-of-a-kind jewelry.

BOTTOM LINE ADVICE:

Ever hear the expression "small but mighty"? It could have been written for jewelry designers. A single piece of jewelry has been known to bring in thousands of dollars. Here's your opportunity to cash in on your one-of-a-kind creations. Since not everyone's tastes are the same, you can create until you're out of ideas (which, hopefully, will never happen). Keep in mind, however, that if you decide to go for GIA certification, the program takes six months to complete and it is offered only in New York and California.

KNITTING/CROCHETING LESSONS

Startup cost:	$100–$300
Potential earnings:	$3,000–$5,000
Typical fees:	$5–$10 per person, per lesson
Advertising:	Craft shows, local library, fliers
Qualifications:	Knowledge of knitting and crocheting
Equipment needed:	Needles and crochet hooks, yarn, simple patterns, scissors
Home business potential:	Yes
Staff required:	No
Hidden costs:	Fluctuating materials costs

LOWDOWN:

Handcrafted baby blankets and booties, sweaters, scarves, and afghans have an heirloom quality in addition to their warmth factor that goes way beyond practicality. Over the years, you've put a lot of time and love into crafting such items for friends and family. Why not turn your talents into a business that allows you to make a little money from something you already know you enjoy doing? You can teach others your craft if you have patience and an eye for detail. You already know how much time it takes to complete a project and you can read intricate patterns; the trick now is to teach someone else what you know without doing it all yourself. You'll most likely have the greatest success marketing your availability through craft shops and networking with friends and family. Sell some of your handmade creations at art and craft shows to showcase your abilities, and always have plenty of business cards on hand.

STARTUP:

If you've been practicing the craft yourself for years, you most likely have all the equipment you need. Initially, your students can use your scraps of leftover yarn for practice. Pick an easy pattern, then have your students purchase the appropriate supplies before they come to your next class, that way you won't have to shell out your own money and wait for reimbursement. Plan on grossing only about $5,000 per year; this is a sideline business, not a full-time career.

BOTTOM LINE ADVICE:

This can be a very relaxing venture to do in your home. It's an opportunity for you to be creative and to pass down these centuries-old techniques to others. Be prepared to hold class at hours that are convenient for your students, including weekends and evenings. Try to fill your classes with more students than you think you can accommodate; there is always the possibility that more than one may drop out without notice.

LACTATION CONSULTANT

Startup cost:	Under $1,000
Potential earnings:	$25,000–$40,000
Typical fees:	$40+ per hour
Advertising:	Doctor's offices, Yellow Pages, visiting nurse centers
Qualifications:	Nursing or related degree adds credibility; some states require certification
Equipment needed:	None
Home business potential:	Yes (but you'll be working with clients on-site)
Staff required:	No
Hidden costs:	Mileage

LOWDOWN:

The womanly art of breastfeeding is not always an easy one for new mothers to master. For one thing, many of them are frightened by the prospect of having to be completely responsible for another human being; for another, many hospital professionals are either not well-trained in teaching new moms how to breast-feed properly or simply don't have the time to devote to it. As a result, there are many women out there who give up on breastfeeding altogether or, who stick with it but breastfeed incorrectly—and often quite painfully. Your prospects look good for this consulting business if you are patient and caring enough to show them the way. And with hospitals increasingly being forced to release mothers and their newborns within a short period of time after the birth, there will be plenty of room (and need) for the services of outside professionals like yourself. Word-of-mouth is likely to bring in quite a few referrals, since many new moms are eager to share their positive experiences with others.

STARTUP:

Your startup costs are minimal; mostly, you'll need to make sure you have an adequate amount of resource materials and dependable transportation. For marketing purposes, invest in professionally designed business cards—you'll want something that conveys a warm, caring feeling. Your fees should start at $40 per hour, and you should ask for them at time of service.

BOTTOM LINE ADVICE:

Dealing with frightened new mothers and helpless fathers can be stressful; you'll need a cool head and plenty of patience to deliver your service. On the bright side, once you've accomplished your mission of teaching a mother how to feed her baby properly, her stress level will sharply subside and you'll have created at least three happy customers, two of whom will, hopefully, spread the good word.

ADVICE FROM THE EXPERTS

What sets your business apart from others like it?

Service is what sets apart International Board Certified Lactation Consultant Barbara Taylor's Breast-feeding Specialties in Lake Jackson, Texas. "I offer the added bonus of breast pump rental services as well as one-on-one work with new moms. Also, I have an extremely high referral rate."

Things you couldn't do without:

"My own business line with an answering machine; also, my own office space in my home for professionalism and confidentiality."

Marketing tips/advice:

"Network with other professionals . . . being in a small town, I often feel cut off. Most of my networking involves a long-distance call! Also, you need to find out what mistakes others have made and share ideas about how to promote your businesses as an industry."

If you had to do it all over again . . .

"It would be much easier to succeed in this business if I had been a Registered Nurse."

LAUNDRY/IRONING SERVICE

Startup cost:	$100–$1,000
Potential earnings:	$20,000–$30,000
Typical fees:	$10 per pound of clothes (this includes "The Works": wash/dry/iron)
Advertising:	Local papers, bulletin boards, fliers, Yellow Pages
Qualifications:	Knowledge of fabric care, attention to detail
Equipment needed:	Extra-large capacity industrial washer/dryer; iron/board or a professional press
Home business potential:	Yes
Staff required:	No
Hidden costs:	Insurance or "mistake money"

LOWDOWN:

With so many women in the workforce, who has time for laundry detail? Keep some business cards handy to promote your services and count on lots of happy customers for referrals; before too long you'll have more business than you can handle. There is no other business where word of mouth can make or break you as much as this one. You'll need to be a perfectionist and pay attention to every detail: People are picky about their clothes and if you make a mistake, they'll take it personally. Have a room in your house specifically devoted to this venture. Have clotheslines available for drip-dry and keep special laundry soap, softeners, and starches on hand. If you elect not to invest in a professional steam press, have more than one iron available; if one breaks, you'll have a backup just in case. You can't afford an equipment failure, so be sure to keep all of your warranties up to date on your machines; they are the lifeline of your business.

STARTUP:

Startup costs are potentially quite low (under $500) if you already have the necessary machines. Any washer or dryer in good working condition will do, but the extra-large capacity will cut your time in half, allowing you to do larger loads, and consequently more laundry in a shorter period of time. The large capacity also allows you to handle big-ticket items like comforters, bedspreads, and pillows. Since your startup costs are low, you can expect to easily clear $20,000 working 40-hour weeks.

BOTTOM LINE ADVICE:

You can learn to love doing laundry when you're paid for it. Since this is a home-based business, you will have time between loads to catch a soap opera or talk show and feed your baby. This is a business that's not without risks, however. Be prepared to correct any mistakes, even those that are not your fault; in the course of your work, you may have to replace missing buttons, reattach shoulder pads, even completely replace a garment that is damaged during washing or ironing. For this reason, you should always keep a little extra "mistake money" on hand. Make small repairs at no charge; it tends to be good for business, and the word will get around.

LAWN CARE SERVICE

Startup cost:	$500–$1,500
Potential earnings:	$25,000–$50,000
Typical fees:	$12–$15 per hour or a flat rate of $50–$100 per job
Advertising:	Flyers left in front doors, ads in local or community newspapers
Qualifications:	Love for working outdoors and some knowledge about lawn care
Equipment needed:	Power mower, rakes, leaf blower, power trimmer and spreader, pickup truck or station wagon
Home business potential:	Yes
Staff required:	No
Hidden costs:	Insurance, transportation, some equipment rental

LOWDOWN:

Many people could find the time to mow their own lawns if they wanted to, but it's the weeding, trimming, fertilizing, aerating, and leaf removal that are difficult to squeeze in. By providing these services, plus the mowing, you can rake in the profits. There's a lot of competition out there, from neighborhood kids who mow lawns on the cheap to the expensive professional lawn services that include landscaping and related services. But if you plant your seeds in the right places, develop your niche, and cultivate the business, your lawn care service can grow.

STARTUP:

Let's assume you already have a truck to carry your equipment. You'll need to shell out at least $300 for basic tools, such as rakes and edgers; more if you need to upgrade the power lawn mower you probably already have. Consider renting some of the items you don't use regularly. Double or triple your costs if you decide to have a team of workers mowing a lawn simultaneously (you'll make more money that way). You can charge roughly $50–$100 per job in a residential lawn care business; more if you handle corporate accounts. Keep in mind, however, that your income isn't limited to flat fees; many happy customers also include a tip for your trouble.

BOTTOM LINE ADVICE:

By scheduling some or all of your services with customers in the same neighborhoods, you can save on transportation and rental costs. One day you might be mowing lawns and another you'll be aerating. You might have to rent an aeration roller at a cost of $25 or more a day, but if you schedule aerations in one neighborhood for the same day, you'll easily recoup the investment. In many parts of the country lawn care is a seasonal business. To pick up the slack in winter, you might consider adding rock salt, shovels, and snow blowers to your equipment inventory.

LITERARY AGENT

Startup cost:	$500–$1,500
Potential earnings:	$20,000–$100,000
Typical fees:	10 to 15 percent commission on domestic sales, 15 to 20 percent for foreign or film rights
Advertising:	Listing in the *Guide to Literary Agents, Literary Market Place,* and *Art/Photo Reps*; ads in *Writer's Digest* and *The Writer* magazines, networking at writer's conferences
Qualifications:	Be able to recognize a marketable book; have connections in the publishing community
Equipment needed:	Computer, printer, fax/modem, copier, phone
Home business potential:	Yes
Staff required:	No
Hidden costs:	Insurance, copying, postage, phone expenses

LOWDOWN:

The literary life is indeed a glamorous one, especially if you're a literary agent. Imagine entire days filled with power meetings at large publishing houses, where you're negotiating for the best deal for one of the many writers you represent. You'll be offering everything from book rights to film options and foreign sales (for publication overseas). Your business may also include book promotion, as you can negotiate book tours and publicity for your client in addition to the sale of the book project itself. Of course, you would hope to represent that one previously unknown client whose book becomes a blockbuster, like Dan Brown of *The Da Vinci Code* fame or J. K. Rowling with her Harry Potter series. Be on the lookout everywhere for talent—even in remote cities or small rural towns. And realize that not every author you decide to represent will turn out to be a Stephen King. Approach every manuscript and query that crosses your desk with an open mind. The successes could really surprise you.

STARTUP:

Your startup is relatively low ($500–$1,500) and mostly covers your initial advertising costs and basic office equipment setup. With hard work and an eye for what editors want, you stand a good chance of earning a respectable income of at least $20,000 the first year—but look forward to making as much as $60,000 or more as you become more experienced and perhaps even get that "big break."

BOTTOM LINE ADVICE:

On the one hand, you'll be making a good chunk of change hanging around the best media minds in the business. On the other hand, you'll have to know when to give up on a particular project, even if it seems totally worthwhile. Often in the publishing world, trends take over and dominate what's likely to be published (remember, for instance, the Mafia book craze a few years back?). You'll need to constantly stay on top of what's hot.

ADVICE FROM THE EXPERTS

What sets your business apart from others like it?
Marie Dutton Brown, president of Marie Brown Associates literary agency in New York City, says her business is unique because her agency primarily represents African-American authors: "We connect clients to the publishing industry and provide counsel for writers . . . we focus on black life and culture as well as books of general interest."

Things you couldn't do without:
Phone, fax, copier, computer, and typewriter.

Marketing tips/advice:
"Start small, think big, and follow your niche," says Brown. She enjoys the process of bringing an interesting creative project to fruition, and thrives on positive publicity. She has been profiled by the Associated Press, and that has certainly been a profitable marketing tool.

If you had to do it all over again . . .
"I would have started with more capital. As it was, I started at home with only $1,000. It takes more than that to get things rolling."

MAGICIAN

Startup cost:	$500–$1,000
Potential earnings:	$6,500–$20,000 or more
Typical fees:	$50 for a two-hour children's party, $300 for a two-hour adult event
Advertising:	Yellow Pages, entertainment section of newspapers, bulletin boards, networking with civic organizations
Qualifications:	Ability to perform magic tricks convincingly, outgoing personality, stage presence
Equipment needed:	Magic trick equipment, business cards
Home business potential:	Yes
Staff required:	No
Hidden costs:	Advertising, props

LOWDOWN:

To be a good magician, you must have the ability to learn magic tricks and perform them quite convincingly (despite the audience's willing suspension of disbelief). You can buy magic kits from party centers/entertainment retailers; a better option is to create your own illusions. To learn the tricks of the trade, enroll in a continuing education course at your local university/college, serve as a magician's apprentice or assistant, and/or attend conventions and local chapter meetings of groups like the Society of American Magicians and the International Brotherhood of Magicians. An engaging personality and the ability to work well with people are strong selling points.

STARTUP:

Startup costs will be minimal, unless you decide to purchase magic kits or extensive props. Visit your local library to find books on magic that contain tips for inexpensive ways to learn the art. Attendance at conventions and enrollment in college classes will boost your startup costs. At some point, you'll need promotional materials—a brochure and business cards should suffice for starters.

BOTTOM LINE ADVICE:

Perform for free at your friends' parties or children's school functions to get exposure. Once your name gets known, you can start charging for your services. Look to your city's parks and recreation department for leads or to the convention and visitors bureau to snag gigs at conferences that come to your city. Working with an events planner or advertising agency is another good way to get your own name pulled out of the hat.

MAKEUP ARTIST

Startup cost:	$500–$1,500
Potential earnings:	$20,000–$40,000
Typical fees:	$25–$100 per hour
Advertising:	Newspapers, beauty salons, bridal consultants, funeral homes, department stores
Qualifications:	Eye for color and contour
Equipment needed:	Makeup samples, kits, brushes, cotton swabs, a director's chair
Home business potential:	Yes
Staff required:	No
Hidden costs:	Insurance

LOWDOWN:

If you enjoy making eyes for people, or just plain giving them lip, you'll revel in the opportunity to be a professional makeup artist. Your services may be needed in extremely diverse areas, from the lively theatrical stage to the stately composure of the funeral home. You can do the makeup for entire wedding parties or offer makeovers for brides-to-be, new moms, college graduates, and anyone simply in the mood for a new look. Or, you could specialize in helping those who are disfigured due to accident or illness. Whomever you choose as your clientele, you will need to be familiar with all skin types and problems, matching your products carefully with each client's basic needs. With the astounding array of cosmetic products currently available (even at wholesale prices), you can produce professional and fabulous-looking results for just about any client in no time. Study facial structure to know where to shade and what to hide, and you're on your way to a beautiful new beginning!

STARTUP:

Your costs are relatively nominal. Start out with some makeup kits and samples, supplies, and a sturdy chair for your clients to sit in—then add your brochures, business cards, or fliers. All of this should cost you no more than $1,000—but add a little more if you decide to sell some of the products you're using, because you'll need to secure a vendor's license.

BOTTOM LINE ADVICE:

While you may enjoy the freedom and creativity of being a professional makeup artist, you may also find the lack of predictable income unnerving. Try to offer your services to groups to maximize your marketing moments, because the one-customer-at-a-time approach won't earn you big bucks. Weddings can be a real profit center. Charge a flat fee of $150–$175 for the bride and $65 for each bridesmaid; add in a fee for traveling to the ceremony and sticking around for touchups. Make yourself available for two or more weddings in a weekend and you can walk away with some serious money!

MALL PROMOTION

Startup cost:	$500–$1,500
Potential earnings:	$30,000–$45,000
Typical fees:	$500–$1,000+ per project or a monthly retainer of $1,000–$3,000
Advertising:	Networking with the corporations that own shopping malls
Qualifications:	Background in events planning, promotion, merchandising, and/or advertising
Equipment needed:	None
Home business potential:	Yes (but you'll mostly be working on-site)
Staff required:	No
Hidden costs:	Travel (reimbursement may take 30 to 45 days)

LOWDOWN:

In the competitive retail sector, professionals with merchandising experience are needed to constantly reel in potential customers with exciting events (such as bridal and fashion shows or antique fairs) and special promotions (discount programs for multiple purchases made within the mall). Although some mall promoters work as permanent staff at a single mall, you can make a business of working as a consultant to several malls if you have the right connections in the corporate world. Meet with executives at companies that own multiple malls to maximize your earning potential in this ever-challenging market. When you land your first client, you'll spend several days with a calendar, planning the best times of the year to bring creative events and promotions to each mall on your client list. Then you'll work with the mall staff to ensure that everything comes off without a hitch; in addition to planning meetings, you'll more than likely also attend post-event meetings to evaluate each program's success or failure. Naturally, you will need to be able to work in two worlds at all times—both corporate and consumer. You'll need to satisfy your corporate client, while at the same time demonstrate your keen understanding of what makes people want to buy.

STARTUP:

This is a great business to start with little cash, largely because you'll be working out of your clients' offices and several malls across the country. You'll need to spend your own money ($500–$1,500) on self-promotion; business cards and networking are your primary ways of getting the word out about your services. Be prepared to shell out your own cash for travel expenses, then wait up to 45 days for reimbursement. If you have the right connections, this can be a profitable business, enabling you to pull in $30,000–$45,000 in no time.

BOTTOM LINE ADVICE:

Being on the road all the time can get real old, real fast, even if you are a self-confessed "mall rat." Just remember that, on the plus side, you're getting paid to put together fun events that will be profitable for the mall—and in the long run, for you as well.

MERCHANDISE DEMONSTRATOR

Startup cost:	$500–$1,000
Potential earnings:	$20,000–$35,000
Typical fees:	$150–$1,000 per event
Advertising:	Yellow Pages, direct mail to manufacturer's representatives or marketing departments, networking
Qualifications:	Good people skills and selling ability, corporate contacts
Equipment needed:	None
Home business potential:	Yes (but you'll be on the road)
Staff required:	No
Hidden costs:	Insurance, slow reimbursement for travel expenses

LOWDOWN:

This is definitely a "who-you-know" sort of business; if you know a key marketing official at a large automobile manufacturer, for example, you've got it made if you want to be a merchandise demonstrator at one of the big auto shows. Many "product specialists" (as some prefer to be called) can travel year-round to trade shows demonstrating products for one specific company, while others circulate their talents to many different types of product manufacturers. More than likely, you'll start small—handing out samples at your local grocery store (the pay will be small, too, usually $25–$50 per day). As you gain experience, you can work toward establishing relationships with larger corporations in order to demonstrate their products at trade shows. Keep in mind that the days of the gimmicky product demonstrator are virtually over; today's consumers want an intelligent presentation and answers to all of their questions. You'll need to learn as much as you can about the products you demonstrate so be willing to talk with everyone from the engineering team to the marketing department.

STARTUP:

You can get started in this business for less than $1,000, because all you really need are some terrific self-promotion pieces (such as business cards, a professional photograph of yourself, and perhaps a postcard for direct mail purposes). Be sure to allow a few extra dollars for advertising, but really limit what you spend since your success will ultimately depend on how well you network. If you have good presentation skills and better-than-average promotional savvy, you can make a fairly respectable $20,000–$30,000 per year—and get to travel all over the country on someone else's tab.

BOTTOM LINE ADVICE:

Travel gets tedious, even for the adventurous. You'll be expending huge amounts of energy up there on stage, and you'll have to work at sounding extremely knowledgeable about everything you show off. Get some rest, drink plenty of fluids, and be sure to collect an advance when possible. Companies are notoriously slow to reimburse for travel expenses.

MOBILE BOOK/MAGAZINE DISTRIBUTOR

Startup cost:	$100–$500
Potential earnings:	$15,000–$25,000 (more, if your market is large)
Typical fees:	$3–$5 per stop
Advertising:	Word of mouth, ads in trade journals, business cards
Qualifications:	Excellent driving record and valid license
Equipment needed:	Delivery vehicle (car or truck)
Home business potential:	Yes
Staff required:	No
Hidden costs:	Mileage (be sure it's covered in your contract), insurance

LOWDOWN:

Many locally generated weekly publications need to hire delivery subcontractors to make sure their distribution base is covered. If you find this kind of work appealing, you should have no problem securing customers, because turnover is often quite high. Why is that? Because these publications tend to rely on a staffer's grandparent or retired parent to make deliveries; that person gets tired of the job because it gets stressful when press runs are late and quits. You can set yourself apart by your positioning as a delivery professional. Start by acquiring business cards, then make the rounds of different publishers. While the work is demanding, it has its perks. You'll be delivering weekly to the same bars, restaurants, and bookstores. Before long, you'll know all the town's movers and shakers—and that can be helpful in ways that go well beyond your delivery service.

STARTUP:

Your initial costs will be low, especially if you already have a delivery vehicle (a station wagon or small pickup is perfect for this job). Expect to earn $15,000–$25,000 (depending on the size of your market and the number of publications you deliver for).

BOTTOM LINE ADVICE:

This is a cool job, with lots of independence and autonomy; basically, you're in and out of a great many places in one day. On the downside, you may have to endure the complaints of customers whose publications arrive late through no fault of your own. If you learn to keep things in perspective and not take the complaints personally, you'll do fine.

Mobile Notary Public

Startup cost:	$100–$200
Potential earnings:	$6,000–$10,000
Typical fees:	$10 per requested service (average) + mileage
Advertising:	Yellow Pages, networking, possibly direct mail
Qualifications:	License as notary public, usually upon recommendation of two lawyers
Equipment needed:	Seal, cell phone, car
Home business potential:	Yes
Staff required:	No
Hidden costs:	Gas to get you from client to client

LOWDOWN:

A surprising number of transactions—everything from loan documents and property deeds to wills and affidavits—must be notarized, and not always in the most convenient places where a notary public just happens to be standing by. You can solve that dilemma by taking your notary public seal on the road. Armed with the seal, a cell phone, and a car, you can provide notary services, at a moment's notice, wherever and whenever they're needed. You won't make big money at this, but you'll meet some interesting people, pick up a few extra dollars, and enjoy a flexible schedule. You can set your own hours and work as much or as little as you like.

STARTUP:

You probably already have a car and a cell phone, so startup costs are minimal, aside from the license fee and whatever the notary seal will cost you (not more than $500). You will need to get the word out about your services, of course. A Yellow Pages ad and some targeted networking with business contacts will probably do the trick. You can schedule stops or work strictly "on-call." Your fees will be low—$10 per signature is standard, but you can add a charge for your mileage and out-of-pocket costs such as tolls or parking. To keep your costs under control, you may want to set a limit on how far you are willing to drive.

BOTTOM LINE ADVICE:

Notary publics aren't all that unusual; the fact that you take your service to the customer rather than vice versa is. No two of your days will be alike. In the course of one afternoon, you might notarize an affidavit at a law firm, a power of attorney at a nursing home, and loan documents in the departure lounge at the airport. To boost your income, consider adding other services, such as paralegal or fingerprinting.

MORTGAGE LOAN BROKER

Startup cost:	$600–$700
Potential earnings:	$15,000–$50,000
Typical fees:	Commission equal to 4 percent or less of the value of the mortgages placed, paid by the borrower
Advertising:	Classified ads, real estate magazines, newspapers, referrals, Web site
Qualifications:	Extensive knowledge of real estate finance; some states require a license
Equipment needed:	Computer, printer, phone, fax
Home business potential:	Yes
Staff required:	No
Hidden costs:	Advertising is necessary on an ongoing basis

LOWDOWN:

Borrowers (people and firms) who want second mortgages come to you to find a lender. Third, fourth, and even higher levels of mortgages are possible in certain cases. You may operate entirely independently or work as a subcontractor for a real estate agent or attorney. You will need to keep putting your message before the public because, for the most part, every transaction you handle will be on behalf of a new client. In some cases, you may be asked to find borrowers for lenders, but that is the exception to the rule.

STARTUP:

Costs to start are very low (around $600); factor in an additional $1,500 or so if you need to purchase a computer and mortgage processing software. You could earn your first $15,000 easily enough on two or three transactions, charging just 4 percent of each total mortgage.

BOTTOM LINE ADVICE:

Once you develop a reputation for service and effectiveness, you may find that repeat business from one or more lenders will garner an excellent income. The majority of your work, however, will likely focus on finding would-be borrowers and then linking them with the dollars, which will take a little more effort on your part. To widen your scope, you may want to consider developing a Web site. You'll need an ability to inspire confidence and to speak the language of the people on both sides of the transaction. Patience and active listening are skills you'll call on regularly.

MOTOR VEHICLE TRANSPORTATION

Startup cost:	$1,000
Potential earnings:	$5,000–$10,000
Typical fees:	$8–$12 per hour plus tolls, gas, lodging, and food expenses
Advertising:	Yellow Pages, fliers to colleges, vacation communities, mailings to auto dealerships
Qualifications:	Good driving record, valid driver's license
Equipment needed:	None
Home business potential:	Yes
Staff required:	No
Hidden costs:	Insurance

LOWDOWN:

Mrs. Smith in Portland, Oregon, wants a very specific vehicle: a peach-colored Cadillac with whitewall tires and a white leather interior. The problem is, the only one like it is in Sarasota, Florida. If the dealer really wants to make the sale, he'll have to send someone down to the Sunshine State to pick up that one-of-a-kind Caddy. That's where a motor vehicle transportation service comes in; typically, a car dealership calls on such a service to make "runs" for customer-specific vehicles, in exchange for an hourly fee plus incidentals (such as tolls, parking, and food/gas/lodging). Likewise, an individual who's flying to another city but wants his car when he gets there might hire a motor vehicle transportation service to drive it down and meet him. In this business, you'll be driving across the country, from one car dealership to another, and, more often than not, you'll be expected to deliver the new vehicle within a fairly short period of time. In other words, you won't have the opportunity for much sightseeing along the way. Still, it's a great way to travel the country while you earn a supplemental income, particularly if you're retired, can pick up and go at a moment's notice, and have plenty of time to spare.

STARTUP:

You won't need to spend a dime to get yourself started in this business, except perhaps on some preliminary marketing. If you're working with several different dealerships, you could make the high end of $10,000—but, more than likely, you'll be in the $5,000 range, because this work is so sporadic and specialized.

BOTTOM LINE ADVICE:

The good news is, you get paid to do a little traveling . . . the bad news is, you won't ever be able to make a full-time living at this business. If income is what you're looking for, you'll need to add this business on to another, such as automotive detailing, which is in the same general line of work.

MOVIE SITE SCOUT

Startup cost:	$500–$1,000
Potential earnings:	$10,000–$25,000
Typical fees:	Usually a retainer fee of $3,000–$5,000 per month
Advertising:	Industry trade publications, word of mouth
Qualifications:	Ability to visualize; general knowledge of history and geography
Equipment needed:	Computer, Internet access, cell phone, business cards
Home business potential:	Yes (but, of course, you'll be on the road a lot)
Staff required:	No
Hidden costs:	Passport; union dues

LOWDOWN:

For every beautiful landscape in a film, there was a site scout who searched for the perfect spot. As a movie site scout, you'll need to be well-connected and able to sell yourself to some pretty high-powered folks, but once you get one job, the others become easier to snag. What will you do all day? You'll likely start by reading a script, doing a little research (especially if it's a period film or the subject involves some historical event), then scanning the globe. Sometimes you'll be able to find a single place for the entire film to be shot. More often, however, you'll be working on two coasts, maybe even in several different countries, in order to meet all of the script's required shots. And your choice of setting won't necessarily be the most obvious one, either. Take for example, the classic film *Dr. Zhivago*. The story was set in Russia during the Revolution, but the movie was shot almost entirely in Spain! The ability to visualize is incredibly important in this profession, because you are responsible for selecting the absolute perfect setting for a movie that costs millions of dollars to produce. You'll take into consideration the architecture of the area, as well as its geography, weather conditions, and people when selecting your site. A background in the movie industry is helpful. This is definitely a "schmoozing" position, as you'll be forming relationships with people all over the world.

STARTUP:

Most of your initial cash outlay will go toward socializing; this is a business that depends on who you know. Get your face out there and start passing out those business cards. Snagging that first job will be the hard part, so plan on spending at least $500 to secure it.

BOTTOM LINE ADVICE:

This is not the kind of business you can simply jump into on a whim. You will likely have started in a lower position in the movie industry and worked your way up. Hopefully, you'll have made a lot of friends along the way who can help you break into scouting.

MULTILEVEL MARKETING

Startup cost:	$500–$1,000
Potential earnings:	$20,000–$50,000
Typical fees:	Percentage, plus bonus for new distributors
Advertising:	Networking, memberships in business and community groups, direct mail
Qualifications:	Salesmanship
Equipment needed:	Basic computer setup, phone
Home business potential:	Yes
Staff required:	No
Hidden costs:	Marketing materials like catalogs or leaflets may become necessary, membership dues

LOWDOWN:

Some products aren't appealing unless they're demonstrated. The classic example is Tupperware, which just sat on store shelves until the company hit on the idea that buyers needed to be shown how the top could be burped to create a vacuum seal. Many other products, with vitamins being an outstanding example, are today sold person to person. Often, a business starts when someone develops enthusiasm for, and commitment to, a product or company. The sales process then seems to simply evolve, almost naturally. If you have recognized something like a line of cosmetics that is especially effective for you, or a nutritional supplement that has made a difference in your sense of well-being, you should consider opportunities in multilevel marketing. By definition, multilevel marketing is a two-tiered approach: Not only do you sell the product, you sell others on the opportunity to sell it as well. Unlike direct sales, where you make commissions from your sales of a product, in multilevel marketing, you maximize your income potential by earning a percentage off the product sales of other salespeople you recruit.

STARTUP:

This is another business you can launch with little more than your own energy and commitment. Potential earnings can reach $20,000 easily, and much higher if you are willing to put in the time and effort.

BOTTOM LINE ADVICE:

Do you know that you can sell? More importantly, do you love the sales process? Do you enjoy helping your customers discover products that will improve their lives? If so, you can make an excellent living in the multilevel marketing world. Keep in mind, however, that far more people have tried multilevel marketing than have made the easy millions that are sometimes promised. Nothing comes free; you really do have to work very, very hard at this to succeed. You can't give up when your first 74 efforts end in no sale because it might just be the 75th that turns the tide. You will need to manage your time well, and find a company whose products are worth the kind of commitment it will take for you to succeed.

MYSTERY SHOPPER

Startup cost:	Less than $500
Potential earnings:	$10,000–$20,000
Typical fee:	$25 to $50 per "shop"
Advertising:	Personal contact with stores, hotels, corporations
Qualifications:	Knowledge of area to be evaluated, acting abilities, keen observation
Equipment needed:	None
Home business potential:	Yes
Hidden costs:	Mileage

LOWDOWN:

Customer service is the name of the game these days and mystery shoppers are the tools for testing it. Disguised as ordinary customers, mystery shoppers "visit" a variety of settings: retail stores, hotel chains, restaurants, charitable organizations, government organizations, collection agencies, and banks. Their purpose is to observe the business from a customer's point of view and to report to management its shortcomings and strengths for the sake of improving service. A mystery shopper acts like a customer, observing the quality of the service and overall employee performance, with a special eye out for theft. Mystery shoppers also "shop" the competition for valuable information. Companies use mystery shoppers because they are less expensive—and less obvious—than electronic surveillance.

STARTUP:

You won't spend very much money at all for launching this business, but you probably won't become a Rockefeller, either—earning $10,000–$20,000 per year would probably be as good as it gets, and you'd be doing a lot of shops to get there.

BOTTOM LINE ADVICE:

You might want to stick to a particular industry where you already have experience or knowledge. If you've been a waitress, for instance, you'd know what to look for at a restaurant. Chains provide multiple opportunities to shop in one geographic area without danger of your being recognized, and they are a good source of continuing business. Typically, you will be asked to provide a written and/or oral report of your findings; in many cases, that will mean simply filling out a form. In some states mystery shoppers are considered private investigators and therefore must be licensed; you'll want to look into your state's laws regarding licensing before launching this career.

NUTRITION CONSULTANT

Startup cost:	$500–$1,000
Potential earnings:	$20,000–$40,000
Typical fees:	$15–$30 per hour
Advertising:	Brochures, direct mail, ads in health-related publications
Qualifications:	Knowledge of nutrition and healthy diet; some states may require degree in dietetics or related discipline
Equipment needed:	Computer, printer, reference books
Home business potential:	Yes
Staff required:	None
Hidden costs:	Make sure legal and health ramifications are understood

LOWDOWN:

Nutrition is increasingly important to Americans these days—and most people are still not eating a healthy diet. Since so many are seeking better, healthier foods and guidance in selecting them, you can share what you know about nutrition with others via classes, seminars, individual counseling, articles, and cookbooks. Nutrition consultants often work on staff at hospitals, health clubs, and large corporations, but you can also work as an independent contractor. If you enjoy helping and motivating others, this might be a great business for you.

STARTUP:

Startup costs are minimal. You can easily run this business from your home with little more than a computer, printer, and basic office supplies. You will need to investigate your state's licensing and certification requirements; some require that you be a Registered Dietitian. Expect to spend some time and money on marketing materials to promote your business. At the very least, you will need a brochure and sales letter for a direct mail campaign and business cards for face-to-face networking with hospitals, health clubs, and human resources managers.

BOTTOM LINE ADVICE:

Depending on where you live and the area of nutrition you choose to specialize in, you may need certain credentials (such as a degree in dietetics or certification as a Registered Dietitian). Even if a formal degree is not required, keep in mind that you cannot instantly become an expert on nutrition; you will need up-to-date knowledge of physiology, food, management, marketing, and psychology. However, if motivating and assisting people to become healthier would be satisfying for you, this field may be a perfect choice.

PACKING/UNPACKING SERVICE

Startup cost:	$500
Potential earnings:	$25,000–$40,000
Typical fees:	$20–$30 per hour or a flat rate by the job
Advertising:	Bulletin boards at apartment complexes and grocery stores, classified ads
Qualifications:	Strong back, patience
Equipment needed:	None
Home business potential:	Yes (but you'll be traveling to the client's site)
Staff required:	None
Hidden costs:	Insurance, just in case something you packed doesn't survive the move in one piece

LOWDOWN:

Today's society is an extremely mobile one; the average family makes twelve moves, some of them across the country, others just across town. In times past, there were always relatives or friends nearby to lend a helping hand with a move, but that's no longer the case, which is one reason why packing services are becoming more popular. Another reason is that our society as a whole has become increasingly dependent on convenience services; we love—and are willing to pay for—services that save us time or aggravation so that we can spend what little free time we have doing things we truly enjoy. Your job will be to carefully pack items for the pending move, labeling every box so that each item can be easily located at any time during the move. If the move is a close one, you'll probably do the unpacking too; if it's a long-distance move, you may be packing items for someone else to unpack or, if you're on the receiving end of a move, unpacking the work of another. Ideally, you'll want to provide the boxes and packing materials for your clients so you must be sure to cover the cost of those items in your fee.

STARTUP:

You can start your packing and unpacking service for practically nothing. All you need are some fliers to spread the word—and you can place those yourself at Laundromats, apartment complexes, and possibly even at truck rental agencies where do-it-yourself movers make arrangements for their vehicles. You might also contact real estate agencies to let them know of your services so they can pass the word along to their clients. Charge either by the hour ($20–$30) or a flat fee. If you choose the latter, be sure to adequately cover your time and don't forget to add in the costs of packing materials if you supply them.

BOTTOM LINE ADVICE:

If you're well-organized and know how to pack delicate items for a sometimes bumpy ride, you will likely enjoy and prosper in this line of work. Developing a system, including an inventory sheet so you know what each box contains, will help you manage each project efficiently and keep your hours reasonable and your fees attractive. On the downside, some clients can be difficult to work with—particularly if their move is due to a bad situation such as a divorce or unanticipated job loss. Try to keep a cool head.

PARTY PLANNER

Startup cost:	$500–$1,000
Potential earnings:	$20,000–$40,000
Typical fees:	Hourly rate of $50–$75 or a percentage of total cost of the arrangements you handle (typically 15 to 20 percent)
Advertising:	Yellow Pages, direct mail, fliers, referrals/networking
Qualifications:	Resourcefulness, creative ability, exceptional organizational skills
Equipment needed:	Planning system (PDA or a good planning book), computer, cell phone, pager, answering machine, fax, camera or camcorder (to record parties so that potential clients can see your work)
Home business potential:	Yes
Staff required:	No
Hidden costs:	Travel expenses

LOWDOWN:

A party planner tends to all the details for any given social function—from hiring the caterer, florist, and musician(s) or entertainer(s) to addressing and mailing the invitations. Planners should have a creative flair and be able to suggest a variety of party themes to fit the occasion. For instance, you could come up with a Caribbean theme where all the partygoers must dress in tropical attire, all the music is calypso-inspired, and giant papier-mâché palm trees sprout from various corners of the room. Or, you might plan a surprise party for your client's family—with a little Sherlock Holmes-style caper for guests to solve upon arrival. Whatever the theme and your plan to carry it out, you'll need to be extremely well organized and attentive to every detail. Your business will grow primarily based on referrals from satisfied customers, so you'll want to make sure that everything comes off without a hitch. More than likely, you'll put in way more hours than you originally anticipated for each job, but the return will be worth it.

STARTUP:

You probably wouldn't consider this business unless you have thrown a few good parties yourself. Still, everyone gets stuck for ideas once in a while, so start by building a personal library of party planning guides. Advertising costs will be your biggest startup expense; be sure to get a Yellow Pages ad ($30–$100 per month, depending on ad size) since this is where many people who don't know you personally will be apt to look. You can charge either by the hour or on a percentage basis (15 to 20 percent of the total cost of the arrangements you handle). As your reputation grows, the bulk of your business will come from word-of-mouth.

BOTTOM LINE ADVICE:

To get started, you might want to plan some friends' parties for free. This will give you valuable experience and help you build a portfolio, so to speak, of your successes and innovations. Keep a photo album or video record of your parties so that you have something to show potential clients. Nothing sells better than demonstrated success. On the downside, expect there to be difficulties in dealing with the personalities involved in planning a party; there will be glitches and last-minute changes. Keep a cool head and remember that it's your client's party after all.

PERSONAL CHEF

Startup cost:	$500–$1,000
Potential earnings:	$35,000–$50,000
Typical fees:	$200–$250 a day, plus the cost of groceries; or, a per-serving charge based on what the same item would cost in a moderately-priced restaurant
Advertising:	Networking/referrals, Yellow Pages ad, Web site, cooking demos
	Qualifications: Cooking skills and knowledge of menu planning and nutrition; organizational skills
Equipment needed:	Computer and printer to keep track of clients' food preferences; a travel set of favorite utensils, pans, and pots
Home business potential:	Yes, but you'll be cooking in your clients' kitchens
Staff required:	No
Hidden costs:	Disposable containers for storing and reheating meals

LOWDOWN:

Do you like to cook? Maybe you should become a personal chef. With more and more dual-income families who have less and less time to spend in the kitchen preparing meals, there's a real market for what you have to sell. Personal chefs are not caterers; they cook in the clients' kitchens instead of their own. And they're not private chefs either who whip up gourmet meals for a single family. As a personal chef you'll cook as little as once a month or as often as once a week for several families using menus you develop based on a particular family's favorite foods and dietary preferences. You may even be asked to prepare meals that reflect the latest diet craze or to address a specific health issue, such as diabetes or heart disease. Taking all these factors into consideration, you pick the recipes and put the menus together. You shop for the ingredients, then bring everything back to your client's kitchen and go to work, creating enough meals to last until it's time for you to come back and cook again. By the time you've finished your feeding frenzy for one family, everything is packaged, labeled, and neatly tucked away in the refrigerator or freezer for them to dine on throughout the coming week or month, complete with reheating and serving instructions.

STARTUP:

Chances are, you already own a computer and printer and have a filing cabinet full of recipes and menu ideas. If so, all you'll need to start this business are some business cards and a brochure that explains your services. You can build your business by networking face-to-face and promote your skill as a cook by offering demonstrations or classes. This is a labor-intensive business and your opportunities for growth are somewhat limited. You can make a respectable living as a personal chef, but you probably won't get rich.

BOTTOM LINE ADVICE:

This could be a great job for amateur and professional cooks alike. Amateur cooks will like the gratification they get, and professionals will enjoy the chance to be creative in a more relaxed environment. Remember, the primary appeal of your business to your clients is as much the convenience of leaving the shopping and cooking to someone else as it is your delicious meals.

PERSONAL INSTRUCTOR/ FITNESS TRAINER

Startup cost:	$100–$1,000
Potential earnings:	$25,000–$65,000
Typical fees:	$50–$200 per session; $25–$50 per hour for classes
Advertising:	Business cards, brochures, fliers, bulletin boards in health clubs, nutrition and athletic equipment stores; networking with chiropractors, orthopedic surgeons, physicians specializing in sports medicine
Qualifications:	Experience, physical fitness, knowledge of equipment and CPR; possible certification as a personal trainer
Equipment needed:	Membership in a gym; your own equipment if you want to provide your service directly out of your home
Home business potential:	Yes
Staff required:	No
Hidden costs:	Travel time needed to meet clients where they work out

LOWDOWN:

Do you keep yourself physically fit, have an energetic personality, and enjoy teaching others? If you answered "yes" to all three, you might be the right candidate to start a personal trainer business. You'll have to market yourself like a pro—give seminars about being fit and the benefits of working out to get your name and face known in this highly competitive occupation. Experience will be on your side. Remember, you are marketing yourself and motivating others to become physically fit at the same time, so you must also be in excellent physical shape and condition. No one is going to be persuaded by an overweight, out-of-shape trainer. Be prepared to work out right alongside your clients if they request it, teaching them all the latest ways to get and stay in shape. It may be helpful to carry before and after photos of yourself and others whom you've helped tone and shape. Consider putting together an exercise video that you can sell through local health clubs. Although a college degree is not necessary, it may help your credibility to have some textbook knowledge of exercise physiology, kinesiology, sports medicine, or a related field. You may also want to consider the certifications offered by various professional organizations; for information on individual programs, go to *www.google.com* and type in "personal trainer certification."

STARTUP:

Startup costs vary, depending largely on where you will provide your services. If your client has his or her own in-house gym, all that's required is a vehicle to get you there. If you plan to meet your client at a health club, you'll need to purchase a membership. If, on the other hand, you want your clients to come to your home, you'll need a full set of equipment including free weights and Nautilus or other strength training devices. That could easily send your startup costs into the $100,000 range. In all cases, you will need to lay out some cash for promotional tools—business cards, brochures, and flyers—to get the word out about your services. In many ways, becoming a personal trainer is a win-win situation. You have the potential to stay in shape while you make a decent living in the range of $25,000–$65,000 or more, depending on how hard you are willing to work and how often your clients require your services.

BOTTOM LINE ADVICE:

How many people can say that going to work relieves their stress? As a personal trainer, you not only get to have fun and stay in shape, you make a decent living and possibly even improve your social life. Working out is the new way to meet people and just about everyone is a potential client. The downside is, while a client may start out gung-ho, he or she can quit without warning. Some people consider working out to be seasonal, so, to stay afloat, you'll really have to get out there and establish a strong base of steady, committed clients.

PERSONAL MENU SERVICE

Startup cost:	Under $1,000
Potential earnings:	$10,000–$30,000
Typical fees:	$20–$50 per project
Advertising:	Brochures, advertisements in newspapers and food/health magazines
Qualifications:	Knowledge of basic nutrition and dietary requirements
Equipment needed:	Computer, Internet access, nutrition resource materials
Home business potential:	Yes
Staff required:	None
Hidden costs:	Licensing if your state requires it

LOWDOWN:

Most people recognize that good nutrition is important, but they lack a sound understanding of how to achieve it. They're also often too busy with work and family responsibilities to learn about the components of a good diet. If you have a solid background in this field, and a computer with Internet access, you can fill that need. You simply create weekly or monthly meal plans, based on the specific requirements and preferences of your clients. And not only do individuals need such services; so do hospitals, retirement centers, schools, and restaurants.

STARTUP:

Other than the cost of a computer and advertising, this business can be started on a shoestring. Surf the Web for a wealth of recipes and menu ideas.

BOTTOM LINE ADVICE:

Creating a steady stream of new menu ideas on a constant basis can become tedious; look for creative ways to vary your menus with unusual foods and seasonal themes. Be aware that unless you have a degree and the necessary credentials in dietetics you may have difficulty selling your services to some institutions, such as hospitals and schools. Any business that relates to food consumption has legal and health ramifications; be sure to check out your state's licensing requirements before embarking on this career.

PERSONAL SHOPPER

Startup cost:	$500–$1,000
Potential earnings:	$10,000–$35,000
Typical fees:	$20–$40 per hour; you can also charge per job, but that's risky
Advertising:	Brochures, classified ads, personalized notes to busy executives
Qualifications:	An eye for a great deal and the ability to match gifts to personalities
Equipment needed:	Dependable transportation, computer, Internet access
Home business potential:	Yes
Staff required:	No
Hidden costs:	Watch your mileage and be sure that you bill on an hourly rate rather than a per-job basis; otherwise, people may try to take advantage of you and you'll end up losing money

LOWDOWN:

Do you consider yourself to be a "shopping goddess"? Are you able to consistently choose tasteful and well-received gifts? If so, this business could be your dream come true. Many of today's executives are simply too busy to spend an hour or two shopping for the perfect gift, so you can do it for them by offering your services at an hourly rate. You'll need to make sure that the client provides you with some method to purchase the gifts—or arrange for the items to be held for pickup by the client. Build a strong network of places to shop; familiarize yourself with every gift/specialty store, retail store, and florist in your area; surf the Web regularly for mail-order merchandise and gift ideas. You'll need better-than-average shopping experience (and plenty of catalogs) to come up with refreshingly new approaches to gift-giving. Another part of your business might be purchasing items for busy executives themselves. In either case, you'll need to know sizes and personal preferences (colors, styles, brand names, etc.); you may find a computer spreadsheet program handy for keeping track of clients and individual details such as these.

STARTUP:

Brochures and personal notes sent to managers of large corporations are a good way to introduce yourself and your services. Be sure to stress the advantages of using a shopping service (chiefly, the time- and money-saving factors) and be clear about your fees and what they cover (time vs. out-of-pocket costs). Start by collecting catalogs, visiting malls and unusual shops, and combing the newspapers for sales. Your clients will expect you to know good value and where to find it—so take the time to prepare!

BOTTOM LINE ADVICE:

You can choose to work only with individuals and make this a part-time job, but you won't make as much as you would working full-time for large companies. Difficult situations can arise when a client isn't happy with your purchase, so always approach an assignment knowing that you may have to return anything you buy. All in all, however, if you love shopping, the joy of spending someone else's money is hard to resist—it gives you all the pleasure with none of the guilt.

PERSONAL WEIGHT LOSS MANAGEMENT CONSULTANT

Startup cost:	$500–$1,000
Potential earnings:	$20,000–$60,000
Typical fees:	$15–$20 per session, or $600–$1,000 for a 12-week program
Advertising:	Direct mail, brochure, Yellow Pages; networking with physicians, trainers
Qualifications:	Degree and/or background in health, nutrition, or fitness; personal experience in weight loss is desirable; some states may require licensing or certification
Equipment needed:	Computer and printer for preparing menu plans and recipes; phone; tape measure, accurate scale, reference books on diet, nutrition, and exercise, a camera for before and after photos
Home business potential:	Yes
Staff required:	No
Hidden costs:	Insurance, mileage, if you meet with clients off-site

LOWDOWN:

Obesity is a big problem in the United States, and getting bigger. Experts agree that the best approach to combating obesity is a program that combines exercise, nutritional education, behavior modification, and accountability. As a personal weight loss management consultant, you can provide all four as you help overweight adults shed unwanted pounds and improve their overall health and well-being. But wait—what about all the diet books, plans, programs, pills, and supplements that are already out there? You offer something all the rest of those methods do not—personalized attention. You'll work with clients one-on-one to come up with tailor-made diet and exercise plans designed to accommodate their individual schedules, needs, and preferences. You'll get together with your clients once or twice a week, in your home office, to weigh in, set goals, answer questions, assess progress, and address individual concerns.

STARTUP:

Expect to spend between $500 and $1,000 getting your business off the ground. At the very least, you will need business cards, a brochure, a direct mail campaign, and a Yellow Pages ad. Network with physicians and other health care professionals, personal trainers, wellness instructors, and dietitians for referrals. You may want to consider giving talks or writing articles on weight management and healthy lifestyles. Develop a print or online newsletter you can distribute to clients and prospects.

BOTTOM LINE ADVICE:

Require all clients to bring written approval from a physician before agreeing to accept them as clients. Avoid making promises about the number of pounds or inches a client can expect to lose within a specific time. Try not to focus on the numbers; instead, stress the importance of changing behaviors and developing healthy lifestyles. And by all means, practice what you preach.

PETSITTER

Startup cost:	$150–$200
Potential earnings:	$10,000–$25,000
Typical fees:	$15 per day for one pet, one visit; add $5 for every additional pet and/or visit. Additional services such as walking, house training for puppies, or administration of special medications justify additional charges; so do visits on holidays or after-hours.
Advertising:	Word of mouth and referrals; Yellow Pages listing; post fliers at veterinarians' offices, pet supply stores, pet trainers and groomers
Qualifications:	Love of animals; knowledge of basic animal care and first-aid; reliability, organizational skills
Equipment needed:	Reliable vehicle; crate or carrier in case you need to take an animal to the vet; computer, cell phone, answering machine
Home business potential:	Yes (although you will be traveling to pet owners' homes)
Staff required:	No; but designate a back-up in case of emergency
Hidden costs:	Insurance and bonding; emergency trip to the vet

LOWDOWN:

Increasingly, pet owners are looking to petsitters to attend to the dogs, cats, birds, hamsters, rabbits, turtles, fish, potbellied pigs, even lizards and snakes they can't bear to leave but can't take along when they go out of town. If you like animals and know how to care for them, this could be an excellent business for you. You'll need to meet with the owners and their animals in advance to discuss expectations, go over your fees, and get to know the little critters firsthand. You can be picky too—agree to handle just dogs and cats, or animals under a certain size or above a certain age. With most animals, including cats, you can probably get by with just one visit a day; dogs will require two or more so you'll want to price your services accordingly.

STARTUP:

Expect to spend practically nothing to get your petsitting business off the ground. Your first clients will probably be friends who in turn will tell their friends and so on. Network with veterinarians, pet groomers and trainers, even the clerks at pet supply stores. You never know who might soon need to take advantage of your services. You probably won't get rich caring for pets, but with hard work and careful scheduling, you can make a nice chunk of change. And even if you don't, you're still sure to find the work both fun and rewarding.

BOTTOM LINE ADVICE:

While you can probably handle several petsitting assignments at a time, don't get too greedy and overload your schedule so much that you're rushing from one job to the next. You're the only human these pets see all day and they probably miss their owners, so allow a little extra time for play and petting. Keep in mind that your business depends largely on referrals; treat your clients' pets and homes as if they were your own. Maintain a list of emergency numbers and know how to reach your clients, just in case. Get to know other petsitters, too, so you can swap jobs when you want to go out of town yourself or need a backup in the event of a personal emergency.

PLANT MAINTENANCE SERVICE

Startup cost:	$800–$1,000
Potential earnings:	$10,000–$60,000
Typical fees:	$25–$50 per day; some work on monthly retainers of $500 and up
Advertising:	Referrals, Yellow Pages, direct mail, affiliations with nursery businesses
Qualifications:	Knowledge of plants' requirements
Equipment needed:	Portable ladder, watering cans/mister, pruners, scissors, fertilizer, soil, vehicle for traveling to client businesses
Home business potential:	Yes
Staff required:	No
Hidden costs:	Gas to get you from one client to the next

LOWDOWN:

Interior plantings are more popular in some parts of the country than in others, but almost all large businesses maintain some kind of greenery to soften their offices. Once you show these organizations that you can care for their plants and make them stay healthy and attractive, you will have the opportunity to develop an ongoing business that brings you a steady income stream.

STARTUP:

Startup costs are minimal. You will need a few tools of the trade, such as a watering can and scissors, a car or truck to drive from client to client, and perhaps some business cards that you can leave near the plants to generate more business. Most larger plant maintenance services charge a flat monthly rate of $500 or more; if you're smaller, however, this will likely be a part-time job, earning you between $25 and $50, per client, per day.

BOTTOM LINE ADVICE:

This is definitely a business for plant lovers. If you enjoy making things grow (and you're good at it), you'll find plant maintenance to be a rewarding enterprise. However, there isn't much change from day to day, although you are in and out of different environments as you go from customer to customer. This is not a business for people who thrive on excitement—and not exactly a get-rich-quick enterprise, either.

PRIVATE TUTOR

Startup cost:	$500
Potential earnings:	$15,000–$20,000
Typical fees:	$15–$60 per hour
Advertising:	Classified ads, Yellow Pages, word of mouth, networking (school principals are a good place to start)
Qualifications:	Teaching experience or degree in area of expertise
Equipment needed:	Educational materials, textbooks; desks, computers, and supplies if you plan to tutor in your home
Home business potential:	Yes
Staff required:	None
Hidden costs:	Watch your mileage

LOWDOWN:

Increases in class size and stiffer competition for college admission means that many students are falling behind. Your services may be needed to bring a struggling student up to speed or to help a teenager get a higher score on his or her college entrance exam—and the best part about this type of business is that it's recession-proof! As long as there are students, there will be a strong need for capable individuals to guide them to scholastic success. Determine where your expertise lies (is it in history? English? mathematics?) and meet with teachers in this subject area or their principals to ask for referrals. Once you get a few clients, word of mouth will grow your business, and you may find that you need to network with other tutors to build referral systems of your own. As a tutor you will start out with each client (student) by finding out his or her needs (probably in a written report from a teacher), then develop lesson plans tailored to address those needs. Be as creative as you like; your challenge is to make the lessons interesting and to empower each student so that every success feels like his or her own.

STARTUP:

To be a good inspiration to your student, you'll need to demonstrate your own willingness to learn. You can start by building a good personal library of used textbooks (preferably with teacher's guides) as well as several books on learning challenges and motivation to succeed. Your only other startup cost will be advertising (classified and Yellow Pages ads), which will generally stay under $500.

BOTTOM LINE ADVICE:

Encouraging a young student's success while fostering a thirst for knowledge can be richly rewarding if you are genuinely interested in education. Helping a student overcome what seemed like an obstacle offers you—and the rest of the world—optimism about your own possibilities. Aside from an occasional obnoxious child, what's there to not like about that? Since you'll most likely be taking your tutoring to the student, do pay attention to your mileage; adjust your hourly fees to cover it as needed.

PROFESSIONAL ORGANIZER

Startup cost:	$500–$1,000
Potential earnings:	$25,000–$45,000
Typical fees:	$35–$85 per hour, or per-project ($1,000 to organize an executive's office, for example)
Advertising:	Contribute articles or a regular column to your local newspapers on time management and organizing space; direct mail coupons; conduct seminars through local community continuing education; network
Qualifications:	You must be a highly organized person by nature, with a drive for efficiency; knowledge of systems, furniture, products, supplies, and accessories is a must
Equipment needed:	Pager or cell phone, computer, Internet access
Home business potential:	Yes
Staff required:	No
Hidden costs:	Mileage and phone bills

LOWDOWN:

Are you the kind of person who thrives on having a place for everything and everything in its place? This could be the business for you. Professional organizers, although a relatively new breed, are in ever-greater demand. You can bill yourself as a organizational generalist, but you may find it more efficient to specialize in one of five areas: space planning (organizing office arrangement of furniture, traffic, lighting, noise, and leisure space); time management (setting goals, developing action plans, scheduling, and delegating tasks); paper management (organizing the steady flow of information materials by setting up filing and retrieval systems, sometimes with the aid of a computer); clutter control (finding the proper and efficient placement of things to keep clutter to a minimum); closet/storage design (organizing closet and storage space). Choose one or two and market your services accordingly. This business would be most likely to thrive in highly urban areas where busy professionals want their homes to run as smoothly as their offices.

STARTUP:

Since what you'll be selling is your time and expertise, your startup expenses will be minimal, in the neighborhood of $500 or so for business cards and perhaps a promotional brochure that you can leave with the prospects you call on. You'll get most of your clients through word-of-mouth and networking. Don't bother with a direct mail campaign. The people who need your services are likely to set your letter aside for later consideration and lose it in the clutter; you'd do better to focus on face-to-face contact. You'll need places to put the "stuff" you organize, so begin collecting catalogs and surfing Web sites for the supplies you might need—boxes, baskets, cabinets, shelving, and the like.

BOTTOM LINE ADVICE:

Consider aligning yourself with the National Association of Professional Organizers; at the very least, consult the Web site (*www.napo.net*) for more information and tips on becoming a professional organizer. Approach your local newspaper or business journal about becoming a columnist or regular contributor and consider conducting seminars in your community.

REAL ESTATE AGENT/ HOME RESEARCHER

Startup cost:	$500–$1,000
Potential earnings:	$25,000–$40,000
Typical fees:	$25–$65 per hour
Advertising:	Yellow Pages, memberships in local business and charitable organizations, local newspapers, penny savers, referrals from real estate agencies
Qualifications:	Real estate license
Equipment needed:	Cell phone, computer, printer, fax, copier,
Home business potential:	Yes
Staff required:	No
Hidden costs:	Travel, marketing

LOWDOWN:

If you enjoy the field of residential real estate, but hate the nitty-gritty details of closing a sale, consider zeroing in on just one aspect of the real estate agent's job: home research. As a home researcher, you will thoroughly research the market rather than see the entire real estate sale through to closing. You will develop a range of choices based on a comprehensive interview with the buyer(s). The information you glean from that interview, along with your knowledge of the community and subsequent research into the properties available, will give your clients—the agent and buyer—an opportunity to plan, clarify wants and needs, and consider the financial implications of a particular real estate purchase. It is reassuring for a family preparing to make a transcontinental move to know the choices available to them within their price range, and the types of neighborhoods they might consider in an unfamiliar community. Your job, essentially, is to match your clients to their "perfect" home. Unlike the real estate agent, you don't have a financial stake in selling a particular property to your client. Nor are you like a relocation specialist; your territory is limited to your own immediate community. You provide information on the homes in your specific geographic area as opposed to helping clients relocate anywhere around the country.

STARTUP:

Startup costs are low (you could get by for $500), but your marketing efforts will be ongoing unless referrals or subcontracting can bring you adequate business. With hard work and persistence, you can easily earn $25,000–$40,000 annually.

BOTTOM LINE ADVICE:

You will need to prove, consistently, that your services add value, don't threaten agents, and make sense to transferees. Keeping good records of your effectiveness and feedback from families for whom you have found the "perfect" home will support your marketing efforts. This is a good choice for someone who loves houses and enjoys thinking about what type of family would choose each one, but who finds the "sale" process unappealing. As a home researcher you can create a service that suits your real estate interests while providing a valuable service for your clients.

REMINDER SERVICE

Startup cost:	Under $1,000 ($500 to cover fliers and advertising); add $1,500 if you buy a computer
Potential earnings:	$10,000–$25,000
Typical fees:	An initial set-up fee of $75–$100, then $20–$35 per month; or, $35–$65 per hour
Advertising:	Bulletin boards, direct mail, networking at business meetings
Qualifications:	Strong organizational and time-management skills
Equipment needed:	Computer and software program with built-in reminders, a PDA or detailed planning system, cell phone
Home business potential:	Yes
Staff required:	No (although you may want someone to cover the late shift and your vacations)
Hidden costs:	Telephone costs may be high if you're not careful; also, be sure to keep accurate records for billing purposes

LOWDOWN:

If you consider yourself exceptionally well-organized and have the ability to stay on top of a million details at once, then setting up a reminder service will come naturally to you. Your days will consist of talking with clients to determine the scope of their needs, entering their data into a computerized tracking system, and keeping on top of what you need to remind them of and when. Set regular hours to maintain continuity; this cannot be a job that you work at only when you feel like it. Also, since many of your customers are too busy to remember important details of their lives (such as when to pay bills, birth dates of family and friends, and other such data), they may forget to pay you. You will probably want to collect at least half of your fee up front, offering standard hourly rates and/or specific packages geared toward themes. For instance, you could offer a "Birthday Blitz" package, where the only service the customer buys from you is that of being reminded of important birthdays as they occur throughout the year.

STARTUP:

There are quite a few good time-management and reminder-type software packages out there, so do yourself a favor and buy the best one you can afford. You'll also need a powerful computer; expect to spend about $1,500 for the hardware. Once your computer is up and running, your only major expenses will be for marketing materials (fliers and business cards).

BOTTOM LINE ADVICE:

Helping others keep track of the important details of their lives, both personally and professionally, can be interesting work, but you'll never get rich from it. Nor will you be allowed to make mistakes. Mess up once by forgetting to remind your client of an important meeting or, even worse, his wife's birthday, and your business could go down the tubes. That's why you should protect yourself with a good software program that will automatically remember what you might be apt to forget.

ROOMMATE REFERRAL SERVICE

Startup cost:	$500–$1,000
Potential earnings:	$10,000–$25,000
Typical fees:	20 to 50 percent of one month's rent
Advertising:	Yellow Pages, fliers at apartment complexes, coin-operated laundries, coffee shops, and supermarkets, newspaper classified ads
Qualifications:	Excellent organizational skills, ability to "read" people
Equipment needed:	Database management software, computer, e-mail, printer, phone, credit card processing equipment
Home business potential:	Yes, but you will need a place to meet with clients
Staff required:	No
Hidden costs:	Liability insurance

LOWDOWN:

With the rising cost of living in many major cities, and the rise in displaced folks who need to share rent with the ideal roommate, you could make a fine living playing matchmaker for live-ins. Ideally, you would have a method for screening each of the candidates (character references and police background checks at the very least) and a method for securing your payment ahead of time (credit card processing equipment would be helpful; accepting personal checks is risky). Advertise in places where the people looking for a place to live are likely to hang out, and you'll have found your special niche. Develop a good questionnaire that really asks the kinds of questions a potential roommate would want answered. To boost your income potential, consider offering other services such as mediation between "rumblin'" roomies and budget development assistance. The best advice is to focus on the roommate referral aspect first, then branch out your services as your business grows. And don't limit your market to "twentysomethings"; newly single middle-agers and seniors on fixed incomes may need roommates too.

STARTUP:

Your costs are incredibly low when compared to most other businesses, mainly because you can create your own fliers to post in noticeable, highly trafficked areas. With low overhead, most of your income ($10,000–$20,000) will be sheer profit, a perk that makes this an attractive opportunity.

BOTTOM LINE ADVICE:

Be sure you carefully screen your applicants—bad matches are sure to happen you if you don't.

Scrapbooker

Startup cost:	$150 or less
Potential earnings:	$3,000–$6,000
Typical fees:	Flat fee of $150–$200 to design and assemble each scrapbook; or hourly rate of $15–$20+ materials
Advertising:	Word-of-mouth/referrals; post fliers at places where busy moms are likely to be
Qualifications:	Creative ability; knowledge of scrapbooking supplies and experience in various scrapbook designs and techniques
Equipment needed:	Scissors, glue, felt-tip pens, stickers, and other scrapbooking supplies; computer so that you can access the Web sites of *Simply Scrapbooks* magazine and other scrapbookers for ideas
Home business potential:	Yes
Staff required:	No
Hidden costs:	Make sure you include the cost of supplies in your fees; don't dip into your personal supplies unless you charge for them

LOWDOWN:

Every few years a new crafts craze comes along and the latest one is scrapbooking. If you have a knack for creating scrapbook pages that tell a story and catch the eye, and if you know your way around the materials that will keep family mementos in archival condition over generations to come, then you can open up shop as a professional scrapbooker. Your clients will be moms and grandmoms who yearn to have a meaningful memory book, but are too busy juggling career and family responsibilities to sit down and make one on their own. After a face-to-face meeting to bounce around a few ideas, you'll walk away with that empty album, blank scrapbook pages, plastic protectors, and the box of loose photos, souvenirs, journal pages, and other miscellaneous "stuff" this busy mom or grandmom has collected. A month or so later you'll return with a beautifully designed, fully assembled scrapbook. What job could be easier or more fun?

STARTUP:

You'll need very little money to launch your scrapbooking venture. The bulk of your supplies will come from your clients; the rest—like scissors, stickers, and glue—you undoubtedly already have on hand. Most of your business will come by word-of-mouth. Paid advertising would be a waste of money, but you might put together a simple flier and post it at craft stores or places where busy moms are likely to be—day care centers, pediatricians' offices, kids' consignment shops, and the like.

BOTTOM LINE ADVICE:

You probably already enjoy scrapbooking and are good at it, or you wouldn't consider this as a possible business venture. You might make a couple thousand dollars a year helping others complete their scrapbooks or create them from scratch, but don't expect this to be a big moneymaker or a lasting craft craze. Sure, quilting and knitting have been around for generations, but scrapbooking? Only time will tell. In the meantime, enjoy the ride.

SILK FLOWER ARRANGER

Startup cost:	$500–$1,000
Potential earnings:	$20,000–$50,000
Typical fees:	$25–$300
Advertising:	Yellow Pages, newspapers, bridal salons, restaurants
Qualifications:	Some training with flower arranging, creativity
Equipment needed:	Phone, floral accessories (vases, baskets, floral tape, access to a wide variety of silk flowers); you may also need a vehicle for deliveries
Home business potential:	Yes
Staff required:	No
Hidden costs:	Watch materials costs

LOWDOWN:

There's nothing in the world like fresh flowers, but they only last a short while. That's why silk flowers have become the mainstays of interior decorating; with little or no care, they retain their beauty for years. You'll have plenty of customers for your services, from brides who don't want to worry about wilting bouquets, to mourners who want to give the bereaved family a lasting token of their remembrance. You'll stay busy, putting together the arrangements that have been ordered by your customers, but you'll have to work hard to get some business, since there are plenty of other silk flower arrangers out there. Think about what makes you different, and let your customers know your unique marketing point. Network with funeral homes, churches, bridal shops, hospitals, and interior decorators for cross-marketing opportunities. Display your wares at bridal, home, and craft shows.

STARTUP:

Obtain a vendor's license (approximately $25) so you can buy your supplies at a wholesale store. Check with local craft stores to see if they offer additional discounts to customers with vendor's licenses. Invest a few hundred dollars up front in floral supplies and silk flowers so you can make arrangements to display and sell at craft shows. And be sure to set aside the money for booth space rental ($25–$100). Your products can be priced anywhere from $25–$300 depending on their size and complexity.

BOTTOM LINE ADVICE:

Gain experience by working with florists or taking classes at craft stores. Once you have some knowledge of floral arranging, sign up to sell your goods at holiday craft fairs. Always have plenty of business cards/brochures to accompany each sale, and keep an album with pictures of your work to show prospective clients.

STORYTELLER

Startup cost:	$100–$500
Potential earnings:	$5,000–$15,000
Typical fees:	$15–$25 per storytelling event
Advertising:	Boards of education, day care centers, libraries
Qualifications:	Ability to tell and retell stories with enthusiasm
Equipment needed:	None (except a great archive of stories)
Home business potential:	Yes
Staff required:	No
Hidden costs:	Books

LOWDOWN:

Do you have a flair for telling (and retelling) stories? Can you paint pictures in listeners' minds as they hear every exciting detail? You may be skilled in the ancient art of story-telling; it's a tradition that's been popular since before Homer's *Odyssey*. Now, storytellers for children are especially popular; many schools regularly bring in professional storytell-ers and parents increasingly hire them for parties and special events. Storytelling isn't just reading well from a book; it's memorizing the stories, adding your own personal touches where necessary, and enlivening them in a way only you can do. You'll need a good repertoire of stories to choose from, and you'll have to practice regularly to ensure that your vocal abilities and versatility stay up to the job. More than likely, this will be a part-time business opportunity; you won't make a lot of money, but you're sure to find it rewarding in other ways.

STARTUP:

You'll have virtually no startup cost except business cards or fliers and the books from which you'll glean your tantalizing tales. Spend about $100–$500 on these items and subscribe to magazines that contain storytelling tips and/or new stories. At $15–$25 a pop, this is not a get-rich opportunity, but if you really love storytelling, the joy of sharing with your audience, most of whom will be children, will be reward enough.

BOTTOM LINE ADVICE:

Get involved with libraries in your area that feature children's activities. Place your busi-ness card at toy stores and bakeries—in short, anywhere parents might go to make arrangements for a child's birthday party.

STRESS MANAGEMENT COUNSELOR

Startup cost:	$500–$1,500
Potential earnings:	$50,000–$65,000
Typical fees:	$25–$65 per session
Advertising:	Newspapers, magazines, bulletin boards, associations, physician referral, direct mail
Qualifications:	Some states require certification or license
Equipment needed:	Materials such as books, videos, audio tapes
Home business potential:	Yes
Staff required:	No
Hidden costs:	Certification can cost you anywhere from $200–$500, depending on your area. Also, corporate clients may have a 45-day payment delay policy, which can play havoc with your cash flow; insist on at least 50 percent in advance

LOWDOWN:

In the high-tech, high-intensity, fast-paced twenty-first century, we're all stressed out to the max—and that's why stress management counselors are cropping up everywhere, from churches and schools to corporate America. Large companies hire such professionals to keep their employees sound, sane, and productive—recognizing that a well-balanced worker is as much as 45 percent more effective on the job. As a stress management counselor, you'll work with individuals and groups, assessing problem areas and using innovative, inspiring materials and exercises to help your clients perform at their happiest, healthiest best.

STARTUP:

Considering the widespread need for stress management, you may be tempted to promote your services to literally hundreds of people; your marketing efforts will be more effective, however, if you pinpoint your top 50 or so prospects and exhaust your efforts there before moving on to capture the attention of the rest of the world. Buy or develop your own list of human resources professionals to whom you can mail your information—and don't forget to secure a vendor's license if you plan to offer resource materials for sale.

BOTTOM LINE ADVICE:

You'll feed off of the creative energy you generate by helping others solve stress problems; the more you work with stressed-out individuals and groups, the easier it will become for you to quickly identify what's working and what's not. Sadly, after a few years of practicing intense stress counseling on others, you may burn out yourself . . . make sure you have a support person who can help you maintain perspective and remind you to practice on yourself what you preach to your clients.

TASTE TESTER FOR FOOD COMPANIES

Startup cost:	$500
Potential earnings:	$10,000–$15,000 (most work part-time hours)
Typical fees:	$15–$25 per hour
Advertising:	Direct mail to food product manufacturers
Qualifications:	A good culinary sense and discerning tastebuds
Equipment needed:	None
Home business potential:	Yes
Staff required:	No
Hidden costs:	Mileage can become a problem; make certain that you are reimbursed or that you have covered any out-of-pocket costs in your pricing structure

LOWDOWN:

This is the ultimate dream job for anyone who loves food! Companies that manufacture and package food products often employ individuals outside of the company as taste testers. And although this is not a particularly lucrative field, it can be an interesting and satisfying one, filled with variety. As a taste tester, you will sample new or improved food products and record your impressions, usually on a predesigned checklist supplied by the company. You may be asked to wear a blindfold for some tests, while others will require only a simple thumbs-up or thumbs-down. It is important that you be able to communicate to others the palatability of food; its taste, texture, and desirability are all of critical importance to the developers of new food products and the professionals who market them.

STARTUP:

Invest in a comprehensive list of companies that manufacture and/or package food items and you're off to a great start! With as little as an introductory letter detailing your interest in becoming a taste tester, you can let companies know of your availability. Be sure to include your special qualifications (such as having worked in a restaurant, or as a professional chef). Since you will rarely be allowed to taste the food in your own home, you will need to have dependable transportation for trips to and from company sites.

BOTTOM LINE ADVICE:

While working as a food tester can be easy to digest, it can also cause heartburn if you are seeking to build a large nest egg. Nowhere will you find a wealthy taste tester basking in his or her just desserts. Still, if financial reward isn't as necessary or important to you as job satisfaction, you can really sink your teeth into this small business opportunity. The menu's pretty good, and the hours aren't all that bad, either.

TRAVEL CONSULTANT

Startup cost:	$250–$500
Potential earnings:	$10,000–$20,000
Typical fees:	$50–$100 per hour
Advertising:	Word of mouth/referrals, networking with travel agents
Qualifications:	Extensive travel experience, especially overseas; strong organizational skills, attention to detail; foreign language fluency is desirable but not absolutely essential
Equipment needed:	Computer and printer, Internet access
Home business potential:	Yes
Staff required:	No
Hidden costs:	Long-distance charges for phone calls and faxes; deposits required to hold reservations

LOWDOWN:

If you've done a fair amount of travel on your own in foreign countries, have a knack for finding those out-of-the-way places and people that make a trip so memorable, and would like to share your experience with others who are bound for distant shores, you're a perfect candidate to become a travel consultant. Using your firsthand knowledge of a particular city, country, or region, combined with research you do on the Internet and in guidebooks, you'll create customized travel itineraries for clients who are willing to pay you $50–$100 per hour to do so. Depending on the needs of your client, you may put together everything from a one-page overview of must-see churches in Milan to a detailed, hour-by-hour itinerary for a three-week driving tour of southern Italy. You may or may not be asked to book rental cars or accommodations, but be prepared just in case, and adjust your rates accordingly to cover the cost of long-distance phone calls, faxes, and deposits. Since you are not a bona fide travel agent, it's unlikely you will qualify for commissions.

STARTUP:

Assuming you already have a computer and Internet access, you'll need only a small amount of money to get started. Network by asking everyone you know if they know someone who could use your expertise; your clients will come to you largely by word-of-mouth. You might also try contacting a few travel agents for referrals. You could also try hanging around the travel guidebook section of your favorite bookstores and striking up conversations.

BOTTOM LINE ADVICE:

Anyone with a computer can put together a pretty complete travel itinerary these days. You'll want to set yourself apart by offering services and expertise no one else can. Take the time to get to know your client and be ready to make those special suggestions that show you understand and appreciate his or her unique preferences and traveling style. You'll want to know your destinations backwards and forwards, of course, so be prepared to plow much of your income right back into your own personal travel fund.

VACATION RENTALS BROKER

Startup cost:	$500–$1,000
Potential earnings:	$45,000–$60,000
Typical fees:	Usually a percentage rental income, typically 10 to 15 percent
Advertising:	Advertising in real estate magazines and real estate section of newspaper, Yellow Pages, referrals, Web site
Qualifications:	Experience in real estate rentals, good organizational skills
Equipment needed:	A basic office setup for record keeping
Home business potential:	Yes
Staff required:	No
Hidden costs:	Insurance, vehicle maintenance

LOWDOWN:

A vacation rentals broker keeps track of all the details related to renting property for absentee owners. Many people with second homes rent them for the better part of the year, reserving a week or two for themselves and their families. Renting helps defray the cost of maintaining an additional residence, but it also can create a number of headaches and problems that are difficult for an absentee owner to deal with. On behalf of the owner, your service finds the renters, writes the rental contract, and makes sure that agreements are carried out, and that the property is protected. You dispense the keys, collect the rent, check for damages, answer the million and one questions renters always have, and just generally keep an eye on things.

STARTUP:

Your startup costs are minimal; you simply need an effective way to keep track of information and money. Since your business depends directly on how much time you put into it, expect to earn as much as you are willing to work for (and that could be anywhere from $45,000–$60,000 or more).

BOTTOM LINE ADVICE:

Consider becoming a vacation rentals broker if you live in an area that has a high appeal for renters and a large stock of available summer (or winter) homes to rent; the Florida Gulf coast, the Outer Banks of North Carolina, and Colorado's ski country are prime examples. Once you develop a reputation for dependability, referrals from satisfied clients will bring other homeowners to you. The amount of advertising you need to do will vary depending on your area and the presence or absence of competing services; for widest possible reach, a Web site is essential.

WELLNESS INSTRUCTOR

Startup cost:	$500–$1,500
Potential earnings:	$25,000–$40,000
Typical fees:	$25–$50 per hour
Advertising:	Human resource association newsletters, Yellow Pages
Qualifications:	Some states require certification
Equipment needed:	Computer, copier, fax, phone, pager or cell phone
Home business potential:	Yes
Staff required:	No
Hidden costs:	Photocopying materials for classes can add up—be sure to include them in your price or cost analysis

LOWDOWN:

Rising medical costs have driven many companies to wellness programs as a preventive measure for cost containment. You can provide seminars for these companies on topics such as stress-reducing foods, the importance of drinking water throughout the day, and even breathing exercises. You'll rely on resource materials such as audiocassettes, books, videos, and DVDs that give added credibility to what you teach. The fact is, most of us are leading potentially destructive lifestyles (drinking too much caffeine and smoking, for example); we need to be given some instruction in our lives to conquer these bad habits. As a wellness instructor, your job will be to help clear out the cobwebs in mind, body, and spirit—and to do it in such a way that your students feel empowered to tackle their own bugaboos.

STARTUP:

You can start a healthy business with a minimal investment if you have the right credentials (a degree in nursing, social work, psychology, exercise physiology, or some related field). Advertising will initially cost you in the neighborhood of $500–$1,000, because you need to be where human resource managers and other professionals can readily find you (more specifically, in their trade association newsletters). One easy way to get your foot in the door is to attend professional functions (local, regional, or national) and pass out your brochure or business card; most associations will allow nonmembers to attend meetings at a slightly higher cost than members. Take advantage—and promote the positive benefits of your work! You might also try advertising in your local newspaper or business journal and post fliers at community centers and health clubs.

BOTTOM LINE ADVICE:

Inspiring others to take charge of their lives and play active roles in their health and longevity can be a richly rewarding field. But you'll need to make sure you follow your own rules; be a good role model and never, ever let them see you sweat!

STARTUPS BETWEEN $1,000 AND $5,000

ABSTRACTING SERVICE

Startup cost:	$2,500–$8,000
Potential earnings:	$25,000–$45,000 per year
Typical fees:	At least $5–$15 per article (full abstract with index)
Advertising:	Solicit database publishers, corporations, respond to newspaper ads for abstract work
Qualifications:	Knowledge in the areas you are abstracting, ability to research a wide range of topics, ability to organize and consolidate data, good writing and communication skills, knowledge of database services and CD-ROM publishers
Equipment needed:	Computer and high-speed Internet access, fax, printer, scanner, copier, word processing software, a comfortable chair, reference books, dictionaries
Home business potential:	Yes
Staff required:	No
Hidden costs:	Abstracting can be highly labor intensive, so be mindful of your time, especially when researching online

LOWDOWN:

Abstracters read and summarize articles from various publications, then store the data on a computer. Some abstracters also index the articles by key words or terms that help the computer locate them quickly. Abstracters may specialize in areas such as engineering, science, and other technical fields; some work in medical and legal fields. A keen interest in reading is very important to your success, as is the ability to retain what you read. Good writing skills and knowledge of the topics you are abstracting is essential, especially for condensing the material. This business could stand alone or fit well with an existing editorial services or technical writing business. If you don't have actual paid experience as an abstracter, you can select articles of interest to certain potential clients, create a portfolio of samples, and pitch your services to them. You might also talk with database publishers to discuss how you might help them, and vice versa.

STARTUP:

Aside from basic computer equipment and word processing software, you need little other than office furniture and reference books to get started. Your business can be launched for as little as $2,500. Charge $5–$15 per article; those with knowledge/experience in a specific scientific discipline, such as chemistry, may command higher fees.

BOTTOM LINE ADVICE:

Many larger corporations, in particular, rely on abstracting services to keep them updated about their competitors and innovations in products and services relating to their businesses. This work allows considerable flexibility in your schedule and requires only a modest investment. Abstracting demands great concentration and careful organization, but also exposes you to a wealth of knowledge and contacts. In addition, you will have the satisfaction of knowing that your work provides a valuable service to your clients.

ACCOUNTANT

Startup cost:	$2,000–$6,000
Potential earnings:	$25,000–$80,000
Typical fees:	$35 and up per hour, or flat fee for specific services such as tax preparation or auditing
Advertising:	Networking through membership and active participation in community groups, Yellow Pages, ads in newspapers and publications for local fundraisers, referrals
Qualifications:	College degree, CPA, some experience in the specific services on which you choose to focus
Equipment needed:	Computer, spreadsheet and accounting software, printer, fax, copier, scanner, Internet access, calculator
Home business potential:	Yes
Staff required:	No
Hidden costs:	Errors and omissions insurance, subscriptions and membership dues, continuing education

LOWDOWN:

Virtually everyone understands the importance of accounting. The challenge comes in showing potential clients how you can improve their lives by helping them better manage their financial affairs and convincing them to pay you for the privilege. Solo accountants generally take one of two approaches: They either work with individuals on tax issues and personal financial planning, or they serve the burgeoning small business market with bookkeeping setup, payroll, tax planning, and all the other financial activities that business enterprises require. Accounting is a rather crowded field and you will need to be creative in order to distinguish yourself from the pack. Start by asking the following questions: How are my accounting services better than those of the six other accountants who have called a particular business this week looking for work? How can I show an individual that I can serve him or her better than the big storefront operations ?

STARTUP:

Will you meet clients in your office, or will you travel to their homes or businesses? These decisions will directly impact your startup costs, which could be as little as $2,000 depending on how much hardware/software and advertising you need to purchase to get up and running. With the right combination of effective networking and carefully placed ads, you can expect earnings of $25,000 or more your first year.

BOTTOM LINE ADVICE:

Being an excellent accountant and being able to establish a profitable business require two entirely different sets of skills. Your education focused largely on numbers; now, as an entrepreneur, you'll need to hone your people skills as well. You'll have a leg up if you've worked for a large firm and have experience in servicing clients. Gaining the confidence of potential clients requires more than excellent accounting abilities. You'll need to present your services in a way that appeals to people who want your help but don't really understand numbers. You can make a nice living as an accountant, but be aware that there is a seasonality to your services; you'll be busiest in December (year-end for most businesses) and during tax season in March and April.

ADVICE FROM THE EXPERTS

What sets your business apart from others like it?

Personalized service and affordable rates are what set apart the business owned by Kelly M. Zimmerman, CPA, in Cuyahoga Falls, Ohio. "I take a genuine interest in my clients' businesses. I really care about whether or not they succeed."

Things you couldn't do without:

Zimmerman says she couldn't do without a computer, telephone, and calculator.

Marketing tips/advice:

"Get involved in an organization that you believe in personally and where you can also promote your business. Marketing for accountants is basically word of mouth, so be sure to do everything you can to keep your current clients happy. They'll send you more clients if they know you've gone out of your way for them."

If you had to do it all over again . . .

"I would try to be more organized and focused on the types of clients I really want to serve."

ADOPTION SEARCH SERVICE

Startup cost:	$2,000–$3,000
Potential earnings:	$25,000–$40,000
Typical fees:	$150–$250 per job or an hourly fee of $20–$35 per hour
Advertising:	Yellow Pages, referrals from social service agencies and associations
Qualifications:	Experience in the field; sensitivity; understanding of state laws, rules, and records regarding adoption; persistence; a social work background is helpful but not required
Equipment needed:	Computer, printer, copier, scanner, Internet access, telephone
Home business potential:	Yes
Staff required:	No
Hidden costs:	Phone bills; some searches can take longer than others so watch your time to make sure you are adequately compensated

LOWDOWN:

Adoption search services provide opportunities for birth children or birth parents to retrace the steps that separated them from their blood relatives and reconnect. This is a challenging business, still entangled with complex regulations that vary from state to state and subject to the infinite variations of human nature. While many reunions are filled with joy, not all discoveries are happy ones and some people would rather not be found. Keep in mind, too, that a vocal minority of the population strongly opposes the adoption search process and you may be subject to some harassment. Overall, however, bridging the chasm caused by adoption decisions can be a viable service and, ultimately, a profitable small business.

STARTUP:

Although some of the searching process may be done online, the telephone and shoe leather will be your major tools. Expect to spend $2,000–$3,000 to equip your office with a good computer, printer, copier, and scanner; opt for a high-speed Internet connection to make your online searches quicker. Charge a flat rate of $150–$250 if your client provides some information for you to go on, but watch your time to make sure you are adequately compensated. If the job looks like it might turn into a wild-goose chase, consider an hourly rate plus related expenses instead; $20–$35 per hour is not unreasonable.

BOTTOM LINE ADVICE:

Marketing will be one of your biggest challenges. How will adoptees and birth parents come to know about your service? And since you won't be getting repeat business from your clients, you'll have to continually pay attention to your marketing to ensure a steady stream of business. Linking people often heals old and painful sores, so you are likely to get more than monetary rewards from your successful searches. On the other hand, the sudden reappearance of a son or daughter who was put up for adoption years ago can reopen a wound that had partially healed. Before you launch an adoption search service, stop and ask yourself this: How will turning someone's life around, for good or ill, affect me? Can I handle the consequences?

ADVERTISING SALES REPRESENTATIVE

Startup cost:	$2,000–$5,000
Potential earnings:	$40,000–$150,000
Typical fees:	Commission-only is standard; commissions range from 5 to 25 percent
Advertising:	Direct mail, trade journals, referrals
Qualifications:	Experience with an advertising agency or as a newspaper/magazine advertising sales rep
Equipment needed:	Computer, printer, copier, Internet access, cell phone, media directories, vehicle
Home business potential:	Yes
Staff required:	No
Hidden costs:	Expect high phone bills and mileage costs; subscriptions to media directories are costly, too.

LOWDOWN:

This business can best be built if you already have extensive experience in the field of advertising sales. Your expertise lies in matching the client's need to ad space availability. If you know how, you can sell ad space in several magazines and newspapers to the advertisers who need it. Your job is to find a buyer who might never have discovered this advertising venue unaided and present him or her with a good price. You'll need contacts and experience to make a success of this enterprise, but there's plenty of room for the independent rep and, possibly, good money to be made ($100,000 or more). Much depends on the specific publications for which you are selling ad space; for instance, if you're selling ads in a prestigious trade journal or nationally circulated consumer magazine, your income can be quite high. However, if you're selling ads for a community newspaper with a limited circulation, your income may reach its peak at $35,000.

STARTUP:

The telephone is your primary tool, and you will probably want both a land line and cell phone. You'll need access to reference books, such as those available from Standard Rate and Data Service, which list newspapers and periodicals, along with circulation figures, advertising rates, and closing dates. A year's subscription to the SRDS directories in just one category (i.e., consumer magazines, trade journals, daily newspapers, etc.) runs around $750. Expect to spend a minimum of $2,000 and probably more to get this business up and running.

BOTTOM LINE ADVICE:

If you love to sell, you'll love this business; it's selling in its purest form. No limitations bind you to one focus, one time, or one perspective. Businesses need to advertise, and finding space for their commercial messages can be both delightful and challenging. Your services are the perfect answer to their needs. The prevailing "but we've always done it this way" attitude will likely be your biggest obstacle. Established advertising agencies are your competitors, and you will need to market your services vigorously.

Aquarium Maintenance and Setup

Startup cost:	$1,000–$2,000 (but may rise significantly if you need to purchase a vehicle)
Potential earnings:	$15,000–$30,000
Typical fees:	$25–$65 per job (depending on tank size)
Advertising:	Fliers, bulletin boards, Yellow Pages
Qualifications:	Knowledge of freshwater and saltwater fish and aquarium maintenance and setup
Equipment needed:	Cleaning equipment, including nets, tongs, siphons, and algae pads; buckets, plastic tarps, and towels; saltwater test kits; fish food; a vehicle to haul it all around
Home business potential:	Yes, but your actual work will be on-site
Staff required:	No
Hidden costs:	Vehicle costs, mileage

LOWDOWN:

This is a great business opportunity for a person with the right combination of patience and enthusiasm for underwater creatures and self-marketing ability. Aquariums, whether freshwater or saltwater, are lovely to look at, but they can require a surprisingly high level of maintenance. The tanks must be cleaned regularly, replenished with fresh water, and treated with chemicals to ensure that the fish remain healthy. Your clients will be those businesses and individuals who love their fish, but would appreciate being relieved of the tiresome, ongoing chore of caring for them and their environment. Experience caring for your own fish, or prior work in a store that sells fish and aquarium supplies, will help you recognize the needs of each aquarium that you service.

STARTUP:

Startup costs are minimal for a maintenance service; if you already have a vehicle, you can probably equip your business for around $1,000. Your costs will increase if you decide to move into sales and setup of aquarium equipment. You should charge $25–$65 per cleaning job, and remember to include your mileage as overhead; out-of-pocket costs for saltwater test kits, fish food, and medications, if needed, should be passed on to your clients.

BOTTOM LINE ADVICE:

This can be a nice part-time job for a self-starter. Many people are simply happy with the opportunity to earn a little extra money from their hobby. If you live in a metropolitan area where many businesses are likely to have aquariums and you are willing to pound the pavement in search of clients, you can earn a full-time living at this. For maximum efficiency, be sure to plan your service calls so you don't spend too much time traveling between clients or backtracking from one side of town to the other on any one given day. Remember, too, that marketing your services will take up a significant amount of your time.

ARBITRATION SERVICE

Startup cost:	$2,000–$6,000
Potential earnings:	$40,000–$75,000
Typical fees:	$35–$65 per hour
Advertising:	Referrals from courts and law firms; Yellow Pages; memberships in legal, business, and community organizations
Qualifications:	Law degree, extensive experience in arbitration, ability to market and sell your services
Equipment needed:	Computer, Internet access, fax, cell phone, printer, copier, scanner
Home business potential:	Yes
Staff required:	No
Hidden costs:	Errors and omissions insurance, membership dues

LOWDOWN:

Arbitration is an essential facet of the American legal process. Increasingly, it is a required step in the effort to find a resolution to legal conflicts. Lawyers are officers of the court, and as an arbitrator you will be too. You'll work as a go-between for parties who can no longer communicate directly but who still seek an equitable solution to their problem. Once you become known for your ability to achieve a consensus between opposing parties, you should have a steady stream of referrals. Commercial conflicts, especially, often cannot wait the years that are now required for a case to pass through the clogged court system. Sometimes you will be able to sell your services before a case even goes to the lawsuit stage. Coming up with a solution that works effectively for both sides in a dispute is a valuable—and rare—ability.

STARTUP:

You're selling yourself, not your premises, so don't put a lot of money into office furnishings. You'll need just enough equipment to prepare your own paperwork and do your bookkeeping; expect to spend under $3,000. Earnings of $40,000–$75,000 are possible.

BOTTOM LINE ADVICE:

Becoming established as an arbitrator will take time and persistence. Keep careful records of your successes to use in future marketing efforts. A supportive network will be vital; you can't build an arbitration service through cold-calling. Wisdom about people, knowledge of the law, and the ability to clarify issues are all essential to success. In effect, you are doing what a lawsuit ought to do but often can't today because of the high costs and long time frames involved. Excellent arbitrators are in high demand, but it may take many years for you to establish your reputation and achieve financial success.

ART BROKER/CORPORATE ART CONSULTANT

Startup cost:	$1,000–$2,000
Potential earnings:	$35,000–$100,000
Typical fees:	$50 per hour
Advertising:	Trade publications, business periodicals, service on corporate boards or in community-based charitable organizations, networking, referrals
Qualifications:	Degree in art or related field, extensive gallery or museum experience, interior design credentials helpful
Equipment needed:	Phone, answering machine or voice mail, computer with Internet access for e-mail
Home business potential:	Yes
Staff required:	No
Hidden costs:	Membership dues, subscriptions to art periodicals, travel

LOWDOWN:

The corporate art consulting business is where connoisseurship and corporate image issues come together. It's a rarified combination, and you'll need a strong eye for art and a reputation for awareness of business requirements to create a successful enterprise. Artistic temperaments often have trouble communicating with business minds. Your ability to move in both worlds is a major factor in your success. To a large degree you will be selling yourself, and you will do this by listening well, grasping the needs of your client's corporate culture, and presenting business organizations with choices that will enhance their workplaces and images. You will transform your own appreciation for art into a service that adds value to your clients' enterprises.

The ability to locate the perfect piece of art for the corporate environment is rare. You'll need to visit every art show or trade convention you can, and collect catalogs from dealers worldwide. Then, you'll negotiate fair prices to the benefit of both sides of the transaction. As an art expert, you can help the newly discovered artist price his or her work to sell.

STARTUP:

Since you'll be working at your clients' premises, in galleries, etc., there's no need to out-fit your office to impress. Buy only the equipment and supplies you absolutely need to support your day-to-day work. You can get by with a telephone, answering machine or voice mail, and letterhead and business cards at first (about $1,000). You may want to add a computer later. Depending on your clients and how hard you want to work, you can easily earn up to $100,000.

BOTTOM LINE ADVICE:

Establishing yourself as an art broker or corporate art consultant will take time, deter-mination, and persistence. Your geographic locale will directly impact your avenues of approach; operating independently will probably be possible only in a major U.S. city, such as New York, Chicago, or Los Angeles. Elsewhere, you'll need to align yourself with a commercial interior design firm or an art gallery.

ASSOCIATION MANAGEMENT SERVICES

Startup cost:	$2,000–$9,000
Potential earnings:	$24,000–$48,000
Typical fees:	Monthly retainers of $2,000–$4,000 are not uncommon (directly dependent upon the association's size)
Advertising:	Network with professional and trade associations, advertise in related publications
Qualifications:	Good organizational, writing, marketing, communication, and motivation skills; an eye for detail; office management or administrative experience is helpful
Equipment needed:	Computer, printer, phone, fax, copier, Internet access
Home business potential:	Yes
Staff required:	None
Hidden costs:	Membership in associations; subscriptions to related publications

LOWDOWN:

From the International Association for Association Management (yes, there really is an association for everyone!) to the Association for Children for Enforcement of Support, most organizations need help in managing their operations. Especially well-suited to a management service are groups too big to rely solely on volunteers but not big enough to justify hiring someone to handle their day-to-day activities on a full-time basis. Your services for each client could vary, but might well include maintaining membership lists, publishing a newsletter, mailing out information about the organization, keeping records, collecting dues, and handling meetings, events, and fundraising activities. Not only could you work for an existing organization, you might also start an association of your own. In that case, your best bet is to build your group from within your own profession or focus on something with which you have personal experience, such as a hobby or similar activity.

STARTUP:

Office and computer equipment is your biggest expense (about $2,000). You may be able to get the organization(s) you represent to pay for some supplies, but that is not something to rely on at the business plan stage. Charge a monthly retainer of $2,000–$4,000 for your services to make sure you cover all of your expenses; since many of these associations work with volunteers, they may try to take advantage of your time, too. Don't let them. You are providing professional expertise and services, so charge accordingly.

BOTTOM LINE ADVICE:

Association management provides a great variety of duties and an opportunity to interact with interesting people. You will also get opportunities to learn about an array of topics at meetings and conventions. This is a great opportunity for those with philanthropic tendencies.

AUDIO RECORDING FOR TRADE SHOWS AND SEMINARS

Startup cost:	$2,000–$5,000
Potential earnings:	$25,000–$50,000+
Typical fees:	$100 per hour to tape a show/seminar, $2 per dub; or, you can tape for free and sell the tapes directly to attendees for $10–$35 a pop
Advertising:	Industry trades, fliers, direct mail
Qualifications:	Knowledge of audio equipment
Equipment needed:	Duplicators/CD burners, small soundproof recording booth, mixing board, computer, printer, labeling software
Home business potential:	Yes
Staff required:	No
Hidden costs:	You may eventually need to move to a studio (see if you can rent space before buying it)

LOWDOWN:

Hundreds of people give seminars every day and seminar attendees often like to take home tapes for their colleagues to hear later. That means the field is ripe for your audio taping services. You may tape on a contractual basis (charge an hourly fee) for a particular association, or you may tape each seminar at a trade show and dub tapes or burn CDs as quickly as possible to produce copies of the sessions for sale on-site at your own booth. This unique business requires that you have knowledge and skill in the audio trade. Read up on your industry and buy the best equipment you can afford; buy used equipment only if you really know what you're doing. A degree or certification in the radio industry may be helpful. Your challenge will be to market your service to seminar speakers—people who are themselves the biggest marketers of all. They know all the sales gimmicks—they've probably even used some themselves—so your best bet is to take an honest approach. Avoid the hard sell and focus instead on the benefits of your services.

STARTUP:

Equipment will be your biggest expense (minimum of $2,000–$5,000); if you need to build a soundproof room, tack on an additional $10,000. Don't limit yourself to hotel-based conventions and seminars; think hospitals, schools, churches, and businesses, too. If you tap into every possible market in your geographic area, you could easily earn a steady annual income of $50,000 or more.

BOTTOM LINE ADVICE:

Be prepared to give up your weekends and evenings. Many seminars take place when the majority of people are able to attend; if you get a free night, spend it dubbing at home. On the plus side, this job will give you a somewhat flexible daytime schedule; it's unlikely you'll be working many regular 8 A.M. to 5 P.M. shifts.

ADVICE FROM THE EXPERTS

What sets your business apart from others like it?

For Kathy Vanaman, co-owner (with husband Jonathan) of Listen Again Recording in Tallmadge, Ohio, it's immediacy that makes her business unique. "We do on-site recording and duplicating, so that conference attendees can purchase tapes of seminars the day of the seminar. They can take them home and listen to them right away."

Things you couldn't do without:

Vanaman's business depends on a duplicator, tape recorders, microphones, a computer and printer, and a labeling program.

Marketing tips/advice:

"Networking has been the most effective method of marketing by far," says Vanaman. She is a member of at least one organization that has used her services for large conferences.

If you had to do it all over again . . .

"We'd do it all the same way over again . . . there's actually not much you can change about this type of business."

Auto Maintenance

Startup cost:	$2,000–$5,000
Potential earnings:	$25,000–$50,000
Typical fees:	$25 and up per job (usually an hourly rate of $45 plus the cost of parts)
Advertising:	Newspaper, radio, Yellow Pages, billboards, neighborhood fliers, direct mail, location
Qualifications:	Certified automobile mechanic
Equipment needed:	Automotive repair tools; inventory of wipers, motor oil, belts, and filters; garage space (rented or owned)
Home business potential:	No
Staff required:	No
Hidden costs:	Inventory, insurance, ongoing advertising

LOWDOWN:

On average, every American spends half of one year's wages on his or her car. To put it another way, we value our autos quite highly, and we want excellent care for them. An auto maintenance service can be a wonderful and profitable way to reach this large group of potential customers, most of whom are keeping their cars years longer than they did in the past. You can limit your business to minor maintenance and leave the complicated computer diagnosis and repairs, not to mention the big parts inventory, to the dealers and garages. You can even be more specialized, focusing on a particular make, such as VW Beetles, or vintage autos which do not require computer diagnostics. Limiting your scope will allow you to have a repeated set of procedures to follow, and you can build a loyal clientele if you keep people's cars running well in a way that is both cost-effective and convenient.

STARTUP:

Costs will be fairly high to equip your business, unless you already own the necessary tools or can buy a set from another business for a reasonable sum. It will take some expensive marketing to launch your enterprise, and you will need to keep a certain level of advertising going throughout each year. If you are good, word of mouth could net you at least $25,000 the first year; repeat business and referrals will continue to grow your business.

BOTTOM LINE ADVICE:

So, what makes you think you can compete with those we'll-change-your-oil-while-you-wait operations you see at major intersections? The answer, of course, is personal service. You're not just a well-trained teenager in a clean uniform, you're an experienced, well-organized, customer-oriented maintenance person. You're the answer to the dreams of the little old lady on the corner who relies on her car for safe travel, of the incredibly busy executive who demands rapid, accurate service, and of the car nuts who drop in and want to "talk cars" with someone else who cares about them as much as they do.

ADVICE FROM THE EXPERTS

What sets your business apart from others like it?

Paul Taylor, owner of a Midas Muffler franchise in Lawrence, New York, says his business is set apart because it's run by him. "I believe in the highest standards of equipment and service, and my customers know that about me."

Things you couldn't do without:

"It really depends on the types of services you're providing. If it's just a muffler shop, you'll only need an air compressor, cutting torches, a MIG welder, and lifts; you'll need more equipment if you start adding brake services and other automotive repair services." Taylor says he couldn't do without multiline phones, and an answering machine, fax, and printer in his office.

Marketing tips/advice:

"As an independent, you'll need to do more guerrilla-type marketing, going after wholesale work within a trade as a subcontractor for body shops or transmission services. If you're in a franchise operation, you should be getting all the marketing and technical support the home office can offer; after all, that's really the only reason for buying into a franchise."

If you had to do it all over again ...

"I think I've done all the right things, but the climate is awfully discouraging for newcomers due to heavy environmental and government regulations. If I had to do it all over again, I'd probably think twice."

BOAT MAINTENANCE/
CLEANING SERVICE

Startup cost:	$2,000–$10,000
Potential earnings:	$30,000–$60,000
Typical fees:	$25–$50 per hour, depending on the service
Advertising:	Marinas, boat retailers, Yellow Pages, brochure
Qualifications:	Know the mechanics of a boat and different types of boats
Equipment needed:	Tools, cleaning supplies, dock, storage space
Home business potential:	No
Staff required:	No
Hidden costs:	Repairs, insurance

LOWDOWN:

Boat owners are nuts about their boats and while they enjoy being out on the open water, they sometimes hate the time they have to spend cleaning and maintaining their vessels. After all, boating is about getting away from it all, right? Clients who can afford to own a boat usually have some disposable income, so they won't mind spending a little more of it to pay someone like you to take care of their investment. Consider this business only if you like boats yourself and you don't mind getting a little grease under your nails or working out in the hot sun. Know your boat types (fiberglass, wood, steel, aluminum) and the chemicals you can use on each without causing damage. Certification as a boat mechanic will be helpful but not required. Advertise your services where people buy dock space and at boat retailers. Try to get the businesses along the shore, such as restaurants where boaters may be likely to congregate, to carry your brochure.

STARTUP:

If you are already a competent mechanic and own your own tools, your startup costs could be minimal (less than $1,000 for a Yellow Pages ad, business cards, and brochures). You'll need storage space, possibly a dock unless you travel to where your clients keep their boats, and all types of cleaners, paints, and detergents. Your basic fee for a tune-up would likely be $50 per hour; add another $25 per hour for cleaning. Depending on how hard you work and the length of the boating season in your area, you can expect annual earnings in the $30,000–$60,000 range.

BOTTOM LINE ADVICE:

This is not a business to be taken lightly; boat owners are very picky about their boats. You have to be conscientious and truly committed. If you like tinkering with engines and take pride in well-maintained, smooth-running vessels, this would be a great opportunity for you. The payoff could be great, too, as there are thousands of registered boaters all across the United States. If you space your jobs out well and pick a prime location, such as the Great Lakes, Gulf coast, or Atlantic seaboard, this could be a full-time job, and you could be making big money, not to mention adding staff, before you know it.

BOOKBINDER

Startup cost:	$1,500 and up
Potential earnings:	$25,000–$40,000
Typical fees:	$3–$5 per page or a flat fee per project
Advertising:	Yellow Pages, newspaper classified, book dealer newsletters and industry publications, direct mail or business cards to libraries
Qualifications:	Apprentice experience and/or formal training
Equipment needed:	Press, page cutter, stamping machines
Home business potential:	Possibly, but you'll need room for the equipment
Staff required:	No
Hidden costs:	Materials costs, insurance

LOWDOWN:

While many book binders actually assemble new books, the majority specialize in repairing them. Damage can be the result of many things: misuse, vandalism, fire, water, simple wear-and-tear. To save books that are rare or out of print, libraries and book dealers often need the services of a book binder who can restore the natural beauty of the original binding and keep the book intact. That can mean sewing together pages by hand or machine and producing a replacement cover that looks remarkably like the old one. Why go to so much trouble for old books? Because many have sentimental value to the owner; others are worth money, a fact of particular importance to rare book dealers. The best way to get started in this field is to apprentice yourself to an experienced book binder. After you have learned the trade and feel confident enough to break out on your own, start networking with owners of bookshops and library administrators, who are always looking for reliable help in maintaining the quality of their products.

STARTUP:

Launching a book-binding business can be expensive if you purchase new equipment ($10,000 or more); look, instead, for used equipment at auctions or in newspaper classifieds to keep startup costs to a minimum. Most book binders charge $3–$5 per page for smaller projects and a per-project fee (varies according to level of damage) for more complex jobs, such as replacing a cover.

BOTTOM LINE ADVICE:

Like carpenters, weavers, and other skilled artisans, your work is highly specialized and requires long years of training and practice; not just anyone can do it or do it well. Be careful not to get too bogged down in detail because you can easily burn out and lose your enthusiasm for this sometimes tedious work. On the other hand, if you like working in solitude and would enjoy a business that reflects your pride of workmanship, this profession could be tailor-made for you.

BOOK PACKAGER

Startup cost:	$1,000–$5,000
Potential earnings:	$45,000–$80,000
Typical fees:	Sometimes a percentage of total production costs; often, a flat consultant's rate
Advertising:	Writers' publications, industry trade magazines, direct mail, word of mouth
Qualifications:	Editorial background and top-notch organizational skills; broad understanding of publishing process
Equipment needed:	Computer, printer, fax, phone, Internet access, desktop publishing software, copier, scanner
Home business potential:	Yes
Staff required:	Not necessarily, as you can rely largely on freelancers; however, you may want to add staff as you grow
Hidden costs:	Insurance, cost of sales (it may take a lot of socializing to get some types of work)

LOWDOWN:

Book packagers are often hired by publishers whose staffs are too limited to work on a multitude of projects simultaneously; in other words, they are maxed out on projects and need outside help in handling additional ones. Some book packagers handle as much as 75 percent of a publishing house's projects, allowing the in-house staff to concentrate on future projects and expansion. You would do well as a book packager if you have an editorial background, a knack for organizing and pulling together all the details of a book project, and the foresight to set realistic goals about accomplishing publication. You will likely handle everything from hiring writers and photographers to copyediting, design, production, and sales/marketing management. About the only thing you might not be involved in is the actual distribution of the book; the publisher usually handles that end. To be successful as a book packager, you would do well to pick an area of expertise, such as high-quality illustrated books, since many publishers don't have that kind of in-house expertise and will gladly pay you for yours.

STARTUP:

Expect to spend between $1,000–$5,000 on your startup, which will cover your initial advertising in addition to your complete computer setup (with printer, fax, Internet access, and desktop publishing software). You'll need to work hard to make $45,000–$75,000 or more in this field, but it isn't uncommon (especially for those in close proximity to the publishing capitals of New York and San Francisco).

BOTTOM LINE ADVICE:

Things could easily get out of hand when you are pulling together many different creative forces for a special project; try to work out your worst-case scenarios early enough to form a game plan around them—and set deadlines that are, in reality, far ahead of when you actually need a project to be turned in. You'll see why after only one project.

ADVICE FROM THE EXPERTS

What sets your business apart from others like it?

Andy Mayer, president and co-owner (with Jim Becker) of becker & mayer ltd. in Seattle, Washington, says the ability to produce very complicated, production-intensive books is what sets his business apart from others like it. "My partner and I both have backgrounds in toy invention and design, and we can produce really interesting books as a result."

Things you couldn't do without:

"Our staff! We couldn't do anything without them . . . so many good ideas come from them. From an equipment standpoint, we couldn't do without a phone, a computer, and a color printer to produce mockups for publishers."

Marketing tips/advice:

"Bring a lot of who you are to your company. Find out what your passions are and try to put that into the things you produce. Also, don't listen to people who try to tell you there's only one way to do something. Freely break the rules and see what happens."

If you had to do it all over again . . .

"I would have focused the business on book packaging much earlier . . . we tried to do both book packaging and toy invention, and that didn't work as well."

BOOKKEEPING SERVICE

Startup cost:	$2,000–$9,000
Potential earnings:	Typically $25,000–$50,000 per year
Typical fees:	$15–$55 per hour; more for financial statements and other tasks. Certain clients may pay a flat monthly fee rather than hourly charges
Advertising:	Ads (Yellow Pages, trade publications), networking, referrals (from CPAs, for example)
Qualifications:	Knowledge of basic bookkeeping principles, some legal and tax knowledge, ability to use a computer, accounting/spreadsheet software, eye for detail, honesty, good communication skills
Equipment needed:	Basic computer and office equipment, a financial calculator, and accounting software
Home business potential:	Yes
Staff required:	No
Hidden costs:	Organizational dues, if applicable; errors and omissions insurance

LOWDOWN:

Small business owners, in particular, use bookkeeping services to keep up with the ever-changing tax laws and the constant flow of bookkeeping details they don't have time for. Clients need help with such tasks as making deposits, reconciliation of bank statements, and the preparation of financial reports, payroll, billing, and accounts payable and receivable, to name a few. What's the difference between bookkeeping and accounting? Bookkeepers are the actual record keepers; an accountant's job is to analyze and audit the records. If you have a clear, logical mind, common sense, and an affinity for numbers, this may be a great business for you. It is recession-proof, essential work that can be challenging and fun.

STARTUP:

The required computer and office equipment can be acquired for as little as $2,000. Add another $500 or so for your first six months of advertising, and you'll be off and running. You might consider joining business owners' associations or your local chamber of commerce to generate business. Charges for your services will vary according to the extent of the project, but the fees typically range from $15 to $55 per hour.

BOTTOM LINE ADVICE:

This work gives you a great opportunity to learn more about the business world—and about specific fields of business. The work requires close attention to detail and necessitates your staying current about tax-law changes related to payroll and record keeping. But beware—mistakes could get your client into hot water with the government and you are likely to shoulder the blame. If you like numbers and enjoy working independently to solve problems, bookkeeping may be a great career for you.

BROADCAST SALES/ ADVERTISING BROKER

Startup cost:	$2,000–$3,000
Potential earnings:	$20,000–$40,000
Typical fees:	Commission, typically 10 to 25 percent
Advertising:	Business publications, Yellow Pages, referrals, networking
Qualifications:	Wide experience buying air time for advertising, good connections with the media, marketing savvy
Equipment needed:	Computer, fax, printer, Internet access, cell phone
Home business potential:	Yes
Staff required:	No
Hidden costs:	Dues to trade/business organizations, phone charges, mileage

LOWDOWN:

Very few businesspeople have enough knowledge of advertising to shop for the best deals for the ads they plan to place. Small business owners must especially make the most of every dollar they spend. Your knowledge of the broadcast opportunities available (e.g., rates, frequency, discounts) will enable you to act as an agent for your small business clients, getting them the best deal in the right medium for their product. You can help each business deliver its message to the appropriate target market, and educate business owners against costly long-term contracts that seem like good deals but turn out to not be cost effective. Many exceptional deals are available for knowledgeable bargainers who understand where advertising slots may be available for a fraction of the usual cost. Some advertising brokers carry their service one step further and negotiate the media contract on behalf of a business as well.

STARTUP:

No need to buy expensive office furniture or a fancy computer system; most of your time will be spent on the phone or in your car. Set aside at least $200–$300 per month for phone charges and gasoline. You may also want to invest in a subscription to Standard Rate and Data Service for a listing of broadcasting outlets, which will run approximately $750 annually per directory. Since your income is derived solely from commissions on your sales (typically 10 to 25 percent), how much you make depends largely on how hard you are willing to work.

BOTTOM LINE ADVICE:

Media reps for specific radio and television stations typically try to sell an advertiser the moon—at a far higher cost than necessary. And that is what makes them poor advisors to their customers. Businesses can achieve much more at less cost by going through someone like you who doesn't have a vested interest in any particular media outlet. Before going out on your own, however, you will need to have considerable media-buying experience under your belt. It helps to be a quick learner, too, as you must be fast at scoping out where the target market really is for a range of different businesses. The organizations that need your service the most are probably the least aware of it, so expect to spend a lot of time marketing your business.

BUSINESS BROKER

Startup cost:	$2,500–$7,000
Potential earnings:	$100,000 (based on one sale a month for ten months of the year)
Typical fees:	Standard 10 to 12 percent of the selling price of the business ($10,000 minimum)
Advertising:	Direct mail, telemarketing, networking, referrals, ads in Yellow Pages and business publications
Qualifications:	Ability to understand financial reports, solid business background, considerable legal knowledge, good sales and "people" skills
Equipment needed:	Computer, printer, scanner, fax; telephone answering service or voice mail; a digital camera can be a handy sales tool
Home business potential:	Yes
Staff required:	No
Hidden costs:	Some states require a real estate broker's license

LOWDOWN:

Business brokers match clients interested in selling a business with those who want to buy—and many are home-based. This field is growing; many people think it's less risky to buy an existing business than to start a new one. Nearly all brokers represent the client who is selling a business; a few choose to represent buyers instead. Specializing in a particular size or type of business, or in a particular geographic area, brings success to many home-based brokers. Excellent communication skills are vital, particularly empathy and an ability to listen carefully. Strong sales skills, coupled with the essential legal knowledge and business background, will help you establish what may become a most lucrative business.

STARTUP:

Computer, printer, and software (some specialized) will cost an average of $3,500. Add to this at least $700 for basic office furniture, phone, letterhead, and supplies. Your earnings will hinge on whether you're able to strike a deal; if so, take a 10 to 12 percent cut on the selling price.

BOTTOM LINE ADVICE:

Network, network, network! Talk to people who own businesses, figure out what associations they belong to, and join them. Enroll in classes, if necessary, to help you learn more about the unfamiliar aspects of your new business. Get referrals from lawyers, accountants, and bankers. Getting businesses to sell is hard work (although specialization helps) and you don't get paid until you sell something, but it's fun to act as matchmaker and satisfying to help your clients succeed. Your expenses and startup costs are low, and the opportunity to make a great living is excellent. Nothing succeeds like success, so once you make a great match, you'll have a basis on which to build future business.

BUSINESS CONSULTING

Startup cost:	$2,000–$3,000
Potential earnings:	$50,000–$100,000 per year
Typical fees:	$75–$150+ per hour
Advertising:	Networking and referrals, Web site
Qualifications:	Significant experience and expertise in a particular industry and/or job
Equipment needed:	Computer, word processing and spreadsheet software, copier, fax, printer, Internet access, cell phone
Home business potential:	Yes
Staff required:	No
Hidden costs:	Insurance, travel expenses

LOWDOWN:

If you've spent 15 or more years in a particular field and have the ability to share your firsthand knowledge and well-honed skills with other businesses, you could be sitting on a gold mine. Business consultants are in high demand by individuals and organizations looking to grow their markets and improve their productivity; startup businesses can use your help too as they work to develop their business plans and seek financial backing to carry them out. Your credibility as a consultant depends on a combination of experience and expertise. It's not enough to have book smarts alone; you must also be able to back up your recommendations with practical, real-world proficiency. You will need to have stellar communication and people skills, plus the ability to present your ideas clearly and concisely whether on paper or face-to-face. Depending on your background, you can focus on a particular industry, such as automotives or electronics, or a specific skill, like marketing or employee benefits planning, which you can apply to many different types of businesses. Business consulting is an excellent second career for a retiree (you can work as much or as little as you choose); it's also a good way to continue making a living off of what you know following a job loss.

STARTUP:

Your startup costs will be relatively low; most of your investment will go toward equipping a home office with a computer, printer, word processing and spreadsheet software, copier, and fax. Consider incorporation if you are writing business plans so that you are protected personally in the event of liability for misrepresentation. The bulk of your business will come as the result of networking and referrals. You won't need to set aside funds for paid advertising; however, at some point, you may wish to develop a Web site so that companies outside your immediate geographic area can easily learn of your services.

BOTTOM LINE ADVICE:

It's practically impossible to become a successful business consultant without first putting in at least 15 years toward mastering a particular industry or skill. Businesses are essentially paying you for what you know—and you can only glean that kind of information from many years of firsthand on-the-job experience. Don't be afraid to charge a minimum of $75–$150 per hour (more for large corporations). And be sure to factor in travel expenses, if your work takes you beyond your immediate geographic locale.

BUYER'S INFORMATION SERVICE

Startup cost:	$3,000–$6,000
Potential earnings:	$30,000–$50,000
Typical fees:	$25–$35 per hour
Advertising:	Trade journals, local and national business periodicals, Yellow Pages, memberships in business associations and community groups, networking, referrals
Qualifications:	An understanding of and experience in the purchasing world
Equipment needed:	Computer, high-speed Internet access, fax, printer, cell phone
Home business potential:	Yes
Staff required:	Yes
Hidden costs:	Phone charges

LOWDOWN:

With new products, parts, and materials constantly coming onto the market, it's tough for purchasing departments to stay abreast of what's available and to be aware of the features of each. That's where a buyer's information service can help. Outsourcing this specialized work makes sense for many organizations, and your business fulfills the need. In all likelihood, you will specialize in a business type (electronics manufacturing, sports retail, etc.) or in a materials area (chemicals or lumber, for example). Having an excellent network of industry contacts in place will enable you to quickly and thoroughly gather the information your clients want and need.

STARTUP:

Communications are vital; you'll be on the phone a lot, and the Internet will supply much of the information you need; expect to spend $3,000 to start. Make one of your early purchases a comfortable chair; you'll be sitting in front of your computer a lot. Once you build your network, you should have no trouble earning $30,000 and up.

BOTTOM LINE ADVICE:

This business is a facet of the "information age." Yes, there's a wealth of information out there, but putting your hands on what you need, when you need it, is harder than ever before. Sorting through the blizzard of product data, materials sources, prices, and requirements for the relevant facts is a real challenge. As the eyes and ears of your purchasing department clients, you'll need to be persistent, detail-oriented, and focused on your clients' needs to make a success of this business. Once you become known as the "go-to person" for the latest parts and materials, you'll have a steady stream of repeat business and referrals.

CALENDAR SERVICE

Startup cost:	$3,000–$5,000
Potential earnings:	$10,000–$25,000
Typical fees:	$150/year for each subscription
Advertising:	Business and trade periodicals, organization membership, networking, direct marketing
Qualifications:	Energy, exceptionally high level of organization, outgoing personality, good writing skills
Equipment needed:	Computer, spreadsheet and database software, high-speed fax and Internet access copier, printer
Home business potential:	Yes
Staff required:	No
Hidden costs:	Attendance at functions, organization dues

LOWDOWN:

You know there are tons of events happening every month in your community. Wouldn't it be nice if there was just one source for listing them all? This business can make it happen. You'll create a master monthly calendar of public events for your community, or perhaps even an annual publication, that you send to your client list of hotels, motels, restaurants, and other high-traffic businesses where guests are likely to be asking for information about local events. Then, on the same day each week you fax a reminder-and-update sheet to everyone on your list. As you become established, gathering the information will get easier, as planners, public relations practitioners, and event sponsors will want to be on your calendar and with time, they'll become more and more proactive about informing you of their dates and events. Why does this work? Because many individuals and businesses get requests for this kind of information, yet they don't have time to gather it themselves. They appreciate that you do and they're willing to pay for that privilege so that they can better serve their customers. Everyone from florists to front desk personnel needs to have event dates at their fingertips, and they will come to rely on your weekly fax for the latest information.

STARTUP:

You will need a good computer system and spreadsheet software to compile and print the information, and above all, high-speed fax capability to broadcast it to your clients weekly. Expect to spend between $3,000 and $5,000 to get your business off the ground. It's a significant investment up front, but by billing $150 per year per client for subscription to your service, you can easily earn back your investment and make a small profit within the first year.

BOTTOM LINE ADVICE:

Keeping track of dates is time-consuming. You'll need to be personable and able to talk to all kinds of people, both for info-gathering and sales of your service. You'll also need to be detail-oriented and accurate. Remember, too, that you'll be competing against a myriad of free arts and entertainment newspapers and similar publications, so your writing style has to be distinctive and fun. And while you're helping to market events all around your community, don't neglect your own marketing efforts. Until you get established, you'll need to spend a lot of time promoting your service.

CARPET/UPHOLSTERY CLEANING

Startup cost:	$1,000–$3,000 if leasing equipment initially; $4,000–$10,000 if buying equipment
Potential earnings:	$35,000–$50,000
Typical fees:	20 cents per square foot first room; $40 or more each additional room, depending on size
Advertising:	Direct mail, Yellow Pages, newspaper ads, coupon books
Qualifications:	Physically able to do manual labor, some prior experience
Equipment needed:	Cleaning machine, large quantity of chemical cleaners, a van or truck for transporting materials and equipment
Home business potential:	Yes
Staff required:	No
Hidden costs:	Fuel for vehicle, insurance

LOWDOWN:

If "Out, out, damned spot!" is your battle cry, getting others to enlist your services in the carpet/upholstery cleaning business shouldn't be too hard. After all, we've all spilled seemingly nonremovable food or drink on at least one piece of furniture in our homes, and we've all thought of paying a professional every once in a while to freshen up the house with a clean-smelling carpet, right? That's why this is such a recession-proof business; the need for clean places to live in never goes out of favor with consumers. You could offer your cleaning services to everyone from individuals to apartment complexes and corporations, and the best way to get your name out there is through excellent, timely service and its resultant positive word of mouth. You'll sweep the surface dirt from furniture and floors, perform an overall general cleaning, and use industrial-strength spot removers on tough stain areas. Since each room takes approximately an hour to service (if there are few stains and no extra attention required), there is the potential for making lots of money once you learn to work quickly and efficiently while maintaining high-quality standards. One final note: You'll have to pay a little more for environmentally safe cleaning fluids; on the other hand, that can be a selling point since many people prefer "green" cleaning products, especially for health reasons. Customers will feel safer and more satisfied when they know there are no toxic residues in their homes and offices.

STARTUP:

Deciding whether to buy or lease equipment at first will depend upon how much capital you have available to invest. A carpet cleaning machine alone will cost from $600–$3,500, while leasing will run about $300–$400 per month. Rotary shampooers and steam extractors are the two types currently available, and each has its advantages and disadvantages, but rotary shampooers are preferred because they clean more deeply. A good, strong vacuum cleaner is your next most vital tool; a sturdy canister model with a variety of attachments will cost $400–$600 to buy or $100–$200 per month to lease. A reliable vehicle large enough to tote your equipment and supplies (and the gasoline to run it) is another expense to consider; if you already have a station wagon/truck/van, you're money ahead. Include advertising in your budget, which could run anywhere

from $600–$3,000 for half a year. Coupon books seem to be fruitful ground for carpet cleaning businesses as a starting point for bringing in new customers. For carpets,
expect to charge fees of 20 cents per square foot plus an additional $40 or more per
each extra room depending on size. Upholstery cleaning is usually priced per piece, with
fees ranging from $50–$150.

BOTTOM LINE ADVICE:

Working for a carpet/upholstery cleaning company before launching your own may
give you a good idea of what's needed to get started and how to proceed from there. As
in most trades, experience is essential to success; knowing which contracts to take and
which are just impossible, how to set appropriate fees for your area, how billing works,
and other aspects of running a business will make your startup smoother. Sales skills
are a plus since people may not even know they need your service, or how often they
need it. Calling former customers to find out if the work was performed satisfactorily and
offering to repeat it on a regular schedule will keep you busy.

CHIMNEY SWEEP

Startup costs:	$1,500–$5,000
Potential earnings:	$35,000–$60,000
Typical fees:	$60–$80 per job is common
Advertising:	Yellow Pages, local newspapers, direct mail
Qualifications:	Knowledge about cleaning chimneys and willingness to get dirty
Equipment needed:	Brushes, tarps, high-pressure dust collectors
Home business potential:	Yes
Staff required:	No
Hidden costs:	Insurance; vehicle to haul equipment and supplies

LOWDOWN:

Many homes have wood-burning fireplaces or stoves with chimneys that should be cleaned at least once a year—for both safety and health reasons. As a chimney sweep, you will work with many customers on a short-term basis. If variety and flexibility appeal to you and you don't mind dirt or working on your own, this business could be an ideal choice. Using specially designed brushes, a skilled sweep can clean a chimney in a maximum of an hour and a half; an efficient, experienced sweep can accomplish the job in even less time. By doing up to eight cleaning jobs per day at about $60–$80 each, you can really "clean up" on profits.

STARTUP:

Your primary expenses will be for brushes and related cleaning equipment ($1,000 or so) and for advertising your services in the Yellow Pages or by distributing fliers. Try to get repeat business by leaving behind a promotional item with your company's name or logo on it—people need to have a physical reminder of your service, since they can't necessarily see the results of your work! And don't be afraid to ask your current customers for referrals; they may have friends and relatives with chimneys in need of your special touch.

BOTTOM LINE ADVICE:

Many people aren't aware of the need to clean chimneys annually. But this is a vital service, since house fires often originate in the chimney. Reminding your clients about the danger of a dirty chimney can help ensure repeat business. And consider dressing the part. In Dickens's time, sweeps wore tails and top hats. Although it's a little gimmicky, that crazy costume can add to your appeal and help people remember you and your business. Whatever brings in the money....

CITY PLANNER

Startup cost:	$3,000–$6,000
Potential earnings:	$40,000–$200,000
Typical fees:	Varies according to length and extent of project
Advertising:	Referrals, membership in civic, charitable, and trade organizations
Qualifications:	Degree in related field, proven track record of success, ability to deal with overlapping governmental structures, excellent oral and written communication skills
Equipment needed:	Computer; Internet access; fax and copier; word processing, spreadsheet, graphics, and presentation software; laser printer; cell phone
Home business potential:	Yes
Staff required:	No
Hidden costs:	Errors and omissions insurance, membership dues, conferences for networking and continuing education

LOWDOWN:

City planning takes into consideration the use of land, the development of neighborhoods, the implementation of incentive programs for new factories, and many other factors that directly impact on the welfare of a community. As an independent city planning consultant, you will work on large and small projects for a number of different communities rather than serving on the staff of one municipality as an employee. Each new project will require a significant amount of learning time as you familiarize yourself with the needs, challenges, infrastructure, and unique politics and culture of a specific community. As with most types of consulting, cookie-cutter approaches to city planning do not work, which means you'll be drawing heavily on your creativity and problem-solving skills.

STARTUP:

You will need to stay in communication with your clients, especially when projects overlap; invest in a good cell phone plan. Professional-looking reports are also essential, so you will need to spend at least $3,000 on a complete computer system with graphics capability, perhaps even a 3-D software program, too. The startup costs may seem steep, until you consider that because cities are always growing and changing, you should have no shortage of work. Depending on how much work you are willing to handle, an income between $40,000 and $200,000 doesn't seem all that unreasonable.

BOTTOM LINE ADVICE:

Marketing yourself and your services will be very demanding. Excellent work will lead to referrals, but you should probably not rely on repeat business to carry you. Small municipalities typically contract for one big project, then wait a considerable time before embarking on another one. To pick up the slack, you will need a small but steady stream of new clients. Dealing with fickle, politics-driven city governments can be challenging. Decisive action comes hard in a democracy sometimes, and you may find yourself the victim of a delayed decision-making process. Plan ahead so that you do not get suddenly caught in a negative cash-flow situation.

CLIPPING SERVICE

Startup cost:	$1,500–$3,000
Potential earnings:	$10,000–$20,000
Typical fees:	$2–$4 per clip or $12–$18 per hour
Advertising:	Local newspapers, business publications
Qualifications:	Attention to detail, better-than-average observational abilities
Equipment needed:	Computer, printer, copier, subscriptions to newspapers and other relevant publications, high-speed Internet access
Home business potential:	Yes
Staff required:	No
Hidden costs:	Subscriptions could run high; try to negotiate the best possible rates or use online services; postage

LOWDOWN:

Are you an avid reader who's always clipping and mailing articles to people you know? Or, do you like to clip articles and file them away for your own future use? You might be able to make a living with what others may have always seen as your obsessive behavior. A clipping service finds and copies articles of interest to various businesses, including those which contain a mention of the company itself and/or its products and employees, as well as features about the industry in general, competitors, and related subjects of interest. Being familiar with library resources is helpful, but even more critical is your ability to search the Internet using the proper keywords. Good research skills and knowledge of how to use periodical indices and search engines are necessary skills for success in this business. Patience and curiosity are important personal traits.

STARTUP:

A powerful computer with high-speed Internet access, a pair of scissors, and a copier are the tools you need to get started in this business. You can charge by the clip ($2–$4 is an average rate), but beware—you may have to spend an hour or more to find just one clip, which means you'll be working for less than minimum wage! A better option is to charge by the hour; $12–$18 is a reasonable rate. A good place to start searching for clients is with the public relations departments of local corporations. They often need proof that their efforts are working and a stack of clips provides it. Network with the local chapter of the Public Relations Society of America (PRSA) for possible clients, too.

BOTTOM LINE ADVICE:

The most positive aspect of this business is its versatility; you'll become a quick "expert" in lots of different fields. Having your own subscriptions to several publications can be costly; visit the library and make copies instead and use online sources whenever possible. This is a very labor-intensive business, unlikely to ever become a big moneymaker; think of it as an extra source of income, not a full-time occupation.

College Internship Placement

Startup cost:	$1,500–$3,000
Potential earnings:	$20,000–$50,000
Typical fees:	$75–$175 (paid by student/parents)
Advertising:	College newspapers, campus bulletin boards, direct mail to parents
Qualifications:	Background in placement services would be helpful
Equipment needed:	Computer, printer, Internet access, fax
Home business potential:	Yes
Staff required:	No
Hidden costs:	Insurance

LOWDOWN:

It used to be that companies offering internships contacted colleges to find students for summer or short-term work. But, in today's ever-competitive marketplace, companies increasingly rely on services such as yours to make them aware of talented students who are qualified and willing to work for very little pay in exchange for experience in the field of their choice. There are lots of internships out there; the challenge comes in matching students and companies. You'll have to scan dozens of directories at your local library and spend many hours on the Internet searching for possibilities. Your market is likely to be parents rather than the students themselves, as Mom and Dad are typically the ones with the foresight to see the importance of an internship; they're also the ones with the money to pay for your services!

STARTUP:

You'll need to spend at least $1,500 for your computer system and another $1,000 or so for advertising in your first six months of operation. Charging customers $75–$175 (depending on the size of the university or college market you're serving) will likely lead you to an annual salary of $20,000–$50,000 per year.

BOTTOM LINE ADVICE:

Your work will be different every day, and there will be challenges on a regular basis, too. From time to time, you may find yourself working with parents you simply can't seem to please, or students who don't come across as highly motivated. Part of your job will be to sell the student on the importance of an internship in terms of securing a full-time job following graduation. Be careful to not make promises you may not be able to keep. While you hope to successfully place every student with whom you work, the ultimate decision about who snares an internship rests with the company. Make sure from the outset that parents understand the limits of your responsibilities.

COLOR CONSULTANT

Startup cost:	$2,000–$4,000
Potential earnings:	$35,000–$50,000
Typical fees:	$50–$75 per hour, per analysis
Advertising:	Local newspapers, business publications, direct mail
Qualifications:	Professional training in color theory and analysis (offered through cosmetic firms, paint companies, or similar businesses)
Equipment needed:	Color swatches, color charts
Home business potential:	Yes
Staff required:	No
Hidden costs:	Travel expenses

LOWDOWN:

Have you ever wondered exactly how the major automobile manufacturers and appliance makers decide which colors to use on their products? Or where the world of fashion comes up with its latest hues? They use color consultants—experts who know the entire spectrum of the rainbow, including minute variations and redefining nuances that are invisible to the untrained eye. It is essential that a color consultant have a strong understanding of color dynamics (how color affects people) in addition to the natural ability to distinguish slight color variations. The former is a learned skill, while the latter is an inherent talent that must be present for acceptance into a training program and ultimate success in this field. Once established in this business, your days will consist of working with anyone from cosmetic companies and appliance/furniture manufacturers to individuals who want to spruce up their personal images. You may be called upon to provide corporate consultations or you may offer group workshops. In all cases, people will be looking to you for advice and expertise in determining the color trends of the future.

STARTUP:

Training with a company that is heavily dependent upon color and color dynamics is the biggest initial expense involved in becoming a consultant. Most often, the program is a week of intensive instruction on color theory and analysis, marketing techniques, and applications; expect to spend around $1,500 on classes and certification (if available in your area). Other costs are directly related to the visual materials you will need to use in your consultations and demonstrations; these can run anywhere from $25–$1,000. Consultations typically last an hour, with the average fee being $50–$75, depending upon the industry with which you are dealing and what the market will bear in your specific geographic location.

BOTTOM LINE ADVICE:

Working with people is always a challenge, but more so when it involves subjective, personal issues such as what's aesthetically pleasing and what's not. Staying on top of what's new in the ever-changing worlds of fashion and design can be an exciting challenge, but if you like the idea of helping other people look good and making money while you do it, this could be the career for you.

COMMERCIAL ACTOR

Startup cost:	Put away at least six months' worth of living expenses (minimum of $1,000–$5,000)
Potential earnings:	$5,000–$100,000 or more (depending on your "star" quality)
Typical fees:	Extremely varied; actors are usually paid union rates for commercials, guest appearances, and feature film work; per diems are varied according to "screen time" (amount of time you're actually on camera)
Advertising:	Resumes, photos, and videos profiling your work or talents
Qualifications:	Dramatic ability; perhaps singing or dancing talent as well
Equipment needed:	None
Home business potential:	Yes, but work is done on location
Staff required:	No
Hidden costs:	New photos, professional wardrobe

LOWDOWN:

There are hundreds, perhaps even thousands, of actors in this country—and not all of them are working on a regular basis. Of course, anyone who's interested in acting as a profession has already heard about the competitive, cutthroat nature of show business (if not from books, then most definitely from family members who think you should get a "real job"). Yet despite the incredible odds against making it, year after year, many new wannabes enter the scene, and some are actually lucky enough to succeed. The best way to break into this business is to work with local advertising agencies, production companies, and public television stations; they need actors of all ages and types for television and radio commercials, corporate films, public service announcements, and voiceovers. From these sources, you can gain the experience and exposure required to build your portfolio and lead to higher-paying work. You'll need to have a professional presentation, including star-quality photographs of yourself, a strong resume, and samples of your work (on video or DVD). Acting is a hard way to make a living, but not impossible if you set your goals in manageable portions.

STARTUP:

Your startup will mainly be your living expenses; you'll need to figure out exactly how much you'll need to survive until that first big break comes. Tally up your monthly expenses, then multiply by six and stash it away before you quit your day job, so you'll have six months to land your first job. Union dues (and you will have to join the union if you want to be considered for many jobs) are typically $200–$500. The union will provide you with a list of typical fees for each kind of acting job you may encounter.

BOTTOM LINE ADVICE:

If you've been bitten by the acting bug, nothing except a lack of funds will keep you from pursuing your dreams. No amount of discouragement . . . no disheartening unemployment figures . . . will quell your determination. Nothing, in fact, will hold you back until you're out of money and have to take another job. But even then, you can keep your hand in, working whatever hours you have available. Oddly enough, the ability to generate some income, no matter how meager, is a great benefit to pursuing this profession.

COMMERCIAL PHOTOGRAPHER

Startup cost:	$3,000–$5,000
Potential earnings:	$35,000 and up
Typical fees:	$35–$50 per hour
Advertising:	Classifieds, Yellow Pages, trade publications, business groups, referrals, direct mail, Web site
Qualifications:	Photographic skills, excellent time management skills, ability to market and sell your services
Equipment needed:	State-of-the-art camera equipment (35mm and digital), computer, printer, copier, scanner, fax, Internet access, cell phone. You will also need darkroom equipment if you choose to process the film yourself; lights and props if you go the studio route.
Home business potential:	Yes
Staff required:	No
Hidden costs:	Equipment upgrades and repair, travel costs

LOWDOWN:

Commercial photography is the type of business that can take many different directions. You can choose to limit your services to studio portraiture, or specialize in photograph-ing weddings, children, pets, or even houses, cars, artwork, or gardens. If you can "see" the images needed by a business segment in your community, and produce them on time for a competitive cost, you can generate an ongoing stream of income as a business photographer. Photos always seem to be needed, but often at the last minute, so you will need to be flexible, skilled, and well-organized. You will often have to work under pressure, and you will need to grow your reputation for getting it right the first time; in photography, there are rarely second chances to get that perfect shot. Commercial pho-tography requires an interesting combination of technical, artistic, sales, and business skills. If you have this mix, or can develop it—no pun intended—you can go far.

STARTUP:

The photographic equipment you use is, of course, the vital component of this business; expect to spend at least $3,000 initially for cameras, lenses, and filters; more if you plan to set up a darkroom. Having an effective home office is also necessary for supporting the "business" side of your business: receiving assignments, preparing invoices, and so on. You could earn upward of $35,000, depending on how hard and often you want to work.

BOTTOM LINE ADVICE:

Most successful commercial photographers specialize. And some have gone beyond providing the photographic image alone to offering related services—preparation of brochures, scanning and retouching images, restoring old photographs, or working in close association with graphic artists and copywriters to provide a completed piece. If you become known for excellence in photography within a particular business segment, say of construction projects, retail store installations, or company board retreats, you will have a leg up on the competition. Photography is another one of those crowded fields, but there's still plenty of room at the top.

ADVICE FROM THE EXPERTS

What sets your business apart from others like it?

Tom Uhlman, owner of Tom Uhlman Photography in Cincinnati, Ohio, says that he stands apart from other commercial photographers by offering sound editorial judgment in addition to providing quality photographic work. "I'm dependable at finding interesting situations, giving publications the kinds of unusual photos they want and need without having to wait for assignment." Uhlman's photos have been picked up by the Associated Press and have appeared in *Newsweek*, the *New York Daily News*, and *USA Today*.

Things you couldn't do without:

Uhlman says he couldn't do without top-quality cameras with motor drives, flash equipment, better-than-average lenses, and dependable transportation. "I would also buy a police scanner, so you can shoot 'hard' news as it happens. It's the best way to break into newspapers, because they often don't have the staff or time to get these shots."

Marketing tips/advice:

"Look at the work of others and learn from it. But you'll probably learn the most from being out there and getting your own experience. Find photos that tell good news stories, and you should never have a problem selling."

If you had to do it all over again . . .

"I pretty much did everything in the right way and time, mainly because I didn't know any better. I learned early on that doing is what gets you there."

CONSTRUCTION MANAGEMENT SERVICES

Startup cost:	$3,000–$6,000
Potential earnings:	$40,000–$60,000
Typical fees:	$50–$75 per hour or a flat monthly retainer ($1,000–$2,500)
Advertising:	Business publications, membership in business and civic groups, referrals
Qualifications:	Extensive background in commercial construction, excellent management ability, attention to detail, selling skills
Equipment needed:	Computer, Internet access, fax, printer, cell phone
Home business potential:	Yes
Staff required:	No
Hidden costs:	Errors and omissions insurance, vehicle maintenance

LOWDOWN:

As a specialist in construction management, you guide the building process through to completion on behalf of an expanding business. The word *construction* covers many different processes, steps, plans, purchases, subcontractors, and schedules. To an outsider, integrating all of these elements in time, space, and design may seem like an impossible task. An effective manager takes it all in stride, easing the process and thus making an enormous difference in the cost and quality of the final resulting structure. The best market for your consulting services will be small-to-medium businesses that are growing rapidly. These enterprises have a great need for support in the construction process because they do not have sufficient staff to keep track of everything in-house. You will need to develop a reputation for effectiveness and the ability to build cooperative relationships with all sides in what can become a contentious process when deadlines loom and things start to go wrong, as they inevitably will.

STARTUP:

In all likelihood, you'll spend more time on the construction site than in your office. Nevertheless, the planning and tracking functions you are being paid to oversee need to be supported by computer and communications equipment; expect to shell out a minimum of $3,000 for a good computer and peripherals, as well as a cell phone or pager system. If you're good at what you do and earn a reputation for keeping projects on time and within budget, referrals will bring you lots of business, and you could soon begin earning $40,000–$60,000 annually managing projects.

BOTTOM LINE ADVICE:

Toughness, decisiveness, and superior organizational skills are absolute musts for success in construction management. You have to be able to see the big picture—what is going well and what is not and how to handle the situation to the satisfaction of all sides. You'll need to stay on top of your subcontractors' needs so that decisions are made in a timely manner and be able to offer a reasonable compromise when things can't be done as planned. Reliability and outstanding work will get you referrals.

CONSUMER RESEARCHER

Startup cost:	$2,500–$5,000
Potential earnings:	$25,000–$60,000
Typical fees:	$25 per hour
Advertising:	Ads in business periodicals and trade journals, Yellow Pages, networking, referrals, membership in business organizations
Qualifications:	Business background, experience in consumer research, proven track record, excellent written and oral communications skills
Equipment needed:	Computer, laser printer, Internet access, fax, cell phone
Home business potential:	Yes
Staff required:	Probably
Hidden costs:	Preparation of materials, utility bills

LOWDOWN:

Your experience in communicating with consumers will allow you to provide essential information to your corporate clients. How do people feel about a particular washing machine? How often do they buy insecticides and what brands do they prefer? What other options would they like to have in that new car they're considering? How were they treated when they stepped up to the counter to make a purchase? Would they be interested in trying a different type of running shoe or baby stroller? Which type of window treatment do they prefer—shades, blinds, curtains, draperies? Thousands of questions like these are the grist for your mill, and you'll find your answers via phone, mail, or face-to-face surveys. You'll need to do a fair amount of marketing yourself in order to show that you can find the answers your clients most need to know. Managing the workflow, along with estimating costs and setting your fees accordingly will be constant challenges, but take heart—every project completed successfully will lead to further work.

STARTUP:

Gathering answers, tracking data, and reporting information clearly are essential functions of your business, and the equipment you select for your office needs to support them. Expect to spend at least $2,500 up front. You can anticipate earnings of around $25,000 after the first year, building to $60,000 as you gain experience and a reputation for excellent service.

BOTTOM LINE ADVICE:

Writing an effective questionnaire or interview script is no easy task. Clarity, simplicity, and effectiveness are vital components to consider. You must be careful at all times to not inadvertently skew your questions in such a way as to deliver answers that support a particular point of view. The gathering and interpreting of data must be carefully handled, too. You will be helping your clients decide what they need to know about their customers and structure a questionnaire accordingly, then you'll present the results of your research in a clear, concise form. Your business will build slowly but surely as companies become more confident about your skills.

Cooking Class Instructor

Startup cost:	$1,000–$5,000
Potential earnings:	$10,000–$20,000
Typical fees:	$35–$50 per student, per class
Advertising:	Newspaper ads, brochures, fliers
Qualifications:	Cooking experience, teaching ability, some marketing skills
Equipment needed:	Cooking equipment and supplies, a place to teach (if not in your home)
Home business potential:	Yes
Staff required:	None
Hidden costs:	Facility rental; demonstration kitchen must have adequate stove(s), generous counter space

LOWDOWN:

Gourmet cooking and dining are popular pastimes these days. Many television shows feature chefs and cooks whose creativity pleases the palate, and gourmet restaurants and cooking supply stores abound. If you have (or can learn) the basics of cooking and have an interest in teaching others to do the same, this could be a profitable business for you. One of your biggest challenges will be finding a place to hold your classes. If your own kitchen is spacious, you can keep operating costs to a minimum by offering classes in your home. If not, you might check into the possibility of teaching in a home economics classroom at your local high school.

STARTUP:

Startup costs can be minimal if you already have the necessary cookware, utensils, and appliances. You can probably get by with your own kitchen range at first, but you may eventually want to consider the purchase of a professional stove. You will also need to factor in the cost of facility rental if you don't want to teach at home. Teaching at home is only recommended if you have a reasonably large kitchen and don't mind having a lot of novice cooks around. Set your class fees high enough to cover the cost of the ingredients you will need to purchase for your demonstrations.

BOTTOM LINE ADVICE:

A cooking class business can be rewarding and fun. Everyone loves to eat, and learning to produce delightful meals will please your students. Marketing is one of the biggest hurdles you'll face in launching this type of business. You will need to advertise; you might also seek sponsorship from related businesses (a cooking supply store, for example) or volunteer to demonstrate cooking techniques on-site as a way to build recognition. Check out the adult education opportunities available through your local public school system, too. You may be able to offer evening cooking classes in your high school's home economics department.

COUNSELOR/PSYCHOLOGIST

Startup cost:	$3,000–$5,000 (not including college expenses)
Potential earnings:	$45,000–$85,000
Typical fees:	$50–$125 per hour
Advertising:	Newspapers, referrals from physicians, Yellow Pages
Qualifications:	Degree and certification
Equipment needed:	Phone, fax, and answering service to field calls when you are not available; computer and printer for preparing patient bills; software for tracking insurance claims
Home business potential:	Yes, but a "real" office may increase your credibility
Staff required:	No (possibly an assistant for scheduling and processing insurance claims)
Hidden costs:	Keep scrupulous records of every meeting you have with a client— emergency meetings/phone consultations are not uncommon and could slip through the cracks if you aren't watching; continuing education classes and seminars are necessary but sometimes costly

LOWDOWN:

Are you a good listener? Do you have a knack for getting to the heart of a problem? Would you enjoy helping others explore problems and find their own solutions? If so, you are well-suited to the profession of counselor/psychologist. You will not only listen to your clients' problems, you'll guide them to identifying the deep-seated sources of the difficulty and arriving at their own healthy solutions. You'll offer resources to expand their abilities in problem-solving and provide creative exercises designed to help them relax and open up their lives to you. There will be more to this job than directly working with clients, of course. You must also keep accurate records of your meetings, and spend time reviewing your notes before and after each meeting so that you can make the appropriate recommendations for treatment. Therefore, you must love detail and be able to budget your time appropriately in order to stay on top of your workload as you help your clients take ownership of their situation and greater control of their lives.

STARTUP:

Assuming that you already have the necessary education and licenses required by your state, your initial expenses will go toward office equipment, supplies, and advertising/ promotion. You'll need business cards and stationery, of course, as well as a computer and printer for preparing patient bills and tracking client histories and insurance claims. Add to that the cost of continuing your education via seminars and conferences (at least $1,000–$2,000 annually). Finally, if you do not have the knowledge to process medical claims, you will need to hire someone who does.

BOTTOM LINE ADVICE:

You may relish the opportunity to help someone else make sense out of his or her life, but keep in mind that being a successful counselor or psychologist often means giving with a capital "G." Your clients will be heavily dependent upon you at first, then possibly disappear altogether as soon as they feel they are better. These up-and-down cycles can be unnerving, so be prepared to experience your own periodic bouts of depression and euphoria as you build a successful practice as a counselor/psychologist.

CREDIT CONSULTANT

Startup cost:	$2,000–$3,000
Potential earnings:	$30,000–$50,000
Typical fees:	Percentage of debt from client and from creditor (usually 10 to 15 percent from each)
Advertising:	Yellow Pages, seminars, speeches to community groups, classified ads, newspapers, radio spots
Qualifications:	A background in finance would be ideal
Equipment needed:	Computer, printer, fax, scanner, copier, spreadsheet software
Home business potential:	Yes
Staff required:	No
Hidden costs:	Insurance, secretarial support if needed

LOWDOWN:

It's no secret that Americans are deep in debt. Whether because of bad planning, identity theft, unexpected setbacks like the sudden loss of a job or catastrophic illness, or injudicious use of credit cards, thousands of individuals and families are in over their heads. As a credit counselor you will work with people who are overextended financially. Your clients will come to you for help in dealing with an unmanageable credit burden. How big is this market? Huge. The Federal Reserve estimates consumer debt in the trillions of dollars. No doubt about it—credit card debt is at an all-time high right now, and many people are struggling to make even their minimum payments. Your job will be twofold: to counsel your client about budgeting and responsible spending and to negotiate with creditors to develop a manageable payment plan. Likewise, your income will be derived from two sources: the client, who pays you a small percentage of what is owed; and the creditors, who are appreciative of the plan you work out because it prevents the debt from most likely being a complete loss.

STARTUP:

Your startup costs can be quite minimal at first; you should be able to get away with spending $3,000–$5,000 maximum for basic office equipment and spreadsheet software. Your business depends on the number of clients you can secure and retain until their debt is eliminated. You should, however, be able to make an annual income in the neighborhood of $30,000–$50,000.

BOTTOM LINE ADVICE:

You're providing a valuable service to desperate, guilt-stricken and frustrated people; it is vital that you remain nonjudgmental throughout the process. This situation can be rewarding or draining, depending on the individuals involved. For most debtors, facing up to the situation and dealing with it is painful, but ultimately they feel much better as they see their debt no longer spiraling out of control. You will have the opportunity to provide educational and psychological support as an integral part of your services. This will allow you to gain the satisfaction of knowing that you have improved an individual's or family's financial standing.

CUSTOM SEWING/ALTERATIONS

Startup cost:	$1,000–$5,000 (depending on whether you have to rent space)
Potential earnings:	$20,000–$40,000
Typical fees:	For alterations: $5–$75, depending on the complexity of the job; for custom-made garments using a pattern: check retail prices of similar garments, then add 15 to 25 percent, depending on fabric and complexity; original designs command higher prices
Advertising:	Newspapers and Yellow Pages; bulletin boards, fashion shows, networking via business cards
Qualifications:	Exceptional sewing skills; the ability to create fashions and apparel without patterns would be useful
Equipment needed:	Sewing machine and basic sewing supplies
Staff required:	No
Hidden costs:	Remakes can take a lot of time so charge accordingly. Make sure your work meets even the toughest standards; your reputation and the possibility of referrals are at stake.

LOWDOWN:

If all you need is a needle and thread to design a business you feel comfortable in, then custom sewing/alterations is a perfect match. In this relatively recession-proof business, you will repair or alter clothing that belongs to your client as well as construct custom-sewn clothing for busy executives who appreciate fine threads designed and fitted expressly for them. To succeed, you'll need sewing experience, plus creativity and the desire to make good clothes even better. The higher the quality of your work, the more your business will prosper. Word of mouth is nearly always the best way to grow a custom sewing/alterations business, although you will also want a Yellow Pages listing and may consider posting your business card on bulletin boards all around your community. Also, leave some extra cards for owners of dress shops and dry cleaners—they often refer their customers to good tailors or seamstresses for alterations.

STARTUP:

If you are even considering this business, you probably already own a good sewing machine. If not, your biggest up-front cost will be the machine (up to $1,000 or more); you might consider buying a used commercial sewing machine, because they are more durable and can be purchased for as little as $400. Be sure to invest in professional-looking business cards, because you'll need a lot of them to spread the word about your service. Use a rate card to keep track of what you're charging per job; some alterations are simple and inexpensive ($5–$10), while others are time-intensive and may require you to charge $75 or more. The pricing of custom-made garments can be tricky; use similar retail garments as a guide, then tack on an additional percentage taking into consideration the complexity of the design and the fabric you will use.

BOTTOM LINE ADVICE:

If you enjoy spending a good deal of time by yourself, you'll love this type of work. However, the hours can be long and the rewards not as frequent as you might like. Sewing is tedious work except to those who truly enjoy it—so make sure that you like this type of work enough to spend 65 percent of your workday with a needle and thread.

DANCE INSTRUCTOR

Startup cost:	$1,500–$5,000
Potential earnings:	$25,000–$50,000
Typical fees:	$20 per student, per lesson
Advertising:	Yellow Pages, entertainment sections of local papers, brochures, dance-wear retailers
Qualifications:	Experience, a degree to teach at the college/conservatory level
Equipment needed:	Studio, sound system, mirrors, railing
Home business potential:	Yes
Staff required:	No
Hidden costs:	Insurance, advertising

LOWDOWN:

Fred and Ginger made it look so easy that everyone wanted to try it—and that's pretty much how the Fred Astaire School of Dance got its start all those years ago. If you are an excellent dancer/choreographer yourself, and don't mind being patient with younger folks who aren't yet as focused as you are on the movement arts, you could literally dance your way into a respectable living. Physical strength, endurance, coordination, and creativity will help your business take off; referrals will keep it thriving. Most dance instructors have years of training themselves; many are retired from performance. Some instructors choose to specialize in one area of dance such as tap, jazz, or ballet in order to develop a cohesive following; others offer special packages which allow students to learn several different dance types over a period of six to eight weeks.

STARTUP:

Startup costs include the rental of studio space if you do not have a large room in your home in which to hold classes, plus a sound system and various dance-related accoutrements such as mirrors and railings. The other significant expense will be advertising your services. Expect to spend a total of $1,500–$5,000, depending on your specific needs. Earnings, however, are pretty decent if you develop a good reputation and get regular referrals. At the college level, a dance instructor can make $40,000+; a private instructor can easily gross $25,000–$50,000.

BOTTOM LINE ADVICE:

The long hours, especially evenings and weekends, may hinder some from pursuing this career. However, the grace, beauty, and strength of dancers are admired by many. Patience and the ability to critique without being hypercritical are vital traits if you want to be successful in this business.

DATA RETRIEVAL SERVICE

Startup cost:	$3,000–$5,000
Potential earnings:	$25,000–$60,000
Typical fees:	$50–$75 per hour
Advertising:	Networking, contacts in fields where you have experience, referrals
Qualifications:	Familiarity with business software in your specialized field
Equipment needed:	Computer, printer, cell phone/pager, vehicle
Home business potential:	Yes
Staff required:	No
Hidden costs:	Business insurance, magazine subscriptions and training to keep abreast of changes in the field, gasoline

LOWDOWN:

Lost data can spell disaster for any business, but especially for those involved in banking transactions, inventory control, and premium fulfillment. Even the best-maintained information systems can experience breakdowns and glitches from time to time. Mechanical failures, electrical glitches, and human error are problems that you can turn into opportunities if you have the expertise to retrieve lost data. This is a business that requires instant response because when your clients need you, they really NEED you. It is also a specialized computer consulting field requiring a combination of high-level computer hardware/software knowledge and excellent communication skills. If you have both of these qualities, plus the ability to manage your clients' stress levels at a very trying time, the sky's the limit.

STARTUP:

You'll need a powerful computer and peripherals of your own to launch this business; expect to invest $3,000 to $5,000 for equipment alone. A cell phone is an absolute must since clients must be able to reach you in a hurry. Your work is of a short-term, emergency nature, so do not be afraid to charge what your expertise is worth; $50 to $75 per hour is standard.

BOTTOM LINE ADVICE:

You'll be the hero of the hour when you recall the first-quarter sales data from oblivion. Data retrieval expertise is highly valued, and you can easily find enough challenges to keep your active intellect fully occupied. The risks are fairly high here (what if you can't retrieve the data?), but so are the rewards, if you can establish a relationship of trust with a few clients and then build on their referrals. You'll need to have the personality type that thrives under pressure, even enjoys chaos, and the patience to work with people and organizations that may not understand exactly what they have hired you to do. This is not a business for the lazy or laid-back; you must be ready to hit the ground running as soon as a call comes in.

DAY CARE SERVICE (CHILDREN)

Startup cost:	$1,000–$3,000
Potential earnings:	$25,000–$40,000
Typical fees:	$20–$45 per child per day; $35–$50 per day for infants
Advertising:	Referrals, bulletin boards, classified ads
Qualifications:	Patience and a genuine affection for children; training in pediatric CPR and basic first aid; most states require a license and insurance
Equipment needed:	Cribs, toys, movies, and games
Home business potential:	Yes
Staff required:	Not necessarily (however, many states impose stringent adult-to-child ratios; for example, in Ohio you may have no more than six children to one adult)
Hidden costs:	Insurance and licensing; child-proofing your home if you have not already done so for your own children

LOWDOWN:

The day care business has continued to grow in direct relation to the rising numbers of dual income households. Busy moms and dads are anxious to find safe and nurturing environments where they can leave their young children throughout the day while they work. If you have a love of children and the willingness and space to accommodate several of them all day, every day (Monday through Friday at least), this could be an enjoyable and profitable business for you. You can easily start a day care center in your home if you meet the necessary zoning requirements of your community. This business works best if you have a large, fenced yard and an extra room (perhaps a finished basement) so there is plenty of room for the kids to play. You'll need to be clear about your rates/policies up front (especially about regular hours, vacations, and payment due dates), and be careful not to let the parents treat you like a babysitter who is at their beck and call. Be assertive about protecting your personal time with your own family. Set a time for dropoffs (no earlier than 7:30 A.M., for example) and a specific deadline for pickups at night, and don't be afraid to charge extra, say $5–$10, for every 10 minutes a parent is overdue without prior notification.

STARTUP:

Since it's doubtful that you would even consider this business unless you had children of your own, you probably already have much of the equipment you'll need. Shop garage sales and baby/child consignment stores for additional cribs and toys as needed. Your main startup cost will be getting the word out about your service. Classified advertising, bulletin boards, and mothers' groups are a good way to build word of mouth. In addition, you may need to update your home to meet zoning regulations; your home may also have to pass inspection before you can be licensed to provide in-home day care. If licensing and insurance are optional in your state and you decide not to go with either one, be sure to let the parents know. Remember, too, without insurance, you will be held personally liable in the event of an accident or disaster. And while we're on the subject, do take a class in pediatric CPR and basic first aid, even if your state does not require it, and post emergency numbers near your phone, so you won't be scrambling for data in the middle of a crisis.

BOTTOM LINE ADVICE:

If you love to be around children, you'll relish the opportunity to do so daily. And if you have children of your own, this is a way for you to get paid for watching them play with others, which is not a bad position to be in. On the downside, although you are responsible for the children you watch, you are not their parent—a fact the parents themselves may constantly remind you of. Be sure to regularly meet with the parents of the children you are tending to avoid the possibility for misunderstandings and to keep the lines of communication always open.

DAY CARE SERVICE (ELDER ADULTS)

Startup cost:	$1,000–$3,000
Potential earnings:	$20,000–$35,000 per year
Typical fees:	$15–$25 per person, per day
Advertising:	Referrals, bulletin boards, classified ads
Qualifications:	Patience and the ability/desire to work with senior adults; training in CPR and basic first aid; a background in geriatrics and/or health care is helpful
Equipment needed:	Arts and crafts supplies, books and magazines, movies, puzzles, games
Home business potential:	Yes
Staff required:	No
Hidden costs:	Insurance and licensing; vehicle costs

LOWDOWN:

By the year 2020, an estimated one in six Americans will be over the age of 65; close to seven million will be 85 or older. And while it's true that Americans are living longer than ever before, it's also true that not all of them are able to remain independent or be left alone for long periods of time. For better or worse, elder day care is a business whose time has come. As an elder day care provider, you will be offering a service that is vital to two types of clients: the seniors themselves who cannot be left alone, and their families who, because of work or other responsibilities, are unable to remain at home all day to watch them. For a minimal cost, you can easily set up an elder day care center in your home, if you meet your community's zoning requirements. This business works best if you have a good-sized yard and plenty of ground floor space (no stairs!) indoors where your elders can spread out and get comfortable. You'll want to have a large table they can gather around for games, meals, and crafts, and a large-screen TV for watching DVDs and their favorite daytime programs. If you want to plan field trips—outings to the nearest mall, library, or movie theater, for example—you will need a van. You'll need to apprise the families of your rates and policies with regard to hours, vacations, and payment due dates up front; they, in turn, will need to make you aware of their elders' specific physical and mental health issues, special dietary needs, and medications. Ask a lot of questions! They are, after all, entrusting you with the safety and well-being of a mother or father who may no longer be competent to make decisions on his or her own.

STARTUP:

You probably already have most of the equipment—books, games, puzzles, etc.—you will need to launch this business. Thus your primary startup expenditures will be for getting the word out. A combination of classified advertising, bulletin boards, and networking with senior centers, home health care agencies, and physicians serving the geriatric community will help build word of mouth. You may need to update your home to meet zoning regulations and to pass a licensing inspection. If licensing and insurance are optional in your state, you may elect to do without; however, keep in mind that should an accident occur in the course of your elder care, you will be held personally liable. If you do not come from a healthcare background, you should take courses in CPR and basic first aid.

BOTTOM LINE ADVICE:

Working with elder adults, particularly those with symptoms of Alzheimer's or dementia, can be both difficult and depressing. You will need to exercise extreme patience and maintain a positive attitude at all times. The families of the elders under your care may prove equally challenging. They are probably most grateful for the service you are performing, but they may also feel guilty that they are forced to "leave" their mom or dad for the day with a stranger. Keep in mind that because they are caught between the responsibilities of work and child-rearing and the growing needs of their aging parents, they may not always be the most pleasant people to deal with. Handle them with care.

DIRECT MARKETING/SALES

Startup cost:	$1,000–$3,000
Potential earnings:	$20,000–$50,000
Typical fees:	Percentage of sales
Advertising:	Word of mouth, direct mail, cold calling
Qualifications:	Energy, persistence, ability to manage time well
Equipment needed:	Telephone, vehicle
Home business potential:	Yes, but you will be calling on prospects face-to-face
Staff required:	None at first
Hidden costs:	Some organizations charge for catalogs and other sales materials, attendance at meetings, inventory replacement

LOWDOWN:

Lots of people try their hand at direct sales, but only a few of them make it big. Why? Because, right from the start, they approached direct marketing in a businesslike manner. Before you launch a business of this type, consider your goals. Do you just want to make a few bucks and sell a line of products you like to family, friends, and acquaintances? Is your primary goal to make your own purchases of a favorite product at a discount? Or are you willing to put the effort and commitment into direct sales that you would into establishing any other type of small business? Many products are best sold person-to-person because they benefit from demonstration. Finding an excellent product line to work with is vital, and you should feel confident in the company as well. The rest is up to your selling skills and personal drive. Many direct sales–oriented companies encourage their salespeople to create networks, bringing in additional salespeople from whom the recruiter (in this case, you) derives a percentage of sales. This practice acts as an incentive to everyone in the sales force and is a way to earn even more money.

STARTUP:

Costs to start are very low (around $1,000), but watch out for hidden charges and fees from manufacturers. Some unscrupulous firms make more money off of gullible sales reps than their actual products. Your income depends largely on how much time and energy you are willing to put into your sales effort.

BOTTOM LINE ADVICE:

How many opportunities are left in this country in which your own hard work will define your success? Direct sales is one of them. Are you comfortable with cold-calling? Are you committed enough to keep yourself going with no one to answer to but yourself? Do you genuinely like people and enjoy helping them find products that will add value to their lives? Or, on the other hand, would you be satisfied with direct sales as an add-on to some other activity? Be sure you're clear about what you want from this business, and what you will need to do to achieve it. If you have big ambitions, you'll need an equally big commitment to reach them in direct marketing and sales.

DISABILITY CONSULTANT

Startup cost:	$2,000–$3,000
Potential earnings:	$50,000–$75,000
Typical fees:	$60–$80 per hour
Advertising:	Direct mail, referrals, membership in business organizations
Qualifications:	Extensive experience in the field, college degree in related area, knowledge of the needs of disabled individuals (you may even be disabled yourself), ability to communicate well with employers and employees, good writing skills
Equipment needed:	Computer, printer, fax, phone
Home business potential:	Yes
Staff required:	No
Hidden costs:	Insurance, membership dues, attendance at conferences and seminars

LOWDOWN:

As a disability consultant you will advise corporations on disability claims and assist them in meeting the requirements of all government and regulatory bodies. Nothing is cut and dried about the disability field, and rapid changes have left even the best-intentioned employers confused about what they must do to be in compliance. Disability claims made by employees are a major expense for some industries; your recommendations for alterations in the setup of the workplace or refinements in work processes could be seen as extremely valuable and cost-effective.

Managing medical claims is an adjunct function of your job. The conflicts arising from the most common worker problem—back pain—need expert management with regard to both insurance claims for treatment and maintaining good employee relations. A third aspect of this field centers on federal requirements that businesses make reasonable accommodations for disabled workers. Creative consultants can often find ways to make small alterations that do not require large outlays of cash; for example, the height of a counter may be adjusted so that a wheelchair-bound person can be hired to fill a particular position that might not otherwise have been available to him or her.

STARTUP:

Most of your work will take place on-site at the companies you are working with. However, you will still need to have your own office to handle paperwork, field calls, and possibly meet with clients from time to time. Expect to spend $2,000–$3,000 for your computer system, office furniture, and supplies. Your fees of $60–$80 per hour will seem quite reasonable when companies consider that your services may well save them thousands of dollars per year.

BOTTOM LINE ADVICE:

If you have experience in this complex field and can communicate with both sides, the disabled individuals and their employers, you can build a business as a disability consultant. In fact, many disabled people have enjoyed success, using their own perspectives to enrich the services they can offer to other organizations. Enabling challenged people to land and hold jobs while keeping employers on the right side of the law are services in which you can take pride.

DOG TRAINER

Startup cost:	$1,000–$2,000
Potential earnings:	$35,000–$50,000
Typical fees:	$25–$75 per hour; classes typically command up to $150–$300 for six sessions
Advertising:	Fliers, direct mail, Yellow Pages, classifieds, referrals from vets, free "clinics"
Qualifications:	Experience with different breeds; track record of success, patience, and credibility
Equipment needed:	None, other than space for pets to practice their skills. You can use your own backyard or a public park.
Home business potential:	Yes, but you will likely be traveling to clients' homes
Staff required:	No
Hidden costs:	Advertising, travel

LOWDOWN:

Dogs may be considered man's best friend, but if not properly trained, they can wreak havoc on a household in a hurry. Most pet owners wake up a bit late to the need for training (usually after half of the carpet has been eaten or peed upon!), but you can present your service as the solution to those nagging problems that make pet dogs so frustrating at times. Some trainers give classes for owner and dog together while others go to the pet's home and provide individual sessions. Network with veterinarians; they are usually the first to hear about animal problems.

STARTUP:

Your main startup cost is for whatever marketing and advertising approaches seem best for your community. Somewhere between $1,000–$2,000 would be an average amount to spend on launching this business. Remember, however, that you'll be charging an average of $50 per hour or up to $300 per dog for a six-session class, which can add up to a tidy profit early in the game.

BOTTOM LINE ADVICE:

This job is immensely enjoyable if you love dogs and can tolerate their owners (remember, you'll be training people, too). Gaining the trust of an animal is an essential part of any training process, but some trainers find that getting the human side of the equation to cooperate is an even bigger challenge. But once the pets under your tutelage begin to give up eating the curtains and jumping all over Grandma, you will seem like a genius. With those pesky behavior problems in check, you can proceed to teaching the really hard stuff such as coming when called (the pet) and being patient (the owner). Dog training is not a route to wealth, but a decent living can be made if you keep up your marketing; a track record of positive results will help spread the word.

ECONOMIC DEVELOPMENT CONSULTANT

Startup cost:	$1,000–$3,000
Potential earnings:	$50,000–$75,000
Typical fees:	$50–$75 per hour
Advertising:	Yellow Pages, affiliations with civic and government agencies (particularly chambers of commerce)
Qualifications:	College degree, with an emphasis on business development and municipal planning
Equipment needed:	Computer, printer, fax, scanner, cell phone
Home business potential:	Yes
Staff required:	No
Hidden costs:	Travel expenses

LOWDOWN:

For a city experiencing a major financial tailspin, economic development consultants provide the compass by which businesses can gain new ground. As an advisor to such businesses, and often through a Chamber of Commerce, you will provide guidance and direction to higher profitability, and perhaps even offer the city developers new ideas or opportunities to cash in on their geographic location. The economic development consultant typically suggests such potential moneymakers as convention centers, sports arenas, and other key profit-boosters. Recognize, however, that economic development can be a sensitive topic, eliciting strong emotional responses on both sides of the issue. While the city may be primed for change, some residents may not be. You could be entering into a potentially volatile environment (politically speaking). Keep a cool head, stick to the facts, and be prepared to demonstrate the value of economic development and to show the decision-makers where the money's really at.

STARTUP:

Your startup is low because your service depends mainly on your brains and experience. Set aside $1,000–$3,000 for basic office equipment and furnishings, and be sure to invest in a cell phone or pager—you'll need it. Your earnings will likely range from $50,000–$75,000, depending on your reputation, proximity to cities in need, and the time you are willing to devote to this business.

BOTTOM LINE ADVICE:

Build a name for yourself by doing some volunteer work in your community; that will help you network with key people who, in turn, may be able to introduce you to people like themselves in other communities. Once you get your name out there and get one or two projects under your belt, you should have little trouble making the phone ring.

EMPLOYEE HARMONY CONSULTANT

Startup cost:	$3,000–$6,000
Potential earnings:	$40,000–$60,000
Typical fees:	$2,000–$3,000 per engagement, or $25–$50 hourly for consultation
Advertising:	Trade publications, business newspapers, association memberships, community activity, seminars and public speaking, referrals, word of mouth
Qualifications:	Background in related field; proven track record in consulting, human relations, total quality management, or related specialty; ability to market your services; excellent presentation and facilitation skills
Equipment needed:	Computer; word processing, graphics, and presentation software; fax; printer; Internet access; copier; marketing materials
Home business potential:	Yes
Staff required:	No
Hidden costs:	Time and support for marketing efforts, cost of materials, travel

LOWDOWN:

Although this is a business whose time has come, don't go into it thinking you're going to be able to call the vice president for human resources at Mega Corp, Inc., and immediately get an assignment as an employee harmony consultant. Your initial marketing efforts will probably have to focus on educating potential clients about the nature and value of your work. More and more demands are being placed on employees in large organizations today, and along with those demands come increased tension and the possibility for conflict. Life for many employees is one of more discord than harmony, and the quality of the customer service they provide is suffering as a result. This is a problem you can turn into an opportunity. The workshops, exercises, and self-discovery projects you offer will meet a direct need in many organizations, and your persistence in selling your services will allow you to build a profitable business.

STARTUP:

Your startup expenses will encompass the cost of a computer system, plus whatever you need to prepare professional-looking presentation materials; $3,000 should get you started. Charge by the hour for consultations with company executives or a flat fee per engagement to cover your preparation, presentation time, and materials.

BOTTOM LINE ADVICE:

Every new business startup presents challenges. As an employee harmony consultant, you will have the additional challenge of making people understand exactly what it is you do and why they need your services. This idea is quite viable, but only if you sell it effectively. Skills in interpersonal relations and team building will be vital to your success.

ENVIRONMENTAL CONSULTANT/ CONTRACTOR

Startup cost:	$3,500–$5,000
Potential earnings:	$50,000–$100,000
Typical fees:	$150 per hour and up (depending on area or field of expertise)
Advertising:	Association memberships, referrals, networking
Qualifications:	Advanced degree in a related field; at least five years of firsthand experience in mechanical engineering, architecture, construction or similar occupation; excellent research/writing skills; ability to work well with people of many different views
Equipment needed:	Sophisticated computer and software, Internet access, printer; additional heavy equipment/supplies, depending on specialty, such as materials for oil-spill clean-up; collection methods for lab samples and a lab for analysis
Home business potential:	Yes and no
Staff required:	No
Hidden costs:	Insurance, publication subscriptions

LOWDOWN:

This is a growing field in most parts of the country. Environmental regulations are becoming more stringent and concern for the welfare of the natural world around us motivates public and private organizations alike to call experts in for specialized advice. Even a seemingly simple decision such as the siting of a factory can have environmental consequences, depending on the effect of the building process on the flow of ground water, the need for safe disposal of effluents, and possibly the need for highway upgrades to handle increased traffic. Farmers and commercial fishermen must have a clean environment to operate successfully, yet their practices can have a harmful effect on the same resources that support them. Even individuals and families looking for their dream homes are calling on environmental consultants for help in spotting contaminants and mold before they sign on the dotted line. Creative environmental consulting can help balance competing interests and clarify the issues upon which political decisions must be made. Your ability to draft and complete an effective report will be an important selling point for your skills.

STARTUP:

Even at the basic level, this field is relatively expensive to enter, particularly when you factor in the cost of your education. An environmental consultant can easily work out of his or her home. Environmental contracting, on the other hand, may require considerably more space and capital expenditure for the necessary heavy equipment and supplies. Do not hesitate to bill your services at $150 per hour or more; after all, you're a highly credentialed professional.

BOTTOM LINE ADVICE:

People with the background to consider becoming environmental consultants usually have a deep personal commitment to this type of work. As a result, each project has special meaning and offers rewards that go well beyond the fees earned. If you can help create a government policy that improves man's relationship to the environment, you are achieving something of which you can be rightfully proud. If you can help a business act responsibly, work effectively, and stay competitive, you will probably receive enthusiastic referrals and repeat business as well. Be aware, however, that getting established in this field is very difficult. You will need to build trust and earn the respect of politicians and/or business people, some of whom likely wish that the whole environmental movement would just quietly fade away.

ADVICE FROM THE EXPERTS

What sets your business apart from others like it?
Anne Hayden, environmental consultant for Resource Services in Brunswick, Maine, says her company stands out because of the value of its particular focus: There are not a lot of other people doing marine-related work. Her clients are typically government agencies and nonprofits.

Things you couldn't do without:
A computer, Internet access, and access to a well-stocked library, as Hayden's work is largely research-intensive.

Marketing tips/advice:
"I try to promote myself as an objective expert in my field. Many of the issues I'm dealing with are controversial. Also, I offer my first hour pro bono (free) to tell what I know about a particular environmental issue. It's been an effective marketing tool."

If you had to do it all over again . . .
"I would buy time-management software. Ideally, it would track time for planning purposes to give a more accurate estimate of my time spent on any particular project."

ERRAND/MESSENGER SERVICE

Startup cost:	$1,000–$5,000
Potential earnings:	$15,000–$55,000, depending on your geographic locale and the number of hours you work
Typical fees:	$15–$25 per hour, or a flat fee per errand
Advertising:	Yellow Pages and newspaper ads, fliers, networking and referrals, possibly a Web site
Qualifications:	Organization and attention to detail; time management skills, knowledge of the area and location of stores and services
Equipment needed:	Cell phone and/or pager, land line with answering machine or voice mail, reliable vehicle (car or van in a large metropolitan area; bicycle downtown)
Home business potential:	Yes
Staff required:	No
Hidden costs:	Mileage, insurance, bonding

LOWDOWN:

Do you sometimes feel as though there just aren't enough hours in a day to get everything done that needs doing? You're not alone. With so many dads and moms working outside the home, who's available to drop off the dry-cleaning, shop for groceries, or pick up that prescription at the pharmacy? A professional errand/messenger service can take the pressure off busy families by handling all those necessary little tasks that can eat up tons of time and energy. You'll market your services to dual-income households, shut-ins, new moms, and others who either can't find time to run their errands or are physically unable to do so. You'll also target local businesses like printers, advertising agencies, lawyers, accountants, and real estate firms that frequently need to deliver or pick up items all over town, but don't have the staff available to do it. You will need to know your way around your community and have the patience to cope with the inevitable traffic tie-ups you are sure to face as you make you way around the streets. You'll spend a lot of time in your car (or on your bike), so make sure your vehicle is comfortable and in good working order.

STARTUP:

Your largest expense to get started in this business will, of course, be the purchase of a vehicle. If you already own one, make sure it's in good running order and that your insurance policy is updated to cover any possible liability that might be related to using your car for business. Other startup costs will include a Yellow Pages listing, newspaper ads, and fliers; ask the businesses you visit frequently—dry cleaners, shoe repair shops, etc.—if you can post a flier or leave a stack of business cards near the cash register.

BOTTOM LINE ADVICE:

You can eat up a lot of gas and time running quick errands for several different clients as opposed to making lengthier trips across town for one or two. Learn how to budget your time and map out the most efficient routes so that you are not backtracking or covering the same territory multiple times a day. If you are quick, prompt, and reliable, you can make a nice living in this business, but keep in mind that there's a limit to how many errands you can physically run yourself in a single day; the key to greater income is adding staff.

EXTERIOR (HOUSE) PAINTING

Startup cost:	$2,000–$3,000
Potential earnings:	$45,000–$75,000
Typical fees:	By the job or square foot
Advertising:	Yellow Pages, newspaper ads, fliers, networking with homeowners' associations and historic preservation groups; yard signs
Qualifications:	Experience with different types of primers and paints, physical stamina, people skills, ability to estimate a job accurately
Equipment needed:	Ladders in various sizes, drop cloths, rollers, brushes, paint trays, sprayers, scaffolding (optional); computer and printer for billing and tracking customers/suppliers; telephone with answering machine or voice mail; vehicle
Home business potential:	Yes
Staff required:	No
Hidden costs:	Vehicle; loss of time due to weather; inaccurate estimates (it may take you a few jobs to get the hang of accurate bidding)

LOWDOWN:

With the resurgence of interest in old houses and neighborhood restoration, more and more homeowners are opting for exterior paint over vinyl siding. This trend toward historic preservation could mean money in your pocket if you like to work outdoors and would enjoy the satisfaction of transforming a previously shabby old Colonial, Victorian, or 1920s-era bungalow into the best-looking house on the block. Exterior painting is hard work and once you start a project, you have to see it through, no matter how hot or cold the weather turns. The only thing that can stop you is rain, but even that is temporary; you'll still have to finish the job even if it means readjusting your schedule and pushing other projects back. Always bid on a job ahead of time and be sure to make allowances for the time and materials you'll need to prep the house for painting. Become a kind of color expert too. When you first meet with homeowners to discuss a job, bring along paint swatches and suggest complementary colors for the background and trim. To get started, you'll need to market aggressively with a Yellow Pages listing, newspaper ads, and fliers you distribute in the neighborhood or post on bulletin boards; word of mouth and a few successfully completed projects are sure to bring additional business. And don't forget to market even while you work: Paint your business name and phone number on your truck and post signs in the yards of the houses your working on. You'll be surprised how much interest you can attract from nearby residents and people who just happen to be walking or driving by.

STARTUP:

Assuming you already have a truck to haul the necessary tools of your trade, you can launch this business for as little as $2,000–$3,000. You will need basic equipment, such as ladders in various sizes, drop cloths, rollers, brushes, and paint trays. Later, when your business begins to make a profit, you may wish to acquire sprayers and scaffolding; in the meantime, you can rent them as needed. Charge by the job or square foot and make sure that you include prep work (scraping, sanding, and caulking) and materials; check around your community for the going prices and set your rates accordingly.

BOTTOM LINE ADVICE:

This is a business you can handle entirely on your own, but if you choose to do so, keep in mind that you will severely limit your income; you can only paint one house at a time and the job will take you much longer if you are working solo. To grow your business, you may consider adding staff during peak seasons. And speaking of which, unless you live in the sunbelt, you will be able to paint houses only about six months out of every year; the other six are too cold and wet. On the upside, your startup costs are low and there's a real feeling of accomplishment, not to mention additional referrals, from a job well done.

FACTORY SITE LOCATION CONSULTANT

Startup cost:	$1,500–$3,000
Potential earnings:	$50,000 and more
Typical fees:	$35–$50 per hour or a monthly retainer of $500–$1,500
Advertising:	National business periodicals, memberships in trade associations and manufacturers' organizations, networking referrals
Qualifications:	Extensive business real estate experience, understanding of manufacturing, knowledge of urban geography, wide network of contacts, excellent oral and written communication skills
Equipment needed:	Computer, high-speed Internet access, fax, printer, cell phone or pager, copier
Home business potential:	Yes
Staff required:	No
Hidden costs:	Travel, telephone charges

LOWDOWN:

The search for a new factory site can often be difficult and long. As a factory site location consultant, your first step will be to outline your client's specific requirements, which include workforce availability, transportation needs, amount of land needed for the facility, availability of power, and environmental concerns. Given the differences among the laws of the fifty states, researching legal issues alone can be a major challenge. In addition, you will need to determine what state and local business development programs are available, and how these offerings compare from site to site. Your ability to outline the desired factors, gather data, and present several alternatives for consideration will help you establish a successful track record as a site location consultant. Your work will be like putting together a gigantic jigsaw puzzle in which you must handle thousands of pieces. And while you won't find the field crowded with competitors, you will soon learn that the potential market for your services is national, perhaps even international, rather than local, so your promotional efforts must be aggressive and far-reaching.

STARTUP:

You will need a computer and high-speed Internet access for your research efforts, as well as to generate reports and invoices. Depending on your knowledge, experience, and networking skills, you could soon be earning $50,000+.

BOTTOM LINE ADVICE:

You'll need to know when a company is considering a new factory site so you can market to them. This means having a network of people in the know who can tip you off. If you live in a geographic area that is open to industrial development, you might also consider aligning yourself as a subcontractor with your state's business development department. You could become the liaison between the state and businesses that are considering relocating or building new factories with regard to available sites well suited to their businesses. A few factory site location consultants operate internationally. Getting established in this business will be challenging, but once you have proven your abilities, referrals may bring a steady stream of interesting and profitable projects.

FAN CLUB MANAGEMENT

Startup cost:	Minimal, if artist pays for expenses; $3,000–$5,000 if you're totally self-sufficient
Potential earnings:	$10,000–$30,000
Typical fees:	$10–$25 each for memberships; you can also derive a percentage from merchandising products
Advertising:	Direct mail and word of mouth
Qualifications:	Membership in the National Association of Fan Clubs
Equipment needed:	Computer, printer, fax, copier, database/label and desktop publishing software, phone system with voice mail capabilities, Internet access
Home business potential:	Yes
Staff required:	Not initially
Hidden costs:	Postage and printing costs

LOWDOWN:

When a celebrity becomes a celebrity, the last thing he or she wants to do is sit around answering fan mail. Still, many celebrities recognize that their fans are the one who put them where they are, and they don't necessarily want to ignore them. That's why it makes sense for popular artists to hire fan club managers to keep in touch with their many admirers; stars recognize the importance of staying where they are by staying in touch with those whose opinions (and pocketbooks) ultimately matter the most. If you have the right skills (such as writing ability) or prior experience as a publicist or a background in radio or television, then you might be able to convince a celebrity to let you take charge of his or her mail. In addition to opening and answering huge bags of mail, you'll offer services such as a quarterly or semiannual newsletter and merchandising (offering promotional products like T-shirts, posters, and autographed photos for sale on which you take a small percentage for yourself). Like the celebrity, if you're in the right place at the right time, this could be the right opportunity for you.

STARTUP:

You won't need very much at all to get started if you can convince a celebrity to foot the bill for his or her fan club; some celebrities actually do see the worth of paying someone else to handle the mail and requests for signed photos. Many fan clubs operate independently without celebrity endorsement, but it's obviously easier to have the blessing of the star. If you have to foot the bill yourself, expect to spend $3,000–$5,000 at the outset. You can recoup this cost and begin to make a profit by selling fan club memberships for $10–$25 each, and offering incentives for joining, such as a free T-shirt or baseball cap. Your duties will include producing newsletters (at $500–$1,000 each) so you'll need to be sure you've sold enough memberships to cover printing and postage rates. You may want to start out with a quarterly newsletter, then go to every other month and monthly as you build your membership base. If all goes well, you could make $10,000–$30,000 per year doing something high-profile that you enjoy; it's not enough to make you rich, but it is certainly enough to make you smile.

BOTTOM LINE ADVICE:
This seems on the surface to be a glamorous job, and it is—until you get barraged with unreasonable requests, tight deadlines on newsletters, and egomaniacal celebrities who think it's okay you to treat you like an "underling." It might help if you continually remind the celebrity just how much more money the fan club is ultimately making him or her in terms of boosting record or ticket sales and what it might mean if you walk away from it.

ADVICE FROM THE EXPERTS

What sets your business apart from others like it?
"We are an authorized fan club management company and I have a highly specialized background in radio," says Joyce Logan, president of Fan Emporium, Inc., a Branford, Connecticut-based firm representing entertainers such as Michael Bolton, Carly Simon, John Mellencamp, and Mariah Carey. "I put myself in the fan's shoes and give every fan the personal touch . . . we produce newsletters, answer fan mail, sell authorized merchandise, and even have a 900-number service for fans to get concert updates and messages from their favorite superstars."

Things you couldn't do without:
Computer with a good database management program, printer and labeling program, fax, and high-speed Internet access.

Marketing tips/advice:
"Start with just one celebrity, and know that you can't just run a fan club for a little while. This is a serious commitment to the celebrity and the fans. You're dealing with people's emotional links to their favorite celebrity . . . you are a 'merchant of emotions.'"

If you had to do it all over again . . .
"I would have made contracts with the artists a little bit differently, so that they would assume all the costs of printing and mailing. We are a public relations firm just like any other, and we need to be recognized as such to stay profitable."

FARMSITTING

Startup cost:	$1,000–$5,000
Potential earnings:	$19,000–$25,000
Typical fees:	$1,500–$2,000 per month
Advertising:	County fairs, farm equipment shops, personal contacts
Qualifications:	Certification as an accredited farm manager (optional); knowledge of agriculture, equipment, and livestock; familiarization with state/federal regulations
Equipment needed:	None
Home business potential:	Yes
Staff required:	Possibly
Hidden costs:	Bonding, insurance, licensing fee

LOWDOWN:

Even farmers need to get away once in a while, but who's going to look after their crops and livestock in the meantime? A farmsitter! If you know something about farming and have the physical stamina to do the work involved, you could make a nice living as a farmsitter. Because you're only doing the job on a short-term basis, perhaps while an owner is on vacation, you have all the benefits of running a farm minus the regular daily headaches. Rural communities are tightly knit, so word of mouth will become your major source of new opportunities. It helps, of course, to have grown up on a farm and to have the knowledge about what needs to be done each day. Being in good physical condition will come in handy when it's time to slop the pigs and clean the stalls. Be prepared for any emergency (keep the veterinarian's phone number close at all times) and know how to handle livestock. Organization and dependability are also key ingredients to success, and be prepared to work from dawn to dusk. The best part is, you can farm only when you choose to. When the farmer comes home, you turn the burdens of running a farm full-time back over to him.

STARTUP:

You'll be headed for well-stocked farms, so all you'll really need to take along are a good pair of boots, and plenty of work clothes. Your biggest expenses will be for bonding and insurance, plus the cost of becoming an accredited farm manager should you decide to go that route. Expect to earn roughly $20,000 annually; more if you have certification.

BOTTOM LINE ADVICE:

This temporary assignment will demand that you give up virtually all of your time until the job is done. A farmer's work is 24/7. Don't lull yourself into thinking that this is a glamorous job; it's hard work! But it's also a good way to get your feet wet if you're considering becoming a full-time farmer yourself. Farming on a temporary basis allows you to see firsthand the inner workings of a farm without making a huge personal investment of money or time.

FARMER OF FRUITS OR VEGETABLES

Startup cost:	$1,000–$5,000
Potential earnings:	$20,000–$45,000+
Typical fees:	Prices are based on what the market will bear for each particular item. A rule of thumb is to charge four times what it costs you to grow the crop; organic foods can be priced up to 30 percent higher.
Advertising:	Newspaper ads, word of mouth, grocery stores, catalogs
Qualifications:	Knowledge of growing fruits/vegetables, marketing skills
Equipment needed:	Planting and harvesting equipment, soil, implements, packing materials, land
Home business potential:	Yes
Staff required:	None at first
Hidden costs:	A cash reserve or other income is needed to get through weather-related setbacks; competition may be stiff in some areas, crops are usually seasonal; fees for space at farmers' markets

LOWDOWN:

If you enjoy working the land and watching fruits and vegetables grow, this may be a satisfying business for you. How much land you need depends on the crop you're growing and the amount of profit you want to realize. Americans are hungry for homegrown (especially organically grown) produce; farmers' markets are gaining popularity everywhere. You will find a market for your crops in groceries, gourmet shops, health-food stores, and even, in some cases, mail-order catalogs. This business spells hard work, but the opportunity for success is excellent.

STARTUP:

Startup costs depend on the crop you wish to grow. Unless you have a very large yard, you will require a plot of land (up to several acres to start), located near a well-populated area. You will also need plants, seeds, or trees (depending on what you're growing), planting and harvesting equipment, farm tools and implements, fertilizers, etc. In addition, plan on using or purchasing a truck or other vehicle for deliveries, and be sure to check out any applicable zoning or health regulations which might impact the growing and sale of your products. You may also need to lease farm equipment, such as a tractor or rotary tiller. Keep in mind, too, that fruit-bearing trees generally require more than one season to mature. It may take two years or more before you have apples, peaches, pears, cherries, oranges, or mangoes available to sell.

BOTTOM LINE ADVICE:

Growing fruits and vegetables is hard, dirty, physical work. It is often frustrating, as well, due to weather and seasonal conditions. You must safeguard your plants with tender care, which means you have little time off (unless you have help with your business). You may eventually have to lease or buy additional land in order to expand. On the upside, if you love the outdoors and enjoy watching plants grow, this endeavor will be a very satisfying one. You will get the chance to live a country lifestyle, while selling your produce in cities. You can take satisfaction in supplying people with one of the basic necessities of life—fresh fruits and vegetables.

Feed Consultant/Broker

Startup cost:	$1,500–$3,000
Potential earnings:	$20,000–$35,000
Typical fees:	10 to 15 percent from dealers and $300 per day from individual clients or small farms
Advertising:	Farm journals, local newspapers, direct mail, Yellow Pages, referrals
Qualifications:	Degree in animal nutrition or extensive experience with livestock or poultry, awareness of agricultural economics, wide network of contacts in your region's farming community
Equipment needed:	Basic office setup, cell phone
Home business potential:	Yes
Staff required:	No
Hidden costs:	Travel between farms, cell phone bills

LOWDOWN:

You can use your understanding of animal nutrition and proven ability to work with the farming community to establish a solid and profitable business as a feed consultant/broker. The science of animal nutrition is growing ever more complicated, and even the most sophisticated and knowledgeable farmer can benefit from the advice of a specialist in making feed decisions. Different mixtures of feed must be designed depending on the intended result—fattening beef cattle is quite different from feeding milk cows—and the cost of each feed mix must be considered as well. Add in seasonal variations and you have a potentially challenging situation. Profit margins on many farms are so low that a change in cost or productivity of even only a few percentage points can have a big effect. As a consultant, you will advise your clients which feed mix to choose. As a broker, you will help them buy feed at the best possible price from the most reliable source.

STARTUP:

Since your success will rely more on your knowledge and contacts than on equipment, your startup costs will be in the neighborhood of $1,500–$3,000 for a basic computer system and peripherals. Your money will be earned from two sources: a daily fee of $300 or more for consulting with livestock owners and a percentage (usually 10 to 15 percent) of the actual feed sale from dealers. With low initial investment and high profits, you can use your know-how to make a reasonable living.

BOTTOM LINE ADVICE:

As with so many consulting businesses, you cannot jump into this cold; you need to know your stuff about livestock and feeds. You will come to be known for your expertise, and you will, in turn, earn the respect of the larger community in which you live. Agriculture is a tough business dependent on many factors (weather included), and you must have enough capital and/or adequate cash flow to ride out the low times.

FINANCIAL AID CONSULTANT

Startup cost:	$2,000–$4,000
Potential earnings:	$15,000–$40,000
Typical fees:	Flat fee of $150–$500 per student, or hourly rate of $15–$35
Advertising:	Yellow Pages, classified ads, direct mail, membership and participation in community organizations related to education, seminars and speeches for community groups, networking, referrals from high schools
Qualifications:	Experience as a school guidance counselor or college admissions officer, extensive knowledge of the field, ability to relate well to college applicants and their parents
Equipment needed:	Computer, word processing and spreadsheet software, high-speed Internet connection fax, printer. If you do not choose to meet with your clients in their homes, you will need an office with a conference table.
Home business potential:	Yes
Staff required:	No
Hidden costs:	Subscriptions, Internet connection, dues

LOWDOWN:

The cost of higher education continues to escalate. And while many types of financial aid are available, finding them is quite another matter. Families need guidance and assistance in preparing the paperwork and in locating the funding sources for which they are eligible and can apply. Your services as a financial aid consultant will be in great demand once your name gets known to the community at large. Word of mouth from the parents and students you have helped will bring you a steady stream of new business. In order to make a success of this business, you will need two basic qualifications: ready familiarity with financial aid options (or the ability to find that information) and excellent people skills. Much of your research will take place online, so a high-speed Internet connection is vital. Although some families seek financial aid to cover secondary and even elementary school tuition, the bulk of your business will focus on students entering college.

STARTUP:

Expect to spend about $2,000 on computer equipment and the usual office supplies to get started. Although the bulk of your business will come from networking and referrals, you will need to purchase a Yellow Pages listing and a few classified ads. Working part-time, you could easily earn $15,000 by setting your flat rates for a financial aid search at anywhere from $150–$500 per job. But be careful. You can eat up a lot of time surfing the Web; you may soon find that charging an hourly rate is more profitable.

BOTTOM LINE ADVICE:

Many parents experience major sticker shock when they first realize how much it costs to put a child through college. Financial aid is available, but the sources can be obscure and even the so-called "simple" forms for determining basic financial need are far from easy to decipher. With your extensive knowledge and better-than-average research skills, you can identify the multitude of special scholarships available to students with a specific cultural heritage, special academic interest, or other unusual characteristic.

FLEA MARKET ORGANIZER

Startup cost:	$1,000–$5,000
Potential earnings:	$25,000–$50,000
Typical fees:	$15–$100 from vendors per day, depending on size and reputation of market; from attendees, some flea markets charge an admission or parking fee of $3–$5 per carload
Advertising:	Fliers, classified ads, rent-a-sign
Qualifications:	Basic knowledge of the area and merchandise
Equipment needed:	Large piece of land (rented is better than owned), insurance, some form of shelter in case of rain
Home business potential:	No
Staff required:	Not at first
Hidden costs:	Liability insurance, crowd control, promotion

LOWDOWN:

Are you the type who simply cannot pass up a bargain? Do you consider yourself an authority on decent used or collectible items? If so, you might make a terrific "head flea." As a flea market promoter/organizer, you would round up as many vendors as you can safely fit into a designated area, and advertise everywhere your clientele (largely flea market aficionados like yourself) would be likely to look for flea markets. The main jobs of the organizer are to promote the event to sales people and customers alike and sched-ule the flea market so there are no conflicts with large competitors running theirs nearby at the same time. Another opportunity for the promoter is in selling goods directly to the public, and even to other dealers who've run short. This won't be easy work, but the good news is you can make as much money as you have the energy to generate.

STARTUP:

Two large expenses up front are the land/space rental and insurance coverage, each of which will run approximately $300–$500 depending upon the area. Advertising is key, but should not be very expensive since small ads will do; average quarterly advertis-ing budgets are typically around $500–$1,000). Creating and making copies of a flier is a good way to get the word out, as well as posting signs on local bulletin boards and en route to the site itself. Buying a supply of goods to sell yourself is not necessary, but could increase your profits by as much as 40 percent. Finally, two or more police offi-cers acting as crowd control/problem prevention should be hired at a cost of at least $15 per hour. Charge anywhere from $15–$100 per table for vendors who wish to rent space; some flea markets also tack on an admission or parking fee for attendees ($3–$5 per carload is typical).

BOTTOM LINE ADVICE:

The number-one priority in considering this business is organizational skills. A well-run flea market can make a great deal of money. Conversely, a poorly run event can be a disaster financially and logistically. Make sure all of your vendors have valid vendors' licenses, or you could be subject to hefty fines.

FOOD DELIVERY SERVICE

Startup cost:	$1,000 or more
Potential earnings:	$25,000 and up
Typical fees:	$5–$15 per item, which includes the cost of the food, plus a slight add-on for the convenience of door-to-door delivery
Advertising:	Brochures in office buildings, newspaper ads
Qualifications:	Ability to create attractive, healthy, portable meals
Equipment needed:	Kitchen, cooking supplies and equipment, food packaging materials, computer, printer, answering machine, cell phone
Home business potential:	Yes
Staff required:	Part-time delivery person, if needed
Hidden costs:	Delivery vehicle and gasoline. Check out legal and health requirements; you may need a license.

LOWDOWN:

Food delivery to the home or office is an idea whose time has come. Delivering lunches to office workers is especially lucrative. Harried working moms and dads will love seeing your delicious dinners brought to their door as they arrive home after a long day at work. The menus need not be extensive, which simplifies the operation. You can "pick up" from a variety of local restaurants, or prepare your own meals. Challenges include safe food handling practices "on the road," keeping foods hot or cold, as appropriate, and maintaining on-time deliveries.

STARTUP:

This business isn't costly to start up, especially if you opt to offer a lunch-only service, which is a good way to test the waters. If you offer sandwiches and soups, salads and rolls, beverages and simple desserts, for instance, you need very little equipment to prepare the meals. You will need to invest in packaging for the foods (disposable plastic containers, cellophane or foil wrapping, for instance); the cost will vary depending on the foods you're selling. Create a flier that can be posted in heavily populated office complexes to get started; always deliver the next day's menu with the meals you drop off (you can generate the menu on your computer and print copies as you need them). Make sure your insurance policy will cover your vehicle while it is being used for deliveries and, if you hire a delivery helper, make sure too that your insurance covers his/her use of your car.

BOTTOM LINE ADVICE:

Most people in the food delivery business get up early in the morning to bake and/or cook; night owls may not survive! Expect a long day of work, especially if you intend to make dinnertime deliveries. Offer a set menu each day, so that you're not having to make just one or two servings of any one item, and have a cutoff time for placing lunch and dinner orders, especially if you're doing both the food preparation and delivery. In addition to cooking skills, you'll need the ability to deal successfully with vendors and suppliers to keep your costs down and the food quality consistent. On the upside, the future is bright for food delivery businesses. More and more people have less and less time to cook; everyone is tired of the typical "fast food." Startup costs in most cases are modest, and you can net $70–$100 a day right from the start (the sky's the limit after that, as you add more routes).

FOOD MANUFACTURING CONSULTANT

Startup cost:	$1,500–$5,000
Potential earnings:	$45,000–$80,000
Typical fees:	$125 per hour is common; some opt for flat, per-job rate
Advertising:	Industry/trade publications, direct mail, word of mouth, Internet
Qualifications:	Extensive manufacturing or food industry background
Equipment needed:	Computer with printer and online services, fax, phone with answering machine or voice mail, cell phone (you'll be on the road a lot!)
Home business potential:	Yes
Staff required:	No
Hidden costs:	Insurance, travel costs

LOWDOWN:

If you decide to become one, you'd better have a background in the food industry; you'll need that just to walk into a trade show and appreciate everything you see. As a food manufacturing consultant, you'll study how the best food producers get their products to market; you'll relish sumptuous facts such as how a particular company decided on a product name or chose an innovative label to sell a particular product more effectively. You'll know all of the major food success stories, too, and you'll eagerly share that information with your client, the budding entrepreneurial food manufacturer. You will assist a company in everything from production to marketing, and you will likely charge an hourly consulting fee of about $125 to take advantage of your extensive knowledge and expertise.

STARTUP:

You'll likely spend $1,500–$5,000 launching this very specialized business; your dollars will be split between equipment and advertising costs. Count on purchasing a computer/printer with high-speed Internet and fax capabilities (approximately $2,000). You'll also want to spend some money on a dynamic direct mail piece that will "wow" your prospects and set you apart from your competitors. Get one or two success stories of your own under your belt and you could soon be making $45,000–$80,000 or more in this high-energy, highly competitive field.

BOTTOM LINE ADVICE:

If you're already so into this industry that you want to be a food manufacturing consultant, then it's probably too late to tell you the downside, but here it is, anyway: You will work long hours and never be able to walk into a grocery store again without checking every aisle for new ideas.

FORENSIC CONSULTANT

Startup cost:	$2,000–$3,000
Potential earnings:	$40,000–$60,000
Typical fees:	$50–$75 per hour
Advertising:	Referrals, professional memberships, networking
Qualifications:	Medical degree with specialty in pathology or related field, extensive experience, law degree desirable as well
Equipment needed:	Computer, printer, fax, copier, cell phone/pager
Home business potential:	Yes
Staff required:	No
Hidden costs:	Errors and omissions insurance, continuing education, professional memberships

LOWDOWN:

Forensic consultants straddle an interesting line in American culture, between the exponential growth in technological tools on the one hand, and the inability of governments and police forces to keep up with the demands of criminal investigations on the other. The O. J. Simpson trial highlighted this contrast, pitting sophisticated DNA evidence against the apparent ineptness and mismanagement of the Los Angeles police lab. As a forensic consultant, your services will be needed by both sides of the criminal justice system: overburdened prosecutors and police departments, as well as defense teams (albeit only those representing defendants wealthy enough to pay for extensive pretrial preparation). You are the expert who looks at the physical remains of a crime scene—analyzing wounds, estimating time of death, establishing identity, and providing factual supporting details for a criminal investigation. With a never-ending stream of crimes to solve and prosecute, the need for your services is great; the challenge in these days of municipal budget cutbacks will come in finding clients who have the money to pay your fees.

STARTUP:

You will need a basic computer system and peripherals, as well as a cell phone and/or pager to support the "business" side of your endeavor. Lab work and other services will be contracted out. Your primary products are your time and expertise, so you will want to set an hourly fee that ensures you adequate compensation; $50–$75 per hour is standard. If you are able to generate a steady stream of work, you can expect annual earnings of $40,000–$60,000.

BOTTOM LINE ADVICE:

You will need to be both streetwise and book smart to make a success of this business. You'll be selling your expertise and your ability to analyze the crime scene and resulting technical data in order to produce results that support one side or the other in a criminal investigation. The forensic expert is a familiar character in dozens of TV dramas, but the real-life work is much less glamorous, and much more tedious. There's a lot of "hurry up and wait" to this job. But if you are skilled at assessing evidence and the courtroom decisions go your way, you'll have all the business you can handle, once your name gets known. You must, however, have strong credentials to even consider making a go at this profession. The field of forensic consulting is no place for amateurs.

FREELANCE ILLUSTRATOR/ARTIST

Startup cost:	$2,000–$5,000
Potential earnings:	$25,000–$60,000+
Typical fees:	$50–$150 per hour, depending on your location and experience level
Advertising:	Personal contacts, trade publications, direct mail, Web site
Qualifications:	Artistic talent, attention to detail and time management, ability to juggle several projects simultaneously, training in basic graphics and design principles and techniques
Equipment needed:	High-end computer with light pen or graphics tablet and a high resolution graphics video card, Internet access, scanner, copier, laser printer, design, and contact management software, fax, office furniture (a drawing table is a plus), reference books
Home business potential:	Yes
Staff required:	No
Hidden costs:	Maintaining personal contacts (business lunches, etc.), memberships in trade organizations, software upgrades

LOWDOWN:

Do you like to draw? Do you have an eye for design and color? Would you enjoy taking a client's marketing plans from conception to printed product? If so, you may find free-lance illustration a satisfying and profitable career choice. To succeed in this business, you will need more than artistic talent. You will also need excellent communication skills and the willingness to work long and hard to create printed materials—ads, brochures, letterhead, logos, etc.—that will best showcase your client's products and/or services.

As a freelance illustrator/artist, you will market your work to ad agencies, small businesses, corporations, nonprofit organizations—in short, anyone who might need graphic design services. You might also target publishing houses with the ultimate goal of a contract for steady work with at least one. If you do secure such a contract, you may design and produce book covers as well as any artwork that would go into a book itself. This area of expertise is particularly lucrative for those who can produce lively, entertaining illustrations for children's books. Should you decide to stay unaffiliated with a large publishing house, your projects will always be varied and you'll have the challenge of getting to know what each of your client companies wants—over and over again. Many illustrators thrive on that kind of variety.

STARTUP:

Even if you don't plan to meet with clients in your home office, you will want to make your work space both attractive and functional. After all, you'll be spending a lot of time there. The high-end computer equipment you will need to produce professional results is costly, averaging $2,000–$5,000. Your hourly rates should cover all of your overhead, including utilities, taxes, insurance, and supplies, so price yourself competitively in the $75–$150 per hour range. Advertising should not be a huge expense as most of your work will come as the result of personal contacts and referrals. At some point, however, you will want to develop a Web site to showcase your talent and experience.

BOTTOM LINE ADVICE:

The freelance illustrator/artist is proof that a working artist need not be a starving artist. If you're always dreamed of making a living from your artistic talent, this business could be just the ticket. Unlike the traditional artist who paints a picture in the hopes that someone will buy it, you'll rarely even start a drawing without knowing there will be a paycheck upon completion. There will be challenges, of course. You'll have to listen carefully and work hard to build the trust of your clients and you may find that pricing your services so that you are adequately compensated for your time and yet still remain competitive in the marketplace can be difficult. But if you thrive on creativity and don't mind working alone or under sometimes stringent deadlines, the life of a freelance illustrator/artist could be a perfect match for your interests and skills.

FREELANCE WRITER/EDITOR

Startup cost:	$1,000–$5,000
Potential earnings:	$25,000–$60,000+
Typical fees:	$20–$75 per hour, depending on location, experience, and service provided (i.e., writing commands more money than editing); expect to be paid a flat fee or per word for magazine articles
Advertising:	Personal contacts, trade publications, direct mail, Web site
Qualifications:	Writing and communication skills; attention to deadlines and detail, organizational ability, an eye for graphics and design
Equipment needed:	Computer, copier, scanner, printer, word processing software, fax, office furniture (a comfortable chair is a must!), reference books, Internet access
Home business potential:	Yes
Staff required:	No
Hidden costs:	Maintaining personal contacts (business lunches, etc.), memberships in trade organizations, software upgrades, Web site management and development

LOWDOWN:

Many people have made careers out of freelance writing and editing—and many more are trying. Success will come for you when you can distinguish your services from those of others who, unfortunately, are willing to work for peanuts. Excellent communication skills are required to discover exactly what your clients want and need. You then turn those skills around to produce the corrected materials and written texts that will support your clients' marketing plans. This is a personal business that requires building up trust slowly and carefully before you can obtain the big projects that bring in enough income to make you successful. Creativity and goal-directedness are both essential. No detail can slip by your eye. Successful projects will bring you referrals, and each small step can lead to a bigger one.

As a writer, you will work on special editorial projects for clients ranging from small business owners to universities to newspapers—and you may even be lucky enough to snag a corporate client or two in the meantime. Your projects might be as varied as a trade journal article, monthly newsletter, informational brochure, press releases, or a corporate history. You may choose to specialize in a particular field, such as health care, higher education, or computers. Or, you could become a generalist who writes articles on a wide variety of topics for various magazines and newspapers. Your best bet, at least in the beginning, is to work with local publications and small businesses. As you build a portfolio of "clips," you can expand to larger markets and more profitable projects.

As an editor, you will work primarily for publishers, checking the galleys and page proofs of articles, books, and other written materials to make sure that they are error free. You will find and correct grammatical, spelling, and punctuation mistakes, as well as paragraph order and poor sentence flow. Your job is to ensure that all the words on the page make sense and have a certain rhythm to them, so that the reader is carried logically and concisely along through the text. You may end up writing/editing thousands of pages and projects, everything from annual reports, brochures, and menus to magazine articles and book-length manuscripts.

STARTUP:

You'll be spending a lot of time in your office, so whether you plan to meet clients there or not, you'll need to make it an effective, comfortable work space. If you're starting from scratch, expect to spend $2,000–$5,000 for your equipment and supplies. Your hourly rates should cover all of your overhead, including utilities, taxes, and insurance. Typical fees range from $20–$75 per hour depending on your experience and the particular service you are providing. You will not need to spend much on advertising; most of your work will come as the result of networking with potential clients and querying editors. As you gain experience, however, you may want to have a Web site to promote your services.

BOTTOM LINE ADVICE:

You can indulge your love of words in this field. You will be learning something new with each project, and you will have the satisfaction of seeing everything you produce end up in print (unlike poets and novelists). Working to support your client businesses can result in a satisfying partnership. However, pricing your services can be very difficult. Non-writers often do not appreciate the time and effort that goes into producing an effective piece of writing, and there are many writers out there in the marketplace who are likely to undercut you. Writing is a solitary occupation; you'll spend long hours alone, staring at your blank computer monitor and then sometimes rushing at the last minute to complete a project you have fought long and hard to get. Deadlines are always too short, and sometimes it can be difficult to obtain the necessary background information from clients.

ADVICE FROM THE EXPERTS

What sets your business apart from others like it?
Ruth Dean, owner of the Writing Toolbox in Akron, Ohio, says her business is unique because she listens well and helps clients clarify their ideas and plans. She specializes in technical marketing communications and gets her best results by writing to appeal to the client's intended audience, not just to the client.

Things you couldn't do without:
"The fax and e-mail are essential. Clients want instant communication." A computer and laser printer are also necessities.

Marketing tips/advice:
Dean markets by networking. "I just ask clients about their business and listen. That's all it takes. It's important to have writing samples available in simple 'packages' so that clients who are not accustomed to working with writers can figure out how to hire you."

If you had to do it all over again . . .
"I wouldn't have waited so long to go out on my own."

FUNDRAISER

Startup cost:	$2,000–$3,000
Potential earnings:	$25,000–$35,000
Typical fees:	Some fundraisers charge a flat fee (varied) while others are paid 10–20 percent of the total funds they raise
Advertising:	Direct solicitation, networking, referrals
Qualifications:	People skills, selling ability, excellent writing ability
Equipment needed:	Computer, printer, copier, fax, Internet access
Home business potential:	Yes
Staff required:	No
Hidden costs:	Telephone charges

LOWDOWN:

Just knowing that your efforts may be helping to find a cure, feed a family, or put a smile on a child's face can make fundraising a gratifying business. The primary skill you will need is the ability to make the general public so appreciate the worthiness of the causes for which you are raising funds, they are willing to reach into their pockets to support them. Fundraising is similar to marketing any intangible product. Fundraisers know a lot about the organizations they support and they believe in the value of their missions. In addition to marketing skills, you will need to be friendly and personable—someone that people like, respect, and with whom they feel comfortable. They are effectively taking your word about the charity you represent, so you must be sure that your word is rock-solid and convincing. A range of public and private organizations survive on fundraising, so once you can demonstrate success, you will have a large market for your services. Much of your work will be on the telephone, but if you have stellar writing skills and can put together an appealing direct mail campaign on behalf of a charitable cause, you can easily broaden your client base.

STARTUP:

The cost of equipping your office will be your primary startup expense here, and there's no need to go overboard at first. Your telephone is your most important tool; you can add the other elements over time. If you don't already have a computer and printer, expect to spend about $1,500 for a decent system and the appropriate software. Your earnings will largely depend on the funds you're able to bring in—not an easy way to earn a living, but it can be a profitable one for the most tenacious.

BOTTOM LINE ADVICE:

Fundraising is done by charities and service organizations of all types, and even government-funded groups need to supplement their annual budgets with funds gathered from donations. If you can help bring in donations, you can take your business wherever you want it to go. Unfortunately, a lot of other people have had the same idea, and some of them have been so dishonest as to cast the whole fundraising profession in a very bad light. Separating yourself from the sleaze will be an ongoing task for you. And don't expect a welcome reception every time you call. Americans are pretty fed up with telemarketers these days, so be prepared for some nasty words and a lot of hangups. You'll have to develop a very thick skin to survive.

GOVERNMENT CONTRACT CONSULTING

Startup cost:	$2,000–$3,000
Potential earnings:	$40,000–$65,000
Typical fees:	$50–$150 per hour or a flat rate of $175+
Advertising:	Trade journals, association memberships, direct mail, networking, referrals
Qualifications:	Experience in obtaining contracts in Washington, writing skills
Equipment needed:	Computer, word processing and spreadsheet software, fax Internet access, copier, printer, scanner, cell phone
Home business potential:	Yes
Staff required:	No
Hidden costs:	Telephone charges, high-speed Internet connection

LOWDOWN:

As companies downsize, they no longer employ full-time personnel who can thread their way through the complex world of government contracts. Yet these contracts can be a source of significant income for many companies. As a government contract consultant, you can guide your clients into the uncharted territory of business opportunities that government contracts represent. Your experience with the special language that government agencies use (not to mention the red tape involved in each transaction) plus your contacts in various departments and agencies will help you help your clients do business with the federal government. This is a specialized field, but it can be quite lucrative if you are willing to work at it. Often, success in gaining one contract and seeing it through to completion will smooth the way for future work. If you can demonstrate your facility for government contract work, a potentially large market of companies that would love to have your services awaits you.

STARTUP:

Equipping your office will be your main startup expense; expect to spend $2,000–$3,000. Considering that some government contract consultants charge as much as $150 per hour for their valued service, you'll be able to recoup your expenses in no time.

BOTTOM LINE ADVICE:

When it comes to securing government contracts, it's not so much what you know, but who you know. Hopefully, you're an insider already; if not, you'll need to sell yourself as one. Don't worry—as you begin to achieve success, you will definitely earn the title. To ensure positive relationships with your clients, you need to exercise good business sense from the get-go. Always remember to ask yourself the following questions: What approach to obtaining a government contract would be most appropriate for this particular client? How can I guide this specific business organization through the process? You may often find yourself under a time crunch, but the fact that you are doing a lot of good for your clients each time you are successful should more than make up for the frequent and stringent deadline pressures.

GRANTS/PROPOSAL WRITER

Startup cost:	$2,000–$3,000
Potential earnings:	$50,000–$150,000
Typical fees:	$500+ per project or an hourly rate of $25–$75
Advertising:	Networking, direct mail, word of mouth
Qualifications:	Knowledge of the regulations governing formal proposals, knowledge of technology and industry, ability to write clearly and logically
Equipment needed:	Computer, spreadsheet, database, and desktop publishing software, Internet access, laser printer, scanner, copier, fax
Home business potential:	Yes
Staff required:	No
Hidden costs:	Printing and publishing documents

LOWDOWN:

Organizations that want to do business with the government often must respond in writing to a request for proposal (RFP). Writing an effective proposal is a highly skilled activity, and businesses rarely have someone on staff who can handle it well. The same is true of grant applications which charitable organizations must complete in order to secure funds. In either case, the writing must conform to specifications outlined in the RFP or grant application, and generally must describe, in detail, the methods to be used, needs to be met, financial background of the agency applying, and expected outcomes of the project. This is a highly specialized type of writing and if you have the ability to do it, you can make a tidy sum as a grants/proposal writer.

Some proposal writers are generalists, while others focus on one field, such as education, energy, or health care administration. Clear organization, logical exposition, and excellent grammar are musts. Aptitude for handling numerical data is also required, along with business communication savvy so that you are able to work with your client's employees who are overseeing the bid or funding request.

STARTUP:

Since you will be the one responsible for preparing the final copies of all the necessary documentation, which may include graphs, charts, and tabular data, you must have a computer system with high-resolution and graphics capabilities, as well as spreadsheet, database, and desktop publishing software. Expect to spend $2,000–$3,000 for your equipment. This is a labor-intensive job (some grant proposals take several months to research and write), so your physical office needs to be both functional and comfortable. Don't be afraid to fork over $200 on a chair; you'll be spending a lot of time in it! You can bill hourly ($25–$75 per hour) or on a per-job basis ($500 and up).

BOTTOM LINE ADVICE:

A skilled grant and proposal writer provides the essential link between the client and the funding, whether it is a grant for a nonprofit organization or a federal contract for a business. It's challenging work that involves constant learning and creative solutions. It can take a long time to gain enough experience and contacts to be effective. Pricing is always a challenge unless you can negotiate an unlimited hourly rate. An upside to this business is that the longer you are in it, the easier it becomes to sell yourself.

HERB/FLOWERS FARMING

Startup cost:	$1,000–$5,000 (presuming you already have the land)
Potential earnings:	$10,000–$60,000 per year
Typical fees:	Usually between $3–$125 (from single item/plant to large dried flower arrangement)
Advertising:	Ads in catalogs; signage in grocery and specialty stores
Qualifications:	Knowledge of plant growing, fertilizers, etc.; marketing/bookkeeping skills
Equipment needed:	Land, fertilizers, seeds, pots, supplies; optional: greenhouse, computer, and office equipment
Home business potential:	Yes (but may outgrow your available land)
Staff required:	None at first
Hidden costs:	Vehicle to transport your products to market

LOWDOWN:

A backyard, basement, or just a few acres may be all you need to begin growing herbs and flowers for resale. Americans have a growing appetite for exotic, unusual, and healthy foods. Restaurants, groceries, and health-food stores are anxious to stock such products. Farmers' markets have grown increasingly popular recently, too, and herb growers can charge premium prices for their produce. Potpourri, fresh and dried flowers, and produce grown without the use of pesticides are also "hot" items to consider. A business like this is great if you want to get "back to nature" or live in a rural area but still have city access. And if you'd rather not be subject to the vagaries of weather, build a greenhouse! You can grow your herbs and tropical plants even when it's snowing outside.

STARTUP:

Unless you go the greenhouse route, you will need a plot of land on which to grow your products; the amount you will need depends on the crop, whether you wish to earn a full-time paycheck from your plants, and whether crop rotation is an issue. You will definitely need seeds, fertilizers, plant boxes and pots, hoses, and general gardening equipment and supplies, which can cost from $500–$2,000 to start. A greenhouse can run you $500–$20,000, depending on its size and the materials used to construct it. You will need a vehicle to service your accounts; to save money, consider purchasing a used truck for as little as $4,000 (new vans or trucks cost $15,000 and up). At some point, you may also wish to purchase a computer and office furniture (approximately $1,500), but these are not necessary to get started.

BOTTOM LINE ADVICE:

Herb farming offers you many choices of products in which to specialize. You have the freedom of working close to the earth while still remaining close to cities. In addition, you can meet many others who have similar interests through the marketing of your goods. The plants are small, which means you don't need a lot of land to get started. However, if you grow your plants outdoors, your income is seasonal and dependent on the weather. You may also face stiff competition; many others are trying to cash in on the current popularity of certain "trendy" herbs and flowers. Land near cities can be expensive, which can shrink your profit margin. Keep in mind, too, that growing any kind of crop is hard, dirty, physically demanding work.

IMAGE CONSULTANT

Startup cost:	$1,500–$5,000 (depending on equipment choices)
Potential earnings:	$25,000–$50,000
Typical fees:	$50–$200 per session
Advertising:	Classified advertising or ads in women's or business newspapers, bulletin boards, coupon books, direct mail
Qualifications:	An innate sense of color and style; a background in the fashion or cosmetic industry is helpful
Equipment needed:	Color swatches and makeup samples; a computerized video system (optional) to demonstrate what your suggestions will look like on your client
Home business potential:	Yes
Staff required:	No
Hidden costs:	Mileage costs; personal wardrobe and accessories—remember, you are a walking advertisement for your services

LOWDOWN:

How many times have you seen a misguided soul wearing colors that should only be on a flag—or makeup that dates back to Cleopatra? Did you have the guts to pull that person aside and offer suggestions on self-improvement? Probably not. Yet that is exactly what image consultants are paid to do. Particularly in the business world, people are increasingly concerned about the way they come across. Your most likely clients will be persons embarking on career changes or job searches, recent college graduates, and brides. Your mission: to help them make a more positive impact on others through look and attitude. In some respects, you will be like the mother who tells it like it is: "You should wear cool blues instead of muddy browns, which make your face look yellow." If you are fashion-minded and have an impeccable sense of balance and color, you are likely to find clients nearly anywhere.

STARTUP:

If you're just starting out, you really needn't invest in much more than mirrors, color swatches, and makeup samples. Once you become a little more established, however, you might add on innovative pieces of equipment such as a computerized video system that "morphs" changes on a picture of your client. You can work entirely from your home. However, a good place to set up shop in a heavy-traffic area would be a mall kiosk; the carts are expensive ($300–$500 per week), but the visibility you gain might be worth it. Also, wouldn't it be interesting to form a cooperative marketing venture with a related (but noncompeting) business, such as a hairstylist or resume service? You could each offer discounts for the other's service as an incentive for clients to buy your own.

BOTTOM LINE ADVICE:

It can be fun to play "dress-up" with people who are in the mood for a change, but keep in mind that the people most likely to seek your services are probably going through emotional changes that have prompted them to think about their looks and take action. Be gentle and take care to not hurt their feelings . . . advice is always easier to take if it sounds encouraging rather than critical.

ADVICE FROM THE EXPERTS

What sets your business apart from others like it?

Janet Neyrinck, Image Consultant and Certified Color Analyst in Akron, Ohio, says her business is set apart by the fact that it offers many services. "We're not just trying to sell makeup; our goal is to create a total harmonious image, including everything from dress and makeup to hair color. We believe in 'personality' dressing."

Things you couldn't do without:

"I need to have my makeup kit and, most important, my fabrics (for color draping). These are the basis of everything I do."

Marketing tips/advice:

"Be out there, be everywhere you can and introduce yourself. Also, be prepared to do a lot of research before buying your equipment."

If you had to do it all over again . . .

"I think that before I'd commit to one method or company's approach to image consulting, I would investigate all of the options out there. I would check the Directory of Image Consultants and ask others what's worked for them."

INTERIOR DESIGNER

Startup cost:	$3,000–$5,000
Potential earnings:	$35,000–$80,000
Typical fees:	$50–$125 per hour or a flat, per-job rate; add a service charge to the price of items purchased on behalf of a client
Advertising:	Yellow Pages, newspapers, networking with builders/contractors, furniture retailers, real estate agents
Qualifications:	Formal training in interior design is an asset, but not absolutely necessary; some states require certification. To boost your credibility, become a member of at least one professional association related to this field
Equipment needed:	Swatches, sample books, catalogs, computer, fax, cell phone, Internet access
Home business potential:	Yes
Staff required:	No
Hidden costs:	Getting set up with distributors and manufacturer's reps can boost your phone bills at first; budget accordingly

LOWDOWN:

Do you have a flair for turning a ho-hum room into a spectacular living space? Do you drop everything and sit down to read when your copy of *Metropolitan Home* arrives in your mailbox? Are you addicted to the latest home fashions and accessories? If so, you may make a fine interior designer. But beware—this career involves more than choosing the right sofa or drapery fabric; you'll need the ability to work with a variety of people— homeowners, builders and contractors, real estate agents, furniture retailers, even corporate executives looking to spruce up their offices. Before going out on your own, try becoming an apprentice to an established interior designer first, you'll gain much more detailed knowledge about the intricacies and nuances of this incredibly subjective business than you could ever learn from a book. Personalities are the most difficult aspect of the job and you may well find that getting others to cooperate and work as a team with a unified vision is your biggest challenge. Keeping up with fast-changing trends is another. Still, if you like meeting with people and helping to create the (interior) home of their dreams, you'll learn to overlook the difficulties and embrace the challenges.

STARTUP:

Your startup costs with an interior design service will be in the $3,000–$5,000 range, most of which will go to cover your first six months of advertising. You'll need classy business cards and brochures about your service, so set aside a minimum of $1,000 for these items alone. Your fees can range from $50–$125 per hour, depending on the client, complexity of the job, and your level of expertise. Interior designers who are formally trained and/or certified command larger fees. As you build your business and reputation for quality design, re-evaluate your prices. The more prestigious clients you land, the higher your prices can go.

BOTTOM LINE ADVICE:

If you truly like working with people in their most intimate surroundings, this is the job for you. However, expect there to be difficulties such as timing (what if you get too many clients at once?), and fussy clients who request so many changes, they wind up costing you money. Learn to set some policies in writing ahead of time to cover yourself in case of problems like; add a surcharge for any work that goes above and beyond your initial agreement.

ADVICE FROM THE EXPERTS

What sets your business apart from others like it?

"I seem to be the remedy person," says Linda Chiera, president of Studio Space Design in Akron, Ohio. "People usually come to me after they've experienced a problem elsewhere . . . I'm working on getting them to think of me first!" Chiera feels that her business is unique in that it provides expert service and assistance with complex projects. "We learn a person's work style and incorporate that into whatever we do for them, whether it be redecorating a home or redesigning their office space."

Things you couldn't do without:

Chiera couldn't do without a computer and CAD system, fax, phone, sample books/resources, tape measure, scale, and business cards.

Marketing tips/advice:

"Get sales training and get out there . . . join networking organizations such as the chamber of commerce, and if there's a mentoring program available in your area, enlist in it. Offer yourself as a speaker, advertise wisely (knowing your exact market), and hire seasoned professionals to do the things you can't." Finally, says Chiera, don't be afraid to make mistakes.

If you had to do it all over again . . .

"I would have been wiser about target marketing and advertising. I should have been more careful about selecting the right niche and also should have tried to become more comfortable earlier on about the selling aspect of my job. I'm trained as a designer, and sales and self-promotion have been a bit of a challenge for me until recently."

INTERVIEWER

Startup cost:	$2,000–$3,000
Potential earnings:	$30,000 and up
Typical fees:	$35 and up per interview + the cost of developing the questions, or an hourly fee
Advertising:	Referrals, trade association memberships, networking
Qualifications:	Master's degree in organizational psychology or related field, experience in human relations with a focus on interviewing, a proven record of effectiveness
Equipment needed:	Basic office setup, marketing materials
Home business potential:	Yes
Staff required:	No
Hidden costs:	Ongoing marketing to maintain workflow, membership dues in professional associations

LOWDOWN:

It costs money to hire and train new employees, which is why business organizations are placing more and more emphasis on selecting the right people and placing them in the most suitable positions. As organizational structures become flatter and managers must take on a wider range of duties, they have less time to perform the vital interviewing functions that allow them to find and hire the most appropriate people. As a professional interviewer, you can fill this corporate need. Your training in interviewing techniques, combined with your background in organizational psychology, enable you to do a far better job of selecting appropriate employees than the overworked executive who has no formal training in hiring techniques. You can design a series of questions related to the company's mission and the job functions of the position that will allow a meaningful comparison to be made among the candidates interviewed. To secure clients, you will need to be able to show that you can save the company money by reducing turnover and increasing employee effectiveness.

STARTUP:

Since you will be meeting clients and performing employee interviews on-site, your own office setup need not be fancy or costly; no more than $2,000 should suffice for a basic office setup and marketing materials. Charge a flat fee per interview or an hourly rate.

BOTTOM LINE ADVICE:

Every business designates someone to handle the personnel interview process, so selling your prospects on hiring you may well be your biggest challenge. Keep in mind that many business people, particularly small business owners who don't have the luxury of a human resources department, assume (in spite of all evidence to the contrary) that they can "take someone's measure" quickly and make the right staffing decision purely by instinct. It will be your job to convince them otherwise. Getting your message out about the value of a more scientific and systematic approach to hiring will take determined marketing. Ideally, you will build a client base that offers ongoing assignments and a steady income flow.

INVENTION CONSULTANT/BROKER

Startup cost:	$3,000–$5,000
Potential earnings:	$30,000–$50,000+
Typical fees:	Up-front fee of $500–$1,500 plus percentage of invention's final sale price (usually 15 to 20 percent)
Advertising:	Yellow Pages, business/trade publications, direct mail to inventors' associations or online services, Web site
Qualifications:	Degree or extensive background in product development; eye for what might become the next "big" thing
Equipment needed:	Computer, phone, fax, high-speed Internet connection
Home business potential:	Yes
Staff required:	No
Hidden costs:	Web site development and maintenance

LOWDOWN:

Where would we be without inventors? There would be no streetlights without Edison, no telephone without Bell, no elevator without Otis. Inventors have quick, creative minds all right, but they often lack business savvy, which is where you come in. As an invention consultant/broker who helps bring an inventor's idea to the marketplace, you can take an up-front fee plus a percentage of each idea sold. The area most ripe for invention these days is in personal furnishings and creature comforts (the massaging chair, for example). Think of the things people buy and why they buy them. Consumers want something unique, don't they? A product that does something no other product on the market does. Your challenge is to be able to spot such potential moneymakers, and the best way to do that is to stay in constant touch with inventors' associations and museums (such as the National Inventors Hall of Fame in Akron, Ohio). Since many inventors live overseas and want to sell products or ideas to the United States, you'll definitely need a Web site to advertise your services. The hardest part of your job won't be finding the inventions—your Web site will soon have ideas rolling in from all corners of the globe. Your challenge will be finding suitable outlets for each invention. But then again, you're a natural-born salesperson or you wouldn't have considered this business in the first place, right?

STARTUP:

Your startup will consist of a basic office setup (computer, printer, fax, high-speed Internet connection, and sales-tracking software package), plus the development of a professional-looking Web site; you'll spend $3,000–$5,000 total for these items. Considering the double-faceted nature of your earning potential (up-front fee plus percentage), you could easily be making $30,000–$50,000 once you get established in your field.

BOTTOM LINE ADVICE:

You're on the cutting edge of product development—that's the best part of your chosen profession. The downside is many inventions never quite make it to market (and that's why it's so essential that you charge an up-front fee to cover your time and marketing expenses); you may never realize that additional percentage from the sale of the invention.

INVESTMENT CLUB ORGANIZER

Startup cost:	$1,000–$5,000
Potential earnings:	$10,000–$40,000+
Typical fees:	A percentage (usually 5 to 15 percent) of the total dividends earned by the club, plus your full share of the dividend as an investor; in lieu of a percentage, you might charge a flat fee for your services ($150–$250)
Advertising:	Classified ads, bulletin boards, and (most importantly) networking
Qualifications:	An interest in the stock market, organizational and research skills; you are an investor/facilitator, not a broker, so certification is not required.
Equipment needed:	Computer with high-speed Internet access, software programs that can generate financial projections, cell phone, fax, TV with cable (to watch special financial programs), and subscriptions to the top financial newspapers
Home business potential:	Yes
Staff required:	No
Hidden costs:	Your own income may fluctuate with the market; be sure to plan for ups and downs

LOWDOWN:

It takes a lot of money to make a real impact on Wall Street, but for those who don't have thousands of dollars to put at risk, investment clubs are a way to dabble in the market without getting burned. Many people have read about investment clubs and would like to start their own, but don't know how. That's where you come in. You're a person who enjoys following the ups and downs on Wall Street and, in all likelihood, you've had some success in the market yourself—perhaps you're even a retired broker. As an investment club organizer, you can put that experience to work assisting others in learning and mastering the art of speculation. You'll help put the club together, then keep it going by taking on the burdens of research and bookkeeping that would normally fall to the volunteer members. It will be your responsibility to study the stock market on a regular basis, keep abreast of trends, and identify likely stocks for purchase. You'll attend the club meetings, keep track of the bank account, make the actual stock purchases, and report on the progress of individual stocks purchased. It's a win-win situation—the club members get to play the market with little risk or hassle, you get to indulge in an activity you enjoy, and, hopefully, you all make some money doing it. There's economy of scale and the chance to make a decent income by handling the details for several investment clubs.

STARTUP:

You'll need some computer strength to crunch numbers and identify "happening" markets. Expect to spend around $2,000 for a powerful computer system and high-speed Internet access (so you can keep tabs on the most up-to-date financial information). Advertising will be minimal; most of your new clients will be the result of networking and referrals. Your earnings could be as little as $5,000 the first year, but expect that number to grow as word gets out about your investment successes. The more clubs you run, the more money you'll make. Once you're more established and have several clubs running simultaneously, you could earn $40,000 or more.

BOTTOM LINE ADVICE:

If highs and lows don't frighten you, go for it! You have an affinity for numbers, you're in constant touch with the markets, and you have the best interests of your clients in mind . . . now all you have to do is make money for them, and once you do, referrals should be no problem. Be prepared to do a lot of hand-holding up front, because the thought of potentially losing money tends to frighten many folks away from investing until they learn more about it and become comfortable with the process. That's why investment clubs are such a good idea—they break people in on key concepts and methods of investing without high risk.

JEWELRY/CLOCK/WATCH REPAIR

Startup cost:	$1,000–$5,000 (more if you need a storefront)
Potential earnings:	$1,800 per month for jewelry; $1,500–$3,000 per month for watches/clocks
Typical fees:	Depends on the jewelry/clock/watch and what is being repaired (can be as low as $5 and as high as several hundred)
Advertising:	Jewelry trade shows, craft and antique fairs, newspapers, jewelry retailers, Yellow Pages
Qualifications:	Gemological Institute of America (GIA) certificate is helpful but not required, knowledge of jewelry and clocks
Equipment needed:	Vises, pliers, jeweler's loupe, magnifying glass, jeweler's tools
Home business potential:	Yes
Staff required:	No
Hidden costs:	Replacement stones, parts

LOWDOWN:

Nothing takes a licking and keeps on ticking forever. Even the best watches, clocks, and pieces of jewelry need to be repaired every once in a while. You will need steady hands and good eyesight to practice this trade well. You'll also need to be exceptionally skilled at detailed work, and enjoy the solitude of working alone with a strong light and a magnifier. Your customers will find you through the Yellow Pages primarily, but you can seek out additional customers at jewelry trade shows, craft shows, and antique fairs. It would be helpful, but not absolutely necessary, to have a GIA certificate. Not only does your GIA training teach you about gemstones, it qualifies you as a licensed appraiser as well—and that can bring you extra dollars.

STARTUP:

Your basement would make the perfect work area for your repair shop; expect to spend about $500 for the necessary equipment. Otherwise, most of your startup expenses will go toward advertising. Spend some time networking with jewelry shops. Those that do not offer repair services are likely to make referrals. Your income could range between $25,000 and $40,000 depending on the type of work you do. Antique clocks and jewelry will command higher fees than watch repair. A combination of all three is probably your best bet.

BOTTOM LINE ADVICE:

Here's a chance to work with fine jewelry, semiprecious/precious stones, and valuable watches or clocks worth hundreds, even thousands, of dollars. Some jewelry repair services have given this business a bad name by using deceptive practices, so you may want to consider registering your service with the Better Business Bureau. Be honest in your dealings, deliver on your promises, and treat your customers with courtesy; you should be able to overcome any lingering public distrust.

LABOR RELATIONS CONSULTANT

Startup cost:	$2,000–$4,000
Potential earnings:	$50,000 and up
Typical fees:	$35–$50 per hour
Advertising:	Referrals, memberships in professional associations and trade groups, advertisements in business publications, direct mail
Qualifications:	Degree in related field, extensive experience in labor relations for a well-respected corporation, ability to gain the confidence of potential clients
Equipment needed:	Computer, fax, printer, Internet access, cell phone
Home business potential:	Yes
Staff required:	No
Hidden costs:	Errors and omissions insurance, utility bills, travel expenses

LOWDOWN:

This is a field for a few outstanding individuals who can show that their expertise in labor relations is applicable to an organization's specific labor challenges. Many companies still operate in a mode of opposition and suspicion between management and employees. Dangers of this approach include unionization, reduced productivity, and an inability to focus as a team on achieving the organization's goals. You will need to reach the top executives of organizations with these or other labor problems and convince them of your ability to bring the two sides together to forge better working relationships. Successful projects will launch your enterprise forward.

STARTUP:

Keeping yourself available to your clients is vitally important to the success of this business. Having an impressive office is not, as you will be working at your clients' premises. You'll need around $2,000 to launch your business, which will cover basic equipment, including a computer, printer, fax, and cell phone. Earnings of $50,000 could be achieved after the first year.

BOTTOM LINE ADVICE:

Setting up a business as a labor relations consultant is not for the faint of heart. You will need boundless self-confidence, an ability to work with angry people to achieve compromise, and excellent teaching skills. Essentially, you will be teaching groups of people how to pull together and in the same direction, for the mutual good of their organization. Even in this age of teamwork and employee empowerment there is still a great deal of need for the services you can provide.

LICENSING AGENT

Startup cost:	$3,000–$6,000
Potential earnings:	$50,000–$100,000
Typical fees:	Percentage of the deal (typically around 15 percent)
Advertising:	Referrals, association memberships, networking
Qualifications:	Salesmanship, outgoing personality, confidence, technical knowledge and/or the ability to communicate with technical "types," and manufacturing specialists
Equipment needed:	Computer, fax, Internet access, copier, scanner, laser printer, cell phone
Home business potential:	Yes
Staff required:	No
Hidden costs:	Insurance, attorney's fees to draw up contracts

LOWDOWN:

The licensing agent acts as a go-between, helping technology-driven companies find manufacturers for their inventions. Conversely, you might also help manufacturers or service companies find organizations that offer the technology they need. The service provided by a licensing agent is often transnational. You may, for example, be finding technology for a Chinese company that cannot develop its own locally. Licensing agents usually specialize in one industry—shoes or electronics, for example—in which they have developed extensive experience and contacts. This saves time and aggravation because the agent already knows many people on "both sides of the street" before negotiations begin. Some technical competence in the field is required, but this can be gained through experience. The other important quality a licensing agent must have is patience. You may work for a long time on several deals, but find, in the end, that only one of them actually pays off.

STARTUP:

Equipping your office to produce professional-looking reports and keep in touch with the rest of the world is the main startup cost; expect to spend at least $3,000 on that alone. However, considering that your 15 percent commission will be spread across a wide range of potentially lucrative projects, your earnings could be as high as $100,000.

BOTTOM LINE ADVICE:

Becoming a licensing agent is an excellent way for a newly laid-off person to make use of his/her industry expertise and contacts. It can be a welcome alternative to simply struggling to get the same job with a competitor. If you have the sales skills, the contacts, and the ability to communicate with "techie" dreamers as easily as hard-nosed business types, you can build a successful enterprise. Keep in mind that you will be paid a percentage of the final deal. This can mean you wait a long time for your money. Be forewarned, too, that client memories can fade with time, so it is essential that you have the specific terms of your compensation agreement in writing from the start. It's when that percentage turns into big money, that the disputes are likely to begin.

LIQUIDATOR

Startup cost:	$2,000–$6,000
Potential earnings:	$20,000–$60,000
Typical fees:	Percentage of sales
Advertising:	Trade publications, memberships in business organizations, direct mail, classifieds, networking, referrals
Qualifications:	Salesmanship, a knack for knowing what goods are worth and the price they'll command
Equipment needed:	Computer, fax, printer, Internet access, cell phone
Home business potential:	Yes
Staff required:	No
Hidden costs:	Storage fees, high phone bills, loss insurance

LOWDOWN:

Liquidators are people who are fast on their feet, can see gold where others see only sheetrock, and don't take "no" for an answer. You will be dealing with the merchandise no one else wants to work with—the odd lots that didn't match, the leftover inventory from bankrupt businesses, and the reclaimed goods ready to be sold after a contract dispute. What sets you apart from a barter service is the plain and simple fact that you are an unloader—getting rid of stuff as quickly as possible without bothering to match your needs to anyone else's. Often, you'll be selling directly to wholesalers or to the general public. You need the confidence to assess the possibilities quickly, develop a pricing and sales strategy in difficult circumstances, and persist until the goods have been liquidated. You also need excellent connections and the ability to engender trust in difficult situations.

STARTUP:

Your office needs to support the intensive marketing-by-phone that a liquidator must practice in order to find a buyer/seller match. You don't need a walnut desk, but the chair had better be comfortable. And you do need to have excellent communications equipment, all of which could generate a nice income of $20,000–$60,000 annually.

BOTTOM LINE ADVICE:

You're working hard to provide a necessary service, but you're not stepping into a bed of roses with each new customer either. Like any good salesperson, you won't be offering as much as the seller hoped to get for the material, and you're going to turn around and sell it for as high a price as you can get. But none of your transactions will have the mellow, customer-service kind of feeling that can develop over the long term in a traditional supplier-customer relationship. The excitement of the chase and the need to be on one's toes at all times are pluses for most liquidators, who thrive on the adrenaline of this fast-paced business. Liquidation can be a great way to make good money if that's the kind of environment in which you feel most alive.

LOBBYIST

Startup cost:	$3,000–$6,000
Potential earnings:	Varies; some lobbyists earn as much as $100,000 or more
Typical fees:	Whatever clients will pay you to further their cause
Advertising:	Networking, word of mouth, and friends in high places
Qualifications:	People skills, knowledge of your specialty area
Equipment needed:	Computer, fax, Internet access, printer, cell phone, pager, professional wardrobe
Home business potential:	Yes
Staff required:	No
Hidden costs:	Travel expenses, phone bills

LOWDOWN:

It is fashionable to assume that lobbyists somehow cause all the problems we experience with our democratic form of government. The reality is that lobbyists help different groups within the country put their views forward. Without the assistance of lobbyists, many state legislatures would have a difficult time producing effective bills. Even the U. S. Congress draws on the expertise of lobbyists for a range of services related to the preparation of legislation. Lobbyists may specialize in a single field or industry, or even represent one company alone, and they must have the ability to develop relationships with the people they hope to influence. To become an effective lobbyist, you'll need to be a good listener and know how to master large amounts of information quickly. Being able to explain issues clearly, with regard to the interests of your listener, will make you an effective representative for your clients. Patience, strong familiarity with the legislative process, persistence, and a sense of humor are other necessary ingredients for lobbyist success.

STARTUP:

You'll need to dress the part of someone who deserves to be listened to, so count clothes as a business expense. And you'll need every possible means of keeping in touch with your clients, including cell phone, pager, and answering service. Expect to spend a maximum of $6,000 on your startup costs to cover a computer system, high-speed Internet connection, the latest communications tools, and a fashionable wardrobe. Sounds like a lot until you consider that it may not be long before you're making a six-figure income.

BOTTOM LINE ADVICE:

If you're effective as a lobbyist, you can pretty much write your own ticket. It will take a lot of hard work and many long hours to achieve that level of success, though. Getting started is hard, and finding ways to have your clients' messages be heard above the roar is even harder. Still, lobbying can be a very stimulating business. You'll be learning all the time, and your studies of human nature will not go unrewarded. Expect to work a lot of nights and weekends; nine-to-fivers need not apply.

MANUFACTURER'S REPRESENTATIVE

Startup cost:	$3,000–$4,000
Potential earnings:	Up to $150,000 (minus travel expenses) within first three years
Typical fees:	Commission basis, usually 3 to 15 percent of product sale (amount depends on product, level of difficulty in selling it, size of territory, and other factors)
Advertising:	Cold-calling, networking, presentations, reference publications
Qualifications:	Sales experience or expertise in a particular field, good people skills, an ability to negotiate
Equipment needed:	Laptop computer with faxing and Internet capabilities, cell phone
Home business potential:	Yes
Staff required:	No
Hidden costs:	Travel expenses

LOWDOWN:

Companies are operating with leaner sales forces these days, creating a need for other alternatives in marketing and selling their products. Independent reps can take on an interesting variety of products to sell—everything from gifts and sporting goods to chemicals, adhesives, and heavy machinery. Many experts recommend that manufacturing agents handle eight to ten lines of goods in order to make a nice profit. In addition to a thorough understanding of your product's features and benefits, you will need to build a solid customer base for each line and have enough money in your personal bank account to carry you while you get established, a process which can take up to a year to accomplish. Having prior experience with the product(s) you "rep" is the easiest way to succeed in this business. Look for opportunities with emerging companies, such as those profiled in entrepreneurial publications and local business newspapers. Be sure to make a client list or personal background sheet available when approaching new companies—they appreciate and often require this level of professionalism.

STARTUP:

Expect to spend around $3,000–$4,000 to cover the cost of your basic home office setup, including computer, printer, copier, and furniture. Since you'll be on the road much of the time, it makes sense for your computer to be a laptop with Internet and faxing capabilities. You'll need a cell phone, too, so that clients can reach you and you can stay in touch with your suppliers. Working for commissions of 3 to 15 percent, it may take a while for you to develop positive cash flow. Do not be discouraged; one good sale is all you need to turn things around and to generate additional business.

BOTTOM LINE ADVICE:

Sales can be an extremely lucrative home business, but you must be willing to pound the pavement—to search for new clients and to service the ones you already have. Meeting and working with people can be rewarding, as can the freedom of choosing the products/companies you will represent and setting your own hours. On the downside, "repping" for a living often means long periods of time away from home and, sometimes, a long wait to be paid for your services. Keep in mind, too, that sales in some fields will require you to be aggressive and highly competitive in order to succeed. Can you swim with the sharks—or will you be eaten alive?

MASSAGE THERAPIST

Startup cost:	$2,000–$5,000 (minus the cost of training)
Potential earnings:	$25,000–$50,000
Typical fees:	$45–$60 per client, per one-hour session
Advertising:	Newspapers, Yellow Pages, bulletin boards, direct mail to corporations
Qualifications:	Training from an accredited school and national certification; many states require licensing
Equipment needed:	Massage table and/or chair, linen, oils; tape or CD player/relaxing music, cell phone or pager
Home business potential:	Yes (but corporate massage therapists work on-site)
Staff required:	None
Hidden costs:	Liability insurance

LOWDOWN:

If you derive satisfaction from helping people and you believe in the power of personal contact, a career in massage therapy could be just the ticket. Gone are the days when the term "massage therapist" was a euphemism for an entirely different "profession." Massage therapists are finally coming into their own as certified professionals and key participants in the overall health and wellness movement. A massage therapist must study human anatomy and physiology as clinically and carefully as a paramedic. In addition to manual dexterity and sensitivity to the needs of others, the massage therapist must be a bit of a sleuth, finding a client's "trouble spots," then applying just the right touch in just the right places for maximum relaxation and stress relief. With many of us leading increasingly stressful lives, massage therapists are welcome additions to all kinds of venues—from health clubs and wellness centers to metaphysical bookstores and even corporate executive suites. Many massage therapists visit harried executives on-site to work out the kinks in their backs and necks. Still others work out of their homes or from small offices in quiet neighborhoods.

STARTUP:

A home office is your most economical choice, but if you decide to lease a small space elsewhere, expect to spend at least $350 per month on rent alone. Add to that the cost of your massage table and/or chair ($350–$500), a tape or CD player and some relaxing music, soothing oils, and supply of linens. You'll need a cell phone, too, so that you can always be in touch with clients when you're away from your home base. Finally, you must get the word out via advertising and/or direct mail to individuals and corporate clients, so be prepared to spend about $500–$1,000 on your initial marketing, too. You can charge a pretty hefty rate per one-hour massage ($45–$60), but keep in mind that massage therapy is physically demanding work; realistically, your body probably won't be able to handle more than four one-hour sessions per day.

BOTTOM LINE ADVICE:

Working in a relaxing atmosphere while helping others relieve stress can be positively exhilarating for you—but it can also be tiring. You'll be on your feet most of every day. Can you stand up to the physical demands of this business? If the answer is yes, the rest of your job will, like those tense muscles you knead, fall back into place.

MEDICAL PRACTICE MANAGEMENT CONSULTANT

Startup cost:	$3,000–$6,000
Potential earnings:	$30,000–$75,000
Typical fees:	$5,000–$10,000 per contract
Advertising:	Referrals, trade publications, memberships and participation in professional groups, networking, seminars and public speaking
Qualifications:	Academic degree in related field, extensive experience in medical practice development and management
Equipment needed:	Computer, with word processing, database, and spreadsheet software; printer; fax; copier; cell phone; marketing materials
Home business potential:	Yes
Staff required:	No
Hidden costs:	Research, membership dues, subscriptions, errors and omissions insurance, additional secretarial services

LOWDOWN:

As the health care marketplace becomes more challenging, the demand for professional assistance in setting up and/or maintaining a medical practice increases. Few medical graduates have received adequate training in the business side of providing health care services. In addition, meeting government regulations and managing the complexities of insurance billing require sophisticated office planning and staff training. Medical practice management consultants offer the services that most physicians require to make a financial success of their practices. You will need a demonstrable record of success, along with excellent referrals, to market yourself effectively. Knowing how to make a physician's office run well, and being able to persuade a busy doctor to engage your services are two completely different skills. Some medical practice management consultants put together a package designed specifically for doctors who are establishing their practices for the first time; others specialize in working with group or multilocation practices.

STARTUP:

Most of your client interactions will take place in their offices, so your own workplace can be furnished for function rather than show; expect to spend around $3,000 for the necessary equipment. Your earnings could be as much as $30,000 the first year.

BOTTOM LINE ADVICE:

Physicians are not the easiest people to reach; they are always pressed for time, and they receive an avalanche of marketing messages every day. The word has gotten out, however, that to be effective and profitable, a medical practice needs to start out with an excellent business structure, staff, and strategic plan. Your marketing strategy should be to point out that you will be helping your clients focus on what they are trained to do—provide patient care—so they can stop wasting time on management and start making money.

MEETING PLANNER

Startup cost:	$2,500–$5,000
Potential earnings:	$25,000 to start per year; possibly as high as $100,000 per year after you get established
Typical fees:	$40–$60 per hour or $400–$500 per day; planners handling large events such as multiday conventions may get 15 to 20 percent of the overall projected budget for the entire event
Advertising:	Networking with convention and visitors' bureaus, caterers, and travel agents to learn about conferences and conventions coming to your area; paid advertising in meetings magazines
Qualifications:	Excellent organizational and negotiation skills; detail-orientation; solid business background; communications and troubleshooting skills
Equipment needed:	Basic office setup with computer, project management software, printer, Internet access, fax, and copier; cell phone or pager; reference books
Home business potential:	Yes
Staff required:	No
Hidden costs:	Phone charges, insurance

LOWDOWN:

If you like handling the myriad details that go into planning meetings, conventions, and other formal events, and if you have the organizational, negotiation, and communications skills necessary to pull them off, you can have a great career as a meeting planner. It will take a little legwork to get started, but you may be surprised how many sources of business you are able to uncover. Corporations and associations of all sizes need to bring their employees/members together from time to time, and conventions and trade shows are probably happening right now in your own community. In many organizations, meetings and events are increasingly viewed as great sales and marketing opportunities, but as companies become "leaner," employees can no longer be spared to oversee all the necessary details. Creative professional meeting planners are in demand, and that's where you come in.

You will need to be knowledgeable about many facets of the meeting process—everything from booking hotels and selecting menus to making travel arrangements to and from the event. The life of a meeting planner is never dull. On any given day, you may be negotiating for the best room rates, researching exotic locales in which to hold a company meeting, booking speakers and after-dinner entertainment, setting up promotions, and fine-tuning the many large and small details that make for a successful event. As a bonus, you may get to travel to exciting locations, stay at exclusive resorts and hotels, and meet interesting people from many walks of life. Best of all, you will have the satisfaction of actually seeing people enjoy the event you have put so much time and energy into planning.

STARTUP:

You'll need a basic home office setup, including a computer, project management software, printer, copier, fax, high-speed Internet access, and reference books; expect to spend $2,500–$3,500 to get started. Your fees will typically be $40–$50 per hour or $400–$600 per day. To gain valuable experience when you're just starting out, try volunteering your services to plan a few small civic or charitable events; from there, word of mouth will help build your business.

BOTTOM LINE ADVICE:

Meeting planning can be very rewarding, and, from the outside, it may look more glamorous than it really is. You will work hard and put in some very long days. If you are good at handling details, you have a leg up already, because every little piece of the puzzle is crucially important to the overall success of the event. In addition to making sure you have adequate money for your startup, bear in mind that a meeting planner's income is directly tied to economic conditions; in down times, companies may tighten their meeting budgets to cut costs. Nevertheless, there will always be a need for meetings and conventions that are productive and well-run, and the trend toward outsourcing these events to professional meeting planners will continue—good news for you!

MOBILE HAIR SALON

Startup costs:	$1,000–$5,000
Potential earnings:	$25,000–$50,000
Typical fees:	$15–$75, depending on the service (haircuts cost less than perms or color)
Advertising:	Local newspapers, direct mail, coupons, contacts with nursing homes and hospitals
Qualifications:	Must be a licensed cosmetologist
Equipment needed:	Scissors, electric trimmers, rollers, combs, brushes, portable hair dryer, blow dryer, curling wands, towels, capes, and supplies (shampoo, conditioners, color, perms, etc.); vehicle for hauling it all
Home business potential:	Yes (but you'll be mobile, of course)
Staff required:	Yes
Hidden costs:	Insurance, continuing education, cell phone, mileage

LOWDOWN:

A hairdresser who makes house calls? What could be more convenient? Or profitable, perhaps, considering that you're not saddled with the overhead of maintaining a stationary salon. You will, of course, need a vehicle to transport your equipment; a station wagon or van should do. And just think of all the likely customers for this convenient service—busy executives, stay-at-home moms, shut-ins, nursing home residents, and hospital patients, to name a few. You'll want to schedule your appointments carefully, so that you're not wasting time backtracking or zipping from one side of town to the other and back. If you set a day of each week to service a specific area, you'll reduce time and travel expenses. Clients will appreciate your in-house service and you can expect to earn some nice tips in addition to your usual fees.

STARTUP:

You'll spend between $1,000–$5,000 getting this show on the road, so to speak. Your money will mainly go to cover equipment and supplies (as a licensed cosmetologist, you pay wholesale, of course). Your charges will vary from $15–$75, depending on the service you are providing, but, in all cases, be sure to incorporate your vehicle costs into your fee structure.

BOTTOM LINE ADVICE:

If you're in the middle of a perm or coloring job, you can't very well stop to take a phone call or book an appointment. You'll need to either hire a receptionist or contract with an answering service to take those incoming calls.

MONEY BROKER

Startup cost:	$1,500–$3,000
Potential earnings:	$40,000–$60,000
Typical fees:	Commission/percentage (usually 5 to 15 percent)
Advertising:	Direct mail, classified ads
Qualifications:	Familiarity with financial news reporting, detail orientation, persistence
Equipment needed:	Computer, fax, high-speed Internet access, word processing and spreadsheet software, printer, copier
Home business potential:	Yes
Staff required:	No
Hidden costs:	Printing materials for reports, utility bills, high-speed Internet access fees

LOWDOWN:

Tracking down money can be surprisingly challenging and time consuming. Yet many businesses depend on loans, either directly or as part of their customers' buying process. Real estate agencies and automobile dealerships, for example, need up-to-date information on the availability of loans because almost all of their transactions will depend on this source of money. Your service saves countless phone calls and prevents missed opportunities because you gather this information and report it to your client companies. They can then transmit it to their buyers. Loan rates, money rates, exchange rates, and a wealth of other financial listings are printed in magazines and newspapers, and online. You will be spending a lot of time on the Internet and at the library gathering the data your clients need. You'll then generate reports, which you distribute to them monthly.

STARTUP:

Your clients probably won't ever see your office, but you'll spend a lot of time there reading, compiling, and writing reports, so you want it to be both functional and comfortable. Since much of your information gathering will take place online, buy the best computer and software you can afford and spring for the fastest Internet connection. Expect to spend $1,500–$3,000 setting up this business. With commissions of 5 to 15 percent, you could make $40,000–$60,000 if you work hard and deliver the information your clients need in a timely manner.

BOTTOM LINE ADVICE:

Consider becoming a money broker if you find finance a fascinating world of shifting relationships and monetary opportunities rather than simply dry, meaningless numbers. You'll need a love of the details to sustain the tedious fact-gathering required to succeed. Financial acumen is reasonably rare, so if you've got it, build a business around it and market yourself effectively.

MOTIVATIONAL SPEAKER

Startup cost:	$1,000–$5,000
Potential earnings:	$40,000–$100,000 (depending on the scope and appeal of your message)
Typical fees:	These vary widely according to experience level and your own personal magnetism; individuals will pay $100 and up to hear speeches they feel will change their lives
Advertising:	Newspapers, Yellow Pages, business publications, networking with associations
Qualifications:	Engaging message, excellent presentation skills, and a communicative ability that truly inspires
Equipment needed:	Computer, printer, and word processing and presentation software only if you intend to provide handouts or visuals; if necessary, you can rent overhead and slide projectors from the facilities you speak at
Home business potential:	Yes
Staff required:	No (unless you're selling tapes, books, or other materials)
Hidden costs:	Travel expenses; make sure you cover these in your fee structure

LOWDOWN:

Dale Carnegie did it . . . so did Les Brown, Lee Iacocca, and Anthony Robbins. They spoke to millions of people from all walks of life and business, and inspired them to feel empowered . . . able to accomplish things they never thought possible and to win friends and influence people. The most renowned motivational speakers got their starts speaking to small groups at the local and regional levels, collecting testimonials, and growing their speaking businesses to nationwide appeal through related books, tapes, and other workshop products. Do you enjoy public speaking? Do you have an engaging style, a unique story to tell and/or an unusual spin on how to improve oneself or one's relationships? If so, you may have the makings of a motivational speaker. Study the many programs that are already out there, watch how the other guys (and gals) do it, then work every day at making your presentation better. Be sure that you have something of value to offer—a personal experience others can learn from or a step-by-step program they can use to change their own lives for the better. Don't just try to sell a trendy idea or a meaningless topic; make your presentation something your audience can truly apply. Your ability to lift people to greater personal fulfillment is what will ultimately lift your sales to new heights. Be prepared to travel, and consider marketing your presentation to one of the many large seminar promotion companies that can get your name out nationwide. You will have to give up a piece of the profits in exchange for bookings, but it may be worth your while to let someone else do the legwork in rounding up audiences so that you can concentrate on the presentation.

STARTUP:

Unless you decide to produce your own slick visuals and handouts, startup costs are pretty low for this business; you'll need to invest approximately $1,000–$5,000 for advertising/promotion. Beyond that, the only equipment you must have is a pager or cell phone to stay connected to those who are willing to hire you. As a motivational speaker, you can charge anywhere from $25–$150 per person for a seminar, depending on your experience level, audience size, and uniqueness of your message.

BOTTOM LINE ADVICE:

Your business hinges on your ability to stay busy—plan to offer at least one speaking engagement per month to start. Organize your speech well, and videotape it for your own viewing so that you can correct your mistakes before you put yourself in front of a live audience. Get opinions from others, iron out the details, and practice, practice, practice!

ADVICE FROM THE EXPERTS

What sets your business apart from others like it?

"Mine is a high-energy presentation that leaves audiences with messages they can use in everyday living," says Barbara Greavu, owner of Something Else & More in Canton, Ohio. "I present them with things they can remember in a humorous format that's easily understood."

Things you couldn't do without:

"I'm finally buying a fax machine. I have believed for the longest time that, if you have a passion for what you do, you don't really need much technology."

Marketing tips/advice:

"Read, read, read—anything and everything that's pertinent to your speaking business. You don't have a tangible product with this kind of work, so speak to other speakers to get the ins and outs of the business."

If you had to do it all over again . . .

Greavu wishes she had spent more time networking with other speaking professionals. "I would have researched better in the beginning, and I would have made a greater effort to talk with others in the business. They would have warned me or given me a better sense of direction, I'm sure."

MOVER

Startup cost:	$1,500–$5,000
Potential earnings:	$20,000 and up
Typical fees:	Varies; charge by the hour or by the number of rooms and distance to be moved (don't forget to factor in stairs!)
Advertising:	Classified ads, radio spots, direct mail, fliers, community bulletin boards, referrals
Qualifications:	Physical strength, packing ability
Equipment needed:	Truck, pads, straps, packing materials
Home business potential:	Yes
Staff required:	Yes
Hidden costs:	Insurance, truck maintenance

LOWDOWN:

The phone directory is filled with listings for moving companies. So to be successful in this business, you will need to carve out a niche. Start by asking yourself a few questions: What can I specialize in—short distance moves perhaps, maybe apartments or offices only? What type of moving service is not readily available in my community? How can I fill that void? The companies that move households across the continent in enormous vans are too expensive and too difficult to schedule for a move within the same community. That's good news for you. Short distance and small household moves are an underserved market, and meeting these needs in a flexible, cost-effective way could allow you to fulfill your entrepreneurial ambitions as you use your knowledge of how to get heavy stuff up and down stairs and from here to there. Another wide open local market is commercial relocation: moving the contents of an office or store from one location to another within the same community.

STARTUP:

Purchasing a truck and paying a reliable staff could cost you big bucks. You could, however, start out for as little as $1,500 if you rent a truck and take on help only when you absolutely need to. Your physical endurance—how many moves your body can stand—will determine your earnings, but you should be able to make at least $20,000, more if you can handle multiple moves each week.

BOTTOM LINE ADVICE:

Your primary market will probably be those people who had originally planned to handle their moves themselves, then realized at the last minute that the task was just too big. You will need to position your business in such a way that these frustrated, desperate people can find you easily and recognize that the value of your service far outweighs its cost: less breakage, no backaches, a quicker, more orderly move, and so on. To inspire confidence in your customers so that they trust you with their valuables, you will need to treat every item as if it were your own. Every move you complete in a professional manner and without any breakage or damage, will mean another recommendation you can use to secure additional business; word of mouth will fuel your continued success.

MURDER MYSTERY PRODUCER

Startup cost:	$1,000–$5,000
Potential earnings:	$20,000–$40,000
Typical fees:	$35–$50 per person, which includes dinner (more if providing overnight accommodations)
Advertising:	Entertainment publications, newspapers, bulletin boards, city magazines, Yellow Pages
Qualifications:	Creativity and a flair for the dramatic; writing ability; theater experience is helpful but not mandatory
Equipment needed:	Costumes, props
Home business potential:	No
Staff required:	Yes (actors who can convincingly stage a "murder")
Hidden costs:	Advertising could get expensive; if you are not a writer, you will have to hire one to create your scripts

LOWDOWN:

Imagine, if you will, a quaint restaurant in the middle of a quiet neighborhood. You and your guests are seated at a lavish table, complete with Victorian amenities and delicious food. You don't know all of the people around you, nor do you know that some of them are "plants." A dark figure walks into the room and begins arguing with your dinner mate, an actor in disguise. Suddenly, your dining companion is "shot" and "killed"—and you and your remaining tablemates are thrust into the role of amateur sleuths in order to solve the "mystery." Sound like fun? Many people think so, and that has fueled the popularity of the murder mystery production business, particularly among those with backgrounds in theater. The challenge for you as a producer is your ability to stage a "murder" that is so convincing the guests feel compelled, and just a little thrilled, to solve it. The evening is all in good fun, of course; right from the start, the guests know it's not real and that everything will come out just fine in the end, but, until then, they're willing to buy into the fantasy and play along. You'll need to provide them with clues (don't forget the infamous "red herrings" to throw them off the trail!) and give them free rein to take the plot in any number of different directions. To ensure repeat business, you'll need to constantly come up with innovative twists and thicker plots. Feel up to it? Good, then let's get started.

STARTUP:

Theatrical events such as murder mysteries are headed for disaster without sufficient advertising. Plan to spend at least $1,000–$3,000 on this expense alone; set aside another 2,000 or so for costumes, props, and a good script. Charging $35–$50 a head for these charming little dinner theater adventures could net you a tidy sum. Your actors can double as servers, but keep in mind that you will have to pay them something—half the minimum wage plus tips at the very least—unless you can find university students willing to work for nothing in exchange for the acting experience.

BOTTOM LINE ADVICE:

There is a huge market out there for entertainment that is interesting and different. Murder mystery productions fill that bill, and they can be staged quite cost-effectively if you work out arrangements with a local restaurant or hotel. Offer the venue a percentage of the take in exchange for the food and space, and you will be off to a profitable start!

NEWSLETTER PUBLISHER

Startup cost:	$3,000–$5,000
Potential earnings:	$25,000–$60,000
Typical fees:	Subscription newsletters: $25–$50 per subscription + advertising revenues, if applicable; newsletters produced for others: $25–$60 per hour or $125–$250 per page
Advertising:	Direct mail, advertising in magazines and trade journals, networking, Web site
Qualifications:	Excellent writing abilities and news judgment; design, typography, layout skills; organization
Equipment needed:	Computer, printer, scanner, copier, desktop publishing software
Home business potential:	Yes
Staff required:	No
Hidden costs:	Generating new subscribers and renewals

LOWDOWN:

Thanks to the proliferation of computers and the ease of using desktop publishing software, newsletters are more readily available and less expensive to create than ever before. You can start your own newsletter, or contract with a business or organization to design, write, and distribute its monthly publication directed at clients or members. You'll need an eye for design, exceptional writing skills, and the ability to determine the types of information that will most likely grab the attention of your readership. If you are creating your own newsletter, you're in complete control of the focus and content; on the downside, you're also in charge of the mailing list and you will have to spend a good deal of time selling both new subscriptions and renewals to ensure a steady income.

Producing newsletters for others, on the other hand, allows you to devote the bulk of your time to the publishing process rather than to distribution. The subscriber list is determined by your client, the business or organization that contracts for your design and writing expertise. You may charge by the hour or per newsletter page. As a marketing device, you might consider soliciting clients in a particular industry or profession in which you already have contacts and experience, such as banking, health care, insurance, or real estate; churches, trade and professional organizations, and homeowners' associations are also potential clients for your newsletter publishing services.

STARTUP:

You will need a powerful computer and special desktop publishing software to create your finished product, in addition to a laser printer, desktop scanner, and fax. Expect to spend approximately $3,000 to get up and running. Your marketing costs will depend on whether yours is a subscription or contracted newsletter. If you are seeking paid subscribers to underwrite your costs, you will need to advertise by direct mail and in magazines and trade journals; a Web site would also be useful. For securing contracted newsletter assignments, you'll find that networking is your most effective marketing tool. Depending on newsletter size and frequency of distribution, you may be able to handle several different publications, but keep in mind that readers come to expect that their newsletters will show up in their mailboxes at around the same time every month. You will have to generate a lot of story ideas and be exceptionally well organized in order to meet multiple deadlines on a continuing basis.

BOTTOM LINE ADVICE:

The purpose of a newsletter is to provide interesting, cutting-edge information about a subject that a reader might not be able to find elsewhere. Before launching a subscription newsletter, consider carefully whether you can fulfill that purpose in every issue for several years to come. And don't expect that once you snare a subscriber the first time, you will automatically be able to retain him or her from one year to the next. Finding new subscribers and generating renewals will be a continuing challenge. Be careful about setting your subscription price too low; too many subscribers can drive you right out of business (remember what happened to *Life* magazine!). Price your product to cover the costs of printing and mailing, then allow a little something extra for yourself. You are in this business, after all, to make money.

NEWSPAPER DELIVERY SERVICE

Startup cost:	$1,000–$5,000
Potential earnings:	$10,000 or more
Typical fees:	Usually a flat rate
Advertising:	Cold-calling
Qualifications:	Ingenuity and persistence
Equipment needed:	Van, canvas bags
Home business potential:	Yes
Staff required:	Yes
Hidden costs:	Maintenance, fuel

LOWDOWN:

Working as a subcontractor, you can provide newspaper delivery within a specific geographic area. With the move toward morning newspapers in many localities, it has become more difficult for newspaper publishers to find reliable carriers. The preteens who used to fulfill this role are no longer available to get up before dawn, deliver papers, and still get through a full day of school. You'll fill that void, delivering one or more routes yourself and hiring a crew to complete the rest.

STARTUP:

You will need a van or pickup truck to pick up bundles of newspapers and to drop them off at your assistants' routes; if you don't already have a vehicle, you should be able to pick up a used one for $3,000 or less. Your other expense will go toward paying your assistants. This isn't easy work—you'll have to be a morning person—but for a part-time job, $10,000 a year to start is pretty darn good money.

BOTTOM LINE ADVICE:

Newspaper delivery might well be the embodiment of the classic American dream: a job that depends on hard work (and an excellent alarm clock) rather than on education, social position, or good luck. To earn an adequate return on your efforts, you'll need to have others working for you, and managing others brings its own set of challenges. You'll need to always be on top of your employees to make sure they are as attentive to their responsibilities as you are to yours. There's no glamour to the job of delivering newspapers, but it's good, honest work, and you'll get plenty of exercise to boot.

NOVELTY MESSAGE SERVICE

Startup cost:	$2,000–$4,000
Potential earnings:	$15,000–$35,000
Typical fees:	$65–$100 per delivery; more if you provide special entertainment like a song or tap dance
Advertising:	Yellow Pages, newspapers, fliers, referrals
Qualifications:	Imagination and a highly developed sense of fun; some acting, dance, or comedy experience is helpful
Equipment needed:	Distinctive costumes and props; phone with answering machine or voice mail; dependable vehicle; cell phone
Home business potential:	Yes
Staff required:	No
Hidden costs:	Mileage, costume purchase or rental

LOWDOWN:

Do you have an outgoing personality and a flair for the dramatic? Would you like to play dress-up and pull off a surprise? If so, then you may be the perfect candidate to launch a novelty message service. You can use your acting or comedic talents to deliver a gift, card, box of chocolates, balloon bouquet, a teddy bear, or even just a simple message, song, or poem in a unique and unforgettable way. Your clients will designate the unsuspecting recipient, who might be a birthday honoree, new parent, recent graduate, newly engaged couple—in short, anyone who is celebrating a milestone or special occasion. You can show up with your greeting dressed as a gorilla, the Easter Bunny, one of Santa's elves, a clown, a storybook favorite, or any costumed character you can think of (as long as it's not copyrighted!).

STARTUP:

The bulk of your startup costs will go toward costumes and props. And unless you think you'll get several uses out of a particular get-up, it's probably more cost-effective to rent rather than purchase. Aside from that, you'll need a phone with an answering machine or voice mail (your message is a sales tool so make it an entertaining one!), plus a dependable vehicle and cell phone. You'll spend the rest of your startup funds on marketing. At the very least you'll need a Yellow Pages listing and selectively placed newspaper ads and fliers. Be sure to carry business cards and leave one behind whenever you deliver a message. If your deliveries are in public places, you're sure to draw a crowd and, if you pull things off, you'll probably also generate a few referrals as a result.

BOTTOM LINE ADVICE:

Novelty messaging is not a business for the timid or uptight. To make this work, you have to be willing to enter into the occasion and to make yourself look a little silly in the process. This is all in good fun, so always remember to act professionally and in good taste. Be sure to confirm your appointments with your clients a day or two ahead of time; nothing could be more embarrassing (or sink your business faster) than showing up at the wrong place, date, or time!

OIL AND GAS FIELD SERVICES

Startup cost:	$2,000–$4,000
Potential earnings:	$30,000–$40,000
Typical fees:	Hourly rate of $150 or daily rate of $500+
Advertising:	Relationships with energy companies, referrals, advertising in trade journals
Qualifications:	Extensive experience, scientific training in geology or related field, good negotiating and people skills
Equipment needed:	Computer, printer, word-processing software, digital camera, cell phone
Home business potential:	Yes (not that you will be home much!)
Staff required:	No
Hidden costs:	Travel, telephone bills

LOWDOWN:

America runs on energy, primarily oil and natural gas. You can make an excellent living if you have the skills and experience to find new sites where wells should be drilled to capture more of these vital resources. You'll need to be a trained geologist, and you'll need that "sixth sense" that tells you where the black gold lies. But you'll need more than science to succeed. Developing the contracts for securing drilling rights will require good people skills, too. You will probably be working in many different parts of the country, each with its own landscape and human culture.

STARTUP:

Although you'll be out in the field most of the time, you will need to write up your reports in a professional manner, so a basic computer with word-processing software and printer may be all the equipment you need, along with a mobile phone or pager and a digital camera to visually record your findings. Expect to lay out approximately $2,000–$3,000 for startup expenses. Bill by the hour ($150 per) or by the day ($500 and up).

BOTTOM LINE ADVICE:

Although oil and gas exploration is essential in order to maintain our comfortable way of life, in the past, this field has had its shady practitioners, and the reputation for hoodwinking naive farmers out of their cow pastures tends to linger today. You are in charge of your own reputation, and you will slowly build up your name for accuracy and honesty as you work. You may set up a cozy home office, but since you won't be spending much time there, you had better develop an enjoyment for your own company and a knack for making friends with strangers.

ONLINE AUCTION SALES

Startup cost:	$1,000–$2,000
Potential earnings:	Depends on what you have to sell and how aggressively you promote it
Typical fees:	Varies; you set your own prices and decide which bids you want to accept
Advertising:	Auction sites offer basic listings at no charge; for additional fees, you can add a snappy headline, graphic design elements like boldfacing, a photo, etc., to make your listing stand out
Qualifications:	A feel for what individual items are worth and the ability to recognize what's likely to sell
Equipment needed:	Computer and Internet access
Home business potential:	Yes
Staff required:	No
Hidden costs:	Federal and state income taxes; in some states, your transactions may be subject to sales tax; state licensing may be required in order to sell some items (i.e., real estate)

LOWDOWN:

Garage sales long ago proved that what one person considers trash, another just might call treasure . . . and, what's more, be willing to fork over a handful of cold hard cash to own. While the interest in garage sales seems to have peaked a bit these days, the desire to drive a hard bargain is every bit as strong. Except now, instead of cruising the neighborhood on Saturday morning looking for garage sale signs, thousands of people are logging on 24/7 to go bargain-hunting online. At dozens of online auction sites—eBay being the largest and easily the most famous—everything from classic cars and custom clothing to fine art and fragile antique glassware are trading hands right now at an amazingly swift pace. For a capsule introduction into how the online auction process works, go to *www.eBay.com* for details and step-by-step instructions.

Most people who get into online auction sales in a big way start out as hobbyists, selling a few personal items for a profit, then moving into the sale of goods they specifically purchase for resale. Setting your prices can be a challenge. If you decide to specialize in a particular category or type of goods, you're probably either a collector or connoisseur and already have a pretty good idea of market values. If not, try searching the "buy" side of the auction Web site for similar goods; you'll be able to check asking prices and see how the items are being presented, then adjust your own price and presentation accordingly. Remember that you are allotted a limited amount of space in which to describe your item. Point out the features (and flaws, if necessary), but avoid broad descriptors like "wow" or "fantastic." Buyers looking for a particular item search these sites by certain keywords, and adjectives are not likely to be among the search terms they select.

STARTUP:

You can get started in the online auction business for next to nothing; you will, of course need a computer and Internet access (a high-speed connection is recommended). You'll pay a small nominal fee simply for listing your item; the amount of that fee is based on the minimum sale price you set. If your item doesn't sell, you pay nothing more; if it does, you'll be charged a final value fee, which is a percentage of the closing price you receive for the item. How you collect payment is between you and the buyer; once again, eBay can show you, step-by-step, how to oversee the finer details of payment and shipping. Pay attention to this information because how you handle customer service can affect your "feedback score" (a rating customers give to you based on your performance), which, in turn, can directly impact your future sales.

BOTTOM LINE ADVICE:

Playing the online auction game is a lot like gambling; it can easily become addictive. If you're like most people who decide to make a business of online auction sales, you probably started by casually selling off some minor piece of "junk" from your own home on eBay. You made a little money, so you looked around the garage and found something else to list. Before too long, you'd run out of personal possessions to sell and began snapping up goods at flea markets and garage sales with the sole intention of reselling them online. There's nothing wrong with that—and you might even make some decent money—just be aware that by doing so, your online sales have become a business and, as such, subject to taxation. Any profits you make off of online auction sales, whether as a hobby or full-fledged business, must be reported to the IRS. And depending on the state you live in and where your buyer is located, you may also have to contend with sales tax.

ONLINE JOB SEARCH

Startup cost:	$3,000–$6,000
Potential earnings:	$25,000–$50,000
Typical fees:	$25 or more per hour
Advertising:	Web site, referrals, electronic and personal networking, Yellow Pages
Qualifications:	Human resources or other job search/hiring experience, extensive familiarity with online searches, ability to draw people out and help them assess their career goals
Equipment needed:	Computer with sufficient memory for high-speed operation, high-speed Internet access, printer, fax, word processing, database, and spreadsheet software
Home business potential:	Yes
Staff required:	No
Hidden costs:	Telephone charges, high-speed Internet access fees

LOWDOWN:

Most people know that the Internet has practical applications for their lives, but they don't know how to access much of the information that is available to them, particularly with regard to job hunting. You can provide a valuable service to job seekers by guiding their paths through the many online career databases available and helping them prepare resumes suitable for an electronic job search. The scannable resume, which focuses on the keywords that allow computerized searching and sorting, is quite different from the graphically attractive hard copy resume that has until recently been the standard. As an online job searcher, you will serve as the link between your client and a very large but invisible world of potential employers. Anyone can search for their own jobs online, of course, so you will want to stress the advantages of using your service, not the least of which is the value of a search by someone (like you!) with exceptional knowledge of the various career database options currently available.

STARTUP:

For maximum efficiency, you'll want to spend the extra money for a powerful computer and high-speed Internet access. Expect your startup costs to be in the neighborhood of around $3,000. Since you'll be spending a lot of time in front of the screen, you'll need a comfortable chair and a monitor that is easy on the eyes. A good first-year income to shoot for is $25,000; expect to double that as you become more adept at surfing the Web and matching your clients to job availabilities.

BOTTOM LINE ADVICE:

Online job searching is still a relatively new field, which makes it fun and exciting if you like being on the cutting edge of developments in the business world. On the flip side, that means your marketing efforts will have to be more intensive and will have to contain an element of education. The people who can use your help the most are exactly the ones who won't immediately understand what an online job search can do for them and why they should pay you to do it. Keep careful track of your successes to support your later marketing and sales claims.

PARALEGAL

Startup cost:	$2,000–$4,000
Potential earnings:	$45,000–$65,000
Typical fees:	$40–$65 per hour
Advertising:	Yellow Pages, local business periodicals, direct mail, association memberships
Qualifications:	Degree in the field, experience, proven track record, excellent organizational skills, service orientation
Equipment needed:	Fully equipped home office with computer; word processing, spreadsheet, and database software; laser printer; fax; scanner; copier; Internet access
Home business potential:	Yes
Staff required:	No
Hidden costs:	Office supplies, software upgrades

LOWDOWN:

More and more lawyers are striking out on their own these days, setting up small firms or even starting single-shingle practices. And while these "lone wolves" often need support services from time to time, they soon find that keeping a person on staff full-time to handle these tasks is both impractical and just too expensive. Independent paralegals can find a niche in this market by offering to complete many of the routine legal tasks that can drain a lawyer's time and energy but still must be done. As an independent paralegal, you will be providing the services that large firms and corporate legal departments retain full-time staff to perform. For a small law firm, the ability to have effective paralegal services on hand only when needed means clients can be serviced for much less cost than if all the necessary quasi-legal tasks had to be performed by the lawyer. In an age where legal bills are being scrutinized closely and clients are striving to reduce fees, your ability to provide efficient, cost-effective support services can be an important selling tool.

STARTUP:

You will need a top-drawer computer, software, and peripherals to get started in this business; expect to spend $2,000–$4,000 up front. For some clients, you may need to work on-site; others will allow you to work from your own home office. Keeping in mind that many attorneys in small firms charge $100 and more per hour, you should not be afraid to command $40–$65 for your knowledge and expertise.

BOTTOM LINE ADVICE:

One look in the phone book would seem to suggest there's a glut of lawyers these days and that they couldn't possibly all have enough work to keep yet another paralegal busy. Not so. The opportunities for paralegal work are on the rise. To be successful, you will need to offer excellent service, complete tasks correctly, ask questions about the areas that are unclear, and deal efficiently with the time crunches that always seem to go hand-in-hand with the practice of law. Once the lawyers in your community come to know your work, they will see you as a solution to the staffing problems they face and your business will grow exponentially.

PARENTING SPECIALIST

Startup cost:	$1,000–$5,000
Potential earnings:	$5,000–$50,000+
Typical fees:	$30–$50 per hour
Advertising:	Networking with nursery schools, play groups, day care centers, YMCA, hospitals, bulletin boards; post fliers wherever parents with young children are likely to gather
Qualifications:	Common sense and parental experience; a degree in childhood development or psychology is helpful but not mandatory
Equipment needed:	Good resource materials, i.e., books, magazines, tapes, etc.
Home business potential:	Yes
Staff required:	No
Hidden costs:	Travel expenses

LOWDOWN:

There was a time in our society when parental advice was passed down from generation to generation. But in today's high-tech, dual-income families, who often live thousands of miles away from relatives, there doesn't seem to be time or the opportunity for mothers and fathers to teach their daughters and sons how to be parents. Good parenting is not necessarily an innate skill; some new moms and dads especially need to be shown how to be parents. Your job as a parenting specialist will be to ease their "parent-anoia." With the patience of a saint you will go into homes with young children and teach the bewildered parents everything from changing a diaper and taking a temperature to handling a tantrum in public and planning a birthday party for a two-year-old. You'll find plenty of prospects for your services in big cities, but don't overlook the suburbia or rural areas, either.

STARTUP:

Your biggest expense will be for marketing yourself and keeping a library of up-to-date reference material on hand for help in unique situations. Since your startup cost will be relatively low (under $2,000), you could earn an easy $25,000 in your first year, no matter where you live.

BOTTOM LINE ADVICE:

You really must love children of all ages to be in this business, and you have to be an excellent example for other parents to follow. When you watch previously frazzled parents turn calm, loving, and caring with their kids, you'll truly appreciate the importance of your work. On the downside, even though you never claimed to be a Dr. Spock, you may be looked upon as one and called upon for advice in all kinds of situations; expect to be on call 24/7. Time has no meaning for babies and children, who often pick the least convenient hours to drive their parents crazy.

PAYROLL ADMINISTRATIVE SERVICES

Startup cost:	$3,000–$6,000
Potential earnings:	$40,000–$60,000
Typical fees:	$25–$40 per hour
Advertising:	Trade publications, direct mail, networking, memberships in community and business groups
Qualifications:	Bookkeeping skills, expertise in payroll technicalities, taxes
Equipment needed:	Office furniture, computer, suite software, fax, modem, printer, business cards, letterhead, envelopes
Home business potential:	Yes
Staff required:	No
Hidden costs:	Errors and omissions insurance, software upgrades

LOWDOWN:

Those accounting software packages that came on the market a few years ago were supposed to make payroll easier for small business owners to manage themselves. In reality, if price tags were placed on the time and energy it takes to set up one of those systems and learn how to use it, those same small business owners would likely find that the cost of having someone like you take over the payroll management chore would be lower. And this is the selling point you'll need to stress as you build your payroll administrative services business. You'll need to first convince business owners of your value, which can be quite a challenge but once you do, you'll have a steady stream of ongoing, regular business. As long as federal, state, and local governments keep making their rules and regulations with regard to payrolls more complicated, you will have plenty of opportunity to make positive differences to your customers' bottom lines. You will need, of course, to be completely accurate and totally reliable. Make a mistake that ends up costing your client money, and you'll be out the door. This is a business for the detail-oriented, conscientious person who likes numbers and just loves to see all those columns add up neatly.

STARTUP:

Your office/computer setup needs to support the accounting and bookkeeping nature of your work (usually $3,000 to start). Once you're up and running and get a few steady clients under your belt, you'll be on your way to an annual income of around $40,000.

BOTTOM LINE ADVICE:

Feelings can run high over payroll issues. Maintaining secrecy, ensuring accuracy, and just getting all the information you need to do your job will pose ongoing challenges. But the complexity of the task works to your advantage; you're the payroll expert and your small business clients will appreciate the time and money you save them. Doing an excellent job for one client is likely to bring you referrals for many more.

PERSONAL COACH

Startup cost:	$2,000–$5,000
Potential earnings:	$50,000–$80,000
Typical fees:	$50 per half-hour phone session, or monthly retainer of $400–$600
Advertising:	Networking, Web site, public speaking, writing bylined articles on coaching
Qualifications:	A background in psychology, human resources management, or career counseling is helpful but not mandatory; life skills, an inquiring mind, and the ability to ask leading questions, then really listen to the responses and distill their true meanings are more important than "book smarts"
Equipment needed:	Computer, printer, scanner, copier, fax, Internet access, cell phone
Home business potential:	Yes
Staff required:	No
Hidden costs:	Training to start, then continuing education

LOWDOWN:

Do you believe that many people are living below their potential, and that given positive guidance and access to the right tools, they have the ability within themselves to change their lives for the better? Would you like to be the person who shows them how? Then you may have a future as a personal coach. Personal coaching is still a relatively new concept, but it's catching on fast. Think of it as a cross between traditional counseling and psychotherapy. Like a counselor, you'll be working one-on-one with your clients. You'll listen, ask questions, and offer advice now and then, but mostly, you'll encourage them to tap into the core knowledge they already have about many fields and use what they know to transform their own lives. You'll explore current patterns of behavior that may be blocking a person from realizing his or her full potential and then, drawing on your own life experience and professional skills, suggest new approaches that can translate into a more satisfying life. You'll concentrate on the "whats" and "hows" of human behavior, but, unlike the psychotherapist, you won't be delving deeply into your clients' psyches to determine the "whys." Nor will you need a couch. In the early stages of coaching, you may meet face-to-face with your client once or twice, but then most of your sessions (typically 30 minutes each) will take place over the telephone.

STARTUP:

One of the most attractive features of this business is that it doesn't require an advanced degree or a huge outlay of cash to get started. You'll need a basic home office setup, of course, including a computer, printer, copier, scanner, and fax, plus a cell phone so that you can counsel your clients from wherever you happen to be. Aside from that, training will account for the most significant portion of your startup costs. The International Coach Federation (ICF) has chapters in nearly every state; check the Web site (*www.coachfederation.org*) for information about accredited training programs. Most of your clients will come as the result of targeted networking and referrals. And since the term "personal coaching" may still be unfamiliar to some, expect to spend a good deal of your marketing efforts on education; public speaking engagements and writing articles for publication in your local newspapers, magazines, and business/trade journals are good ways to get the word out.

BOTTOM LINE ADVICE:

Personal coaching is a feel-good kind of business. You're helping people live happier, more productive lives and what could be better that that? And did we mention the fact that you don't have to "kill" yourself to make a pretty good living at this? Since you'll be coaching by telephone, you can work from virtually anywhere, logging in as many or as few hours as you like. You can even schedule your phone appointments in such a way that you're working just a couple of days a week yet still earning the equivalent of a full-time salary. Personal coaching can be the springboard to other moneymaking opportunities, too. Many successful personal coaches have gone on to full-time careers as motivational speakers and bestselling authors.

PERSONALITY ANALYSIS/
TESTING SERVICE

Startup cost:	$1,000–$5,000
Potential earnings:	$35,000–$50,000
Typical fees:	$125–$300 per test/interview
Advertising:	Direct mail, human resource publications, networking with executives
Qualifications:	Degree/background in psychology or sociology
Equipment needed:	Computer, standardized tests, a system for recording results
Home business potential:	Yes
Staff required:	No (unless you grow quickly or have several corporate clients)
Hidden costs:	Insurance; telephone bills may be high due to long-distance interviewing for corporate clients; keep accurate records and hold your terms at 30 days

LOWDOWN:

With every alarming news story about a disgruntled employee who suddenly opens fire on his or her former boss and colleagues, more and more businesses turn their attention to security and policies and practices aimed at preventing violence in the workplace. One of the best ways a company can protect itself is to hire a personality analyst to interview all current and prospective employees. Determining individual personality types (using a standard psychological test such as the Briggs-Meyers) and identifying employees' potential hot buttons can be the first step in preventing violent behavior. As a personality analyst, you will administer the standardized tests and spend a minimum of three hours with each individual, either on the phone or in person, to assess their ability to cope under pressure. As your business grows, you may decide to take on additional staff so that several interviews may be conducted at once.

STARTUP:

Most of your initial investment will go toward the cost of resource materials (there may also be a licensing fee involved for your use of some tests). In all likelihood, the face-to-face interviews will be conducted at your clients' offices; if not, you may need to rent office space for this purpose. You can probably conduct most of the phone interviews from your home office, but, again, you may prefer an off-site space. Your other major expense will be for the placement of ads in professional publications (average cost: $500 each) to reach key management and human resource professionals in need of your services.

BOTTOM LINE ADVICE:

With your background in psychology or sociology, you will no doubt enjoy the diversity of the people you interview. But you may find the actual testing and interview process repetitive and somewhat tedious. Make sure you protect yourself from potential lawsuits later by eliciting adequate details from your interview subjects, possibly even securing a second opinion from another professional. Not everyone will appreciate being hired (or fired) on the basis of a single professional opinion!

PERSONNEL SAFETY CONSULTANT

Startup cost:	$3,000–$6,000
Potential earnings:	$30,000 and up
Typical fees:	$35–$50 per hour
Advertising:	Business publications, membership in business and trade groups, referrals, networking
Qualifications:	Degree in organizational psychology or related field, experience in corporate security or industrial hygiene, proven track record, ability to market and sell your own services
Equipment needed:	Computer; Internet access; fax; laser printer; word processing, database, and spreadsheet software; cell phone; marketing materials
Home business potential:	Yes
Staff required:	No
Hidden costs:	Travel, errors and omissions insurance, attendance at seminars or conferences for ongoing education, membership dues

LOWDOWN:

The American workplace is changing . . . and, in some cases, not necessarily for the better. Tensions arise and sometimes, they blow up into major crises; we read about the worst of these in the news media. But even if a situation does not deteriorate into open conflict, hostility and negative attitudes may still simmer below the surface in many organizations. Your business is founded on your ability to recognize the triggers for potential violence, be they physical/structural problems or management issues, and then mediate conflicts. This is a high-profile, high-stress form of consulting. It requires outstanding presentation skills, the ability to communicate effectively with all types of people, and the self-confidence to be an effective change agent. Unlike employee harmony consultants (who specialize in making sure everyone gets along) and labor relations professionals (who primarily translate corporate policies), you will be working to resolve employee conflicts before they have the opportunity to escalate into full-blown crises with tragic results.

STARTUP:

Conflicts don't happen according to a schedule, so you'll need to be in communication with your clients as you travel, and a cell phone is a must. And even though most of your work will be carried out at the client's site, you will need the basic office setup to support your efforts (a computer, printer, fax, and Internet access); expect to spend $2,000–$3,000 for your equipment.

BOTTOM LINE ADVICE:

Crises will be a regular part of your work, so you'll need to feel comfortable dealing with potentially volatile situations and people. Ideally, companies will bring you in to prevent hostility from arising in the first place, but realistically, that's probably not what will happen. More than likely, you'll be called in when the crisis becomes full-blown. On the other hand, you should encounter no difficulties in getting clients to appreciate the importance and value of the services you provide. Marketing is likely to be one of your biggest challenges. Getting established will not be easy, but once you have a few successful resolutions to your credit, word of mouth and referrals will bring in more business.

PHARMACEUTICAL RETURNS CONSULTING

Startup cost:	$1,000–$3,000
Potential earnings:	$20,000–$40,000
Typical fees:	Percentage of value of returns
Advertising:	Trade journals, participation in professional organizations, association with health care management consulting firms, direct mail
Qualifications:	Pharmacy degree
Equipment needed:	Basic office setup, Internet access, manuals, pharmaceutical listings
Home business potential:	Yes
Staff required:	No
Hidden costs:	Errors and omissions insurance, ongoing marketing, continuing education to remain abreast of the latest developments in the field

LOWDOWN:

Hospital pharmacies could save enormous amounts of money, and meet tightened quality standards, by reviewing the inventory in their pharmacies and returning expired drugs that can still be returned to the manufacturer. Busy hospital pharmacies, with thousands of different drugs to track, almost always have an extensive quantity of such expired material that cannot be administered to patients and should be returned. Your expertise in the field of drug returns can be marketed directly to hospitals, or you can subcontract your services to health care management consulting firms with projects related to pharmacy operations. Cutbacks in funding mean that no health care organization can ignore any means of recovering dollars, and your business could provide them with an excellent way to achieve this goal.

STARTUP:

Your primary product is your expertise, so you won't need much in the way of equipment. Since you will, however, need the ability to generate a professional report, you will probably want to invest in a computer, printer, and word processing software. Internet access will be helpful for keeping up on the latest developments in the pharmaceutical industry and the expiration of specific products. Potential earnings of $20,000–$40,000 are possible depending on how aggressive you are in snaring clients.

BOTTOM LINE ADVICE:

Success breeds success. Your challenge from the outset will be to get your foot into the door of the clannish world of health care administration. Most hospital pharmacists would be only too glad to have your assistance in clearing up the inventory in their departments, but a vice president of administration who is relatively unfamiliar with the issues involved will probably be the one making the decision about whether to engage your services. As with so many businesses that rely on individual expertise, you will have to be an aggressive marketer in order to become known and to gather a small nucleus of clients.

POLITICAL CAMPAIGN MANAGEMENT

Startup cost:	$2,000–$3,000
Potential earnings:	$40,000–$100,000
Typical fees:	Extremely varied according to level of government, but can range from $40,000–$75,000
Advertising:	Networking; paid ads are a waste of money
Qualifications:	Organizational and communication skills, persistence, energy, a track record of success
Equipment needed:	Office with phone, fax, computer, Internet access, copier, cell phone and/or pager
Home business potential:	Yes
Staff required:	Possibly
Hidden costs:	Phone bills

LOWDOWN:

Political campaign management is a combination business and crusade. Campaign managers are usually identified with a political party; they almost never work for more than one. And unless you are able to join the select few who work at the national level, your success is strongly related to your familiarity with the attitudes, issues, and expectations of your city, state, or region. This is a profession for dynamic, incredibly energetic, intuitive, and very well-organized people who want to act out their commitment to causes and issues by supporting candidates who share their beliefs. The cynical manipulator who can package some faceless candidate to hoodwink the electorate is a myth. That is not to say that the process of getting someone elected is entirely pretty or pleasant. Money, influence, constituent demands, and attacks from the opposition can all make a campaign manager's life miserable. But winning the election is an incredible high—and your automatic ticket to the next challenge in two or four years.

STARTUP:

You probably won't be working much out of your own office, but you need to be available when you are. Factor both a land line with answering machine or voice main and cell phone into your startup costs, along with a computer so that you have Internet access and e-mail. The time you put into a campaign may equal a year's worth of work or more, so don't think in terms of flat fees or hourly rates; it's easier to count your earnings by annual salary ($40,000–$100,000, depending on who you represent). If you are managing a large campaign, you will probably need to hire staff.

BOTTOM LINE ADVICE:

Ahhh . . . politics. You either love the game or hate it. Some people thrive on the exciting give and take of the political process, the opportunity to meet public figures, and the possible chance to affect public policy. Other people hate the hysteria. One good way to see which type of person you are and whether campaign management would be a good business for you is to volunteer for several campaigns. You'll do the menial tasks, like answering the phone, licking the stamps, and blowing up the balloons for the victory celebration, but you'll get a taste for what political campaigns are all about. You'll need to be a risk-taker and an unabashed self-promoter to make political campaign management your career. But be forewarned—if you do, expect politics to take over your life.

POLLSTER

Startup cost:	$2,000–$3,000
Potential earnings:	$15,000–$40,000
Typical fees:	$15–$25 per hour or a flat rate of $250 and up
Advertising:	Connections, referrals, networking, newspaper ads
Qualifications:	Energy, patience, people skills
Equipment needed:	Computer, word processing, database, and spreadsheet software, printer, fax, phone, copier
Home business potential:	Yes
Staff required:	Yes (number depends on the size of the poll)
Hidden costs:	Time is money, so plan well; phone charges; if you are polling by phone from your home office, you may need more than one line

LOWDOWN:

To become a pollster you will need an ability to get people to talk to you. If you have energy, the determination to keep going in the face of rejection, and a genuine interest in what people have to say, you can make a success of this business. As a pollster, you may be constructing the questions to ask for one client and finding the right people to ask the questions devised by someone else for another; in all cases, you'll be working with your clients to determine the "cohort," the group of people from whom you want to elicit responses to your questionnaire. Typically, pollsters focus on one geographic area or demographic category.

STARTUP:

You will need a computer and printer to create your questionnaires and reports. Tabulating results will be much easier with a good spreadsheet program. Expect to spend $2,000–$3,000 to get up and running. This is a time-consuming business, so you will find it more profitable to charge by the hour ($15–$25 per). However, if your client prefers a flat fee, a good starting point is $250 to design and conduct a simple poll; don't forget to add in the cost of long-distance phone charges, if applicable.

BOTTOM LINE ADVICE:

Polling can be a fascinating field. You will be gathering and analyzing information that can be gleaned no other way. You may find, however, that marketing your services can be both challenging and time-consuming. Polling requires connections in government as well as industry, so your networking and communication skills need to be top-drawer. Once established, your network will lead you to further referrals. One other word of caution—polling is a business that ebbs and flows depending on the electoral season, the weather, and other factors out of your control, so make sure you have adequate financial reserves to cover your slow times.

PRINTING BROKER

Startup cost:	$1,000–$3,000
Potential earnings:	$35,000–$50,000
Typical fees:	10 to 15 percent commission on sales
Advertising:	Yellow Pages, trade publications, direct mail, cold calls
Qualifications:	Printing sales background, knowledge of the printing process
Equipment needed:	Cell phone, computer, printer, fax, copier, land line
Home business potential:	Yes
Staff required:	No
Hidden costs:	Insurance, mileage

LOWDOWN:

For those who are inexperienced in the world of printing and publishing, a printing broker can be a godsend. Relying on his or her extensive background in printing sales, a printing broker can actually save the client hundreds of dollars in printing costs by shopping for the best (and most current) rates. The broker does not work for any one specific printer, but rather represents all of them, and as a result, clients can rest assured that they are getting the best possible rate without sacrificing quality. As a printing broker, your clients could be anyone from advertising agencies and small businesses to community newspapers and book publishers. To be successful, you'll need to have a natural sales ability and technical know-how about printing in general as well as specific techniques. You'll be working with two sides of the printing process: the customer who needs a brochure, catalog, or book printed, and the printer. As an outside representative, you will have no vested interest in a particular printing house; you will, however, need to establish positive working relationships with printers of all types and sizes. If ink is in your blood, this could be a terrific opportunity for you. All types of businesses need printed materials and they all want quality work at a reasonable cost, but don't know where to find it. You are the conduit for putting them in touch with the right printer at the right price.

STARTUP:

Your startup costs are low ($1,000–$3,000), because you'll need just a basic office setup (computer, printer, fax, copier, and phone), plus some advertising to get things off the ground. (This assumes that you already have a printing background and contacts in the industry.) With some heavy shoe action, you could make $35,000–$50,000 per year—especially if you can build a solid reputation for finding quality workmanship at affordable prices on behalf of your clients.

BOTTOM LINE ADVICE:

Your contacts will make or break you in this business; if you are always honest, reputable, and deliver on your promises, you will reap the benefits threefold. Why threefold? Because your satisfied clients will tell at least two other potential clients about your services and the money you saved them. On the sour side, all you have to sell is your time and expertise; you make money only when you close the deal. Be careful that you don't wind up spending a lot of time trying to negotiate deals that never actually materialize; you'll have to eat the related costs.

PRODUCT DEVELOPER

Startup cost:	$3,000–$5,000
Potential earnings:	$25,000 and up
Typical fees:	$500+ per project (could be as high as several thousand dollars)
Advertising:	Referrals, networking, memberships in business and trade organizations
Qualifications:	Record of success, business background, creativity, ability to be a self-starter
Equipment needed:	Computer, Internet access, word processing, spreadsheet, and presentation software, fax, laser printer, marketing materials
Home business potential:	Yes
Staff required:	No
Hidden costs:	Research, subscriptions to newspapers and trade journals

LOWDOWN:

Tens of thousands of new products are introduced every year into the American economy. The consumer items we use each day were once someone's bright idea for a new product. And then there are the fads. . . . We all laughed about the pet rock, but we bought it, and the people who developed and sold it got very rich in the process. As a product developer, you'll bring together the needs of your corporate clients, the temper of the marketplace, and your own creativity to develop new products that will capture the public's attention, along with a healthy share of their dollars. This is not a game for sissies. You'll need a major dose of self-confidence and a generous helping of right-brain creativity to succeed as a freelance product developer.

STARTUP:

Are you just thinking, or are you tinkering? The answer to that question will directly impact that amount you need to get started as a freelance product developer. Expect to spend about $3,000 for the hardware and software you will need to produce professional-looking materials for your marketing efforts. You could make $25,000 your first year.

BOTTOM LINE ADVICE:

There is a big gap in the field of product development between the many voices crying for attention and the few who can actually generate valuable ideas. Some product developers are truly freelance, while others focus on serving one or two corporations with which they have long-term contractual relationships. Your personal reputation for creativity, reliability, and awareness of the perspective of the consumer will be central to your success.

PROFIT SHARING PLAN CONSULTANT

Startup cost:	$2,500–$4,000
Potential earnings:	$25,000–$50,000
Typical fees:	$50–$75 per hour
Advertising:	Participation in business-oriented community groups, trade publications, direct mail
Qualifications:	A general business or financial background, certification as a financial planner, industry experience as a benefits advisor
Equipment needed:	Basic office setup, including computer, printer, copier, fax, phone, and Internet access
Home business potential:	Yes
Staff required:	No
Hidden costs:	Continuing education, subscriptions and membership dues

LOWDOWN:

Profit sharing is becoming an increasingly important employee benefit, but designing an effective plan requires expertise and experience. Goal setting is vital. Questions like: What is the purpose of the profit-sharing plan? What level of employee will we target?, and How will the specific elements of the plan be designed? must be asked up front. Preparing the cost-benefit analysis alone is often a major challenge, and evaluation of the effectiveness of the chosen plan over the short- and long-term is absolutely essential. As a consultant in this field, you will target companies that are growing rapidly but are not yet large enough to have a human resources staff capable of designing and implementing a profit-sharing plan. A history of successful plan design will be your major marketing tool.

STARTUP:

You will need the kind of marketing materials and professional image that appeal to your corporate market. Although you'll be calling regularly on prospects and clients, you will need a functional office in which to conduct research and design the actual plans; set aside approximately $2,500 to start. An hourly fee of $50–$75 for your services should easily net you $25,000 your first year in business.

BOTTOM LINE ADVICE:

This business appeals to a narrow but potentially very profitable market niche: growing companies with a vision for the future. Unfortunately, you'll have many competitors, but your record of success, along with your ability to present your ideas in terms that will appeal to these clients, will help set you apart.

PROPERTY MANAGEMENT SERVICE

Startup cost:	$2,000–$3,000
Potential earnings:	$25,000–$50,000
Typical fees:	$25 per hour or a monthly retainer of $500–$2,500
Advertising:	Classified ads, referrals, memberships in community and business real estate groups
Qualifications:	Experience in property management or a related field, related degree helpful but not mandatory, outstanding management skills, ability to communicate and work well with people, knowledge of basic bookkeeping, understanding of building maintenance issues
Equipment needed:	Computer, word processing and spreadsheet software, possibly specialized property management software, printer, fax, copier, Internet access, cell phone
Home business potential:	Yes
Staff required:	No
Hidden costs:	Insurance, bonding

LOWDOWN:

Property management is ideally suited to someone who isn't afraid of details and likes juggling several balls at once, pulling many different pieces together, and keeping track of people and data on a continuing basis. If you're good, you'll become indispensable to the owners of the properties you manage, and your well-established reputation will bring you enough business to keep you busy and well-rewarded indefinitely. Property managers take a huge burden off the shoulders of property owners. As a manager, you will maintain all the financial records for each property, which include keeping track of income and expenses, paying bills, and filing taxes. Skill at auditing bills and collecting rents, as well as the ability to keep repair and maintenance schedules up to date, are essential assets for effective property management. The right person for this position is one who isn't afraid to pay attention to the most minute details and who has the people skills necessary for relating to both tenants and those who carry out work on the buildings.

STARTUP:

At the minimum, you will need a cell phone, computer, Internet access, and word processing and spreadsheet software; specialized property management software would be useful, too. Your basic office setup will run $2,000–$3,000. Depending on your location and how many properties you manage (be careful not to overextend yourself!), you should be able to make $25,000–$50,000 annually.

BOTTOM LINE ADVICE:

The owners of properties—your prospective clients—will be placing a great deal of responsibility on your shoulders. Things can degenerate quite quickly in a poorly managed building. You are asking your clients to trust you to take care of their significant investments, and marketing your services successfully may depend on how well you can engender a sense of trust. It may well be that you find you only want or need a few clients. Once you arrive at a comfortable number, each of whom you can service well, constant marketing will no longer be necessary.

RECREATION ACTIVITIES CONSULTANT

Startup cost:	$1,000–$2,000
Potential earnings:	$30,000–$50,000
Typical fees:	$500–$1,000 per job (plus travel expenses)
Advertising:	Recreation associations (for networking and advertising in their publications)
Qualifications:	Creativity and a sense of fun; a degree in recreation management or hospitality would be extremely helpful but not absolutely necessary
Equipment needed:	Good resource materials and perhaps some road atlas software (with points of interest mapped out and profiled)
Home business potential:	No (you'll be on the road a lot or may work on-site at a particular resort)
Staff required:	Usually a low-paid (or no-paid) staff of college interns majoring in hotel or sports management, on an as-needed basis
Hidden costs:	Association dues

LOWDOWN:

What does a recreation activities consultant do besides get paid to show others a great time? Not too much, actually. You may be hired as a regular consultant to a particular resort, where you handle the details and finer points of guest programs aimed at hospitality and fun. Or, you might be hired by corporations sending groups of people on trips to interesting places; you'll go along to make sure that everything goes smoothly for the travelers, from dining and room arrangements to activities and sightseeing. Whichever route you choose, you'll enjoy the challenge of finding interesting, offbeat things for people to do—with the added bonus of getting to travel to interesting places yourself. What could be more fun than that? On the downside, you won't always get to "play." You'll be putting in long days, and you will generally need to be up and at 'em in the wee morning hours, well before any of your clients. You'll need to have patience, better-than-average organizational skills, and high attention to detail. You're being paid to worry and fuss over these people, constantly making sure that their every need is met. In that sense, you're in the same league as a concierge except you get to go on the road and play outside, too.

STARTUP:

Your startup expenses are low ($1,000–$2,000), and your income potential will be driven by your ability to network. If you get out there and make yourself available (especially over holidays and weekends), you could reap $30,000–$50,000 annually. The icing on the cake is that you'll get the chance to travel on someone else's money; in addition to paying for your time, the hiring company will cover your travel costs.

BOTTOM LINE ADVICE:

Who could blame you for wanting to get paid for having fun? Expect to be harassed by your family and friends, because yours is truly an enviable job. Little do they know that it's not all fun and games. There's at least one disgruntled traveler in every group and it will be your job to keep him or her happy. You'll have to learn the fine arts of perpetual patience and kindness.

Recycling

Startup cost:	$1,000–$5,000 (depending on whether you already own a vehicle)
Potential earnings:	$10,000–$20,000
Typical fees:	None; you are paid by the recycling center for the goods you drop off
Advertising:	Fliers, referrals, networking
Qualifications:	Driver's license, knowledge of state and federal guidelines; some states require certification
Equipment needed:	Pickup truck
Home business potential:	Yes
Staff required:	No
Hidden costs:	Mileage, insurance, vehicle maintenance

LOWDOWN:

Tossing your daily newspaper into the trash is like tossing away money. Toss out a ton of newspapers, and you're talking big bucks. A ton of newsprint these days can be worth $50 to $75, and it's yours for the gathering. So are cans, cardboard, office paper, aluminum, and glass and plastic bottles. The increasing popularity of recycling means that you may be able to make a good living picking up these materials and selling them to a recycling center. Many large cities now offer recycling as part of their waste management programs; however, opportunities are still available for the small contractor who isn't afraid to get his or her hands just a little dirty. To become a recycler, you will need contracts with regular customers and a vehicle that can carry relatively heavy loads. As you travel your regular routes, picking up unwanted materials, you're not only earning a little pin money, you're also making the world a better and cleaner place.

STARTUP:

Assuming you already own a truck, your only startup cost will be for the design, printing, and distribution of fliers to let homeowners and businesses in your service area know about your business. If you do not have a vehicle, you will obviously need to purchase one; since your vehicle is for function not show, you can probably find a used pickup for $5,000 or less. Your income will vary depending on how much you gather and on what the recycling center is willing to pay you; rates fluctuate according to the item and market. Unless you have hundreds of customers under contract and a fleet of trucks, recycling is not a business that will make you the big bucks.

BOTTOM LINE ADVICE:

Recycling is outdoor work. The good news is, you're not stuck sitting behind a desk all day; the bad news is you have to work in all kinds of weather. For active, friendly people, recycling can be an ideal occupation. While some go into it purely for the profits, meager as they may be, others have a higher purpose; they feel strongly about the wise use of resources and the importance of reusing what we can. Many people who are unable to recycle their own waste materials will be grateful for your assistance so that they can easily participate in this worthwhile activity. From an environmental point of view, you may feel good about being a recycler, but there is nothing glamorous about this job. The routine of picking up and sorting, whatever the weather, can be numbing. Carrying heavy loads is both back-breaking and tedious.

REFERRAL SERVICE

Startup cost:	$3,000–$5,000
Potential earnings:	$5,000–$40,000
Typical fees:	Percentage of what a recommended business charges its customers and/or flat fee per recommendation
Advertising:	Yellow Pages, newspapers, bulletin boards, Web site
Qualifications:	Attention to detail
Equipment needed:	Telephone, computer, business and database software, Internet access
Home business potential:	Yes
Staff required:	No
Hidden costs:	Annual updates to your database; insurance

LOWDOWN:

Suppose you're new to a community, or just not all that familiar with the services available, and you need a particular product or service—a petsitter for the weekend or a ceramic tile in your kitchen needs replacing—who do you call? A referral service, that's who. One phone call puts you in touch with reputable businesses in any given category and within a specific geographic area. As a referral service operator, you would prescreen the businesses in communities, gathering every piece of information you can about their reputation, workmanship, and reliability, perhaps aligning yourself closely to chambers of commerce and the Better Business Bureau to ensure the credibility of each company you recommend. Your money would come from either a commission paid by the companies you represent, or a small fee paid by the folks in need of referrals; some referral services use a combination of both. In all cases, you will need to establish yourself as an authority on a wide variety of businesses, and the only way to do that is through careful, methodical research. Check and recheck your information; one bad referral—a customer gets "conned" by a company you suggested—and you're sunk.

STARTUP:

You will need to keep meticulous files and update them regularly. Expect to spend anywhere from $3,000–$5,000 on a computer and business and database software to handle that job. You can tap into many sources for your recommended businesses: the Internet, phone book, bulletin boards, word of mouth; ask friends and family for suggestions, then check them out yourself. You'll need a Yellow Pages ad yourself for sure, and, later perhaps, a Web site, where, for a fee, consumers in need of services can log on and search your list by category. Your income will depend on the size of your database and how you charge—commission, fees, or a combination of the two.

BOTTOM LINE ADVICE:

If you like dealing with people and vast amounts of data, and if you're skilled at matching the two, you'll likely succeed in this business. Remember, however, that unless people know about you, they won't call . . . be sure to advertise in the most high-profile places you can afford. And always be careful what you say. Badmouthing a business could have legal ramifications if word gets around; carry insurance.

REFLEXOLOGIST

Startup cost:	$1,000–$4,000
Potential earnings:	$25,000–$40,000
Typical fees:	$25–$35 per half-hour session
Advertising:	Yellow Pages, newspaper ads, fliers, networking and referrals
Qualifications:	Formal training in reflexology; there are no licensing requirements for reflexologists at this time; however, some states/cities classify reflexology as a form of massage and thus require certification
Equipment needed:	Lounge chair/recliner; computer, printer, scheduling and bookkeeping software; telephone and answering machine or voice mail
Home business potential:	Yes
Staff required:	No
Hidden costs:	Training and continuing education; remodeling of a room in your home to specifically accommodate your practice

LOWDOWN:

Reflexology may well be a business whose time has come. While not widely known or practiced in the United States, this ages-old therapy traces its roots at least as far back as ancient Egypt. Evidence of reflexology being applied has been found inside an Egyptian tomb dating to 2300 B.C.E. Reflexology is based on the principle that certain reflex areas (zones) in our hands and feet are directly linked to glands and organs in other parts of our bodies; the application of pressure to these zones may relieve pain in specific areas of the body as well as generate an overall feeling of well-being and relaxation. While this therapy has been shown anecdotally to have a positive effect on numerous chronic health conditions, including back pain, migraine, and arthritis, it is primarily used as a stress reduction and relaxation technique. Using your home as a base and offering appointments of 30 minutes each, you can make a decent living as a reflexologist working just 20 hours a week. Keep in mind, however, that although reflexology is not as physically demanding as massage therapy, it does require that you be on your feet for long periods of time. You probably won't want to schedule more than six to eight half-hour appointments per day.

STARTUP:

Even though there are no formal licensing requirements at this time for the practice of reflexology in most cities and states, you can't just call yourself a reflexologist and start offering this therapy, either. You must have some training, either a formal course in reflexology or an informal apprenticeship with a practicing reflexologist. The Reflexology Association of America (*www.reflexology-usa.org*) maintains lists of practicing reflexologists and schools that offer training programs; expect to spend $500–$1,000 to learn the techniques. The only pieces of equipment you absolutely must have are a recliner/lounge chair and a telephone with answering machine or voice mail capabilities. At some point, you'll probably also want to add a computer, printer, and scheduling and bookkeeping software to your basic office setup. You can easily operate this business from your home; if you decide to remodel a room specifically to accommodate your reflexology practice, your startup costs will be significantly higher, of course. To broaden your client base, consider aligning yourself with a massage therapy business, health club, or health care provider in a related specialty such as chiropractic or orthopedics.

BOTTOM LINE ADVICE:

Reflexology is widely recognized in Europe, but has been slow to catch on in the United States, perhaps because it is often confused with massage. Although both fall under the broad category of "touch therapies," they are, in fact, quite different. Massage therapy is directed at the entire body, with particular emphasis on the shoulders, back, and neck. Reflexology, on the other hand, focuses on reflex areas of the hands and feet which are believed to correspond to other parts of the body. While reflexology is never promoted as a cure for any particular health condition, its proponents contend that proper stimulation of reflexes in the hands and feet may be effective for back pain, migraine, arthritis, sleep and digestive disorders, infertility, hormonal imbalances, sports injuries, and stress-related conditions. As a reflexologist, you will face the continuing challenge of educating your potential clients with regard to the purpose and benefits of this centuries-old therapy.

RELOCATION CONSULTANT

Startup cost:	$1,500–$3,000
Potential earnings:	$15,000 and more
Typical fees:	$25–$35 per hour
Advertising:	Networking, memberships in real estate and general business organizations, referrals
Qualifications:	Real estate experience helpful but not mandatory; extensive knowledge of your area's neighborhoods, attractions, amenities, schools, etc.
Equipment needed:	Computer, printer, fax, Internet access, cell phone
Home business potential:	Yes
Staff required:	No
Hidden costs:	Telephone charges, membership dues, entertainment

LOWDOWN:

Americans are always on the move, and many of them are relocating from one state or metro-politan community to another. Imagine how much smoother their moves would go if they had access to an "insider" at their new home base to help them settle in. As a relocation consultant, you will play that very important role. Your ideal market will be those companies that relocate employees from time to time, but are too small to provide much assistance in-house to the families they transfer into your community. Moving is always a challenging and often unsettling experience, and enlightened employers will see the value of your assistance in making the transition go as smoothly as possible. You will begin your work early in the relocation processing, meeting in-person or by phone, with the affected family to answer questions and offer advice as they begin making decisions with regard to their move. Be prepared to answer such questions as: What neighborhood will we like best? Where can we find eldercare or child care? What sports are played at local high schools? Can we find a house big enough for our belongings? You may work with the transferees before they are even ready to choose a real estate agent, or you may receive referrals from the real estate agents themselves.

STARTUP:

Your primary startup expense will be equipping your office for business. You may have to explore different areas of your local community by car or on foot, or meet with transferees over a restaurant meal. You will need to purchase a computer, printer, and fax for basic office tasks, and you'll want Internet access for research and e-mail, as well as a cell phone so you can be in constant touch with your clients. An annual income of $15,000 is realistic for part-time work.

BOTTOM LINE ADVICE:

As a relocation consultant, you're really doing two kinds of marketing: first, for your own service, and second, for your community. Many organizations hire relocation consultants to help them persuade a prospective employee to take a job they are offering. How the prospect and his/her family perceive your community can be a major factor in their moving decision. Your most likely clients are hospitals hoping to snare a certain physician and companies recruiting for upper-management positions. Watch your local newspaper and business journals for companies that may be expanding their local operations.

RESPIRATORY EQUIPMENT REPAIR

Startup cost:	$2,000–$5,000
Potential earnings:	$30,000 or more
Typical fees:	$20–$50 per service call, plus parts and labor
Advertising:	Direct mail to hospitals and other inpatient health care facilities and medical equipment dealers (sales/rental), trade journals, business publications, referrals, participation in professional organizations
Qualifications:	Technical training with the related equipment, familiarity with all brands used in your service area, a can-do attitude, aptitude for mechanical tinkering
Equipment needed:	Van for pickup, delivery, and on-site service; tools, parts, and repair equipment; answering service, cell phone
Home business potential:	Yes
Staff required:	No
Hidden costs:	Training in new equipment brands, mileage

LOWDOWN:

In the health care equipment industry, service is everything. Lives are on the line and the escalation of costs means that equipment is being stretched further and further. Your business, which keeps vital respiratory therapy equipment in top working order, has a ready and eager market with few competitors. You will have to find the people (and machines) that need you, and to get to them "stat" when things break down. If you can quickly identify and resolve equipment problems, fix things correctly the first time, and keep your transportation expenses in check, you'll have an excellent enterprise, ripe for early expansion. As our population ages, the need for respiratory therapy grows, yet fewer dollars are available for buying new equipment. Keeping everything in tip-top running order is not a "nice-to-have" service for health care providers and equipment dealers, it's a "must," and in today's volatile marketplace a business that deals in "musts" is the ideal kind to be in.

STARTUP:

Your business may be slow to take off at first, but once you establish a reputation for quick, quality service, word of mouth and repeat customers will keep you going. To generate business, you will need to be able to demonstrate that you can handle a complete service job from beginning to end, and that means you'll need to have the necessary tools and parts on hand. Expect to spend about $2,000 just in tools to start. If you do not have a van, you will need one, of course, and that will significantly add to your startup costs; however, you should be able to find a used vehicle for under $3,000–$4,000.

BOTTOM LINE ADVICE:

Making a profit in this field will take both business savvy and mechanical know-how. Many people who are wonderfully talented at the delicate work necessary to repair a sophisticated piece of equipment lack the people skills essential for servicing their clients and marketing their abilities. If you are one of them, don't despair; these skills can be learned, and even if you have to shell out a few dollars for some formal training, you are sure to find it money well spent as your business grows. As with any service business, a key factor to your success will be how well you manage your time and expenses.

RESUME SERVICE

Startup cost:	$1,500–$2,000
Potential earnings:	$20,000–$50,000
Typical fees:	$50–$100 per hour or $150–$500 per resume (depending on the job candidate and your geographic locale)
Advertising:	Yellow Pages, newspaper classifieds, referrals
Qualifications:	Writing ability, attention to detail, organizational and proofreading skills
Equipment needed:	Computer, laser printer, fax, Internet access, high-quality paper on which to print the final product, extra floppy disks or blank CDs
Home business potential:	Yes
Staff required:	No
Hidden costs:	Insurance; watch your time—make sure your flat fees are high enough to cover the interview and writing, or charge an hourly rate

LOWDOWN:

At any given time, thousands of people are looking for new jobs, and they all have one thing in common: Each one needs a dynamic resume. Those who truly desire to put their best foot forward will seek professional help in creating and printing their resume and cover letters. Your resume service will provide products that are both visually appealing and businesslike . . . a complete and polished package that is likely to get more than a single, quick glance from even the most jaded hiring professional. Today's resumes are not like those of a decade ago, and that means you may need to do a little research up front to learn more about how technology and the Internet have influenced the latest job search techniques. You'll need to know about career Web sites and how job search databases scan resumes for keywords.

Your days will be spent meeting with a wide variety of clients from all walks of life (everyone from foundry supervisors to attorneys is in the job market these days). You'll interview each client to learn about his or her employment history and educational background, as well as pertinent on-the-job experiences and skills that would likely attract the attention of a potential employer. You will provide your client with a finished product—a printed resume on high-quality paper. You can then either turn over the resume file to your client on a floppy disk or CD, or make arrangements to print resumes as needed from your computer for an additional charge. And don't forget to offer an updating service. As your client's employment situation or job focus changes, you can adapt his or her resume file for a nominal fee. Yours will be a time-consuming job that gets easier the more you work at it. And just think of the satisfaction you will derive when one of your clients lands his or her dream job as the result of your efforts!

STARTUP:

Your startup costs will be relatively low ($1,000–$5,000) because all you will really need is a good computer setup and a small advertising budget to get the word out. You can expect to earn $20,000 or so in most medium-size markets; in New York City and other large metropolitan areas, where you can command higher fees for your services (up to $500 per package), you could easily make $50,000 per year.

BOTTOM LINE ADVICE:

If you're an accomplished writer, resume writing can be a pretty easy way to make a full-time living or to bring in additional income while you build a freelance writing business or pen the "Great American Novel." However, you must be knowledgeable about both hard copy and electronic resumes and keywords. To be successful at this business, you will need to enjoy working with people, most of whom are anxious about their employment situations and who may hound you day and night until their materials are completed. If you'd rather not be bothered by angst-infested clients, stick to fiction writing.

ADVICE FROM THE EXPERTS

What sets your business apart from others like it?

Katina Z. Jones has a nontraditional resume service called Going Places Self-Promotions, Inc., in Akron, Ohio. She says that her business is unique because it breaks many of the traditional rules of resume writing. "We do resumes that are not only eye-catching, but also go beyond providing a mere rundown of a client's job history. We like to add a sense of not only what a person has accomplished in his or her career, but also who he or she is and how he or she might fit into an organization. We have a 98 percent success rate in helping clients secure interviews because of that personalized approach."

Things you couldn't do without:

"I couldn't do without my computer, laser printer, phone, pager, and fax. My clients want fairly quick turnaround, and these items help me to accomplish that. Also, I need to have plenty of paper catalogs on hand, as I use a ton of specialty preprinted stationery to produce resumes on."

Marketing tips/advice:

"Set yourself apart from the people who are glorified typists . . . recognize that the resume industry is changing rapidly, and the resumes of the past (with cookie-cutter objectives and meaningless buzzwords) are just not getting people results anymore. After you've found your niche, network like crazy. Anywhere you go, introduce yourself; you're bound to meet someone who either needs a resume or knows someone who does."

If you had to do it all over again . . .

"I would have started networking much sooner and would also have put together a more meaningful marketing plan; I don't think I strategized nearly enough in the beginning."

RETAIL BAKERY/
SPECIALTY DESSERTS

Startup cost:	$1,000–$5,000
Potential earnings:	$2,000–$5,000 per month
Advertising:	Newspapers, fliers, brochures, direct mail, press kits
Qualifications:	Knowledge of baking, sanitation, and food safety; tasty recipes and the ability to prepare a specialty food item; licensing may be required
Equipment needed:	Oven, mixer, baking utensils; knowledge of sanitation and food safety; packaging; delivery vehicle or storefront
Home business potential:	Yes
Staff required:	Not initially; may be needed to grow
Hidden costs:	Licensing; vehicle costs, rent

LOWDOWN:

People are hungry for homemade baked goods and specialty desserts (such as fancy cakes, pies, and cookies). No one has time to bake these days; yet, the "personal touch" is greatly desired by consumers who are tired of mass-produced, commercially processed foods. You'll soon find that presentation, packaging, and marketing are every bit as important as taste in this business, so you will need to be both an astute marketer and an excellent baker or pastry chef. You may be able to start out completely on your own, but as your business grows, you will probably need to add staff; don't forget to include this additional cost in your budget projections. Maintaining top quality by using the finest ingredients is important; so is consistency. Your customers will come to expect a certain level of quality, which means every chocolate torte or key lime pie you make this week should look and taste exactly like the ones you made last week. Some stores make their name by offering a single category of baked goods; they may specialize in only pies, cakes, or muffins, for example. Others succeed as generalists offering everything from chocolate fudge layer cakes and apple pies to macaroon cookies and oat bran muffins.

STARTUP:

Establishing your niche as a baker of pies, cakes, cookies, muffins, or other sweet treats can be accomplished on a shoestring budget. All you need are the ingredients and a few supplies you probably already have, such as a mixer and mixing bowls, spatulas, spoons, pans, and an oven. Considering that the cake which may have cost you as little as 60 cents to create can be sold for an average of $10–$15 per cake, you'll begin making money quite quickly.

BOTTOM LINE ADVICE:

Creating a food product that looks and tastes twice as good as its commercial counterpart will give you a loyal following with customers who are willing to come out of their way to buy your wares. There's a huge market out there for tasty foods with the personal touch. On the downside, marketing will require a chunk of your budget, as will staffing as you grow. Food safety considerations and zoning regulations can be potential headaches, too.

RETIREMENT PLANNER

Startup cost:	$1,000–$2,000
Potential earnings:	$20,000–$40,000
Typical fees:	Set fee of $150–$1,000 (depending on scope of project)
Advertising:	Newspapers, publications of local interest groups, membership in community organizations, word of mouth, direct mail
Qualifications:	Expertise in financial planning (certification helpful), experience in a related field
Equipment needed:	Computer, printer, fax, phone, copier, marketing materials, Internet access
Home business potential:	Yes
Staff required:	No
Hidden costs:	Conferences for continuing self-education

LOWDOWN:

It's hard to convince a twenty- or thirty-something that now is the time to begin planning for retirement, but convince them you must. With rising health care costs and widespread fears about the future of Social Security, retirement planners are finding a growing demand for their services. And while there are thousands of financial planners in the marketplace, retirement planners are still a relatively new breed. Instead of offering the full gamut of services that financial planners offer, you will focus on a single piece of the complete financial puzzle. Just like a lawyer, accountant, or other professional who operates as a small business, your challenge will be to gain the confidence of your clients so that they prefer your personal touch and individualized service over the perceived security of dealing with a large financial institution that claims to offer the same type of advice. You'll sell your clients on your knowledge and meticulous attention to detail that can be used to develop financial strategies tailored specifically to their own unique situations. In each case, you'll take a good look at their current financial situation, suggest the appropriate alternatives for retirement planning, and work out a sensible schedule and budget for setting aside the necessary funds. You may suggest specific investment options, such as mutual funds, Treasury bonds, or annuities, but you will not represent any one particular product.

STARTUP:

Your startup costs are minimal (about $1,500) to cover the cost of a computer, printer, copier, spreadsheet software, and Internet access. Since you will likely meet with your clients at their offices or in their homes, your own office setup need not be elaborate.

BOTTOM LINE ADVICE:

The difficulty in selling retirement services is that, while everyone needs them, few people are anxious to contemplate the reality of one day retiring or to begin saving more, spending less, and keeping to a budget. Your "hook" for this market may be to find a way to send the reassuring message that "yes, you can plan for retirement and still have fun today."

REUNION ORGANIZER

Startup cost:	$2,000–$3,000
Potential earnings:	$15,000–$50,000
Typical fees:	Hourly rate of $35–$50, or a percentage of total cost of the arrangements you handle (typically 10 to 15 percent)
Advertising:	Word of mouth and warm calling
Qualifications:	A big network of friends and acquaintances in your community; patience, determination, organizational ability
Equipment needed:	Computer, database and business software, printer fax, copier, Internet access, cell phone
Home business potential:	Yes
Staff required:	No
Hidden costs:	Telephone bills

LOWDOWN:

Reunions have long been a popular way to reconnect with family and friends. But chang-ing life patterns and the fact that more and more women are working outside the home means that fewer people are available who have the time and inclination to pull such events together. This leaves the market wide open for competent reunion organizers, who are willing to plan the events and handle all the details required to pull them off. High school reunions will be a major focus of your business and tracking down "lost" classmates an important part of the process. Your efforts are likely to begin at least a full year ahead of the event, and you will need persistence and sheer determination to keep going with your search against sometimes incredible long odds. Former employees of some organizations occasionally hold reunions too, as do the members of disbanded military units; there's a definite niche market in putting together events for these far-flung "families." And while we're on the subject, multigenerational families—both large and small—hold reunions, too, and you may be able to get a share of that business as well. Uncovering the whereabouts of long-lost friends or family members is only the beginning; you will also be responsible for planning and carrying out the event itself, arranging for catering, photos, band, decorations, take-home mementos, and more.

STARTUP:

You will need a basic office setup with computer, database and business software, printer, copier, and fax. You may have to search nationwide for long-lost friends or rela-tives, so high-speed Internet access is a must. Some reunion organizers charge a flat rate ($5–$15 per attendee), but this can be dangerous. If you have to spend a lot of time tracking people down, you'll quickly eat into your profits. You may want to charge an hourly rate instead, or a percentage (typically 15 to 20 percent) of the total cost of the arrangements you handle.

BOTTOM LINE ADVICE:

Almost every community can be an excellent market for this service; your job is to let potential clients know it. Reunion organizing is one of those obvious services that peo-ple are simply not expecting to be available. Consider the organizations and groups in your immediate geographic location that might have reunions, such as high schools, colleges, and military units. Get a foothold with one, do an excellent job, and you'll find that the referrals just begin to roll in. After all, classes are graduated every year from high schools and colleges; somewhere—even in your hometown—there is always at least one getting ready to hold its reunion. Your success will depend to some extent on the material and information you are given to work with, but once you refine your people-searching skills, you'll have a service to offer that amateurs will be hard-pressed to match. Thanks to Internet search engines and online phone books you can easily locate nearly anyone in the country these days.

SALES OF NOVELTY AND PROMOTIONAL PRODUCTS

Startup cost:	$1,000–$5,000
Potential earnings:	$30,000–$60,000
Typical fees:	Percentage of sales (10 to 15 percent); products typically sell anywhere from a few dollars to several hundred each
Advertising:	Trade publications, business periodicals, direct mail, catalogs, Yellow Pages
Qualifications:	Sales ability
Equipment needed:	Computer, Internet access, fax, laser printer, marketing materials
Home business potential:	Yes
Staff required:	Possibly, as your business grows
Hidden costs:	Inventory, reprinting of catalogs and other sales materials

LOWDOWN:

This is a great business for those who recognize what will amuse people (namely your clients' customers) and catch their attention. You are providing one facet of the activity that is essential to every business: marketing. Novelties and promotional materials put the name and message of a business out before the public. You've seen these items, and probably own a few yourself. They're the pens, magnets, mugs, calendars, hats, jackets, etc. that carry the name and address of a business, and they can be an enormously effective way of keeping that business in front of its customers and prospects. As a seller of novelty products, you are more than just a writer of orders. You know which novelties people are likely to keep around and you suggest ideas for new and different products that reflect the business they promote. Promotional materials can take many forms, and fitting the object to the message requires a special kind of business insight. You'll need to have an enthusiasm for sales and marketing, and you'll need to be both creative and a little offbeat in order to attract the attention of companies that want to attract attention for themselves. If you're exceptionally energetic and creative, you may grow your business from one of selling other people's novelty products to developing a line of your own.

STARTUP:

The relationship you establish early on with your distributor will control your need for inventory, which ideally should be kept to a minimum. Demonstration samples and catalogs can be quite expensive, so try to secure an arrangement with your manufacturers and their reps before trying to produce your own. You can earn a tidy living selling novelty products and if you don't believe it, just look at how well companies like Successories are doing. There's definitely a market for your services and it's a profitable one.

BOTTOM LINE ADVICE:

Your devotion to the needs of your clients will make you stand out from the crowd. There's a good deal of competition in this field, but many of the other businesses just throw catalogs at prospects and expect them to make a creative choice. You, on the other hand, develop a presentation tailored to each client's distinctive needs and expectations. You suggest several appealing options, and you carry out the detailed ordering and delivery process. It's work all right, but it's also fun and potentially quite profitable.

ADVICE FROM THE EXPERTS

What sets your business apart from others like it?
"We have not only created a specialty product, but something that has a life and character all its own," says Mark Juarez, President and CEO of *Tender Loving Things, Inc.,* in Oakland, California, which produces tiny wooden creatures with message capability.

Things you couldn't do without:
"Birch or maple wood, drilling machine, glue, smiley-face brander and office equipment to run shipping, production, art, marketing, customer service, and administrative departments."

Marketing tips/advice:
"We turn profits into social responsibility; we donate 10 percent of our product to non-profit organizations and other groups that might benefit from the caring touch."

If you had to do it all over again . . .
"One of our biggest external challenges has been combating knockoffs and copycats." Juarez suggests protecting yourself as early as possible within federal trademark regulations.

SECRETARIAL AND OFFICE-SUPPORT SERVICES

Startup cost:	$3,000–$5,000
Potential earnings:	$25,000–$40,000
Typical fees:	$15–$35 per hour (depending on size of the company and specific services you provide)
Advertising:	Classified ads, Yellow Pages, phone contacts
Qualifications:	Good typing and clerical skills; detail orientation; organization
Equipment needed:	Computer; word processing, database, and spreadsheet software; printer, copier, scanner, and fax; basic office supplies
Home business potential:	Yes
Staff required:	No
Hidden costs:	Freelance proofreader, as mistakes could cost you repeat business

LOWDOWN:

The executive stretches in his chair, puts his feet up on his desk, and calls for his secretary . . . only, in the age of downsizing, he's likely to be kept waiting—because he's sharing her with ten others who are already in line with their requests. The good old days where every executive had his own personal secretary are gone; many office-support functions are now being handled by small secretarial pools and/or machines. Still, however, the need for personalized service has not gone away, and often a beleaguered company, its small administrative force stretched to the max, needs to farm out work. So do sales reps who are on the road and single-person operations that can't afford to hire support staff full-time. That's where you come in. You can assist an office for a short period of time and at the last minute with a myriad of tasks—such as typing and writing letters, transcription, dictation, general bookkeeping, copying, assembling manuals and reports, etc. In short, you provide the same level of support that would simply be too costly to employ a full-timer with benefits to handle. Training and/or experience as a secretary will help you understand the types of skills that are needed and an idea of which companies you should target. This business offers a lot of flexibility: everything from after-regular-hours work for out-of-towners to temporary fill-ins for local companies caught in crunch-time situations.

STARTUP:

You will need a complete computer system, including word processing, database, and spreadsheet software, as well as a printer, copier, scanner, and fax. Expect to spend $2,000–$3,000 for the necessary equipment. You'll need to advertise, too—in the Yellow Pages for about $50–$100 per month and in the newspaper classifieds for around $10 per week; put together a flier describing your fees and services and network with hotels where businesspeople from out-of-town who might need occasional secretarial help are likely to stay. Since the amount of time it will take you to finish a particular assignment can vary and is not always known at the start of a job, charging a set price per task may not prove profitable. Instead, set an hourly fee of $15–$35, depending on the services you are asked to provide.

BOTTOM LINE ADVICE:

Since it's likely that this job will involve working with many different people, your ability to tolerate personality quirks will make the jobs—and time—go more quickly and smoothly. Your hours will sometimes vary from one day to the next, which, in terms of cash flow, can become stressful; budget carefully and plan ahead to avoid getting caught short when the bills come due. This business requires a high-energy, go-getter type of person. Do you have what it takes, and, more importantly, are you willing to always take orders from others?

ADVICE FROM THE EXPERTS

What sets your business apart from others like it?

"I'm incredibly fast, accurate, and affordable," says Jana McClish, owner of Paragon Word Services in Akron, Ohio. "I can offer a quicker turnaround than most of my competitors."

Things you couldn't do without:

McClish needs a computer, answering machine, and a 10-key adding machine to run her business effectively.

Marketing tips/advice:

"You have to be persistent and market almost constantly. You must be confident and be able to sell that confidence in order to get in the door. You really need to have a special skill that sets you apart, too."

If you had to do it all over again . . .

"I'd research my equipment purchases better. I needed to buy new equipment a year and a half into my business because I did not purchase wisely. Also, I would've started with a much bigger base of prospects . . . . I got kind of discouraged in the beginning because I didn't have huge amounts of work."

SIGN PAINTING

Startup cost:	$2,000–$3,000
Potential earnings:	$25,000–$75,000 (depends on your geographic locale, production methods, and sign types)
Typical fees:	$25–$35 per hour for a drawing; $40–$50 per hour for hand lettering; $55+ per hour for a mural
Advertising:	Yellow Pages, newspaper classified and display ads, direct mail to new businesses, networking, Web site; always sign your work
Qualifications:	Artistic talent and an eye for design, mechanical aptitude; previous work in a sign-painting shop or apprenticeship with a master sign painter
Equipment needed:	Assorted brushes and other basic art supplies, paints, special tools such as an air-brush or sandblast stencil
Home business potential:	Yes
Staff required:	No
Hidden costs:	Time spent doing sketches for jobs you never get; make sure you retain the sketches or charge for them

LOWDOWN:

Even in this day of neon and computer-generated art, signs that are painted, etched, or carved by hand are still in high demand. With the right combination of artistic talent and sign-painting experience, you can satisfy your creative urges and make a nice living at this business. You will need artistic talent, of course, but you should also be a people person. Your prices will depend on the techniques you incorporate into the finished sign; lettering takes more time and a steadier hand than drawing, so charge accordingly. Use your original sketches and photographs of the actual finished signs to create a portfolio of samples that you can show to prospective customers. Be sure to keep track of how long it takes you to create a sign, from concept through completion, so that you can better estimate the time you will need for future projects. Also, make notes of any discoveries you make along the way—surfaces that give you trouble, materials that are easy to work with, etc. As a general policy, when it comes time to deliver your preliminary ideas, provide your client with several sketches of signs in a variety of price ranges. Offering a choice of options may help ensure that you get the job.

STARTUP:

Budget for startup expenses of approximately $2,000–$3,000 to cover the costs of basic art supplies and advertising. Add another $1,500 if you decide to add a computer and peripherals to your basic office setup. There's no need to keep a large inventory of paints and other materials; you can acquire them for specific projects as needed.

BOTTOM LINE ADVICE:

Your customers will want to see a written estimate and a sketch of the finished product before giving you the go-ahead, and sometimes, that's as far as the project goes. If a prospect for whom you have prepared a sketch decides to go no further, make sure that you get your sketch back or that you are compensated for it. Be firm about this and persistent in collecting what is due.

SOFTWARE CONVERSION SERVICE

Startup cost:	$2,000–$3,000
Potential earnings:	$20,000–$30,000
Typical fees:	$50–$75 per job or $25–$30 per hour
Advertising:	Referrals, advertising in trade journals, public speaking, networking
Qualifications:	Expertise in a wide range of systems and programs
Equipment needed:	Computer, printer, fax for your own office
Home business potential:	Yes
Staff required:	No
Hidden costs:	Risk and error insurance

LOWDOWN:

Software conversion is a narrow but vital field. When a business upgrades its computer equipment, installs different software, or merges with another company, systems clashes can occur and information can be rendered inaccessible or seem to be lost altogether. Files may need to be merged or converted from one program to another. Business owners and managers frequently fail to grasp the implications of decisions to change systems, and the resulting apparent loss of files quickly throws them into major crisis mode. If you have expertise in computer systems, you can serve this niche market by converting files so they can be read by the new system. As technology and software programs continue to change at a rapid pace, the need for this service is likely to grow well into the foreseeable future.

STARTUP:

If you're even considering the software conversion business, you probably already have all the computer hardware and software you will need. And considering that most of your work will be conducted on your clients' premises, your startup costs will be relatively low. You will need to have high-speed Internet access and subscriptions to several computer magazines in order to keep on top of software developments; set aside at least $250 annually for the subscriptions alone. Charge your clients $50–$75 per job—but if the hours start to get long and the bills mount up, consider switching to an hourly rate of $25–$30, or charge a flat fee.

BOTTOM LINE ADVICE:

Once established as a software converter, a detail-oriented person can easily develop a satisfied clientele. You understand disk architecture and the means by which electronic information is stored in files; use your knowledge to keep your clients' information systems up-to-date and operating smoothly. Your work can be both satisfying and profitable, but it can also be tense. Clients who know little or nothing about technology are likely to panic when their systems do not function as they expect them to. Be prepared to drop everything and rush to the aid of a frustrated client who doesn't understand the problems he's having and isn't at all sure that what you are doing will resolve them. Patience and the ability to explain highly technical issues in everyday terms will take you far in this business.

SPECIALTY FOOD PRODUCTION

Startup cost:	$500–$5,000 (depending on the food product)
Potential earnings:	$30,000–$75,000
Typical fees:	As high as $50 for some items, but most range $2–$25 each
Advertising:	Mail-order catalogs, brochures, direct mail, groceries, farmers' markets
Qualifications:	Knowledge of how to manufacture and market the item
Equipment needed:	Depends on the item
Home business potential:	Yes; at least until the business outgrows your home
Staff required:	None
Hidden costs:	Legal advice, licensing

LOWDOWN:

The sky is truly the limit in food production—anything from eggs, organically grown tomatoes, and bottled water to candy, cookies, jellies, and condiments can be produced by a home-based entrepreneur. The details of starting and running a specialty food production business vary greatly, depending upon which product you choose, but whether you offer a unique food item or market a tried-and-true favorite in a new way there's a great possibility for success. The package of pasta you can produce for as little as 46 cents can be sold for $3.50 or more. Want more ideas? There's food by mail order, preserved foods, specialty breads, sassafras tea, mustards and vinegars, holiday cookies, maple syrup . . . the list goes on and on. If you are willing to work hard and learn the ins and outs of producing and marketing a particular food product, you can establish a profitable business.

STARTUP:

Startup costs depend on the food product you choose. If you need ovens or an assembly line to manufacture your products, you may have to spend some big bucks up front. On the other hand, candy, baked goods, even soup can be started on a shoestring. Packaging and marketing costs for any product must be carefully considered; explore your market area, examine the packaging and pricing of similar products, and research the costs of production and marketing.

BOTTOM LINE ADVICE:

If your product is home-grown outdoors, your income will be greatly affected by weather and the seasons. In addition, you may need considerable knowledge about soil, fertilizers, plant diseases, etc. If you are making a product from scratch in your kitchen, you must have a continuing supply of ingredients and a consistent manufacturing method to ensure that your products always taste the same. Food products are subject to safety and health regulations, too. You may need a special license to produce your product. The good news is that many food manufacturing operations are quite simple, requiring few ingredients and no great technical skills. Everyone loves to eat, so food products are always in vogue. If you have a favorite family recipe you think others would enjoy, why not give it a go?

Speechwriter

Startup cost:	$1,000–$1,500
Potential earnings:	$20,000–$60,000
Typical fees:	$30–$125 per hour or a flat rate of $500 or more
Advertising:	Referrals, networking
Qualifications:	Excellent writing and presentation skills
Equipment needed:	Computer, printer, fax, Internet access
Home business potential:	Yes
Staff required:	No
Hidden costs:	None

LOWDOWN:

Excellent speechwriters are like trusted advisors to their clients. If you can develop speeches that work well for different speakers, you can earn an impressive living in this field. Depending on the topic of the speech, you may need to do extensive research in the library or online. Success will depend on your sense of what is effective in a spoken format, and what kinds of language and ideas can best be delivered by your clients. Businesses executives, politicians, and public figures often give many speeches each year, but they lack the time and skill to write the presentations themselves. Write a speech that really moves people—or better yet puts your client in office—and your career will advance quickly.

STARTUP:

Startup costs are low, but you will need a computer and printer (approximately $1,500). You can bill anywhere from $30–$125 an hour for your service, depending on the client and audience, or charge a flat rate for 10-, 30-, and 60-minute speeches.

BOTTOM LINE ADVICE:

Many speechwriters develop a sense of partnership with the people who will be delivering their speeches. Once you prove yourself, you become invaluable to your clients. Yet this can be a very hard business to break into. Many writers offer speechwriting as just one of their services, and you must find a way to distinguish yourself from all the rest. Expect to put in a lot of long hours and late nights. This work is often done under tight deadlines and extreme pressure.

STANDARDIZED TEST PREPARATORY SERVICES

Startup cost:	$1,000–$5,000
Potential earnings:	$30,000–$45,000
Typical fees:	$75–$175 per client
Advertising:	Yellow Pages, direct mail to students/parents
Qualifications:	Familiarity with the major standardized tests (including SAT, ACT, GED, GRE, LSAT), a degree in education and/or classroom teaching experience is helpful (a teaching certificate may be required in some states)
Equipment needed:	Workbooks/sample practice tests, pencils, timers
Home business potential:	Yes (but you may be able to rent testing space from schools at minimal cost)
Staff required:	No
Hidden costs:	Insurance

LOWDOWN:

Thousands of students each year are required to take standardized tests for entry into college, and they usually must spend weeks preparing for them. The tests typically include sections designed to assess math, reading, and writing skills. You can help students prepare for individual sections or the entire test by presenting them with sample questions/problems as practice guides. You will score their responses, then, as you go over the results, answer their questions and assist them in improving their scores. You may focus on the tests all entering college freshmen are required to take, or elect to work with a more specialized test such as the LSAT which undergraduates must pass before being accepted into law school. You can work with students one-on-one or, for the most profitable approach, work with groups of students in test preparation classes.

STARTUP:

Your startup costs will be low, because the only tools you'll need are workbooks/sample test booklets, pencils, and timers. And since your clients will be paying up front for your services, you needn't worry about maintaining an inventory; you can purchase them according to your needs. You can conduct your training in your home; however, if you truly want to simulate the test-taking experience, you will probably want to rent classroom space. Check with your local school system for after-hour rates; you may be able to get by for as little as $35. Set your fees at $75–$175 per student to cover your time and expenses, and expect an income potential of $30,000–$45,000 depending on how many practice sessions you conduct.

BOTTOM LINE ADVICE:

If you don't mind repetition, a standardized test-prep business can be a relaxing and comfortable way to make a living; you simply provide the same services over and over and collect your checks for the privilege. On the other hand, you may find this business too repetitious, and therefore not challenging enough. If so, you might try combining it with a private tutoring service or incorporate test preparation into a primary business as a college application consultant.

STENCILING

Startup cost:	$1,000–$2,000
Potential earnings:	$1,000–$3,000 per month
Typical fees:	$25–$1,000 per project or finished piece
Advertising:	Business cards, bulletin boards, craft stores, specialty clothing shops, paint and wallpaper stores; Yellow Pages and small newspaper ads
Qualifications:	Some artistic flair, ability to handle repetitious work
Equipment needed:	Various paint brushes, sponges, stenciling patterns, tracing paper, paint and varnishes, towels and rags
Home business potential:	Yes
Staff required:	No
Hidden costs:	Insurance

LOWDOWN:

The centuries-old technique of stenciling is believed to have started in the Fiji Islands. Even today it remains popular among folks who want to add special touches to their walls, floors, and furniture, but don't have the skill to do the stenciling themselves. If you are adept at this craft, you should have no problem getting plenty of business. There are as many techniques of stenciling as there are surfaces to stencil. You can stencil floors, furniture, and all types of fabrics. If you want to cash in on the potentially lucrative home interior stenciling market, start by hooking up with custom builders and interior designers who can provide referrals or contract the work out themselves. Take along some pictures of stenciling you've done in your own home or for friends and family. Another possible source of income is to sell the furniture or fabrics you have already stenciled at craft shows. As a general rule of thumb, the more unique the item, the better it is likely to sell.

STARTUP:

Your startup costs will largely depend on the direction in which you decide to take your business. For jobs you do on-site, you probably already have the basic equipment; the cost of any supplies you need to purchase for a particular job, such as a unique pattern or special paint, can be incorporated into your fees. If you decide to sell stenciled products, you'll have the additional cost of the fabric or furniture, plus rental fees for table or floor space (typically $150–$400 a pop). In either case, you'll want to do some advertising—Yellow Pages and small newspaper ads. Nonprofessional stencilers are content to remain hobbyists and never earn a penny from their art; those who choose to turn their hobby into a business, however, can make $1,000–$3,000 per month.

BOTTOM LINE ADVICE:

You can stencil on practically everything, from furniture to kites to cars. And if you don't see a pattern out there for a stencil you like, you can make your own with minimal effort. All you need is a package of tracing paper and a library card; your local library probably has shelves of books full of stenciling ideas. Stenciling may require long periods of standing, bending, or sitting. And because the paint and varnishes you'll be working with give off fumes, be sure that your work area is well-ventilated.

STENOGRAPHY SERVICE

Startup cost:	$2,000–$4,000
Potential earnings:	$30,000–$40,000
Typical fees:	$15 per page, or $25 per hour
Advertising:	Newspapers, Yellow Pages, publications targeting the business community, referrals
Qualifications:	Secretarial skills, good organizational ability, proficiency in spelling and grammar
Equipment needed:	Computer with word processing software and e-mail capabilities, dictation machine, laserprinter, fax
Home business potential:	Yes
Staff required:	No
Hidden costs:	Software upgrades, office supplies

LOWDOWN:

Even in today's high-tech world of computers and word processing software, there's still a need for stenography skills. Stenography is a service that can be marketed widely to businesses that are understaffed or have lean organizational structures. Your ability to transcribe dictation accurately onto paper and deliver it on time, can be a valuable addition to your clients' work processes. Senior managers have assumed that the introduction of the computer removed the need for stenographic services, and consequently, they're no longer available in many corporations. The need still exists, however, and you can fill it. In addition to large corporations that have trimmed their in-house support staffs, you may find work with small business establishments that have no support staff at all.

STARTUP:

Your office setup must allow you to work comfortably; you'll be spending a lot of time at your computer keyboard, so invest in a comfortable chair. You will need word processing software and dictation equipment that is compatible with that of your clientele; expect to spend $2,000–$4,000 to get up and running. A stenography business won't make you rich, but it will earn you a reasonably comfortable income of around $30,000 to start.

BOTTOM LINE ADVICE:

Depending on your geographic location, you may find plenty of competition for the services you offer. Pricing your work so that you can be competitive and still make a profit can be a challenge. It may take you a few jobs before you master the knack of estimating your time accurately and setting appropriate prices. To succeed, you'll need to be a self-starter, able to work without much direction or the stimulation of a busy workplace to keep you on task. The fact that you'll be flying solo much of the time is not necessarily a drawback. Many people find it easier to get work done without the hubbub of the social scene that's usual in a large organization.

SYSTEMS INTEGRATOR

Startup cost:	$1,000–$5,000
Potential earnings:	$37,500–$100,000
Typical fees:	$100+ per hour
Advertising:	Referrals, direct mail, publications, networking
Qualifications:	Technical knowledge and expertise in systems, time-management skills
Equipment needed:	Computer, software, high-speed Internet access, fax, cell phone and or pager,
Home business potential:	Yes
Staff required:	No, but subcontracting may be required depending on project needs and timetable for completion
Hidden costs:	Time and expense of staying current in this demanding field

LOWDOWN:

Computers are wonderful business tools, yet there are bound to be glitches from time to time and there is always room for improvement. Operations and compatibility problems can be sometimes enormous, and as businesses grow, so too must their information systems. If you have the expertise to be a systems integrator, you won't have any trouble finding enough work to keep you busy; nearly every growing company in the United States, possibly even the world, needs your services, and the more successful projects you complete, the greater your reputation will grow and the more business you will have. You'll need more than "tech smarts" to succeed in this business, however; you will also need some people skills to work effectively with the employees assigned to oversee information systems at your client's offices. The primary asset you bring to the marketplace is your detailed understanding of how the latest computer systems work, and how old and new systems can be brought into effective integration.

STARTUP:

Most of your work will take place on-site at your client's premises; you'll be working primarily on their equipment, not your own. Keep in mind, however, that you'll need to be familiar with many different types of equipment, some of which you may already have on hand and some of which you will need to lease. Your skill is highly unique and technical; do not be afraid to bill at a rate of at least $100–$150 per hour.

BOTTOM LINE ADVICE:

If you live within commuting distance of an urban area, you ought to be able to create an excellent and profitable business. A long-term commitment to one client, which is often necessary to complete many projects in this field, can limit your contacts. On the other hand, successful completion of the job should also provide you with an excellent referral base. Systems integration is an extremely challenging field, and one problem you are likely to face is that the people making the decision to hire you often have little understanding of what their information system needs or how much services like yours should cost. Thus, education with regard to both your services and your fees will play a major role in your sales effort. Systems integrators are often called in at the last minute, so be prepared to work against the clock and under a great deal of pressure.

Taxidermist

Startup cost:	$1,000–$3,500
Potential earnings:	$17,000–$25,000
Typical fees:	$45–$60 per animal
Advertising:	Yellow Pages, referrals from gun shops, fishing tackle and bait suppliers, and outdoor equipment stores, location
Qualifications:	Experience with taxidermy
Equipment needed:	Chemical preservatives, scalpel, inventory of replaceable parts
Home business potential:	Yes
Staff required:	No
Hidden costs:	Mounts and supplies

LOWDOWN:

Your major market will be hunters and fishermen, although some taxidermists special-ize in pet preservation and/or museum exhibits. Location is an important factor to con-sider. Taxidermy is often a home-based business, but you will need a way to make your business visible. The easiest way is to post a sign in your yard, but check your city's zon-ing laws to make sure that it is legal to do so; some ordinances prohibit the posting of business signs in residential neighborhoods. Proximity to a hunting or fishing area will improve your flow of business. The popularity of hunting and fishing continues to increase, so if you are capable of creating an attractive mounted trophy or specimen, you could earn a steady although probably not spectacular income. Taxidermy is more than a craft. You will need to have a certain artistic sense and an understanding of the unique characteristics of specific wild creatures in order to produce effective results.

STARTUP:

Your startup costs consist primarily of the chemical preservatives that keep the animal looking lifelike after death. These chemicals and related items of equipment could run between $1,000–$3,500 to start. Sounds expensive until you consider that you'll be using them on more than a few animals. Charge at least $45 per animal to cover your time and the cost of supplies.

BOTTOM LINE ADVICE:

Building your market will be slow at first. Many hunters and fishermen are fundamen-tally conservative people who do not jump on the latest trend. You will need to provide excellent work over several years before referrals keep a steady clientele coming to your door. Taxidermy is not easy or quick, and it will require diligence on your part to develop a pricing structure that compensates you adequately for the time, materials, and labor involved in your business.

TIME-MANAGEMENT SPECIALIST

Startup cost:	$1,000–$6,500
Potential earnings:	$20,000–$40,000
Typical fees:	$75–$100 per hour or a set fee (i.e., $100+ per person) for classes you offer
Advertising:	Free workshops/seminars and other public speaking opportunities, word-of-mouth referrals, networking, news releases, bylined articles in local newspapers and trade journals
Qualifications:	High level of organization (you must be a good time manager yourself!), analytical ability, punctuality, ability to deliver on your commitments, an open mind
Equipment needed:	Computer, fax, Internet connection, printer, phone, word processing and time-management software, handout materials
Home business potential:	Yes
Staff required:	No
Hidden costs:	Preparation time if you are not using a prepackaged time management program, licensing fees if you are

LOWDOWN:

Bringing relief to people under inordinate stress is just one of the many benefits of being a time-management specialist. In addition to making the workplace less of a sweatshop, you'll be assisting clients in goal-setting, developing action plans, defining priorities, and scheduling/delegating tasks and activities. You may work as a freelance consultant, identifying and helping to correct problems for harried company executives in search of techniques for improving productivity, or you may present your ideas in stand-alone seminars you conduct for large groups or as part of a personal productivity training program. The opportunities to make money from time are certainly out there, you just need to get your name out to the people most in need of your services (and they are nowhere near as limited as you might think). Quick profitability is a definite possibility in this low over-head business, but be careful not to underprice your product. You need to be sure that you charge appropriately for your time and expertise. One last tip: Don't forget to offer periodic refresher courses as a way to build repeat business; you'd be surprised how many customers slip back into their old habits and say they'd benefit from another session.

STARTUP:

Word-of-mouth advertising will keep your startup costs low; your credibility and a suc-cessful track record will grow your business. You'll want to present a professional image, so be prepared to spend a minimum of $250 for business cards, letterhead, and bro-chures. You'll need a computer and printer, plus word processing and time manage-ment software, to prepare your handouts and presentation materials; costs can range from $1,500–$3,000. Remember, too, that you'll need to join and participate in as many professional organizations as possible in order to continually network and prospect for clients; set aside at least $250 per year for this valuable lead-generator. Charge at least $75 per hour for individualized corporate consulting; more ($1,000 per day is typical) to conduct seminars for groups of professionals.

BOTTOM LINE ADVICE:
The idea that one needs to be trained to manage time is still a relatively new one to many businesses. Hence, competition may not be a significant problem . . . yet. If you enjoy leading others to dramatic results in a short period of time, this career can be extremely gratifying ad enjoyable. But you should be advised that you'll have to expend a good deal of your own time and energy to get started. Are you able to practice what you preach? Do you manage your own time wisely? Are you willing to be patient? It may take as much as a year or two before you are able to make a full-time income.

ADVICE FROM THE EXPERTS

What sets your business apart from others like it?
Jennifer Annandono, managing partner of the Kent, Ohio-based Progressive Leadership Center, says her business is unique because she is. "I greatly enjoy demonstrating to others how to have a more balanced work and personal life. My feeling is that time management is about setting goals, and the implementation of new tools, which will promote achievement."

Things you couldn't do without:
Annandono says she could not do without a second telephone line with answering or voice mail capability. "My computer and laser printer allow me the convenience of professional correspondence."

Marketing tips/advice:
"It is always more effective to market your service as the 'benefit' customers will receive rather than focusing on various features you might offer. Much of my marketing success is based in community interaction and word-of-mouth referral. The best advice is: Always be a product of the service you provide!"

If you had to do it all over again . . .
"I would have spent the months preceding the opening of my business selecting centers of influence. If you are not already established in the community, it is never too early to identify and communicate with those individuals who know and trust you and clearly understand what service you provide."

TRADEMARK AGENT

Startup cost:	$1,000–$1,500
Potential earnings:	$40,000–$65,000
Typical fees:	Usually a flat fee of $175–$250 (more for larger corporations)
Advertising:	Business publications, direct mail, referrals, networking, Web site
Qualifications:	Extensive experience in field, familiarity with computer searches, proximity to the U.S. Trademark Office in Washington, D.C., may be helpful
Equipment needed:	Computer with fax and high-speed Internet connection
Home business potential:	Yes
Staff required:	No
Hidden costs:	Insurance

LOWDOWN:

It is often said that perception is 99 percent reality. Whether you agree with that statement or not, you no doubt recognize that the image of a product or service is undeniably a factor in its value. Since medieval times, a trademark has been a way of protecting an essential element of that image, the name. How important is a trademark? Ask the people who first marketed aspirin. They neglected to protect their brand name and, before too long, it had become the generic term for a certain type of pain reliever. Throughout the centuries, an incredibly large number of names have been trademarked, and your clients need to know if, for example, "Angelic Skydiving Service," the name they have selected for their Hawaii-based stunt act, is already in use and trademarked by someone else. As a trademark agent, your primary job will be to search the records of the U.S. Trademark Office in Washington, D.C., as well as records maintained by all 50 secretaries of state, to make sure a specific name is available before your client invests significant money in the labeling, packaging, and marketing of a new product. Since the electronic databases containing the information you need are largely proprietary—owned by your giant competitors—you will have to rely largely on time-consuming manual searches. For economy of scale, you may want to limit your services to a specific industry or product type. Some trademark agents specialize, for example, in automotive products, such as tires.

STARTUP:

Your startup costs will be relatively low, especially if you already have a computer; if you do not, expect to spend around $2,000 for the necessary equipment. Searching the listings of trademarks is a highly labor intensive task. If you are an attorney, you'll probably have access to a computer database; if you're not, you'll have to do your searching manually. Time is money, so be sure to charge accordingly. Charge $175–$250 per search/registry for an individual or small business, more if you are working for a large corporation (unlikely, since many large companies have attorneys in-house or on-retainer to handle this type of work).

BOTTOM LINE ADVICE:

Skill, and sometimes even intuition, are required to establish the validity of a given trademark. Finding the proper trademark files requires creative thinking. To protect your client from infringing on someone else's trademark, you can't simply look up a word like *sword* and let it go at that. You must consider all words with similar meanings, such as *rapier* and *saber*, as well as words with similar sounds, like *sod* and *sore*. Then, you must consider graphic designs that include swords. The search process can become quite complicated, so be sure that you enjoy tedious work and minute detail before embarking on this business. And make sure you are adequately covered by insurance, just in case you should happen to miss one of those finer nuances of the name you are researching and inadvertently infringe on some other company's trademark.

TRANSLATION SERVICES

Startup cost:	$2,000–$3,000
Potential earnings:	$20,000–$30,000
Typical fees:	$8–$15 per 100 words; $25–$35 per hour
Advertising:	Trade journals, Yellow Pages, referrals, personal contacts
Qualifications:	Fluency in English as well as the foreign language(s) you offer, including familiarity with colloquialisms and slang; excellent writing and communications skills
Equipment needed:	Computer, copier, Internet access, and fax, software and compatible printer that will reproduce the appropriate foreign language characters and accents
Home business potential:	Yes
Staff required:	Yes, for languages you cannot translate yourself
Hidden costs:	Telephone charges, marketing

LOWDOWN:

Thousands of languages are spoken across the globe, and even within the United States, where English is the official language, texts often need translation into French or Spanish. In today's global marketplace, a translation service can be useful to develop, among other things, a glossary of terms to use in the translation process. Additional services can relate to development of icons and illustrations that are readily understandable across cultures. Your business can specialize in translation for a specific field such as medical instrument sales, or you can focus on one particular language. The ability to produce effective, accurate results under deadline will enable you to build your translation business into a highly successful enterprise. If you or members of your staff are fluent in a particular language and quick on your feet, you may be able to broaden your services to include interpretation of the spoken word in addition to translation of written documents; interpreters may command fees of $250 or more per day.

STARTUP:

Reference materials, such as foreign language dictionaries, and basic office equipment will be your major startup costs. You will need computer software and a compatible printer that can produce all of the characters and accent marks used in your specialty languages; expect to spend $2,000–$3,000. Your earnings will come from fees ($8–$15 per 100 words or $25–$35 per hour). Translation of highly technical, scientific, or medical documents may command higher prices.

BOTTOM LINE ADVICE:

The market for translation services is growing rapidly and will continue to do so in the future as our world becomes a smaller place. English is by no means a universal language, and few Americans are fluent enough in a foreign language to produce their own translations. You'll be learning as you translate while providing a much-needed service for your clients. Translation is not without its difficulties, however. Problems can result when you try to simply plug words into slots (e.g., one foreign word for one English term or vice versa); you may try to translate an idiom word for word and misconstrue its meaning entirely. Communicating the total meaning of a sentence or paragraph accurately is a creative and challenging activity, and your pricing should reflect the time needed to get it right.

TRAVEL AGENT

Startup cost:	$2,000–$3,000
Potential earnings:	$25,000–$45,000
Typical fees:	Commission of 60 to 80 percent of the travel agency's commission from the airlines is standard
Advertising:	Yellow Pages, newspaper ads, direct mail
Qualifications:	Knowledge of the travel industry and particular destinations; certification through an accredited travel school is a plus; prior experience with a travel agency or training on the customized computer systems most travel agencies use
Equipment needed:	Computer with high-speed Internet access, phone
Home business potential:	Yes
Staff required:	No
Hidden costs:	Phone expenses

LOWDOWN:

Do you like to travel? Would you find satisfaction helping others fly the "friendly skies" to exotic places? If you answered yes to both questions, you could potentially succeed as an outside travel agent. As an outside travel agent, you do not have access to a computerized reservation system nor can you actually cut the tickets (FAA restrictions are very strict about that), so you will have to align yourself with a full-service travel agency that is willing to let you search for and book flights, then transfer the information so they can do the actual ticketing. Travel agencies receive commissions from the airlines on the tickets they sell; for the referrals you provide, the agency should be willing to pay you as much as 60 to 80 percent of their commission. And because some networked travel agencies rely almost solely on home-based agents, your options are many if you decide to embark on this exciting and interesting business. The best part is, many travel companies offer incentives and special perks for agents like you, which means you could wind up doing some sightseeing yourself.

To succeed in this business, you will have to be a particularly aggressive marketer. Your potential customers have access to a whole host of Web-based travel services which allow them to easily check fares and book their own reservations. So why should they come to you? Because you know the travel industry and can save them the time and aggravation of searching for the best price. Besides, it's free; you derive your income from the travel agency that does the actual ticketing.

STARTUP:

You'll need a budget for advertising, plus a powerful computer with high-speed Internet access, and a phone. Beware of travel agencies that try to charge you for the privilege of becoming an outside agent; they should be paying you for the business you bring in.

BOTTOM LINE ADVICE:

The travel business is huge—and, despite occasional downturns in the economy, still growing by leaps and bounds. Many opportunities exist to make money in this field. The cost of running a travel business is modest if you are working as an outside agent; little more than a powerful computer with high-speed Internet access and basic office furnishings are required. Compared to opening your own full-service travel agency, which is an expensive proposition, working as an "outsider" allows you to enjoy many travel perks without the expense. Expect to invest a lot of time, however, getting established and to face stiff competition from large, full-service agencies capable of booking tickets for lucrative corporate accounts.

ADVICE FROM THE EXPERTS

What sets your business apart from others like it?

"My agents and I have traveled to almost every destination in the world, so I would say that personal experience sets us apart from other travel agents," says Helen Meek, owner of Helen Meek Travel in Fairlawn, Ohio.

Things you couldn't do without:

Computers with specialized reservation programs (leased from airline companies) and telephones are the primary pieces of equipment needed to run this travel agency. "We also couldn't do without our experienced, wonderful staff."

Marketing tips/advice:

"You need to look at location and market demographics; I knew my area would grow, and now I'm an established leader in my geographic location." Meek also advises entrepreneurs to get their names out there any way possible while building credibility.

If you had to do it all over again . . .

"Nothing. It's worked for thirteen years, and if you can get past those first five, you are probably going to make it."

TREE SERVICE

Startup cost:	$1,000–$5,000
Potential earnings:	$25,000–$35,000
Typical fees:	$120–$350 per day
Advertising:	Classified ads, Yellow Pages
Qualifications:	Experience, formal training in landscaping and/or arborism
Equipment needed:	Pickup truck, ladders, chain saw, small handsaws, axes, hatchets
Home business potential:	Yes
Staff required:	You may need a helper, depending on the size of the job (and the tree)
Hidden costs:	Permission of local authorities, health and liability insurance

LOWDOWN:

A tree service can be a good business for an energetic and relatively fearless person who doesn't mind climbing up where the squirrels run and using heavy, dangerous tools like chain saws when he gets there. In order to ensure that your work does not harm the tree, you'll need to have expertise in tree health. Which limbs are about to fall? How should a tree be pruned so that it will become strong and graceful? If a tree must come down, you'll need to know the art and science of making it fall safely so no one gets hurt and property is not damaged. You'll put a quick end to your career if you take out your customer's carport or the neighbor's backyard fence. If your customer does not ask to retain the resulting logs, you may be able to earn a little extra money by selling them as firewood. Most tree services are generalists (they'll handle any type of tree), but a few choose to specialize. Orchard trees, for instance, require special pruning techniques in order to produce a healthy crop.

STARTUP:

Cutting tools, heavy boots, gloves, and a truck are the essentials you'll need to get started in this business; your startup costs will depend on which of these you already have and which ones you need to buy. You'll do best if you live in a rural area or an older community, where the trees are well-established. Hurricane-prone regions are particularly lucrative because trees need to be trimmed back before the storm arrives, then repaired and the debris removed after the storm has passed. You can expect to bill $150–$350 per job, depending on the number and size of the trees. If possible, keep the wood. You can net as much as an additional $500 per month selling the wood to lumberyards or firewood companies.

BOTTOM LINE ADVICE:

Most people who make a success of the tree service business have a deep love of the outdoors and of growing things. It takes a well-trained eye and knowledge of tree health to determine which limbs to keep and which to cut. If you'd rather climb a tree than sit in an office and look at one through a skyscraper window, this just might be the business for you. The major negative is, of course, the physical danger. You can get seriously hurt handling ladders, chain saws, and axes. Expect your insurance premiums to be steep; you may love the treetops, but insurance companies see them from a slightly different perspective. And unless you live in a place like Florida, where the trees are green and growing all year round, you'll need to plan for seasonal ups and downs.

UPHOLSTERER

Startup cost:	$1,000–$5,000
Potential earnings:	$25,000–$45,000
Typical fees:	Varied; could be as low as $50 and as high as $1,000 per piece
Advertising:	Yellow Pages, community newspapers, coupon books, referral
Qualifications:	Skilled apprenticeship
Equipment needed:	Commercial sewing machine; upholstery tools, tacks, and fabric; delivery vehicle
Home business potential:	Yes
Staff required:	No
Hidden costs:	Insurance, vehicle costs

LOWDOWN:

There's nothing like a terrific-looking accent chair to make any room stand out . . . and, as a quality-driven upholsterer, you can make it happen for your customers. If you have the background and skill in the centuries-old art of upholstery, you could go into business as quickly as you can hang up a sign. Just make sure you're reaching an affluent client base; they're the ones willing to pay top dollar for quality work and to see the value of having furniture re-covered rather than replaced. Once you've established yourself as a trusted name in the business, you'll be surprised how quickly the referrals will start rolling in. Then, instead of spending your days scouting for new customers, you'll be able to concentrate on helping the ones you have choose new and exciting fabrics, style-enhancing accents (such as decorative tacks or tassels), and other details that can change the look and personality of a piece of furniture. You'll provide an estimate for your work up front, secure the necessary fabric and materials, then set about the work itself. For those who truly love and appreciate good furniture, upholstering can be a challenging, but fun, creative business.

STARTUP:

You'll need approximately $1,000–$3,000 to get started in this business, mainly to cover the cost of your equipment and initial supplies. Of course, you'll need to spend $1,000 or so on advertising, too. But if you are conscientious and pay attention to small details, happy customers will spread the word and you could soon be bringing in as much as $25,000–$45,000 per year.

BOTTOM LINE ADVICE:

If you like working alone in a quiet place, and if you are especially task-oriented, this could be a wonderful business opportunity for you. There's plenty of room for creativity, too; some furniture designers look to upholsterers for fresh ideas.

VENDING MACHINE OWNER

Startup cost:	$1,000–$20,000
Potential earnings:	Depends on the machine location and type; a possible annual potential income of $25,000–$40,000
Typical fees:	Monthly revenue ranges from as low as $100 to as high as $500 per machine, less a percentage of sales to the owner of the site
Advertising:	Direct mail, Yellow Pages
Qualifications:	Excellent sales ability, working knowledge of vending machines available
Equipment needed:	Vending machines and the product to fill them
Home business potential:	Yes
Staff required:	No
Hidden costs:	An average of 10 percent on what you earn from each machine goes to the property owner

LOWDOWN:

Although vending machines seem to be just about everywhere these days, it will take some research to determine which types are available and exactly which spots might be most profitable to put them in. Without a doubt, you'll need good marketing and sales skills to succeed in this business. For example, you could place your machines inside large factories that have round-the-clock shifts and a need for "real food" such as soup and sandwiches, or in small firms where only soda and candy machines are likely to do well. Once you've captured the interest of a potential client, he or she should be able to tell you what to stock, but ask to tour the facility so you can get a good idea of where to actually place your machine for maximum revenues. If you go with soda and candy, make sure your client company is willing to place your machine in a high-visibility, high-traffic area.

STARTUP:

Startup costs depend on the type of vending machine you use. Bubble gum machines cost as little as $65 each; a cappuccino machine can run into the thousands of dollars. You'll need to stock your machines, of course, and once again those prices can vary. Enough gumballs to fill your machine can be had for under $10; a sandwich machine will cost about $100 to fill. But regardless of the machine you choose, you'll have a winner if you market correctly. Before too long, you could easily be earning $25,000–$40,000.

BOTTOM LINE ADVICE:

Our recommendation is to go after the big factories and large businesses. They may even be willing to pay you for the privilege of delivering and stocking a machine on-site instead of requiring a 10 percent commission on your sales. Be careful about overextending yourself machine-wise. You will have to follow up on your machines; every day for the ones you place in large businesses and a minimum of once a week for smaller-volume locations. Even so, this can pretty much be a five-day-a-week job, since many businesses close for the weekend.

WALLPAPERING/INTERIOR PAINTING

Startup cost:	$2,000–$3,000
Potential earnings:	$20,000–$50,000
Typical fees:	Wallpapering: by the roll, hour, or difficulty of the job; painting: by the square foot and type of paint used (oil-based is more difficult to apply than latex)
Advertising:	Yellow Pages, newspaper ads, fliers, word-of-mouth, referrals
Qualifications:	Experience with different types of primers, paints, and papers; physical stamina; people skills; ability to estimate a job accurately
Equipment needed:	Stepladder, drop cloths, assorted paint brushes and rollers, papering brushes and rollers, razor blades for cutting paper, knives, computer and printer for billing and tracking customers/suppliers, telephone with answering machine or voice mail, vehicle
Home business potential:	Yes
Staff required:	No
Hidden costs:	Vehicle; inaccurate estimates (it may take you a few jobs to get the hang of accurate bidding)

LOWDOWN:

Wallpapering and painting are pretty straightforward decorating tasks that many home-owners could do for themselves, but why, when there's someone like you, with the expertise and equipment, to do it for them? You can sell your services as a convenience to busy, dual-income families who'd rather spend a weekend relaxing than perched on a ladder with a paper roller or paint brush. In the time these amateur redecorators would spend just assembling all their supplies and getting ready to paint or paper, you could easily have the job halfway to completion. Your customers will always ask for an estimate up front; providing an accurate one could well be your toughest challenge. The paper and paint you use for the job will be charged at cost to the customer, of course, but to be sure you are adequately compensated for your time, you'll want to take into consideration the size of the room and its decorative details (woodwork and moldings take more time to paint), the materials you'll be using (some are more difficult to work with than others), and the current condition of the walls (how much prep time will be needed before you can begin to actually paper or paint?). Work with a professional paperhanger or painter before going out on your own to get a feel for the length of time it should take to complete a job. Recognize, too, that you may have to handle a few jobs on your own and take a few losses before you get the hang of accurate bidding. To snare your first customers, you'll need to advertise in the Yellow Pages and local newspapers; once you complete a few jobs and earn a reputation for quality workmanship, referrals should keep you busy.

STARTUP:

Assuming you already have a van or pickup truck to haul your equipment around in, you'll need a stepladder, drop cloths, assorted paint brushes and rollers, papering brushes and rollers, razor blades for cutting paper, and knives. You'll be using your home office as a base so you'll probably want a computer and printer for billing and tracking customers and suppliers, plus a telephone with answering machine or voice mail. You'll have to spend a little money on advertising at first; once you have a few successful jobs to your credit, referrals should carry you along.

BOTTOM LINE ADVICE:

No matter how hard a homeowner may press you, never give an estimate over the phone. Always make a personal visit to assess the size of the room and get a look at any unusual structural or decorative details that could add to the painting or papering time. Make sure you have a signed contract from your customer in hand before you begin the job so there are no surprises later on when it comes time to collect the money you are owed. Try to make as little mess as possible and pay attention to details—cover the furniture and floors adequately and do the kind of quality work that will lead to referrals.

WATER PUMP REPAIR SERVICE

Startup cost:	$4,000–$6,000
Potential earnings:	$30,000–$45,000
Typical fees:	Often a per-job rate of $200–$300
Advertising:	Yellow Pages, direct mail, classified ads
Qualifications:	Knowledge of pumping systems and machinery repair
Equipment needed:	Pickup truck, tools, spare parts inventory
Home business potential:	Yes
Staff required:	No
Hidden costs:	Insurance, wear and tear on equipment

LOWDOWN:

For homes and businesses that receive their water from wells, a pump breakdown means an immediate call for help. If you have the knowledge and experience to work with these types of systems, you can establish a healthy business. You will need to live in an area where wells are the common mode for water supply, and you must be able to quickly diagnose the reasons for the breakdowns and repair the pumps. Beyond that, your major challenge will be making the availability of your services known to the public.

STARTUP:

As repair services go, a water pump repair business is relatively inexpensive to set up; $4,000–$6,000 should cover the cost of your tools and a used truck, if you don't already have one. With a reliable parts supplier who can get you what you need, when you need it, you'll be able to get by with very little inventory and only a small investment in spare parts. Bill your services at a flat rate of $200–$300 per job, or set an hourly rate of $45 and up.

BOTTOM LINE ADVICE:

It's great to have a business that provides an essential service. Well pumps can be tricky, and when one goes out, the owner will be eager to become your customer. The downside is that you may find yourself working outdoors in unpleasant weather, and more often than not, you'll be responding to a crisis and dealing with agitated customers. You'll need to keep a smile on your face, roll with the punches, and always practice patience.

WEBMASTER

Startup cost:	$3,000–$6,000
Potential earnings:	$40,000–$75,000
Typical fees:	$25 to $75 per hour, or monthly management fee of $1,000–$5,000
Advertising:	Referrals from and/or joint proposals with Web designers and Internet consultants; cold contacts (search the Web for sites that need updating, then make proposals)
Qualifications:	Knowledge of how Web sites work in terms of hit/flow tracking, quality assurance, server administration, etc.; technical proficiency in HTML, CGI, Perl programming, and scripting system administration in UNIX and Windows; understanding of client objectives and how they can be met online; interpersonal communication skills; organizational abilities
Equipment needed:	Computer with 17" or larger monitor; printer, fax, scanner, copier; high-speed Internet access; comfortable chair
Home business potential:	Yes
Staff required:	No
Hidden costs:	Keeping up with new technology; certification from one of the major webmaster professional associations

LOWDOWN:

Every business that wants to be competitive in today's global marketplace must have its own Web site. And the sites that are active—the ones where buying and selling take place on a regular basis, for example—must have a webmaster, a person behind the scenes who is charged with the responsibility of managing and updating the operation of a Web site. Webmasters typically do not design Web sites; rather, they keep the sites that designers have created running smoothly. A webmaster's duties may include everything from converting editorial content to HTML and monitoring the operation of the site on a regular basis to updating content and correcting any technical glitches. And while in the early days of the Internet, an e-commerce business might have relied on a staff member with minimal technical skills to perform simple Web site management and updates, the job is increasingly being turned over to independent webmasters. In some cases, the webmaster may actually perform the technical work required for the maintenance of a particular Web site; more likely, however, he or she acts as a kind of general contractor, overseeing the full operation, but contracting out for specific site management tasks. In other words, as a webmaster, you probably won't have to write code, but you will be responsible for its operation on the Web sites you manage.

STARTUP:

Not surprisingly considering that this is technology-oriented business, you're going to have to lay out some significant cash to get started in this profession. You'll need a computer (surprise!) with a 17" or larger monitor and high-speed Internet access, plus a printer, fax, scanner, and copier. You'll want an especially comfortable chair too, because you're going to be spending a lot of time in it, staring at a computer monitor. Hourly rates for webmaster tasks range from $25 to $75; at an average of $50 per hour and working just 24 hours a week, you could quickly be earning an annual income of $60,000. Not bad for part-time work, eh?

BOTTOM LINE ADVICE:

Webmastering is a great business for a solitary type who likes a flexible schedule. Thanks to specialized software like DeskLINK and pcANYWHERE, there's no need for webmasters to work on-site. A freelancer can access his or her clients' computers remotely, at any time and from any location. So if you're a night person who'd rather work in the wee hours of the morning and sleep all day, no problem. And considering that the Internet continues to grow by leaps and bounds, you can rest assured that if you're technically proficient and reliable, you're likely to have more work than you can handle now and well into the future. Keep in mind, however, that you can't be a complete recluse and succeed at this job. You will need the ability to interact with business owners, technical staff, and contractors, such as graphic designers, information architects, programmers, editors, and Web page developers.

WEDDING PLANNER

Startup cost:	$2,000–$6,000
Potential earnings:	$25,000–$60,000 (depending on volume and location)
Advertising:	Bridal magazines (many areas have their own, local versions), bridal salons, newspapers, word of mouth
Qualifications:	An eye for detail and a cool head; it helps to have a network of wedding suppliers already in place
Equipment needed:	Cellular phone, computer plus software for contacts and clients; wardrobe (traditional business attire + attire suitable for attending the wedding)
Home business potential:	Yes
Staff required:	Sometimes
Hidden costs:	Keep accurate records of the time you spend with each client, or you could shortchange yourself.

LOWDOWN:

Wedding planning can easily turn any reasonable family into a temporary war zone—and that's where wedding planners have entered the picture. With most families spending $15,000 and up on the wedding extravaganza itself, what's a few extra dollars to take the headache out of planning this blessed event? Your rates would range from $50 per hour to a flat fee of $1,500 or more for the entire wedding, so it is easy to see how you could earn a profitable amount of money in a short period of time. But don't think you won't work hard for it. As a wedding planner, you will handle every minute detail, from the number of guests to invite to what kind of champagne to serve. You are essentially in the hotbed of the action, with total responsibility for every aspect of the wedding. And while this is typically a happy occasion, it is also a stressful one; the successful wedding planner knows how to deal with the full range of emotions—from complete bliss to tantrums and tears.

STARTUP:

You will need to develop strong word of mouth (try forging reciprocal referral arrangements with florists and bridal and hair salons) to build a good reputation. Also, since this is a people- and image-oriented business, you will need to make sure you look like you're worth it; dress professionally and carry yourself with poise and an air of diplomacy. The bulk of your startup expenses will go toward producing business cards and brochures in addition to placing ads in newspapers and magazines likely to reach brides (count on forking over $1,000 or more for those items); you'll also want to exhibit at bridal shows and fairs.

BOTTOM LINE ADVICE:

The flash and excitement of impending nuptials can be intoxicating, as can the power involved in directing others to perform their best. This is a business that requires higher-than-average diplomacy and tact. Be careful not to offend anyone or step on any toes. Listen to what your customers tell you they want—and have the good sense to make them think all of the good ideas were theirs. While such ego-suppression is hard to accomplish in a high-profile job like this one, remember that this is the bride's day not yours; the customer is always queen.

WELCOMING SERVICE

Startup cost:	$1,500–$3,000
Potential earnings:	$15,000–$20,000
Typical fees:	Flat monthly fee paid by the businesses you promote to newcomers, or fee based on the number of responses a business receives as a result of your visits (this can be tricky unless you have set up a reliable tracking mechanism in advance)
Advertising:	Ads in real estate booklets and newspapers, Yellow Pages, direct mail/networking with real estate agencies, businesses
Qualifications:	Enthusiasm, poise, professional demeanor, knowledge of businesses and services available in your community
Equipment needed:	Basic office setup, including a computer, printer, copier, and fax, business telephone with answering machine or voice mail; cell phone; professional wardrobe; reliable vehicle; packaging (a supply of gift boxes/baskets in which to deliver your "goodies")
Home business potential:	Yes
Staff required:	No
Hidden costs:	Mileage, attorneys fees for drawing up contracts with merchants

LOWDOWN:

Moving from one house to another can be pretty traumatic in and of itself, but if you're relocating to a brand new community where you don't know a soul, the whole experience can be downright overwhelming. Gone are the days when next-door neighbors greeted newcomers with a warm welcome and a hearty casserole; a welcoming service lets you bring those days back. Within a few days of a family's arrival at their new home, you'll show up with a warm smile and a basket or box of welcoming information, coupons, and gifts. You'll be working at three levels: with the businesses that pay you to promote their products and services; with real estate agencies that provide you with the names of incoming families; and with the newcomers themselves to whom you deliver your welcoming gifts. Pack your boxes/baskets with coupons from restaurants, local retailers, and service businesses like dry cleaners, hairdressers, and shoe repair shops; sample copies of the local newspaper; directories from school districts and local government agencies. Don't embarrass the newcomers, who may still be in the midst of their moving-in "frenzy," by showing up unannounced; call ahead to schedule a convenient time for your visit and stay just long enough to pass along your goodies and answer any questions they might have. Leave a business card behind and encourage them to call you for additional information. Make a follow-up call within the month to learn which of your businesses and services they used; this information can help your sales efforts.

STARTUP:

Expect to spend between $1,500 and $3,000 to get started. You'll need the basic office setup—computer, printer, phone, and fax—plus a reliable vehicle and professional wardrobe for making your sales calls and deliveries. And don't forget to include the cost of the boxes or baskets you'll use to contain your "goodies." They don't necessarily all have to look alike; be on the lookout for sales of these items at retail stores, and browse second-hand and consignment shops for gently-used but interesting possibilities. Your money will come from the fee businesses pay to participate in your service; you can charge a flat rate or a fee based on the number of actual customer responses your gift baskets generate. If you choose the latter method, you will need to set up a reliable system for tracking those responses, which could be a little tricky and certainly time-consuming.

BOTTOM LINE ADVICE:

Be creative—not every box or basket you deliver has to look alike or contain exactly the same items. If possible, try to learn a little something about the newcomers in advance of your visit and tailor your delivery accordingly. Add a package of balloons or a couple of whistles for the kids, a refrigerator magnet for mom, some golf balls for dad. And encourage your businesses to be creative, too. Coupons will certainly be appreciated, but try also for novelty items like pens, mugs, calendars, and the like. If you're outgoing and enjoy meeting new people, you'll thrive in the welcoming business. But don't expect to get rich. Think of this as a part-time or second income opportunity.

WINDOW TREATMENT SPECIALIST

Startup cost:	$1,000–$5,000
Potential earnings:	$25,000–$35,000
Typical fee:	$20–$35 per hour, or charge per job
Advertising:	Personal contacts with interior decorators, fabric and drapery stores, Yellow Pages, newspaper ads
Qualifications:	Basic sewing skills, ability to accurately measure
Equipment needed:	Heavy-duty sewing machine; scissors, tape measure, thread, and other basic sewing supplies
Home business potential:	Yes
Staff required:	No
Hidden costs:	Fabric and supplies; buy wholesale, if possible

LOWDOWN:

Few things make a home look more inviting from the outside or more cozy within than beautiful window treatments. Armed with a heavy-duty sewing machine, the space to create, and an interest in interior decorating, you can satisfy your love of sewing while you generate a steady income as a window treatment specialist. With the continuing influx of new housing developments and condominium complexes, you should have no shortage of customers in need of fine window detail such as draperies, curtains, valances, and swags. Network with condo associations and apartment complex owners; they may provide you with regular referrals and a steady flow of business. Cultivate contacts with local fabric stores and interior designers, too. Remember, accuracy is a must; any mistakes you make in measuring can quickly add up if you have to replace ruined fabric.

STARTUP:

Even if you already have the necessary equipment and basic sewing supplies, you'll still need to spend between $1,000 and $5,000 to get started. Your biggest cost will be advertising. You'll need to get the word out about your business in community newspapers, the Yellow Pages, and through coupon books, keeping in mind that ad size is not as important as frequency. Studies show that consumers typically need to see an ad a minimum of six times before they act on it. Set your hourly rate at what the market will bear; around $20–$35 per hour is standard.

BOTTOM LINE ADVICE:

You probably wouldn't launch this type of business unless you had a good deal of experience under your belt already. So put together a portfolio with photographs of your previous work to show prospective clients; add to it regularly as you gain experience. Display some of your photographs in fabric stores, and make business cards available to the store owners and to interior designers.

WINDOW WASHING SERVICE

Startup cost:	$1,000–$5,000
Potential earnings:	$25,000–$45,000
Typical fee:	$25–$50 per hour (slightly more for corporate work; add an extra fee for high-rise work)
Advertising:	Yellow Pages, local newspapers, coupons through direct mail and welcoming services, word of mouth
Qualifications:	Enthusiasm, willingness to work hard—and no fear of heights
Equipment needed:	Ladders, scaffolding, platforms, cleaning solutions, squeegees, buckets, rags
Home business potential:	Yes
Staff required:	Perhaps as business grows, especially for high-rise buildings
Hidden costs:	Insurance; workers' compensation if you hire staff

LOWDOWN:

How many times have you heard that classic line, "I don't do windows"? If you choose this business as your line of work, you will. As a window washer, you'll be working outside at various heights and in various locations. The work is pretty straightforward: You come, you clean, you move on; in a few weeks, you repeat. With a little elbow grease, this can be a business with few startup costs, especially if you target the small jobs. If you plan to go after more lucrative commercial work, however, you'll need more equipment and you may need to hire personnel, which means you'll have to pay wages, workers' compensation costs, perhaps even benefits like health insurance. Still, this is a fairly recession-proof business and with some targeted marketing and a few well-placed ads, you should have plenty of work. After all, no one really likes to clean windows . . . except maybe you!

STARTUP:

Set aside about $100–$150 for your business cards, then add $3,000 or so for advertising in the Yellow Pages (both the business and consumer books are recommended). Use the remainder of your startup funds to get your vehicle packed with rags, squeegees, buckets, and cleaning chemicals. Ladders, scaffolding, and other equipment can be leased until you're more established and start to turn a profit.

BOTTOM LINE ADVICE:

Everybody's windows get dirty—homeowners and businesses alike, so you shouldn't have any problem finding customers. The biggest bucks are probably to be made cleaning the windows of high-rise apartments, condominiums, and commercial office buildings. Decide on the niche you want to fill, then plan your business accordingly. You'll need different tools and use different methods of advertising depending on whether you target your business to commercial buildings or homeowners.

STARTUPS BETWEEN $5,000 AND $15,000

ACCIDENT RECONSTRUCTION SERVICE

Startup cost:	$10,000–$15,000
Potential earnings:	$50,000–$100,000
Typical fees:	Hourly rate of $50–$75, or flat fee of $500–$1,500 per job
Advertising:	Law journals, referrals, direct mail
Qualifications:	Extensive experience, technical training in accident reconstruction, writing skills, ability to give effective testimony in court; a legal background is helpful
Equipment needed:	Computer, Internet access, fax, word processing and design-building software for accident reconstruction, laser and photo printers, copier, scanner, digital camera
Home business potential:	Yes
Staff required:	No
Hidden costs:	Travel, insurance

LOWDOWN:

Automobile accidents happen every day, and the serious crashes often result in court cases. Yet even when there are several witnesses to a collision, it can be surprisingly difficult to establish the facts of what happened. Bystanders offer different stories based on their different perspectives, and memories can be clouded by shock, the sheer suddenness of the accident, and the passage of time. Passengers in the vehicles involved often remember little beyond the first terrifying sounds of the crash. A person who specializes in accident reconstruction can help fill in the blanks. Typically, an accident reconstruction service is hired, either by the police department or by one of the parties involved in the crash, to develop a picture of what took place at the time of the accident in order to support the claims made by one side or the other. As an accident reconstructor, you will use a combination of drivers' recollections and bystanders' eyewitness accounts, evidence collected immediately after the accident, and the findings from any subsequent fact-gathering trips you make to the crash scene itself in order to build a vivid, convincing reconstruction of the accident from your client's point of view. Accident reconstruction is a skilled activity, requiring accuracy, persistence, and patience. The written report you prepare based on a compilation of your findings from many sources will be used to determine if the case should go to court; in some instances, you may be asked to provide a formal deposition. If the case does indeed go to trial, you may be called upon again for "expert" testimony in order to support the presentation of your client's case.

STARTUP:

Although the majority of your work will be done in the field, you will need a place where you can put all the pieces together and prepare your reports. You'll want a powerful computer and laser printer, as well as both word processing software and the specialized design-oriented programs you will need to build computer models of the accident site. You will also want to have a digital camera and photo printing capabilities. Expect to shell out around $10,000 for state-of-the-art technology and related office equipment. Many accident reconstruction services charge $500–$1,500 per job, but considering the time it can take to generate a clear image of what has occurred, you may find an hourly fee of $50–$75 to be more cost-effective. Straightforward cases with plenty of witnesses are obviously the easiest to re-create, so adjust your fees accordingly (possibly as low as $250).

BOTTOM LINE ADVICE:

Attention to accuracy, the ability to focus on small pieces of evidence, and a creative imagination are the key qualities you will need to re-create past events and build a convincing picture on behalf of your client. Every case is different, and each comes with its own set of challenges. Accident reconstruction is never a dull job, but it is not an easy one either. You will need to be persistent in your marketing efforts in order to build your reputation and establish the value of your services in the eyes of the legal community.

ACOUSTICAL SERVICES

Startup cost:	$5,000–$15,000
Potential earnings:	$25,000–$45,000
Typical fees:	$150–$1,000+ per job (depending on size of work area) plus materials costs
Advertising:	Yellow Pages; direct mail to schools, auditoriums, and concert halls; cold calls
Qualifications:	Background in noise control and some working knowledge of architecture, basic business and marketing skills
Equipment needed:	Van for transporting materials and tools
Home business potential:	Yes
Staff required:	Not initially
Hidden costs:	Insurance, fluctuations in materials costs

LOWDOWN:

Because they rely so heavily upon quality sound effects and reverberation during per-formances, school auditoriums, performing arts centers, and other concert venues often need the services of a skilled acoustical professional. Your services will typically begin with an initial consultation (you might need to attend a rehearsal or performance to experience the room's true acoustics and how sound gets absorbed by a full house, for example). After you've made notes about the sound quality in the performing venue or rehearsal room, you will offer suggestions on how to improve tonal qualities and general acoustics. Your recommendations could be as simple as hanging carpet squares over old speakers no lon-ger being used, or as extensive as the application of sound-dampening foam insulation throughout an auditorium. In all cases, you will need to be both technically proficient—extremely familiar with every type of available sound barrier material—and adept at cus-tomer service. Your reputation for creating superior sound will bring you more business.

STARTUP:

Your startup costs ($5,000–$15,000) will go toward the purchase of tools and materials, plus a van to carry them all. Your income will vary depending on the size of your client venues (multiplex performing arts centers will be the most lucrative, of course); expect to charge $150–$1,000+ per job. Your earnings will likely be in the $25,000–$45,000 range.

BOTTOM LINE ADVICE:

Once you've helped a venue boost its acoustical efficiency and quality, where do you go from there? You're not likely to have repeat sales—although the potential does exist for you to make a small income servicing your client base—so you will have to market aggressively and continually expand your service area. While the positive side of this business is that you can make a pretty decent income from each installation, the down-side is that you're going to be constantly on the lookout for new business. This business does not lend itself to small towns; you need to be located in a large metropolitan area with a lively performing arts scene, where there are likely to be many theaters, concert halls, and school auditoriums requiring superior acoustical systems.

ADVERTISING AGENCY

Startup cost:	$5,000–$12,000
Potential earnings:	$40,000–$85,000
Typical fees:	$50–$85 per hour for creative services, $40–$65 for administrative tasks/account supervision; a monthly retainer, or flat fee per project
Advertising:	Networking, cold-calling, trade publications, Web site
Qualifications:	Knowledge of design, layout, and typography; writing skills; previous advertising agency experience
Equipment needed:	Computer with Internet access, dual CD-ROM drives, and high-resolution laser printer; word processing, presentation, desktop publishing, and photo software; scanner, fax, copier
Home business potential:	Yes
Staff required:	No; you may need to hire out for specific services you aren't capable of providing yourself
Hidden costs:	Organizational dues, "schmoozing," updating equipment

LOWDOWN:

Businesses of all sizes use advertising to get the word out about their products and services. *Fortune* 500 companies like General Motors, General Foods, American Airlines, and Microsoft hire agencies on Madison and Michigan Avenue to handle their multimillion-dollar accounts. But there are still plenty of smaller businesses that need the help of an advertising agency. If you are motivated and highly skilled in copywriting and design, you can build a home-based ad agency serving clients in your own immediate area. To get a foothold in the ad agency business, it's a good idea to already have some experience with a larger agency, or, at the very least, proximity to businesspeople who know your abilities and respect your interest in what they do. Potential clients are everywhere, just look around you. The guy you see on the treadmill next to you at the health club every morning owns a small software company; he could probably use some slick new sales literature. Or how about the dry cleaners, where you drop your shirts for laundering once a week? A few well-placed print ads could boost that business. And doesn't your daughter's softball coach own a natural foods store? She'll need regular advertising to compete with the supermarket that's just come to town. If you're located in a large enough area, you might choose to specialize in promotional campaigns for one type of store or product, or service, or in a particular type of advertising, such as print ads only (leave the radio ads to someone else; otherwise, be a generalist. Whichever direction you choose, get to know your client organizations well, and be prepared to draw on all of your creativity, both verbal and graphic. New ways of getting a commercial message out to the public are revolutionizing the advertising field, so you'll need to stay on top of innovations in the advertising industry as well. Few businesses can succeed without some type of advertising, so you shouldn't worry about having a shortage of potential clients. You may, however, need to educate some of them about the value of advertising—even in times when there's so little business they think they can't afford to advertise, or conversely, when there's so much, they think they can't possibly handle any more.

STARTUP:

The high-end computers with graphics and print-production software now available enable even small agencies to produce the kind of ads that once required the skills of an entire big agency art department. Getting up to speed with your equipment is expensive, however; expect to spend $5,000–$8,000. In the interest of attracting new clients, you may be surprised to learn that ads don't work so well for advertising agencies; most of your new business will be the result of networking and cold-calling. Once you're up and running, and, more importantly have some samples to show, you'll want to develop a Web site. And unless you have particular expertise in Internet marketing, don't try to design it yourself; pay an expert ($2,000–$5,000). Bill out between $40–$85 per hour depending on the services you offer and your geographic locale, or determine your rates on a per-project basis that takes into account the amount of time/work actually involved in all of the activities required to complete the job. Many ad agencies also work on monthly retainers of $500 or more, but be careful about setting your fees. Take a close look at the time and expertise that will be involved in each project you are likely to work on in any given month on behalf of a particular client, then set your retainer accordingly. Specify to your client exactly what is covered in the fee and have a contingency plan for any additional charges if you go above and beyond those specifications within any given month.

BOTTOM LINE ADVICE:

Advertising is a rewarding occupation because it incorporates both creativity and concrete, measurable results. You'll know if your ads are working—sales will go up. Successful ad agency personnel (in this case, you) develop close relationships with their clients; you're members of the same team, working toward the same goals. You'll be serving people you know and a product or service you enjoy, and you'll be using all of your talents to do so. Keep in mind, however, that this can be a labor-intensive business. As a one-man (or -woman) band, you must be able to handle all facets of the advertising process, from concept to writing and design to actual ad placement. You'll have to be a good salesperson too—not just for your client's product or service, but also for your own. The pressure never lets up—and the competition for clients is shark-like.

ADVICE FROM THE EXPERTS

What sets your business apart from others like it?

For Carol Wilkerson, owner of Wilkerson Ltd., in Portland, Oregon, it's experience that sets her business apart. "I have over twenty-three years of experience in advertising and public relations, and I have dealt from the bottom up with any kind of promotional effort there is. Also, I'm small and selective about who I work with, because I want to make sure I can really provide the top-notch service the client's looking for, turning things around quickly enough to keep them coming back for more."

Things you couldn't do without:

Wilkerson's business depends on a computer, laser printer, fax, telephone, and overnight delivery services.

Marketing tips/advice:

"Before you start, determine what your strengths are and identify them for your clients. You really run into problems when you start promising things you really can't do . . . you can't fake knowledge and experience. Farm out what you can't do to others who can, and you'll gain a lot more respect."

If you had to do it all over again . . .

"Oddly enough, I didn't promote myself well enough in the beginning . . . I wasn't a big enough cheerleader for my own business. It's so ironic!"

AGRICULTURAL MARKETING

Startup cost:	$5,000–$10,000
Potential earnings:	$35,000–$60,000
Typical fees:	Percentage of goods sold (usually 5 to 15 percent); sometimes an up-front fee of $500–$1,000 in addition to percentage
Advertising:	Yellow Pages, farm publications, networking and referrals, Web site
Qualifications:	Commodities background would be extremely helpful
Equipment needed:	Computer, printer, fax, Internet access, phone, cell phone
Home business potential:	Yes
Staff required:	No
Hidden costs:	Insurance, high-speed Internet access

LOWDOWN:

Farmers are very good at growing crops, but they're not always the best at selling them—that's why they often turn to agricultural marketing services like yours for help. You'll advertise in a respected farming journal and/or the Yellow Pages, and if you land at least one client for whom you can make a difference, you'll be on the road to referrals for others in no time. Of course, trying to get a farmer's goods to market at a profitable (yet competitive) price takes a lot of work and long hours, and you can't expect the farmer to be much help; he or she is too busy seeding, cultivating, and harvesting the crops to spend the time it takes to market them well. You will have to work hard to develop contacts in your immediate area, and if you're really enterprising and have a knack for using the Internet, perhaps all over the United States and in many other parts of the world, too. If you can arrange for the right modes of shipping and know your way around complex customs regulations, you could make a significant amount of money selling farm goods on a global scale.

STARTUP:

Since some of your work will likely be done online, you'll need a powerful computer system and high-speed Internet connection as part of your basic office setup, which should also include a printer, fax, and phones (both landline and cell); add to that your advertising costs and you can expect to spend $5,000–$10,000 to get this business properly launched. Considering, however, that you may quickly be earning $35,000–$60,000 per year, the up-front office expense doesn't seem so out of line.

BOTTOM LINE ADVICE:

You'll enjoy the independence of working solo and pretty much on your own time schedule; your biggest challenge is likely to be the volatility of the agricultural market. Be prepared to spend a lot of time watching the commodities markets for fluctuations and set aside the funds to tide you over during the down times.

AMBULATORY SERVICES

Startup cost:	$6,000–$20,000
Potential earnings:	$20,000–$50,000
Typical fees:	$100–$150 per visit
Advertising:	Direct mail, fliers in health care offices and clinics, referrals from physicians and home nurses
Qualifications:	RN or certification in specific service offered (respiratory therapy, physical therapy, etc.)
Equipment needed:	Small van, medical supplies, and equipment appropriate for your specialty, telephone with answering service or voice mail, cell phone
Home business potential:	Yes
Staff required:	No
Hidden costs:	Business and professional insurance, licensing fees, vehicle fuel and maintenance

LOWDOWN:

Rare in the United States these days is the doctor still willing to make house calls, yet that's exactly what some people need, especially those who are home-bound because of medical conditions. And even if they could get out, there's no place to go. Reductions in federal support for health care in recent years have forced many smaller, neighborhood hospitals and clinics to close their doors. These developments present an opportunity for an individual with the appropriate medical credentials to create a business providing ambulatory care to patients. If you are a registered nurse, physician's assistant, respiratory therapist, or similar health care professional, you can provide an important service to those people who cannot fit the tighter-than-ever-before criteria for hospital admission, and who have no way to get to an outpatient clinic for needed medical services.

STARTUP:

You will need a reliable vehicle (van) that is large enough to carry your equipment and supplies. Your vehicle doesn't have to be brand new, but keep in mind that because your van is a moving advertisement for the services you provide, it must convey a respectable image. You will need to stock your van with the latest health care equipment and supplies, too. The cost of doing so will vary, depending on the services you provide. A portable X-ray machine alone, for example, can run into the thousands of dollars. Expect to spend at least $10,000 for the vehicle, basic diagnostic equipment (blood pressure cuff, thermometers, etc.), and medical supplies.

BOTTOM LINE ADVICE:

Getting the confidence of a few physicians with large practices will be the first step in establishing your client base. A home nursing service may also prove to be a steady source of referrals. Being reliable, accurate, and totally patient-focused is essential. It may take you a while to discover the right market niche for your services, but once you do, referrals and word of mouth will carry you along. This business requires superb time-management skills and a good sense of logistics as well. You will need to schedule appointments wisely so that you do not find yourself driving from one end of town to another, then back again in a single day. Carry a cell phone so that you can be reached at all times.

ANIMAL BROKER/DEALER

Startup cost:	$10,000–$15,000
Potential earnings:	$45,000–$70,000
Typical fees:	Varies per animal, depending on the species and the trouble you have to go to in order to secure it
Advertising:	Trade journals, direct mail, referrals, networking
Qualifications:	Background and/or professional training in zoology or animal welfare; familiarity with CITES, the international treaty on the movement of plants and animals; established contacts with zoo personnel, animal parks, and animal importers
Equipment needed:	Computer, Internet access, fax, printer, cell phone
Home business potential:	Yes
Staff required:	No
Hidden costs:	Travel expenses, conference fees

LOWDOWN:

To build their animal populations, zoos either have on-site breeding programs or they acquire specific animals from other zoos, either by trade or purchase. When an animal simply isn't available by either of these means, a zoo will call upon an animal broker or dealer to fill the bill. Many of the animals acquired by brokers have been bred domestically in private parks and later come on the market for purchase by a zoo. Some are traded across international boundaries, a practice regulated by CITES and various laws and regulations pertaining to the countries involved. To make a go at being an animal broker, you will need to already have many close contacts in the zoo world so you are likely to hear when a particular species is needed and know where you might be able to find it. The animals themselves can be tough to find, and your ability to link a particular creature with the zoo needing it will set you apart from your competition. To succeed in this business, you must like animals and you must be willing and able to care for them in interim situations when they are between places to live. This doesn't necessarily mean you'll be taking a tiger into your home. Some animal brokers don't deal with zoos or exotic animals at all. Some are in the business of locating purebred puppies and rare breeds of cats for families and individual owners.

STARTUP:

The telephone is your lifeline, since networking with zoos and animal handlers will be your most important source of business. You'll want to have a land line with an answering machine or voice mail for when you're in your office, and a cell phone for when you're on the road. You'll also need a computer with Internet access and e-mail for communicating with distant sources. Your biggest expense will, of course, be travel. You can't judge an animal by its picture; you will have to go and look at it yourself. And while your clients will likely pay your travel expenses, you will probably have to lay out the money from your own pocket first and await reimbursement. You'll want to have a fair amount of cash on hand to be able to travel and live in the meantime.

BOTTOM LINE ADVICE:
Trading in animals is today not the fast-growing fad business it was in the 1990s. Nor is it open to just anyone who has completed a course or two in zoology at their local community college. You need to know what you're doing—not just about animals, but with regard to the international rules and regulations that affect their sale/trade and well-being. You also need to have a background and/or professional training in zoology as well as some serious connections. If you have a friend in every zoo in the country, and if you care enough about the welfare of animals to plan their new homes successfully, you can establish yourself as an animal broker. But don't expect to grow rich overnight. Like the many animals you'll represent, this is one business that will take time to grow.

ARCHAEOLOGICAL SERVICES

Startup cost:	$5,000–$10,000
Potential earnings:	$15,000–$45,000
Typical fees:	$50–$75 per hour
Advertising:	Yellow Pages; networking through universities, museums, and historical societies; Web site
Qualifications:	Degree in archaeology, hands-on experience at several "digs"
Equipment needed:	Digging tools, sturdy boots, screens (for sifting dirt), cloth, cell phone/pager
Home business potential:	Yes (but you'll be working on-site)
Staff required:	Probably; you may be able to hire students (cheaply) to work with you on a large dig
Hidden costs:	Insurance, workers' compensation

LOWDOWN:

If you're deeply interested in uncovering the secrets of the past, and if you can stand working long hours in sometimes not-so-great conditions, archaeological services may be the perfect business for you. Just put on your Indiana Jones hat and start digging! Not really, of course. You need to be precise and extremely careful when sifting through layers of sediment in search of works of manmade wonder; the slightest scratch or dent could cost the life (and value) of the pieces you uncover. This is not a business for amateurs. You'll need to have a degree in archaeology to begin with, plus hands-on experience; at the point in your career where you decide to branch out on your own, you'll likely have already been on several digs and recognize the delicacy of the work you're doing. As an archaeological entrepreneur, you'll need to know precisely where to dig (based on historic evidence or detail about a particular culture's habits) as well as how to dig in order to avoid damaging any artifacts in the process. You'll also need to know the proper techniques for cleaning, numbering, and tagging each piece that you find. And, finally, you'll have to wrap the pieces properly, then transport them to the nearest lab for dating and more meticulous examination, taking care to ensure that nothing gets damaged along the way. Museum directors, historians, university professors, and others in your community and beyond will be interested in your findings.

STARTUP:

Your clients—museums, universities, corporations, wealthy patrons—will likely foot the bill for any travel expenses, permitting fees, and/or rental of heavy-duty equipment related to a specific dig. You will, however, still need to spend around $5,000 to equip your archaeological operation with basic tools and supplies for the dig itself; instead of buying expensive ready-made screens for sifting, save a little cash by making your own. Unless your client can provide you with on-site laboratory access, you'll want to spend another $5,000–$10,000 on equipment to create your own testing and documentation facilities. Archaeological exploration is time-consuming and subject to weather-related delays; a single dig can take many weeks and you can only work on one at a time. However, if you are able to work with one or two clients on small projects your first year, you could easily make about $15,000; as you become more proficient in your marketing (develop a Web site!) and are able to snag a fair amount of work at the corporate level, you can expect to see earnings as high as $45,000. Charge $50–$75 per hour for your work.

BOTTOM LINE ADVICE:
If you like being outdoors in different seasons, and you don't mind the dirt or long hours of tedium as you uncover layer after layer of sediment, this could be your dream job. The reward is finding something truly unique or of incredible intrinsic value (such as the oldest human remains in your area or evidence of a pre-existing civilization).

ADVICE FROM THE EXPERTS

What sets your business apart from others like it?
"We have a large in-house staff and the ability to work on multiple projects," says Donald J. Weir, president of Archaeological and Historical Consulting in Jackson, Michigan. "We provide guidance for a complex and confusing process."

Things you couldn't do without:
Weir couldn't do without accounting software, a phone system, and archaeological field and laboratory equipment.

Marketing tips/advice:
Visibility and networking are the best methods of getting more business.

If you had to do it all over again . . .
For Weir, location has been a concern. He would probably move to an area where his services had more of a broad appeal.

ARCHITECT

Startup cost:	$10,000–$15,000
Potential earnings:	$45,000–$65,000+
Typical fees:	Extremely varied; could be $5,000 to $30,000, depending on the size/complexity of your designs
Advertising:	Referrals, Yellow Pages, newspaper advertising
Qualifications:	Architectural degree, license (after schooling and apprenticeship)
Equipment needed:	Drafting table, top-of-the-line computer with computer-aided design (CAD) software, Internet access, laser printer with 11" X 17" paper capacity, blueprint copier, flatbed scanner, cell phone
Home business potential:	Yes
Staff required:	No
Hidden costs:	Insurance, high number of requested changes from uncertain customers (charge for excessive requests), continuing education

LOWDOWN:

You have a knack for designing interesting buildings with plenty of airy, open spaces and aesthetically pleasing features. You know what people want from a building, and how to design one that encompasses many tastes and purposes. Once you've received your license and, perhaps, have a few years of experience under your belt, you can put out your shingle and announce your availability, primarily to builders, contractors, and real estate agents (who are often asked to recommend a competent architect). Depending on where you live, you'll likely have plenty of competition, so be sure to set yourself apart as a specialist in a particular area: For instance, you might enjoy designing ultra-contemporary homes in affluent parts of town, or creating renovations/additions for homes in a registered historic district. More often than not, you'll be dreaming up practical designs for doctors' offices, corporate headquarters, and possibly even manufacturing facilities. The commercial sector will likely provide you with steadier income than residential might; it largely depends on where you are located and how readily your designs are accepted.

STARTUP:

Assuming you come into this business with your degree and licensing already in place, your startup costs will be in the $10,000–$15,000 range. You'll need to purchase drafting and design equipment, including a computer with CAD capabilities, and you'll need to do some pretty intensive networking. However, if you market effectively, you should soon be making $45,000–$65,000 or more; within two to three years you'll be in serious profit-making mode.

BOTTOM LINE ADVICE:

While architectural work is detail-oriented and technically precise, there is room for glamour, too. If you develop a reputation for creative and inspiring designs, you could easily find yourself with more commissions than you can possibly handle.

ART RESTORATION SERVICES

Startup cost:	$5,000–$10,000
Potential earnings:	$20,000–$45,000
Typical fees:	$45–$75 per hour
Advertising:	Yellow Pages, art publications, direct mail, cold calls (networking is almost always the best bet), Web site
Qualifications:	Art history degree and artistic background/experience, knowledge of historic technique and materials
Equipment needed:	Paints, brushes, palette, ladders, easel, van for ease of transport
Home business potential:	Yes, but only if you have a studio
Staff required:	No
Hidden costs:	Insurance, travel costs

LOWDOWN:

When the Mona Lisa's smile starts cracking or Van Gogh's sunflowers begin to flake off, an art museum director turns to a restoration artist who is trained in historic technique and "patch" work, a professional who can touch up a masterpiece without destroying it or adding any of his/her own personal touches to the work. Typically, an art restoration service is made up of one or two artists who are skilled in this type of meticulous work and who, over many years, have built a reputation for fixing great works of art. In other words, you won't have to go looking for clients; they'll come to you by way of referral. You may take a work of art to your own studio so that you can work on it for a period of a few weeks to several months; or, if the museum's policy does not allow you to leave the premises with its precious objects, you'll have to work on-site. In either case, your job will be to painstakingly restore the work, with careful attention to the nuances of each brush stroke, so that you preserve the creating artist's original style. The end product should look as close to the original as possible, as if it has never been touched up at all. You may be forced to spend long hours in unusual positions and you will almost always work alone. But if artistic solitude and the satisfaction that comes from a job well done are what you're looking for, this could be a rewarding job for you.

STARTUP:

If you're skilled enough to take on this kind of work, the chances are pretty good you already have a studio and many of the basic materials you need to get started. You'll need to spend about $5,000–$10,000 for a vehicle, paints, brushes, drop cloths, ladders, and other assorted tools of the trade. On the upside, yours is a highly developed skill, requiring years to perfect, and you should expect to be paid accordingly. On the other hand, great works of art require restoration only intermittently, which means you may not have a steady flow of work. Depending on your portfolio/reference list, you can probably make between $20,000 and $45,000 in art restoration working part-time.

BOTTOM LINE ADVICE:

The hours are long, and the insurance you'll need to carry is very expensive. One mistake could ruin a priceless piece of art, not to mention, cost you your career, so the pressure can be exceptionally high.

ART/PHOTO REPRESENTATIVE

Startup cost:	$5,000–$15,000
Potential earnings:	$25,000–$100,000
Typical fees:	20 percent commission on each sale
Advertising:	Trade publications for artists and photographers, listings in *Photographers Market* and *Guide to Literary Agents/Art Photo Reps*, direct mail to related associations, Web site
Qualifications:	Knowledge of art and photography and/or sales background
Equipment needed:	Computer, printer, fax, Internet access, copier, phone
Home business potential:	Yes
Staff required:	No
Hidden costs:	Insurance, bad risks (artists whom you care about but who turn out to not be very marketable)

LOWDOWN:

Behind every successful artist or photographer is an agent who carts around resumes and slides, seeking to sell works of art to everyone from gallery owners to art catalog publishers and distributors. The key to success as an art/photo representative is to represent several artists and photographers at once, and to spread their work as far as possible. To grow your stable of clients to represent, advertise in the publications that artists and photographers are likely to read. Invite them to respond by sending in a detailed resume and plenty of slides. Select the ones you'd like to represent. then provide a contract that clearly spells out what is expected in the business relationship; for instance, if you expect to earn a 20 percent commission from each sale, state that clearly in the contract so there is no misunderstanding later on.

STARTUP:

You'll need to promote your services in each of the respective professional trade publications, and that will likely cost you in the neighborhood of $3,000–$5,000 (some directories do, however, make free listings available). Next, you'll need to have a set of dynamic, professional-looking promotional materials of your own (letterhead, business cards, and, eventually, a Web site) and a basic office setup (computer, printer, fax, Internet access, copier, and phone system) to keep your business running smoothly. Since you'll be working strictly on commission (20 percent is standard), choose your clients carefully; the more marketable they are, the more money you'll make. You could easily earn $100,000 a year if you represent an artist who ends up becoming the next "big thing"; more likely, your income will fall somewhere in the range of $25,000–$50,000.

BOTTOM LINE ADVICE:

The art world is extremely narcissistic and tight-knit; and if your name isn't well-regarded, you may not succeed as much as you'd like. Work art show openings, trade shows, and other functions if you really want to get your name out there fast. Above all else, be knowledgeable about art and photography—if you're not, it will definitely show and your business will suffer as a result. On the positive side, artists are hungry for sales, and there are far more of them than there are folks like you to represent them—so your income potential may be quite high.

AUDITING SPECIALIST

Startup cost:	$5,000–$8,000
Potential earnings:	$50,000–$75,000
Typical fees:	Percentage of the savings you find for clients; often 50 percent for past savings and 10 percent for two or more years into the future
Advertising:	Business and trade publications, direct mail, membership in business groups, networking, referrals
Qualifications:	Knowledge of area of specialty (utility bills, telephone options), math skills or accounting background, detail orientation, selling skills
Equipment needed:	Computer; word processing, database, and spreadsheet software; printer; calculator; telephone; marketing materials
Home business potential:	Yes
Staff required:	No
Hidden costs:	Ongoing marketing time and materials, continuing education

LOWDOWN:

As bills become more complicated, the opportunity for finding errors and overcharges in them increases. Yet despite the possibility for cost-savings, most businesses find the tedious, detail-oriented work necessary to check each bill and interpret all the data just too time-consuming. An auditing specialist can work through all the paper records, uncover overcharges, collect a percentage of the money saved, and make an excellent living. To be successful in this business, you will need a sharp eye and the ability to consider what lies behind those rows of figures on a telephone or electric bill. Something as simple as a misplaced decimal point can have a huge impact on a company's bottom line; even more difficult to spot are incorrect rate assignments, double billing for small segments of a service, and specific opportunities for which a different (lower) rate structure might apply.

STARTUP:

You'll need a comfortable, well-lighted place in which to work. This business requires a lot of detailed reading, calculating, and thinking, so spring for a powerful computer system and software, a good desk lamp, and an ergonomically designed chair (around $3,000 to start). Earnings could be $50,000 annually.

BOTTOM LINE ADVICE:

Since utility bills are a likely place for mistakes to occur, look for organizations that consume large quantities of electricity—manufacturing operations or businesses that are open 24/7, for example. Government agencies, churches, and other institutions with large buildings and inadequate staffing are excellent prospects also. High-risk businesses that require heavy cash outlays for insurance and firms like call centers or collection agencies that depend heavily on their telephones are another source of business for auditing specialists. In spite of the clear benefits you can offer to a business, you will find that marketing is always a challenge. Many business owners aren't used to the idea of auditing specialists, and they probably have no idea how much money they are pouring down the drain each month paying bills that are incorrect. In other words, while they undoubtedly need your service, they don't realize it. You will succeed when you find a way to effectively market the benefits you offer.

ADVICE FROM THE EXPERTS

What sets your business apart from others like it?
"I don't just punch numbers into a computer . . . I delve deeper to find out more about the customer and how I can help them on a long-term basis," says Dianna Stahl, president and CEO of E.R.S., Inc., in Akron, Ohio.

Things you couldn't do without:
Stahl says she absolutely couldn't do without a computer and a phone.

Marketing tips/advice:
"Find a good mentor in whatever area you're weak in. I was weak in sales, so I found myself a good sales mentor and it helped immeasurably."

If you had to do it all over again . . .
"Know the people you're going to go into business with well before you do it. I was starting my business based on someone else's promises, and they didn't come through. Fortunately, it worked out."

AUTO SWAP MEET PROMOTION

Startup cost:	$10,000–$15,000
Potential earnings:	$50,000–$100,000
Typical fees:	Participant fees of $25 or more each; admission fees of $5 or more
Advertising:	Automotive newspapers, classified ads, bulletin boards, fliers at auto body and repair shops
Qualifications:	Avid interest in cars, organizational skills
Equipment needed:	A parking lot or warehouse to rent for the event
Home business potential:	No (except for handling business details)
Staff required:	Possibly one other person
Hidden costs:	Liability insurance

LOWDOWN:

Auto swap meets, where buyers and sellers gather to buy, sell, and/or trade used vehicles and parts, have been a popular mainstay among car aficionados for several years, and promoting such events can be a profitable business. As a promoter, you would secure the parking lot or large warehouse for those seeking to trade or sell their cars and car parts. Participants would pay you as much as $25 each for the opportunity to showcase their vehicles and other merchandise. In addition, attendees would pay an admission fee of around $5, thereby increasing your income potential even more. And because snack shops fit well with such events, you could earn extra money by taking a cut of the sales of popular "festival" foods like pizza, hot dogs, popcorn, and soda.

STARTUP:

You'll need to rent temporary space for your swap meets; it should be fairly easy to obtain weekend use of a large parking lot, such as space adjacent to an office complex or at the fairgrounds. You'll need enough room for the event itself, plus adequate parking for attendees. Most rentals will cost you a flat fee of around $50–$100 per day, but keep in mind that some of the more savvy business owners may ask you for a small percentage of what you'll earn. Some may be hesitant to rent their space due to liability concerns, so you will need to make it clear that, as the event organizer, you have your own adequate liability insurance to cover any mishaps. Your major startup cost will be for the insurance, plus promotion and advertising.

BOTTOM LINE ADVICE:

Once you become established, you should be able to generate cash flow very quickly for the auto swap meets you promote. However, if you're not advertising in the right places, your participants won't know about the opportunity. Your success will hinge on your ability to get the word out. Visibility is an important consideration, too. Advertising gets the word out prior to the event, but a high-traffic location will boost your attendance on the day of the event and help pile up your revenues significantly.

AUTOMOBILE WINDOW STICKERS

Startup cost:	$5,000–$10,000
Potential earnings:	$15,000–$25,000
Typical fees:	$5–$10 per sticker
Advertising:	Cold calls, networking and direct mail to car dealerships
Qualifications:	Energy, aggressive sales ability; background in auto sales is helpful
Equipment needed:	Mobile printer with preprinted forms, cell phone; vehicle
Home business potential:	Yes
Staff required:	No
Hidden costs:	Insurance, equipment maintenance, vehicle expenses

LOWDOWN:

Success in the used car industry depends on making adequate, accurate information about each car on each lot readily available to consumers. One of the best ways to do that is to have standardized, printed labels on each car window, detailing such critical information about the car's history as mileage, special features, and life cycle of particular items such as tires and timing belts. Credibility is an important component of sales for used car dealers these days, and something as seemingly unimportant as a window label can go a long way toward building customer trust. The buying public is far too smart to be duped by used car salesmen with slick pitches, and many states have laws concerning the sales of so-called "lemon" automobiles. Consumers who don't know a lot about cars are even beginning to hire automotive inspection services to check out a used vehicle before they buy it. Dealers need your product. Your main objective is to sell them on-site, print out the labels immediately, and collect your cash.

STARTUP:

Unless you have access to the specialized forms and printer you'll need to produce the window labels, you'll need to buy into a franchise to get started in this business; expect to spend about $5,000–$10,000 toward the franchise fees. Your advertising budget can be rather small, due to the fact that your first sales will come as the result of cold-calling; your subsequent growth will be based on reputation and networking success. Expect to earn anywhere from $15,000–$25,000 as you run around from dealer to dealer, building lasting relationships based on short-term need.

BOTTOM LINE ADVICE:

This is a simple business to manage and run—but you'll need to provide immediate and accurate service to your clients to keep the cash rolling in. Any time you're not readily available, they'll turn to a competitor (and you know what that can do to your bank account).

AUTOMOTIVE MARKETING AND TRAINING SERVICES

Startup cost:	$6,000–$10,000
Potential earnings:	$40,000–$70,000
Typical fees:	$75–$100 per hour or a flat per diem of $500
Advertising:	Dealer publications, business publications, trade association memberships, direct mail, networking with auto dealerships
Qualifications:	Proven track record of success in automotive marketing, sales training experience, outstanding oral and written communication skills
Equipment needed:	High-end computer with graphics capability; color printer; word processing, spreadsheet, and presentation software; Internet access; fax; scanner; copier; cell phone; marketing materials
Home business potential:	Yes, but you'll be on the road a lot
Staff required:	Yes
Hidden costs:	Preparation of presentation materials: workbooks, slides, and overheads; travel time and mileage

LOWDOWN:

Next to a home, an automobile is perhaps the most expensive purchase most people will ever make. And although most Americans will purchase at least four cars in their lifetime, many are uncomfortable just walking into an automobile dealership. If you have sold cars successfully yourself and can communicate with others who work in this field, you have a great opportunity to develop a successful business in the field of automotive marketing and training. Essentially, it will be your job to teach automobile sales personnel how to be more effective at what they do. You may even work with auto technicians, too; after all, once the sale is made, they are the ones who continue to work with customers at the repair level, which is ripe for add-on product sales.

STARTUP:

Your success will depend on the training and support materials you are able to provide to your clients. Expect to spend between $6,000 and $10,000 for the actual presentation materials, slides, workbooks, etc. you will need to conduct your training sessions and the high-powered computer, printer, and software you will need to create them. You'll also want to set aside some of your startup funds for your own sales/promotional materials, such as business cards and brochures for direct mail to automobile dealerships. Potential annual earnings of $40,000–$70,000 can be yours, if you charge $75–$100 per hour for your services.

BOTTOM LINE ADVICE:

Working with sales professionals to improve their methods can be both exhilarating and draining. Everyone, including you, has his or her unique selling style—tread carefully on the egos in every roomful of folks you train. Try to penetrate preconceived mindsets early in the game.

BICYCLE RENTAL

Startup cost:	$7,500–$12,000
Potential earnings:	$50,000–$80,000
Typical fees:	$5–$10 per hour rental; $25–$35 per day
Advertising:	Fliers/brochures (give some to the chamber of commerce or travel agencies), Yellow Pages
Qualifications:	Outgoing personality, knowledge of bike repair, basic business and marketing skills
Equipment needed:	Fleet of bicycles, replacement tires, and repair kits
Home business potential:	Yes
Staff required:	No
Hidden costs:	Liability/theft insurance

LOWDOWN:

Remember the days of the bicycle built for two, when couples rented bikes to explore island areas where cars either didn't exist or were blessedly limited? Those days are still here—but the majority of bicycle rental businesses are clustered around heavily trafficked tourist spots such as Michigan's Mackinac Island and beachside towns in Florida. And in addition to lightweight racers, mountain bikes, tandems, and tricycles—with hand brakes or the old-fashioned coaster kind—many of today's bicycle shops, especially in places like California, rent in-line skates as well. No matter what kind of stock you decide to offer, you're sure to be amazed at how much money you can make in this relatively easy business. Just about any place where tourists are likely to gather, you'll find a market for bike and skate rentals. You can offer short-term rentals—by the hour, half-day, or day—or longer contracts of several days or a full week aimed at visitors who plan to be around for a while. And, since a good share of your rentals are likely to be cash transactions, you'll have instant money.

STARTUP:

Your main startup cost will be acquiring a good fleet of bicycles; you'll need at least 20 to 25 to get started. How much you spend per bike depends, in part, on your geographic locale. In a flat place like Mackinac Island or Key West, you can get by with a fleet of "coaster" bikes; in hilly terrain, you'll need the more costly bikes with multiple gears. Keep in mind that your bikes will be getting a lot of hard wear, so while used bicycles will cost less to purchase, the cost of maintaining them could be quite high. Police auctions—sales of unclaimed stolen merchandise—can sometimes be good sources of gently used bikes. The key to making money in bike rental is high turnover; the more bikes you rent in a day, the more money you'll make. If you're located in a tourist area (especially one that doesn't allow many cars or even any at all), you'll do well.

BOTTOM LINE ADVICE:

Location is everything in this business, so do your homework and choose the right one. Bike rental is a seasonal business in northern climates. Are you willing to accept that? Or would you rather make money from this relatively simple, straightforward business all year long? If so, you'll have to head south. The decision is yours, but either way, you can make a decent chunk of change doing something that's fun.

BOUDOIR PHOTOGRAPHY

Startup cost:	$10,000–$15,000
Potential earnings:	$15,000–$35,000
Typical fees:	$150–$250 per sitting + the cost of the actual photographs that result
Advertising:	Yellow Pages, coupon books, community newspapers, referrals
Qualifications:	Creativity, sensitivity, photographic background
Equipment needed:	Cameras, lenses, filters, soft lighting, touch-up equipment, small studio/darkroom, drapes and props
Home business potential:	Yes (if you have your own studio)
Staff required:	No
Hidden costs:	Insurance, film and processing costs, equipment updates

LOWDOWN:

Many a woman has fantasized about posing for a seductive portrait that she could give to her significant other to mark a special occasion, such as a birthday, wedding, or anniversary, or for no particular reason at all. If you have photographic talent, you may be able to cash in on what is fast becoming a lucrative niche market in the photography business. We're not talking about nude photography here; we're talking about slightly racy, but tastefully executed, formal portraits. Your clients are women who wouldn't normally don a lace teddy or negligee for a formal photograph, but decide to do so just for fun. You'll need to do a fair amount of advertising to find your subjects, and your message will need to be carefully crafted, stressing affordability and the high quality of your images. In addition to a Yellow Pages listing and newspaper ads, you may want to reach out to specialty lingerie shops and bridal salons; leave a stack of business cards or brochures behind, and perhaps offer coupon deals tied to purchases. If you like a creative challenge, you'll find one in boudoir photography as you work to determine the right poses for each of your clients, and make sure that the finished product they receive is both sexy and tasteful enough to be displayed in your studio.

STARTUP:

Expect to spend $10,000–$15,000 to get your business up and running. If you're into photography, you probably already own at least one good camera and several lenses; however, you may need to purchase backup equipment, as well as tripods, lights, and a variety of filters for special effects. And since you'll probably be doing your own processing and touchups, you'll need a full complement of darkroom equipment, too. Remember, these are fantasy photos and you need to have the tools that will help you make your subjects look as sexy and beautiful as they can possibly be. Set aside a chunk of money for advertising too—about $3,000 should get you started.

BOTTOM LINE ADVICE:

This is an extremely sensitive business. Your clients are trusting you with a very private side of themselves, so your reputation must be impeccable. Women are more likely to succeed as boudoir photographers because they are perceived by their female subjects as being a little "safer" than men. If you are a male photographer, you can launch this type of business, but you must be careful. One lapse in judgment could cost you everything in the form of a lawsuit over real (or perceived) amorous advances on your part. Tread carefully.

BRIDAL SHOW PROMOTIONS

Startup cost:	$5,000–$15,000
Potential earnings:	$20,000–$40,000
Typical fees:	$125 per booth rental space
Advertising:	Fliers, radio ads, newspapers, bridal shops, mailings, billboards
Qualifications:	Exceptional organizational skills, interest in brides and bridal planning, basic business and marketing skills
Equipment needed:	Computer; printer; word processing, database, and spreadsheet software; fax; copier; cell phone
Home business potential:	Yes
Staff required:	Not initially
Hidden costs:	Radio ads are expensive; try to work with sponsors to secure airtime and split costs

LOWDOWN:

Bridal shows are popular just about everywhere—there are always young women and their moms shopping for the best in wedding preparations. You should have no trouble securing an audience if you book your shows in the right places (such as shopping malls, banquet halls, and hotels). Your biggest challenge will be to gain the attention, support, and dollars from participating vendors, who likely would include bridal salons, tuxedo rentals, caterers, florists, musicians, cake decorators—in short, any business that gets a share of the wedding market. You must be highly organized to pull all of the pieces together and, ultimately, to pull off a successful event. Lose sight of details and you'll lose credibility with both your audience of brides and their moms and your vendors. If you think you can handle the pressure, our best advice is to secure financial support up front so that you don't have to lay out your own money to cover out-of-pocket expenses—that way, in the event of a no-show vendor, you'll still have your cash.

STARTUP:

The $5,000–$10,000 you'll need to get this business off the ground properly will mainly cover your advertising and promotional costs. You'll need to have professional-looking materials in order to secure vendors, plus appealing ads, fliers, and billboards to attract your audience. Do it right and you can make between $20,000–$40,000 yourself, depending on how many shows you run per year.

BOTTOM LINE ADVICE:

You should be able to secure at least 50 vendors for your first show; if you can't, maybe you should rethink your marketing strategy. Look for a novel approach, or try to get a well-known spokesperson or celebrity to appear (local television personalities are a possibility). Do everything humanly possible to attract the kind of attention that will set your bridal show apart from the rest.

BUSINESS PLAN WRITER/PACKAGER

Startup cost:	$5,000–$12,000
Potential earnings:	$30,000–$100,000
Typical fees:	$2,500–$6,000 per plan (approximately two to four weeks of work)
Advertising:	Teaching courses on business development, networking, memberships in business associations, referrals from bankers and entrepreneurship centers, advertising in local business newsletters/journals, Web site
Qualifications:	Understanding of financial statements, savvy business sense, excellent oral and written communication skills, ability to get people to work together, experience writing business plans
Equipment needed:	Computer; fax; Internet access; laser printer; word processing, business-planning, and spreadsheet software; copier
Home business potential:	Yes
Staff required:	No
Hidden costs:	Organizational dues, business newsletter/journal and newspaper subscriptions, liability insurance

LOWDOWN:

Businesses are springing up all over the country at a phenomenal rate, and those that are likeliest to succeed recognize the two most important benefits of having a business plan in place from the start. First, the plan structures the efforts of everyone involved, listing the goals that need to be accomplished and describing the means by which those goals will be achieved. A business plan highlights the feasibility of the products or services the enterprise intends to market and, more importantly, estimates expenses and revenues, along with sales projections, in order to provide the clearest possible prediction for business success. While wonderful things might well happen down the road, if it's apparent up-front that the revenues won't cover the expenses, the business is almost surely headed for failure. A cash-starved business won't last long enough to reach even the best-intentioned goals. The second primary benefit of having a business plan is to obtain financing. A startup business simply can't obtain bank loans and most other types of outside financing without one.

Sadly, although many new business owners recognize the importance of having a solid business plan, they don't know the first thing about how to put one together. That's where you can help. If you have the right combination of experience, business sense, and writing skills, you can launch your own small enterprise as a writer/packager of business plans for others. Your ability to translate the dreams of fledgling entrepreneurs into financial reality and put it all on paper could earn you a hefty annual income.

STARTUP:

The equipment and materials you will need in order to create final products with a reassuringly professional image are fairly costly; expect to spend between $3,000 and $10,000 for the necessary top-of-the-line computer hardware and software. A polished printout of the final plan will best be achieved using one of the better-quality business plan software packages available, which typically cost about $150–$300. However, since you'll be charging between $2,500 and $6,000 per business plan, it shouldn't take long for you to recoup your startup costs and begin generating a profit.

BOTTOM LINE ADVICE:

Putting together a business plan is time-consuming and hardly the most creative kind of writing you could ever do. But if you have developed the wide range of skills necessary to do this work, you undoubtedly are the kind of person who thrives on detail and can tolerate the tedium. Effective business plans aren't easy to write, which is precisely why there's a market for what you do. Every situation is different, and that means you'll encounter constant opportunities for learning. And there's no repeat business. Once you complete a plan, you will need to find another client, so your marketing efforts must be ongoing. Approximately one-third of new business startups fail within the first two years, mostly due to poor marketing or undercapitalization; however, some fledgling enterprises are shaky right from the start and if they fail before or shortly after you have completed your plan, you might never receive payment for your work. Always ask for at least half of your fee up front, so you're not out the time with nothing at all to show for it if the business fails before it even has a chance to get off the ground.

CAREER COUNSELOR

Startup cost:	$10,000–$15,000
Potential earnings:	$30,000–$65,000
Typical fees:	Hourly rate of $50–$100 or $350 per session
Advertising:	Yellow Pages, classified ads, job fairs, human resource newsletters, Web site
Qualifications:	Empathy and good listening skills; a background in human resources is helpful; many states require certification
Equipment needed:	Computer, printer, Internet access, personal assessment software programs; library of videos, DVDs, and books related to career planning; copier; cell phone or pager; land line with answering service or voice mail
Home business potential:	Yes
Staff required:	No
Hidden costs:	Assessment materials; staying abreast of trends in the employment market

LOWDOWN:

Once upon a time, if you lost a job through no fault of your own, you could simply look for a similar position at another firm in the same general industry. Not so today. Thanks to constantly changing technology and corporate downsizing, the jobs for which a laid-off employee is most qualified may no longer be available at all. Faced with the necessity of finding an entirely new career, many a suddenly unemployed person is left floundering. As a career counselor, you can assist these newly unemployed workers in discovering a new direction for their job aspirations. You'll begin with a personality assessment, then work with your client to match his or her motivations and interests to a potential new career. Together, you'll map out a success plan for landing a new job or launching a business (yes, many people do discover through career counseling that they'd really rather work for themselves). You can use pre-existing, formatted questionnaires or personal interviews (or a combination of both) to arrive at some conclusions that can help your client make important decisions about his or her professional goals. But your counseling efforts needn't stop there; you can also offer such related services as resume and cover letter preparation, role-playing for improving interview skills, and rental of motivational videos, cassette tapes and CDs, and printed resources on topics related to career planning and job searching. Your biggest challenge will be reaching the people who could most use your services but simply don't know that they exist. Tailor your marketing efforts to appeal directly to the career changers themselves, or network with corporations to provide outplacement services for employees affected by downsizing.

STARTUP:

Your startup costs are directly related to equipping your office with a computer system and assembling the necessary testing materials and career-oriented resources. You can charge between $50 and $100 per hour for your services, or a flat fee of $350 per career counseling session. To get your business off the ground, shoot for at least one solid corporate client and a handful of individual job seekers; then grow your business with continued networking and referrals. Your primary product is your personal expertise, so build your credibility by offering seminars on career change and/or providing tips on job hunting and career planning via your own Web site.

BOTTOM LINE ADVICE:

Although you will be working with many different types of people, keep in mind, they all have one thing in common: They have no idea in which direction to take their careers. This uncertainty can be frustrating, even frightening, for your clients, so you can expect your job to be part information-giving, part hand-holding. If you're well-adjusted yourself and can help others get through the often wrenching ordeal of remaking themselves and their careers, you will reap a host of professional and personal benefits from providing this type of service.

CARPET INSTALLATION

Startup costs:	$8,000–$15,000
Potential earnings:	$40,000–$80,000; some installers earn $5,000 or more per month
Typical fees:	A per-job rate between $300–$500; for larger, more difficult jobs, a per-square-foot rate may be more cost effective
Advertising:	Personal contact with flooring stores, Yellow Pages, referrals
Qualifications:	Knowledge of carpeting materials; training and firsthand experience, usually under the direction of seasoned carpet layer
Equipment needed:	Van to deliver and haul away carpet, tools
Home business potential:	Yes
Staff required:	No
Hidden costs:	Insurance, transportation

LOWDOWN:

Carpet is a mainstay in American décor. The good news is virtually every home or business is a potential customer for your carpet installation services; the bad news is, you're not the only one out there. So go into this business knowing that you'll have to find a way to set yourself apart. You can learn this trade by correspondence or by working with an experienced carpet layer. Whichever course you choose, remember that quality workmanship is what ultimately sells your service, along with neatness, reliability, and the ability to leave a good impression on those you're serving. After making contacts with several flooring stores and providing high-quality workmanship, recommendations should flow your way from sales personnel and satisfied consumers.

STARTUP:

You'll need installation equipment and tools ($1,500–$3,000), advertising ($3,000–$5,000), and a vehicle if you don't already have one ($5,000–$10,000 for a used van). However, since you'll be charging per job or by the square foot (average jobs run $300–$500 for carpet laying alone), you should have little trouble earning back what you initially lay out.

BOTTOM LINE ADVICE:

Neatness counts. Part of your service should be removal of the old carpeting and associated debris. And since few people want to deal with the refuse, include the cost of hauling it away as part of your total installation package (covering your costs, of course).

CASTING DIRECTOR

Startup cost:	$5,000–$10,000
Potential earnings:	$5,000 or more per month
Typical fees:	Varies according to size of job; can range from $3,000–$50,000
Advertising:	Industry trade publications, word of mouth
Qualifications:	Experience and contacts in the entertainment industry, creativity, ability to visualize "talent" in specific roles
Equipment needed:	Computer, video and camera equipment, multiple phone lines, cell phone fax
Home business potential:	Not likely because you'll probably need ample space for casting calls
Staff required:	No
Hidden costs:	Insurance, cell phone expenses

LOWDOWN:

As a casting director, you will work closely with a host of talent agencies and artists to find the right actor or actress for a particular role. What fun it will be to be involved in the movie industry, you might think. However, once you get your foot in the door, you'll begin to see what a difficult and stressful situation you've gotten yourself into. If you're one who likes to live on the edge, you'll love the challenges this business will present on a minute-to-minute basis. You'll need the ability to spot potential personality conflicts (those infamous "creative differences") and the creativity to visualize a particular actor in a role that might be a stretch for others to see at first. And you'll probably become the proud owner of a huge address book with hundreds of actors' names.

STARTUP:

A casting director is employed on a short-term, contractual basis and paid by the hiring studio, network, agency, or producer, so the potential earnings will vary greatly—bringing in as little as $3,000 or as much as $50,000 per job; it just depends on whom you're working with and how big the backing studio is. Hollywood is all about show, and to be successful, you must play the game. Be prepared to make a significant investment ($5,000–$10,000) in your personal image, an impressive office setup, and schmoozing with the right people. You can make good money as a casting director, but it won't come easy or quick. Expect a dry period up front as you build your business; set aside ample money to cover living expenses until you land your first contracts and plan your cash flow accordingly.

BOTTOM LINE ADVICE:

Since you are employed by the studio, network, etc., you won't have to pay union dues. Experience and contacts will be your greatest assets. And since you will be working on many different projects simultaneously, be sure your organizational skills are top-notch.

CLASSIFIED ADVERTISING NEWSPAPER

Startup cost:	$5,000–$10,000
Potential earnings:	$30,000–$50,000
Typical fees:	Ad space generally sells for anywhere from $4–$500
Advertising:	Cold calling, neighborhood bulletin boards, fliers
Qualifications:	Energy, selling ability, organizational and desktop publishing skills, eye for detail
Equipment needed:	Computer, desktop publishing software, laser printer, copier, fax, Internet access, telephone with answering service or voice mail
Home business potential:	Yes
Staff required:	No
Hidden costs:	Printing can get costly; develop a relationship with a printer who will work with you to keep production costs down.

LOWDOWN:

Would it surprise you to know that of all the sections in your daily newspaper, it's the classified ads that are the most carefully read? And many different kinds of people peruse the newspaper classifieds on a daily basis. What's more, they're likely to also pick up and read publications that are devoted to classifieds-only. If you are persistent and have a certain eye for detail, you can take advantage of this widespread interest by publishing and circulating your own classifieds-only newspaper. To succeed, you'll need a wide variety of skills, not the least of which is the ability to sell; you must convince your advertisers that an ad in your publication will get results. Putting the paper together will demand desktop publishing skills, of course, but, since classified ads are more utilitarian than creative, you won't need much in the way of artistic design or layout abilities. You will, however, need to come up with an effective method for circulating your newspaper; publications like these are often simply made available free of charge wherever there is heavy foot traffic.

STARTUP:

You can launch this business from your home with little more than a telephone, but you'll probably do better if you have a more visible location; the people who plunk down money to place a classified ad like to know exactly where their money's going. Expect to spend at least $350 per month for office space. You'll need adequate computer equipment and desktop publishing software to support the production side of your enterprise and you'll definitely need to set aside cash for producing the first six months' worth of issues ($10,000). On the upside, if you promote your paper and make sure it gets distributed in the right places, you could soon be making $30,000 or more per year.

BOTTOM LINE ADVICE:

This is the kind of business you build out of your own energy, determination, and drive. Consequently, you'll have a real sense of ownership and pride. On the other hand, this is a lot of work for one person. Your commitment to complete each issue will be tested and tested again—miss a deadline or turn out a substandard product and your customers will not only notice, they'll take their business elsewhere.

COLLECTIBLES/MEMORABILIA

Startup cost:	$5,000–$15,000
Potential earnings:	$500–$35,000
Typical fees:	Vary depending on the items you are selling and their market rates
Advertising:	Booths/tables at flea markets, swap meets, antique fairs, etc; fliers; business cards; newspaper classified ads
Qualifications:	A keen interest in collectibles, an eye for what will sell
Equipment needed:	A stock of collectibles to start, pricing resource guides, a vehicle to haul your "stuff" to flea markets and fairs
Home business potential:	Yes, but at some point you may want to open a storefront
Staff required:	No
Hidden costs:	Table/space rental fees, transportation to and from events

LOWDOWN:

Everything old is new again! Remember the Morton Salt Girl or those Brady Bunch lunch boxes with radios? They are in demand right now and commanding top dollar ($100 or more each). So is anything retro: salt-and-pepper sets, board games, clothing, limited edition plates, presidential items, cereal boxes—you name it and you can probably make money from it. But not without some heavy-duty marketing of your services. You can specialize in one era like the 1940s or '50s and carry items exclusively from that time period. Or, you can specialize in an item category, like movie posters or toasters through the century. You'll find your items at garage sales, flea markets, dealer conventions, out-of-the-way antique shops, and fairs. Try to hit as many events as possible, first as a buyer and later as a seller; you'll spend a little, but earn a lot.

STARTUP:

To get started, you'll need a healthy stock of collectibles, a way to display them—portable tables, shelving, glass cases, etc.—and a vehicle to haul it all around in. How much you have to spend to get up and running depends on what you currently have on hand and how elaborate a display you want to create. You'll need to set aside some money for marketing, too. Around $1,000 should be enough for a simple flyer, business cards, and a few classified ads. Plan on paying $15–$100+ to rent a table or space at antique fairs and flea markets to showcase your merchandise. Initial earnings will be low—$500 or less per event—but once you get established and collectors come to associate your name with the specific items they seek, your income can jump substantially.

BOTTOM LINE ADVICE:

People are crazy for the past. And perhaps because certain items remind them of a simpler time in their lives, they're willing to pay to acquire them. Collecting has become a $6-billion-dollar-a-year business, so if you have a collection you're willing to part with or an interest in acquiring memorabilia you can turn around and sell, you could make some serious money. Collecting interests tend to run in 20-year cycles, so this business has long-term possibilities if you have an eye for what is collectible now and what will sell in the future. The danger is getting so caught up in acquiring certain pieces that you aren't willing to part with them yourself. Beware—collecting can be downright addictive for those who enjoy it!

COLLECTION AGENCY

Startup costs:	$3,000–$10,500
Potential earnings:	$30,000–$60,000
Typical fees:	25 percent commission
Advertising:	Phone solicitation, networking and referrals, writing articles for local publications, public speaking
Qualifications:	Good communication and budgeting skills, patience, high self-esteem; clear understanding of the Federal Fair Debt Collection Practices Act and relevant state laws; knowledge of health insurance policies and billing practices if working in the medical field
Equipment needed:	Computer with Internet access, printer, fax, word-processing and spreadsheet software, specialized collection software, phone, headset
Home business potential:	Possibly; some states have regulations against home-based collection agencies
Staff required:	No
Hidden costs:	Organizational dues for networking purposes; state, city, and/or county licenses; bonding

LOWDOWN:

Are you a fan of mysteries and whodunits? Do you have a thick enough skin to handle a regular dose of verbal abuse by phone? Then you may have the makings of a debt collector. As the owner of a collection agency, it will be your job to track down elusive debtors on behalf of your clients, who may be individual merchants, credit card companies, utilities, and health-care providers. State laws typically require that people who do collections be bonded and licensed; some states do not allow home-based collection agencies. It is generally not difficult to obtain the proper license, just be sure that you check on the location requirements that apply to your situation. Using special collections software and a computer, today's collection services can be far more efficient and less costly than the old-fashioned agencies that depended primarily on direct mail to go after debtors. Internet access and online searching have cut the cost of tracking debtors considerably.

STARTUP:

It is essential that you take advantage of the many high-tech devices that will make the collection process easier. A computer and Internet access are essential, as is customized collection software. Expect to spend $2,000–$7,000 for these office basics. And since all of your work is done by phone, shop around for the best rates on local and long-distance phone calls and invest in a headset for hands-free use; you'll be spending too much time on the phone to try and prop the receiver against your shoulder. You'll need to be almost as aggressive about your marketing as you are about collecting on your clients' bills. Networking and cold-calling will get you started, and once you're up and running, referrals will help grow your business.

BOTTOM LINE ADVICE:

The collection process is often frustrating. Keeping your self-esteem intact in the face of rejection and verbal abuse is difficult but necessary. Although confronting someone with the reality of unpaid bills can be emotionally draining, this work never ceases to be challenging and rewarding. In some cases, you are able to resolve a debtor's financial problems and keep him or her from bankruptcy. When all parties agree on a suitable payment plan, everyone wins.

ADVICE FROM THE EXPERTS

What sets your business apart from others like it?

"There are a lot of good agencies, and we all basically do the same things," says Deloris C. Lewis, president of Debt Credit Services and Associates in Akron, Ohio. "I cater to the needs of my clients and go out of my way to help them. I try to be fair to both the creditors and the debtors."

Things you couldn't do without:

Items such as an excellent, well-trained staff, speed dialers, computers, integrated skip tracing and bookkeeping software, a phone system, and mailing equipment, Lewis says.

Marketing tips/advice:

"Go after the large-dollar, small-account commercial business that's out there. Stay away from health care; if you're new, it will be too demanding and intense for you. Use networking and advertising to bring in new business, but depend heavily on referrals."

If you had to do it all over again . . .

"I'd have started with more capital . . . that means developing a sound business plan, which I didn't do in the beginning and which has held me back. I winged it—and now I'd be more organized so that I could get better funding."

COMPUTER CONSULTANT

Startup cost:	$5,000–$13,000
Potential earnings:	$40,000–$100,000
Typical fees:	$75–$150 per hour
Advertising:	Referrals, direct mail, publications, networking
Qualifications:	Technical know-how, specialty knowledge, people, organizational, and time-management skills
Equipment needed:	High-end computer, hardware, software, and peripherals; copier, scanner, and fax; high-speed Internet access; cell phone
Home business potential:	Yes
Staff required:	No; must be able to subcontract outside of specialty
Hidden costs:	High-speed Internet access; time and expense of staying current in a fast-changing field

LOWDOWN:

It's downright impossible to operate any business these days without a computer, so if you know how to match up a computer system with a company's needs, just about anyone is a potential client for your services. Computer consulting is a field that's big and getting bigger. Many computer consultants become as essential to their clients as the systems themselves, earning a steady income in the process. This field is for individuals with wide expertise in computer hardware, software, and peripherals. But you will need more than technical know-how to succeed. Even more important is the ability to see issues from the client's point of view. What are the problems this business faces on a daily basis, and how can those problems best be addressed using computer technology? Although it's possible to be a jack-of-all-computer-trades, you will probably do better if you focus on one area of specialization, such as networking computers, or on one type of business, such as retail outlets or physicians' offices. That way you can develop a reputation as the reigning "expert" in a particular field or type of technology.

STARTUP:

Your own business must have a computer system, including software, that is comparable to that of your client. This will be a major expense, but if you have the expertise necessary to call yourself a computer consultant, you probably have some pretty heavy-duty hardware and software, as well as high-speed Internet access, already. You'll want to add a high-quality copier, scanner, and fax to your office equipment, along with a cell phone so that you are readily available to your clients. Most of your clients will come as the result of networking and referrals; set aside some money for the essential organizational dues and a targeted direct mail campaign. Your high-level expertise can easily translate into fees of $75–$150 per hour, which means you should be able to earn back your initial investment in as little as six months to a year.

BOTTOM LINE ADVICE:

Computer consulting is for big-picture people who are equally adept at keeping track of details. Each client and situation is different, which makes for a challenging and stimulating work life. You will be able to function outside of normal time-space restrictions and you won't find competitors undercutting you with cookie-cutter services. On the downside, computer consulting is extremely demanding. You will often be working under a deadline or in a crisis situation; you must produce what you promise and be able to train your clients' employees to make the system work under real conditions. Bidding jobs may be challenging at first, but you will soon get the hang of it as you build your business. Since you are working on an hourly basis, keeping track of your time is essential.

ADVICE FROM THE EXPERTS

What sets your business apart from others like it?
Lee Hughes, systems engineer at Hughes Information Systems in Cloquet, Minnesota, says his business is successful because it streamlines and automates other businesses' operations. "We take an engineering approach to solving problems."

Things you couldn't do without:
"A personal computer, printer, high-speed Internet access, and phone."

Marketing tips/advice:
"It is virtually impossible to accurately estimate project costs. Try to build in a cushion when you provide an estimate."

If you had to do it all over again . . .
"I would educate myself much more in business management, sales/marketing, and presentation/negotiation skills."

COMPUTER REPAIR AND MAINTENANCE

Startup cost:	$5,000–$10,000
Potential earnings:	$50,000–$70,000
Typical fees:	$35–$50 per hour
Advertising:	Word of mouth, Yellow Pages, fliers, business card, Web site
Qualifications:	Knowledge of computer hardware, interfaces, and operating systems; ability to deal with upset clients in a diplomatic and sympathetic manner; licensing and/or certification may be required in some states
Equipment needed:	Computer with high-speed Internet access, printer, and fax; tools, cleaning supplies, diagnostic software, spare parts, reference books and repair manuals
Home business potential:	Yes
Staff required:	No
Hidden costs:	Staying abreast of new technology; training and certification, vehicle expenses

LOWDOWN:

Computers and dust don't mix. Seems like a simple idea, but many people have little appreciation of this concept. Nor do they understand that, without regular maintenance, computers can break down. But once you develop your clientele and gain their trust, you'll be able to negotiate ongoing service contracts that will give you a steady flow of work and regular income. Yours is a skill that thrives on repeat business. Twice a year you can service each client on your list. Along the way, you may also develop connections to possible add-on services you can offer, such as training, software installation, file back-ups, and other types of computer-related services.

STARTUP:

Your largest expense may well be the training you will need to undergo in order to become a knowledgeable and, eventually, certified computer repair technician. The actual tools you'll need to clean and repair the machines are quite simple and not very costly; you will, however, want to have a computer system for your own office, plus high-speed Internet access, in order to stay abreast of the latest technological developments. Fees for computer repair and maintenance are typically in the $50 per hour range, so you can make a nice living, as long as you have steady work. Your biggest challenge will be to make potential clients aware of the benefits of maintaining their systems. Set aside approximately $2,000–$3,000 per year for advertising and sending "it's time for your annual checkup" reminder cards.

BOTTOM LINE ADVICE:

If you have the ability to clean and repair computers and peripheral equipment, you can provide a service needed by almost every business and many individuals as well. Satisfied customers will probably provide you with plenty of referrals; but keep in mind that much of your work will be with distraught clients whose machines have suddenly broken down. Most of your work will be done on-site, so careful planning is necessary to make the best use of your travel time.

COMPUTER SOFTWARE SALES

Startup cost:	$5,000–$15,000
Potential earnings:	$15,000–$40,000
Typical fees:	Software retails anywhere between $5–$500; your commission can be as high as 20 percent (depending on your markup)
Advertising:	Computer magazines, bulletin boards, direct mail, Web site
Qualifications:	Knowledge of what is new and hot in consumer software
Equipment needed:	Computer, fax, printer, copier, scanner, high-speed Internet access, multiline telephone system
Home business potential:	Yes
Staff required:	No
Hidden costs:	Depends on your approach, but may include high phone bills and advertising costs; Web site design

LOWDOWN:

A number of avenues exist for the creation of a small business that sells already established software. A mail-order business requires considerable advertising, a Web site, and an 800 number for customers to call. Your ability to convert phone calls into orders may depend on how you match callers with the packages they need. Use your wide familiarity with different types of software to serve customers better than they can be served by mass-market outlets—and keep your prices competitive as well. Some small software sellers might open a retail store, while others find selling opportunities in a range of areas, including flea markets. Combine your knowledge of what is available in software with carefully honed selling skills to help your customers find the package that is right for them, and you can expect to develop a successful business.

STARTUP:

Your startup costs depend largely on the direction in which you decide to take your business. For mail order, you'll need a computer, multiline phone system, 800 number, and Web site. A retail outlet will require you to rent or buy space, then stock it with expensive inventory to meet the needs and expectations of a fickle, fast-changing market; and, of course, you'll need a cash register, display shelves and counters, and computers where you can demonstrate the different types of software you have available. Your commission will depend on what you are able to negotiate with your supplier as markup; for planning purposes, count on between 5 and 20 percent.

BOTTOM LINE ADVICE:

It's fun to put products into the hands of customers who need them. More computers than televisions are sold in the United States each year, and all of these machines require some type of software and their upgrades. The market is definitely out there. Your challenge is to establish the right connections with it. To make a profit you'll need to offer better, more knowledgeable service and competitive prices. Keeping up with all the new packages will be an ongoing test of your abilities, and keeping track of what your competition is up to will demand a great deal of your time.

COMPUTER TRAINER

Startup cost:	$5,000–$15,000
Potential earnings:	$40,000–$100,000
Typical fees:	$50–$75 per hour for private instruction; $150–$200 per hour for a group session
Advertising:	Speaking at business meetings, referrals from software companies, networking, direct mail to specific companies, computer and trade publications, Web site
Qualifications:	Computer skills and/or certification by software manufacturers, writing and presentation skills, ability to handle group dynamics, background in teaching or educational design
Equipment needed:	High-end computer, desktop publishing and presentation software, laser printer, copier, scanner, fax, comb binding machine (optional) for handout booklets, brochures and/or presentation folder; laptop computer, desktop projector, and laser pointer for classroom demonstrations
Home business potential:	Yes
Staff required:	No
Hidden costs:	Certification and training in order to teach specific programs; continuing education to stay abreast of new developments, professional organization dues

LOWDOWN:

As computers become ever more vital to effective business operations, so does computer training. New software is powerful, but added features mean that almost every employee needs training to be able to take full and productive advantage of its features. To be a successful computer trainer, you will need a range of skills, beginning with expertise in the software packages for which you provide training. It goes without saying that you need to be proficient in using the software yourself, but beyond that, you need to be able to instruct others in how to use it. Computer trainers may work as tutors with one or two individuals at a time, but more often they teach classes to groups at a business location; good teaching and presentation skills are essential to prosper in this business. Computer training can be a successful business for people with better-than-average computer skills who find teaching to be a creative enterprise and who like working with adult learners. For maximum effectiveness, focus on the areas that are in greatest demand and where your expertise can most easily be updated: word processing, database, and/or accounting programs, for example.

STARTUP:

Your computer, software, and laser printer will represent the largest single category of startup expenses, totaling as much as $5,000. In all likelihood, you'll be producing your own training materials, and adapting them to the needs of specific clients and to new versions of software packages. Since training is usually conducted on clients' premises, your own office setup can be minimal at first; you'll need just enough to be able to create your handout materials. Although you can use traditional transparencies and your client's overhead projector for classroom demonstrations, you may find that it's worth the extra expense (another $5,000 or so) to bring along your own laptop computer, desktop projector, and laser pointer. Charge an adequate hourly rate to cover your expenses and make a tidy profit.

BOTTOM LINE ADVICE:

If you are good at teaching, you can make a big difference in the work lives of the people you train. They must use computer equipment to complete their tasks, and knowing how the programs operate will greatly increase their efficiency. So you can walk into a training situation knowing that the services you provide are important to the employees you train and to the businesses that depend on them. You'll need to be good at defusing computer anxiety, however. People who don't understand the intricacies of a program are sometimes intimidated and impatient as they try—and fail at first—to make things happen with new software. You will need to coax them gradually through each skill level until they gain confidence and proficiency. Students who are new to a skill often don't ask clear questions; anticipate that and listen carefully so that you can give the right responses. Remember, you are teaching adults, many of whom may find it very difficult to become students again; be patient, but be careful to not be condescending in your speech or teaching manner. You're likely to encounter a good deal of competition in this field today, so you will need to look for ways to distinguish what you have to offer from other computer trainers. Keep in mind, too, that preparing training materials can be time-consuming and labor-intensive; for best results, keep your materials simple and use step-by-step approaches to writing instructions.

CONSTRUCTION SERVICES

Startup cost:	$5,000–$10,000
Potential earnings:	$25,000–$65,000
Typical fees:	$35–$50 per hour or a flat rate depending on the project ($1,000–$1 million)
Advertising:	Newspapers, real estate magazines, local periodicals, Yellow Pages, radio, fliers; networking with hardware and home improvement stores
Qualifications:	Extensive experience with all phases of the type of construction in which you specialize; excellent marketing, pricing, multitasking,and management skills; some states require licensing
Equipment needed:	Tools and a vehicle to haul them around in; computer, printer, cell phone
Home business potential:	Yes
Staff required:	Probably
Hidden costs:	Costs for materials; insurance, licensing. Nonpaying customers can be a major problem in this area.

LOWDOWN:

Remodeling is big business these days and construction services are widely needed. Some construction companies are one-person operations that build entire homes from start to finish almost single-handedly; others employ several people and handle multiple projects at the same time. There are even firms that focus on just one element of the construction process, like kitchen remodeling, decks, or skylights. Nor is commercial construction limited only to homes; small businesses also have remodeling needs that a construction services business can readily address. If you are handy with tools and able to juggle all of the elements that go into a remodeling project, this could be a profitable business. Whether you choose to focus your efforts on individual homes or commercial enterprises, marketing will be central. How will you reach that well-heeled homeowner dreaming about a state-of-the-art kitchen? Or the family that wants to add a deck out back? If you focus on the small projects that are just beyond the skill level of a typical handyman, neighborhood fliers could be an effective way to send out your message. Get a few projects and happy customers under your tool belt, and referrals are sure to keep you busy. In addition to basic construction skills, you'll need to be an excellent estimator and a good judge of people.

STARTUP:

Even if you aim for just a couple of simple jobs at first, your startup costs will be fairly high (at least $5,000); at the very least, you'll need tools and a vehicle. You'll want to have a cell phone for sure, plus a computer and printer to prepare your written estimates, contracts, and invoices. With more and more people wanting to remodel their homes and offices these days, you could earn $25,000 fairly soon—possibly on your first job! Be good at what you do and keep your materials costs down; you could work your way up to making an exceptionally fine living.

BOTTOM LINE ADVICE:

It takes more than solid construction skills to succeed in this business. Many excellent builders are not able to make their businesses profitable because time and cost overruns defeat them. Being able to find customers, helping them clarify what they want to have done, and then fulfilling their expectations within a specified time frame and at the right price are essential qualities for continued success.

CORPORATE INSURANCE BROKER

Startup cost:	$5,000–$8,000
Potential earnings:	$50,000–$100,000
Typical fees:	$35–$50 per hour
Advertising:	Direct mail and/or cold calls, Yellow Pages, ads in newspapers and business or trade publications, networking through local business organizations
Qualifications:	Extensive experience in the insurance industry and specialty lines
Equipment needed:	Computer; printer; Internet access; word processing, spreadsheet, database, and presentation software; cell phone; copier; fax; marketing materials
Home business potential:	Yes
Staff required:	No
Hidden costs:	Marketing, organization dues

LOWDOWN:

The insurance field is crowded, but there is always room for the agent who can offer qualities that are available from no other agent out there. Many voices are clamoring for the attention of your potential customers, but far fewer have a real understanding of the effects of insurance on a business organization. For example, if you specialize in employee benefits, your expertise and willingness to assemble the best combination of benefits for your client's specific employee group will set you apart. Assistance with claims processing is another selling point. You will need to go into this business with general knowledge of the insurance field, as well as a specific understanding of insurance costs and benefits; your expertise in these areas will allow you to handle everything from group information intakes to claims. Don't forget that you are primarily a salesperson—your job is to sell peace of mind to your corporate clients, who depend on you for the most thorough, comprehensive, and competitive insurance plans available. They want the best insurance at the most reasonable price; what they don't want is to spend the time it would take to track it down for themselves, and that's why they need you.

STARTUP:

You'll need a computer and printer, Internet access, and a full complement of office software to support your marketing and insurance research efforts. Set aside approximately $2,000 up front for your marketing efforts, including a direct mail campaign, Yellow Pages listing, and ads in newspapers and publications specifically directed to businesses.

BOTTOM LINE ADVICE:

The key to success here is a good business sense. Although your primary goal is to sell insurance and earn a commission, don't let that show. Focus instead on the benefits you can bring to your clients; show them how working with you can meet their strategic goals. As with so many service-oriented enterprises, success comes down to having a clear focus on the service you're providing and a dedication to marketing as an ongoing part of your business life.

CORPORATE TRAINER

Startup cost:	$5,000–$11,000
Potential earnings:	$35,000–$100,000
Typical fees:	$500–$2,000 per day
Advertising:	Networking with local personnel managers, speaking before professional organizations and local groups, compiling a detailed portfolio
Qualifications:	Experience as a corporate trainer and/or expertise in a specific area of interest to businesses, such as sales or team management; communication skills, and/or facility with group dynamics; ASTD certification is not required, but adds credibility
Equipment needed:	Computer, printer, Internet access, fax, scanner, and copier; word processing, desktop publishing, and presentation software
Home business potential:	Yes
Staff required:	No
Hidden costs:	Living expenses for first six months while building a client base; continuing education and certification; cost of producing seminar handouts and other materials

LOWDOWN:

Even though more and more employees receive formal training these days, fewer large companies keep a professional trainer on their payroll. Perhaps they simply don't want to spend the money; sadly, however, they pay for their lack of foresight in other ways. Employees that aren't up to speed with regard to changing techniques, technologies, and procedures can mean big losses for companies trying to compete in a global market-place. As a corporate trainer working on a contractual basis rather than on-staff, you provide a cost-effective solution. Your ability to jump in and lead successful training sessions will not only build your reputation as a corporate trainer, it can be a foothold to other moneymaking opportunities, such as books, tapes, manuals, and seminars.

STARTUP:

The American Society for Training and Development (ASTD) and the American Management Association can be useful resources for developing your corporate training programs. You will need to spend a significant amount of time and money (at least $5,000 to start) in order to create a specific and professional-looking presentation that will fill an existing niche in the industry. If you are good at what you do and develop a solid reputation for your training programs, you can easily earn $35,000 and more depending on how well you market your services and how many hours you are willing to work.

BOTTOM LINE ADVICE:

Top trainers make excellent money, but be prepared to devote a lot of time to selling yourself and your seminars. Remember that companies are often looking for short-term benefits rather than the long-term value a comprehensive, ongoing training program would provide. However, once your reputation is established, there is excellent opportunity for repeat business.

ADVICE FROM THE EXPERTS

What sets your business apart from others like it?
For Mike Robinson, managing partner of Triad Training and Consulting in Kernersville, North Carolina, it's customized service delivered at great value that sets his business apart from others like it. "With many clients, we'll offer a money-back guarantee."

Things you couldn't do without:
"You'll need a powerful computer system with a good multimedia setup for on-site productions and near-published quality training materials. Also, you'll need audiovisual equipment."

Marketing tips/advice:
"Work on your teaching skills, delivery, and training ability. You'll need to have the ability to read a crowd and fantastic communications skills to get the kind of word of mouth necessary to build business."

If you had to do it all over again . . .
"I didn't have enough clients lined up before I left my previous company. Also, if you're not good in certain areas of business, surround yourself with people who are. Finally, remember that the first few years are going to be difficult—but, if you're persistent, it could snowball soon thereafter."

COST REDUCTION CONSULTANT

Startup cost:	$5,000–$8,000
Potential earnings:	$50,000–$75,000
Typical fees:	Percentage of the cost savings, for a contracted time
Advertising:	Business and trade publications, direct mail, memberships in business organizations and community groups
Qualifications:	Business experience, some financial background, excellent selling and people skills, attention to detail
Equipment needed:	Computer, word processing and spreadsheet software, printer, Internet access, calculator, copier, fax, marketing materials
Home business potential:	Yes
Staff required:	No
Hidden costs:	Dues to community organizations, publication subscriptions

LOWDOWN:

All businesses want to keep costs down, but with flatter organizational structures and fewer people doing more work, searching for savings often has to take last place behind the needs of the day-to-day operations. As a cost consultant, you can use your creativity and your "nose for money" to keep your clients in the black. Are they really getting the best deal on copier paper? Would it be cheaper to outsource the cleaning? Can orders be batched for a discount? Energy savings can be a significant subspecialty all on its own. You keep a percentage of the savings you find, just as a bill auditor would, and both you and your client profit by your work. This is a great business for people who love a challenge and who are extremely persistent and detail-oriented. You're not only looking at reducing current bills; you're also on the lookout for any savings opportunities that might lie ahead.

STARTUP:

You will probably do most of your work on your clients' premises, so a basic, functional office will serve you well; expect to spend $3,000–$5,000 for a complete computer setup, including laser printer, Internet access, and software, as well as a copier and fax. You'll probably spend a lot of time at your desk poring over financial records, so invest in furniture that is both functional and physically comfortable; an ergonomic chair is a must! Networking will be your primary marketing tool, which means you'll need to be visible in your community and active in local business organizations where you are apt to come in contact with potential clients; set aside plenty of money for dues and subscriptions to local business-related publications. Your earnings will depend on how aggressively you pursue cost-saving opportunities. If you are good, you could easily reach $50,000 quickly.

BOTTOM LINE ADVICE:

Aside from the qualities necessary to look beneath the surface and find savings, you'll need excellent people skills. Allowing someone from the outside to be as involved in the workings of a company as a cost consultant must be can be uncomfortable for many businesspeople. You'll need to gain their confidence not only in the service you offer but in your personal character as well.

COSTUME DESIGN AND CONSTRUCTION

Startup cost:	$5,000–$15,000
Potential earnings:	$35,000–$65,000; more for a large costume rental business
Typical fees:	$50–$100 per hour for design/construction of costumes; $45–$100 per rental
Advertising:	Networking with performing arts centers and theater companies; direct mail to schools, theaters, and churches; Yellow Pages and newspaper ads; Web site; referrals
Qualifications:	Training/experience in clothing design and construction, background in theater, knowledge of clothing from different historical periods and cultures, creativity, ability to read a script and visualize the necessary clothing
Equipment needed:	Sewing machine and miscellaneous sewing supplies; fabric and notions; adequate space for fittings and storage; library of period and present-day clothing and costume books; pencils, sketchpads, and other miscellaneous art supplies; phone
Home business potential:	Yes
Staff required:	No
Hidden costs:	Cost of materials

LOWDOWN:

Remember what fun it was to play dress-up as a kid? If you have the right combination of sewing and design skills, you can carry some of that same fun over into your adult life with a business in costume design and construction. We're not just talking about kids' Halloween costumes here (although that could be a lucrative market for you); we're talking about the costumes that are needed year-round by individual entertainers and/or for stage productions, dance recitals, skating tournaments, ballroom dancing competitions, church pageants, historical re-enactments, ceremonies, parades, and other special events. Somebody has to stitch up all those sequined gowns and period clothing. It might as well be you. If you live in a metropolitan area with a lively arts scene and make the right contacts, you'll have plenty of opportunities to sell your services.

STARTUP:

If you have the skills to pursue this business, you probably already have most of the equipment and supplies you need to get up and running, including a sewing machine; consequently, your startup costs will be on the low end of the scale. Keep in mind, however, that since you'll be giving your sewing machine a heavy-duty workout, you may want to invest in a sturdier model. Although referrals will grow your business later on, you will need to do some intensive marketing up front to get the word out—a few carefully placed newspaper ads, plus direct mail and networking with theaters, schools, churches, and other groups that would likely need costumes should do the trick. Consider aligning yourself with an adult education program or perhaps a local fabric store to offer classes in basic kids' costume construction. And since some of your creations may be worn just once or for the brief run of a single production, you might want to think about renting instead of selling your costumes outright; this will, however, require that you have adequate storage space. Don't forget to build the cost of dry cleaning and any alterations that might be necessary into your rental fees either.

BOTTOM LINE ADVICE:

Costumes aren't just for Halloween any more; they're popular for holiday parties and around Mardi Gras time too. You'll do best if you're located in a community with a thriving theater scene or where a major special event and its minor spinoffs require costumes—i.e., the Gasparilla Parade in Tampa or Fantasy Fest in Key West. Be willing to take on the challenge of creating authentic period costumes or designing to your customer's specifications and don't be afraid to show up in costume at a community function or fair. Just think of the marketing possibilities!

DATABASE CONSULTANT

Startup cost:	$5,000–$13,000
Potential earnings:	$50,000–$100,000
Typical fees:	$75–$100+ per hour
Advertising:	Referrals, business publications, trade journal advertising, Web site
Qualifications:	Experience in database management and analysis, programming skills are helpful but not required, awareness of business information needs, excellent communication and project management skills, attention to detail
Equipment needed:	State-of-the-art computer, printer, database software, high-speed Internet access, printer, fax, phone
Home business potential:	Yes
Staff required:	No
Hidden costs:	Business insurance, incorporation to protect your assets against risk, software updates, continuing education to keep up with technological developments

LOWDOWN:

Companies create databases in order to store the information they need to make critical decisions and develop corporate strategies. For example, a mail-order retailer could effectively use a database to garner interesting information about the buying habits of its customers, such as what they purchase by mail, the time of year, week, or day they call to place an order, the size and quality selections they make, and the types of catalogs they find most appealing. If you have the knowledge to create database systems that will present the needed information correctly, efficiently, and accurately, you can command a high hourly rate. Depending on your background and skills, you may actually write the program for a database, oversee the work of database programmers, supervise the customization of existing software in order to fulfill your clients' needs.

STARTUP:

Although you may spend much of your time working on-site, you will still need your own state-of-the-art computer equipment and database software to support your work. Your computer must be powerful enough to store and manipulate huge amounts of data; expect to spend $5,000–$10,000 for your complete system. Considering that your hourly rates may top $100, you should be able to recoup your investment and begin to see a profit within a relatively short period of time.

BOTTOM LINE ADVICE:

This is an enormously challenging business for people who love working at a high level with abstract ideas. Central to your success will be your ability to understand the information your clients really need and to design a database system that will collect and store it for later access. This involves learning in detail how a specific business operates, then using your imagination to determine how a database might support that mission, now and well into the future. Your projects will be both large and lengthy, involving many steps and multiple personalities. You will need to be exceptionally well-organized to pull all of the pieces together and to work with several people, each of whom may have a different agenda.

DECKS/OUTDOOR FURNITURE

Startup cost:	$5,000–$15,000
Potential earnings:	$25,000–$65,000
Typical fees:	Can range anywhere from $150–$3,000 for each piece or finished deck
Advertising:	Yellow Pages, local newspapers, direct mail, home and flower shows, hardware stores, Web site
Qualifications:	Carpentry and sales skills
Equipment needed:	Basic carpentry equipment, including saws, blades, hammers, nails, etc.
Home business potential:	Yes
Staff required:	Yes (for decks)
Hidden costs:	Insurance and workers' compensation

LOWDOWN:

There's nothing like sitting out on a deck in the summertime, sipping a soda and enjoying a fresh, cool breeze. Many homeowners yearn to add decks to their homes, along with practical, tasteful custom-made outdoor furniture. Many retirees have begun businesses like this one; it's the perfect way to parlay an interest in woodworking into a secondary income, or even a primary one, if you're industrious. You'll be working with homeowners on everything from concept and design to the actual construction of each custom deck and/or piece of furniture, so you must have strong listening and customer service skills. Keep in mind that even simple home construction projects require building permits in many locations; get to know the rules in your community. In most parts of the country, this is a business that's seasonal. In high season, you could easily end up with more work than you can handle on your own, and to meet the demand, you may have to hire additional help.

STARTUP:

Your startup fees will include your equipment (saws and other tools needed for custom carpentry) and a vehicle to carry it all, so be prepared to spend $5,000–$10,000 getting started. Advertising will be another main cost (roughly $3,000). If you're building furniture, you'll need a large workspace; rent may become a consideration if you don't have room at home or if you decide you need a storefront. Fees will vary from $150 for a small piece of wooden furniture (such as an end table) to several thousand dollars for decks.

BOTTOM LINE ADVICE:

If you live in a cold climate where you can't work outdoors at deck-building all year-round, use the winter months to build a stockpile of furniture, and to promote your deck-building business and line up clients for the coming summer. Don't rely solely on homeowners to grow your business—cultivate contacts with developers, too. Decks and handcrafted outdoor furniture can add value to new homes and condos.

DESIGNER/RETAIL ITEMS

Startup cost:	$10,000–$20,000
Potential earnings:	$50,000–$150,000+
Typical fees:	Varied according to project; can be as low as $500 for a simple design sketch to several thousand for a complete design/technical layout with product specifications
Advertising:	Referral and direct mail
Qualifications:	Product design experience and/or degree in product design, creativity, ability to work as part of a team
Equipment needed:	Computer, printer, Internet access, product design software (CAD)
Home business potential:	Yes
Staff required:	No
Hidden costs:	Insurance, excessive client changes to product specifications (make sure you're clear on what's expected—and get it in writing!)

LOWDOWN:

Behind every good product is a strong design team, and you could offer your services to such a team on a contract basis. If you can bring to the table a reputation for quality product design done on a quick-turnaround basis and within budget, you stand a very good chance of building lasting relationships with product manufacturers who will come to depend on your flair and expertise to pull off products that at first seem almost too challenging to make. Your experience in design for manufacturability (i.e., designing products with the manufacturing team's constraints in mind) will be a valuable commodity among the clients you seek to attract; they appreciate working with professionals who understand that good design must be more than artistic, it must be practical, too.

STARTUP:

You'll need to invest a minimum of $10,000 in a high-end computer with a large monitor and a computer-aided design (CAD) software package. Aside from some carefully targeted direct mail, your advertising budget will be virtually nonexistent; your area of expertise depends heavily on referrals and word of mouth. If you are successful in building the kinds of contacts you'll need to survive on your own, you'll be making anywhere from $50,000–$150,000 or more; obviously, if you're working for large, well-known manufacturers, your earnings will be on the high end because these companies appreciate quality design and are more apt to pay big bucks to receive it.

BOTTOM LINE ADVICE:

This business affords plenty of opportunity for creativity, but keep in mind that the work you do will not always be your own. Since you'll be working on a contract basis most of the time, you will often be brought in to solve design problems or to pick up where another designer left off; your own ideas may have to take a backseat to the consensus of the team. Still, the work is solid, challenging, and potentially quite profitable if you are both quick and talented.

DOULA/MIDWIFE

Startup cost:	$5,000–$15,000++, depending on the level of certification you're shooting for
Potential earnings:	$25,000–$65,000
Advertising:	Parenting newsletters, doctors' offices, word of mouth
Typical fees:	$300–$500 per client
Qualifications:	Training and certification required
Equipment needed:	Dependable car, pager, cell phone or answering service
Home business potential:	Yes (although you'll be traveling a lot to birth sites)
Staff required:	No
Hidden costs:	Liability/malpractice insurance can be costly, but you can't do without it; make sure you have good coverage

LOWDOWN:

If you appreciate the joy of bringing a new life into the world, becoming a doula or midwife could be an ideal career for you. Deciding which path to follow depends largely on how much time and money you want to invest up front. You have the following three options: certified doula, certified midwife, or certified nurse midwife. Each has specific training and certification requirements, with doula requiring the smallest investment of money and time.

A *doula* (Greek for "woman's helper") is trained to provide emotional and physical support to a mother during childbirth and to offer assistance immediately after the baby comes home. She doesn't deliver babies and, in fact, may not even be present during the birth. Typically, a doula either helps out during labor or with postpartum care, but rarely both; certification is available for either stage of the birthing process. Doula training takes the form of a formal workshop lasting three to five days, plus hands-on experience with new mothers. Check with Doulas of North America (*www.dona.com*) for information about doula training.

At the other end of the birthing care spectrum is a certified nurse midwife. To become a CNM, you must be a Registered Nurse (RN), which requires graduation from an accredited baccalaureate or associate's degree program in nursing. Nurse midwives provide primary prenatal and maternity care and, in some cases, may deliver the baby without the presence of a physician; in most states, CNMs may also write prescriptions. In between the two, there's the certified midwife, a credential only just approved in 1994 and not yet recognized in all states. CMs are not registered nurses, although they might have formal training in some other health care specialty such as physical therapy or as physicians' assistants.

After receiving your certification as a doula, CM, or CNM, you'll need to meet with family physicians and obstetricians to let them know about your services. Although midwifery and doula services are gaining in popularity among patients, some medical professionals remain slow to catch on; be aware that not all doctors will react favorably to your overtures. Still, the rise in popularity of home births and homelike birthing centers in hospitals is a trend that could easily contribute to your success. One thing is certain: In this field, your best advertising will come from networking and word of mouth.

STARTUP:
Your training costs will vary depending on the level of certification you seek. You can become a certified doula for less than $1,000; training to become a certified nurse mid-wife will cost significantly more. In all cases, you will need to have liability and/or mal-practice insurance, which can run into the thousands of dollars. Keep in mind, too, that most insurance companies do not cover doula services—so you will have to work out payment plans (and collection methods) directly with your clients.

BOTTOM LINE ADVICE:
The demands of being on-call for much of your career can take its toll—as can the occa-sional life-or-death emergency. Obviously, if you enjoy the challenges and aren't afraid of the risks, you can make a difference in the lives of a new family—and that may be your biggest reward.

DRAFTSMAN/BLUEPRINTING SERVICE

Startup cost:	$5,000–$10,000
Potential earnings:	$35,000–$65,000
Typical fees:	$150–$500 per blueprint
Advertising:	Yellow Pages, networking and referrals, ads in trade publications
Qualifications:	Degree in drafting, professional experience as a draftsman, connections to architects and builders
Equipment needed:	Blueprint copier, drafting table, pencils, erasers, and other related small tools
Home business potential:	Yes
Staff required:	No
Hidden costs:	Insurance, equipment maintenance/upgrade

LOWDOWN:

You're detail-oriented, with a flair for putting the finishing touches on someone else's work. You've also likely studied drafting in college or worked professionally as a drafts-man before embarking on this entrepreneurial endeavor; you have the book smarts and experience that your customers will eventually come to rely on. As a draftsman/blueprinting service, you will ultimately produce the blueprints that architects and builders need to complete their dynamic new projects and provide whatever number of copies of each blueprint they need as well. Although individuals may hire you for smaller projects, most of your customers will be architectural firms and building professionals, so you'll need to be well-connected to get any share of the work that's out there. Set yourself apart by adding additional services or special treatment (such as free delivery to worksites).

STARTUP:

You'll need between $5,000–$10,000 to get started in drafting and blueprinting, primarily to cover your equipment costs for such items as a blueprint copier (approximately $4,000) and drafting table with drafting pencils, etc. You'll likely earn $35,000–$65,000 for your efforts.

BOTTOM LINE ADVICE:

Yours is a precise, behind-the-scenes, and often thankless job (seeing as how the more visible architects and builders take all the glory). Oh, well ... just keep in mind that without you, those projects might never be completed. Develop a list of contacts and stay close to the builders and architects in your area; they will ultimately make up your referral system and be a continuing source of repeat business.

EFFICIENCY EXPERT

Startup cost:	$5,000–$10,000
Potential earnings:	$35,000–$75,000+ (depending on your market)
Typical fees:	$75–$100 per hour or a monthly retainer of $3,000–$5,000
Advertising:	Trade publications, Yellow Pages, direct mail, business newspapers
Qualifications:	Broad background in business operations; management experience; ability to spot potential problems and time-wasters before and as they occur
Equipment needed:	Computer; fax; Internet access; printer; word processing, database, spreadsheet, and presentation software; resource materials
Home business potential:	Yes
Staff required:	No
Hidden costs:	Liability insurance, underbilling for amount of time spent (watch your own clock!)

LOWDOWN:

Time is money and in many corporations there are CEOs who want the company to run like clockwork, particularly if production goals have been set which must be met regularly. As an efficiency expert, you will come into a company for a period of about two to four weeks and carefully monitor exactly how things are being done. You will ask workers questions such as, "Why are you repeatedly moving across the room to accomplish one simple task?" and "Is there any other way to minimize the steps involved in your particular process?" You are, in a sense, a detective searching for answers to the big question (which is, of course: "How can this company achieve its goals in a better and more economical way?"). Once you have gathered all the necessary information and have put together your recommendations, you will print up a report and/or make a formal presentation, pinpointing for the CEO where he or she can improve operations. To succeed as an efficiency expert, you will need a broad background in business operations, significant management experience, and a strong eye for detail. Your client companies will be paying you big bucks to figure out where they could make improvements in their facilities and operations; you must convey the idea that you're worth it, so watch your own image and always give 110 percent to your work.

STARTUP:

You'll be preparing formal written reports and oral presentations of your findings and recommendations for your clients. You'll need to have the computer, printer, and software to support those services. Expect to spend $5,000–$7,500 to get up and running. Set aside another $2,000 or so for a Yellow Pages listing and ads in trade publications and business journals.

BOTTOM LINE ADVICE:

While corporate moguls will be hiring you to tell them what's wrong with their organization, some may not be willing to actually listen. Beware of potential liability issues; don't make promises about things over which you have no control. You'll need to be clear from the beginning that you are merely offering your professional opinions and advice, not guarantees of higher profits or improved productivity.

ELECTRICAL CONTRACTOR/ ELECTRICIAN

Startup cost:	$10,000–$15,000
Potential earnings:	$40,000–$60,000
Typical fees:	$20–$35 per hour (labor only, parts are billed at cost)
Advertising:	Yellow Pages, classifieds, neighborhood fliers, community bulletin boards, word of mouth, radio spots
Qualifications:	Skill and experience as an electrician, ability to manage time and expenses, good people skills; most states require certification and regular credit hours toward career development
Equipment needed:	Tools, parts, and equipment related to the nature of the work; truck or van; marketing materials.
Home business potential:	Yes
Staff required:	No
Hidden costs:	Inventory of parts, vehicle maintenance, insurance, continuing education

LOWDOWN:

Skilled electricians are always in demand, especially ones that can work with homeowners who can't make up their minds and small business owners who are impatient to get the work done. As the general population becomes less handy with tools and wires, your electrical knowledge and expertise will become more and more valuable. This is a classic one-person business, and you may face considerable competition. You will need good estimating skills to assess the cost and complexity of the work you are asked to do. Some of your jobs will be pretty straightforward, but you're also sure to encounter those times when you have to play the role of a detective in order to interpret the hidden wiring in an old house or trace the cause of a short "somewhere in the wall." Of course, you'll need to be familiar with code standards in all the communities located within your service area.

STARTUP:

Startup costs are relatively high as you must equip yourself to be ready for whatever electrical job you are called upon to perform; if you don't already have a vehicle in which to haul your equipment, you'll need to acquire one. You'll also need to secure your initial certification, and take regular refresher courses in order to keep your skills and certification up to date. Set aside at least $7,000 for your equipment, certification, and liability insurance; add another $8,000–$10,000 for a reliable used truck or van.

BOTTOM LINE ADVICE:

Many electricians have made an excellent living by focusing on upgrading the wiring in old houses. If your area has a charming neighborhood of old Victorians, 1920s bungalows, or quaint cottages that are in the process of being restored, you have a golden opportunity to build a client base. Other electricians work closely with independent builders to install wiring in new structures. Your ability to get these new wiring jobs completed according to the overall construction schedule will have a big influence on the builder's profits and your reputation. With exceptional planning and time-management skills, you can help build a steady stream of referrals and repeat projects from busy builders.

EMPLOYEE BENEFITS CONSULTANT

Startup cost:	$5,000–$8,000
Potential earnings:	$35,000–$70,000
Typical fees:	$25–$50 per hour
Advertising:	Direct mail, networking, memberships in business and community organizations
Qualifications:	Extensive experience in insurance sales, ability to reach business owners, detail orientation, communications skills
Equipment needed:	Computer, high-speed Internet access, fax, laser printer, copier, scanner, cell phone
Home business potential:	Yes
Staff required:	No
Hidden costs:	Preparation of presentation materials, errors and omissions insurance

LOWDOWN:

An effective employee benefits program is an important factor in building a loyal workforce. The challenge is to create a combination of benefits that meets the needs of the organization and also fits its budget. As an employee benefits consultant, you will help growing businesses survey their employees to determine their needs and wants regarding employer-paid insurance. You will work with the business owner to design the best combination of benefits for the dollars available. The likeliest market for your services will be businesses with 20 to 200 employees, which are large enough to offer employee benefits but too small to have the kind of human resources department that can handle this type of work.

STARTUP:

Most of your client contact will take place at their locations, so your office can be functional rather than impressive; $4,000 should be enough to get you up and running with a computer, printer, high-speed Internet access, copier, scanner, and fax. You'll need to be readily accessible to potential and current clients, so carry a cell phone. You should plan to earn about $35,000 in the beginning; networking and referrals will help your business grow.

BOTTOM LINE ADVICE:

Many insurance agents have terrible sales approaches. They seem very eager for their commissions, but then do not follow up with ongoing service throughout the year. Then, as annual review time rolls around, these agents show up again with a plan to switch providers in order to save the client a few dollars. Implementation and employee education are lacking in this approach. You will be able to easily set yourself apart if you can demonstrate that your focus is on customer service, and not on personal profit (at least outwardly). Experience in assisting with claims and with any conflicts that may arise is an important selling point for your enterprise.

EXECUTIVE RECRUITER

Startup cost:	$5,000–$10,000
Potential earnings:	$40,000–$150,000 (gross)
Typical fees:	Vary, but often equal 25–30 percent of first-year earnings of person placed with client
Advertising:	Cold calls, attending trade shows, newsletter to potential clients, direct mail, ads in publications, Web site
Qualifications:	Excellent people skills, patience, self-confidence, knowledge of specialized fields to be able to select appropriate candidates for jobs, good hiring instincts
Equipment needed:	Computer, printer, Internet access, copier, scanner, fax, telephone with headset, cell phone
Home business potential:	Yes
Staff required:	None
Hidden costs:	Phone expenses and advertising costs could exceed budget early

LOWDOWN:

Executive recruiters (also known as headhunters) are paid by companies to fill management, professional, and technical slots within their firms. Most of a recruiter's work is done via phone and e-mail, so you can perform this job from anywhere; from time to time, however, you may still need to make face-to-face contacts. Finding job candidates is the easy part of this business. They will typically come to you, via your Web site or as the result of the carefully targeted ads you place; you may also do some searching for them yourself at online career Web sites or by scanning business publications where the names of up-and-comers are mentioned. Client companies will be a little tougher to come by. You will have to be aggressive in your marketing efforts—make cold calls, attend trade shows, place ads. Some executive recruiters specialize in recruiting for a particular industry, such as technology or telecommunications; others focus on a job category across all industries—they recruit for marketing or human resources positions, for example. A sales personality is helpful in this business, as is the ability to be self-motivated and persistent. You will need self-confidence, tenacity, and good networking skills to make it as a recruiter. This career choice gives you a great deal of flexibility and personal freedom; as long as you have access to a phone, you can work from any location.

STARTUP:

A computer and printer are essential, as is database, word processing, and communications software. These items will cost from $2,500 to $5,000. You will need telephones (land line and cell phone), a headset, copier, scanner, and fax, along with office furniture and business cards, brochures, and a Web site to promote your business, for an additional cost of $1,500–$5,000. You'll earn an average 25–30 percent of the new hire's salary—so it behooves you to search for high-end, top-level management positions.

BOTTOM LINE ADVICE:

Competition for the best companies and top-notch candidates is stiff, and you get paid only when you successfully match a company with a candidate. But the financial rewards in this business can be considerable, and the satisfaction of helping a good candidate find a job and filling a key position for your client makes your efforts worthwhile.

EXPERT WITNESS

Startup cost:	$5,000–$7,000
Potential earnings:	$50,000–$100,000
Typical fees:	Varied (but can be as high as $1,000 per day)
Advertising:	Legal periodicals, referrals, networking, association memberships, Web site
Qualifications:	Selling ability, expert knowledge about a particular subject and/or wide range of contacts in technical and business areas
Equipment needed:	Computer, word processing and database software, fax, scanner, copier, Internet access, laser printer
Home business potential:	Yes
Staff required:	No
Hidden costs:	Travel expenses, telephone bills

LOWDOWN:

Expert testimony is frequently required in civil cases where the actions of a person, deliberate or otherwise, or a consumer product that may or may not be defective are believed to have caused injury to a plaintiff. Your business can be a source for lawyers to call when they have clients with claims that require substantiation from a person knowledgeable in a particular field. The expert witness has specific training or experience that would allow him or her to support a claim about defective products or shoddy workmanship. You can serve as the expert yourself, or you can provide from your database the names of appropriate expert witnesses for cases involving subjects outside of your expertise.

Being an expert witness can be an excellent source of income, especially for someone newly laid off or recently retired. This job is a perfect sideline for doctors and other medical practitioners. In addition to making yourself available to provide courtroom testimony, you can help connect people with technical or business expertise to the lawyers who need them. Expert witnesses must be able to pull complex facts together into clear, concise sentences that may be readily understood by a jury made up of people who may have no prior knowledge of a sometimes highly technical subject. In addition to relaying important details, expert witnesses need to be able to see the big picture; they must be adept at thinking on their feet and dealing calmly with cross-examination.

STARTUP:

Up front, you'll need to shell out $2,000–$3,000 for a computer, printer, and word processing software for producing credible, professional looking reports to offer as background information or to be entered as evidence. And if you intend to become a source for witnesses beyond your personal area of expertise, you'll need database software, too, for keeping track of them; add another $500–$1,000 to your tab. There may well be hundreds of court cases on dockets throughout the United States that could benefit from your expertise. In order to make attorneys nationwide aware of your services, you will need to post your availability on the Internet by way of your own Web site; expect to pay a minimum of $2,000 for the services of a professional Web site designer. Many expert witnesses charge $1,000 a day or more for their services; whether you can command that kind of fee depends on the nature of your testimony and the extent to which you must prepare for your court appearance.

BOTTOM LINE ADVICE:

This business can thrive on your ability to be an expert witness or to find others with technical or business expertise who can articulate clearly and credibly to a jury. Expert witnesses testify in a wide range of cases daily, and they can be very difficult to find sometimes. If you have a particularly unusual specialty, you could be sitting on a gold mine. Once your business is established, referrals should keep an excellent income rolling in.

E-Zine Publisher

Startup cost:	$5,000–$15,000
Potential earnings:	Depends on the number of subscribers and/or advertisers
Typical fees:	$10–$35 per month for subscriptions; varied fees for ads depending on size and frequency
Advertising:	Direct e-mail, Internet ads, Web site, print ads in publications that target your specialized audience
Qualifications:	Creativity, writing and desktop publishing skills, experience and/or strong interest in a specific hobby, sport, lifestyle, profession, etc.
Equipment needed:	Top-of-the-line computer, word-processing and desktop publishing software, high-speed Internet access, laser printer, scanner, copier, fax, phone
Home business potential:	Yes
Staff required:	No, but you may need to hire freelance writers and editors
Hidden costs:	Mailing list; research to find unusual/valuable/exclusive content worthy of your subscription price

LOWDOWN:

If you've ever had a hankering to get into the magazine business, but held back because of the cost, here's your chance to publish a periodical for the proverbial song. Whereas you might have had to spend several hundred thousand to launch a hard-copy magazine, you can start an e-zine for under $15,000. Why the huge difference? Because you don't have to pay for slick glossy paper or postage to do it; your magazine is entirely online. Other than that, setting up an e-zine is a lot like launching a traditional magazine. You'll choose a market niche on which to focus your content, build a list of subscribers, and sell ads. If you intend to produce your electronic magazine entirely on your own, be sure to choose a content focus in which you have a good deal of experience or knowledge; otherwise, you may have to pay experts to feed you a steady stream of ideas and articles. And while we're on that subject, keep in mind that you have a schedule to keep and, to draw subscribers in the first place and retain them year after year, you must give them a reason to read your magazine. Coming up on a regular basis with new and engaging articles that are chock full of up-to-the-minute facts they can't find anywhere else, will be a constant drain on your creativity.

STARTUP:

You'll need some heavy-duty hardware and software to launch your publication—a top-of-the-line computer, word-processing and desktop publishing programs, high-speed Internet access, laser printer, scanner, copier, fax, and phone. Expect to spend a minimum of $5,000 to get up and running. Your money to publish, and ultimately your profits, will come from a combination of subscription fees and advertising revenues; some e-zine publishers offer free subscriptions, letting advertising dollars foot the entire bill.

BOTTOM LINE ADVICE:

E-zine publishing can be a lucrative field, but don't expect to be making the big bucks anytime soon. Just like traditional magazines, which sometimes take several years to really catch on, you probably won't be turning a profit for a while. But if your content is interesting and on the cutting edge, you'll retain your subscribers and, in turn, attract the advertisers who want to reach them. Publishing an e-zine can be both fun and down-right nerve-wracking; once you establish a publication schedule, you have to stick with it. The immediacy of electronic publishing can be both a plus and a minus. You can share late-breaking news almost as it happens, but you can't use postal snafus as an excuse for the late arrival of your publication either. Your subscribers will come to expect their issues of your e-zine to show up by e-mail at the same time and on the same day every week or month.

Fabric Wallcoverings

Startup costs:	$5,000–$10,000
Potential earnings:	$25,000–$50,000
Typical fees:	Varied according to project and square footage; can be as low as $150 or as high as several thousand
Advertising:	Contacts with fabric stores and interior designers, news releases to home improvement editor of local newspaper, Yellow Pages
Qualifications:	Creativity, training in and/or eye for interior design, physical stamina, firsthand experience applying fabrics to walls
Equipment needed:	Heavy-duty sewing machine, shears, yardstick and tape measures, fabric paste and application tools, sample books galore
Home business potential:	Yes
Staff required:	Not initially (maybe for larger installations)
Hidden costs:	Insurance and unexpected fluctuations in materials costs

LOWDOWN:

Fabric is a creative alternative to wallpaper for the discerning customer for whom money is no object when it comes to redecorating a room. In fact, many Victorian homes used fabric as a wall covering to provide a lush, almost ethereal appearance, and now that many of these old homes are being restored, their new owners are eager to re-create the original look. Covering a wall with fabric is a little trickier than papering, so you'll want to have a fair amount of experience at it before you try to sell your services. Practice on your own walls or those of friends and family to perfect your skills and build a portfolio. You'll need special pastes and tools to smooth bumps and trim edges, and you'll need to have plenty of sample materials to show your clients to assist them in selecting the best patterns and fabrics. Network closely with interior designers and fabric store owners to gain some immediate business; consider waiving the fee for the first few jobs (or until you have a strong portfolio and a stable of satisfied customers). Offer a wide variety of styles and designs to choose from, and keep up with trends in the fabric industry by reading every textile-related publication you can get your hands on.

STARTUP:

You'll spend $5,000–$10,000 in your first year of business, primarily to cover your training and materials. Sample books should be easy enough to come by (many are offered by manufacturers free of charge). Your own fees will vary widely, depending on the square footage of the room and the intricacy of its details (broad expanses of wall take less time and skill than little indentations and nooks). Take the fabric into consideration when making estimates, too; some fabrics are more difficult to work with than others.

BOTTOM LINE ADVICE:

This job requires accurate measurements and careful treatment of unusual, and often expensive, fabrics. You can't afford to let your mind wander, as mistakes can be both costly and aesthetically disastrous. Practice, practice, practice—on your own walls first before tackling someone else's home.

FACIALIST

Startup cost:	$7,000–$15,000
Potential earnings:	$35,000–$50,000
Typical fees:	$50 per session
Advertising:	Personal contacts, direct mail, Yellow Pages, networking with health clubs and salons
Qualifications:	Training/licensing in cosmetology and skin care techniques and treatments; thorough understanding and practice of good hygiene and sanitation techniques; outgoing personality and desire to pamper people
Equipment needed:	Treatment table, steamer, sterilizer, towels, skin-care products
Home business potential:	Yes, but check zoning laws in your area
Staff required:	No
Hidden costs:	Insurance, licensing

LOWDOWN:

Take a quick stroll down the cosmetic aisles of your nearest drug or department store and it's pretty easy to see where a lot of Americans are putting their money these days—into skin care products. The baby boom generation is aging rapidly and men and women alike want to keep their faces looking as healthy and young as possible. As a facialist, you can help them do just that. Using a combination of pressure, electricity, and chemistry, you can offer an array of skin-care treatments, including peels, masks, waxing, collagen, lash and brow tinting, and facial massage. Your primary clients will be women and men for whom a youthful appearance is not just a matter of vanity; it's a case of occupational survival. Entertainers, business executives, professional speakers, flight attendants, and others with jobs that emphasize personal appearance will look to you for ongoing advice and treatment. Exceptional customer service should be the hallmark of this business. Skin care is an ongoing process; if your customers are satisfied, they'll likely return for regular visits and tell their friends about the results.

STARTUP:

You can't touch a person's skin unless you're licensed, and you can't be licensed unless you're trained and certified as a cosmetologist or beauty therapist. Expect to spend up to $15,000 for your training and the equipment you'll need for skin cleaning, hydrating, exfoliating, and toning. At $50 per session, you could easily make an annual income of $40,000–$50,000.

BOTTOM LINE ADVICE:

With more than half of the American population over the age of 35 these days, you should have no shortage of prospective clients; the trick is not only getting them in your door the first time, but signing them up for a long-term skin care regimen. Start by networking with friends and acquaintances, professional organizations, health clubs, and full-service salons. Consider hosting an open house, where you demonstrate your services, or offering coupons for complimentary facials. Make someone feel better about his or her appearance and you're likely to reap the benefits in repeat business.

FINANCIAL PLANNER

Startup cost:	$5,000–$8,000
Potential earnings:	$40,000–$60,000
Typical fees:	Flat fee to put together a plan, typically $250–$500 depending on investments; you may make commission on the sale of certain investment products
Advertising:	Referrals, networking, memberships in community and business groups, local magazines and newspapers, programs of fundraisers
Qualifications:	Registration with the National Association of Securities Dealers; most states require licensing to handle health/life insurance and securities; Certified Financial Planner (CFP) designation is recommended; familiarity with financial products and trends; excellent people skills for marketing, and for creating a plan suitable to the client's needs; ability to inspire trust
Equipment needed:	Computer; printer; word processing, database, and spreadsheet software; fax; scanner; copier; high-speed Internet access; phone
Home business potential:	Yes
Staff required:	No
Hidden costs:	Subscriptions to newspapers and financial periodicals, continuing education, registration and licensing, errors and omissions insurance

LOWDOWN:

The market for financial planning services is growing by leaps and bounds, especially now that the baby boom generation is beginning to retire. Your difficulty in establishing your business will be that so many others have done it before you. It helps if you have a close network of family, friends, and acquaintances you can draw on to build your client base. Your friends and family can become your first clients and, in turn, they can refer you to their friends and families. Financial planning is a very personal business, and your ability to inspire confidence will be vital. Creativity in helping your clients plan their financial futures and skill at helping them achieve the goals you establish together will set you apart. Pay attention to your environment and look around for niche markets that are currently underserved. Could you design plans specifically for self-employed people, the elderly, or investment clubs? Could you work in association with related businesses such as accounting firms to add value to the services they are already offering?

STARTUP:

If you decide to enter the field of financial planning, you should know that this is not a business you can simply launch on the spur of the moment. In most states, you will need to be licensed in health/life insurance and securities; to discuss and distribute securities, you must be registered with the National Association of Securities Dealers, which requires passage of a difficult test. Figure into your startup expenses the cost of training and testing, plus a computer, printer, software, fax, phone, copier, and scanner. And don't forget to include the cost of high-speed Internet access so that you can stay abreast of minute-to-minute changes in the markets.

BOTTOM LINE ADVICE:

Most people manage their money very poorly, if at all. They don't plan well or budget, and they haven't faced up to the reality of their eventual retirement. These are difficult topics, which often make people uncomfortable to discuss; tread carefully. With a reassuring attitude and careful attention to financial details, you'll be able to provide a much-needed service for your clients and make a nice income for yourself.

ADVICE FROM THE EXPERTS

What sets your business apart from others like it?

Dianne Winnen, a Certified Financial Planner in Akron, Ohio, says she is different because her business caters to middle-income people rather than focusing on seniors with retirement funds. "I'm one of 31,000 CFPs in the country, and I'm proud to be a part of a select group."

Things you couldn't do without:

"I couldn't do without my computer, telephone, and copier."

Marketing tips/advice:

"You really have to want to be in this field to make it successful for you. Read and educate yourself about business matters."

If you had to do it all over again ...

"I would've gone in with more realistic expectations about what it would take to survive the first couple of years."

FIREWOOD SERVICE

Startup cost:	$5,000–$15,000
Potential earnings:	$25,000–$35,000
Typical fees:	$65 per cord, delivered and stacked
Advertising:	Local newspapers, bulletin boards, fliers
Qualifications:	Knowledge of wood, good physical condition, ability to manage accounts and records
Equipment needed:	Log splitter, chain saws, various other saws, axes; trailer and/or truck
Home business potential:	Yes
Staff required:	Yes
Hidden costs:	Equipment maintenance

LOWDOWN:

Some folks just don't relish the idea of getting up on a cold morning and splitting firewood à la Abe Lincoln; others simply don't have the time and would appreciate the convenience of a service like yours. Good physical condition is an absolute must for this position. You can't be afraid to work with your hands for long hours, and hoist loads up to and out of your vehicle. Know the different types of wood that you are handling. There's a difference between hardwoods and softwoods, and your job depends on your knowing which varieties burn better than others. Yours is a seasonal business; you'll be busiest in fall and winter. Use your down months to prepare your marketing materials for later distribution, and line up opportunities to sell small bundles of firewood through local lumberyards, hardware stores, and home improvement centers. Make sure you have product in place and available well ahead of the season; many people like to start buying wood before the cold sets in so they're ready to strike a match when it actually does.

STARTUP:

Your initial investment will be relatively low. About $5,000 should cover the cost of your equipment (axes, chain saws, etc.); you'll need another $5,000–$10,000 if you need to purchase a small used truck. This business won't be a huge moneymaker, and keep in mind that it is seasonal, so to make the most you possibly can (probably no more than $35,000), you really need to get the word out early.

BOTTOM LINE ADVICE:

This business could be a great second income, and you don't necessarily need to start out like gangbusters. After you've been working for a few seasons and get a steady clientele of homeowners and retailers in place, you could make a decent living as a full-time woodsman.

FLOWERSCAPING

Startup cost:	$5,000–$10,000
Potential earnings:	$30,000–$45,000 in a growing season
Typical fees:	$25–$40 per hour, plus markup on the wholesale price of flowers
Advertising:	Yellow Pages, newspaper ads, fliers on community bulletin boards, networking with landscapers and garden centers
Qualifications:	Degree or training in ornamental horticulture; extensive knowledge of flowering plants, soils, growing seasons, and regional climates; previous work experience with a nursery, garden center, or greenhouse; physical stamina; eye for color and design
Equipment needed:	Full complement of gardening equipment, including spade, hoe, rakes, pruners, clippers, edger, trowels, wheelbarrow, watering can; computer with bookkeeping and billing software; design software; printer; Internet access; cell phone; vehicle; greenhouse (optional)
Home business potential:	Yes, but you will be working mostly on-site
Staff required:	Possibly
Hidden costs:	Liability insurance, workers' compensation if you hire staff, vehicle expenses

LOWDOWN:

As a flowerscaper, you will plan and design the placement of flowering plants, shrubs, and perhaps even decorative structures such as floral arbors, birdbaths, and benches. Unlike a gardening consultant or landscaper, your focus is extremely narrow—you deal solely in flowers. In most cases, you'll plant the gardens, too, either from seed or using plants you have raised yourself or secured from gardening centers; you may also maintain those gardens throughout the growing season. Your primary market will be dual-income couples, elderly adults who love the look of flowers but can no longer maintain their own gardens, and businesses that want to add color to their more traditional landscaping. Look for ways to provide distinctive services—specialize in roses or wildflowers, or design gardens that will bloom from early spring to first frost. Be prepared to offer advice on dealing with insect infestation and plant disease, too.

STARTUP:

To get started in this business, you'll need a full complement of gardening tools plus a vehicle in which to carry them all; expect to spend up to $10,000 if you're starting from scratch. While you can certainly handle your accounting and design tasks the old-fashioned way by hand, a computer and software for bookkeeping and design will speed the process. Advertise in the Yellow Pages and local newspapers, and network heavily with garden centers and landscapers that do not handle the type of work you do.

BOTTOM LINE ADVICE:

Flowerscaping is a perfect business for someone who loves flowers, has an eye for color, and likes to spend the bulk of every day outdoors. Keep in mind, however, that this is no hobby; your customers are depending on your expertise, so you'll really have to know your stuff. To build awareness for your business, consider teaching a class at your nearest community college or adult education program, and offer your services as a regular gardening columnist to your local newspaper.

FRANCHISE IDEA CENTER

Startup cost:	$5,000–$15,000
Potential earnings:	$25,000–$55,000
Typical fees:	$20–$35 to conduct a search
Advertising:	Yellow Pages, ads in national entrepreneurial publications, local newspapers, Web site, direct mail
Qualifications:	Business background helpful; should be an excellent resource person
Equipment needed:	Computer with printer, high-speed Internet access, fax, phone, copier, scanner, extensive collection of (or ready access to) resource materials on franchising
Home business potential:	Yes
Staff required:	No
Hidden costs:	Insurance, constant updating of information (new materials), Web site management

LOWDOWN:

Thousands of folks with entrepreneurial dreams set out to find the perfect moneymaking opportunity, and franchising is appealing because it offers immediate support and a sense of stability. But not everyone knows which opportunities will work best for them, or how to go about researching franchises to determine their feasibility and/or market potential. That's where you come in. Your service may be limited to simple printouts of specific franchises available in the United States today, or it may include detailed contact and financial information on one or more franchises. For maximum visibility, you'll want to have a Web site for sure; budding entrepreneurs are among the most prolific "surfers." To succeed in this business, you'll need to be an expert on the ins and outs of franchising (firsthand experience is golden!), and to monitor the constant changes occurring in this dynamic and growing area of opportunity.

STARTUP:

You'll spend $5,000–$15,000 launching a business that helps others go into business, in order to cover all of your resource materials (magazine subscriptions, directories, and high-speed Internet access, in addition to your office setup (computer, printer, fax, copier, and scanner). You'll earmark at least $2,000 for the development of your Web site, plus another $2,000–$3,000 for your first year of advertising, most of which will be directed to markets well beyond your immediate locale.

BOTTOM LINE ADVICE:

Your biggest challenge will be to collect your fees up front, particularly as most of your business will come via the Internet. You should have a system in place for credit card processing (PayPal, for example) and make sure that you don't give anything away without securing payment first. On the positive side, you'll enjoy the fact that the information you're selling need only be produced once—and can be sold and resold (profitably) an infinite number of times.

FURNITURE REFINISHER

Startup costs:	$5,000–$20,000
Potential earnings:	$30,000–$60,000
Typical fees:	$20–$35 per hour; or flat fee per item—i.e., $50 for a straight chair; $400 for a dining table and six chairs
Advertising:	Yellow Pages, local newspapers, contacts with antique shops, interior decorators
Qualifications:	Thorough knowledge of woods, stripping techniques, stains and varnishes; training/experience in furniture refinishing
Equipment needed:	Dipping tanks, specialized refinishing tools
Home business potential:	Possibly—but be careful about disposal of hazardous chemicals; renting space is probably a better option
Staff required:	No
Hidden costs:	Insurance

LOWDOWN:

Antiques and other priceless pieces of furniture don't always keep their beauty—especially if they're being used rather than simply displayed. As a furniture refinisher, you can recapture the beauty of an old and treasured mahogany chest of drawers or cherry-wood end table. Furniture refinishing requires specialized knowledge and skill. Using the wrong stripping agent, technique, or tool might ruin someone's priceless antique forever. But if you have an appreciation for fine woods and the patience to restore them, this business can be both enjoyable and lucrative. When it comes to the stripping alone, 50 percent of what you can charge will go toward materials, overhead, and operating costs, so high volume is the key to big profits. Stripping a simple chair usually takes a veteran only about 15 minutes, which means you'll have to strip a lot of them to make a living at this.

STARTUP:

You'll need to spend $5,000 or so getting started, mainly to cover your advertising fees and initial supplies. You can run this business out of your home, but you will need a well-ventilated space and enough room to allow you to be working on several pieces of furniture at any given time. Renting space away from your home is probably a better option, since you will also need customer parking; expect to shell out $300–$600 per month for rent. Charge at least $20 per hour for your services, or flat rates per piece; develop a price list you can share with customers.

BOTTOM LINE ADVICE:

If you plan to locate this business in your home, be sure to check out zoning restrictions before you hang your shingle. The chemicals you are using may be corrosive or flammable; handle with care and be sure you're very familiar with government regulations regarding their disposal to avoid hefty fines.

GARDENING CONSULTANT

Startup cost:	$5,000–$10,000 (more if you need to purchase a vehicle)
Potential earnings:	$35,000–$50,000 (during the growing season)
Typical fees:	Varied; can be as low as $125 or as high as several thousand per project (depending on square footage and whether you're working for an individual or a corporation)
Advertising:	Yellow Pages, community newspapers, city magazines, direct mail, bulletin boards, networking, speaking to community organizations
Qualifications:	Extensive knowledge of plants, soils, growing seasons, and regional climates; training and/or experience in landscape design
Equipment needed:	Gardening tools, hoses, seeds/seedlings, small truck or van; nursery catalogs and landscaping design resources; computer with Internet access for shopping online
Home business potential:	Yes
Staff required:	Possibly; you can handle small projects on your own, one at a time; to handle full-scale landscaping or multiple projects, you will need to hire staff
Hidden costs:	Liability insurance, workers' compensation if you hire staff

LOWDOWN:

There's nothing lovelier than a perfectly planned garden in bloom. If you know your green and flowering plants, can effectively plan a garden where something is always in bloom, and don't mind digging in the dirt for long periods of time under the hot sun, have we got a business for you! As a gardening consultant, you will meet with homeowners, and perhaps business owners too, to work out the details of what will bloom where. Taking into account the overall climate as well as variations in soil and light, you will draw up a plan, which incorporates the best trees, shrubs, and flowers for a particular plot of land, as well as decorative touches such as birdbaths, fountains, and benches. You may simply turn over the plan and let your client carry it out, or you may actually plant the garden yourself. Your work may end once the garden is in, or you may continue to tend it over the full course of the growing season for an additional fee. Develop a portfolio of your best work, then use it to entice additional clients one-on-one or through presentations you make to community organizations that are always looking for speakers. Be sure that you make the scope of your services clear to your clients up front. Many well-meaning folks may confuse your services with those of a professional landscaper; if you don't cut grass, say so.

STARTUP:

You probably wouldn't be considering this business at all if you weren't already into gardening, so there's a good chance you have many of the tools you'll need to get started. Keep in mind, however, that you'll likely be adding staff once the phone starts ringing, so you'll need to double or possibly triple the number of tools you have on hand. You'll probably also need a van or small pickup truck. Instead of buying a vehicle, consider leasing one; apply a magnetic sign to the door to advertise your services and phone number. Park it outside a job site and you'll be amazed at how many referrals you get just from people driving or walking by. Although you can grow your own plants or purchase them from local gardening centers, you may find it more cost effective to order what you need from specialty nurseries. Keep a stack of nursery catalogs on hand and consider purchasing a computer and Internet access for shopping online. When all is said and done, you'll shell out about $5,000–$10,000 to get up and running—more if you add staff right away.

BOTTOM LINE ADVICE:

In most parts of the country, gardening is a seasonal activity. Plan your speaking engagements and other promotional efforts during the off-season. Use the winter months to line up jobs for the coming spring and summer; once growing season arrives, you'll be too busy planting and tending other peoples' gardens to worry about growing your own.

GIFT BASKET BUSINESS

Startup cost:	$5,000–$15,000
Potential earnings:	$25,000–$50,000
Typical fees:	Baskets are individually priced depending on the contents, usually $25–$85 per basket; tailor-made baskets could be priced as high as $350 each
Advertising:	Local newspapers, fliers, bulletin boards, direct mail to busy executives, Yellow Pages, Web site
Qualifications:	Natural creativity mixed with a strong business sense; organizational and time-management skills
Equipment needed:	Baskets, filler, gift materials, glue gun, shrink wrap machine, tables/counters for assembly; delivery vehicle
Home business potential:	Yes
Staff required:	No, although you may want to hire help during peak holiday periods—Christmas, Easter, Valentine's Day
Hidden costs:	Shipping costs/vehicle expenses; you may need a liquor license if your baskets contain wine or champagne

LOWDOWN:

There's nothing nicer to receive than a basket full of goodies meant especially for you . . . that's why gift basket businesses continue to grow in popularity. Some are offered as franchise opportunities, but you can certainly set one up on your own. On the surface, a gift basket business seems like a no-brainer: You just round up a bunch of neat items, place them in a basket, put ribbons and shrink wrap around it all, and voilà! But there's much more to this business than pretty ribbons and baskets; you must also be a gifted buyer (to get the best bargains on gift items and materials) and a real sales go-getter to bring in the constant flow of business you will need to stay afloat. In other words, you should have all the marketing skills of a seasoned retailer, plus a dynamic and creative mind. If you have those qualities, you will likely succeed as long as your market area isn't already saturated with gift basket businesses. Gift baskets have become a billion-dollar industry nationwide; the competition is fierce and you'll lose out if you don't carve an interesting niche for yourself. Think about ways you can make your baskets stand out from the rest. Perhaps you can fill them with an exclusive type of product, such as items manufactured only in your state, or create baskets geared around special themes, like a booklover's basket or a trip to the beach. Consider tailor-made gift baskets too—your client gives you a list of things a specific recipient enjoys and you create a basket just for him or her.

STARTUP:

Your startup costs hinge largely on whether you need to purchase a delivery vehicle or will be using your own car or van. You'll need to keep a pretty sizeable inventory of baskets and gift items on hand; shop for specialty items as you need them. Some gift basket businesses rent storefronts, but for the amount of walk-in business you are likely to generate, you're probably better off to run this one out of your home; you can use a Web site and/or brochures to describe your services and display samples of finished products you have created. Just make sure you have plenty of room at home to spread out; gifts and baskets have a way of taking over! You'll need to advertise heavily—in the Yellow Pages, newspapers, local magazines, and via direct mail to busy executives; expect to spend $2,000–$4,000 on your initial promotional efforts. Your money will come from the gift baskets you sell (minus overhead and the cost of the gift items themselves); gift baskets are typically priced between $25–$85; specialty baskets may run as high as $350.

BOTTOM LINE ADVICE:

It seems as if everyone is trying to get into the gift basket business these days. The competition is bound to be tough, but if you feel you can create gift baskets that truly stand apart in some way, you have a good chance of earning a nice living. If you're not sure you have something unique to offer, think things over carefully or better yet rewrite your business plan before taking the plunge.

GRAFFITI REMOVAL

Startup cost:	$5,000–$10,000
Potential earnings:	$10,000–$20,000
Typical fees:	$150–$300 per job, or $50 per hour
Advertising:	Fliers, door-to-door solicitation, Yellow Pages, classifieds
Qualifications:	Persistence, physical stamina, knowledge of chemical cleaning agents
Equipment needed:	Chemical cleaning agents, scrub brushes, buckets, rags, power washer, vehicle
Home business potential:	Yes
Staff required:	No
Hidden costs:	Vehicle expenses

LOWDOWN:

Graffiti is everywhere, and it's not a pretty sight. Find the owner of the defaced property, or the person authorized to contract for work on such property, sell your removal service, roll up your sleeves, and go at it. You won't lack for opportunities. Graffiti is a serious problem all over the country—in densely populated places, and, oddly enough, in relatively deserted spots, too, where the spray-can artists feel free to let loose. Letting graffiti remain is an open invitation for more vandalism, so it pays to have the mess cleared up as soon as it occurs. Clear a site and you might be able to develop an ongoing contract for regular checking and cleaning if the graffiti is severe enough. Onlookers may even provide additional referrals on the spot.

STARTUP:

Your strong arm is your main tool, but you will also need to buy cleaning chemicals, scrub brushes, and possibly a power washer, plus a vehicle for transporting them all to the jobsite. Look for a used van or small pickup truck with storage capacity. Charge $150–$300 per job, unless you anticipate a significant investment of time, in which case, you should charge by the hour; $50 is reasonable.

BOTTOM LINE ADVICE:

This is a classic American bootstrap-type business. Hard work will be the main ingredient in your recipe for success. This is mostly outdoor work, so expect it to be more pleasant in some seasons than in others. While this work isn't particularly difficult, it is repetitive; after a while the sameness of the task may begin to bore you. Keep in mind, too, that you'll be working with some heavy-duty cleaning chemicals. Make sure that you handle them with care and abide by federal regulations for their disposal to avoid injury or fines.

GRAPHIC DESIGNER

Startup cost:	$6,000–$10,000
Potential earnings:	$30,000–$75,000
Typical fees:	$50–$75 per hour or average retainer fees of $1,000 per month
Advertising:	Networking and cold calls, ads in business publications, direct mail, referrals, Web site
Qualifications:	Background/training in graphic design, typography, color, and print production; communication and marketing skills; artistic ability/eye for good design
Equipment needed:	High-end computer with quality graphics design and desktop publishing software, color scanner, large-screen monitor, laser printer; fax, high-speed Internet access, light table
Home business potential:	Yes
Staff required:	No
Hidden costs:	Training in new software programs, equipment updates

LOWDOWN:

Graphic design is a competitive field, but if you're skilled, creative, and able to meet sometimes stringent deadlines, you can easily stand out from the crowd. Experienced graphic designers who want to work independently can make an excellent living producing work for a wide range of clients from a home-based studio. Freelance graphic designers work for a variety of different businesses, including advertising agencies, book publishers, newspapers, and consumer product manufacturers. Even other small startup businesses are a source of projects; they need logos, letterhead, and business cards to get up and running. You can remain home-based and on your own for the duration of your career, or you can open an office and employ others to work with you. In either case, you'll need artistic and production skills as well as an ability to communicate effectively with clients. It is not enough to create designs that appeal to your own aesthetic sense; you must produce designs that will satisfy your clients, and for that, you will need to be part marketer, part psychologist.

STARTUP:

Gone are the days when a graphic designer could get by with a drawing table and a T-square. Today you will need some heady-duty computer power capable of supporting graphic design and desktop publishing software. You'll want a large-screen monitor, too, plus a color scanner and laser printer. Your office furnishings should include a light table, drawing board, and comfortable chair. Total price tag: $6,000–$10,000. Figure your charges at the $50–$75 per hour range to start. Be careful about bidding on a perproject basis; many companies will demand that you do only to take advantage of your time later by eating up the hours. If you go the per-project route, put a cap on the number of hours included in your bid; charge extra for anything above and beyond the cap.

BOTTOM LINE ADVICE:

You can make an excellent living as a graphic designer once you distinguish yourself from the competition and build up a reputation for excellence and on-time delivery. Good working relationships will lead to a satisfied group of clients who will return to you again and again. It can be difficult to bid jobs accurately and clients can sometimes be slow to pay. This is a deadline business, so working under rush conditions will often be the norm. For the most part, your working relationships will.be pleasant ones, but occasionally you will run across a customer you simply can't seem to please; making the decision to cut your losses in such a case may be painful, but could turn out to be more cost-effective in the end.

ADVICE FROM THE EXPERTS

What sets your business apart from others like it?

Kelvin Oden, owner of Oh Snap! Design in Brooklyn, New York, says he's had to pay his dues to get where he is. "On the positive side, I'm a young company and can work without limitation or restriction. I can go against the norm."

Things you couldn't do without:

A computer, top-of-the-line laser printer, and clients are all Oden says he needs to survive.

Marketing tips/advice:

"The most important thing is to build really good relationships with your clients. If they're comfortable with you as a person, they'll come back to you."

If you had to do it all over again . . .

"I wouldn't change anything . . . I'm extremely happy doing what I'm doing."

GREETING CARD SENDER

Startup cost:	$5,000–$10,000
Potential earnings:	$20,000–$30,000
Typical fees:	$2–$3 per card
Advertising:	Direct mail, Yellow Pages, networking, business publications
Qualifications:	Highly organized, good time-management skills
Equipment needed:	Computer with database and labeling software, laser printer, fax, phone, greeting card sample books or brochures
Home business potential:	Yes
Staff required:	No
Hidden costs:	Postage can be tricky, as can untimely price increases from vendors

LOWDOWN:

In this age of electronic communication, a personalized piece of mail really stands out. Busy executives barely have the time to run personal errands of a critical nature, let alone send out holiday greetings to their full list of customers or birthday cards to their most important clients. That's where you come in. As a professional greeting card sender, you will develop a database of card recipients for as many clients as you can muster (and adequately handle)—then mail the cards to everyone on the list. It sounds quite simple, really, and it is—except that you need to be exceptionally skilled at organization and time management to be able to stay on top of every holiday, birthday, special occasion, and company announcement that comes along. Buy a software program that features a large calendar that can hold many events. Better yet, buy a software organizer with an alarm system to remind you of your deadlines. The success of your business will depend not only on the quality of what you send out, but, more importantly, on your ability to stay on track. Collect brochures and/or samples from greeting card companies and have a wide assortment available to show your customers; offer competitively priced package deals to snag the big contracts that pay better than piecemeal assignments.

STARTUP:

Your startup costs will primarily cover the computer system (about $3,000) you'll need to maintain mailing lists and customer information. Expect to spend another $2,000 or so on advertising. Your charges will vary, but will likely be around $2–$3 per card. Add on a database maintenance fee to cover periodic updates.

BOTTOM LINE ADVICE:

Since mailing cards is your business, the best way to market is by direct mail; send creative announcements to businesses on your "hit" list, inviting them to do business with you in the same manner you would extend a wedding invitation. The more creative you are, the more likely you'll be to win their business.

ADVICE FROM THE EXPERTS

What sets your business apart from others like it?
"I feel my company best helps businesses maintain contact with their clients and customers," says Jo Adamczyk, owner of Cards in the Mail in Akron, Ohio. She says that the most interesting and challenging aspects of her business are acquiring customers and explaining her business.

Things you couldn't do without:
Computer, high-quality laser printer, fax machine, and telephone.

Marketing tips/advice:
"It takes time to build business and there is no profit while you are building. Networking will ultimately help you achieve a profitable customer level, as will sending cards of your own to potential customers on a regular basis."

If you had to do it all over again . . .
"I would better identify my target market. Also, I would offer complete packages that companies could purchase in order to bring each client to a more profitable level."

HARDWOOD FLOOR REFINISHER

Startup cost:	$5,000–$12,000
Potential earnings:	$40,000–$65,000
Typical fees:	$2–$2.25 per square foot; add a surcharge for added services like dark stains
Advertising:	Yellow Pages; newspaper ads; fliers in older neighborhoods where houses are likely to have hardwood floors; networking with interior designers, remodeling contractors, and home improvement stores; referrals
Qualifications:	Knowledge of wood, including ability to recognize dryness and moisture; experience/skill in sanding, use of heavy equipment, and finishes; ability to move furniture and lift heavy loads
Equipment needed:	Drum floor sander, small rotary sander, and buffer with steel wool pads; paint rollers and brushes; polyurethanes, varnish, and wood stains
Home business potential:	Yes
Staff required:	No
Hidden costs:	Equipment maintenance and repair, materials, vehicle expenses

LOWDOWN:

In the early 1900s, the heavy carpeting that covered hardwood floors in fine homes was a sign of wealth; if you didn't cover your floors with carpeting, it was because you couldn't afford to. Today, the situation is quite the opposite. Hardwood floors are highly prized these days. Buyers of new homes specifically ask their builders to install wood flooring; those who buy older homes rip up the carpeting to expose it. As a result, there's plenty of work out there for a skilled hardwood floor refinisher, just don't expect this job to be easy or fun. As anyone who's ever handled a drum floor sander or dealt with the dust it leaves behind will tell you, this is hard, hot, messy work. But it's also quite gratifying to watch as a dark, dingy hardwood floor is restored to its former beauty.

STARTUP:

You can't refinish hardwood floors without the right equipment, in particular a drum floor sander; you'll also need a small rotary sander and buffer, plus a vehicle large enough to haul it all around in. Expect to spend around $10,000 for your equipment and supplies, plus another $2,000 or so for advertising and promotion. Print up a healthy stack of fliers and leave them on doorsteps in neighborhoods where the homes and apartment buildings are old enough to have hardwood floors in need of your services; you may be surprised how quickly your phone starts to ring. Once you get a few jobs to your credit, the referrals are likely to come pouring in. Make sure that your van has your business name and phone number prominently displayed so, when you're in working in one house, the neighbors in others know it and can take note.

BOTTOM LINE ADVICE:

Hardwood floor refinishing is good, honest work, but it's not exactly glamorous. In the process of restoring a floor, you will work up a sweat and get very dirty, but you'll also be appreciated and well-paid. Few homeowners will quibble about your prices when they see what it takes to do this job!

HAULING SERVICE

Startup cost:	$5,000–$15,000
Potential earnings:	$20,000–$40,000
Typical fees:	$30–$75 per haul (depending on size and content)
Advertising:	Yellow Pages, community newspapers, coupon books, direct mail
Qualifications:	Physical strength and stamina; possibly hazardous waste certification
Equipment needed:	Hauling vehicle (preferably the largest you can afford); dollies and straps/ropes; work gloves
Home business potential:	Yes
Staff required:	Yes (it often takes more than one person to load/unload the truck or lift heavy items)
Hidden costs:	Insurance, workers' compensation, equipment maintenance

LOWDOWN:

People are always looking to get rid of things and you can help them do it. if you have a large enough vehicle and the physical strength and/or manpower to lift heavy loads, you can haul just about anything—from dead trees and ratty old furniture to broken appliances and leftover construction materials. The only restrictions that might apply would be those concerning hazardous materials or waste products—for these items, you'll need to have training and certification with regard to safe disposal and Environmental Protection Agency (EPA) regulations. Don't expect this to be easy work, but do expect it to be straightforward: You get the call, you pick up the load, you deliver it to a designated area. Not too difficult, right? Except that your knowledge of what can go where (i.e., appliances containing freon can't just be dumped into any old landfill) needs to be up-to-date, and your ability to work on-call needs to be top-notch. You must be dependable in this business if you want to make it work, because you only get paid when you show up and if you don't arrive within a specified period of time, your potential customers will call the next guy on their list.

STARTUP:

Most of your startup expenses ($5,000–$10,000) will go toward the purchase of a used vehicle and its related upkeep. You may want to consider leasing a truck at first, until you get a feel for the business and decide if it's for you. If you work hard and promote yourself well via the Yellow Pages and some low-cost classified ads in newspapers and "shoppers," you can easily make $20,000–$30,000 charging $30–$75 per haul.

BOTTOM LINE ADVICE:

You could make a decent enough living doing this type of work, but keep in mind that it may mean working in hazardous environments or inclement weather. Pack dozens of warm gloves for those cold days and lots of bottled water for summertime heat and humidity.

HERBAL PRODUCTS DISTRIBUTOR

Startup cost:	$5,000–$10,000
Potential earnings:	$25,000–$35,000
Typical fees:	$25–$75 per herbal product package
Advertising:	Direct mail, networking, trade shows
Qualifications:	Sales ability, basic business and marketing skills
Equipment needed:	Phone, vehicle
Home business potential:	Yes
Staff required:	No
Hidden costs:	Liability, possible licensing fees, vehicle expenses

LOWDOWN:

More and more health-conscious Americans are looking to herbal products as healthy alternatives to traditional medications, for everything from energy-boosting to sinus troubles. You will purchase a distributorship of established herbal products, then market them to a predetermined list of potential clients (or perhaps come up with a list of your own). From sports-minded professionals and fitness fans to working moms and health-conscious seniors, your clients will cover a wide range of humanity, all with varying levels of open-mindedness to your products. The biggest hurdle you'll have to overcome may well be the negative, fad-like perceptions of the health food and herbal nutrition industry; you'll need to provide detailed information regarding the features and benefits of using your products as opposed to others with seemingly similar claims that can't be substantiated. Your product line could include herbs in pill, tablet, or drink mix form. In all cases, don't make claims you can't back up or try to sell any one of them as "wonder drugs." Consumers aren't easily hoodwinked these days and the more cynical ones are sure to speak up and tell their friends.

STARTUP:

To get started in this business, you'll need to put down some investment capital or make an outright distributorship purchase of anywhere from $5,000–$10,000. Most of your business will come as the result of cold calls and referrals, so you needn't worry about a hefty advertising budget. Pounding the pavement is what counts here. With persistence and some aggressive marketing on your part, you could make $25,000–$35,000 per year.

BOTTOM LINE ADVICE:

This is a hard way to make a living, unless you're lucky enough to find a specialty health food store willing to stock your product and let you collect a percentage of the sales. If you aren't successful in selling to a built-in market, you'll have to do it customer by customer, and that can take an infinite amount of time. Don't expect to be making big bucks at this anytime soon.

HOME ENTERTAINMENT SYSTEM INSTALLATION AND SERVICE

Startup cost:	$5,000–$10,000
Potential earnings:	$35,000–$50,000
Typical fees:	$20–$45 per hour for labor; parts are billed at cost
Advertising:	Classified ads, entertainment magazines and newspaper sections, referrals, neighborhood fliers, direct mail, networking with local dealers and mass market stores
Qualifications:	Electronics skill, knowledge of entertainment systems operation and hookups
Equipment needed:	Tools, cell phone, vehicle
Home business potential:	Yes
Staff required:	No
Hidden costs:	Vehicle maintenance

LOWDOWN:

Today's home entertainment systems are nothing short of amazing—but only if they're operating properly. Simply getting them installed is beyond the skills of many people, taking one component out so that it can be delivered to a store for repair is downright impossible. Just think about all those people who had a VCR for years, yet never taped a favorite television show because they simply couldn't figure out how; now they're having an equally tough time grappling with their new DVD players. What these technologically challenged folks need is someone like you who understands home entertainment systems and can help them put theirs together and then keep it running right. As a home entertainment system installation and service person, you have a ready-made market in the dozens of people who bring their plasma TVs, surround-sound speakers, and DVD players home in boxes and then don't know what to do. Every successful job you complete is sure to lead to referrals.

STARTUP:

You'll need tools, a small inventory of parts, and a van to haul everything around in. Carry your cell phone, so that you'll be readily available for "emergency" calls.

BOTTOM LINE ADVICE:

Referrals from individual customers will take you far, but establishing a relationship with a dealer or two for service and repairs on the systems they sell should keep you working steadily. As more and more families purchase high-end equipment purely for entertainment, you should have no lack of business, especially if the components are purchased at mass market outlets, or even by Internet/mail order. The purchaser who boasts he can set the system up himself may well soon be calling on you for both the setup and subsequent repairs. Your electronics know-how should easily find a ready market.

HOME-BASED BUSINESS CONSULTANT

Startup cost:	$5,000–$10,000
Potential earnings:	$30,000–$50,000
Typical fees:	One-time consultation fee of $125–$200 or $50–$75 per hour
Advertising:	Networking with entrepreneurial assistance organizations (such as Service Corps of Retired Executives), Yellow Pages, newspapers, presentations on starting a home-based business for community organizations and women's groups, teach courses on starting a business
Qualifications:	Business degree and/or home-based entrepreneurial experience
Equipment needed:	Computer, printer, fax, Internet access, copier, pager or cell phone
Home business potential:	Yes
Staff required:	No
Hidden costs:	Slow payment for your services as many beginning entrepreneurs have cash-flow problems

LOWDOWN:

Home-based businesses represent a significant segment of the burgeoning entrepreneurial marketplace—and you can cash in on the ground floor if you have the expertise needed to help a home-based business get off on the right foot. Your biggest challenge will likely be locating those who are thinking about working from home; there's no directory you can consult for names and phone numbers. One excellent way to find clients is through online services and work-at-home computer forums, where you can offer your expert advice free of charge in an effort to get your name and company information out there. You can also comb the business, professional, and entrepreneurial groups that meet in your community for potential clients. You might also consider offering a class on starting a business (your students could become clients!) or make presentations on home-based businesses to community organizations and women's groups. Once you establish a client base, you will sit down with each individually to discuss topics of interest to his or her particular business situation. For one, that might mean help with selecting a computer system, for another, mapping out a marketing strategy or full-blown business plan. To succeed at this, you need to be well-rounded in your realm of experience, as you'll be called upon for advice on everything from finances and sales projections to setting up an efficient workspace and purchasing supplies. Make sure that you focus heavily on the types of equipment a home office might need, as well as tips on balancing work and family life under the same roof. Most home offices only launch once, so your likelihood of having repeat customers is pretty low. You will have to stay on top of things in your community and be constantly on the lookout for new prospects, many of whom will come via referral, in order to make a living as a home-based business consultant.

STARTUP:

Your launch fees ($5,000–$10,000) will go primarily to cover your own basic office setup and marketing expenses, including a Yellow Pages listing and a few carefully placed newspaper ads. Expect to earn $30,000–$45,000 once you get established; charge a one-time consultation fee of $125–$200, or $50–$65 per hour for services as needed.

BOTTOM LINE ADVICE:

While it may be interesting and even exciting to be in on the ground floor of an innovative young company's beginning, due to cash flow, you may have to wait a while to secure payment for your services. If you can charge up front (consider accepting credit cards), you'll have a much better chance of collecting what your services are worth and improving your own cash flow in the process.

HUMAN RESOURCES SERVICES

Startup cost:	$5,000–$10,000
Potential earnings:	$40,000–$70,000
Typical fees:	$35–$50 per hour
Advertising:	Referrals, membership in trade associations and business groups, business periodicals, cold calls
Qualifications:	A proven track record of effectiveness in human resources department management for a medium-sized or larger company, degree in related field, excellent selling skills and ability to interact with people
Equipment needed:	Computer; printer; word processing, database, and spreadsheet software; desktop publishing software if you'll be preparing employee handbooks; Internet access; fax; cell phone; marketing materials
Home business potential:	Yes
Staff required:	No
Hidden costs:	Errors and omissions insurance, nonreimbursable costs for development of informational materials for clients

LOWDOWN:

If you have a proven track record in successful human resources department management, providing human resources services on a freelance basis is an excellent business except for one thing . . . the enormous marketing efforts that will be required. Getting your foot in the door of a business will be really tough. But once you're established, the ongoing relationships you develop with clients should ensure a steady income, year to year. If you can get your sales message through to growing companies with expanding workforces and no human resources departments, you can begin building your business. Some consultants specialize in one area of this complex field, such as developing, writing, and updating employee handbooks. Others function more as recruiters, identifying potential job candidates and assisting in the hiring process. The training side of human resources work can be marketed effectively if you can show how your presentations are tightly linked to the client company's missions and the specific job responsibilities of their workforce.

STARTUP:

You'll be working on-site at your client companies, so your own office can be more functional than impressive; approximately $5,000 should get you up and running. A computer system, with word processing, database, spreadsheet, and possibly, desktop publishing software, is vital. Potential earnings of $40,000–$70,000 are possible.

BOTTOM LINE ADVICE:

Many business owners just fumble along with the human resources challenges of their organizations until a crisis forces them to think about how they could do a better job. How can you present your services to these busy people as the solution to their problems and not just a fuzzy, fluffy, feel-good waste of time? This is a marketing challenge all right, but one in which you can apply your track record of success to support your claims. Referrals will probably be your best sources of business.

IMPORTING/EXPORTING

Startup cost:	$5,000–$15,000
Potential earnings:	$60,000–$100,000
Typical fees:	Commission on each transaction (typically 2–3 percent on consumer goods, 5–15 percent on software and other proprietary items)
Advertising:	International business publications, direct mail, referrals, Web site
Qualifications:	Extensive knowledge of foreign business operations, including letters of credit and legal issues; familiarity with U.S. regulations regarding import/export of products; Internet proficiency; verbal and written communication skills; patience; foreign language fluency would be helpful
Equipment needed:	Computer with high-speed Internet access; fax, copier, scanner, cell phone, reference books
Home business potential:	Yes
Staff required:	No
Hidden costs:	Insurance, telephone charges, travel expenses

LOWDOWN:

Import/export businesses have been on the rise since the late 1980s, when U.S. companies began to benefit from the dollar dropping against foreign currencies and foreign countries became more receptive to the idea of doing business with Americans. Now, with the global marketplace open for business on the Internet, there have never been greater opportunities for folks who have high-quality or high-demand products to sell to other countries. You can import or export everything from ball bearings to furniture. At first, this may seem like a no-brainer—just call on foreigners to talk about business exchanges. In reality, however, the import/export business is quite challenging, not to mention exceedingly competitive now that virtually anyone with Internet access can announce that they're open for business. Nevertheless, if you are willing to spend the time it will take to stay on top of economic developments in other countries, and have a knack for getting along with people of different cultural backgrounds than yours, this can be an exciting—and potentially quite profitable—business.

STARTUP:

Your startup costs ($5,000–$15,000) will go toward the purchase of a computer with high-speed Internet access and fax, plus laser printer. Since you'll be dealing with clients around the world, your phone bills are likely to be pretty expensive; shop around for the long-distance plan that offers the best international rates. Thanks to advances in technology, international business can largely be conducted over the Internet these days. There may be times, however, when you need to meet face-to-face with foreign clients, so be sure to factor the cost of some overseas travel into your initial business plan. An import/export business takes time to build, but if you establish good connections and deal in high-quality goods that are in demand, you could be earning a six-figure income within three years.

BOTTOM LINE ADVICE:

This type of business seems like an easy way to become wealthy; in reality, it takes time and effort to build the kinds of contacts you'll need to make a profit at this. If you go into this business, make sure you have adequate living expenses set aside to carry you for a while.

INCENTIVE PROGRAMS/ PROMOTIONAL MATERIAL

Startup cost:	$6,000–$10,000
Potential earnings:	$45,000–$75,000
Typical fees:	$35 per hour or a flat fee of $300–$700 per incentive program
Advertising:	Business periodicals, trade journals, memberships in business and community groups, direct mail, referrals
Qualifications:	Extensive experience in advertising, promotions; proven track record in structuring successful incentive programs
Equipment needed:	Computer with graphic arts capability, laser printer, Internet access, fax, cell phone
Home business potential:	Yes
Staff required:	No
Hidden costs:	Development of your own promotional materials, supplies, software upgrades, association dues

LOWDOWN:

Effective incentives and promotions require skill and experience to produce. Everyone wants something new, something that works like magic, something that's cost-effective. Your creativity in designing a program that harmonizes with the mission, goals, and corporate image of your clients will be central to your success in this enterprise. Yes, this business can be fun. But it's also high-risk and marketing-intensive. People do not really value the jacket or mug you give them so much as they like the feeling of being "in" that promotional products represent. This is a business for those who have a good sense of what's currently "cool," what people want to own. Your expertise may make you responsible for incentive products all the way from conception through manufacturing and/or delivery (if you choose).

STARTUP:

Client presentations are very important, and the best ones require a lot of time and effort to prepare. Your support systems need to be adequate from the start so that you can present your services in a professional, appealing manner; expect to spend $6,000 for the necessary computer, software, and peripherals. Potential earnings can reach $45,000–$75,000.

BOTTOM LINE ADVICE:

Incentive programs can take many forms. You may specialize in internal motivation, focusing on programs that recognize and reward employee achievement. Or your work may assist companies in reaching out to their customers with special incentives and promotional programs from time to time. You'll need good relationships with distributors and with the business community in general as you build your reputation for effectiveness and creativity.

INFORMATION CONSULTANT

Startup cost:	$5,000–$11,000
Potential earnings:	$50,000–$75,000
Typical fees:	$35–$125 per hour
Advertising:	Trade groups, public speaking, writing articles for local and trade publications, networking and referrals
Qualifications:	Interest in almost any type of fact or question, skill in database research and knowledge of the most efficient Web surfing techniques, ability to market yourself, patience and persistence, organizational and time-management skills
Equipment needed:	Computer with large hard drive and plenty of memory; high-speed Internet access; laser printer; word processing, database, and spreadsheet software; ergonomic office furniture, fax, copier, scanner
Home business potential:	Yes
Staff required:	No
Hidden costs:	Memberships, equipment updates, subscriptions to online databases

LOWDOWN:

Managing information is not something most businesspeople include as a line item in their annual budgets—but they should. Every organization accumulates mountains of data each day, and just about every one of them could use some help sorting through it. Scientific data to support R&D efforts, articles on the activities of competitors, background information for lawsuits—these are just some of the types of information companies need most. Sometimes they have the data, but don't have time to distill it; more often, they simply don't know where to find the facts they need. As an information consultant, you will locate what they need and put it in a form they can readily access. Your sources will include online databases, reference books, periodicals and trade journals, even interviews with experts in the field. You can offer your services as a generalist or specialize in serving a particular type of client/industry or in finding a specific type of data. And you certainly won't lack for potential places to sell your services or findings. Take demographic information, for example. Marketers, advertisers, and city planners, to name just a few, are likely potential clients. Or consider a subject like recent research on addiction issues. Health care professionals, counselors, hospital administrators, court officials, law enforcement agencies, and many others may be interested in what you find. As an information consultant, you are limited only by your creativity in pulling information together, then presenting it in a way that best to serves your client.

STARTUP:

Much of the information you seek is available online and you will spend the majority of your time at your computer searching for it. You will want a computer system that has plenty of power and memory, plus high-speed Internet access for maximum efficiency and faster downloads. You'll need word processing, database, and spreadsheet software, too, as well as a laser printer for preparing your reports. And since you'll be spending hours in front of your terminal, don't forget ergonomic furniture, especially a comfortable chair. Plan on spending $5,000–$11,000 to get up and running. Market your services through networking, referrals, and public speaking engagements; you could easily earn $50,000 or more.

BOTTOM LINE ADVICE:

You'll need to track information relentlessly, follow many tangents, and look for the subtle clues buried in what at first looks to be irrelevant material. At the completion of your search, you'll have piles of paper and you may find that pulling it all together is tedious, but at the same time, exciting too. There's a lot of talk about information overload in our country these days, but we're missing the point. What we really have is information disorganization. Beware of giving your client too much information. It is your ability to sift through reams of data and make sense of it that adds value to your clients' business efforts and will put cold, hard cash in your pocket.

ADVICE FROM THE EXPERTS

What sets your business apart from others like it?

Timothy P. Baynham, Esq., president of TPB Information in Winston-Salem, North Carolina, says his business is known as the "public records specialist. We separate ourselves from others by concentrating on providing the highest quality public records report for the least money. My company repackages information and tries to make it easy to comprehend."

Things you couldn't do without:

A computer, laser printer, and fax machine are essential components to Baynham's business.

Marketing tips/advice:

"Despite your basic assumptions, most information is not free. You'll need to be on the Internet a great deal. Most people are still not aware of the vast amounts of information that is available through fee-based online databases. Clients cannot buy something they don't know exists—and that is a marketing problem for you."

If you had to do it all over again . . .

"The biggest lesson I've learned is that less is more. When I started, I wanted to show clients every single thing I could get online, hoping they would fall in love with the idea of unlimited information. I now focus on problem-solving; this approach is much more effective, and you don't spend as much on catalogs, copies, etc."

INSURANCE AGENT

Startup cost:	$10,000–$15,000
Potential earnings:	$45,000–$60,000
Typical fees:	Commissions range from 20 to 35 percent
Advertising:	Cold-calling, membership in community groups, radio and newspaper ads, community publications, billboards, direct mail
Qualifications:	Training and licensing, experience, outstanding selling ability, affiliation with a particular company
Equipment needed:	Computer; word processing, database, and spreadsheet software; printer, copier, fax, and cell phone
Home business potential:	Yes
Staff required:	No
Hidden costs:	Membership dues, errors and omissions insurance

LOWDOWN:

As a single agent, you will need to develop a focus or specialty to set yourself apart in the crowded field of insurance sales. One possibility is business insurance, with a special focus on insuring home businesses. Dedicated service to your customers is essential in distinguishing your business from the competition. You will be working closely with individuals and small organizations, and you will depend heavily on your financial expertise and your ability to listen to the wants and needs of the buyer. If you can find a way to help people and companies manage their risk appropriately (which is what insurance is all about) without making them feel pushed or confused, you will be performing a useful service. You will be earning your agent's commission many times over.

STARTUP:

Knowledge and experience are far more important than equipment, although you will need a computer system that can be networked to your corporate headquarters if you're affiliated or own a franchise. In that case, your startup costs will be considerably higher (potentially $50,000–$75,000 for training, licensing the company name, and heavy advertising), but you'll get the support you need instead of having to go it alone. However, should you decide to go solo, you can expect to spend between $10,000–$15,000 for your basic office setup, some advertising, and the fees you'll need for training and to take your exam. Either way, your commissions should net 20 to 35 percent and ultimately lead to an income potential of $45,000–$60,000 or more.

BOTTOM LINE ADVICE:

Being an insurance agent can be tough—but people make fun of lawyers and accountants, too. Once you become established, you will have an excellent business that can support your family and possibly make you rich. Being successful in this type of enterprise requires excellent selling skills, up-to-date information on financial issues, persistence, and many hours of hard work. You'll be using people skills and numerical facility intensively. Tenacity and determination are your most important assets; you have to be willing to hang in there—through the first 100 sales calls all of which end in no if that's what it takes—because number 101 just might be the break you're waiting for.

INVENTORY CONTROL

Startup cost:	$5,000- $12,000
Potential earnings:	$35,000–$50,000
Typical fees:	$50–$100 per hour, or $3–$5 per thousand dollars of merchandise
Advertising:	Business periodicals, direct mail, memberships in trade groups
Qualifications:	Inventory experience, efficiency, excellent organizational and people management skills
Equipment needed:	Handheld or laptop computer; desktop computer with inventory and data collection software, Internet access, fax, and printer; pagers or cell phones
Home business potential:	Yes
Staff required:	Yes
Hidden costs:	Record-keeping materials, staff wages

LOWDOWN:

Your inventory control service is another one of those businesses that have grown up in response to the needs of today's downsized corporation. Taking inventory requires many hours of labor that can no longer be wrung out of an already overburdened corporate staff. Instead of handling this chore in-house, the work is outsourced to you and your group of part-time employees, who track and record the necessary information for your clients. By applying people exactly where and when they are needed, rather than keeping them on the payroll, your client gets the information he or she needs and saves time and money in the process. Your ability to manage people and data is what enables you to perform these services in a cost-effective manner.

STARTUP:

The actual work is done at the client's worksite. However, you'll still need to equip your own office for the effective management of people and projects. For purposes of conducting the inventory on-site, you'll want a laptop computer or handheld units, and since you'll need to generate data in electronic and/or printed form for transmission to head offices, you'll want a printer and desktop computer with inventory and data collection software back in your office. Total tab: $5,000–$12,000.

BOTTOM LINE ADVICE:

The ability to convince businesspeople to trust you with this vital aspect of their record keeping will be necessary for the launching of a successful inventory control service business. Higher-level management skills are an absolute must. You must track person-hours, data, and client needs accurately and inexpensively in order to succeed in this type of enterprise. The potential market is broad; your challenge will come in reaching it.

INVISIBLE FENCING SALES/ INSTALLATION

Startup cost:	$10,000–$15,000
Potential earnings:	$35,000–$50,000
Typical fees:	$8–$10 per square yard
Advertising:	Newspapers, Yellow Pages, direct mail, fliers, referrals from vets
Qualifications:	Salesmanship, ability to do light digging, some electrical competence
Equipment needed:	Pickup truck, digging tools, inventory of fencing supplies and transmitters
Home business potential:	Yes
Staff required:	No
Hidden costs:	Wear and tear on vehicle

LOWDOWN:

Invisible fencing is growing increasingly popular as more people have dogs but less time to walk them. Many homeowners don't want to solve this problem by making their yards into fortresses. A fence tall enough to keep in a big dog and tough enough to block a digging dog can be a real eyesore, and is, in fact, prohibited in many communities that are governed by homeowners' association rules. Here is your market. The invisible fence works like this: An electric line is buried a few inches beneath the soil around the perimeter of the yard and a transmitter is placed on Fido's collar; whenever the dog tries to cross that line, the transmitter delivers a slight shock. It's not enough to harm the animal, but just enough to remind him that he's supposed to stay within his own yard.

STARTUP:

You will need some inventory of fencing supplies and transmitters, plus digging equipment, which could cost as much as $15,000. But if you're competitive and charge between $8–$10 per square yard, you should be able to make a sizable profit. Network with vets; they're often the first to know when a dog is "straying." And since your product can't be seen, post a small sign advertising your services in your client's yard during the installation and for a week or two after the job is complete. A line like "Invisible fence training in progress by [your business name and number]" may be enough to pique the curiosity of passersby.

BOTTOM LINE ADVICE:

Your charm and ability to convey a sense of caring for the welfare of your customers' pets will make you successful in this business. Some people start by going door to door, but you may find the negative reactions from some homeowners to an unexpected knock on the door disheartening. Referrals are a better approach. Talk to veterinarians and be sure to leave a stack of your business cards behind.

IRRIGATION SERVICES

Startup cost:	$5,000–$10,000
Potential earnings:	$15,000–$30,000
Typical fees:	$100–$200 per hour; $500+ per day, or charge per job
Advertising:	Newspapers, Yellow Pages, direct mail, interest-group meetings, seminars
Qualifications:	Knowledge of irrigation systems and plants; mechanical knowledge
Equipment needed:	Drip irrigation systems, tools for installation
Home business potential:	Yes
Staff required:	No
Hidden costs:	Permission of local authorities, business insurance

LOWDOWN:

Your business will be directed at two distinct market segments: individual gardeners and commercial operations. Many individuals love plants and want their premises to look beautiful and well maintained, but they lack the time to water their gardens on a regular basis. You can set up a drip irrigation system that will replace hours of fussing with muddy hoses and bulky sprinklers. Once the drip system is set up properly, it requires little attention, making it ideal for you and for your customer. Another potential source of business are homes that already have irrigation systems, but need new ones in order to deal with water runoff and avoid watery basements.

On the commercial side, garden and nursery operations have a large investment in plant materials; their trees, shrubs, and plants must be kept in peak condition to be salable. It would take many people with hoses to keep these plants healthy and with the rising cost of labor in most communities, a drip irrigation system will make business sense to these establishments.

STARTUP:

You will need an inventory of drip irrigation materials and the tools to set up these systems. A pickup truck or van will allow you to deliver the bulky materials to your customers' locations. Bill out at an hourly rate of $100–$200, a daily rate of $500 or more, or a per-job rate based on your estimate of the time involved.

BOTTOM LINE ADVICE:

This is a great business for a friendly person with a love of the outdoors and growing things, and a knack for tinkering with machinery. Drip irrigation systems are not heavy or high-tech, but setting each one up will require some customization to suit the specific location. In many geographic areas your business will be seasonal, so to fill out the year, you may want to add a service that complements irrigation, such as snow removal. There is limited profit potential in this kind of enterprise, but you may find that the steady income from regular customers compensates for the modest return.

LAWYER

Startup cost:	$5,000–$15,000
Potential earnings:	$50,000–$100,000+
Typical fees:	$125 per hour outside of major cities; $150–$250 per hour in large metropolitan areas
Advertising:	Yellow Pages, networking, referrals, newspaper and television ads (some states may have restrictions on attorney advertising), organization memberships
Qualifications:	Law degree, persistence, people skills
Equipment needed:	Office space decorated in a professional (but not necessarily ostentatious) manner, access to law library, computer, Internet access, fax, laser printer
Home business potential:	Yes
Staff required:	Not initially (if you can type)
Hidden costs:	Drain on your billable time from people wanting free advice, insurance, support services

LOWDOWN:

Abraham Lincoln set up his own law firm, why can't you? It has been fashionable in some legal circles to mock the "single shingle" lawyer, but opportunities to join huge firms right out of law school—and make big bucks—just aren't as common as they used to be. One way to make use of the degree you struggled so long and hard to earn is to start your own business. You determine the clientele, you develop the specialty, you reap the rewards. But unless you can afford to hire a secretary, you also answer the phone, do the typing, and mail out the bills. Single shingle lawyers may decide to focus on a particular legal specialty, but they typically start out as generalists. Can you find a way to advise small businesses in your area? Are you able to help wealthy individuals write their wills and plan their estates? Can you deal with the animosity that often accompanies divorce and help manage the separation process through mediation and negotiation? If you answered yes to any of these questions, you can give up the frustration of trying to land a job with a big firm and make a go of your single-shingle operation.

STARTUP:

Many solo practitioners share office space, support staff, and the other necessary costs of running a business with one another. You can certainly work out of your home, but, at some point, you may need a conference room in which to meet your clients and a place to produce and store the extensive paperwork that goes along with the practice of law. Expect to spend at least $5,000 setting up your office and its contents (include enough money for a powerful computer and high-speed Internet access to make online searches less time-consuming). You can bill out at around $125 to start; more if you live in a large metropolitan area. And unless you want to do the typing yourself, be sure to set aside some funds for support services.

BOTTOM LINE ADVICE:

Probably the most important factor in your success will be your connections to the community you hope to serve. Let's be honest, lawyers don't enjoy the best reputation among average folks, and you're going to have to struggle against this stereotype. Building trust is such a challenge these days that you will have little chance for success unless you start with a network of people who already know and like you. Hopefully, you'll come to be known in certain circles as the helpful, skilled lawyer to go to. Another difficulty you are likely to face has to do with your fees; it's not that you're overpriced, it's that some people think they're entitled to get legal advice for nothing. Just about everyone needs a lawyer at one time or another, but many are reluctant to pay what your experience, expertise, and skills are worth. If you are to survive on your own, you'll have to keep an eagle eye on your billable hours, then send out the bills and make sure they're collected. This can be a tedious, time-consuming process, but it's essential. One suggestion: Consider offering prepaid legal services, which work much like insurance; clients pay a monthly fee whether they use your services or not.

ADVICE FROM THE EXPERTS

What sets your business apart from others like it?
Stanford M. Altschul, sole practitioner based in Long Island, New York, says he picked a niche and set about servicing it with free information (in the form of marketing materials such as brochures and newsletters). "I market myself regularly to my clients, keeping my name in front of them via newsletters, brochures, and other direct mail pieces I produce myself."

Things you couldn't do without:
Altschul could not do without a computer and laser printer, telephone, copier, and fax machine.

Marketing tips/advice:
"You should definitely be networking with certain industries that will bring you referral business, such as accounting, real estate, and banking. All of these professionals are in regular contact with those who need your services."

If you had to do it all over again . . .
"I made a mistake in being in a partnership that wasn't a good partnership . . . It took me over twenty years to figure out that I prefer working alone."

LEGAL COST CONTROL/LITIGATION MANAGEMENT SERVICES

Startup cost:	$5,000–$10,000
Potential earnings:	$40,000–$75,000
Typical fees:	Equivalent to the prevailing fee level for lawyers in the community (for example, small firms outside of major U.S. cities charge about $125 per hour)
Advertising:	Local business associations, advertising in trade journals and business publications, networking and referrals
Qualifications:	Law or accounting degree and/or background, experience in case management and billing assessment, litigation experience
Equipment needed:	Business office, computer, Internet access, fax, word processing and spreadsheet software, printer, copier, scanner, fax
Home business potential:	No
Staff required:	No
Hidden costs:	Insurance, office rent

LOWDOWN:

The movement is under way to rein in legal costs and in particular, those pertaining to litigation. For business organizations with a small in-house legal staff or none at all, you can provide this important cost-management service. Your assessment of ongoing billing can spotlight waste, duplication of services, overbilling, and incorrect entries. This can be painstaking work, which is why it is often overlooked; busy in-house lawyers simply do not have the time to comb through the bills their organization receives from outside counsel. The economic benefit of having a service like yours perform this function should far outweigh its cost to the organization.

STARTUP:

Equipping your office to be functional and to present a professional image will be expensive ($4,000–$10,000), but necessary. This business is not the kind you can operate from a corner of your dining room; you will need to have a "real" office and you'll need to equip it with all the necessary tools of your trade—computer, software, and peripherals; copier; scanner; fax; and phone. Still, considering that you'll be able to charge around $125 an hour for your services (more, if you live in a large metropolitan area), you should be able to afford the monthly rent for professional quarters in a decent location.

BOTTOM LINE ADVICE:

This service is a creative way to utilize a background that combines legal training with financial and accounting skills. More and more lawyers are competing for the shrinking number of jobs, but few have the combination of expertise and experience that will make you a success in this tightly focused service niche. Marketing your services will be challenging as this concept is still relatively new. Allow yourself considerable time to build the business through networking and participation in business and professional associations. Keep in mind that the lawyers around town may not be too thrilled to have someone looking over their shoulders. You'll need thick skin to face up to possible negative reactions from the attorneys whose accounts you are checking.

ADVICE FROM THE EXPERTS

What sets your business apart from others like it?

Edward J. Charlton, Esq., chief operating officer of Legalgard in Philadelphia, Pennsylvania, says his company ensures that purchasers of legal services are billed fairly and reasonably. "We're the oldest and largest business of this kind, and we have a national capability."

Things you couldn't do without:

Office equipment (computer, fax, phone) and furniture are all Charlton says he couldn't do without.

Marketing tips/advice:

In this emerging field, Charlton suggests that you go in recognizing that you'll be fighting an uphill battle at times. "Dealing with law firms that refuse to change their practices is challenging," he says. "We're changing the way law firms deliver their services."

LOCK BOX SERVICE

Startup cost:	$5,000–$10,000
Potential earnings:	$35,000–$50,000
Typical fees:	$35 per box (includes one spare key)
Advertising:	Direct mail, brochures, trade journals, networking with real estate firms, construction companies, auto dealers, car rental agencies, etc.
Qualifications:	None
Equipment needed:	Lock boxes, adapters, spare keys, tools
Home business potential:	Yes
Staff required:	No
Hidden costs:	Spare keys

LOWDOWN:

This is one of those businesses that has applications to only a small market segment; not everyone needs a lock box and so your job is to be the best at servicing those in your area who do. Who are your clients? People who need to secure property or vehicles. Real estate agents, construction companies, and anyone who owns a fleet of vehicles, such as car dealers, utility companies, and car rental agencies are your likeliest customers. Although this is not a very common or for that matter obvious, service, it is a necessary and useful one for businesses that need to keep the wrong people out and let the right people in. Solicit your client industries in person and try to give them the best deal you can; if you can't budge on price, make up for it by offering the best service and follow-up care you can muster. Build relationships with your clients to obtain repeat business.

STARTUP:

Lock boxes are generally sold by gross units at $20 each; spare keys go for $6 each. At a bare minimum, your startup cost will be $5,000, not including advertising; you'll want to add another $3,000–$5,000 for a direct mail campaign, Yellow Pages listing, and selectively placed print ads. With the right contacts and a good reputation, you could earn in the neighborhood of $30,000–$45,000.

BOTTOM LINE ADVICE:

Several obstacles await you in this service business; first, it's by no means glamorous, and second, the cost of securing your initial inventory of lock boxes and keys will have to come out of your own pocket. After you've dealt with these two concerns, you can begin to enjoy the relationships that you build with your clients. You might even get to enjoy a few perks—like a good deal on a new car or being the first to hear about that gem of a house that's about to go on the market in your neighborhood. Small fringe benefits like these abound in the lock box business.

LOCKSMITH

Startup cost:	$5,000–$10,000
Potential earnings:	$20,000–$35,000
Typical fees:	Varied depending on the service; for example $1.50 per key or a per-job lock replacement fee of $15–$45
Advertising:	Direct mail, Yellow Pages, bulletin boards
Qualifications:	Mechanical aptitude, training (usually a correspondence course)
Equipment needed:	Key cutting machine, lock picking implements, product stock/supply, vehicle
Home business potential:	Yes, but check zoning regulations
Staff required:	No
Hidden costs:	Equipment maintenance costs, insurance, vehicle expenses

LOWDOWN:

You probably know that a locksmith makes keys, but did you know he or she is capable of much more? In addition to duplicating keys, you can change lock tumblers, open locked cars, pick locks, even sell new or reconditioned locking devices. This isn't the most exciting business—in fact, once you get the hang of it, locksmithing may seem downright mundane—but it's good, honest work and a necessary service as anyone who's ever been locked out of his or her house can tell you. And if you do house calls regularly enough, you might even find yourself in some interesting situations.

STARTUP:

Startup costs will vary depending on which services you choose to provide and where you decide to locate your business. Unless you have learned the trade by working alongside an experienced locksmith, you'll need to invest in a locksmith training course, either by correspondence or online. Tuition is typically just under $1,000, which includes a textbook and the keys, tools, and other items you will need to practice your newly acquired skills. Upon completion of your training, you will want to purchase a key duplicating machine and a set of blank keys to work from; if you plan on selling new locking devices, you will need to invest in some inventory. And don't forget to set aside funds for advertising; at the very least, you will want a Yellow Pages listing. Locksmithing can be a home-based business, but be sure to check your local zoning requirements before hanging your shingle, especially if you are offering key duplication services. Parking and signage can present problems in some residential neighborhoods. You may be better off with a storefront; the monthly rent ($350 and up) will likely be offset by the increased business due to greater visibility. If you intend to come to the aid of persons who are locked out of their cars or homes, you will need a vehicle to travel to the lock-out site.

BOTTOM LINE ADVICE:

This is a trust-based business; persons with criminal records need not apply, unless, of course, you intend to use your burglary experience as a springboard for providing insightful tips on how break-ins happen. Check with local law enforcement to determine any requirements or laws you need to know before launching your business. For example, should you obtain signed documents from a property owner before proceeding with a lock change?

MAID SERVICE

Startup costs:	$10,000–$20,000
Potential earnings:	$35,000–$150,000
Typical fees:	$12–$35 per hour, or $50 per room
Advertising:	Yellow Pages, local newspapers, direct mail couponing, personal contact with apartment and office building superintendents, and real estate firms
Qualifications:	Management skills, ability to motivate personnel and improve their efficiency with superior products
Equipment needed:	Mops, rags, buckets, cleaning solutions, vacuum cleaner; vehicles
Home business potential:	Yes
Staff required:	Yes
Hidden costs:	Insurance, workers' compensation, bonding

LOWDOWN:

This business can really turn a profit if you hire a crew of trustworthy employees. You can run the business from a desk in your home, if you have sales ability and the knack for managing others. Train them to clean thoroughly and efficiently, and you can earn a tidy sum. You will probably have to arrange for your employees to be bonded and insured since they will be working, unsupervised, in other people's homes and workplaces. Always follow up with the client to make sure your employees have accomplished the assigned task, and be willing to accept feedback from both clients and your cleaners in order to improve your business. It's important to offer stellar service, because word of mouth will be your best form of advertising. Overhead is relatively low if you're not buying into a franchise; once you have an established business with a steady clientele, you will be able to buy cleaning supplies in bulk.

STARTUP:

You'll spend between $10,000 and $20,000 to launch your own cleaning service, much more if you buy into one of the established franchises, which typically require an initial investment of $50,000 or more. Your startup costs will go toward cleaning equipment and supplies, plus the vehicles in which to haul everything from one jobsite to another. Charge by the hour ($12–$35) or by the room ($50) for routine cleaning services—dusting, mopping, bathroom cleaning, vacuuming. Add a surcharge for heavy-duty jobs you don't do every week, such as cleaning the oven or stripping and waxing the kitchen floor.

BOTTOM LINE ADVICE:

Make contacts with real estate agents to help new homeowners clean their house before they move in. If you do a good job, odds are they'll retain your services on a weekly basis. Set up your clients on a regular cleaning schedule—but make sure you send enough people to do each job. Your reputation depends on thorough and efficient service. Treat every household as if it were your own and always provide a written estimate for your work.

MAILING LIST SERVICE

Startup cost:	$5,000–$11,000
Potential earnings:	$40,000–$100,000 per year
Typical fees:	Vary; 15 to 25 cents per entry (name, address, city, state, Zip); about $1 per entry per year to maintain the list. Mailing out 10,000 pieces of mail could earn you $800–$1,200
Advertising:	Contacting local businesses, retailers, associations, churches, clubs, etc. to offer to maintain their mailing lists; networking in business organizations, Yellow Pages, direct mail
Qualifications:	Detailed knowledge of postal rates and regulations; computer skills; fast, accurate typing skills; ability to meet deadlines
Equipment needed:	Computer, Internet access, printer, database and specialized mailing list software, postal permits, postage meter, copier, scanner
Home business potential:	Yes
Staff required:	None
Hidden costs:	Computer backups (in the event of disaster; you don't want to have to re-create a list from scratch!)

LOWDOWN:

Much as we all complain about the amount of "junk mail" that gets dumped into our mailboxes each day, direct mail continues to be one of the most popular forms of advertising. Why? Because it works. Direct mail is big business and getting bigger, especially now that more and more people are opting to list their names on the federal government's "do not call" list for telemarketing. Companies that once relied on telemarketing to boost sales are switching to direct mail. The opportunity to succeed in running a mailing list service for the companies sending out all those materials is tremendous. Startup costs are low, the necessary skills are easy to acquire, and money is there to be made. Your business can provide: list maintenance, letter shop services (i.e.—assembling the actual mailings), list creation, list brokering, and even teaching others about mailing lists. Deciphering current postal regulations and keeping up with U.S. Postal Service changes may well be your biggest challenge. You'll need to monitor the USPS Web site and avail yourself of the many pamphlets and seminars available at your local post office to stay abreast.

STARTUP:

You're going to need a fair amount of equipment to get started in this business: a computer with Internet access, printer, mailing list and bar coding/sorting software; fax; scanner; and copier. If you elect to offer letter shop services, you will need postal permits and/or a postage meter. Expect to spend from $5,000 to $11,000 to get up and running. You can operate a mailing list service out of your home, but keep in mind, that if you are doing the actual mailing, you will need plenty of space for assembly and sorting. Charges will vary depending on the specific service. For example, for list creation/maintenance, you'll need to set two rates: a per-entry fee (usually 15 to 25 cents per name) and $1 per entry, per year, to maintain the list.

BOTTOM LINE ADVICE:

Mailing list businesses are relatively easy to start and to promote. And rather than rely on just a few key clients, you can have as large a customer base as you can handle. The actual work of creating and maintaining the lists is pretty routine, although it does require great attention to detail and accuracy. A thorough understanding of postal regulations is vitally important—and those regulations keep changing, so you must stay current. You have to be sure you know what you're doing to gain and keep your customers' business; otherwise, the minute those envelopes start bouncing back as undeliverable because of incorrect addresses or insufficient postage, your business is headed for the nearest "dead letter box."

MANAGEMENT CONSULTANT

Startup cost:	$5,000–$15,000
Potential earnings:	$30,000–$60,000 (average); some make as much as $300,000 per year
Typical fees:	Varies by market and client needs: average of $500–$1,500 per day (charge by hour, day, or job)
Advertising:	Networking, referrals, creating audio- or videotapes showing your skills, ads in professional organizations' magazines and newsletters, brochures, direct mail, Web site
Qualifications:	Technical knowledge, expertise, and experience; good problem-solving skills and people skills; excellent communication skills (written and oral)
Equipment needed:	Computer, printer, business software, Internet access, fax, cell phone, reference books
Home business potential:	Yes
Staff required:	No
Hidden costs:	Errors and omissions insurance, continuing education to keep your skills up-to-date (techniques, technology, etc.), travel expenses

LOWDOWN:

Professional management consulting remains a fast-growing field as leaner U.S. companies increasingly rely on outside consultants, especially in the areas of government compliance and the introduction of new technologies. Consultants provide many services, from strategy-planning and implementation to market analysis and problem-solving. Many who choose to become consultants have top-level skills and many years of firsthand management experience. They want the freedom and greater variety of working for themselves and recognize the world of opportunity that exists in assisting smaller, entrepreneurial companies get their businesses off the ground.

STARTUP:

Startup costs will vary according to the requirements of the specialty you choose. No matter what you decide, however, you will require the basic office and computer equipment (costing as little as $2,500); however, depending on the quality and extent of computer equipment needed, this figure could reach $12,000. You will also need to budget a minimum of $2,000 for continuing education, organizational dues, and reference books.

BOTTOM LINE ADVICE:

To succeed in this business, you must first analyze yourself: Decide what sorts of problems you can solve for a client, based on your background and expertise. Research the companies (or types of companies) to which you might want to offer your services in order to help you discover needs you can fill. Network with every contact you have in your target areas. Remember, however, that not everyone with good technical skills can be a successful consultant. You need excellent listening and counseling abilities—and patience. Not only does it take time to "grow" your consulting business, but it takes considerable time to determine if your efforts have paid off for the client. Meeting the challenges of working as a consultant can be financially rewarding. You will have the opportunity to work on a wide variety of projects and enjoy helping clients find creative, successful solutions to their problems.

ADVICE FROM THE EXPERTS

What sets your business apart from others like it?

Norma J. Rist, owner of the Boardroom Group based in Akron, Ohio, says her business assists women business owners to become clear about their goals and to achieve them in a shorter period of time and in an easier way by providing resources and business information in a group setting.

Things you couldn't do without:

A business phone line, fax, copier, and personal computer. Also, a meeting/conference room is useful for generating group discussion and participation.

Marketing tips/advice:

"Segment your niche even more . . . I started 'Spirit Groups' for home-based business owners at the same time so that I could serve a broader population of women owners and generate more income potential simultaneously."

If you had to do it all over again . . .

"I would have segmented much earlier."

MANICURIST/PEDICURIST

Startup cost:	$5,000–$10,000
Potential earnings:	$15,000–$35,000
Typical fees:	$50 per set of nails (for length additions) and $15–$20 for a simple manicure or pedicure
Advertising:	Newspapers, coupon books, bulletin boards, Yellow Pages
Qualifications:	Training and certification in cosmetology or as a nail technician (required in most states)
Equipment needed:	Manicuring table with a strong light, foot bath, credit card processing equipment (if you decide to accept plastic, and you really must), nail maintenance tools, nail enhancement and beautification products, nail polish in a variety of shades
Home business potential:	Yes
Staff required:	No
Hidden costs:	Liability insurance and materials

LOWDOWN:

Luxurious nails are no longer for the rich and famous only—teens, brides, professional women, moms, grandmoms, even men want beautiful hands and feet. But while there's no lack of people willing to pay for professional manicures and pedicures, the competition for their business is tough. Gone are the days when the only place you could get a professional manicure was in a hair salon. Today's manicurists are opening their own stand-alone shops and there are lots of them. But if you can provide exceptional service at a reasonable price, you should have no problem staying busy. Look for creative ways to set your business apart—choose a specific market niche, like senior citizens, or link up with a jeweler and offer discount coupons to engaged women who'll be showing off their newly acquired diamond rings.

STARTUP:

Your biggest expense will be for training and certification; you can't open your own nail salon (or even work as a manicurist in someone else's hair salon for that matter) without it. The necessary equipment is minimal. Essentially, you'll need a good, strong table, foot bath, and bright light to work under, in addition to assorted nail polishes and nail maintenance tools. Charge at least $40–$60 for a set of acrylic, fiberglass, or gel nails; $15–$20 for a simple manicure or pedicure.

BOTTOM LINE ADVICE:

If you like working with people from several different walks of life, this could be your kind of business. Expect to be more than a manicurist, however. Just like a hairdresser, you'll be part psychologist too—a sounding board for your customers who will air their problems, not to mention the latest juicy gossip, while you smooth away calluses, trim cuticles, apply polish, and buff.

MARKET MAPPING SERVICE

Startup cost:	$5,000–$15,000
Potential earnings:	$30,000–$50,000+
Typical fees:	$1,200–$5,000 per project
Advertising:	Yellow Pages, business/trade journals, newspapers, direct mail, cold calls
Qualifications:	Background in strategic marketing and/or list rental
Equipment needed:	Computer with Internet access, database software, printer, fax
Home business potential:	Yes
Staff required:	No
Hidden costs:	Insurance

LOWDOWN:

Companies need to know certain critical information from the get-go, such as where their potential clients are located and how close they are physically to competitive markets. You can assist businesses in their tracking needs by providing a detailed map or listing of names, addresses, phone numbers, and contacts. Your listing can take several forms: a database and/or mailing labels (which you sell on a one-time-use-only basis), an actual map pinpointing areas of opportunity, or a simple list of contact names/addresses/phone numbers with ample space for follow-up notes next to each column. Offer your services via direct mail or cold calls after producing a market map of your own to locate your potential clients (usually small- to medium-sized businesses). Once you sell a market map, you have the potential to resell to the same client, especially if the company expands its product line or market areas.

STARTUP:

Your startup costs ($5,000–$15,000) will cover your computer system, printer, fax, copier, Internet access, and database software, along with some preliminary advertising. Don't forget to figure in your cost of building lists, which can take considerable time and plenty of outside resources. You can expect to earn at least $30,000 and possibly more than $50,000—if you target market your own services as well as your customers'.

BOTTOM LINE ADVICE:

Make sure that you secure payment up front or upon delivery of your market map because the value of your services will diminish significantly upon receipt of your product. In other words, get your money before the client has a chance to actually use your product—otherwise, you could be giving your services away.

MARKETING CONSULTANT

Startup cost:	$5,000–$10,000
Potential earnings:	$60,000–$150,000
Typical fees:	$50 to $200 per hour; $2,000–$4,000 for leading a workshop
Advertising:	Referrals, word of mouth, networking
Qualifications:	Degree or work experience in marketing, business savvy, high energy level, excellent written/oral communications skills, creativity, persistence, problem-solving ability
Equipment needed:	Computer, laser printer, fax, Internet access, copier, and scanner; word processing, spreadsheet, and presentation software
Home business potential:	Yes
Staff required:	No
Hidden costs:	Membership dues, phone bills

LOWDOWN:

Customers are the lifeblood of any business—and marketing is the means for attracting them. Everything from developing ad brochures, and newsletters to creating promotions, generating publicity, and designing sales strategies fall under the umbrella of marketing activities. Putting together a targeted marketing plan is a demanding activity, and most executives need the services of a marketing professional to create one that produces effective results. Marketing consultants are in great demand to fill in the gaps left by downsizing at large organizations and to boost sales at small companies. Opportunities abound if you have the right mix of skills and experience and can generate results.

STARTUP:

You will need a sophisticated and flexible computer setup in order to produce the professional-looking reports and presentation materials necessary for your work. Although you probably won't be preparing the camera-ready versions of ads or brochures (your client's art department or ad agency will be responsible for those), you will need to be able to generate drafts that clearly reflect your recommendations for the final product. You'll need to set aside a fair amount of money for your own marketing efforts, too. Among your expenses will be dues for professional associations and community organizations in which you can build a strong network of potential clients.

BOTTOM LINE ADVICE:

Effective marketing takes skill and imagination. You'll be looking for the answers to two very important questions on behalf of your client: What do my potential customers want? What kind of message must I deliver in order to grab their attention? Knowing how to match your client's product or service to the right market will make you a success as a marketing consultant. To prove your worth, be creative. You will need to put together a marketing plan that not only establishes goals, but lays out the specific steps for achieving them; then you'll have to get buy-in from the executives. The plan itself is just the beginning; implementation may take many months. Be sure to secure a contract that allows you to receive incremental payments; otherwise your cash flow will suffer.

MEDIATOR

Startup cost:	$5,000–$10,000
Potential earnings:	$40,000–$65,000
Typical fees:	$75–$300 per hour (usually split between the disputing parties)
Advertising:	Yellow Pages, newspapers, bulletin boards, networking with legal groups
Qualifications:	A legal background and/or expertise in a specific area; some states require license/certification
Equipment needed:	Office with comfortable furniture, phones, computer
Home business potential:	Possibly
Staff required:	No
Hidden costs:	Some cases are more complicated than others; try to see the writing on the wall when it comes to the bigger jobs

LOWDOWN:

Once considered an experimental approach, mediation is today a widely accepted method for resolving conflict for two primary reasons: The courts are overloaded and attorneys cost just too darn much. Mediators have an important role to play in the modern legal system. While attorneys are paid to reach an eventual court settlement, a mediator looks for ways to settle disputes with compromise and without going to court. With so many marriages ending in bitter divorce these days, mediators have some of their ripest ground in the domestic sector, where they can save the parties literally thousands of dollars in litigation by getting to the heart of the matter through mutual conciliation. Identifying what each party truly wants out of a deal is the most critical part of successful mediation. Keeping the parties from "killing" each other might well be the next. Are you skilled at bringing people back to the issues at hand from a point of hurling pointless accusations at one another? Can you help them see the big picture instead of zeroing in on the smallest of details? If so, you would make a fine mediator. Your job, essentially, is to help fighting folks stay out of court. It's an admirable profession—and, if you're good at it, more and more profitable in our increasingly litigious society.

STARTUP:

You can use your home office for administrative chores, but you will need a neutral space for meetings with your clients; expect to lay out at least $3,000 for your "digs." Next, spend some money advertising in places potential clients typically look for help (namely, the Yellow Pages). Network with attorneys for referrals and give speeches before business and community organizations to promote mediation in general and your services in particular. Hourly rates vary. Plan on $75–$100 per hour if the court mandates mediation; $150–$300 if you are hired by private parties.

BOTTOM LINE ADVICE:

While this is an admirable profession and is more respected than some others in the legal field, it is still a personally challenging one. Can you listen all day to folks fighting over trivial, petty things (like who gets the washing machine or the collection of Tupperware)? If you're able to keep the opposing sides focused on the goal of an amicable settlement, you'll do well. But do take time for yourself—you'll need it.

ADVICE FROM THE EXPERTS

What sets your business apart from others like it?

Albert H. Couch, a Family, Divorce and Community Mediator for Akron Family Mediation in Akron, Ohio, says three things set his business apart from others like it. "We have a full-time commitment to mediation, and a lot of mediators don't have that. Second, we cap our fees so that our customers know there's a limit to what they'll spend with us. Finally, we have experience in our field and are aggressive in promoting mediation in general. When I'm not mediating, I'm talking about mediating somewhere."

Things you couldn't do without:

Couch says he couldn't do without a computer, phone and, most important, the training he's had in his field.

Marketing tips/advice:

"Learn mediation inside and out, that's first and foremost." But the second most important thing you can do, according to Couch, is to talk mediation with just about anyone who'll listen. "This is primarily a word-of-mouth business."

If you had to do it all over again . . .

"I'd spend less money up front on advertising, since so much of my business comes from referrals. I advise others to get involved in their community and give as many speeches as you can to promote your business."

MEDICAL BILLING SERVICE

Startup cost:	$5,000–$15,000
Potential earnings:	$20,000–$85,000
Typical fees:	$1.50–$3 per claim or flat fee of 7–10 percent of claims collected; some billing services charge by the hour ($15–$50 depending on the service provided)
Advertising:	Referrals, cold calls, direct mail, networking, Web site
Qualifications:	Knowledge of insurance billing procedures and Medicare and Medicaid regulations which change frequently; familiarity with the diagnostic-and-procedure codes doctors use to designate specific services on claim forms; computer proficiency; accuracy; organizational and time-management skills; ability to work with health care providers and their staffs
Equipment needed:	Computer with oversized monitor, Internet access, printer, copier, scanner, medical billing software, fax
Home business potential:	Yes
Staff required:	Not at first; you may want to add staff later as your business grows
Hidden costs:	Professional liability insurance, training. If you are new to the insurance claims arena, it is strongly recommended that you attend classes in medical billing and coding procedures at your local community college or adult education facility; contact your nearest Medicare office for information about classes related specifically to electronic claims processing for Medicare

LOWDOWN:

Medical billing is a complicated process. Due to an aging population and a 1990 federal law requiring that physicians rather than patients submit claims for Medicare reimbursement, many medical offices are inundated with paperwork. While some physicians have chosen to establish their own in-house billing services, many more are hiring outside medical billing assistance to process the claims and, in many cases, provide various other services such as invoicing, collecting the co-payments the patients themselves are required to pay, tracking past due and uncollectible accounts, and answering patient inquiries with regard to their claims. While medical doctors remain the primary source of business for billing services, opportunities are also available for work with other health care providers, including chiropractors, dentists, osteopaths, optometrists, physical and respiratory therapists, psychologists, nurse practitioners, and podiatrists, to name a few. If you are looking for a challenging opportunity that utilizes computer technology and sharp interpersonal skills, medical billing can be a very promising field.

STARTUP:

Considering that most claims are filed electronically these days, you absolutely must have a computer, Internet access, and the latest medical billing software to compete in this market (costs range from $3,000–$5,000). And since you'll be spending a lot of time in front of your computer entering data and reading fine print, opt for a comfortable chair and an oversized monitor (at least 17"). Set aside approximately $1,000 for your initial marketing budget and allow for hourly wages of additional staff as your business begins to grow. Medical billing services typically charge by the claim—either for filing

($1.50–$3 per claim) or for collecting (a flat fee of 7–10 percent of claims collected). Those that provide more extensive services, such as invoicing and collection, charge an hourly rate, depending on the particular service performed. In all cases, you will need a minimum of eight to 10 doctors or practices to be profitable.

BOTTOM LINE ADVICE:

Medical billing requires patience and attention to detail. The work can be interesting, but challenging due to the ever-changing nature of health insurance and Medicare. Although selling your services may be difficult at first, good communication skills and persistence will result in lasting relationships with those doctors or practices you serve. Once your business is established, processing individual claims electronically takes little time and can be done at your convenience. You must, however, stay on top of it; your client's cash flow depends, in part, on how quickly you file the claims. Most importantly, you must be accurate. Mistakes can mean delays in reimbursement and, in the case of Medicare, even fines.

MEDICAL CLAIMS ASSISTANCE PROFESSIONAL

Startup cost:	$5,000–$9,000
Potential earnings:	$35,000–$50,000
Typical fees:	$25–$75 per hour; $200–$400 per person, per year, to process and review new medical claims; or 10–15 percent of benefits paid
Advertising:	Networking (ask friends and family for referrals), Yellow Pages, ads in community newspapers and local publications aimed at seniors, presentations to community groups, Web site
Qualifications:	Knowledge of health insurance industry, especially how claims are processed, why they might be denied, and how to appeal the decision; attention to detail and eye for mistakes; good communication and negotiation skills; empathy; organizational and multitasking abilities
Equipment needed:	Computer, printer, Internet access, fax, scanner, copier, manuals, phone with headset
Home business potential:	Yes
Staff required:	No
Hidden costs:	Keeping abreast of changes in the insurance industry and Medicare regulations

LOWDOWN:

If your health insurer has ever denied one of your claims, then you know the frustration experienced on a daily basis by hundreds of individuals, many of them senior citizens, who can't get the reimbursement they were counting on for expensive medical treatment and diagnostic procedures. As a medical claims assistance professional—CAP for short—you can help. Unlike the medical billing service which works with health care providers, you will work directly with the patients themselves, filing and following up on their claims to private insurance companies. Physicians are required by law to file Medicare claims on behalf of their patients; however, since there is no such requirement with regard to private insurance, patients are pretty much on their own when it comes to securing reimbursement from private carriers. It's a frustrating process, and for those patients who are seriously ill or easily confused, downright impossible. Being able to call on a professional who understands the inner workings of the system and who can "talk the talk" of the health care insurance industry can be a source of tremendous peace of mind. To work as a CAP, you will need to understand the claims filing process and have dogged determination to follow a claim through to reimbursement, a process which can take several weeks and sometimes even months. If a claim is denied, you'll be the one who investigates the reason why and works to get the decision overturned. Your people skills will need to be superb and wide-ranging. In a single day, you might be asking a doctor to lower his or her fee on behalf of one client and disputing a denied claim with an insurance company representative for another; in between, you could be comforting a family in crisis or simply listening to a frustrated patient vent about his or her insurance carrier.

STARTUP:
Although you must have a better-than-average knowledge of the health insurance industry and medical claims processing, no formal training is necessary to get started in this business. You will, however, want to have a computer with Internet access, so you can stay abreast of changes in the insurance industry in general and Medicare regulations in particular. You'll also need a printer, fax, copier, scanner, and phone, and since you may be spending long periods of time on hold with insurance providers, you'll want a headset too. Set aside some money for marketing ($1,000–$1,500); at the very least, you'll want a Yellow Pages listing and a few carefully placed ads in community newspapers and/or local publications that circulate primarily to senior citizens. The bulk of your business will come from networking with family and friends, referrals from satisfied customers, and the contacts you make speaking to community groups. Consider a Web site once you get established and have testimonials you can post online.

BOTTOM LINE ADVICE:
This is one of those businesses you can really feel good about pursuing. You are performing a much-needed service for people who would likely drop a disputed claim or not bother to go after the reimbursement they deserve in the first place simply because the paperwork is too complicated. There's no shortage of potential clients for your services out there and you could easily make $35,000–$50,000 per year as a CAP. In addition to hourly rates or annual fees, consider charging an initial processing fee to cover the cost of registering a new client and obtaining all the details regarding his or her insurance coverage and prior claims.

MEDICAL CODING

Startup cost:	$5,000–$15,000
Potential earnings:	$30,000–$45,000
Typical fees:	$20–$5 per hour; piece rates for insurance company appeals and hospital work
Advertising:	Cold calls, networking, referrals
Qualifications:	Knowledge of basic anatomy, physiology, and pharmacology; understanding of medical terminology and medical coding procedures; ability to decipher physicians' handwriting; accuracy and attention to detail; certification is desirable (requires minimum of two years' experience)
Equipment needed:	Computer, printer, medical coding software, fax, scanner, copier, coding manuals
Home business potential:	Yes
Staff required:	No
Hidden costs:	Liability insurance, training and certification. If you have no experience in medical coding, you will need formal training; home-study options are available.

LOWDOWN:

In order to be reimbursed by insurance companies and Medicare/Medicaid for the diagnostic procedures and treatments they provide, physicians and other health care practitioners must follow certain, very specific rules. Every procedure has a designated medical code, and in order to receive full and prompt payment from a third party (the insurance company, Medicare, and Medicaid), each code must be assigned accurately. Coding for less than the actual treatment provided (down-coding) can mean a delay in reimbursement and/or a loss of income for the health care provider. Coding for more than the actual treatment (up-coding) can result in fines of up to $50,000 from Medicare, and private insurance companies may demand reimbursement of any overpayment. The accuracy of coding is vital to the health and well-being of any medical practice, which is why many individual health care providers, clinics, hospitals, nursing homes, and others are contracting out to professional medical coders. As a medical coder, you will review the doctor's clinical notes, then assign the appropriate procedural or diagnostic code, according to guidelines established by the American Medical Association (procedural) and World Health Organization (diagnostic). While you will not be required to memorize the codes (there are so many it would be impossible anyway!), you will have to be extremely familiar with the coding manuals in order to find them quickly; an understanding of medical terminology is essential.

STARTUP:

If you do not have a medical background or experience in medical claims processing, you will need to get training in medical coding; check the Internet for home-study options, which typically take 12 to 18 months to complete. When you are ready to launch your business, you will need a computer and medical coding software, as well as coding manuals, a printer, fax, scanner, and copier. Set aside approximately $1,000 for your initial marketing efforts (primarily networking and cold calls to physicians' offices and health care facilities); once you are established, referrals will bring steady work. Coders typically earn $20–$45 per hour; certification will bring higher earnings.

BOTTOM LINE ADVICE:

Professional medical coders can help physicians improve office efficiency, cash flow, and revenue; your challenge is to convince them of your worth. You will likely have to make many cold calls by phone and in-person before landing your first account. Be persistent; once you have demonstrated your ability to provide accurate and dependable service for one medical practice, word of mouth will bring you additional clients. If you are serious about making a living as a medical coder, do get certified. The American Health Information Management Association offers two options for certification: hospital coding and physician-based coding. You will need a minimum of two years of experience in order to qualify for either certification specialty.

MEDICAL TRANSCRIPTIONIST

Startup cost:	$5,000–$13,000
Potential earnings:	$30,000–$80,000
Typical fees:	$15–$40 per hour (hourly rate varies according to difficulty of understanding a speaker due to speech idiosyncrasies or heavy accents); some transcriptionists charge by the line (10–20 cents per) or page ($5–$6 per), but this can be difficult due to variations in font size and formatting
Advertising:	Advertise in publications of local medical societies, direct mail, cold calls, networking
Qualifications:	Excellent listening skills and good eye, hand, and auditory coordination; knowledge of word processing, dictation, and transcription equipment; understanding of medical diagnostic procedures and terminology; good typing skills; an aptitude for science and language; impeccable spelling
Equipment needed:	Computer and printer; specialized medical word-processing software; fax; scanner; copier; transcribing unit; reference books (medical dictionary, medical-transcription stylebook; drug references, etc.)
Home business potential:	Yes
Staff required:	No
Hidden costs:	As many as one to two years of formal training, plus firsthand experience in a hospital or other health care facility before going out on your own may be necessary

LOWDOWN:

Medical transcription is a $50 billion industry and growing. This job is in demand primarily for two reasons: The practice of medicine is getting more complicated by the day and litigation is becoming more frequent. Transcribed copies of dictated notes related to physical examinations and diagnostic procedures provide health care professionals with the necessary documentation for review of patient histories, legal evidence of patient care, data for research, and facts on which to make a diagnosis/evaluation and subsequently render the appropriate continuing patient care. In addition, many insurance companies want transcribed reports before they will pay doctors or health care facilities. Transcriptionists must be speedy typists, have superior listening skills, and sufficient knowledge of medical diagnostic procedures and terminology in order to be able to spell them correctly. There is no room for error in this field; a seemingly simple misspelling—substituting "hypotension" for "hypertension," in a patient's medical record, for example—could mean the difference between life and death. Independent transcriptionists typically receive work from two sources: individual physicians in private practice and/or overload from hospitals. Transcriptions are made from notes either dictated onto tape or into a computer using voice recognition software. In the latter case, editing skills are more important than typing speed. Since turnaround time of transcribed notes is a primary concern for health care providers, you can increase your competitiveness by offering extras, such as pickup and delivery as well as seven-day-a-week, same-day, and phone-in dictation services.

STARTUP

To get started in this business, you will need a computer and printer, plus word process-ing software that is specifically designed for preparing medical documents. You will also need to have a transcribing unit with foot pedals and conversion capabilities (to handle different sizes of tapes). In addition, you will want to have a full complement of reference books within reach, including a medical dictionary, drug references, a medical-transcription stylebook, and books related to the specific medical special-ties you cover. A copier, scanner, fax, and phone with headset round out your basic office setup. And since this job requires hours sitting in front of a computer, a comfort-able chair and desk at the proper height are smart investments, too. Expect to spend $5,000–$13,000 to get up and running.

BOTTOM LINE ADVICE:

Medical transcription can easily become monotonous. You must possess high levels of self-discipline and focus as you work in order to maintain the highest levels of accu-racy. The demand for faster turnaround times occasionally necessitates working nights and weekends. On the other hand, medical transcription work is steady and resistant to recession! This field is rapidly expanding with more work than there are trained tran-scriptionists to complete it.

MIDDLEMAN

Startup cost:	$5,000–$10,000
Potential earnings:	$20,000–$80,000 (net)
Typical fees:	A percentage, varying widely by type of product and manufacturer
Advertising:	Direct mail to obtain line to sell; cold calling, and networking to complete the sales process
Qualifications:	Extensive experience with the type of product you plan to represent; a wide network of friends, associates, acquaintances, and people who might be buyers; sales skills; persistence and personal drive
Equipment needed:	Laptop computer; Internet access; fax; printer; word processing, spreadsheet, and database software; cell phone; business directories and maps; reliable vehicle
Home business potential:	Yes
Staff required:	No
Hidden costs:	Development of sales materials, travel expenses

LOWDOWN:

What does a middleman do? In today's economy, this role is expanding. Sales must be central to the operation of all manufacturing businesses, yet in-house sales forces are shrinking. Someone needs to bring the market and the product together—and there you are, right in the middle. Deciding to start a middleman business means that you love this process, and that you are both committed to it and excellent at it. You can explain anything, so that someone who needs what you have to offer will immediately grasp the idea and jump at the opportunity to buy your product. First, you persuade the manufacturer to work through you. Then you identify his market for him or her. You could be involved at one or several steps in the process of producing a final consumer product, from selling raw materials to finished parts, or you could be smack dab "in the middle" between a wholesaler and a retailer.

STARTUP:

You'll need an office that supports your efforts, and, of course, a reliable vehicle since you'll be traveling extensively. You could net $20,000 in the beginning, and as much as $80,000 later on.

BOTTOM LINE ADVICE:

Your success will depend on your sales skills, organizational abilities, and knowledge of the specialty chemical market, or whatever line you have chosen to sell. "Choice" is the optimum word here; people who are employed by large organizations tend to have little choice. They have rigid quotas to meet, memos from on high to consider, a set pattern they are expected to follow, and an endless stream of tedious reports to write during time that might better be spent calling on customers. You, on the other hand, are your own boss, with responsibility for managing your own time and expenses. You have your own sense of who needs what you've got, and how you can present that information most effectively. This is not an enterprise for people who hate, or even mildly dislike, cold calling. This is an enterprise for people with outstanding personal charm, persistence, and a huge appetite for work.

Mini-Blind Cleaning Service

Startup cost:	$10,000–$15,000
Potential earnings:	$25,000–$35,000
Typical fees:	$10–$20 per blind for standard-sizes, more for oversized blinds
Advertising:	Yellow Pages, local newspapers, direct mail, coupon books
Qualifications:	Commitment to providing quality service, familiarity with equipment
Equipment needed:	Ultrasonic cleaning system, phone with answering service or voice mail and/or cell phone, vehicle
Staff required:	No
Home business potential:	Yes
Hidden costs:	Vehicle expenses, insurance

LOWDOWN:

Mini-blinds are a versatile and popular window treatment for offices and homes alike. To be kept in pristine condition, they must be cleaned regularly, but who likes to do it? When you try to just dust the blinds off or, better yet, use soap and water, the static electricity only pushes the dirt from one side to the other. Professional cleaning by a service armed with the right equipment is the answer. Ultrasonic cleaning systems use sound waves to remove dust, grease, and grime from your mini-blinds. The system is compact and portable, so you can take the cleaning process right to the customer in a van or station wagon. On the downside, your equipment will cost a pretty hefty chunk of change up front. You'll have to work hard to build a high volume business as quickly as possible in order to recoup the cost.

STARTUP:

Your ultrasonic cleaning equipment will run between $10,000–$15,000; the rest of your startup funds will go toward a vehicle if you don't already have one (try leasing at first to save money) and advertising. But, if you do a high enough volume at $10–$20 per blind, you could recoup your investment within the first two years.

BOTTOM LINE ADVICE:

You'll be out and about most of every day, so make sure you use a reliable answering service or carry a cell phone so you don't miss calls from potential clients. Consider aggressive advertising aimed at homeowners and businesses alike. This is still a relatively new service, and many people may not be aware that such a thing even exists. Your ultrasonic cleaning system may take some getting used to, so give it a few practice runs on your own mini-blinds or those belonging to friends and family. You want to create the best possible impression when you go into someone else's home or office; fumbling around with equipment you've never tried before is a sure-fire way to not receive an invitation to return next month.

MOBILE AUTOMOTIVE DETAILING

Startup costs:	$5,000–$15,000
Potential earnings:	$30,000–$60,000
Typical fees:	$100–$250 per job
Advertising:	Newspaper ads, Yellow Pages, automotive publications, networking with auto dealers and body shops
Qualifications:	Auto detailing experience, knowledge of waxes and finishes, physical stamina
Equipment needed:	Wet/dry vacuum; buffer/polisher; hose; buckets; cleaning supplies, such as wax/polish, upholstery and tire cleaners, rags, chamois, brushes, toothbrushes, cotton swabs; access to electrical outlet and water spigot; truck or van
Home business potential:	Yes
Staff required:	Not at first
Hidden costs:	Liability insurance, vehicle expenses, hourly wages of additional assistants, if necessary

LOWDOWN:

Automotive detailing can be done anywhere and at your convenience. Although the number of auto detailers has grown significantly in recent years, you can remain competitive by taking your service directly to the consumer. A smart marketing plan, superior service, fair prices, sound management skills, and always keeping a watchful eye out for services you can provide that your competition has overlooked are strategies that will build your business.

STARTUP:

Launching a mobile auto detailing business can cost anywhere from $5,000 to $15,000. The difference lies in whether you already have a vehicle in which to haul your equipment or need to purchase a used one. In either case, you'll need to acquire the basic tools of your trade: a wet/dry vac, buffer, hose, waxes, upholstery and tire cleaners, buckets, chamois, etc. You should also set aside at least $1,000 for advertising—a Yellow Pages listing and small newspaper ads. The rest of your business will come by referral and networking with auto dealers and body shops. Your best customers are likely to be the owners of high-end vehicles, who have paid a lot of money for their cars and want to keep them looking sharp. Keep in mind, however, that these are their "babies," so be sure to protect yourself against damages with adequate liability insurance.

BOTTOM LINE ADVICE:

If you have dreamed of working at your own pace, automotive detailing can be a rewarding occupation. Individuals with an appreciation for well-kept automobiles are always in demand—by automobile dealers and body shops that farm out their detail work, as well as busy auto owners who want to keep their pricey vehicles looking good but don't have the time to do it themselves. Creativity is the key to keeping the competition at bay and mobility is what sets your business apart. Why should a consumer have to waste precious time dropping his or her vehicle at the auto detailer when you can do the work on-site? Auto detailing is a physically demanding job, sometimes in hot, sticky conditions, but considering that no two days are quite the same and you can charge fees of $100–$250, there's a lot to like about this business.

MOBILE DISC JOCKEY SERVICE

Startup cost:	$5,000–$10,000
Potential earnings:	$25,000–$80,000
Typical fees:	$50–$150 per hour
Advertising:	Classified ads, bulletin boards, referrals
Qualifications:	Knowledge of popular music, strong personality
Equipment needed:	Compact disc and cassette players, professional turntable, sound/mixing systems, cordless microphone, theatrical lighting (optional), and a large and varied CD and cassette collection; records, if you go the turntable route
Home business potential:	Yes (but your work will always be on-site)
Staff required:	No
Hidden costs:	Cost of CDs and tapes; buy used or try to get on record company/DJ-only promotional mailing lists

LOWDOWN:

If you've always harbored a secret desire to spin records and entertain an audience with lively patter in between, you may have a future as a mobile disc jockey. Because live bands can be pretty costly, many party-givers book DJs to handle the entertainment needs of their party or celebration; sometimes they even ask the DJ to play "host" for a theme party. Disc jockeys have been around as long as there have been records to play, and they will no doubt continue even as equipment gets more sophisticated. Today's systems for producing excellent sound quality are getting smaller and more portable, which is good news for mobile DJs. You and your equipment can easily travel in a station wagon or mini-van to several locations in any given weekend. As a DJ, you'll need to develop your own patter for building rapport with the audience; study the techniques of professionals you respect and try to emulate them if you can't come up with your own material. Your music collection should include the widest possible variety to appeal to all ages and musical tastes. Read industry publications such as *Billboard* and *Rolling Stone* to learn what's new and what's hot; scour secondhand stores and flea markets for used CDs and cassettes to build your collection.

STARTUP:

Your startup costs are tied up in the equipment and your music collection itself; expect to spend around $5,000 for a basic setup. No need to spend a lot on advertising; most of your business will be the result of referrals and classified ads. Look for used equipment and CDs before plunking down the big bucks for new; you could easily save several thousand dollars that way. Since you'll be working an average of 3 to 5 hours per job, it's not unrealistic to set your fee at $50–$150 per hour.

BOTTOM LINE ADVICE:

Your work cycles will be extremely varied, with heavier loads typically in the spring and summer and around the holidays. Most of your work will be done on weekends, which can seriously cut into your social life. If you're a 9-to-5 kind of person, being a DJ is not for you. On the other hand, if you love music, don't mind the erratic hours, and enjoy being with people in a celebrative mood, you'll look forward to each new gig.

MODELING SCHOOL/AGENCY

Startup cost:	$5,000–$10,000
Potential earnings:	$40,000–$150,000 (of course, larger and better-known agencies command millions)
Typical fees:	Models earn $25–$1,000 per hour; you get 15 to 20 percent of their income
Advertising:	Direct mail, Yellow Pages, networking/"scouting" on college campuses and at nightclubs, Web site
Qualifications:	Ability to recognize a photogenic face; good marketing skills
Equipment needed:	Cameras, backdrops, makeup kits, lots of lights
Home business potential:	Yes
Staff required:	Not initially
Hidden costs:	Insurance

LOWDOWN:

Rounding up a bevy of beauties is the easy part, but truly marketing your models is the real challenge. If you start out with just a few terrific (and fresh) faces, and aggressively market them in the right places, you'll build credibility much quicker than you would by filling up your agency with a lot of men and women all dressed up with no place to go. In other words, don't overextend yourself in the beginning—start slow and steadily increase your stable of models over a period of months. Arrange to staff the fashion shows at local malls/retail stores, and make contact with area advertising agencies in order to secure modeling gigs for your stable of talent in newspaper and television ads. Let department stores know about your business—and don't forget that many companies seek models to act as demonstrators or serve as spokespersons at special events, such as trade shows.

STARTUP:

Startup costs should be relatively low (in the $5,000 range, mostly to cover basic office setup). If you have the space and adequate lighting for photo shoots, you can run this business out of your home; for the sake of credibility, however, you will probably want to rent office space elsewhere. Think about the infamous casting couch, and you'll understand why a home office may not be the best idea. Top-of-the-line camera/video equipment is another wise investment; expect to shell out at least $2,000 for these items alone. If you succeed at building a solid, reputable agency, you could make between $40,000 and $150,000 or more if one of your "girls" turns out to be the next Christie Brinkley or Cindy Crawford.

BOTTOM LINE ADVICE:

Determination and persistence will get your business off the ground. When first starting your agency, you will most likely need to charge the models who enroll in your modeling school. Try to keep your sign-up fees low to attract a broad range of hopefuls. Later, you can offer modeling lessons free of charge. To build your stable of talent, try offering two-for-one specials, or give dollar incentives to anyone who brings in new models.

MONOGRAMMING SERVICE

Startup cost:	$5,000–$15,000
Potential earnings:	$20,000–$50,000
Typical fees:	$3.50–$100 per item, depending on the item being monogrammed and the monogramming technique; offer volume discounts when possible
Advertising:	Yellow Pages, networking with local school districts, direct mail to companies and organizations, Web site
Qualifications:	Silk-screening and sewing skills; ability to operate monogramming equipment
Equipment needed:	Monogramming equipment, basic office setup
Home business potential:	Yes
Staff required:	No
Hidden costs:	Insurance

LOWDOWN:

You've seen them everywhere . . . baseball caps, sweatshirts, and jackets sporting company logos. You have a knack for working with many types of fabric and for transferring a company's identity to the appropriate material. Or maybe you simply want to monogram initials onto towels, blankets, and other home accessories for the marriage-minded. Whatever your specialty area, you'll need the right equipment and marketing savvy to get your business off the ground. Silk screening is a good place to start; check your local art supply shops for information and creative options. For the more advanced monogrammer, there's thermal transfer or computer-aided machine embroidery; check business and trade publications before making an expensive equipment purchase.

STARTUP:

This business can be started on a relatively modest budget; depending on the equipment you select, you could spend anywhere from $5,000–$15,000 to get started. Since the equipment is your livelihood, you will want to insure it, along with your inventory of monogramming supplies. Expect to earn back your initial cash outlay in about two to three years, based on an income potential of $20,000–$50,000 per year.

BOTTOM LINE ADVICE:

Advertising and marketing will play an important role in making this business a successful venture. You can start with a Yellow Pages listing and direct mail to companies, organizations, and schools; eventually, you'll want to have a Web site to show samples of your finished products. Monogramming is much more than just initialing towels—and you'll need to convey that in every piece of literature you send out, including your business cards.

MOTION PICTURE RESEARCH
CONSULTANT

Startup cost:	$10,000–$15,000
Potential earnings:	$35,000–$60,000
Typical fees:	$150–$300 per hour
Advertising:	Industry trade publications, networking/"schmoozing," word of mouth
Qualifications:	Knowledge of and/or interest in history, ability to conduct research, inquisitive mind
Equipment needed:	Computer with high-speed Internet access, library card, reference books and other resource materials of your own
Home business potential:	Yes
Staff required:	No
Hidden costs:	Travel expenses

LOWDOWN:

You are the fact man (or woman): Your mission is to research a person, place, event (or all three) and put that information together so that actors and moviegoers alike can understand it. If you are a history buff in general, inquisitive about events, and nosy about people or places, then this seek-and-find mission is for you. The motion picture research consultant flushes out all possible angles, much like a reporter; the only difference is you remain behind the scenes. Could you imagine what might have happened with the movie *Gone With the Wind* had no one checked for historical accuracy? A good researcher is invaluable to movie producers and the finished film itself because if there's an error in setting or costumes, a critic is bound to find it and point it out—even if the movie is otherwise flawless. Your services are invaluable to Hollywood all right; now your challenge is to make yourself available and get the word out.

STARTUP:

You'll be rubbing elbows with directors, producers, actors, and other movie people, so plan on making the rounds of all the important trade shows, cocktail parties, and other events that draw the show biz elite. It's at these functions that you'll network—you'll get to know people and they'll get to know you. Plan on dropping a minimum of $5,000 just to get noticed. As for what kind of return you'll yield as a result, that depends on what you charge per hour per project. Generally speaking, you could charge between $150–$300 per hour (more if it's a major studio) and easily pull in between $35,000–$60,000 working part-time.

BOTTOM LINE ADVICE:

Plan on traveling and talking to all types of people to help you in your research. This is one of Hollywood's lowest-profile jobs—it sometimes requires months to complete—and yet it is of critical importance to directors and producers. Plan on using your computer and high-speed Internet access regularly and set aside plenty of cash to cover travel expenses.

NETWORKING SERVICES

Startup cost:	$8,000–$12,000
Potential earnings:	$20,000–$50,000
Typical fees:	$10–$20 per event attendee (mixers); higher fees for seminars and trade shows
Advertising:	Yellow Pages, direct mail (most effective), newspaper ads, billboards
Qualifications:	Creativity, strong organizational skills and follow-through
Equipment needed:	Computer, printer, fax, Internet access, copier, phone, contact management and database software
Home business potential:	Yes
Staff required:	No
Hidden costs:	List rental fees, insurance

LOWDOWN:

How do most business professionals in the twenty-first century meet other influential types who might help them in the future? They go to networking events, such as business trade shows and after-hours mixers. In many cities, it is the larger networking events held at luxurious hotels that bring in the most business. Your business will probably start out much smaller; you could organize a series of small after-work mixers at a local hotel, and advertise them on a regular basis. Charge an admission fee, supply a few light refreshments, and let people simply mingle and exchange business cards. Aim toward holding your events on a regular basis—at the same time and in the same place, say once a month—so people will come to anticipate the mixers and regularly attend. Build a strong enough following to generate more business through referral, and you might move on to organize larger events—dinners, seminars, even trade shows. In the beginning, you will probably want to rent a mailing list and send out invitations. Later, you can save that list rental money by building your own list; offer a discount on admission to those who leave their business cards behind with you. Better yet, find a corporate sponsor and split the profits; you save money and get a boost in credibility besides.

STARTUP:

The $10,000 or so it will take to get you started in the networking services business will mainly cover your basic office setup (computer, printer, fax, Internet access, copier, and phone system) along with the initial outlay for mailing list rentals and labels. You'll also need to set aside money for direct mail and newspaper advertising for each event. With hard work and persistence, you could make $20,000–$50,000 bringing professionals together for the economic benefit of all concerned—including, of course, yourself.

BOTTOM LINE ADVICE:

Your toughest challenge will be getting enough people to attend your functions on a regular basis—and keeping "new blood" flowing in. Your income potential depends on the number of people you are able to draw, so you must continually be looking for prospects and planning interesting enough events to attract them. On the bright side, once you've built a following, you'll have a strong referral base. This business will work especially well in a metropolitan area where you can hold multiple mixers a month in different locations to reach businesspeople in the city center and various suburbs.

NEW PRODUCT RESEARCHER

Startup cost:	$5,000–$10,000
Potential earnings:	$40,000–$80,000
Typical fees:	$50–$75 per hour, flat fee of $1,000–$5,000 per project, or a percentage of gross sales (10 to 15 percent is standard)
Advertising:	Business publications, direct mail, networking with venture capitalists and other investors who can provide referrals, Web site
Qualifications:	Extensive experience in all aspects of product launch (particularly strategic marketing); technical know-how may be helpful
Equipment needed:	Computer, high-speed Internet access, fax, phone, copier, scanner
Home business potential:	Yes
Staff required:	No
Hidden costs:	Time; online searching can eat up a lot of hours. Watch the clock, especially if you are not billing by the hour.

LOWDOWN:

Ever wonder where innovative new products come from? While most major corporations have in-house "think tanks" in place to come up with ideas for new products and improvements to existing ones, even the most progressive small companies can rarely afford such a luxury. For them, hiring a new product researcher to determine the marketability and profitability of a proposed new product can be a cost-effective solution to an age-old problem. We live in a society where innovation is highly prized, so it's a sure bet that even the most established companies are looking for new products to add to their already hugely successful lines. Your job as a new product researcher will entail a significant amount of "detective work" in order to figure out what the competition might be up to, identify customer needs, and break down the cost of producing a particular suggested product into palatable portions for management to swallow. In other words, you'll be looking at an idea and determining whether it's worth it or not to take the product into production.

STARTUP:

Your startup costs will mostly cover advertising your services, either through direct mail pieces to manufacturers or through ads in business publications. Expect to spend at least $5,000 on these items alone. Add to that another $3,000–$5,000 for equipment—a computer, high-speed Internet access, fax, phone, copier, and scanner. Sounds like a lot, until you consider that your earnings per project could be as high as $5,000 for approximately one month's worth of work. Doesn't take a mathematician to see that your own product is worth it, eh?

BOTTOM LINE ADVICE:

On the positive side, you'll be among the first to know about emerging products. You'll likely be sitting at conference tables with some of the greatest engineering minds around, hashing through ideas and weighing the pros and cons of every project. However, make sure you're paid up front for your services, or have a good contract lawyer working with you to protect your interests. Otherwise, should a project lose its backing midway through your work, you could have a tough time collecting what is owed to you.

NEWSPAPER FEATURES SYNDICATE

Startup cost:	$10,000–$15,000
Potential earnings:	$20,000–$45,000
Typical fees:	$10–$25 per month, per article, per publication
Advertising:	Direct mail to newspapers, ads in industry publications—i.e., Editor & Publisher (for newspapers); *Writer's Digest* and *The Artist's Magazine* (for freelancers)
Qualifications:	Knowledge of newspaper operations/needs; ability to recognize "sellable" writing/art; organizational skills
Equipment needed:	Computer, fax, Internet access, laser printer, mailing supplies and postage meter
Home business potential:	Yes
Staff required:	Yes (freelance writers and artists)
Hidden costs:	Production, postage

LOWDOWN:

Newspapers are always on the lookout for new, exciting, and offbeat articles and cartoons to boost readership and fill space. Most, however, don't have the staffs to supply it. That's why features syndicates work so well: They provide a wide array of usable, printable journalism at a fraction of what it might cost to develop such work in-house. Why pay salary and benefits to a movie reviewer when you can purchase syndicated movie reviews for around $20 per month? As a syndicate, you'll need to first build a stable of fine writers and artists, then you'll need to get the word out. You won't be able to sell newspapers on using your services unless you provide some samples of the work you represent. Network with artists'/writers' groups and through universities to scour the journalistic "jungle" for the best in your area. Or, open your doors to writers and illustrators across the country by advertising in the publications they read (*Writer's Digest*, *The Artist's Magazine*, etc.).Describe the syndicate you're building and encourage them to get in on the ground floor. You can offer to pay them a flat fee per piece, or a percentage of sales. Either way, syndication means regular work and many "starving" artists and writers are likely to jump at the opportunity.

STARTUP:

You'll spend between $10,000–$15,000 getting this operation off the ground, largely due to the fact that you'll need to advertise heavily in the beginning (first to build your stable of writers/artists, then to get the word out to papers). Still, you could make between $25,000–$50,000 if you have a solid group of people producing quality work on a regular basis.

BOTTOM LINE ADVICE:

Keep your freelancers happy and well-paid, because if you don't, they'll quickly take their talents elsewhere—leaving you high and dry and minus a good deal of credibility with your newspaper customers. Your best bet is to negotiate a fair deal with your freelancers from the beginning, even if you have to spend a little more money to do so. It's worth it in the long run because you can't build—and keep—a syndicate without them.

NOISE CONTROL CONSULTANT

Startup cost:	$5,000–$10,000
Potential earnings:	$30,000–$50,000
Typical fees:	$50–$75 per hour
Advertising:	Trade publications, business associations, networking and referrals
Qualifications:	Certification as an industrial hygienist, extensive experience with a large employer or consulting firm, quantification orientation, ability to deal with people in a workplace environment, assessment and writing skills
Equipment needed:	Decibel-measuring equipment, computer, word processing and spreadsheet software, printer fax, phone, copier, scanner
Home business potential:	Yes
Staff required:	No
Hidden costs:	Travel, insurance, trade journal subscriptions

LOWDOWN:

Noise control is rapidly becoming one of the most important branches of industrial hygiene. Employers need to track noise levels in their plants because long-term exposure to noise—even the kind that causes no immediate physical pain—can result in hearing loss. Simply requiring employees to wear earplugs has not been found to be an adequate response to the problem. As a noise control consultant, you'll suggest other, better options. You'll measure decibel levels with a sound meter, write a report, and work with the employer to determine ways to reduce the noise level. You may recommend adding baffles to machines, relocating them, running them at different speeds, or replacing them with other, quieter equipment. Technical knowledge and considerable business judgment is required to assess the problem, plan improvements, and present recommendations that meet the expectations of both the employer and the workers.

STARTUP:

You will need to invest in some highly sensitive, specialized equipment to start your business, along with office machines and furnishings. Expect to spend close to $10,000 to get up and running. Charge $50–$75 per hour for your services; more ($500–$750 per day) if working for a large corporation or factory.

BOTTOM LINE ADVICE:

You will need certification in industrial hygiene to gain credibility as a noise control consultant. More importantly, you will need the acoustical ability to locate the source of different workplace sounds. Your analysis must be performed in relationship to the real people who work in the environment and operate the machines. You'll need good people skills and the ability to present abstract measurements clearly on paper and in face-to-face discussions. Your ability to offer creative solutions to any problems you discover will set you apart from mere technicians. In other words, you'll need both technical know-how and a sense of how your recommendations relate to the overall operation of the plant. This is not an easy business to break into nor is it one without risk. Some working conditions may be difficult and hazardous to your own hearing.

ONLINE INTERNET RESEARCHER

Startup cost:	$5,000–$12,000
Potential earnings:	$18,000–$75,000
Typical fees:	$45–$75 per hour
Advertising:	Networking, contacts in fields where you have experience, seminars, newsletters, advertising in trade journals, bulletin boards, Yellow Pages
Qualifications:	Familiarity with the requirements of the databases in your specialized field, ability to scan information rapidly and pick out what is relevant
Equipment needed:	Computer, high-speed Internet access, fax, printer, comfortable chair
Home business potential:	Yes
Staff required:	No
Hidden costs:	Online access, marketing

LOWDOWN:

Companies require many kinds of information, but they often do not have the time or skills necessary to find it. Not everyone has the patience and creativity to be an effective, efficient researcher. Consider, too, that while the so-called "information explosion" has put a wealth of data within reach, sorting through it all and picking out what might be useful to a particular project can be challenging. Thanks to the World Wide Web and the proliferation of computerized databases, you don't have to spend hours in the library to find what you need; you can research successfully from a computer at home . . . and get paid to do so. Keep in mind, however, that while you could easily access information on just about any subject online, for the sake of speed and efficiency, you would do well to specialize. Limit your services to just one or two types of information so that you can draw on your familiarity with specific Internet locations and come up with the facts and figures your clients need in a flash.

STARTUP:

A powerful computer and high-speed Internet access will be your basic tools in this busi-ness. There are lots of options out there for online access, many of which can be costly, so spend some time shopping for the one that best meets your needs and budget. Expect to spend at least $2,000–$3,000 for your equipment; add on another $1,000–$2,000 for your initial marketing efforts. Since you'll be spending a lot of time in front of a computer, be sure to factor in the cost of ergonomic office furniture and, in particular, a comfortable chair. Expect to bill at $45 per hour to start; increase your hourly rate as you develop a strong reputation for stellar researching abilities.

BOTTOM LINE ADVICE:

Finding specific data for a client is a lot like solving a puzzle or tracking down the answer to a mystery. You'll need to pull out your creative thinking cap to discover new approaches to a search or hidden sources of information. Use your intellectual curios-ity and your desire to leave no stone unturned to develop a successful online research business. You'll have the satisfaction of providing information essential to the growth and development of your client businesses. Costs can be difficult to manage, however, because it is hard to predict how long a search will take, and you may not always be able to find every possible piece of data. Online searches can eat up a lot of time, so to cover yourself, charge by the hour rather than the project. And since this field is fluid, you will have to keep learning how to use new databases, and you will have to keep educating potential clients about exactly what it is that you do so that you can justify what might at first look to be an expensive bill for a few facts or figures.

OUTDOOR ADVENTURES

Startup cost:	$5,000–$15,000
Potential earnings:	$50,000–$100,000
Typical fees:	Varied, depending on length of excursion, group size, and corporate versus individual rates (a weekend camping trip could range anywhere from $300–$1,000 per person, for example)
Advertising:	Magazines with an outdoor or fitness focus, newspapers, public speaking on outdoor or environmental issues, direct mail, Web site
Qualifications:	Outdoor leadership skills and experience, knowledge of the natural world, first aid and CPR training, excellent planning skills, ability to roll with the punches
Equipment needed:	Outdoor equipment for yourself and group, van, basic office setup
Home business potential:	Yes
Staff required:	Yes
Hidden costs:	Insurance, equipment repairs and replacement

LOWDOWN:

There are almost as many ways to conduct an "outdoor adventure" as there are individual personalities to enjoy one. Broadly defined, your business will take groups of people into the outdoors to camp, hike, and just generally experience the wilderness. The demand for wilderness adventures today far outweighs the ability of the organizations that have been offering them for many years to supply, and, so, many small organizations are springing up to fill the void. Some focus on helping city folks learn to survive for a week or a weekend with little material support in a wilderness environment. Others offer opportunities for self-development, self-reflection, or fitness. Still more offer group activities designed to build relationships of trust among businesspeople, students, and others who must work closely together for a common cause.

STARTUP:

Your decisions about equipment will affect the cost of your startup as well as expenses related to your continuing operations. Advertising will be an ongoing requirement; expect to spend at least $5,000 on that alone. However, if you find the right niche and market yourself well, especially to corporations, you can carve out a mighty fine living for yourself, perhaps as much as $100,000 per year.

BOTTOM LINE ADVICE:

An outdoor adventures business will rely on a combination of factors: your love of the wilderness, your knowledge of outdoor survival skills, and your creativity in designing effective, appealing programs that allow your customers to truly experience life in the wild. You must also be people-oriented enough to share their expertise with others. Cold, wet campers with painful blisters on their feet facing another night in tents are not as easy to charm as day trippers on a short hike who'll return to their comfortable homes before nightfall. Don't whitewash the experience in your sales pitch, but do emphasize that surviving the full range of challenges a weekend in the wilderness brings can build individual self-esteem, group solidarity, and an enduring respect for the power and beauty of nature.

PACKAGING CONSULTANT

Startup cost:	$8,000–$10,000
Potential earnings:	$40,000–$80,000
Typical fees:	$50–$75 per hour or flat fee per project
Advertising:	Membership in trade organizations, referrals, networking, direct mail, Web site
Qualifications:	Extensive experience in commercial design, advertising and sales promotion; outstanding skill/track record in package design
Equipment needed:	Top-of-the-line computer with graphic design software, color laser printer, high-speed Internet access, fax, phone, copier, scanner
Home business potential:	Yes
Staff required:	No
Hidden costs:	Cost of creating sample packages

LOWDOWN:

Packaging is a separate and very highly developed facet of the product development process. As a consultant, you will work with an advertising agency, manufacturer, and/or product developer to create the ideal package. Do you need to focus on form (perfume bottle) or function (milk carton)? Will the package need to jump off the shelf at a discount store or reach out to an impulse purchaser in a gourmet food shop? Your ability to respond to the market, the materials, the message, and the channel of distribution will make you a valuable addition to the process of bringing many products to market. Consider specializing in the area where you have a record of success to back up your own marketing efforts.

STARTUP:

Equipping your office to support your design work will not be cheap, but it's an expense you must bear so that you have the ability to produce professional-looking results; expect to spend at least $8,000. Use a Web site to display your designs and promote your services beyond your immediate geographic area. At billings of $50–$75 per hour, you'll earn between $40,000–$80,000.

BOTTOM LINE ADVICE:

Creative and practical: That combination is a requirement for success as a packaging consultant. You're producing a design that wraps up what "they" want, what will work, and what will sell. Intuition, skill, and artistic ability must be the hallmarks of your designs. As with many high-end consulting businesses, it will take time to become established, but once you are, referrals will bring you a steady stream of work.

ADVICE FROM THE EXPERTS

What sets your business apart from others like it?

Andrea S. Mandel, President of Andrea S. Mandel Associates, Packaging Consulting Services in Robinsville, New Jersey, says her diverse experience is what counts. "I've worked for a number of different major companies in health care, personal care, foods, medical devices, and household products. This broad product experience facilitates technology transfer between areas. This is not commonly available inside a particular company."

Things you couldn't do without:

"A good computer and printer, Internet access, software, and extras as needed. You need at least one extra phone line, answering device, fax machine, and copier. Also, small measuring devices (calipers), and resource materials."

Marketing tips/advice:

Get on the Internet, says Mandel. "I have a good knowledge of computers and have been utilizing online services for a long time. Many independent consultants do not have this capability yet."

If you had to do it all over again . . .

"I would have come up with a different name for my company. I had felt my name in the title would have some equity, as I am somewhat well-known in the industry. However, the current name makes it too obvious that this is a one-person or very small company. This can be a disadvantage."

PATIENT GIFT PACKAGER

Startup cost:	$5,000–$10,000
Potential earnings:	$25,000–$40,000
Typical fees:	$15–$35 depending on the size and content of the basket
Advertising:	Direct mail to hospital administrators; fliers to health care facilities; Yellow Pages listing; newspaper ads
Qualifications:	Creative flair, ability to market yourself
Equipment needed:	Decorative baskets, boxes, glue gun, shrink-wrap machine, filling, ribbons; personal care products such as toothpaste, soap, and lotion; delivery vehicle
Home business potential:	Yes
Staff required:	No
Hidden costs:	Insurance, vendor's license

LOWDOWN:

Creativity, organization, and the ability to visualize are all you need to make a go of this business. Build your market carefully—pinpoint hospitals, extended care facilities, and even church groups (they often have members who regularly visit hospitalized parishioners). Who doesn't like to take a gift to a friend or relative in the hospital, even if the basket just contains a get-well card and a few well-packaged toiletries? It makes both the gift-giver and the patient feel good. The gift basket business has caught on in the last five years, and this is just a slightly more specialized version of it. Most of your competition will be small shops, perhaps even some large retailers, but few are creating baskets especially geared to patients. Market yourself by networking with your local hospitals and nonprofit organizations. Donate a basket or two to a local charity event to get your name out there.

STARTUP:

The initial startup cost is in the relatively low range (around $5,000 for supplies); you may even have some of the decorative items lying around the house if you're crafty. What will constantly keep you going after more clients is the need to maintain a high profit level—this business will not be substantial enough to support you if you aren't constantly on the lookout for new business. Find the private craft retailer who sells only to vendors; his or her prices could be as much as 40 percent lower than traditional retail craft supply shops. Get busy making and selling gift baskets, and you could wrap up an annual salary between $25,000–$50,000.

BOTTOM LINE ADVICE:

What a wonderful business to be in! Wouldn't it be a great feeling to know that you're making someone's day a little brighter, and getting paid to do it? This can be a very time-consuming occupation, however. If you decide to customize, be prepared to go on the hunt for specific requests. If you offer an assortment from which your clients can pick, make sure you provide enough variety—something to appeal to all ages. And don't forget, somebody has to deliver the baskets, too. If you have a station wagon or van, you could add a delivery fee to your orders and make additional money.

PERSONALIZED CHILDREN'S BOOKS

Startup cost:	$5,000–$15,000
Potential earnings:	$20,000–$40,000
Typical fees:	$15–$25 per book
Advertising:	Direct mail, flea markets, fliers on bulletin boards wherever parents gather, Web site
Qualifications:	Computer proficiency, writing skills
Equipment needed:	Computer, desktop publishing software, color laser printer, binder
Home business potential:	Yes
Staff required:	No
Hidden costs:	Mistakes can be costly; proof your work carefully

LOWDOWN:

Customized picture books can brighten any kid's day—after all, what could be better for a child than reading a story with his or her own name throughout? With personalized picture books, pint-sized readers get to be the leading character in the book they're reading. What a great gift for parents and grandparents to give to their early readers! You'll produce your books using one of a few templates, and then simply drop in the child's name via computer. You'll print the books out on your color laser printer, bind them, and package them up for your customers. Get the word out by advertising in community newspapers or on your own Web site. Consider renting a mall kiosk during weekends or the holiday season to sell your services directly and in a place where you can produce your products on the spot.

STARTUP:

Set your book prices at $15–$25, depending on the length of the book. There will be an initial investment to get the book made (around $10,000 for your basic equipment setup and paper stock). If you have a way with words, you can create your own stories; if not, you'll likely be buying into a franchise which can be pretty costly. Expect to shell out a franchising fee of $30,000–$50,000, which includes the book templates, plus sales and marketing support. In either case, you'll need to generate a few samples to sell your services, so don't forget to include the cost of two or three mockups of the actual books in your startup plan. Market your books via direct mail to preschools and/or direct selling at flea markets and shopping mall kiosks; producing the books on-site can help attract interest and boost sales.

BOTTOM LINE ADVICE:

This is a fun and entertaining venture—who doesn't love to make a child smile and get paid for doing it? The flip side, of course, is the frustration of working with difficult customers, and we're not talking about just the kids here. But hey, you're in the retail/customer service business, just go with the flow and reap the profits.

PET BREEDER

Startup cost:	$5,000–$10,000
Potential earnings:	$15,000–$20,000
Typical fees:	$200–$300 for purebred kittens and puppies; more for very rare or exotic breeds and show/breeding quality animals
Advertising:	Classified ads, specialty periodicals for your breed
Qualifications:	Love of animals; experience with care, breeding, and medical needs
Equipment needed:	Kennels, feeders, space, etc.
Home business potential:	Yes
Staff required:	No
Hidden costs:	Loss of young animals due to birth defects or disease, high vet bills, insurance, breeding fees

LOWDOWN:

Most people breed animals because they love them, and only secondarily to make money. If you really add up the cost in terms of your time and effort, you wouldn't find breeding your beloved shelties or Persians to be a particularly good business deal. Even so, many people still choose to fit breeding into the daily flow of their lives. If you have adequate space (you live on a farm, for example) and healthy purebred males and females, you can produce the adorable purebred puppies or kittens that find their way into more homes in America than children. Some kennels grow to large, full-time businesses providing working dogs, guide dogs, or animals for pet stores. You'll need adequate kennel space for your animals to live in while they are being weaned; some states have mandatory (and unscheduled) inspections of such facilities to root out animal rights violators. Make sure you distinguish your service as a caring one.

STARTUP:

Your startup costs for this business will depend on where you live and the breed you decide to specialize in. It doesn't take a rocket scientist to know that raising Great Danes is quite a different proposition than breeding toy poodles. Be aware that if you advertise your offspring as purebred, your customers may ask you to present a "family tree" for verification of your claim; securing one can sometimes be expensive. But that may well be the least of your expenses. Dog pens and kennels do not come cheap; expect to spend $5,000–$10,000, depending on size and quality. Purebred dogs and cats sell for $200–$300, with rare and exotic breeds going for as much as $500–$1,000 each, so you can make some money if all goes well. And *if* is the optimum word. Vet bills can take a major chunk out of your budget, so be sure you have plenty set aside in the event of illness or injury.

BOTTOM LINE ADVICE:

If you find a deep satisfaction in watching tiny creatures open their eyes and take their first wobbly steps into the world, if you love the idea of putting a warm puppy or a fluffy kitten into the arms of a delighted child, then by all means consider making pet breeding your business. Just remember that the work is not always happy and heartwarming. There are messes to be cleaned up and sometimes a loss of life to be faced; then too, there's the fact that your schedule is no longer your own as the needs of your tiny charges must always come first. Pet breeding is a 24/7 occupation.

PET GROOMING/CARE

Startup cost:	$10,000–$25,000
Potential earnings:	$25,000–$40,000
Typical fees:	$30–$60 per pet, depending on the size and service provided
Advertising:	Yellow Pages, direct mail, community bulletin boards, referrals from vets
Qualifications:	Experience, patience, knowledge of animal behavior patterns, familiarity with the grooming standards of different breeds
Equipment needed:	Grooming table, sinks or tubs, cages, clippers, brushes, combs, bathing tub/shower accessories, shampoos, dryer, detangler, a vehicle if you decide to go the mobile route
Home business potential:	Possibly; check zoning regulations
Staff required:	No
Hidden costs:	Supplies, insurance, licensing

LOWDOWN:

If you enjoy working with pets, you can build a profitable business providing grooming services. Pet ownership increases each year in this country, but people have less free time than ever. What Afghan owners can really manage to comb out their pet's entire coat every day, as the books recommend? The popular white poodles need considerable grooming to present themselves in a clean, fluffy, well-trimmed coat. Aside from the pet's appearance, good health practices dictate cleaning and brushing, and sometimes trimming, the coat regularly. Once you establish rapport with Rover, you are likely to have regular repeat business from his owner. Giving cats their flea baths is another popular service (to the owner, definitely not to the feline). As an add-on, consider selling pet supplies and/or specialty products for the pampered pet, and to set yourself apart from other groomers in your area, consider a mobile operation.

STARTUP:

To make a go of the business, you'll need a businesslike setting and the right equipment—sinks, cages, a grooming table—plus shampoos, flea dips, and all the other supplies necessary to do a professional job. Equipping your operation can easily set you back $10,000–$25,000, but you stand a good chance of recouping your expenses in a year or two if the competition is sparse and you market effectively. Pet grooming can be an in-home business if you have the space, but be sure to check your the zoning regulations for your neighborhood before opening shop. Charge between $30–$60, depending on the size of the animal and the specific services you perform.

BOTTOM LINE ADVICE:

You may not be the only pet grooming service in your community, but you can be the best. You can offer pickup and delivery services, specialize in attending to the idiosyncrasies of particular breeds, and always leave each "patient" happy and sweet-smelling. You'll need to make the pet owners in your area feel that your pet grooming service, in particular, is the one they can't live without. Pet grooming is hard, physical work, but each session leaves a beloved pet looking better—until he or she can get outside again, of course—and then—hooray!—it's back to the groomer again.

PHOTOCOPYING SERVICE

Startup cost:	$5,000–$15,000
Potential earnings:	$40,000–$60,000
Typical fees:	Prices vary; some copy centers charge as little as 4 cents per copy; shop the competition to determine the average rates in your area
Advertising:	Newspapers, Yellow Pages, fliers, direct mail, location
Qualifications:	Some graphics experience
Equipment needed:	High-quality photocopying machines, preferably with large-format capabilities; paper and toner stock
Home business potential:	No
Staff required:	Not initially
Hidden costs:	Repairs, paper inventories

LOWDOWN:

Photocopying is one of those services that just about everyone—businesses and individuals alike—needs from time to time. You will need at least one top-of-the-line machine capable of producing excellent copies, and a customer-focused attitude. Add additional machines as you grow and consider making a self-serve unit available for those who simply need a couple of copies on the fly. Franchises (i.e., Kinko's, Sir Speedy, etc.) for copying services are available, or you can set up your own small, independent operation. Unless you plan to do all pickup and delivery work, you will also need an accessible location. And you must be creative about distinguishing yourself from the competition. Many successful copying businesses offer design and paste-up in addition to basic copying functions. Having a range of papers available will add to the professional look of your products. Quick turnaround and personalized service will help set you apart from the national chains.

STARTUP:

Your startup costs will depend in part on whether or not you choose the franchise route. With a franchise comes a recognizable name, all the necessary supplies, and marketing assistance, but also significantly higher startup costs ($10,000–$50,000 or more for the initial investment). If you choose to remain independent, you will need to purchase your own photocopying equipment and supplies, arrange for maintenance and repair contracts, and develop a marketing plan. Equipment costs alone will run you $10,000–$15,000, which, hopefully, you'll be able to quickly recoup with a combination of the right per-copy rate and high volume. Most copy centers charge around 5 cents per copy (some frequently run 2½-cent specials to build business); your income will be directly contingent upon how many clients you serve per month. Unless you plan to handle only pickup and delivery work, your location will be an important concern. You'll need to be both visible and easily accessible. Look for rental space with plenty of free parking in front.

BOTTOM LINE ADVICE:

The photocopying market is potentially huge, and you need very little technical training or professional experience at it to get started. Your number one concern should be customer service. People who enjoy a stream of customers, each with a different project to be completed, will find a photocopying business rewarding. The downside is the competition, and not just from the giants like Kinko's. Libraries, convenience stores, even supermarkets have photocopying machines available for public use. It will take some serious marketing efforts on your part to lure customers away from the competition.

ADVICE FROM THE EXPERTS

What sets your business apart from others like it?

Connie Delehanty, owner of a Sir Speedy Printing Center franchise in Fairlawn, Ohio, says: "A knowledgeable staff that asks the right questions and is able to get the job done right as a result. We have a commitment to customer service and quality."

Things you couldn't do without:

"We couldn't do without our staff and up-to-date technology such as interfaced computers with digital color output devices and laser printers."

Marketing tips/advice:

"Location, location . . . you need to be in a highly traveled path." Delehanty's print shop is located in a small shopping plaza near a major thoroughfare.

If you had to do it all over again . . .

"I'd start with more capital," says Delehanty. "Equipment costs can skyrocket in this technology-driven business."

POLITICAL MARKETING CONSULTANT

Startup cost:	$5,000–$10,000
Potential earnings:	$50,000–$150,000
Typical fees:	Average fees are anywhere from $75–$150 per hour
Advertising:	Referrals (it's who you know)
Qualifications:	Wide and deep experience with politics, demographics, marketing, statistics, and polling techniques
Equipment needed:	Laptop computer with Internet access and word processing, database, and spreadsheet software; printer, fax, copier, scanner, cell phone
Home business potential:	Yes
Staff required:	Eventually (you'll need a network of subcontractors, associates, etc. as the candidate's popularity grows)
Hidden costs:	Telephone bills, travel expenses

LOWDOWN:

Thanks to the presidential campaigns of recent years, political consultants have achieved an almost mythological status in America. We somehow respect them, even as we resent them for what we see as manipulation of public opinion. The consultants who operate at the national level are, in a sense, just the tip of the political iceberg. Behind the scenes in many a local or regional campaign are skilled, knowledgeable people who help candidates present their messages clearly and effectively to the public. If you are savvy about language, political issues, government, and current affairs, you could become one of them. Politics is a business of very high highs and extremely low lows in which consultants play an important role. Our democratic form of government requires reaching out to the people, and political marketing consultants provide a vital service in helping candidates do just that.

STARTUP:

In this business, communication is the name of the game; you will have to be reachable 24/7. Shop for the best cell phone plan; you'll be eating up minutes like crazy! You'll want to carry a laptop, too, so you can keep up with e-mail and surf the Web whenever necessary. Expect to spend $5,000–$10,000 to cover your basic office setup and communications needs.

BOTTOM LINE ADVICE:

Being involved with the political process is dynamic and interesting, but it is also very hard work. You will need to know as much as you can about your district, the issues voters care about, and the views of your candidate's constituents. During political campaigns, you will be part of a tightly focused team; between elections, you can work independently to keep politicians and parties informed about public attitudes. You'll need excellent connections and an impressive track record to make a go of this kind of business.

PORTRAIT ARTIST/PHOTOGRAPHER

Startup cost:	$5,000–$15,000
Potential earnings:	$20,000–$50,000
Typical fees:	$1,500–$3,000 per finished oil portrait
Advertising:	Brochures mailed to executives, networking, Yellow Pages, Web site, word of mouth
Qualifications:	Artistic talent and the ability to capture a person's "essence" on canvas; salesmanship
Equipment needed:	Cameras, lights, backdrops, film, paint, props, easel, paints, canvas
Home business potential:	Yes
Staff required:	No
Hidden costs:	Refunds may be necessary if customers are not happy with the work; supplies

LOWDOWN:

Ever walk into a large corporate office and see walls adorned with fancy oil portraits of everyone who's ever been anyone at the company? If you have the kind of artistic talent that lends itself to portraiture, you could be the artist selected to render the next painting for the corporate wall. Part of your challenge as a portrait artist will be education: You'll need to help your clients understand that, although portraiture requires artistic talent, it is a highly specialized form of art and not something just any artist can do. Set yourself apart as an artist who is skilled at conveying a person's "essence" in each portrait; you are not in the same league as the sidewalk artist who dashes off a caricature or sketch and hands it to the subject at the end of a 20-minute sitting. Yours is a highly refined art form that takes time to create. You may require several sittings or, if you prefer to work solely from photographs, at least one lengthy photographic session. One last tip: Since you'll be most often working with a wealthy clientele who expect to pay top dollar for goods and services, you can set your fees higher; add at least 20 percent to whatever figure you have in mind.

STARTUP:

You'll need a studio in which to work, as well as photographic equipment and artistic supplies. Plan on spending between $5,000 and $10,000 for your cameras, lights, backdrops, film, paints, props, and canvas. You'll need another $2,000–$5,000 to cover the cost of your marketing efforts, which should include a Web site and brochures to display samples of your work. You'll have to be somewhat aggressive about marketing your services because your income will depend on how many commissions you are able to secure and complete within a year.

BOTTOM LINE ADVICE:

If as an artist you are concerned that to go after the business portraiture market feels like selling out, consider this: Some of Rembrandt's most memorable works, including *The Night Watch* and *De Staalmeesters* (the painting made famous by Dutch Masters cigars) were commissioned portraits of businessmen. Business portraiture is an honorable way to make a living, but if it's still not enough to keep a roof over your head, consider boosting your earning by teaching the art of portraiture at a local university or community college.

PRIVATE DETECTIVE/ INTELLIGENCE SPECIALIST

Startup cost:	$5,000–$9,000
Potential earnings:	$50,000–$75,000
Advertising:	Direct solicitation, Yellow Pages, direct mail, speaking at meetings and seminars, networking with attorneys and law enforcement
Qualifications:	Experience in law enforcement and/or investigative work, people skills, writing ability, creativity, persistence, listening skills
Equipment needed:	Computer with Internet access, printer, and software, fax; small tape recorder, pocket notebooks, cell phone, digital or video camera
Home business potential:	Yes
Staff required:	Not initially
Hidden costs:	Most states require a private investigator's license

LOWDOWN:

Private investigators dig up information that others want to keep hidden. There's a good market these days for solo practitioners who support lawyers working on both criminal and civil cases. As with so many other businesses, however, specialization may be your key to success. For example, computer crime is on the rise, and those who can track it down are extremely valuable to a range of organizations, especially banks and businesses that are worried about employee theft or false workers' compensation claims. Background checks form another non-glamorous but profitable specialty. And then there's the whole burgeoning world of identity theft.

Licensing is required in most states, and, to get one, you will need experience in a related field, such as law enforcement, collections, or claims adjustment. Creativity with regard to finding the answers to puzzles that may have troubled your clients for years and well-developed listening skills are essential.

STARTUP:

Outfitting yourself and your office for duty will be your main startup expense. In addition to the traditional computer and peripherals, you'll want specific tools of your trade, including a digital or video camera for surveillance and a small tape recorder for interviews. Expect to spend around $5,000 to get your business up and running. You should, however, see a return on your investment fairly soon.

BOTTOM LINE ADVICE:

Of course, the real world of private detection bears little resemblance to its portrayal on television or in books. You may desire to be on the crusade for truth, justice, and the American way, but you will soon find that the rest of the world doesn't see things your way. Nevertheless, your clients will come to value your services, and you can build repeat business if you demonstrate your ability to be an honest and effective investigator. The bulk of investigative work is not about taking down a bad guy, it's about genuinely helping people, by finding a lost family member or recovering money they are owed. You may occasionally feel the thrill of the chase, but more often, it is resentment and even direct opposition that will come your way. A P.I.'s hours are awful, and time management is next to impossible.

PROFESSIONAL RESCUE AND RECOVERY DIVER

Startup cost:	$5,000–$8,000
Potential earnings:	$20,000–$35,000
Typical fees:	$25–$50 per hour
Advertising:	Networking, referrals, word of mouth
Qualifications:	Training and certification in open-water diving (advanced level) and rescue diving; aquatic first aid and CPR training; extensive underwater diving experience; physical strength and stamina; emotional stability
Equipment needed:	Full complement of diving gear and related equipment, tanks, diving apparel, cell phone
Home business potential:	Yes
Staff required:	No
Hidden costs:	Insurance

LOWDOWN:

Professional rescue and recovery divers are not just underwater divers looking for recreation; they provide a critical service to police and rescue personnel when emergency situations involving deep water arise. As a rescue and recovery diver, you can have the best of both worlds: you get to pursue a sport that you love, on the one hand, and, on the other, you help save lives and property or solve mysteries by locating people and important items, some of which may be related to a crime. Most of your business will come from law enforcement agencies—police and sheriffs' departments, possibly even the FBI or DEA—who need the kind of help that only your expertise can provide. You won't need to do any advertising to find clients. Once you have made your expertise and availability known to the proper authorities, the business will come to you. If you're just looking for a way to log diving hours and get paid for it, find another outlet for your recreational ambitions. Rescue diving is serious business and it's not for everyone.

STARTUP:

Don't even consider this business unless you are already an accomplished and heavily experienced diver. You will need to have advanced level open-water certification, plus certification in the specialty of rescue diving. Most of your work will be on-call and related to emergencies, which means you'll need to be accessible 24/7 and ready to go at the proverbial drop of a hat. You'll need to have your own diving apparel, SCUBA gear, tanks, and related underwater equipment at the ready (you won't have time to find a place to rent it), plus a cell phone for easy accessibility. Rescue diving is a pretty sporadic occupation, so you might want to consider this only as a secondary source of income, perhaps as an adjunct to a full-time underwater adventure/SCUBA instruction business.

BOTTOM LINE ADVICE:

Imagine getting paid to do something you enjoy and are good at! Diving can be fun, relaxing, even inspiring—but it can also be physically demanding, strenuous, and, in the case of underwater rescue and recovery, incredibly stressful. Are you up to the task—even if it means pulling a dead body out of the water?

PUBLIC RELATIONS

Startup cost:	$5,000–$10,000
Potential earnings:	$35,000–$75,000
Typical fees:	$50–$75 per hour, flat fee per project, or monthly retainer
Advertising:	Networking and personal contacts, speeches before business or community groups, volunteer work for nonprofit organizations, cold calling, Web site
Qualifications:	Creativity, strong verbal and written communication skills, assertive and persuasive personality, ability to deal effectively with abstract concepts, high energy level, photographic abilities helpful but not required
Equipment needed:	Computer with high-speed Internet access; printer, copier, scanner, and fax; word processing, spreadsheet, and desktop publishing software; telephone headset, multiple phone lines with call-forwarding and conferencing features; cell phone
Home business potential:	Yes
Staff required:	No
Hidden costs:	Accreditation; slow starting time (expect two years before profit)

LOWDOWN:

As with so many other fields, the demand for PR is growing. At the same time, however, many corporations are cutting their public relations staffs (PR people are usually the first to go when a company downsizes). Consequently, a lot of PR work these days is being farmed out. If you have the right skills, public relations can be an ideal home-based business. Keep in mind, however, that relationships with clients take time to develop and your success as a freelance PR practitioner will depend in large part on your network of contacts in the media. The opportunities for public relations activities are many: When a small company launches a breakthrough new product, when the advertising budget is too small to make much of a splash, when an organization needs to get its message across to the public in a way advertising cannot do, when a crisis arises or a negative situation needs to be turned around, your PR services can be invaluable. To attract media attention and interest, you will need outstanding writing and speaking skills, a healthy dose of creativity, awareness of how different types of media work and what they're hungry for, and an ability to put all the pieces together to create an effective public relations campaign. PR can be fun, but it's tough too. You must straddle that fine line between promoting your client's product or service and giving the media what it wants. The ability to think on your feet and network effectively with print and broadcast reporters and editors is essential.

STARTUP:

You will need to present yourself and your business at a high level of professionalism, so a well-equipped office is a must. Expect to spend $5,000 on your basic office setup, including a computer, printer, and desktop publishing software, as well as a multiline phone system and cell phone. Bill at a rate of $50–$75 per hour for your expertise.

BOTTOM LINE ADVICE:

For creative, dynamic, and above all energetic people, public relations is a terrific field. If you thrive on relationships with many different individuals and organizations and love the stimulation of constant change, you should consider making PR your business. As a solo practitioner, you'll start with small projects and gradually expand your network and contacts to take on more complex campaigns. PR is not just about "liking people." It's a demanding profession that requires excellent verbal and written communication skills, as well as the ability to network effectively with clients and media representatives. Many people call themselves PR practitioners, but not everyone who does actually has the necessary background or skills; to set yourself apart and to gain credibility in the industry, consider becoming accredited through the Public Relations Society of America. Your success in this business will depend on your ability to produce results. Recognize from the get-go that your business will take tremendous time and effort to grow. Marketing your own services must be a priority even as you complete one project after another on behalf of your clients. Media representatives can be fickle; getting publicity for your clients will require new angles and ideas each time to catch the media's attention.

ADVICE FROM THE EXPERTS

What sets your business apart from others like it?

Eric Yaverbaum, president of the New York City-based Jericho Promotions, says his soaring public relations business is unique because of how often the company itself is in the press. "We're on national TV regularly, and we've been written about in the *Wall Street Journal*. Our customers know we're in a league of our own in terms of creativity."

Things you couldn't do without:

Yaverbaum says he couldn't do without a fax machine, mailing list database, multiple phone lines, and e-mail.

Marketing tips/advice:

"Hire the right people to establish credibility . . . you're buying their experience and capitalizing on it. Doing that has saved me at least ten years of pounding the pavement. Also, when you lose someone, you can turn it into an opportunity to bring in new business. One of my people moved to a company that later became a client as a result of my professionalism in the matter."

If you had to do it all over again . . .

"I probably wouldn't do it . . . starting a business is a tough road for anyone. I guess I liked it best when the company was small enough to have a lot of fun."

PUBLIC SPEAKING CONSULTANT

Startup cost:	$5,000–$10,000
Potential earnings:	$30,000–$45,000
Typical fees:	$75 per hour or a flat rate ($500–$1,500, depending on type of service provided)
Advertising:	Yellow Pages, business directories, association mailings, and direct mail, networking
Qualifications:	Public speaking ability and/or degree in speech communication; writing skills
Equipment needed:	Resource/educational materials, TV/VCR unit, video camera (to tape and subsequently critique your client's performance), basic office setup: computer, Internet access, word processing and desktop publishing software, printer, fax, phone, copier, scanner
Home business potential:	Yes
Staff required:	No
Hidden costs:	Insurance, equipment maintenance

LOWDOWN:

Executives and other professionals are often called on to deliver speeches—only to fall flat on their faces due to inexperience or lack of preparation. That's where you come in. With your background in speech communication, you can help these floundering folks put together a presentation that is not only effective in its content, but also in its delivery. You can assist them in everything from written speech development and outlining to punchy delivery that gets repeated by listeners long after the fact. The best part about this business is, it's fairly easy work once you've established yourself. You can develop and print your own educational materials for coaching professionals, and you'll want to tape their "performance" to be able to critique. You will likely work with a wide array of professionals, from CEOs to physicians to engineers: The list of potentials goes on as far as your imagination permits. This is a straightforward kind of business, with many established rules and strategies for success. You'll probably enjoy it best when you have the opportunity to deliver your own speeches—which you'll need to do from time to time to boost your business. Offer your services to associations and corporate professional development directors.

STARTUP:

You'll need some resource materials (books, tapes, etc.), plus a video camera to tape your subjects' performances and a TV/VCR unit on which to play them back for purposes of review and critique. You'll need a basic office setup, too, including a computer with Internet access, printer, word processing and desktop publishing software (for creating your own educational materials), fax, scanner, copier, and phone. With some hard work in the area of promotion, you can expect to earn $30,000–$45,000 per year.

BOTTOM LINE ADVICE:

Diversify yourself as much as possible—go after CEOs at large corporations, of course, but don't forget to target small business owners, university officials, even local politicos who are just getting started, too. The point is, there's a huge market out there for your services—be smart enough to fully develop it, and you'll do well.

RARE BOOK DEALER/
SEARCH SERVICE

Startup cost:	$5,000–$10,000
Potential earnings:	$20,000–$40,000
Typical fees:	$10–$25 per hour, per book, plus a markup on sale price of the book
Advertising:	Yellow Pages, book industry publications, referrals from bookstores, Web site
Qualifications:	Knowledge of old books and their market values; exceptional research abilities; persistence; good organizational skills and excellent follow-up ability
Equipment needed:	Computer, printer, fax, high-speed Internet access, phone, 800 number
Home business potential:	Yes
Staff required:	No
Hidden costs:	High-speed Internet access; phone bills; time (some searches can really rack up the hours; be certain you are covered)

LOWDOWN:

Some avid readers will go to extraordinary lengths to find a used or rare book that they'd relish having in their private collection. Whether you're providing this service in addition to running a bookstore (as many searchers do) or running it as a separate business, you'll need to be highly detail-oriented and well-organized to make this business profitable. The good news is, there's a wealth of information online as well as plenty of publications that you can subscribe to; you should have no difficulty tracking down the books that are currently available through other dealers. Sometimes, you'll be lucky enough to work out an even trade (and maximize your own profit on the book you're selling to the customer). Most often, however, you'll derive your income from a search fee ($10–$25 per hour) and a sales commission on the book itself (which you will have priced accordingly to reflect market value and a tidy commission for yourself). It should come as no surprise that the older and rarer the book you're looking for, the harder it will be to locate—but if you can manage to find it somewhere in the world, no matter how yellowed or dog-eared the pages, your earnings could be quite high on just one book.

STARTUP:

It will take around $5,000 to equip yourself with a powerful computer and speedy Internet searching capabilities; expect to spend at least another $1,000–$2,000 on advertising in your first year. If you are good at what you do, the word will get around and you could see income potentials of $25,000–$45,000 per year.

BOTTOM LINE ADVICE:

The stress level is actually quite low in this field, and you can pretty much search for a book at your own pace. However, you don't get paid as much for looking as you do for finding—so rely on the Internet heavily to expedite your searches.

REAL ESTATE APPRAISER

Startup cost:	$7,000–$15,000
Potential earnings:	$50,000–$100,000
Typical fees:	$300 per house, more for commercial property
Advertising:	Referrals from banks and mortgage companies, networking
Qualifications:	License or certification based on your state's requirements; knowledge of architecture, construction, and building materials; familiarity with financing options and mortgage equity; writing skills
Equipment needed:	Computer, fax, Internet access, printer, word processing and appraisal software, 35mm and/or digital camera, cell phone, vehicle
Home business potential:	Yes
Staff required:	No
Hidden costs:	Training, insurance, license and renewal fees, organizational dues, vehicle expenses

LOWDOWN:

Real estate investment has made fortunes for people in the recent past—and it has brought down large institutions as well. Appraising the value of land and buildings is always necessary, but it becomes even more so during periods of intensive property turnover and when declining interest rates prompt a tidal wave of refinancing activity in the marketplace. Once you pass your state's required certification process to become an appraiser, you will have the opportunity to provide a much-needed service for home owners, home buyers and sellers, investors, commercial property developers, and the institutions that lend money for real estate transactions. As an appraiser, you will conduct research concerning the trends likely to affect real estate values, much of which can be handled online. Demographic statistics, finance issues, and changes in building construction methods can all be relevant to your findings. Of course you will also physically inspect the site and structures you are valuing. You will need a working knowledge of architecture and building materials to help make good judgments, and your grasp of the big picture will help you compare the property you are appraising to other similar properties and the local real estate market in general.

STARTUP:

As with other professions requiring certification, your startup costs may be as high as $15,000. Equipping an office to create and produce appraisal reports is also an expensive proposition; to cut costs, consider shopping for used appraisal equipment. You'll be billing customers at the rate of $300 per house (and more for commercial properties), so if you are aggressive in your marketing efforts, it shouldn't be too terribly long before you'll begin to generate a profit.

BOTTOM LINE ADVICE:

Real estate appraisers are often caught in the middle between sellers who want the value of their property to be high and buyers who want it to be low. You will need errors and omissions insurance with broad coverage as you could be in some danger of being sued if your assessment results in negative consequences for an investor.

RECREATIONAL COUPON DISTRIBUTOR

Startup cost:	$5,000–$10,000
Potential earnings:	$15,000–$35,000
Typical fees:	Advertising rates vary from $150–$3,000 per client
Advertising:	Yellow Pages, networking with and direct mail to recreational facilities and health clubs, etc.
Qualifications:	Sales ability, good organizational skills
Equipment needed:	Computer with desktop publishing software, laser printer, rate cards/contracts, perhaps a delivery vehicle
Home business potential:	Yes
Staff required:	No (but you will probably need to hire helpers for distribution)
Hidden costs:	Printing and paper; vehicle expenses

LOWDOWN:

Everyone likes to have a good time—and everyone likes a good deal, too. That's why coupon books for recreational activities are such sure bets; they'll be read, kept, and, with the exception of grocery coupons, better used than any other kind of coupon. Your mission is to sell those in the recreation industry on earmarking some of their advertising dollars for your service, then making sure that your package is enticing enough to grab the interest of potential customers. If you try to cut corners and your coupon books end up looking cheap, they'll get tossed like any other piece of junk mail; spend the money it takes to acquire a decent desktop publishing system that allows you to create your own innovative coupons, then work with printers to get the best deals on paper and printing costs. Familiarize yourself with the printing process so that you have a clear understanding of how and where you can save, then ask your printer for additional tips and cost-cutting ideas. Plan your distribution system well, and count on hiring one or two part-time helpers to get your coupons in the hands of consumers; you won't have time to do everything yourself.

STARTUP:

You should be able to stay in the $5,000–$10,000 range to get this business off the ground; primarily, you'll be spending your startup monies on a computer system with a top-of-the-line printer and desktop publishing software and the vehicle and/or phone expenses you'll incur in trying to build sales. However, if you work hard and don't mind putting in lots of long hours, you could make $15,000–$35,000 or more at this one.

BOTTOM LINE ADVICE:

Your ability to find businesses willing to buy into your concept will hinge largely on your reputation; for purposes of networking and credibility you may want to become active in community organizations; at the very least, you should consider joining your local chamber of commerce.

RESTORATION SERVICES

Startup costs:	$5,000–$15,000
Potential earnings:	$30,000–$45,000
Typical fees:	Varied, depending on project and scope
Advertising:	Yellow Pages, local newspapers, business cards and fliers in antique shops, networking with interior designers and buildings/operations managers
Equipment needed:	Floor and rotary sanders, strippers, steel wool, rags to start; add equipment based on type of restoration project
Qualifications:	Thorough knowledge of techniques for and experience in restoring a variety of surfaces, basic business and marketing skills
Home business potential:	Yes
Staff required:	No
Hidden costs:	Insurance, hazardous materials disposal costs, legal fees

LOWDOWN:

Many people value hardwood floors, antique furniture and ceramic fixtures, and vintage floor coverings—and would rather restore them than buy something new. Restoration services may be especially needed after natural disasters—floods, earthquakes, or hurricanes—and fires. For large clients such as offices, apartments, or hotels, repairing carpet and restoring tile and wood floors may be more cost effective than replacing them. Refinishing hardwood floors, especially, can be time-consuming and labor-intensive, and people are often too busy or lack the know-how to bother with the job. That's why there's a market for restoration services. You can start by simply refinishing furniture with strippers, steel wool, rags, and stain, and later move into more complicated projects. You could opt to purchase a franchise; typical costs run close to $20,000. While that's a significant investment, the fact that many offer training, tools, and materials to start you off make these franchise opportunities worth investigating.

STARTUP:

Your startup costs will largely be determined by your decision to go it alone or invest in a franchise operation. If you decide to wing it, be prepared to spend $15,000 or more for equipment in addition to the $5,000 initial investment you will need to make in order to cover basics, including EPA training for disposal of hazardous materials and marketing. Your fees will vary according to the scope of each project, but could be as low as $100 or as high as several thousand.

BOTTOM LINE ADVICE:

Cultivate a variety of contacts—antiques dealers, interior designers, buildings/operations managers of corporations and hotels. Have a ready supply of business cards and a simple brochure or flier outlining your services. If you have a knack for writing, submit articles to regional antiques publications or send news releases to the antiques or home improvement editor of your local newspaper. When dealing with customers, get a deposit to cover the cost of materials so you're not out the money. Submit a proposal detailing the work you plan to do. After coming to an agreement with the customer, have your attorney draw up a contract and get your client to sign it before proceeding with the work.

RUBBER STAMP BUSINESS

Startup cost:	$5,000–$10,000
Potential earnings:	$40,000–$60,000
Typical fees:	Anywhere from $3–$15 per stamp
Advertising:	Mail order, direct mail, newspapers, Web site
Qualifications:	Creativity and an eye for designs that will sell; spelling accuracy; you can be trained in the manufacturing process by a printing professional
Equipment needed:	Computer with laser printer, photopolymer system; subcontract with a stamp manufacturer for larger orders that need to be made of rubber)
Home business potential:	Yes
Staff required:	No
Hidden costs:	Materials

LOWDOWN:

The rubber stamp business gets the stamp of approval from many entrepreneurial resources. Why? Because it's a relatively easy way to make steady money from a simple product. The variety of stamps you can produce is mind-boggling; think of the last time you went into a retail store and saw literally hundreds of choices (from frogs to stars to computers). While there are lots of possibilities in the business world, too (small businesses need return address stamps and stamps that read "Paid," "Handle with Care," and "This Side Up"), they can purchase them pretty readily at office supply stores. The stamps you'll be making are the "art" stamps people use to "pretty up" stationery, envelopes, wrapping paper, even fabric. You can sell your stamps wholesale or retail, by mail order, on the Web, in stores, or at craft shows. Whichever direction you choose, you'll be off to a strong start if you launch your company with introductory specials and discounts for new customers. Making your own stamps is relatively simple; printers and graphics people can provide you with all the background and technical information you need. You can take your designs from the clip art that's available in the public domain or design your own.

STARTUP:

You can make simple stamps using a personal computer, laser printer, and photopolymer system ($2,500–$3,000), but if you want to get into the rubber stamp business, you'll either need to subcontract with a manufacturer or invest in the necessary special equipment (about $5,000 to start). Another option is to buy a franchise version of this business. The advantage is that your purchase price covers all the training you'll need; the disadvantage is that you'll have to spend at least $10,000 on licensing fees. But considering that this is potentially a high-volume business and you'll be marketing your products to the masses at a cost of $3–$15 a pop, you stand a good chance of making a decent living at this one.

BOTTOM LINE ADVICE:

Hmmm . . . the investment's not too big, the income potential is high, what's not to like about the rubber stamp business?

SALES TRAINER

Startup cost:	$5,000–$8,000
Potential earnings:	$40,000–$60,000
Typical fees:	$2,000–$3,000 per engagement
Advertising:	Networking, referrals, trade journals, memberships in business and community groups
Qualifications:	Extensive record of success in sales, demonstrated effectiveness as a trainer, ability to sell your own services
Equipment needed:	Computer; word processing, desktop publishing, and presentation software; laser and/or color printer; cell phone; fax; copier; scanner; Internet access; marketing and training materials
Home business potential:	Yes
Staff required:	No
Hidden costs:	Preparation of training manuals and handouts, overheads

LOWDOWN:

Sales is a skilled profession, and as the hierarchy at most companies gets flatter, the managers have less and less time to train their vital salespeople in the techniques and approaches that really work. Your ability to transfer your wide experience and reper-toire of proven techniques for getting in the door, making a case clearly, and closing the sale will be your stock-in-trade as you respond to this growing corporate need. You may find it effective to focus on companies making the types of products you have sold in the past (pharmaceuticals, toys, etc.), or you may target a certain size of company or region of the country. Getting established as a sales trainer is no easy task, but it's cer-tainly doable with drive and persistence. You're a sales pro, remember? Among the most profitable sales trainers are those who have continuing contracts with one or two large organizations whose confidence they have gained. Be sure to plan for the cost and time you must spend on marketing as you develop your own business.

STARTUP:

Equipping your office to function for your business and produce whatever training mate-rials you plan to supply will be your main expenses (plan on at least $3,000). Travel can also be costly, depending on your range of operations; you may be able to bill your cli-ents for expenses, but even so, you'll have to wait for reimbursements which can wreak havoc on your cash flow. Once you get established and snare a couple of key, regular clients, you can make $40,000–$60,000 a year as a sales trainer.

BOTTOM LINE ADVICE:

An effective sales trainer can make a significant difference in a company's sales figures. But salespeople can be a tough audience. They don't usually want to sit and listen; they want to get up and take over, or take off. You'll need excellent presentation techniques to keep your audience's attention and convince them of the value of your ideas. As you become successful, make sure that you track your results and use them in your market-ing efforts. This will help set you apart from the many competitors in this field. Referrals and repeat business are the real key to a healthy bottom line for your enterprise.

ADVICE FROM THE EXPERTS

What sets your business apart from others like it?

Joan Thomas, a training consultant based in Akron, Ohio, says her ability to work with several different industries is paramount to her success. "I can work with anyone from banking to medical to manufacturing—and really listen to their needs before putting together a program for them."

Things you couldn't do without:

A computer with laser printer, fax machine, and index cards for brainstorming sessions are all Thomas says she needs to keep her business in business.

Marketing tips/advice:

"Network, network, network! Ask for referrals, and help others who can help you."

If you had to do it all over again . . .

"I would have more audiovisual products . . . in this business, you need stuff that's current, easy to transport, and yet economical."

Security Systems Consultant

Startup cost:	$5,000–$15,000
Potential earnings:	$65,000–$85,000
Typical fees:	$75–$100 per hour
Advertising:	Networking, Yellow Pages, direct mail, writing articles
Qualifications:	Security or crime prevention experience, academic degree and/or experience in civilian or military law enforcement, writing ability, ability to draft and read blueprints, knowledge of architectural software, knowledge of electronic equipment and facility with tools
Equipment needed:	Computer with high-speed Internet access, printer, and architectural (CAD) software, fax; digital camera; tools
Home business potential:	Yes
Staff required:	No
Hidden costs:	Errors and omissions insurance, keeping up with changing trends in security technology through publication subscriptions and conferences

LOWDOWN:

Consulting about security systems is a subset of the security field (and of the consulting field too, for that matter) that in today's safety-conscious society has the potential to become quite a lucrative enterprise. If you have the extensive background required, you can develop an extremely successful business in the design phase of security consulting. You will visit the location needing a security system—a museum, store, expensive home—and assess the security issues that need to be addressed. Drafting and writing skills are essential, because your next step is to draw up architectural plans as they affect the security system you are recommending. A well-written report outlines the results of your investigation to your clients and offers recommendations for improving security. If you are skilled with tools and have knowledge of specific security devices, you may also install the system you designed, although this is not a requirement. The prospects for success in security consulting are good, as the need for this service continues to grow faster than the pool of individuals with the skills and experience to meet it.

STARTUP:

Equipping your office with a computer powerful enough to render architectural drawings and produce professional-looking reports is the principal cost of launching this business. You'll typically spend between $5,000–$15,000 on equipment, supplies, and furnishings to get started, and bill out at $75 per hour after you're established.

BOTTOM LINE ADVICE:

Challenges and innovation make security systems consulting an exciting field. You will know that you are providing a much-needed service to your client organizations and individuals. Business success won't happen overnight, however. Plan for several years of development before your business becomes widely accepted and profitable. On top of all the qualifications listed above is the necessity to be very good at what you do. The recommendations you make on paper have to work in the real world. In addition to security knowledge, you will need to have patience and people skills as you will often be working under difficult circumstances or in crisis mode.

SEMINAR (SPEAKERS) SERVICE

Startup cost:	$5,000–$10,000
Potential earnings:	$30,000–$50,000
Typical fees:	25–40 percent of the charge per speaking engagement (speakers typically earn $150–$750 per engagement)
Advertising:	Press releases to newspapers, radio, business/civic organizations; direct mail to a targeted list of likely attendees; ads in newspapers/ trade journals
Qualifications:	Managerial and marketing skills, expertise in planning and promotion, multitasking and detail orientation, ability to recognize trends and put together seminar programs that will address them
Equipment needed:	Computer, printer, database and desktop publishing software, Internet access, fax, copier, scanner; tape recorder and transcription equipment if you decide to sell seminar products
Home business potential:	Yes
Staff required:	No
Hidden costs:	Transcription and tape reproduction costs

LOWDOWN:

If you have a sense of what trends are attracting the attention of the public now and into the future, you may be able to create a business by arranging for speakers on these topics. If you can organize appealing seminars and publicize them effectively, you can make a good living. While you might choose to fill some of the assignments yourself, in order to be really successful in this business, you will need to have a list of speakers available who can make the kind of amusing, relevant, and compelling presentations that stay with the audience long after they leave the meeting. The most enjoyable seminars have an atmosphere of give and take, with a lively speaker and active participation from the audience. Satisfied customers (seminar attendees) will be your best advertising; they'll talk about the seminar they attended and return with their friends for future sessions. As an add-on business, you can sell presentation tapes or transcripts of your seminars on-site as attendees leave the event. If you have a bit of show biz flair yourself, use your talents, combined with good event planning skills, to create a fun, profitable seminar business.

STARTUP:

Each seminar requires extensive planning and publicity. You will need a computer ($1,500–$2,500) with database and desktop publishing software and a laser printer in order to prepare promotional materials and seminar handouts, and to keep track of your stable of speakers and satisfied customers. Expect to spend around $500 on direct mail pieces to promote each event. Initially, you will probably have to purchase a mailing list, but as you build your pool of attendees over the course of several events, you will create your own list. Your speakers can earn $125–$750 for each speech they deliver; your take of that fee will be between 25 and 40 percent.

BOTTOM LINE ADVICE:
Bringing together a group of people for an enjoyable seminar is almost like putting on a play. There is a sense of excitement when a presentation goes well. You can get satisfaction from enabling people to learn something they need or want to know. You are also providing a service to your speakers, who rely on you to organize and support their work. Not all of your seminars may turn out to be well-attended, however, and you need to determine why. Perhaps you chose the wrong topic, or bad weather kept people at home. Analyze the reasons and adjust your seminar offerings accordingly. Running a seminar service requires superior multitasking skills; you will need to be extremely detail oriented in order to make all the pieces come together to create the perfect and memorable event.

SHIPPING/CUSTOMS CONSULTANT

Startup cost:	$10,000–$20,000
Potential earnings:	$50,000–$75,000
Typical fees:	$75–$150 per hour or a per-job rate
Advertising:	Yellow Pages, business publications, referrals
Qualifications:	Extensive background in customs and foreign shipping regulations, international law, and currency issues
Equipment needed:	Computer with high-speed Internet access, fax, printer, copier, scanner, phone
Home business potential:	Yes
Staff required:	No
Hidden costs:	Insurance, high-speed Internet access; keeping up with changes in currency exchange rates and customs regulations can be time-consuming

LOWDOWN:

Product manufacturers know everything there is to know about making their product. What they often don't know, however, is how to get it to their potential markets, particularly when those markets exist overseas. As a shipping/customs consultant, you can help product manufacturers learn the ins and outs of dealing with foreign distribution channels. Your expertise will be applied to everything from letters of credit, exchange rates, and currency conversion to customs regulations (which have a tendency to change according to the political climate in many countries) and shipping considerations. Your work with individual clients will likely be short-lived, perhaps only a few hours. You'll spend just enough time with one manufacturer to explain the finer details of operating in a global marketplace as it relates to a particular product, then move on to the next. You'll have to do some marketing in the beginning to land your first clients, but as you build experience and a reputation for offering timely, sound advice, your business will be heavily dependent upon word of mouth; referrals will soon become your path to greater income potential.

STARTUP:

You'll need about $10,000–$20,000 to get started in this business, mainly to cover your computer equipment and online access in addition to advertising. You will need to keep on top of changes in shipping regulations, exchange rates, and international law, so a high-speed Internet connection is a must. Your income potential is $50,000–$75,000, based on a consulting fee of $75–$150 per hour; in some cases, you may opt for a flat fee per job.

BOTTOM LINE ADVICE:

With all of the changes occurring daily in the world economy, it is difficult to stay on top of every detail affecting international shipping and customs law. You'll really need to be on the ball to succeed in this business, because one mistake could cost you your reputation—quickly. News about good and bad services travels fast via the Internet where companies often post their experiences. Stay in control of what's being said about you by providing stellar service.

Sightseeing Excursions

Startup cost:	$5,000–$10,000
Potential earnings:	$20,000–$45,000
Typical fees:	$5–$20 per person per trip
Advertising:	Local interest magazines, community bulletin boards, neighborhood fliers, newspaper entertainment sections, networking with local convention and visitors bureau/tourism office
Qualifications:	Exceptional driving record and a commercial driver's license that allows you to carry passengers in your vehicle; knowledge of area attractions and history; enthusiasm; love of people, excellent verbal communications skills
Equipment needed:	Van or small bus
Home business potential:	Yes
Staff required:	No
Hidden costs:	Insurance, vehicle maintenance

LOWDOWN:

Conducting a successful sightseeing excursion is more than getting a bunch of people into a bus and driving them around. You need a theme or focus, and you need to carry on a commentary as you travel around with your customers. There are excursion services, for example, that tour Hollywood neighborhoods, pointing out the homes of the stars; others take groups to places of historic interest such as Civil War battlefields. A sightseeing excursion can be a safe and fun way to explore a new city or to venture into the countryside; special tours can be adapted to the season. Depending on your geographic location, you could offer fall foliage tours, visits to an Amish farm, or a drive through ethnic neighborhoods with stops along the way at interesting shops and bakeries. The way you frame your business will define the kind of advertising you will need to bring in customers. Network with your local tourism office or convention and visitors bureau to get on the list of suppliers they call on for services when groups come to town.

STARTUP:

The vehicle you rent, lease, or buy will be your main startup expense; with your advertising costs figured in, you may spend between $10,000–$15,000 getting this business off the ground. However, since you could stand to make between $20,000–$45,000 annually—and have a lot of fun along the way—your return on investment should be both quick and personally satisfying.

BOTTOM LINE ADVICE:

You are going to have the most success at presenting the type of tour that you yourself would like to take. What are your special interests? Are you a history buff? Can you spot a herd of grazing deer at dusk? Have you visited every antique shop within a 50-mile radius? Do you know the twisted streets of the old part of your city like the back of your hand? You are the leader, the planner, the host of this experience. Make it an excursion you would enjoy and your enthusiasm will make it a wonderful one for your riders.

SMALL BUSINESS CONSULTANT

Startup cost:	$5,000–$15,000
Potential earnings:	$50,000–$150,000
Typical fees:	$50–$75 per hour, $750–$2,000 per day
Advertising:	Word of mouth, referrals, presentations made to business groups, audiovisual materials, professional organizations, cold calls
Qualifications:	Experience and expertise in small business management and marketing, business sense, communication skills, research and planning abilities
Equipment needed:	Computer with word processing, database, and spreadsheet software; printer; fax; copier; scanner; cell phone
Home business potential:	Yes
Staff required:	No
Hidden costs:	Slow payment; get some money up front if possible, as many small businesses just starting out experience cash flow problems

LOWDOWN:

As a small business consultant, you are the one with the knowledge and expertise to assess and solve many of the difficulties facing today's small businesses. Between complying with growing government regulations, integrating new technologies, and competing in a tightening economy, most small businesses can use all the help they can get from consultants who have proved their ability to solve problems. This position offers variety, challenge, and respect—because you have a role in improving your client's bottom line.

STARTUP:

A sizable time investment (and at least $5,000) is necessary to identify and approach your clients. Conduct research, send letters, make cold calls, do lunch. With persistence, you should make at least $50,000 your first year.

BOTTOM LINE ADVICE:

You can't "fake it" in this business. You must know what you're talking about at all times because if you don't, it's going to eventually show in declining sales and your client's inability to keep up with changing technology. The companies that hire you are essentially buying concrete solutions to their problems, even though the benefits they derive from your expertise may not always be immediately apparent. In terms of your own small business, take a lesson from yourself. Be able to apply your skills in equal measure to your own business and that of your clients.

SNOW PLOW SERVICE

Startup cost:	$5,000–$15,000
Potential earnings:	$25,000–$35,000
Typical fees:	$25–$40 per job
Advertising:	Yellow Pages, seasonally in newspapers
Qualifications:	Driver's license, physical stamina, ability to withstand cold temperatures
Equipment needed:	4-wheel-drive truck with snow plow attachment, snow blower, shovels, de-icers; cell phone
Home business potential:	Yes
Staff required:	Possibly
Hidden costs:	Liability insurance, equipment maintenance

LOWDOWN:

There's nothing like the convenience of having a snow plow service remove the mountain of snow in your driveway—or on your roof—first thing in the morning in blizzard conditions. And plenty of people in America's snowbelt will pay good money for just such convenience. This is an easy, relatively inexpensive business to start, especially if you've already got a heavy-duty vehicle that needs only a plow attachment to get you up and running. Add some shovels, de-icers, and a couple of snow blowers to your inventory and you're good to go. And if you set up a list of residential and business customers in advance, you won't even have to wait for the calls to come in; an overnight snowfall will have you up and out in the early morning hours fulfilling your prearranged obligations throughout the winter months. And, unlike most people who dread the thought of a heavy snowfall, you'll thrive on it. In fact, if you advertise in the right places and get your name known, you could be in the enviable position of having more work than you can handle; you'll either farm it out to another service like your own or take on temporary help. Obviously, since your livelihood is dependent on the white stuff, you should only consider this business opportunity if you live in a climate with cold, snowy winters. It's a seasonal business, for sure, but by coupling it with a warm-weather business like lawn mowing or exterior house painting you can stay busy year round. Many folks do just that and rake in a healthy annual income.

STARTUP:

You can start your operation small by investing only in a shovel and snow blower at a cost of approximately $500. However, you won't be able to clear anything larger than the average household driveway or sidewalk with this minimal equipment. To clear larger parking lots, you'll need a truck and a snow plow attachment. Don't forget to set aside money for vehicle upkeep and repairs. Bill your services by the size of the job.

BOTTOM LINE ADVICE:

This is a great and necessary service you provide . . . and it can be profitable one, too, if you don't mind being out in "Ice Station Zebra." Keep in mind, however, that this is a seasonal business, so be sure you either make enough in the winter to carry you through the summer, or come up with a complementary business to keep you busy during those hot, humid months.

SOFTWARE DEVELOPMENT/
CD-ROM PACKAGING

Startup cost:	$5,000–$10,000
Potential earnings:	$25,000–$50,000
Typical fees:	$100 per hour, average flat fee of $1,000 per job, or percentage of profits on sales of finished product
Advertising:	Shareware distribution, direct mail, computer bulletin boards magazines and user groups, reselling by consultants, Web site
Qualifications:	Creativity, ideas for software that will work and appeal to a specific market; programming skills
Equipment needed:	Computer, high-speed Internet access, printer, fax, phone, copier, scanner
Home business potential:	Yes
Staff required:	No
Hidden costs:	Attendance at trade shows, keeping abreast of changes in technology

LOWDOWN:

Many software companies that are today household names got their start as small businesses. In fact, some well-known software programs are based on products that were developed by individuals working on their PCs at home. In addition to creating new software programs from scratch, you might also develop an add-on utility for a program that's already on the shelf. You are most likely to have success in one or both of two general areas: creating a software package for a field in which you already specialize or have extensive experience, such as accounting or database-building, or producing and publishing a computer game. Your creativity and ability to make the most of CD-ROM technology will influence your chances for success in this demanding field. The conventional business activities of networking, marketing, and selling are just as important here as in any other type of enterprise. And don't forget the Internet; a Web site may turn out to be the only avenue you need to reach your market.

STARTUP:

To launch this business, you'll need a high-end computer ($2,000–$5,000), of course, but then you probably already have one and you've been experimenting with program design or you wouldn't even think of launching a business like this. Use your startup funds to upgrade your system or add peripherals you don't already have. In all likelihood, you'll be creating and publishing your own software products; however, if you are working for someone else, establish a payment plan that allows you to secure at least part of your fee ($500 or so) up front. The computer software market is extremely volatile, and today's great idea could easily become tomorrow's canned project. If your project gets cancelled midstream, you may not recoup all of the time you've put into it, but at least you won't be left empty-handed.

BOTTOM LINE ADVICE:

If you've always wondered why no one has developed a program to make life easier in your industry, use CD-ROM technology in a dynamic way to illustrate home repair techniques, or blow up the galaxy in 3-D color, now's your chance to try it yourself. You can express your creative, practical, or imaginative side as you develop your program. Recognize, however, that while the software business has been known to pay big bucks, it is not a route to instant wealth. Selling your program via the shareware route can be especially slow. You will need to advertise, market, and network at trade shows to achieve success, and that could be a tall order. Not everyone who's good at writing code enjoys the social scene.

Surveyor

Startup cost:	$5,000–$10,000
Potential earnings:	$35,000–$65,000
Typical fees:	Varies; can be as low as $125 or as high as several thousand per project
Advertising:	Business periodicals, referrals, networking/ongoing relationships with architectural firms, civil engineering companies, planning departments
Qualifications:	Degree/license in surveying, organizational and time-management skills, attention to detail
Equipment needed:	Surveying equipment, such as tripods and measuring devices; vehicle
Home business potential:	Yes
Staff required:	No
Hidden costs:	Travel, vehicle maintenance, errors and omissions insurance

LOWDOWN:

Surveyors are skilled in measuring land and buildings. They help landowners, mortgagors, municipalities, and real estate agents determine the boundaries of parcels of land. Surveyors also assess the elevations of land for planning, construction, road projects, and so on. As a skilled surveyor, you will use your mathematical skills and detail orientation on a contract basis to supplement the work of organizations and governments. Land must be surveyed whenever it is sold, and inaccurate surveying can lead to disagreements and litigation. A mis-located fence or boundary wall can be a major problem to correct. People and organizations anxious to avoid such disputes will be eager to call upon the surveying services you provide.

STARTUP:

Your initial cash investment ($5,000–$10,000) will go toward the purchase of surveying equipment and a vehicle. In addition, you'll need to set aside some funds to market your services, most likely through networking with city or township zoning officials, architectural firms, and civil engineering companies. Carry a decent set of business cards and present yourself well, and you could figure on an income of $35,000–$65,000 or more.

BOTTOM LINE ADVICE:

You will maximize your chance for developing a successful enterprise if you can make connections with active architectural and civil engineering firms, real estate agencies, and other organizations that often require surveying services. Accurate, on-time work will cement these good relationships and generate a steady stream of referrals.

TALENT AGENCY

Startup cost:	$10,000–$15,000
Potential earnings:	$30,000–$50,000+
Typical fees:	10 percent flat fee of what your client makes
Advertising:	Industry trade publications, Yellow Pages, word of mouth, Web site
Qualifications:	You must be licensed by the state in which you operate. Some agencies must also be franchised by the labor union to which their talent belongs (such as Actors' Equity Association or Screen Actors Guild). A background in business, law, and/or entertainment is useful.
Equipment needed:	Computer, printer, fax, camera/video equipment
Home business potential:	Yes
Staff required:	No
Hidden costs:	Insurance, phone/travel expenses

LOWDOWN:

Talent comes in all shapes and sizes; your job is to figure out who's got it and who's hiring. Your representation may consist of actors, singers, instrumentalists, comedians, etc., or you can specialize in one area (such as modeling or animal performers). Once you get established, you'll have no trouble finding people to represent; they will approach you. In the beginning, however, you'll have to go looking and you'll probably need to conduct some open casting calls. Advertise in local newspapers and through networking relationships with community theater directors and advertising agencies (both use the kind of talent you're looking for and may be able to suggest some likely candidates). It may also be helpful to align yourself with acting and vocal coaches, dance instructors, and other teaching professionals. Not only can they provide you with a steady stream of potential clients, they can also help hone the talents of those you're already representing. The more added services you can provide, the better your chances of developing fine (and marketable) talent. In addition to a keen sense of who's hot and who's not, you'll need the ability to negotiate contracts; some business and/or law background is helpful for conducting this side of the business.

STARTUP:

As the owner of a talent agency, you have no say about what you can charge; your fee has been determined for you by labor unions. This is to protect actors and others from getting ripped off by unscrupulous agents. You will receive a 10 percent (nonnegotiable) fee of whatever your talent makes, even if you did not book him or her. The only way you will be able to collect any additional money, such as royalties and residuals, is if you actually booked the talent yourself.

BOTTOM LINE ADVICE:

In the talent agency business, you get to meet people from all walks of life. Hopefully, you'll get to represent at least one who becomes a star and takes you along for what could be a pretty profitable ride. To really make a splash in this industry, you'll have to go where the talent goes and, not surprisingly, that means big cities. Working with theatrical types can be fun, but also frustrating. Be ready to handle unusual (and egomaniacal) personalities.

TAX PREPARATION SERVICE

Startup cost:	$5,500–$15,000
Potential earnings:	$40,000–$100,000
Typical fees:	Flat fee for Form 1040 preparation, plus additional fee for every attached schedule; $25–$50 per hour
Advertising:	Referrals, networking, ads in local publications and Yellow Pages, direct mail
Qualifications:	An interest in people and their financial situations, patience, excellent math skills, thorough understanding of tax laws and calculations
Equipment needed:	Computer, laser printer, high-speed Internet access, phone, fax, copier, scanner, tax preparation software, calculator, reference manuals, insurance
Home business potential:	Yes
Staff required:	None
Hidden costs:	Errors and omissions insurance; time and money for continuing education (annual updates are needed) software upgrades

LOWDOWN:

Income tax regulations and their associated forms are often too complicated for the average person to comprehend. And, since fees for income tax preparation are deductible, many people would rather pay someone else to make heads and tails out of the tax code on their behalf than spend the time it would take to figure it out for themselves. To launch this business, you obviously need to have a thorough knowledge of tax law, tax preparation, and the attendant forms, but you don't need to earn a degree in accounting or study for a license unless you want to become a CPA. That is not to say that you can simply jump into this business. Tax preparation is complicated, detailed work; our tax laws are cumbersome and confusing. It would behoove you to take a comprehensive tax training course before you begin. Not only would the training ensure that your skills are adequate and up-to-date, it would give you a real feel for whether this work is for you. Tax preparation can generate a solid income, but it requires serious attention to detail; a tiny mistake could cost your client interest and penalties and you, your reputation.

STARTUP:

In addition to the usual computer, copier, fax, and phone, you will need tax preparation software, hard copy and CD-ROM tax guides, and a laser printer. And since the IRS now makes it possible to file taxes electronically, you'll want high-speed Internet access as well. Plan on spending a minimum of $3,500 just to set up your office. There are plenty of giants in the tax preparation business and you can't out-advertise them, so don't even try. Instead, look for ways to set your business apart; use direct mail and network with small businesses or within a specific industry to reach potential clients. And don't forget to set aside some money for ongoing education. The tax code and forms change annually; you must be current. Most tax preparers charge by the form—a basic fee for the 1040, then additional fees for every schedule that must be attached to support it.

BOTTOM LINE ADVICE:

Since people will always have to pay taxes, you will never run out of potential clients. IRS guidelines are complex and confusing to most citizens, so knowledgeable tax preparers are in great demand. Tax laws are continually in flux so to be good at what you do, you must constantly upgrade your skills and your software to address the changes in forms and regulations. Tax preparation is seasonal, which means cash flow can be uneven; your busiest time will be the weeks leading up to April 15 (or March 15 for corporate taxes). To fill in the slower months, consider adding other services, such as bookkeeping or tax planning. And don't forget those procrastinators who filed for extensions; their taxes are due on August 15.

TECHNICAL WRITER
(DOCUMENTATION AND ONSCREEN TEXT)

Startup cost:	$4,000–$8,000
Potential earnings:	$30,000–$75,000
Typical fees:	$25–$80 per hour
Advertising:	Networking, trade publications, direct solicitation, Web site
Qualifications:	Writing and organizational skills, knowledge in specific technical areas, ability to translate highly technical information into lay language
Equipment needed:	Computer with high-speed Internet access and ink-jet or laser printer; word-processing, desktop publishing, and online documentation software; fax, phone, copier, and scanner
Home business potential:	Yes
Staff required:	No
Hidden costs:	Time and expense in researching new technologies

LOWDOWN:

Technical writers take highly complex information about a product and translate it into language that can be easily understood by a variety of audiences, including buyers, sellers, users, and those who install and repair the product. Often taking the form of step-by-step instructions, their work may appear in manuals, proposals, software documentation, or even slide presentations for executives needing to explain or teach technical information to others.

The field of technical writing encompasses two broad areas: print publications and online documentation. Both areas are growing explosively, and the supply of skilled writers, although fairly high, does not meet the demand. While there are many kinds of freelance writers in the marketplace, relatively few of them are able to produce technical materials. A technical writer needs technical knowledge (medical, engineering, scientific, electronics, etc.) in addition to verbal and written communications skills. The ability to explain technical products clearly, directly, and effectively sets the technical writer apart. If you have this ability and can market your skills effectively, you may have a rosy future ahead as a member of this "elite" group of communicators.

Online documentation requires even more specialized skills. Anyone who has tried to use a computer "help" program has an inkling of how difficult it is to create one that can respond adequately to every user question. Many technical people—the ones who conceive of and design complex products—are unable to translate their vast stores of knowledge into the simplest of terms, which is exactly what users need in order to be able to take full advantage of a product's features. The technical writer acts as a kind of conduit between the two, becoming a quasi-expert in the technical aspects of a product so that he or she can write documentation that a user with no technical knowledge can understand. To play this role, you must know everything about the technical topic or program and also have an acute awareness of how other people learn, read, and need to receive such information.

STARTUP:

Most of the work of a technical writer takes place on the clients' premises. Typically, you will be brought in, on a contractual basis, prior to the launch of a new product; you will learn about the product directly from the developers, then use what you have learned to create the printed materials that will be needed by the sales department, installation and repair technicians, and, of course, the end users. While the bulk of your work will be conducted on-site, you will still need to have a basic office setup at home, including a computer equivalent to or compatible with that of your client, a printer, high-speed Internet access, and a full complement of software—word processing and desktop publishing programs for hard copy documentation, specialized programs for creating online help. Expect to spend a minimum of $2,500 to equip your office. Set aside another $3,000 or so for advertising, including Web site development.

BOTTOM LINE ADVICE:

This is the ideal field for people with excellent communications skills and a love of learning, but it is not for every writer. Each new project takes you into uncharted territory, connects you with new people in your client business, and asks the most of your ability to create and synthesize. Marketing your services will be hard—and pricing projects can be even harder. It takes time to get established in this field; you must be able to produce good results under demanding, uncertain conditions.

TELECOMMUNICATIONS CONSULTANT

Startup cost:	$10,000–$15,000
Potential earnings:	$40,000–$75,000
Typical fees:	$50–$100 per hour
Advertising:	Referrals are the main source of jobs
Qualifications:	High-level telecommunications experience, business awareness, and interpersonal skills
Equipment needed:	Computer, software, printer, fax, Internet access, copier, scanner, cell phone
Home business potential:	Yes
Staff required:	No
Hidden costs:	Business insurance, equipment maintenance, software upgrades

LOWDOWN:

You can offer what growing companies need but don't have in-house: superior electronic communications. As management flattens out and workers are spread across the country to be close to their customers, companies need more and more services to connect them. As a telecommunications consultant, you will assess each client's needs, and advise them on which of the many services available are appropriate. Cell phones, voice mail, video teleconferencing, and other telecommunications services are more and more in demand, and you will be able to build up a customer base of organizations needing the sophisticated services you can provide.

STARTUP:

Telecommunications equipment is expensive, and you may need to acquire training in some of the growing areas for which you do not already have expertise. Initial investments of $10,000–$15,000 are not unheard of in this field. As a knowledgeable and valued technician, however, you can earn as much as $100 per hour (although, if you're just starting out in this field, you may want to offer a more easily justifiable rate of $50 per hour until you build your reputation).

BOTTOM LINE ADVICE:

People who have skills in the growing telecommunications field can build dynamic businesses offering the connections that their client organizations depend on. You will become a vital part of the businesses you serve, and you'll be operating on the leading edge of technology as you do so. Becoming established will be a challenge as the very organizations that need you the most will be the hardest to reach. Competition exists from a number of different types of services, so always be on the lookout for ways to improve your product and set yourself apart.

Telemarketing Service

Startup cost:	$6,000–$10,000
Potential earnings:	$40,000 or more
Typical fees:	$30 an hour
Advertising:	Yellow Pages, direct mail, business publications, membership in local business and civic groups
Qualifications:	Experience, persistence, ability to market your own service, writing skills for preparing script and reports, patience and a thick skin for dealing with verbal abuse and hang-ups
Equipment needed:	Telephone with headset; ergonomic office furniture; computer with word processing, database, and spreadsheet software; printer; fax; Internet access; copier and scanner
Home business potential:	Yes
Staff required:	No
Hidden costs:	Phone bills, marketing time and materials, insurance

LOWDOWN:

Telemarketing is a specialized and very focused form of marketing . . . and it's gotten a pretty bad rap lately. Still, no business can survive without effective marketing, and your challenge will be twofold: to reach the organizations that need to develop their customer base via the telephone and to cope with the ever-growing numbers of consumers who don't want to be bothered in that way. Telemarketing can be informational—a way of doing market research—but the bulk of it is focused on sales. As a small business, you may choose to offer telemarketing for a specific type of business or industry, such as pharmaceuticals, commercial photography, wedding services, etc. or limit your efforts to soliciting funds on behalf of a not-for-profit organization. This specialization will help you focus on your own marketing efforts. Keep in mind that you must be aware of and follow state and federal regulations with regard to telemarketing; one call to a person who has placed his or her name on a "do not call" list can result in hefty fines.

STARTUP:

You will need top-of-the-line telephone equipment (a headset is essential!) and a reasonably sophisticated computer system to track results and produce reports; plan on spending about $6,000 to start. Once you get the hang of this business, you can make $40,000 or more annually.

BOTTOM LINE ADVICE:

People skills are even more important to success as a telemarketer than they are in other types of small businesses. Listening well, speaking convincingly, and tuning the message to the receiver are all essential. You'll need experience writing effective scripts, and you'll need patience, persistence, and a thick skin. It will probably take some time to develop the client base for your business. You can distinguish yourself from the run-of-the-mill telemarketers because you're a professional at this, not someone just hired off the street. You have experience, you're creating a proven track record, and you have an unquenchable enthusiasm for your clients' projects.

ADVICE FROM THE EXPERTS

What sets your business apart from others like it?

"While there are many marketing and advertising agencies, public relations firms, and telemarketing organizations, my company is a one-stop agency that has the capability of coordinating any and all aspects of a marketing plan," says Cheryl D. Cira, owner of Columbus, Ohio-based Marketing Dimensions. "I cannot stress how important it is to be honest and up front with your customers. Marketing Dimensions looks at each project and account as a long-term relationship."

Things you couldn't do without:

"Essentials include telephone equipment and office furniture. It also helps to have computers in order to enter large lists, track calls, pull up records, and run reports. Computers are also used for simple design work, database management, and mail merges," says Cira.

Staffing tips/advice:

"Telemarketing projects depend on the work and devotion of employees. And, because people are people, there are some aspects that cannot be controlled, such as employees quitting without notice, coming in late, and calling in sick time after time. My office manager is very good at juggling schedules and maintaining a strong pool of telemarketers, but it can get crazy at times."

If you had to do it all over again ...

"I don't think there is any one thing of great importance that I would change or do differently. In general, however, I wish that I had had more hands-on experience in managing a large staff and more working knowledge related to personnel issues."

TELEVISION PROGRAM DISTRIBUTOR

Startup cost:	$10,000–$15,000
Potential earnings:	$45,000–$75,000
Typical fees:	15 percent of the selling price per show
Advertising:	Business card, industry trade publications, word of mouth
Qualifications:	Knowledge of the television industry, extensive contacts at local, national, and cable network levels
Equipment needed:	Computer, printer, fax, cell phone
Home business potential:	Yes
Staff required:	No
Hidden costs:	Insurance, travel/entertainment expenses

LOWDOWN:

In layman's terms, a television program distributor is essentially a program sales rep, hired by program producers to find the right matches in the television industry. Good selling skills and knowledge of how television programs are bought and sold will help you get your foot in the door. In addition, you'll need to have wide-ranging industry contacts at the local, national, and cable network levels. If you find that a particular group of programs is not selling, you can always launch your own network (provided you have the resources, of course). Keep your business cards handy; you never know who you'll bump into at the drugstore.

STARTUP:

Unless you have been with a reputable distributor already, you'll have to spend some money to set up shop and market your services ($10,000–$15,000). Keep a portfolio on the shows you've sold and how they fared in the ratings game; this will provide proof to the new client that you know this business. If you are good at what you do, you could easily earn upwards of $50,000.

BOTTOM LINE ADVICE:

This is probably the hardest job in the broadcasting industry. Pounding the pavement to sell a TV program isn't for everyone. There will be long hours and lots of negotiating with some very high-powered clients. If you can stand the heat, you can work in this kitchen. If not, you'd better seek another profession.

TEXTILE BROKER

Startup cost:	$10,000–$20,000
Potential earnings:	$40,000–$80,000+
Typical fees:	Usually a percentage of the sale (15 to 25 percent is standard)
Advertising:	Trade/industry publications, direct mail, word-of-mouth, Web site
Qualifications:	Background in textile merchandising or wholesaling, knowledge of fabric and clothing manufacturing
Equipment needed:	Computer, Internet access, fax, phone system with separate line for international business (which tends to be a 24/7 prospect), cell phone for when you're on the road
Home business potential:	Yes (but you'll be on the road a lot!)
Staff required:	No
Hidden costs:	Insurance, travel costs; also, fluctuating fabric costs could make it hard to calculate a predictable income

LOWDOWN:

If just looking at traditional and exotic fabrics gets you wrapped up in thinking about their infinite merchandising possibilities, a business as a textile broker could well be the "material" world for you. As a broker, you'll be the liaison between the textile mills and the clothing industry, selling fabrics to designers as well as to manufacturers. You may help a manufacturer get his or her hands on a specific type of cloth at the best possible price, or you may work with mass production houses, supplying specific amounts of fabric on a regular basis. You'll be competing daily on price and quality against other brokers, and you must establish key relationships early on to be sure you have an inside track. To maximize your earning potential, consider working in the global marketplace or over the Internet to strike some deals. Whether you go international or stick with domestic markets only, know that you'll be doing a lot of traveling—to call on suppliers, visit mills, and attend trade shows to check out what's new and hot.

STARTUP:

Right out of the starting gate, you'll need to spend a lot of time traveling to supply houses, and that takes money—possibly as much as $5,000–$7,000. Don't forget to add in your computer equipment and international phone line costs (another $2,000 or so). Spend the rest on advertising and building relationships. If all goes well, expect to earn between $45,000–$80,000 or more (depending on whether you're selling domestically or internationally).

BOTTOM LINE ADVICE:

Traveling sounds glamorous, but it can get to you after a while, as can the discriminating (and often changeable) tastes of the clothing designer/manufacturer. You may get tired of all the "attitude" you'll be expected to put up with, but think positively. Keep a cool head and your income may greatly benefit. This is not a field for the weak.

THEATRICAL LIGHTING SERVICE

Startup cost:	$10,000–$20,000
Potential earnings:	$30,000–$50,000
Typical fees:	$150–$1,000 per show
Advertising:	Industry trade publications, word of mouth
Qualifications:	Electrician, possible licensing and union contract required, maintenance and repair skills, knowledge of lighting techniques, gels and special effects, ability to scan a script for lighting opportunities
Equipment needed:	Light board, lamps, gels, pipes, booms
Home business potential:	Yes
Staff required:	Assistant to keep track of the lighting changes in the scripts
Hidden costs:	None

LOWDOWN:

The show must go on, and the only way it can is with great lighting. While lighting is a facet of the theater rarely noticed by audiences, it is very important to the look and feel of stage production. Lighting determines how an actor looks on stage, sets the mood of a scene, and may even indicate weather conditions and time of day. In order to light the stage effectively, you'll need to have experience scanning a script for lighting opportunities, and carefully choosing the right gels or special effects to create an atmosphere that works for the actors, the director, and the audience. You can get your start as a lighting technician by volunteering to light community theater productions or by working with a professional lighting company before embarking on your own. To make a go of this business, you will need a well-developed eye for design as well as knowledge of lighting gels and how they interact with fabrics and scenery. Not every stage company or theater will have extensive lighting equipment on hand; they'll be counting on you to supply it. Your equipment can be either purchased or rented; in the early stage of your business, you can save money by working out short-term leases with other lighting companies. Networking will always be an important aspect of your profession; you'll never know what or whom you'll need later on, and you may want to farm out additional work as you become more and more in demand.

STARTUP:

You can operate as a freelancer, designing the lighting for individual productions, with practically no startup costs. If you're planning on running your own company and buying all of your own equipment outright, however, you'll need large amounts of capital ($10,000–$20,000 or more) up front. Unfortunately, this isn't one of those "I-can-get-by-on-what-I've-got" kind of businesses. Lighting can make or break a show, so you've got to have all the right stuff. Decide early on whether you want to make your equipment available for rent or purchase. If you want to be in the lighting rental business, you can charge by the show. The success of a theatrical lighting business depends largely on creativity and experience. The longer you work at this, the better you become. If you work hard and develop a fine reputation, you could make at least $30,000–$50,000 per year to start; your fees will vary greatly depending on your geographic locale and the size or complexity of each project.

BOTTOM LINE ADVICE:

Theatrical lighting can involve long setup times. A Broadway show takes several weeks to light; community theater productions require only days. And setup is only the tip of the iceberg. You must light each and every show for the entire run of the production, or train others to do so. Set your fees accordingly and plan your time wisely.

TRAFFIC CONTROL CONSULTANT

Startup cost:	$5,000–$10,000
Potential earnings:	$45,000–$100,000+
Typical fees:	From $1,000–$150,000, according to size and duration of project
Advertising:	Business publications, membership in civic and charitable organization, networking and referrals
Qualifications:	Degree in traffic engineering or related field, traffic control planning experience, ability to market your services, facility/experience with design issues
Equipment needed:	Top-of-the-line computer with oversized monitor, design and presentation software; laser printer; cell phone; fax; copier; scanner; Internet access
Home business potential:	Yes
Staff required:	No
Hidden costs:	Errors and omissions insurance, software upgrades, ongoing education, membership dues

LOWDOWN:

Many municipalities across the United States have poor traffic design. Some towns appear to have "just grown," without regard for overall planning to accommodate the increasing number of vehicles. As the population expands, poor traffic control goes from a simple annoyance to being downright dangerous. Your skills in traffic control can be the foundation for building a successful small business if you can find effective ways of linking what you know to the municipal governments that need it. You should find a market for your services among cities and towns that are large enough to benefit from better traffic patterns, cycled lights, clearer lanes, and improved signage, but too small to afford a full-time traffic control staff. Your challenge will be to get your foot in the door and begin showing how your planning skills can get the people of these communities where they're trying to go.

STARTUP:

Your office must support the design side of traffic control consulting and, at the same time, keep you in touch with your clients. You'll need to spend about $5,000–$10,000 for the necessary computer hardware and software to get started. But since so many cities are experiencing unprecedented growth and the traffic snarls that go along with it, you shouldn't have any trouble commanding a decent dollar for your expertise; charge at least $1,000 for each minor project and several thousand for the major traffic snafus.

BOTTOM LINE ADVICE:

As a traffic control consultant you will be in the same situation as other high-end consultants: having a hard time getting those first clients. It's a classic "catch-22": you need a track record to attract business, which you can't get unless you have a track record. Expect to spend a significant amount of time and effort to become established; once you do, referrals will represent the largest proportion of your total client base. Projects may take you away from home frequently. On the other hand, there isn't a traffic control consultant on every street corner, as there seems to be with accountants and management consultants, so you won't be facing tremendous competition.

TROPHY/ENGRAVING SERVICE

Startup cost:	$5,000–$12,000
Potential earnings:	$40,000–$65,000
Typical fees:	Vary, depending on the item
Advertising:	Direct mail, Yellow Pages, networking with business and civic organizations, schools, and sports leagues; networking with insurance companies and retailers of high-ticket items
Qualifications:	Training on engraving equipment/tools, and practice, practice, practice! An apprenticeship with an experienced engraver may be helpful
Equipment needed:	Handheld engraving tools, air-driven drill engraver, molds, and stencils; inventory of products if you sell engraved items
Home business potential:	Yes
Staff required:	No
Hidden costs:	Insurance

LOWDOWN:

For nearly every school, sports league, association, or organization, there's a trophy or award to be given, and you can do the engraving. There's also a market in engraving high-ticket items for identification purposes in case of loss or theft. Think of the potential, then, for your engraving business—it's a bottomless cup, isn't it? You'll need to be a strong networker, as much of this business has already been soaked up by those established much earlier than you. To compete, you can set yourself apart by offering unique products to engrave—or even by reselling recognition products from other sources. Sell people on your exceptional eye for detail and customer service abilities—and, if you can, throw in quick turnaround. Your clients will often need an award or trophy to be made on a tight deadline—if you handle quick turnaround, you may be able to reap an additional fee for speedy service. Network with insurance companies to learn which items should be engraved for identification, then contact the stores where those items are sold—jewelers, gun shops, art galleries, etc.

STARTUP:

A simple electric engraver will set you back only about $100; an air-driven drill engraver, on the other hand, goes for about $5,000. You'll need to spend about $1,000 on advertising. In terms of earning power, you could make between $40,000–$65,000, if you work hard and build the right contacts.

BOTTOM LINE ADVICE:

You'll be singled out as a winner yourself if you can keep up with your orders in an accurate, timely manner. One of the best things you can do to get the word out about your services is to send samples of your work to folks with their names or company logos already engraved on it—nothing appeals more to a person than a little ego boost. (Wasn't it Dale Carnegie who said that there is no sweeter sound than the sound of one's own name?)

USED INDUSTRIAL EQUIPMENT SALES

Startup cost:	$5,000–$11,000
Potential earnings:	$45,000–$100,000+
Typical fees:	20 to 40 percent commission on each sale
Advertising:	Classified ads in trade journals, Yellow Pages, newspapers, Web site
Qualifications:	Manufacturing experience or sales background in a manufacturing environment
Equipment needed:	Computer, printer, fax, copier, Internet access, cell phone
Home business potential:	Yes
Staff required:	No
Hidden costs:	Insurance, occasional storage costs for machinery, attorney's fees for contracts

LOWDOWN:

Many large manufacturers buy more equipment than they actually need. That's why the big guys unload equipment that may be obsolete according to their needs, but is affordable and usable for the fledgling manufacturer. Your job is to first locate those selling equipment, then placing ads to sell the equipment from Manufacturer A to Manufacturer B. You should be a dynamic, yet extremely knowledgeable sales professional, because manufacturing types just aren't taken in by salespeople who obviously don't know how to actually use the equipment they're selling. You must create the impression that you have dirt under your fingernails. You won't have to keep an inventory of used equipment, but, from time to time, you may have to pay to store individual pieces. If at all possible, try not to get into the storage business, unless it's an extreme emergency on the seller's part; even then, make sure you include a clause in your contract that states that the seller agrees to pay storage fees. One final tip: Be sure you have an "as-is/without warranty" clause in your buyer's contract—the last thing you need is to find yourself facing a lawsuit when a piece of used equipment you sold fails.

STARTUP:

The first $5,000–$6,000 of your startup costs will be all wrapped up in advertising to manufacturers who are looking to unload some of their old equipment on the one side, and to manufacturers seeking to acquire good, used equipment on the other. You'll want to use a combination of classified ads in newspapers and trade journals, plus your own Web site to reach both. In addition, you'll need a basic office setup, including a computer, printer, fax, and phone. You'll typically earn 20 to 40 percent of the asking price on each piece of equipment you sell, and that could easily put $45,000–$100,000 or more in your pocket per year.

BOTTOM LINE ADVICE:

Prior experience in manufacturing, regardless of the product, should be enough to give you the kind of credibility you need in order to sell your service. On the positive side, you could earn a great deal of money simply by placing ads and answering inquiries knowledgeably and professionally. If you're doing business with foreign countries, however, you'll need to spend some time and money learning about international markets and sales in order to make a decent profit.

VACUUM CLEANER REPAIR

Startup cost:	$5,000–$15,000
Potential earnings:	$25,000–$40,000
Typical fees:	$45 per hour, plus parts
Advertising:	Yellow Pages, local newspapers, supermarket and community bulletin boards, direct mail, coupon books
Qualifications:	Knowledge of vacuum cleaners and hands-on ability in repairing them
Equipment needed:	Inventory of replacement parts from a variety of manufacturers, including central vacuum systems (look for places that sell old vacuum cleaners for parts)
Home business potential:	Yes
Staff required:	No
Hidden costs:	Shipping costs (some parts come from overseas); insurance

LOWDOWN:

How many times has the beater bar on your vacuum cleaner been so completely clogged with animal hair it just won't move anymore? The fact is, just about everyone has experienced difficulty with his or her trusty vacuum from time to time. And since nearly every home has a vacuum cleaner that will need service and parts sooner or later, you'll have no shortage of customers. The problem is, your customers probably won't give a thought to your services until they actually need them—so be aware of that in your advertising or marketing plan. Put yourself in the place where most customers are likely to go looking for you, such as the Yellow Pages and coupon books. To build a customer base from the outset, you might consider offering a free six-month checkup for early problem diagnosis. Even if you don't find a problem that needs fixing at the moment, they'll remember you and return when their vacuum quits six months later. Diversify as much as you can, too; by stocking replacement bags for a variety of models, attachments, and commonly used parts, you can make a tidy side profit.

STARTUP:

From the start, you'll need to set up shop in a comfortable place with adequate lighting and a sturdy workbench. You can do this in your home, but you better check zoning regulations first; your neighbors may not be amenable to a steady stream of customers. Opt instead to spend $300 or more per month to rent shop space. You'll need to advertise, of course ($1,500–$3,000 to start), and keep a fairly complete parts inventory. Charge at least $45 per hour for your time to be sure you're covering overhead and expenses.

BOTTOM LINE ADVICE:

You can supplement the money you make on small vacuum cleaner repairs by installing and servicing central vacuum systems, a feature in many new homes. Cultivate contacts among local developers and builders to get in on the ground floor.

VIDEO/DVD TRANSFER SERVICE

Startup cost:	$5,000–$10,000
Potential earnings:	$25,000–$35,000
Typical fees:	$250 for a 12-minute transfer (including music and character generation); conversion of existing video program to DVD, $40 for first copy, $25–$30 for additional copies
Advertising:	Industry trade publications, bulletin boards, direct mail, video retailers, Web site
Qualifications:	Background in video production; experience in working with all types of film and video formats, including 8mm, 3/4", Super VHS, VHS
Equipment needed:	Old movie projector, video camcorder, editing deck, audio equipment, character generator, DVD recorder/burner, computer and DVD/video transfer software
Home business potential:	Yes
Staff required:	No
Hidden costs:	You may eventually need a studio; start setting aside cash as early as possible

LOWDOWN:

People have a strong desire to preserve their memories, and video/DVD memory books have become a great way to keep those memories intact and in an easy-to-view, long-lasting medium. In most cases, you will be hired to simply transfer old film onto VHS tapes or DVDs, or to convert an existing video memory book to DVD. You might, however, also be asked to shoot video of old photographs, which you will then put into documentary format. Work with writers to sell your clients on narration of their cherished memories or family histories; you can charge extra and split the profits with the writer. For the actual voice-overs, you could use the talents of college theater or communications students who might work just for the experience (or for a nominal fee). You must have a strong background in video/DVD production and know how to run audio equipment. If the client wants music behind the video, you must pick the appropriate track(s) and secure the rights to each song you use. Or, you could network with local musicians to provide suitable original soundtracks that you could offer for a lower cost than existing musical selections.

STARTUP:

Startup is high ($10,000 or more), but you could cut your costs by purchasing used equipment. Technology changes quickly in this business, so be sure that whatever you buy is not more than a couple of years old or it will be obsolete. Starting out, your earnings could be in the range of $5,000–$20,000 per year, with a potential of $25,000–$35,000. Most video/DVD transfer services also offer other services such as video/DVD production and audio reproduction.

BOTTOM LINE ADVICE:

This can be a really fun business, but it can also be tedious. You have to be able to sit through lots of family footage (some of it very boring!) and try to pick out the most interesting parts. Remember, you're in the sentiment business here. Your job is to preserve precious memories ... tread carefully, because you're treading on people's lives. In other words, don't discard anything; save every frame for your client.

VIRTUAL ASSISTANT

Startup cost:	$5,000–$8,000
Potential earnings:	$25,000–$45,000
Typical fees:	$30–$45 per hour
Advertising:	Networking and referrals; a previous employer could be your first client
Qualifications:	Strong administrative abilities and/or previous experience as an executive assistant or office manager; exceptional organizational, multitasking, and time-management skills; self-starter who is able to work without a lot of direction
Equipment needed:	Computer; high-speed Internet access; printer; word processing, database, spreadsheet, and linking software; copier; scanner; cell phone/pager; personal digital assistant
Home business potential:	Yes
Staff required:	None
Hidden costs:	Phone expenses; time—keep careful track of your hours; some clients may want you to be on-call 24/7

LOWDOWN:

A recent article in *Entrepreneur* magazine listed virtual assistance as one of the hottest new concepts in home-based business. And no wonder. With so many self-employed sole proprietors out there who could use some help with their administrative work but don't have enough of it to justify hiring a full- or even part-time assistant, this is a real opportunity for someone with strong organizational and time-management skills. Best of all, you can provide administrative services to a busy home-based entrepreneur without ever leaving your own home; thanks to technology, your client, who might be a doctor, attorney, financial planner, writer, real estate agent—in short, anyone who has administrative chores to delegate—could be half a continent away! As a virtual assistant, your days will be spent on everything from making customer/patient contacts, scheduling client appointments, and coordinating travel arrangements to maintaining databases, conducting market research, sending out the bills, and editing/formatting documents. You're like the administrative assistant at a corporation who works just outside the boss' office, except you work from your own office, which may be located just around the block or even a couple of states away. And you may not work exclusively for one person, either. Depending on the workload and your personal capacities, you could serve as a virtual assistant for two or more clients at the same time. Just make sure you're supremely organized. You'll communicate with your clients by fax, phone, e-mail, and online instant messaging and have access to one another's computers using special linking software.

STARTUP:

You'll need to have an office setup that's at least comparable to that of the clients you serve—i.e., if your "boss" is using Microsoft Excel or PowerPoint software, you need to be using it, too. And since you'll be spending a lot of time online e-mailing back and forth and downloading/uploading documents, opt for a high-speed Internet connection.

BOTTOM LINE ADVICE:

Perhaps the best thing about being a virtual assistant is the flexibility this job affords you. Because there's no one looking over your shoulder or watching to see when you come and go, you can pretty much set your own hours, as long as you get the work done. Be careful, however—because you're out of sight and working on your own, some clients may think it's okay to consider your office open for business 24/7. After all, they're working at 9 A.M. on a Saturday morning, why shouldn't you be too? Be sure to make your schedule parameters clear from the beginning and keep careful records of your time, just in case any questions should arise with regard to how you're spending it.

WATER QUALITY ANALYSIS

Startup cost:	$5,000–$15,000
Potential earnings:	$25,000–$40,000
Typical fees:	$60–$150 per job; more for commercial clients ($350+)
Advertising:	Referrals from related businesses, including well drillers, environmentalists, government departments
Qualifications:	Degree in biology, chemistry, or a related science; extensive lab and field experience
Equipment needed:	Well-equipped lab, computer, software, printer, copier, scanner, fax, phone
Home business potential:	No
Staff required:	No
Hidden costs:	Lab supplies, travel costs, mobile phone bills

LOWDOWN:

Individuals and businesses need to monitor water quality for a variety of reasons. Your customers may deliver water samples to you for analysis, or you may gather the samples yourself. Highly developed lab skills are essential as the most refined testing will be required to make an accurate report, which needs to include documentation regarding contamination, its properties, and how to get rid of them. Traces measured in parts per billion are being considered in the most up-to-date environmental plans. You will also need marketing skills to form business relationships, along with the attention to detail and precision that is the hallmark of the professional laboratory scientist. Your ability to write a clear and effective report will help set you apart from your competitors, as will the ability to perform your services quickly and efficiently.

STARTUP:

Equipping a lab is a major outlay and must be completed before you can begin work. Depending on how extensive you want your services to be, you can expect to spend between $5,000–$15,000 on your laboratory and office setup. Once you are established, however, you should be able to find a steady stream of both individual and commercial clients. Charge them at least $60 per job (for individuals) and a larger flat rate for commercial clients.

BOTTOM LINE ADVICE:

Accuracy, on-time reports, and an attitude of strong customer service will help you build your water quality analysis business. You will need to be serious and dedicated to the process so that your lab work is precise; if you are not detail-oriented, this can be a challenge. You'll also need to be good at forming client relationships in order to keep business flowing in. Establishing your credentials and earning trust will take a good deal of time and energy in the early years.

WEB SITE DESIGNER

Startup cost:	$5,000–$15,000
Potential earnings:	$25,000–$100,000+
Typical fees:	$30–$150 per hour
Advertising:	Your own Web site (with links to others you've designed), networking, referrals, cold calls
Qualifications:	Background/experience in graphic design; ability to apply sound design principles to Internet promotion; familiarity with how users interact with Web sites; knowledge of HTML, Java, and other programming languages; experience with Web tools for integrating text, sound, graphics, etc.; ability to evaluate the various Internet Service Providers; exceptional communication skills
Equipment needed:	Desktop computer with Zip drive and high-speed Internet access; color laser printer; graphic design software, plus software specifically for Web site design; color scanner; copier; cell phone; laptop computer for presenting designs to client offline (optional)
Home business potential:	Yes
Staff required:	No
Hidden costs:	Equipment updates and staying abreast of technology

LOWDOWN:

Companies that wanted to get noticed in the twentieth century put their advertising dollars into broadcast media. It's a different story today. While television and radio are certainly not passé, they've definitely taken a backseat to the World Wide Web in many a company's advertising budget. Just about every business has a Web site these days, and those that don't, are looking to get one. If you have the skills to become a Web site designer, the market for your services is big . . . and rapidly getting bigger. Your ideal prospective client is not the little guy who can, and probably will, create his own Web site pretty inexpensively with off-the-shelf Web design software. Your target clients are the companies that recognize the power of the Web in terms of building market share and know the importance of creating a sophisticated Web site that not only catches the eye but closes the sale. They understand that a Web site must be both easy for the user to navigate and versatile enough to grow and change right along with their business. That's where you come in. You have a solid background in good graphic design principles, as well as the technical know-how to put those principles to work on the Internet, which is a medium like no other. You'll meet with your clients to discuss their Web site goals. Then you'll go back to your drawing board—in this case, a computer—and, using your knowledge of programming languages, ISPs, and how users interact with Web sites, design a tailor-made site to address your client's specific needs, whether to sell products, build name recognition, and/or establish credibility within a specific industry.

STARTUP:

You're going to need some significant technology to launch this business; expect to spend up to $15,000 for the necessary hardware, software, and peripherals. Your best sales tool will be the Web sites you've designed, including your own. Make sure that yours has all the latest and most appropriate bells and whistles, and link it to other sites you've designed so that your prospects have a wide-ranging portfolio of your work to review. You'll be charging a hefty hourly rate for your services (as much as $100), and one of your toughest challenges may be convincing clients that you're worth it. Be prepared to prove how the Web sites you've created have increased sales and positively impacted your clients' bottom lines.

BOTTOM LINE ADVICE:

Web site design is a great business for a creative person who isn't afraid to take chances and try new things. Even though the Web has been around for a while, it's still a relatively new advertising medium, affording plenty of opportunities to stretch your imagination and display your finely honed artistic abilities. And considering that so many businesses want to have an online presence, but don't know the first thing about how to get one, there's a real need for what you do. Design a few outstanding Web sites, then market yourself effectively, and you could easily be looking at a six-figure income.

ADVICE FROM THE EXPERTS

What sets your business apart from others like it?
"We're based in the fundamentals of advertising and design," says Larry Rosenthal, president of Cube Productions, Inc., in New York City. "We are also on the cutting edge; if it's new technology, it's been in here for an experimental run. Our clients appreciate the fact that we try everything out first."

Things you couldn't do without:
Rosenthal says he couldn't do without a computer and high-speed Internet access, software tools, and external, peripheral equipment such as scanners.

Marketing tips/advice:
"Get yourself a home page, and make it a well-constructed, easy-to-use one with a clear point of view. Also, use e-mail to market directly to those who might be interested in your services."

If you had to do it all over again . . .
"I would have started working on the Web even earlier. I would've also e-mailed Mark Andreeson from Netscape and asked to work with him!"

WILDERNESS-BASED THERAPEUTIC PROGRAMS

Startup cost:	$6,000–$10,000
Potential earnings:	$15,000–$25,000
Typical fees:	A flat rate of $1,500–$3,000 per client/group
Advertising:	Referrals from therapists, seminars and speeches for community groups, networking, direct mail, advertising in national and area-wide publications, radio spots, Web site
Qualifications:	Degree in recreational therapy or related field, extensive outdoor experience, participation in group dynamics and leadership training, excellent marketing and management skills
Equipment needed:	Camping equipment for self and group, computer and printer, copier, cell phone, high-quality brochures
Home business potential:	Yes
Staff required:	Probably
Hidden costs:	Insurance, equipment repair and replacement, transportation

LOWDOWN:

Setting up a successful small business that offers wilderness-based therapeutic programs will require a number of special talents and enthusiasms. To be more than just another Outward Bound wannabe, you will need to have, and to market, a special conviction concerning the efficacy of the therapy you provide and its relationship to the wilderness. Whether you specialize in rock-climbing programs for adolescents with depression or marine mammal encounters for autistic children, you will be creating a wilderness experience that directly targets the complex needs of a particular patient population. Your geographic location will, to some extent, define the type of experience you are able to provide—kayaking a seashore or mountain lake, hiking and camping in a hidden valley, or a Saturday in the country for kids who have never been outside the city limits. While you can certainly do the preplanning on your own, you will probably need a support system of part-time helpers who can deal with transportation, food supplies, and any challenging therapy situations that may arise. Once the structure of your business is in place, you should be able to draw many clients whose caregivers and/or families can see the power of getting away, changing perspectives, and experiencing the simple and beautiful things of life that can't be seen and felt from the parking lot of a mall.

STARTUP:

Your major expenses will be for equipment and marketing (at least $6,000). Until you become known for your work and for the effectiveness of your wilderness therapy, you will have to spend heavily on advertising and other types of marketing to build your client base. Nevertheless, a profit of $15,000 should be possible by the end of your first full year in business.

BOTTOM LINE ADVICE:

Determining the focus for your business will be your first challenge. To whom do you want to appeal? Secondly, how will you deliver your services? What age requirements and other limitations will you need to place on participants? What form of evaluation will establish the effectiveness of your efforts and support further marketing? How can you carry out your events without doing everything yourself? Finding the right answers to these questions will set the course for your ultimate success in combining your concern for the welfare of your clients with your love of the wilderness and your belief in its infinite power to heal.

WORD-PROCESSING SERVICE

Startup cost:	$5,000–$15,000
Potential earnings:	$30,000–$45,000
Typical fees:	$5–$10 per page, hourly rate of $20–$35 per hour
Advertising:	Yellow Pages, focus advertising within a 5- to 10-mile radius of your business location, direct mail, university bulletin boards, networking with business and professional organizations
Qualifications:	Fast and accurate typing skills (at least 65 words per minute), customer-oriented attitude
Equipment needed:	Computer hardware and software, laser printer, Internet access copier, scanner, fax, transcribing machine (optional)
Home business potential:	Yes
Staff required:	No
Hidden costs:	Equipment and software upgrades; vehicle expenses if you offer pickup and delivery

LOWDOWN:

Despite the abundance of personal computers, demand for off-site word-processing services has steadily increased. Essentially, word processing is a fancier (and, these days, more technically correct) phrase for typing. As a professional word processor, you'll be doing all the same kinds of work as a typist, only you'll be using a computer instead of a typewriter. Customers will come to you with everything from reports and term papers to resumes, letters, dissertations, and technical documentation. Your ability to produce an accurate, attractive product with quick turnaround will ensure your success in this fairly competitive field. Remember that just about any Joe or Joanna with a basic computer system and printer thinks of getting into the word-processing business; you'll have to be able to set yourself apart from these folks as well as the hundreds of secretarial services out there (who likely perform services that go well beyond your own). Position yourself close to a university or in a downtown area, and you'll increase your chances of success by at least 50 percent.

STARTUP:

Your startup costs will be practically nothing if you already own a computer and laser printer; if you don't, it's time to invest in the best one you can afford. Most of your initial expense will go toward advertising and the purchase of new and updated software (set aside at least $3,000 for these). Charge a per-page rate of $5–$10 or an hourly fee for the larger jobs; it may take you a while to get a feel for the bidding process and which projects are likely to be labor-intensive.

BOTTOM LINE ADVICE:

You are providing a valuable service; beware of underpricing it. Consider adding a surcharge for transcribing from handwritten or hard-to-read documents and for adding charts and/or tables to finished documents. If you can stand the repetitive motion that goes along with keyboarding, and of typing other people's work, your income is limited only by your speed and the number of hours you want to work.

WORKERS' COMPENSATION CONSULTANT

Startup cost:	$5,000–$7,000
Potential earnings:	$45,000–$60,000
Typical fees:	Monthly retainer of $1,500–$3,000 (depending on the size of the company)
Advertising:	Business periodicals, networking, referrals
Qualifications:	Investigative abilities in order to root out "cheaters," broad understanding of workers' compensation, ability to shop for the best rates and suggest ways to keep costs down, organizational and communications skills, tenacity
Equipment needed:	Computer, printer, word processing and desktop publishing software, fax, phone, copier
Home business potential:	Yes
Staff required:	No
Hidden costs:	Insurance, membership dues

LOWDOWN:

A workers' compensation consultant is an outside contractor who works with companies to reduce the incidence of workers' compensation claims, find better rates, and suggest innovative ways to save money. You will start by investigating the circumstances of the manner in which the employer deals with these problems. You might also be called upon to actually administer the claims process for a period of time, in place of a company employee. Typical strategies to reduce claims include: 1) more thoroughly investigating the claim to determine whether it is indeed valid; 2) conducting regular reviews of workers' compensation benefits packages; and 3) recommending changes in the workplace to reduce injuries. The bottom line is, your nose for trouble can prevent a company from being taken advantage of—either by invalid claims or high rates.

STARTUP:

To get started, you'll need investigative tools and the equipment to write reports; spend at least $4,000 equipping your office with a computer and peripherals. Your reports will need to be clear and easy to understand (they hired you to clear up the red tape, remember?), so invest in decent word processing and desktop publishing software packages for all of your major communications. Most disability consultants work on retainer (typically $1,500–$3,000 per month).

BOTTOM LINE ADVICE:

This has become quite a lively field. For the sake of credibility, you will probably need to have the experience gained from having been a workers' compensation specialist for an employer, or at least another consulting firm. If you show that you can conduct excellent investigations, write effective reports, and make productive recommendations for improvements in processes, you can build a very successful enterprise. You will not be everyone's favorite person as you uncover cheaters, but the impact of your efforts on your clients' bottom line is sure to make a positive impression on the person who hired you for the job.

Startups Between $15,000 and $40,000

ANTIQUES DEALER

Startup cost:	$20,000–$40,000 (depending on size of inventory and shop location)
Potential earnings:	$25,000–$80,000
Typical fees:	Varied; pieces sell anywhere from $10–$10,000
Advertising:	Yellow Pages, community newspapers, direct mail, show participation, location
Qualifications:	Knowledge of antiques and pricing, basic business and marketing skills; previous retail experience would be helpful
Equipment needed:	Inventory of antiques; storefront with cash register and credit care processing equipment, display cases, counters, and shelves; computer for accounting/inventory purposes, printer, fax, phone
Home business potential:	No
Staff required:	Not initially
Hidden costs:	Insurance, warehousing

LOWDOWN:

The lure of the old and priceless draws many a sentimental customer into an antique store, and you could start such a business with a dozen or so nice pieces of furniture, some antique china, and lots of old books and toys. These types of items tend to sell well, as they are collectible and may be worth increasingly more with every passing year. You'll need to develop a sizable stock of pieces to sell, and that can best be accomplished by combing thrift shops, flea markets, and estate auctions for the best and most interesting old items you can find. Watch the newspaper for garage sales, too—sometimes people will unknowingly unload a fabulous antique dresser for a steal.

Keep in mind that your business will need to be run just like any other retail establishment—and that means you'll need to set your prices high enough to cover your operating expenses in addition to building a profit. Tricky work, because, in the antiques business, there are lots of collectors out there who know the value of certain items and will want to barter with you on price. Don't be suckered into lowering your price . . . unless you want to, of course.

STARTUP:

You'll need at least $20,000–$50,000 to get an antiques business off the ground properly. Most of your startup money will go toward building a significant inventory of many different kinds of items and securing a storefront in the right location in which to display and sell your products. If you're looking to save a little money on your site, look to securing a space in an antiques mall; it's usually cheaper than having your own standalone store. Your earnings will be in the $25,000–$80,000 range, depending on three things: location, quality of product line, and price. Obviously, if you're in a quaint New England village or a town that's historically significant, like Charleston, South Carolina, for instance, you might fare better than with an antiques shop in the middle of Kansas.

BOTTOM LINE ADVICE:
The antiques market is a competitive one, and too many well-intentioned hobbyists-turned-entrepreneurs make the mistake of thinking this will be an easy ride. If you have sufficient working capital to buy the kinds of pieces that will build your reputation for the finer things, then you'll have little trouble making a living. On the other hand, if you're undercapitalized and just stocking a bunch of "old stuff," you could be out of business before you know it.

ART GALLERY

Startup cost:	$15,000–$30,000
Potential earnings:	$40,000–$70,000
Typical fees:	20 to 40 percent commission on each piece sold
Advertising:	Newspapers, city magazines, art guides, universities
Qualifications:	Knowledge of and appreciation for art, basic business and marketing skills; negotiation abilities; previous retail experience would be helpful
Equipment needed:	Cash register and credit card processing system, storefront with ample wall space, hanging materials/tools
Home business potential:	No
Staff required:	Not at first
Hidden costs:	Insurance, promotion

LOWDOWN:

To run a successful gallery, you can't just love art . . . you must also be able to promote it well; otherwise, you run the risk of simply running a museum rather than a retail establishment. Using whatever contacts you may have, you'll need to build a solid stable of artists to represent. Surf the Web and scour national art publications for the work of both prominent modern artists and potential "up-and-comers"; invite the ones whose work you like (or better yet, think will sell) to submit slides and resumes. Of course, if you're relatively new to the art gallery business, the best way to secure a wide assortment of work may be to invite art students to show in your gallery on a consignment basis. In all cases, you'll typically keep anywhere from 20 to 40 percent of the selling price of each item for yourself; the more experienced artists will let you know what they expect to receive for each piece and how much markup they'll allow for your profit. Use your negotiation skills to determine what type of business arrangements you should make with each artist. In today's competitive marketplace, you may want to pick a theme for your gallery instead of trying to offer a little bit of everything; you might, for instance, decide to be a nature gallery or feature only works by local artists.

STARTUP:

Startup costs can be considerably high in this high-profile "image" business. Art is a discretionary purchase and, since you're asking people to spend a pretty penny with you, your gallery better have a classy look about it and be located in the right place. Many gallery owners—and even the artists themselves—are banding together to rent space in warehouses where they can offer their wares in what amounts to an artsy shopping mall atmosphere. If you can locate your gallery in a spot like this, you'll benefit from the high foot traffic and save on rent.

BOTTOM LINE ADVICE:

While you may be tempted to launch special exhibitions at your gallery with fancy receptions for the "hipper-than-thou," tread carefully. How many of those people who come to sip your wine and nibble on your cheese really have the money to buy your art? Qualify your list before you send out those invitations. Otherwise, you could stand to lose money quicker than you make it—and that's not the direction you want to go.

AUTOMOTIVE PARTS REBUILDER

Startup cost:	$20,000–$40,000
Potential earnings:	$20,000–$40,000
Typical fees:	$40–$50 per job
Advertising:	Auto enthusiast publications and membership in enthusiast organizations (look for those dedicated to specific makes and models), Yellow Pages, auto show participation, referrals from re-conditioners, restorers, networking with auto repair shops
Qualifications:	Excellent mechanical aptitude, experience with rebuilding auto parts, ability to manage sales and invoicing
Equipment needed:	Tools, parts, specialized diagnostic equipment
Home business potential:	Yes
Staff required:	No
Hidden costs:	Materials, replacements of equipment and tools

LOWDOWN:

"Motorheads" are everywhere across the United States. Some of these car lovers are rebuilding antique autos, others are just keeping cars with high personal sentimental value alive. Regardless of the reason, people who care about their old cars also care about total authenticity; believe it or not, they want the exact air filter that would have come new on a '79 Monza, even if another one would work just fine. As an automotive parts rebuilder, you'll be addressing that need. You can meet and greet these enthusiasts at car shows, hand them a business card, and build up their enthusiasm for your rebuilding/reconditioning skills. And don't neglect that all-important secondary market for your services: simple replacement parts. Fuel pumps, alternators, and other expensive parts can be reconditioned for resale to people looking to get a few more years out of their expensive vehicles. With a little legwork, you may find that the best auto repair garage in town offers a market for your reconditioned parts.

STARTUP:

The tools necessary to perform this work are relatively expensive, but if you're even half-way considering this business, it's because you've been rebuilding your own parts for a while and so you probably have most of the tools you'll need already. Even so, you'll be giving your tools a heavy-duty workout, so do set aside some funds for replacements. You'll need a place to work, of course; your home garage or basement workshop may be suitable in the beginning, but as your business grows you'll probably need to think about another, larger, and more visible site. You'll charge $40–$50 per job, and more for special parts needed to complete the job properly. Figure on an income potential of $20,000–$40,000.

BOTTOM LINE ADVICE:

A love of autos is usually what fuels the desire to launch a business like this. The pleasure that you take in mechanical devices will translate itself into a successful operation if you also remember to keep a good manager's head on your shoulders. Marketing, pricing, selling, and billing are vital to the growth of your enterprise.

BANQUET FACILITY

Startup cost:	$15,000–$25,000
Potential earnings:	$40,000 and up
Typical fees:	$250 and up for facility rental; per person price for food depending on the menu
Advertising:	Newspapers, wedding planners/publications, direct mail, location
Qualifications:	Cooking experience, people skills, management and marketing experience, multitasking and time management skills
Equipment needed:	A building for banquets, fully equipped kitchen and cooking utensils, dinnerware, cutlery, table linens
Home business potential:	No
Staff required:	Cook(s), dishwasher(s), servers, and cleanup help
Hidden costs:	Meeting legal, zoning, and sanitation/hygiene requirements; insurance

LOWDOWN:

Running a banquet facility can be a satisfying career for the right person. This is a business that will be a good fit for someone who enjoys food and people, who can juggle a lot of small but important details, and who is willing to work hard to get established. Be ready to do a lot of menu planning and cooking. Networking to obtain bookings for wedding receptions, class reunions, and club parties is essential to getting started; you can send brochures or business cards to churches, the chamber of commerce, bridal shops, florists, and others who could make referrals. You might want to start out by volunteering your catering services (working from your home at first) for several large parties to gain exposure and find out if this business is for you.

STARTUP:

Startup costs for a banquet business are not small: in addition to needing a fully equipped kitchen and cooking utensils, you must buy or rent a hall in which to conduct the festivities. Ideally, the hall would contain a kitchen, but if not, you'll have to make other arrangements; research the possibility of sharing a building with someone else at first to cut costs. You'll need expert legal advice to launch this business; there are legal, zoning, liquor, and food handling requirements to meet. Keep in mind, too, that you'll have labor costs (you can't do this by yourself!) and ongoing marketing expenses.

BOTTOM LINE ADVICE:

As long as there are people and occasions to be celebrated, there will always be a need for your banquet business. It can be quite satisfying to provide people with good food and good fun, but it can be exhausting, too. You'll have to work long hours, especially while getting established; you will be required to work evenings, weekends, and some holidays, since that's when most parties take place. Good management skills and an ability to market your business successfully will be essential. Although you will likely have bookings year-round, this business can be "feast or famine," with your busiest time being around the winter holidays.

BIOFEEDBACK THERAPIST

Startup cost:	$20,000–$50,000
Potential earnings:	$30,000–$45,000
Typical fees:	$150 per hour-long session
Advertising:	Yellow Pages, referrals from physicians, psychologists, and other health care providers, advertising in community newspapers
Qualifications:	Biofeedback training, license or certification
Equipment needed:	Biofeedback equipment
Home business potential:	Not typically
Staff required:	No; however, you may want to contract for medical claims processing services
Hidden costs:	Malpractice and liability insurance, equipment upgrades and maintenance

LOWDOWN:

Biofeedback is a treatment technique that teaches people how to improve their health by using signals from their own bodies. Using biofeedback, anxious patients can be taught to relax, stroke victims may be able to regain movement in paralyzed muscles, and patients experiencing chronic pain can learn to better cope with their discomfort. As a biofeedback therapist, you will use highly sensitive equipment designed to detect a person's internal bodily functions. The results of each test you conduct will be used to determine and monitor an appropriate course of treatment. For example, you might use one particular biofeedback machine to measure electrical signals in the muscles of a woman who is experiencing chronic leg pain. Your goal is to get the patient to relax her muscles and thus, reduce the pain. You would work alongside her as she tries to slow down and/or eliminate the flashes or beeps, coaching her performance and making suggestions for improving it. The techniques you teach can then be carried over into her everyday activities, until eventually she is able to automatically relax her muscles without benefit of any signal. Your clients would primarily be referred by physicians and psychologists; from time to time, however, persons simply looking to relax and reduce stress might seek your services directly.

STARTUP:

You will need $20,000–$50,000 to cover the cost of your highly sensitive equipment. To avoid the risk of inaccurate readings, be sure to also set aside an ample amount for regular maintenance. And speaking of risk, you'll need to make sure that you have adequate liability and malpractice insurance, too. If you are well-connected with other health care professionals who can provide regular referrals, you could easily make $30,000–$45,000 per year in this specialized and increasingly accepted profession.

BOTTOM LINE ADVICE:

If you enjoy working closely with people and helping them better respond to stress, pain, and other chronic conditions, this business will give you everything you need (including a reasonable amount of financial security). On the other hand, getting insurance companies to cover your services may be trickier than you imagine; you'll be money ahead if you hire an administrator who knows the ins and outs of filing insurance claims.

BOAT OPERATION INSTRUCTOR

Startup cost:	$25,000+ (depending on whether you own or lease a boat)
Potential earnings:	$23,000–$45,000
Typical fees:	$75–$100 per person for a one-time class of four hours
Advertising:	Marinas, fliers, Yellow Pages, boating publications
Qualifications:	Captain's license, first aid and CPR certification
Equipment needed:	Computer, printer, bookkeeping software; boat; life jackets and other aquatic safety equipment
Home business potential:	Yes (but you'll be out on the water most of the time)
Staff required:	No
Hidden costs:	Insurance, wear and tear on your boat

LOWDOWN:

The water can be a very unsafe place, especially if you don't know what you're doing. Sadly, many people who get behind the wheel of a boat are inexperienced and, consequently, accidents are on the rise due to their lack of knowledge or just plain negligence. As a boat operation instructor, you can teach people the "rules of the sea" before they venture out on open water, and possibly help save lives. You'll need to be familiar with U.S. Coast Guard regulations with regard to lifejackets, life preservers, flares, fire extinguishers, etc., as well as boating safety requirements, map- and chart-reading, and basic meteorology. In addition, you'll need to have general seamanship knowledge and a good dose of common sense. Market yourself to local boat retailers with brochures and fliers—and get to know your neighbors along the water's edge, so they can help spread your word with waves of referrals.

STARTUP:

It's certainly possible to be a boat operations instructor without a boat (you could use your client's boat for teaching purposes), but, even so, it's a good idea to have one of your own. That way, you can get started with brand-new mariners even before they step aboard their own vessels. You will need to carry liability insurance and, to make sure that you are absolved from all responsibility should one of the folks you teach cause an accident later on, have legal counsel draw up the necessary papers for clients to sign in advance of their first lessons. You'll have the best chance for high profitability, obviously, if you live in a place where boating is possible year-round. If not, you can still make a reasonable living teaching 13 to 26 weeks out of the year.

BOTTOM LINE ADVICE:

Spring and summer will be your busiest seasons. If you love boats and love to teach, but hate the confines of a classroom, then this water job is for you! Be prepared to take some flak from people who don't take your instruction seriously ("I can drive a car, what's so hard about a boat?"). Perhaps showing them a photo or two of a boat accident will help encourage them to stay with your program.

BUILDING MAINTENANCE SERVICE

Startup cost:	$20,000–$40,000
Potential earnings:	$45,000–$75,000
Typical fees:	Monthly contract of $150–$350 per client/building per month
Advertising:	Yellow Pages, direct mail to building owners and rental property managers, networking, cold calls
Qualifications:	Handyman experience (preferably with some background in electrical work), organizational and time-management skills
Equipment needed:	Van equipped with tools, cleaning supplies and equipment, chemicals/solvents, ladders and small power equipment; cell phone
Home business potential:	Yes (but you'll be working on-site)
Staff required:	No (but you may need additional staff if your business gets too large for you to handle the workload alone)
Hidden costs:	Insurance, vehicle expenses

LOWDOWN:

Someone has to maintain all those apartment complexes and office buildings in your community. It might as well be you. If you have a technical, hands-on background in building maintenance, or even if you're just known around your neighborhood as a "Mr. Fix-It," you can nicely parlay that talent into a building maintenance service. This business makes perfect sense when you look at things from the point of view of a building owner. Whom would you rather trust with your fix-up needs: a small service with an expert at the top or a large company of transient employees? And that's exactly how you'll need to position yourself in this competitive marketplace—as a small-but-mighty leader with stability and a commitment to keeping things running smoothly. Of course, you can't promise that a light switch will always work or a drain won't get clogged, but you can offer your cell phone number and 24/7 service so that your clients can rest comfortably knowing they can sleep on while you handle those 3 A.M. emergencies (because isn't that the time most things go wrong?).

STARTUP:

Your costs to launch this business will be moderate—about $20,000–$40,000. You'll need a reliable van equipped with everything from wrenches and sockets to small pneumatic drills and large ladders. If you're a hard worker, as most maintenance folks are, you could make $45,000–$75,000, depending on how many clients you serve. Of course, the more clients you have, the more likely you'll need to hire staff, since one person can't simultaneously fix the light switches and circuits in a dozen buildings.

BOTTOM LINE ADVICE:

Be prepared to spend long hours doing the kind of work that tinkerers like to do most of all: figuring out what went wrong with that furnace blower or ceiling fan, and being the hero when the problem is solved. That's not a bad way to end a day, even if it's a long one.

ADVICE FROM THE EXPERTS

What sets your business apart from others like it?
Lillian Lincoln, president of Centennial One, Inc., in Landover, Maryland, says her company distinguishes itself from others by emphasis on quality. "We place a great deal of emphasis on giving our clients a comfort level that assures them that their building maintenance requirements will be adequately addressed."

Things you couldn't do without:
Vacuums, buffers, scrubbing and shampooing machines. "No equipment is needed until some work has been secured. No lead time is needed unless the job requires specialized equipment, so purchase only the equipment needed for each job as they roll in."

Marketing tips/advice:
"Industry knowledge as well as business acumen is a great asset. Too many people have the mistaken impression that this industry is a 'mop and bucket' business. Far from true! It requires knowledge of chemical and equipment usage, time management, human relations, and a number of other skills. For anyone going into this business, I advise them to work in the industry (preferably in the field) for a minimum of six months."

If you had to do it all over again ...
"I would spend more time working in the field to learn more about on-site operations. I made some mistakes early on because I was not as knowledgeable as I should have been about the basics of the business."

BUNGEE JUMPING INSTRUCTOR

Startup cost:	$25,000+
Potential earnings:	$35,000–$55,000
Typical fees:	$50–$100 for the first jump and $10 less for each additional jump
Advertising:	Yellow Pages, entertainment sections of local papers, brochures, convention and visitor bureaus, Web site
Qualifications:	Bungee jumping experience; knowledge of correct form and safety considerations, certification in first aid and CPR. Note: If you use a hot-air balloon, a pilot's license will be required
Equipment needed:	Platform, harness, bungee cords, insurance, cell phone
Home business potential:	Yes
Staff required:	Yes
Hidden costs:	Downtime due to weather, insurance

LOWDOWN:

The bungee jumping craze has got hundreds of people jumping off bridges literally—and, thankfully, they pretty much all live to tell about it. If you are into the craze, and have teaching ability and common sense about safety, you could probably take the plunge and launch your own specialized business. While this may seem like nothing but fun at first, you should remember that liability insurance for this type of business runs very high due to the risk involved. One lawsuit could wipe out your bank account and put you out of business in a nanosecond. You'll be working with customers who are real thrill-seekers: people who simply aren't afraid to take risk in the first place. Your marketing will be minimal because the kind of people who would consider bungee jumping are the kind who'll come looking for you. Take every precaution you can to prevent injuries, but just in case, make sure your certifications in first aid and CPR are up-to-date and carry a cell phone for emergencies. And, by the way, if you use a balloon as a platform, you'll need a pilot's license to operate it.

STARTUP:

Your startup cost will directly relate to the type of platform you use. Hot-air balloons start at around $12,000, cranes may be double that amount. Some people build their own platforms, while others use isolated bridges (this is not recommended and, in some states, it's actually illegal). Your fee will be based on the number of jumps a person wants to take. Most are one-time shots of $50 each. For each additional jump on the same day, reduce your price by $10. Your typical earnings could range from $35,000–$55,000.

BOTTOM LINE ADVICE:

People take up bungee jumping purely for the thrill of it. There is no physical benefit to this activity except the "adrenaline rush" received from jumping, and that alone may be enough to cause your business to jump with steady repeats. A bungee jumping business is not likely to be a huge moneymaker; it would, however, be a good sideline job especially in climates where it might be a seasonal activity. Keep in mind that although bungee jumping has gained in popularity, it has also resulted in some catastrophic accidents, and even deaths. There's always the chance that something could go terribly wrong. Can you handle that?

BUSINESS FORM SALES AND SERVICE

Startup cost:	$20,000–$40,000
Potential earnings:	$35,000–$60,000
Typical fees:	$25–$30 per form; more for complex custom designs
Advertising:	Yellow Pages, classified ads, direct mail
Qualifications:	Super sales skills, organizational abilities, accuracy
Equipment needed:	Printing equipment (or have a subcontractor lined up), extensive color catalog of your goods, inventory
Home business potential:	Yes
Staff required:	No
Hidden costs:	Cold calls

LOWDOWN:

A business form business is so standardized and easy to learn that it's among the top franchise businesses available on the market today. All you need to do is find out the types of business forms potential customers are using (such as inventory records, receipts, invoices, and other important documents). Then, you sell those customers on your ability to provide the forms they need, along with customized service, quick turnaround, and easy terms. Remember, however, that you'll be competing against some pretty large organizations like Office Depot, Office Max, and Staples, not to mention other independents like yourself; you'll need super sales skills to stay on top of the competition and meet your regular goals. Cold-calling will be your primary way of finding new business, and you can expect it to be extremely uncertain—and costly—in the beginning. Still, the income potential is great for those who can stomach the battle—and if you capitalize on your strong points, you should be able to come up with forms that make your customers happy and your business a profitable one.

STARTUP:

You'll need between $20,000–$40,000 to launch this business, particularly if you buy into a franchise operation. Your initial investment will cover catalogs, inventory, and training materials, and possibly even printing equipment (typically including specialized software). You'll charge $25–$30 to create a simple form; more if it's a complex custom design. Add printing charges and, in the end, you'll wind up making between $35,000–$65,000 per year—but that's only if you're working at this full-time and full-throttle.

BOTTOM LINE ADVICE:

There is probably no more straightforward, easy business to learn than this one—but do recognize that you're going to need to be well connected to get regular, dependable business. Network with anyone who's anyone, and make the daily fifty or so phone calls it may take to get just one fresh lead. After all, you're competing against major office store chains, and you need to let people know just what's different about your business—in this case, it's the customized service they can't get from the chains.

CATALOG RETAILER

Startup cost:	$15,000–$60,000 (depends on whether you're marketing your own or someone else's products)
Potential earnings:	$25,000–$50,000+
Typical fees:	Products can sell from $5–$500 or more; you'll charge a third more than list price plus shipping charges
Advertising:	Direct mail; advertising co-ops with other catalog retailers in national publications, Web site
Qualifications:	Sales/marketing background, organizational, time-management, and customer service skills
Equipment needed:	Inventory of items to sell, postage meter, computer, printer, fax, Internet access, phone with 800 number for ease of ordering, credit card processing equipment, boxes and packing supplies, UPS/FedEx accounts
Home business potential:	Yes
Staff required:	Not initially
Hidden costs:	Insurance, purchase/lease of specialized mailing lists, shipping

LOWDOWN:

Catalogs have been around almost as long as there have been products to sell, and, from the looks of most anyone's mailbox these days, they're not going away anytime soon. There's always room for one more, but the days of the one-catalog-fits-all retailer (think Sears and Montgomery Ward) are gone. What seems to work best in the mail order business today is niche marketing; that is, pick an area of specialization and create a catalog that features products related only to that area. For instance, you might sell products just for golfers, or cat owners or fill your catalog with only baby items or travel supplies. Choose an area that is specific enough to grab instant attention, yet broad enough to include a wide variety of products. You'll build your customer base from lists you either rent or purchase; if you specialize, narrowing your list should be an easy process. Your days will be spent mailing out catalogs, then taking and filling orders in the most efficient way possible; you'll also be handling customer service and returns/exchanges. In addition to a sales and marketing background, you'll need some accounting and organizational skills; it all gets to be quite complicated when you're dealing with hundreds of orders (which you'll need to have in order to break even). Make sure you have adequate space for inventory storage and assembly of packages for mailing; your basement will run out of room quickly.

STARTUP:

Your earnings potential is unpredictable because you're dealing with various products at different prices and hoping they all sell well within a short period of time. Because you'll need to send out no fewer than two or three thousand catalogs at a pop, plus launch a Web site, to make your sales efforts pay off, and because you'll need everything from a postage meter to credit card processing equipment and a computer system to maintain and run your business, expect to spend $15,000–$60,000 just to get up and running. Your startup costs will be closer to the high end if you're selling your own product line; it's cheaper to work out agreements with other manufacturers and get a percentage of their take (usually 15 to 20 percent). Don't forget printing costs, either, which could run as high as $10,000–$15,000 per catalog issue. You could potentially earn $25,000–$50,000 or more, depending on your product line and prices.

BOTTOM LINE ADVICE:

On the positive side, you can work in your pajamas if you want to, since you'll be in your office most of the day and your only customer contact will be by computer or phone. The downside is, you are your work and you can't afford to let up—if you're having a bad day, the orders won't get filled, your customers will be unhappy, and you'll wind up losing money. One word of warning: be sure that you're selling quality products, and don't just accept a photograph as proof—ask your suppliers for samples. Knowing the most you possibly can about your actual products just makes good business sense.

Caterer

Startup cost:	$15,000–$25,000
Potential earnings:	$30,000–$80,000
Typical fees:	$800–$15,000 per event
Advertising:	Brochures, press kits, direct mail, Yellow Pages, networking, referrals
Qualifications:	Cooking and menu planning experience, knowledge about sanitation and safe food handling, ability to work well with people, organizational, and time-management skills
Equipment needed:	Fully-equipped kitchen, cooking utensils and supplies, vehicle
Home business potential:	Possibly
Staff required:	Not initially; may be needed to grow
Hidden costs:	Insurance and licensing. In some states, it is illegal to sell food prepared in a home kitchen; a commercial kitchen (which can be rented and/or shared) may be required

LOWDOWN:

If you have the right mixture of cooking know-how, business savvy, and good communication skills, catering can be a profitable and enjoyable enterprise; it's also very hard work. Although a commercial kitchen may eventually be required, most catering businesses begin at home because startup does not require years of training, expensive equipment, or capital investment. One fast-growing segment of this business is food delivery—especially lunches—to offices and corporations. Catering opportunities also abound in preparing private banquets at hotels, furnishing meals to airlines, cooking for parties, fundraisers, and other events, or serving as an executive chef in a company dining room. Specializing in a particular item is another option. Caterers must observe health, safety, zoning, product liability, and other laws and regulations. Detailed record-keeping is a must.

STARTUP:

The cost of setting up a commercial kitchen can take a minimum of $8,000–$12,000; equipping it with the tools of the trade (pots, pans, mixing bowls, heavy-duty utensils, etc.) will require another $2,000–$3,000. In addition, you should allow $3,000–$10,000 for insurance, legal fees, licensing, and advertising. You'll need a delivery vehicle, too. And don't forget the cost of your "raw materials" (the ingredients needed to prepare your recipes); you can charge those back to the customer, but you will still have to shell the money out up front.

BOTTOM LINE ADVICE:

Successful catering is not just about being a good cook; it requires a lot of hard work and careful planning. You will have to devote time to meeting with—and cooking for—potential clients just to bid on the business, and then you may not be chosen to cater the event after all. Catering involves weekend and evening work, and is also often seasonal in nature; you'll be busiest in December. Keep in mind that, in addition to menu planning and cooking, the caterer is also responsible for serving and cleanup. In the beginning, and for small events, you may be able to handle everything yourself; later on, you may want to hire others to take on some of these tasks. On the upside, cooking is fun! It's a creative activity, one that nourishes the cook as well as those who eat his or her food. You can control how much or how little you work, and you'll always be welcome in everyone's kitchen!

CHILD ID PRODUCTS

Startup cost:	$20,000–$40,000
Potential earnings:	$35,000–$50,000
Typical fees:	Varied according to type of equipment sold; can range anywhere from $350–$1,000 per sale
Advertising:	Direct mail to organizations sponsoring child ID programs, Web site
Qualifications:	None
Equipment needed:	Video, 35mm, and digital cameras; fingerprinting equipment; background information forms to sell as a distributor; computer, printer, and desktop publishing software
Home business potential:	Yes
Staff required:	No
Hidden costs:	Insurance, equipment storage and shipping costs

LOWDOWN:

Sadly, too many children go missing every day in America. . . sometimes snatched by a stranger, but more often taken by one parent out of spite for the other due to a bitter divorce or a custody battle that's gone sour. That's why so many parents are making sure that their children can be easily identified by facial features, voice, and fingerprints—and you can supply the equipment to produce such critical information by rounding up the necessary video, 35mm, and digital cameras, and fingerprinting equipment that can be used by police departments, service clubs, and other organizations that sponsor child ID programs through schools, malls, or churches. You'll especially want to include an extensive profile sheet parents can fill out on each child, chronicling such important identification information as birthmarks and/or special medical conditions. You'll market to organizations across the country that offer regular child ID programs to help give parents peace of mind. As a distributor of these products, you can take pride in knowing that yours is a noble profession, that can actually be quite profitable if you can work out exceptional deals with your own product suppliers.

STARTUP:

You'll need to invest in product inventory up front and then always keep some on hand ($20,000–$40,000) so that organizations wanting to sponsor child ID events do not have to wait for their products. Your equipment inventory will include video, 35mm, and digital cameras, fingerprinting equipment, and detailed information sheets that you can produce in bulk via desktop publishing. If you market aggressively, you could make between $35,000–$50,000 per year.

BOTTOM LINE ADVICE:

Marketing your business may be a little tricky at first; you're selling a service that is based on a negative need. One approach might be to tell as many success stories as you can—examples of how your products have located missing children and saved lives—to encourage parents everywhere to take the preventive measures necessary to protect their children against crime.

COFFEE BAR/TEA SALON

Startup cost:	$20,000–$40,000
Potential earnings:	$25,000–$40,000
Typical fees:	$1.50 $4.75 per cup
Advertising:	Newspaper ads, fliers, location
Qualifications:	Retail and/or restaurant experience (especially purchasing and marketing) would be helpful; knowledge and ability to prepare the coffee, tea, and other products
Equipment needed:	Coffee/tea brewing equipment and supplies, including espresso and cappuccino machines; cups and saucers/mugs; spoons/stirrers/straws; flavored syrups and sweeteners; blender (for iced drinks); counters, refrigerator/freezer, storage units, cash register, comfortable furnishings, computer with bookkeeping and spreadsheet software
Home business potential:	No
Staff required:	None at first; several later on
Hidden costs:	Purchase or rental of location for the shop; meeting zoning, legal, and food service regulations

LOWDOWN:

Gourmet beverage businesses, such as tea shops and coffee bars, are high-ticket specialty businesses that can brew big profits. People are tired of the same old coffees and teas, and they want interesting new flavors and lower-caffeine alternatives. Your shop can feature a line of healthy herbal teas to address that desire, as well as attractive add-ons, such as serving your beverages in china teacups and offering sweet snacks like slices of cake, muffins, and specialty cookies. Profit margins are high; repeat customers are almost guaranteed. Be aware, however, that you will likely face stiff competition, especially in urban areas, where the larger chains have taken hold. You will have to look for creative ways to set your business apart.

STARTUP:

Your biggest expense will likely be related to your location. You will need to either rent space or purchase a shop, and it must be in a visible, high-traffic location. You will also need top-of-the-line coffees and teas, brewing equipment, comfortable furnishings so that your customers are eager to come in and "sit a spell," signage, a cash register, and a computer with bookkeeping and spreadsheet software for tracking your sales and income. You'll probably also need to retain the services of an attorney to make sure that you are up to snuff with regard to zoning and health regulations. A well-organized advertising campaign is another must.

BOTTOM LINE ADVICE:

Coffee is big business these days and your biggest challenge may well be setting yourself apart from the crowd. Look for ways to make your shop more inviting than cookie-cutter corporate competitors—invest in some comfortable sofas and easy chairs, for example. Like any small business owner, you will undoubtedly have to work long hours, at least at first or until you can afford to hire trustworthy staff. Your business may be affected by the economy, or by the time of year. It will most certainly be affected by the location. You will want to find a spot that is both visible and readily accessible. Look for locations in areas where pedestrians congregate and are likely to just wander in—near a park or in neighborhood shopping "villages," for example. As you expand, you will experience the usual headaches of staff management. However, this is a business that can generate a very healthy profit, with relatively low overhead and modest equipment requirements. As you become more successful, you may want to offer more than beverages; light sandwiches and pastries, for instance, are a natural adjunct to coffee and tea.

ADVICE FROM THE EXPERTS

What sets your business apart from others like it?
Howard Schultz, chairman and CEO of Starbucks Coffee Company in Seattle, Washington, says that his company's mission is to establish itself as the premier purveyor of the finest coffees in the world, while maintaining uncompromising principles as the company grows. Today, Starbucks has close to 4,700 company-operated coffeehouses in the United States, Australia, Canada, China, Germany, Singapore, Thailand, and the United Kingdom, plus another 2,200 licensed locations all over the world.

Things you couldn't do without:
Carrying more than thirty varieties of coffee beans, plus bottled teas, specialty bottled coffee drinks, chocolates, pastries and sandwiches, and an exclusive line of home espresso machines, coffee brewers, grinders, mugs, and coffee accessories. Retail and restaurant equipment specific to each location.

Marketing tips/advice:
"We are the quintessential product-driven company," says Schultz. "We have the most knowledgeable workforce in our industry, from our head coffee buyer to the skillful baristas in all of our stores. I take great pride in the growth and development of our people." Schultz believes in setting his company apart through its commitment to social responsibility, giving back as much as possible to the community.

If you had to do it all over again . . .
Schultz wouldn't change a thing at his continually growing company.

COMMERCIAL FISHERMAN

Startup cost:	$15,000–$40,000
Potential earnings:	$15,000–$25,000
Typical fees:	The going price that day at your co-op or wholesaler
Advertising:	None
Qualifications:	Experience with and interest in water, boats, and fish; physical strength and stamina; basic fishing license and additional stamps for specific breeds as required by your state
Equipment needed:	Depends on the type of fish you are aiming for: boat, nets, trawl, rods, crab pots, lobster traps, etc.
Home business potential:	Yes
Staff required:	Probably
Hidden costs:	Fuel and bait, boat maintenance and equipment repair, insurance

LOWDOWN:

You become a fisherman because you love the water and have extensive experience with the ways of the type of fish you intend to catch. You do not become a fisherman to get rich, or to have a soft life. This is one of the most difficult and dangerous jobs there is. International markets and domestic regulations have both negative and positive effects on the profitability of fishing. For example, the federal government may impose a short- or long-term ban on harvesting a particular fish; if your business is grouper and the government says you can't catch it for the next five months, you're out of business. Or suppose your primary catch is cod, and imports from Canada are selling for below domestic prices; you can't find a buyer for the boatload you just brought in. Not only can the prices paid for a fisherman's catch be volatile, but so too are the costs of fuel and bait; those two essential items never seem to go down. Yet fishing has a way of getting in your blood and many a seasoned fisherman would not trade the hardships for any other occupation. The commercial fishermen who have grown up with the life can't think of anything else they'd rather do, and the ones who enter this difficult business from another career do so for reasons that make them determined to stick it out, no matter what.

STARTUP:

Startup costs vary enormously, depending on whether you need an ocean-going trawler or a skiff, a simple line with baited hooks, or 150 wire lobster traps. Regardless, you can't get up and running in this business, even with used equipment, for less than $15,000; the boat alone will cost you at least half of that. Don't expect to get rich; in your best year, your income could be as little as $25,000.

BOTTOM LINE ADVICE:

The love of fishing will carry you only so far. You also need insight into both catching the fish and marketing your product profitably. Skill, strength, and endurance are the hallmarks of a successful fisherman. You are at the whim of the weather and market conditions. Commercial fishing is a risky occupation, both in terms of income potential and physical danger, but don't just take our word for it. Hustle on down to the nearest video/DVD rental store for a copy of *The Perfect Storm*. If you can come away from that movie still wanting to be a commercial fisherman, go for it!

COMPUTER-AIDED DESIGN (CAD) SERVICE

Startup cost:	$15,000–$25,000
Potential earnings:	$30,000–$75,000
Typical fees:	$15–$50 per hour; some projects bill on a per-job basis
Advertising:	Yellow Pages, trade journals, referrals, networking
Qualifications:	Degree and/or experience in drafting or design; design expertise in a specific field, knowledge of hardware and software required for CAD
Equipment needed:	Top-of-the-line computer with oversized monitor, CAD software, light pen or graphics tablet with a puck, high-resolution graphics video card, laser printer with 11" x 17" paper capacity, flatbed scanner, blueprint copier
Home business potential:	Yes
Hidden costs:	Continuing education, equipment upgrades

LOWDOWN:

If you have an engineering or design background, you have numerous opportunities to create a successful business. Many fields, from architecture to fashion to civil engineering, use computer-aided design (CAD) extensively to develop prototypes and/or detailed plans. CAD enables a designer to see a design from a more functional standpoint than is possible on paper, thus creating an instant prototype on screen. As a CAD designer, you will be integrating computer hardware and software with the design needs of a field with which you already have extensive experience. And it's precisely this dual nature of your expertise that separates successful CAD freelancers from the rest of the competition. Design skills coupled with up-to-date computer hardware and software expertise and the ability to work well with clients will establish you as the person to call for the next CAD project—and the one after that.

STARTUP:

Startup costs are high because you will need the tools of the trade: a top-of-the-line computer with at least a 3.2 gigabyte hard drive and 32 megabytes of RAM, oversized monitor, CAD software, a laser printer with 11" x 17" paper capacity, and a blueprint copier. Expect to spend a minimum of $10,000 for your computer and peripherals; billings at $15–$50 per hour should help you recoup your expenses within a reasonably short period of time.

BOTTOM LINE ADVICE:

Creativity meets technology in a computer-aided design service. You can earn a high hourly rate in this business once you develop your client base. CAD is a growth field, and the number of skilled people has not nearly met the demand. It will be a challenge to keep your skills current; to be competitive, you'll need to stay abreast of CAD trends as well as developments in the profession or design field in which you specialize.

COMPUTER COMPOSER

Startup cost:	$15,000–$30,000
Potential earnings:	$20,000–$40,000
Typical fees:	Bids can range from $500 for a small project to $10,000 or more
Advertising:	Web site, bulletin board services, trade journals, referrals
Qualifications:	Musical composition skills and ability to apply them to technology; computer programming experience is helpful
Equipment needed:	Computer and peripherals such as CD-ROM player and speakers, tape deck, mixing console, amplifier, sound cards, microphones, printer, high-speed Internet access, fax; library of sample sounds
Home business potential:	Yes
Staff required:	No
Hidden costs:	Software/hardware updates, equipment maintenance

LOWDOWN:

People with musical skill and a love of the leading edge in computer creations can produce the music that accompanies most CD-ROMs and many regular programs, principally games. You'll need experience in musical composition and with MIDI programs, especially at the popular level, and you'll need high-speed Internet connections. It would be most beneficial to produce your own sample or demo that others could download and listen to before engaging your services. There aren't many who are qualified to connect with this developing market, but if you are one of them, you stand to become very successful. Computer composition is definitely on the cutting edge of creativity.

STARTUP:

Your startup costs (as high as $30,000) relate to the level of sophistication in required computer equipment; many composers have extensive MIDI equipment and composition software that is connected to actual instruments. Can you earn it back and eventually make a profit? You bet! But you'll have to have an excellent demo and go after the really big accounts.

BOTTOM LINE ADVICE:

Few people are even capable of entering this field, so it's wide open if you have the talent and computer expertise. Creating the sounds that are heard in millions of homes and businesses each day can be a rewarding experience, not to mention a lucrative one, especially if you enjoy the team aspect of multimedia production. Only a few people and businesses make up the market for this service, so you'll need to be creative in finding them. Focus your marketing efforts on larger companies that have been around for a while; you'll receive better pay for the same kind of work.

ADVICE FROM THE EXPERTS

What sets your business apart from others like it?
Michael Bross, audio producer/music composer for SoundPlanet in Latrobe, Pennsylvania, says his company provides very high quality audio and music for multimedia. "We work fast. I also believe that we understand the needs of multimedia developers better than other companies of this type."

Things you couldn't do without:
Broos couldn't do without the following: both a PC and a Macintosh computer, appropriate software for music composition and audio production, professional mixing console, multitrack recording system, effects processors, storage and backup memory storage for computers, sound modules and at least one sampler, MIDI keyboard, pro-level DAT machine, cassette deck, amplifier and audio monitors, sound cards, headphones, microphones, high-speed Internet access and printer, and a sound source library.

Marketing tips/advice:
"The work seems to pile up between July and December. Most developers are attempting to get their product on retail shelves for the Christmas buying season. The demands are very high during this time because many clients want to have work finished immediately."

If you had to do it all over again . . .
"I would learn computer programming. Also, I would have taken the time to develop a better marketing plan in the beginning."

COMPUTERIZED SPECIAL EFFECTS DESIGNER

Startup cost:	$20,000–$40,000
Potential earnings:	$65,000–$150,000+
Typical fees:	$75–$150 per hour or a flat, per-project rate ($2,500–$30,000)
Advertising:	Yellow Pages, referral, direct mail, industry/trade publications, Web site
Qualifications:	Extensive computer programming experience (in as many programming languages as possible); ability to conceptualize, then execute your ideas in a computer environment; artistic background
Equipment needed:	High-speed computer system with multimedia production studio and oversized, high-resolution monitors; backup tapes; simulation software; high-speed Internet access
Home business potential:	Yes
Staff required:	No
Hidden costs:	Equipment maintenance and upgrades, resource materials and research time

LOWDOWN:

When a computer program needs to have special effects, such as a city-crushing giant spider or a flight simulator, software producers turn to computerized special effects designers for expertise. But your client base isn't limited to just CD-ROMs—the market for computerized special effects in the film industry has been growing at a phenomenal rate. Movies like *Shrek* and *Finding Nemo*, which were produced using computer animation, prove that computers have a bright cinematic future ahead—and so do you, if you have the right skills and can market them effectively. If you're working with a film producer, your turnaround time may be six months to two years; special effects for software producers can sometimes happen in two months or less. In either case, expect there to be changes upon changes—and be sure to build that into the contract so that you are adequately compensated for your extra time and work. Regardless of who your clients are, you'll be spending huge amounts of your time researching (i.e., how exactly does a fighter jet operate?), then, based on your research, developing visuals that look realistic and programming them into a particular project. The best way to get your company's services out there is to produce a dynamic simulation or special effects package you post to your own Web site. Invite potential clients to visit your site via e-mail messages or direct mail (post cards can be pretty effective).

STARTUP:

Your startup is relatively high ($20,000–$40,000), but that's because you'll need to spend a lot of money on a state-of-the-art computer/multimedia station with high-end graphics packages that allow you to program your intricate designs and bring them to life. Expect to update your equipment every year or so, as new developments occur frequently in computer hardware, software, and peripherals. If you're working mostly for small software companies and corporate productions, you can expect to earn at least $65,000; If you're lucky enough to snag film studio work, your earnings could be significantly higher—$150,000 or more.

BOTTOM LINE ADVICE:

There's no doubt that you're good at what you do, but, if you're like most computer geniuses, you're not so wonderful at promoting yourself. Image is everything in this field, particularly if you want to hook up with Hollywood. If you don't feel comfortable selling yourself, bite the bullet and hire a public relations professional to do it for you. It will cost you some money, but if it gets high-paying work, then it's worth it, right? Take your first few jobs and turn them into sample presentations; get your Web site up and running as soon as possible. Designing computerized special effects is intense, complex, and often just plain lonely. Yet when you can finally stand back and appreciate the finished product, you can't help but be proud. You've done something downright cool.

CONCERT PROMOTER

Potential earnings:	$50,000–$100,000+
Typical fees:	25 to 30 percent of the concert gross
Advertising:	Promoters' magazines, industry trades, newspapers, word of mouth
Qualifications:	Extensive background and/or connections in the music industry, go-getter personality, integrity, track record of successful promotions
Equipment needed:	Basic office setup, cell phone
Home business potential:	Yes
Staff required:	Yes
Hidden costs:	Insurance, travel/entertainment costs

LOWDOWN:

Rock, opera, classical, folk . . . there are as many different acts to promote as there are types of music. If you are a real go-getter and have had an extensive background in the music industry, you stand a chance of making it as a concert promoter. You'll need to be supremely well-organized and detail-oriented, since your business hinges on making sure everything runs like clockwork. You will solicit a talent agent by telling him or her that, if a particular group or individual is brought to your town, you'll do the promoting and in virtually every place there's space. Network with local media to ensure good public relations, but don't promise agents the moon if you aren't absolutely sure you can deliver. This business is full of hyped-up promoters who turn out to be rip-off artists. You can't afford to be greedy until after you've established yourself; once you have a solid track record of successful promotions, you can ask for the big bucks.

STARTUP:

Your startup fee ($15,000–$25,000) will be wrapped up in getting your name out there and presenting a professional image. You have to be fairly well-known before someone will turn over the reins of promoting his or her act. Your fee will be 25 to 30 percent of the concert gross; if the act you're promoting is a big name star, you could earn as much as $150,000 per show.

BOTTOM LINE ADVICE:

There are long hours involved in this occupation—and lots of socializing, too. Not necessarily a good deal for a person with a family, but it's workable if you have a strong support staff and don't mind the late nights and weekends. Expect a lot of trial and error in the beginning; learn from each experience and improve yourself with time.

CONSULTING ENGINEER

Startup cost:	$20,000–$50,000
Potential earnings:	$40,000–$85,000+
Typical fees:	Depends on length and extent of project; can be as little as $175 for a "quick-and-dirty" project to as high as several thousand for on-site advice over many months
Advertising:	Trade journals, classified ads, federal publications, networking
Qualifications:	Degree and certification necessary (possibly in each state you do business in)
Equipment needed:	Drafting equipment and reference materials, computer with computer-aided design (CAD) software, perhaps surveying equipment
Home business potential:	Yes (but you'll be mostly working on-site)
Staff required:	Not initially; at some point, you may want to hire an administrative assistant
Hidden costs:	Liability insurance, mileage

LOWDOWN:

When a big project is launched at a corporation or even in a municipal environment, the expertise needed to actually execute the "great idea" isn't always available in-house. That's where you can really carve a nice niche for yourself—as a "hired gun" to pull together all the necessary finishing touches for construction, manufacturing, or technical situations. Consulting engineers offer their opinions and/or "hands-on" abilities to bring special projects to fruition. This could involve anything from creating CAD designs to developing a better means of production for the manufacturing arm of a large corporation. If you don't mind the pressure of coming into a potentially volatile (and often highly political) situation, and particularly if you are amenable to long hours for a short-term project, this could be a perfectly workable business for you. You would likely be called in as an expert; perhaps you'll be solving a snafu between the manufacturing and design departments of a major manufacturer, or ironing out a labor dispute that's holding up production.

STARTUP:

Assuming you already have your degree and certification, your startup costs will consist mainly of basic equipment. Expect to spend at least $20,000 (more if you're planning to have others working along with you). If you're good at what you do, you'll be able to earn a considerable amount of money within the first year or two—perhaps as much as $100,000 or more.

BOTTOM LINE ADVICE:

The key to success as a consulting engineer depends heavily on your ability to establish yourself as an industry expert. The more well-known you are for solving manufacturability problems, for instance, the more calls you're going to get—and the richer you'll become.

CUSTOM CARPENTRY/ FURNITURE MAKER

Startup cost:	$15,000–$20,000
Potential earnings:	$20,000–$65,000
Typical fees:	Varied, depending on the item, wood, and geographic locale; a handmade jewelry box might go for under $100, a chair or chest for $350–$2,500
Advertising:	Web site, catalog, exhibits at high-end shows, ads in specialty magazines, referrals
Qualifications:	Woodworking experience, either as a professional or hobbyist; knowledge of woods and woodworking equipment/tools; patience and pride of workmanship; creativity
Equipment needed:	Miscellaneous woodworking tools, including saws, lathes, levels, drills, sanders, clamps; delivery vehicle (optional)
Home business potential:	Yes
Staff required:	No
Hidden costs:	Equipment maintenance and replacement; fluctuating wood prices, vehicle expenses

LOWDOWN:

There's nothing so beautiful as a handcrafted piece of furniture, and, in this day and age, almost nothing so rare either. While the majority of today's homeowners shop for furnishings in warehouses that offer cookie-cutter styles and next-day delivery, there's a select group of discriminating shoppers who are looking for something a little less ordinary and will shell out top dollar when they find it. If you have woodworking ability and are willing to take the time to create a one-of-a-kind chair, chest, table, or bed from scratch, you may have the makings of a profitable business. Handmade furniture is not for everyone—especially those who are looking to furnish their homes in a hurry or on a limited budget. Still, among a specific market segment that appreciates high-quality workmanship and classic styles, the demand for custom carpentry is strong and growing. Once you are established, word of mouth and referrals will grow your business. Until you get to that point, however, you will need to spend some time and money marketing your services. Invest in a professionally designed Web site and possibly a color catalog to show off your creations. Consider exhibiting some of your work at high-end shows (juried art fairs, for example), too, but be careful not to damage your fragile handcrafted creations in the process.

STARTUP:

You can't make a living building custom furniture without the right tools. Expect to spend a minimum of $15,000 equipping your workshop with the full gamut of wood-working tools, including saws, lathes, levels, drills, sanders, etc. Shop for the best prices, but don't skimp on quality; in this business, your tools are your lifeblood. You may be able to start a custom carpentry business in your home basement or garage workshop, but as you grow, you're probably going to need—and want—a larger and more visible workspace. Keep that in mind as you put together your business plan. If you make delivery a part of your services, you'll need a vehicle; to keep costs down, consider renting a truck only when you need it. The kind of people who will buy your handmade products are not the kind who shop the newspaper classified ads for a bargain; if you decide to put some money into paid advertising, go for specialty magazines like *Yankee* or *Early American Life*.

BOTTOM LINE ADVICE:

Cash flow can be a problem in this business, given the length of time it takes to craft a chair or chest and then receive your check for it. To pick up the slack, consider making smaller items, too, like jewelry boxes, humidors, cedar chests, and toy boxes, which you can sell over the counter or at art fairs. And while we're on the subject of fairs, avoid run-of-the-mill craft shows; the clientele who typically attend these events won't pay the kind of prices you'll likely be asking. Opt instead for high-end events, possibly those associated with museums or historic attractions.

DAMAGE RESTORATION SERVICE

Startup cost:	$15,000–$20,000
Potential earnings:	$40,000–$65,000
Typical fees:	Varied according to damage; can be as little as $500 and as much as several thousand
Advertising:	Yellow Pages, coupon books, networking with insurance companies, real estate agents, and contractors
Qualifications:	Should have extensive knowledge about building structure and repair, codes and regulations regarding hazardous chemicals
Equipment needed:	A complete set of tools, painting/wallpapering equipment, varnishes and woodworking equipment, special solvents for cleaning up waste by-products, vehicle, cell phone
Home business potential:	Yes (but, of course, you'll be working on-site)
Staff required:	Not initially
Hidden costs:	Insurance, vehicle costs

LOWDOWN:

When a hurricane, flood, or other natural disaster strikes, professionals who can fix homes or offices are called in to assess the damage, create an estimate, and work with insurance companies to return the property to a "liveable" state. A damage restoration service is just one of the many services that can help repair the havoc nature has wreaked. But don't limit your services to federal disaster areas; fires and severe thunderstorms leave behind damages that warrant significant repair work too. In addition to structural damage, fire and flood can ruin the appearance of floors and walls. As a damage repair service professional, you'll probably spend the majority of your time fixing and cleaning walls, ceilings, and floors, so you'll need to be familiar with the variety of chemicals available for cleaning, repairing, and/or restoring such surfaces. If peeling paint and water-logged walls are your cup of tea, you'll revel in the kind of restoration projects that come your way. And while every disaster leaves a slightly different outcome behind, one thing is always the same: This kind of work is never without its challenges.

STARTUP:

Your basic equipment and tools, plus a vehicle to haul them all in, could easily set you back $15,000–$20,000. If you're just getting started and don't already own some tools, however, the smartest thing you might do is lease your equipment until you're sure this is a business you want to pursue full-time and that there's enough of it out there to support you. Leasing can cost you between $150–$300 per month. Since disasters can happen anytime, you'll want to be readily accessible to the folks who need you; invest in a good cell phone plan. Your charges will depend on the extent of damage done to the building; some repair jobs bill at a mere $500, while others are much costlier ($1,500–$80,000).

BOTTOM LINE ADVICE:

This business can be quite lucrative if you're in a hurricane- or flood-prone area, but sporadic in other parts of the country. You might consider adding on related services, such as wallpaper installation or faux finishes, to keep the money rolling in during your slack times.

DATING SERVICE

Startup cost:	$15,000–$50,000
Potential earnings:	$40,000–$100,000+
Typical fees:	Monthly retainer or annual fee that is high enough to attract only serious applicants; poll your competitors to determine the going rate for your geographic locale
Advertising:	Yellow Pages, newspaper ads, television spots, local magazines that appeal to your target market (singles of any age looking to meet new people)
Qualifications:	Outgoing personality, ability to make people feel at ease, interviewing experience; a background in psychology or counseling is helpful
Equipment needed:	Telephone with answering service or voice mail; computer and printer; word processing, database, and "matching" software; digital camera and/or video equipment (optional)
Home business potential:	Possibly, but check zoning laws to be sure; you will need parking space and a room for interviewing or videotaping clients
Staff required:	Yes
Hidden costs:	Insurance, ID verification

LOWDOWN:

Matchmaker, matchmaker, make me a living. . . . today's dating scene is vastly different from the old days, when a village woman made matches based on instinct and superstition. But one thing hasn't changed, however. Men and women are still looking for love, and many are still not having much luck finding it on their own. Tired of meeting people in bars and a little reticent to make use of the newspaper personals or online matchmaking sites, many singles would welcome a confidential, efficient way to meet the man or woman of their dreams. Your service would not only put them in touch with prospective partners, you'd do the prescreening for them to help ensure a better, safer match. You gather pertinent data about each client—age, personal and professional interests, what he or she is looking for in a mate, etc.—then you make a match with another client who seems compatible. To protect yourself and your clients, you will need a reliable system for verifying IDs and you'll want to carry liability insurance as well. Your matches can be made using a hard copy questionnaire, computer software, video, or any combination of all three.

STARTUP:

You'll need some high-ticket equipment to open this business; matchmaking technology and the video equipment to support it does not come cheap. Expect to spend a minimum of $15,000 to get up and running. There's a huge turnover of clients in this type of business—hopefully, most of those who leave will be doing so because you found them a match! You'll need to do some heavy-duty advertising to launch your business, plus ongoing newspaper ads and radio/TV spots to keep your name in front of your target markets. Look for ways to garner free publicity, too. There's nothing like a newspaper or television feature story about a wedding between two of your clients to get people talking and more clients coming in. And don't limit your target markets to single twenty- and thirty-somethings, either. Middle-aged divorcées and retired widow-ers are looking for companionship, too.

BOTTOM LINE ADVICE:

A dating service puts you in the love business, so what's not to love about that? You'll be meeting an array of interesting people, and you'll be helping them find new friendships, and possibly even long-lasting happiness with the mate of their dreams. Keep in mind, however, that when it comes to love, there are no guarantees. Be careful not to make promises about circumstances over which you have no control; even so-called "perfect matches" may not always work out. Are you prepared to deal with hurt feelings and bro-ken hearts, all the while encouraging your clients to stay in the game? If the answer is yes, you'll be heartily rewarded for your efforts.

DESKTOP PUBLISHER

Startup cost:	$15,000–$25,000
Potential earnings:	$20,00–$100,000
Typical fees:	$25–$65 per hour, $25–$50 per page, or flat rate per job based on estimated number of hours to complete and allowing for multiple corrections/changes
Advertising:	Direct solicitation of small businesses and nonprofit organizations, Yellow Pages, local publications, word of mouth, networking, advertising in writers' magazines, Web site
Qualifications:	Computer skills; knowledge of and feel for typography, design, and layout; writing and editing skills; verbal communication skills; patience and ability to cope with numerous client changes
Equipment needed:	Computer with large hard drive and full-page monitor; high-speed Internet access; color scanner; high-resolution color laser printer; software for desktop publishing, word processing, page layout, Web-page design, graphics and photo editor, digital photography, drawing, fonts, and clip art; fax; phone
Home business potential:	Yes
Staff required:	No
Hidden costs:	Marketing; keeping up with changes in software

LOWDOWN:

Desktop publishing (DTP) enables people with better-than-average writing and editing skills who also understand graphic design and typography to offer a range of services to clients. Skills with a variety of computer software packages will allow you to produce books, fliers, newsletters, and almost every kind of printed material in between. Many small DTP businesses succeed by specializing; for example, they create newsletters for a specific type of business. Others produce entire books or focus on annual reports. Most provide only the camera-ready master and subcontract the actual printing to a commercial printer. The DTP field includes many small and large businesses, but there is still plenty of room for people who do excellent work, produce it on time, and focus on their clients' needs and expectations. In fact, according to the Department of Labor, desktop publishing is one of today's fastest growing fields. If you have an interest in DTP, and the necessary skills to succeed at it, go ahead and take the plunge!

STARTUP:

One look at the list of computer hardware, software, and peripherals recommended for desktop publishing will tell you that you can't start this business with pocket change. Expect to spend a minimum of $15,000 for the technology alone. Add to that a work space large enough to support the complex nature of some DTP tasks. Then figure in the price of developing and maintaining a Web site, plus networking and selected ads in local publications and writers' magazines. Now you're getting close to a total of $25,000 to get this business up and running. Your income will be dependent upon how many clients you can win in a short period of time, so you'll need to get out there and pound the pavement. A good place to start might be with your former employer. Some desktop publishers bill by the hour ($25–$65 per) or by the page ($25–$50 per); most, however, price their services on a per-project basis, taking into account the number of hours needed to complete the job and factoring in extra time for changes and corrections. Smaller jobs can net $50–$300; larger ones can bring in $5,000 or more.

BOTTOM LINE ADVICE:

Although working on several different creative projects at one time can be interesting and challenging, the pressure can be unbelievable. In these days of instant information and 24-hour turnaround, everybody expects their work done today. That can be a problem when you are juggling projects for 10 or more clients. To avoid a steady stream of all-nighters and stress-filled days, work with your clients to establish realistic deadlines, and be careful to schedule enough time for you to complete the work without killing yourself in the process.

ADVICE FROM THE EXPERTS

What sets your business apart from others like it?
"We produce healthy recipes and a common-sense approach to healthy living," says JoAnna M. Lund, president and CEO of Healthy Exchange, Inc., in DeWitt, Louisiana. "We appeal to the average person and offer quick, healthy recipes that taste good using easy-to-find ingredients."

Things you couldn't do without:
A computer and laser printer, plus a fax machine.

Marketing tips/advice:
It's challenging to stay on top of changes in your field, but it can pay you well to do so, says Lund. Make sure you're an expert on that which you're reporting about.

If you had to do it all over again . . .
"Nothing. I'm quite happy where I am."

DESKTOP VIDEO

Startup cost:	$15,000–$40,000
Potential earnings:	$50,000–$120,000
Typical fees:	Varied, depending on the service—i.e., $50–$150 per hour for editing, $75–$125 per hour for on-site videotaping, $50 per minute of video time for scriptwriting
Advertising:	Direct mail, networking, participation in trade and business associations, Yellow Pages, Web site
Qualifications:	Training and hands-on experience in video production; eye for images and the way they fit together; creativity; technical and mechanical abilities; background in animation or graphic design is helpful
Equipment needed:	Computer with adequate gigabyte hard disk for video editing (5 minutes of video requires 1 gigabyte), printer, nonlinear digital editing card for editing and special effects, backup drive, authorware or desktop presentation software, writable CD-ROM and software, dedicated editing suite software (i.e., Frame Factory, Avid Express), digital camera, two color monitors, multiple video recorders, fax, scanner, copier, cell phone
Home business potential:	Yes
Staff required:	Yes
Hidden costs:	Equipment updates, keeping up with changes in technology

LOWDOWN:

From brides to business owners, everybody loves videos. And now, thanks to computer technology, it's easier—and less expensive than ever before—to professionally edit those tapes, adding animation, sound, music, photos, and other elements to create a more polished product. It's called desktop video—DTV for short—and with an eye for what makes a good visual production, plus the right combination of equipment and skills, you can make a good living with a video authoring and editing service. On the editing side, you'll use sophisticated computer hardware and software to cut and paste video footage and add sound, titles, fades and other effects. You'll also duplicate videos and convert them to and/or from another medium such as film, CD, or DVD. In addition, you may use software authoring systems to create interactive presentations that combine video with music, animation, still photos, and other elements. Does this sound like a business you'd be interested in pursuing? Well, the good news is there are tons of individuals, business owners, and professionals who could use your services—everyone from families wanting personal histories to surgeons seeking to document a complicated procedure and businesses looking for an innovative way to present their new project bids. The bad news is you're going to have to spend some serious bucks to acquire the equipment you'll need to do the job. And even before you do that, you'll need to have a pretty solid background and plenty of hands-on experience in video production.

STARTUP:

One look at the list of equipment needed for desktop video should tell you that this is going to be an expensive business to launch. At the very least, you will need a powerful computer, plus specialized desktop presentation and video editing software, digital camera, multiple video recorders, and at least two color monitors. Expect to spend up to $35,000 for the equipment alone. Thankfully, most of your marketing efforts will not involve large outlays of cash. You'll be doing a lot of networking—with businesses, wedding coordinators, meeting planners, advertising agencies, and even other videographers for their overflow work. Once you're up and running and have a few projects to your credit, look to referrals to grow your business and expect annual earnings of $50,000–$120,000.

BOTTOM LINE ADVICE:

This is not a business you should consider launching on a whim. It's highly technical and you need to really know what you're doing in order to succeed. You'll do best if you come into it with significant hands-on experience in video production. To prepare, hook up with an experienced professional who can show you the ropes or take a job with a cable television station that produces local programs. On the upside, DTV is growing by leaps and bounds. If you're creative and like a challenge, you should have no trouble finding plenty of work to do.

DIGITAL IMAGING SERVICE

Startup cost:	$20,000–$40,000
Potential earnings:	$25,000–$45,000
Typical fees:	$15–$45 per scanned-image product
Advertising:	Yellow Pages, mall kiosks and other high people-volume locations
Qualifications:	Training in equipment, super sales ability
Equipment needed:	Computer with scanner and video imaging capability
Home business potential:	No
Staff required:	No
Hidden costs:	Insurance, equipment maintenance and upgrades

LOWDOWN:

The digital craze is on—and it's not limited to musical instruments or compact disks. You can cash in on the trend by starting your own digital imaging service. You've probably seen such businesses in your local shopping mall or at a community flea market: The proprietor simply takes a video image of a person and places it onto a computer screen for printing on a color printer; the image is then transferred to a product (such as a felt banner, T-shirt, or coffee mug) and a personalized gift has been created. It's that simple, and the product generally sells itself if positioned in a high-traveled area. You can buy a franchise or start your own version if you are familiar enough with the equipment and can work with product vendors. Expect to market your service aggressively; you'll need to talk to people and have excellent sales ability to make enough money to cover your expenses (particularly rent, if you elect to locate inside a mall). Still, your products represent a fun method of gift-giving for many consumers—and they will buy, if you are visible enough.

STARTUP:

You'll need $20,000–$40,000 for your equipment and space rental, slightly more if you buy a franchise. Your equipment will include a computer with color printer, video camera, and software that permits image transfer from video to computer screen to printer. Thermal transfer equipment will also be necessary to produce those personalized coffee mugs and T-shirts. On the plus side, you might see as much as $45,000 for what amounts to very little effort on your part.

BOTTOM LINE ADVICE:

Your business will fluctuate according to season; expect low times in the fall and spring, and a Christmas high (complete with long hours and heavy volume).

EDUCATIONAL PRODUCT DEVELOPMENT

Startup cost:	$20,000–$30,000
Potential earnings:	$45,000–$65,000
Typical fees:	$25–$1,000 per item
Advertising:	Yellow Pages, direct mail and cold calls to educational product distributors, teachers' stores, and school systems, Web site
Qualifications:	Creativity, eye for good design; degree in education and/or classroom teaching experience would be helpful
Equipment needed:	Complete computer setup with laser printer, fax, Internet access, copier, scanner, phone system
Home business potential:	Yes
Staff required:	No
Hidden costs:	Insurance

LOWDOWN:

If you have a background in education and/or publishing, developing and producing a multitude of creative learning materials may be right up your alley. You could produce everything from bulletin board decorations to mathematics workbooks to individualized reading program materials and textbooks, and all of it could be marketed through a catalog and Web site detailing your complete product line. You might, for example, be doing contract work for an educational distributor or publisher who needs your expertise for the development of a specific product, such as a series of overhead projection maps. Find a creative way to set yourself apart from your competitors—capitalize on your unusual personal credentials, or highlight the nontraditional way of teaching children that you've come up with, such as solving problems via storytelling. Whatever your niche, you'll need to make sure that your materials are of the highest educational quality; enlisting a few teachers to use and subsequently endorse your products will certainly help get you started.

STARTUP:

It could easily cost $20,000–$30,000 to establish yourself in the educational product development business, mainly because you'll need a complete computer system with desktop publishing capability and a top-of-the-line color laser printer. You'll need to create and produce a catalog, too, and the quality you're striving for won't come cheap (budget at least $10,000 for your catalog alone). And don't forget your Web site. You'll need to budget $2,000–$4,000 for development by a professional Web site designer. Still, if you have a solid client base and sell regularly enough from your catalogs and Web site, you could soon be pocketing $45,000–$65,000 a year.

BOTTOM LINE ADVICE:

Your clients will want to see innovation and excitement in their educational materials. The market is wide open if you can develop truly unusual materials that actually succeed in educating children. Your biggest challenge will be to tell enough clients about your products to make a sizable profit. Buy targeted lists when you can. One last tip: Since educational materials are for teaching, they should set an example by always being precise and accurate themselves.

EMPLOYEE LEASING

Startup cost:	$15,000–$35,000
Potential earnings:	$60,000–$80,000
Typical fees:	Mark up the going rates by 40 to 50 percent
Advertising:	Direct mail, networking in business and trade associations, publishing a newsletter
Qualifications:	Knowledge of and contacts in a specific field, excellent organizational skills
Equipment needed:	Computer, printer, word processing and database software, fax, copier, scanner, telephone headset, brochure
Home business potential:	Yes
Staff required:	No
Hidden costs:	Liability insurance against employee misconduct

LOWDOWN:

While you may not be able, or for that matter even desire, to compete with the big temporary help firms, your small employee leasing agency can provide workers with specialized skills that are normally not offered through the traditional temp services. This business produces good earnings relative to time and materials: You're not doing the actual work—just the organization required to match employees to employers. Build your database of specialists in a field you have particular experience with, then target your prospective clients through direct mail.

STARTUP:

Although the cost of building your initial database and center of operations is not high, you will need a sizable initial investment ($20,000) to cover the delays in cash flow between your clients and your employees. You could see at least $60,000 at the end of your first year.

BOTTOM LINE ADVICE:

You will probably need to consult an attorney and/or accountant to stay abreast of the laws regarding taxes, workers' compensation, and employment. Some types of temps will need to be bonded, and you will need to measure the advantages of incorporating your business against the extra costs and red tape that incorporation involves.

ENTERTAINMENT DIRECTORY PUBLISHER

Startup cost:	$15,000–$30,000
Potential earnings:	$35,000–$65,000
Typical fees:	Advertising income (rates from $125–$3,000 per issue)
Advertising:	High-profile shelf space (and plenty of drop-off sites), advertisements on buses and taxis, billboards, distribution at hotels, restaurants, and other entertainment venues
Qualifications:	Sales ability, good organizational and people skills; previous publishing experience would be extremely helpful
Equipment needed:	Computer, laser printer, copier, scanner, fax, Internet access, phone
Home business potential:	Yes
Staff required:	One to two with editorial or production skills
Hidden costs:	Rising printing and paper costs, distribution

LOWDOWN:

Where do all the happening folk turn to for entertainment ideas in their community? They pick up a free entertainment directory from restaurants, hotels, nightclubs, and other hot spots around town. Despite the myriad choices they'll have due to an influx of free newspapers and other publications, consumers will choose to read only your publication once you have established it as the source for what's truly hot and happening. You will solicit advertisements from every entertainment-related business you possibly can throughout your community, from video stores to restaurants to concert halls. You'll be able to sell them on the virtues of advertising regularly in your pages once you present evidence of your circulation figures. You will design a publication that looks inviting and entertaining in and of itself, and you'll set up a vast enough distribution channel to make advertising with you worth the money you charge. Words like "more than 500,000 distribution points in the tri-state area" will strike the right chords with potential advertisers. Create the product, get it printed as economically as possible, then wait to build consumer recognition. This could easily take a couple of years, but if you work hard and stick with it, you could see a huge profit down the road. Just be sure you set aside enough capital to pay your bills until your directory begins to pay off.

STARTUP:

It will cost you between $15,000–$30,000 to successfully launch an entertainment directory publishing business, mainly to cover printing and paper costs. Your actual costs really depend, however, on how large your print run is; determine early on what your demographics have to say about your potential market for these directories, and budget accordingly for each issue you produce. If you can generate enough ad sales to cover printing costs, your income could reach anywhere from $35,000–$65,000.

BOTTOM LINE ADVICE:

You're competing against many other media in this field, including other entertainment directories. Set yourself apart by offering regular contests or add-on services for your advertisers, such as a coupon-packaging service.

FISH RESTOCKING

Startup cost:	$15,000–$25,000
Potential earnings:	$30,000–$50,000
Typical fees:	$30–$50 per job
Advertising:	Sport/angling magazines, direct mail, referrals
Qualifications:	Knowledge of fish breeding and nurturing, restocking practices
Equipment needed:	Land for a hatchery, vehicles equipped with fish tanks for restocking, computer, printer, phone, fax
Home business potential:	No
Staff required:	Yes
Hidden costs:	Staff to feed the fish, conduct the restocking procedures, and maintain the property in your absence; insurance

LOWDOWN:

A fish restocking service appeals to two broad categories of clients: governments and private fishing resorts. Governments at different levels have many rigid requirements and can be challenging to work with. However, many government entities conduct fish restocking on a large scale, and this could be a good opportunity for the right business. Private fishing resorts also often need major restocking efforts, and it is possible that one of these might fund your operation's startup costs. Detailed knowledge of fish is essential for success in this business.

STARTUP:

Startup costs are relatively high in this business as you must have not only the land and equipment to support a hatchery, you must also have the vehicles for delivering fish stock across a fairly wide geographic area. Many fish restockers charge $500–$1,000 for their services; your rates will largely depend on your geographic location and the needs of your customers. It is generally a good idea to specialize in only one species of fish: This helps keep your startup costs down, particularly with regard to the first hatchings.

BOTTOM LINE ADVICE:

If you love the outdoors and the world of fishing, this business could be an appropriate one for you. You will be establishing relationships with your clients, whether they are in the public or private sector, that could potentially last for many years. You will also have a close involvement with the natural world. However, you may find it difficult to attract workers who share your enthusiasm for hard outdoor labor, especially in bad weather. And your business will be at the mercy of budget cutters in either the public or private arenas.

FLORAL SHOP

Startup cost:	$30,000–$60,000
Potential earnings:	$1,000–$5,000 per month
Typical fees:	Depends on market price for what you sell (i.e., roses cost more than daisies, a floral arrangement, wreath, or swag more than loose blooms or a potted plant)
Advertising:	Yellow Pages; specialty magazines; business cards at bridal salons, funeral homes, and other places where people buy and use flowers regularly
Qualifications:	Formal training in and/or knowledge of flowers and floral design, creativity, organizational and time-management skills; some states require licensing
Equipment needed:	Storefront; floral tools and supplies; refrigerators; inventory of fresh, silk, and dried flowers and potted plants; baskets, vases, and other containers; balloons (optional); gift cards
Home business potential:	No
Staff required:	Yes
Hidden costs:	Insurance, taxes, spoilage, backup generator (one power outage, even if it's a brief one, could wipe out your inventory)

LOWDOWN:

Nothing compares to the beauty of a single rose—or, better yet, an artfully designed floral bouquet. If you know your daisies from your day lilies, you can start a floral shop. This is truly creative work, and you'll enjoy the challenge of putting together an interesting array of the most gorgeous posies on the planet. You'll use three types of flowers: fresh cut, silk, and dried. A keen visual sense of what is pleasing to the eye and appropriate for the event is required. You must have the ability to preserve and sell flowers, take, fill, and deliver customer orders, and be as knowledgeable as any of your competitors. In this business, you will probably require a staff, especially to help you on the busiest flower days: Valentine's Day, Mother's Day, and Easter. You'll find lots of competition in the flower business; creativity and attention to customer service will help set you apart.

STARTUP:

Your startup costs will be high (at least $30,000), because you will need a storefront, refrigerators, and a comprehensive inventory of flowers and the containers to put them in. Your prices will largely depend on the season, the wholesale price you have to pay for particular types of flowers, and your geographic location. The peak period in the floral industry is November through May; the demand for flowers tends to wither during the summer months, although June and August are especially popular for weddings, so you may be able to pick up some of that slack. Once you've recovered your initial investment, your earning potential will still be slow until you've captured your unique market niche. Expect $12,000–$24,000 the first year.

BOTTOM LINE ADVICE:

Running a floral shop requires standing on your feet for long periods of time—sometimes as much as 10 to 12 hours per day. Expect your hours to be even longer when you're getting the flowers ready for weddings and holidays such as Christmas, Easter,

Mother's Day, and Valentine's Day. Flower shops are typically closed on Sundays and sometimes on Mondays too, but you can count on working a lot of late nights immediately prior to holidays and on Saturdays. Your earnings are directly linked to volume, so the quicker you are in creating beauty, the more money you can make.

ADVICE FROM THE EXPERTS

What sets your business apart from others like it?

Personalized service, high quality, and reasonable prices are what set apart Pam Williams's florist shop, Pam's Posies, in Akron, Ohio. "We also have a pleasant atmosphere that's homey and inviting. We go one step further than any of our competitors by producing the most creative arrangements we can muster." Williams's business is located in a converted home in the middle of a busy commercial real estate parcel.

Things you couldn't do without:

"Employees, of course. But we also couldn't do without our coolers, decorative materials, fresh and silk inventory, knives, and cutters."

Marketing tips/advice:

"Be in an area where you already know a lot of people, first of all. Then, realize that whatever you send out is ultimately going to be your best advertising— so send out your best work!" Williams also participates in Welcome Wagon-type giveaways to bring people into the store for free flowers. "Once they've been inside, they almost always come back, so the free flowers are worth it."

If you had to do it all over again . . .

"I might have gotten more schooling before launching my own business. As it was, I had to learn everything on the job. Still, I think I handled my company's growth in the right way, growing in five- to seven-year increments rather than all at once."

HEALTH/FITNESS CENTERS FOR CORPORATIONS

Startup cost:	$15,000–$35,000 per center
Potential earnings:	$40,000–$65,000
Typical fees:	Monthly retainers of $3,000–$5,000 per project
Advertising:	Business publications, newspapers, direct mail, networking
Qualifications:	Business and/or fitness center background; extensive knowledge of the health and fitness field and fitness center operations; excellent managerial and selling skills
Equipment needed:	Basic office setup, including computer, printer, fax, copier, scanner, phone; high-quality marketing materials
Home business potential:	Yes
Staff required:	Yes
Hidden costs:	Insurance, equipment updates and maintenance

LOWDOWN:

For many employees, a company-sponsored health/fitness center on-site or in close proximity to their workplace would be the ultimate benefit. You can use your excellent managerial skills to develop and manage fitness centers for corporations that wish to make these services more readily available to their employees, thereby increasing their loyalty while improving their health and well-being. The challenge of balancing your costs against the fees you will charge requires an excellent business sense; you'll have to be a good judge of people, too, as you will need to hire outstanding employees of your own to run each center. By centralizing purchasing, marketing, and other business activities, you will be able to offer your services to corporations at a competitive price. Considering the current state of health care in America and what businesses are having to shell out to provide health benefits to their employees, it seems as though this business is one whose time has definitely come; if you can come up with the capital it requires to launch this business, you could make good money down the road.

STARTUP:

Even if your client corporation provides the space, you will still have to incur some significant startup costs to get each center up and running. Expect to spend a minimum of $40,000–$100,000 per center for equipment. And don't forget to factor in the costs of preparing training/resource materials for your personnel and setting up your own office with computer, printer, copier, scanner, fax, phone, and Internet access. You'll earn every cent of the $40,000–$65,000 you are likely to earn each year.

BOTTOM LINE ADVICE:

Once your business is established, you will have an innovative and highly profitable enterprise. However, building the health/fitness center concept into an established business will be enormously demanding. Your marketing and selling skills will be thoroughly tested. Keeping the centers operating well, safely, and profitably, will also be challenging. This is not a crowded field, and with these demands on your time, energy, and pocketbook, it's easy to see why.

HOME INSPECTOR

Startup costs:	$30,000–$40,000
Potential earnings:	$50,000–$75,000
Typical fees:	$200–$400 per home, depending on square footage and geographic location
Advertising:	Yellow Pages, real estate publications, local newspapers, networking with real estate agents
Qualifications:	Thorough knowledge of home construction and building codes and/or experience in contracting and building; writing skills; license or permits may be required, depending on the city or state
Equipment needed:	Electrical tracer, circuit tester, gas detector, basic tools (screwdrivers, wrenches, levels, etc.), flashlights, ladders, computer, printer, fax, cell phone, vehicle
Home business potential:	Yes
Staff required:	No
Hidden costs:	Errors and omission insurance, phone bills, association dues, vehicle expenses

LOWDOWN:

In today's litigious society, home buyers, sellers, and real estate agents are all looking for the best protection they can get. Bringing in an objective party to assess the condition of a home before the deal is closed just makes good sense. For the buyers especially, a home inspector can provide reassurance that the home they're buying is exactly what it appears to be—with no hidden flaws—and that the price they've agreed to pay is a fair one. If you're working for a buyer, you'll typically take two to three hours to conduct a thorough visual inspection, including the roof, foundation, heating and air conditioning, plumbing, and electrical system. You'll prepare a written report and, based on what you find, the potential buyers may simply accept the house as is, require the sellers to fix any problems before the closing, or obtain a larger mortgage so they can make the repairs. A seller may also call upon a home inspector for help in determining a realistic sale price that is based on the actual value of the house as opposed to simply fair market price. Home inspectors can often spot a problem that owners may have overlooked simply because they're so used to it.

The business of home inspection is not without risk and, unfortunately, the inspectors themselves are sometimes targets for litigation. If you go into this field, be sure that you look into the certification and licensing requirements in your area and that you protect yourself by either incorporating your business or affiliating with a franchise organization. Whichever you choose, you are sure to find that home inspection is both interesting and challenging. Your work will change on a daily basis, as you'll be moving from one home to another to inspect everything from the furnace in the basement to the shingles on the roof. Yours is an honorable profession and, in today's "buyer-beware" kind of real estate market, a necessary and valuable service, too.

STARTUP:

You can't just walk into someone's house and start picking it apart; you'll need to have some credentials and, in most states, a license or permits, and they cost money. You can operate independently, of course, but you'll find that this business will be much easier to get up and running effectively—and in a shorter period of time—if you pay a franchise fee (anywhere from $30,000–$50,000) to an already established company in this field. In addition to the networking and support you'll receive, as franchisee, you're protected legally.

BOTTOM LINE ADVICE:

Don't underestimate the value of contact with real estate agents. Many of your best referrals will come from them. Likewise, thorough and honest inspections will result in satisfied home buyers, who, in turn, will become your most valuable source of word-of-mouth advertising. You'll have lots of face-to-face contact with buyers and sellers, so excellent communication and people skills are a must.

HORSE/CARGO TRAILER SERVICE

Startup cost:	$15,000–$30,000
Potential earnings:	$20,000–$30,000
Typical fees:	$40–$50 per horse, per trailer ride, plus mileage
Advertising:	Yellow Pages, word of mouth, business/farming publications
Qualifications:	Experience in horse handling and transportation, clean driving record
Equipment needed:	Trailer with room to accommodate two to four horses; truck or van
Home business potential:	Yes
Staff required:	No
Hidden costs:	Insurance, equipment maintenance, vehicle expenses

LOWDOWN:

Horse owners often need to have their animals transported to shows, county fairs, and even to new owners, and they will pay you $40–$50 plus mileage to transport an animal for them—especially if they've got ten horses and only one two-horse trailer of their own. That's why it's so important for you to network well with local equestrians. Try circulating your business card with equestrian associations and meeting face-to-face with horse owners and trainers. These are the folks who will continually provide you with business.

STARTUP:

You'll need to shell out approximately $15,000–$30,000 for a trailer (slightly less if you lease), but if you promote heavily and subcontract to others like you during the heavy seasons (specifically, summertime—when most county fairs occur), you can expect to begin earning a fairly decent living soon.

BOTTOM LINE ADVICE:

If you don't mind the hosing down you'll need to do after each equestrian delivery (horses can be quite messy when they're nervous or confined), this could be a relatively easy way to earn a living. However, until you get well-known, you won't be able to make enough to support yourself full-time. Plan on two to five years before any real money starts coming your way.

Hot Air Balloon Rides

Startup cost:	$15,000–$21,000
Potential earnings:	$45,000+
Typical fees:	$150–$200 per person in groups of four to six; more for solo/single couple flights
Advertising:	Yellow Pages, word of mouth/referrals, Web site
Qualifications:	Hot air balloon pilot's license, good navigational skills
Equipment needed:	Complete balloon rig, insurance, chase vehicle
Home business potential:	Yes, but flights require open space
Staff required:	Yes, for liftoff and return
Hidden costs:	Liability insurance

LOWDOWN:

Up, up, and away in a beautiful (and profitable) balloon! Hot air balloon rides remain a popular form of entertainment, especially for those thrill-seekers who aren't into bungee jumping, skydiving, or other potentially life-threatening adventures. From tethered rides to free-flying across the countryside at varying altitudes, the range of flight packages you can offer is wide. Many balloon ride businesses provide extras such as a picnic lunch or rides to special places of interest. You'll need to carry some costly insurance and regularly maintain your pilot's license, but think of all the interesting people you'll meet while cruising the friendly skies. Fees for a two- or three-hour tethered ride can be $800 or more, while a short flight is generally priced at $150–$250 per person, depending on the amenities you provide. To make money on a flight, you really need to have four to six paying passengers; you can either offer a group rate for folks who want to fly together as a single party, or you can assemble your own groups from singles and couples who are willing to share the basket with strangers. You can offer flights for just one passenger or a single couple, of course, but charge a premium—say, $525 just to get the basket off the ground.

STARTUP:

The biggest expense in the "launch" of this business is the purchase of a balloon rig (balloon and basket), which can start at $12,000. More luxurious models increase rapidly in price, but the average four-seater runs about $18,000. Obtaining a pilot's license will cost you $2,000–$3,000 (less if you bring your own balloon); insurance premiums will vary according to where you live.

BOTTOM LINE ADVICE:

This business could be seasonal, depending on where you live, and even in season, it is iffy. If the weather is not quite right for ballooning, you're grounded. A love for flying is a must, as well as the ability to enjoy being around people. Skill at helping others calm their fears could be an added benefit in situations when clients experience slight vertigo. There's no telling what can happen when you're flying along at 2,000 feet, so keep a cool head.

HURRICANE PRODUCTS/SERVICES

Startup cost:	$15,000–$25,000
Potential earnings:	$40,000–$75,000
Typical fees:	Varied according to product or service; could be as low as $100 for a consultation or as high as several thousand to install hurricane-resistant windows or protective shutters
Advertising:	Yellow Pages, ads in newspapers/business publications, home shows, referrals
Qualifications:	Thorough knowledge of various protective options and ability to install them; basic business and marketing skills
Equipment needed:	Inventory of protective devices in a wide range of prices; installation tools and accessories; ladders; truck or van; computer and printer with bookkeeping and billing software; cell phone
Home business potential:	No
Staff required:	Yes
Hidden costs:	Insurance, vehicle expenses, escalating product costs, workers' compensation

LOWDOWN:

If recent meteorological events and predictions from the National Hurricane Center concerning future weather patterns are any indication, it looks like the need for hurricane products and services isn't likely to diminish anytime soon. And while the hurricane season officially lasts just six months and directly affects only a limited segment of the U.S. population, there's plenty of opportunity these days for a business devoted to providing hurricane products and services. For the folks who live in a hurricane-prone region, you'll have two important roles to play: You'll advise homeowners and businesses about the measures they should take to protect their property, and you'll sell the devices that will improve their chances of weathering a storm with minimal damage. In order to appeal to the widest possible customer base, you'll want to have a complete stock of protective devices on hand in every price category—from the least expensive (aluminum accordion storm panels) to the most costly (rolling hurricane shutters) and everything in between—along with the necessary hardware and tools to install them. For maximum profitability, strive to do the actual installation, too; at the same time, however, be prepared to simply offer advice and instructions (written or possibly even on video) for diehard do-it-yourselfers who want to tackle the job on their own.

STARTUP:

Keep in mind that you have just a six-month window of opportunity from the end of one hurricane season to the beginning of the next, so you'll need to be prepared to hit the ground running on the day you open for business. Spend whatever it takes ($25,000+ if necessary) to make sure that you have adequate inventory to address the needs of your community; requests for your services are likely to grow the closer it gets to hurricane season and with every land-falling storm, no matter where it comes ashore. Advertise in the Yellow Pages and in local newspapers and business publications, and don't forget home shows; they're a great place to demonstrate your products and meet potential customers face-to-face.

BOTTOM LINE ADVICE:

Hurricane preparedness is a matter of public safety, and you'll do well if you come across as genuinely concerned for life and property. Build visibility for your products and services by making yourself available as the source of information about protection. Work with the local media as they put together their annual hurricane guides, and volunteer to be a speaker at hurricane preparedness seminars and other events. Hurricanes are something people would really rather not think about, but they know they must, and the product you're selling is a vital one. Tread the line carefully between fear-mongering and creating a healthy respect for the power of Mother Nature.

INTERNATIONAL BUSINESS CONSULTANT

Startup cost:	$15,000–$40,000
Potential earnings:	$45,000–$150,000+
Typical fees:	$100–$500 per hour; sometimes a percentage of the deal (15 to 25 percent)
Advertising:	Industry and business publications, Web site
Qualifications:	Solid business background, knowledge of foreign business operations, extensive travel experience, foreign language skills, ability to understand and work within other cultures
Equipment needed:	Basic office setup with cell phone, laptop computer, high-speed Internet access; strong, durable suitcases
Home business potential:	Yes, but you'll be doing lots of traveling
Staff required:	No
Hidden costs:	Insurance, travel and cell phone expenses

LOWDOWN:

Large corporations long ago recognized the importance of the global marketplace; now small- to medium-sized companies are entering the international arena, too. And you can help them get off on the right foot. As an international business consultant, your expertise will be in matching the needs and goals of one particular corporate culture to the culture of one or more foreign countries. In other words, you'll play the role of matchmaker between a company and its possible sites for overseas expansion. You'll need to have a good handle on the economic, political, and especially cultural climate in each country, as well as the ability to communicate well with foreign officials as you try to negotiate intricate contracts. Dealing with other countries can be tricky, and not just in terms of government regulations, as General Motors so painfully learned a few years ago when Chevrolet tried to promote its Nova in Mexico. The car didn't sell well south of the border and you want to know why? Because, in Spanish, "no va" means "does not go." Common sense would tell you that a car carrying the brand name "does not go" isn't going to sell. Keep that story in mind as you approach different countries with products and concepts. Will the particular product you're representing "play" in Russia or Peru or wherever your client wants to take it? Work within cultural boundaries and remember to abide by that time-honored phrase, "when in Rome do as the Romans do." While recent advances in technology make some of your work possible by Internet, you will still have to do a fair amount of overseas travel. Jetting over multiple time zones can get old after a while; on the plus side, just imagine the Frequent Flyer miles you'll rack up!

STARTUP:

You'll need sufficient capital to advertise and travel in the right circles, so that you can meet with high-powered corporate officials who need your services. You might well spend $15,000–$25,000 up front just getting this business off the ground, unless you have several good client possibilities already under your belt. Still, at $100–$500 per hour (depending on your level of expertise and track record), you'll be able to earn a highly respectable income for yourself—and, if the deals are right, you'd be wise to pencil in a commission for yourself as well.

BOTTOM LINE ADVICE:

Traveling all over the world helping companies expand in the global marketplace can be glamorous work when it goes well—and downright dismal when it doesn't. Remember, you're not traveling to sightsee; you'll log a lot of air miles and while you may get to exotic locales, most of your time in foreign countries will be spent in meetings.

LANDSCAPE DESIGNER

Startup cost:	$15,000–$35,000
Potential earnings:	$30,000–$50,000
Typical fees:	$60–$100 per hour for consulting and design; $25–$50 per hour for installation and maintenance
Advertising:	Personal contact with landscaping companies and nurseries, Yellow Pages, ads in local newspapers, Web site
Qualifications:	Thorough knowledge of shrubs, trees, flowers, grass, soils, growing seasons, and regional climate conditions; training and/or extensive experience in landscape design; sense of aesthetics and ability to design plans that please the customer
Equipment needed:	Basic office setup, including computer, printer, CAD software, fax, phone, copier, and scanner; Internet access; nursery catalogs and landscaping design resources; gardening tools and truck for installation and maintenance
Home business potential:	Yes
Staff required:	Possibly, if you decide to go the installation and maintenance route
Hidden costs:	Phone and vehicle expenses

LOWDOWN:

Do you have a love of nature—and the knowledge/skill to transform its beauty into a gorgeous landscape? If the answer is yes, you may be well-suited to the business of landscape design. You'll be selling your services to clients on many different levels: landscape companies that will implement your plans, business owners and developers with grounds to beautify, and/or consumers who want to be surrounded by natural beauty but don't know how to make it happen. You will need excellent listening and communications skills in order to, first, determine what your clients want and, second, translate their desires into an actual landscaping plan. Drawing up plans that fit individual budgets and personal tastes, either working with landscape companies that will implement your ideas or executing the plans yourself, can be a challenging yet rewarding job for those with the eye to see a garden worthy of Monet's paintbrush in an otherwise ordinary grassy knoll.

STARTUP:

Your startup costs will vary, depending on how far you want to take your services. At the very least, you will need a computer, printer, and CAD software in order to be able to put your plans on paper. If your job ends with the delivery of the plan, you can launch this business for under $10,000. But if, like the majority of landscape design firms, you decide to add installation and maintenance to your services, you will need to outfit your business with basic landscaping tools and a van or small truck in which to haul them; expect to spend another $10,000–$15,000. With aggressive marketing and fees of $25–$100 per hour, depending on the services, you should be able to recoup your investment in a relatively short period of time. Some landscape designers charge by the project rather than by the hour; if you decide to go that route, be careful to figure your project fees so that your time and expenses are adequately covered.

BOTTOM LINE ADVICE:

Don't rely on business from homeowners alone—they're likely to think of landscaping only during warm weather months. The large contracts—and significant money—will come from developers and landscape companies. For best results, spring for the cost of developing a professional Web site ($2,000 or more), then advertise your services on the Internet and be prepared to venture beyond your immediate geographic region for work.

MESSAGE RETRIEVAL SERVICE
(ANSWERING SERVICE)

Startup cost:	$15,000–$25,000
Potential earnings:	$20,000–$35,000
Typical fees:	$50–$75 per month based on a set number of calls; add a surcharge for calls above the preset number
Advertising:	Networking and referrals, Yellow Pages, local business publications, newspaper ads
Qualifications:	A good phone voice, good listening skills, organizational abilities
Equipment needed:	Computer with bookkeeping and billing software, high-speed Internet access, printer, fax, multiline phone system with headsets, automated voice mail system (optional)
Home business potential:	Yes
Staff required:	Yes (usually 1–5 employees)
Hidden costs:	Additional phone lines to handle more clients, personnel costs

LOWDOWN:

Answering services have been around for a long time, and while answering machines and voice mail have taken their toll, that real voice on the end of the line still has an important role to play for small businesses that are intensely customer service oriented. If you have a pleasant phone manner and good listening skills, you can take advantage of this excellent business opportunity. Advances in technology have made the answering service business easier to run than ever before. The latest software allows keyboard entry of caller information; pagers and cell phones can quickly connect you to the plumber or freelancer who has hired you to be his or her "home office." For clients that value efficiency, you can offer a higher-tech approach—an automated voice mail system, with an options menu and the capability of recording and sharing long messages. Ours is increasingly a communications culture, and you can succeed by joining forces with automated voice mail rather than competing with it. You might also consider offering e-mail accounts for clients that do not have Internet access as well as electronic forwarding of voice mail messages and faxes.

STARTUP:

Your startup costs will depend to a large extent on the level of service you plan to offer. A traditional telephone system, including a switchboard with multiple phone lines and headsets is, obviously, less expensive than a high-tech automated voice mail system. Add to these expenses a computer with bookkeeping and billing software, printer, fax, and promotional brochures for a total of $15,000–$25,000 to get up and running. If you are able to quickly build a strong client base willing to pay monthly fees of $50–$75, you should be able to realize a profit in a relatively short period of time.

BOTTOM LINE ADVICE:

You have a pleasant voice, care about people, and are organized. You know how to filter out what is important from the background chatter. You're a natural for this business. On the downside, an answering service doesn't offer a lot of flexibility; you're pretty much tied to your desk and phones. Plus, you'll have to work hard at marketing to build a client base large enough to support you and, eventually, a small staff.

MOBILE CAR INSPECTION/REPAIR

Startup costs:	$15,000–$25,000
Potential earnings:	$30,000–$45,000
Typical fees:	$25–$45 per hour for repairs; $125 per inspection
Advertising:	Yellow Pages, local newspapers, news release announcing your service in newspaper automotive sections and/or special publications delivered free to residences, coupon books
Qualifications:	Training/experience as an auto mechanic; some states require certification
Equipment needed:	Basic mechanic's tools, dependable transportation of your own
Home business potential:	Yes
Staff required:	No
Hidden costs:	Insurance, mileage

LOWDOWN:

Convenience sells. Many consumers today are too busy to take their cars into the shop; they'd no doubt welcome a repair service that would come to them, even if it cost a little more. You'd be saving them time—and for many busy professionals, time is money. Not only will you be capable of making minor repairs on the spot, such as replacing windshield wipers and batteries or fixing minor electrical problems, you can offer to inspect new or used vehicles prior to purchase. Assisting buyers with a good once-over before they plunk down the cash can be a valuable service, especially if the car is used and being purchased from an individual owner whom the buyer does not know. Women especially will appreciate the expertise of a mechanic who can inspect a vehicle and help them make a fair offer based on the car's actual condition rather than its "blue-book" value.

STARTUP:

You'll need a good set of mechanic's tools and dependable transportation of your own (preferably something with your logo on the side to get even more for your advertising dollar); expect to spend at least $15,000–$25,000 on launching this innovative yet necessary business. As a mobile car care professional, you can charge an hourly fee ($25–$45) for repairs and a flat fee ($125) for inspecting each vehicle.

BOTTOM LINE ADVICE:

Your honesty and integrity are on the line. Backing those traits with a written, personal guarantee will help sell your service and build a steady referral business.

MOBILE PAPER-SHREDDING SERVICE

Startup cost:	$15,000–$18,000
Potential earnings:	$20,000–$40,000
Typical fees:	$30–$50 per office visit; offer monthly rates for clients that generate more than the usual amounts of paper waste
Advertising:	Local business periodicals, direct mail
Qualifications:	Marketing skills, excellent time management and scheduling ability
Equipment needed:	Van, heavy-duty paper shredder(s), computer, printer, fax, cell phone, vehicle, plastic bags
Home business potential:	Yes
Staff required:	No
Hidden costs:	Vehicle maintenance and repair

LOWDOWN:

We've all heard the horror stories about identity theft—how discarded medical records, bank account statements, and other sensitive documents tossed into the trash receptacles outside of an office building ended up in the wrong hands. No wonder mobile paper-shredding services are popping up all across the United States. As information becomes easier to steal, it becomes more important for certain types of businesses to protect the security of their customers. Banks, for example, have suffered great losses when criminals obtained their discarded paper trash. It's essential that computer codes, product information, even individual customer records be kept confidential. The value of your service is that it guarantees security; the actual shredding is completed on the client's premises, in front of witnesses, so that no possibility exists for data to be lost or stolen. Sure, a business could do its own shredding, but that can be time-consuming and messy. You save a business time and trouble by showing up on-site with your shredding machines on a regular schedule to perform this necessary but tedious task. You shred the necessary documents, bag up the refuse, and, if necessary, haul everything away for disposal.

STARTUP:

A van or truck represents your largest startup expense, at $15,000 or more. Then, of course, you'll need at least one heavy-duty shredder and a back-up machine (about $300 each), plus a good supply of heavy-duty plastic bags for containing the shredded pieces. Charge $30–$50 per office visit; offer a reduced per visit/monthly rate to more regular clients, such as attorneys and government agencies that generate a lot of paper waste.

BOTTOM LINE ADVICE:

As every day brings yet another alarming story of identity theft, this business is growing fast, but if you want to get into it, you better do so soon before the crush of competitors limits your opportunity to make a fair profit. Your marketing will need to include considerable education so that your potential clients recognize the value of paying a mobile shredding service rather than doing the shredding themselves. Excellent customer service and integrity will maintain and increase your hard-won client base.

MULTIMEDIA SERVICE

Startup cost:	$15,000–$30,000
Potential earnings:	$35,000–$80,000
Typical fees:	$50–$75 per hour, or flat per-project fee of $500+
Advertising:	Networking, Yellow Pages, direct mail, portfolio, Web site
Qualifications:	Knowledge of and experience in CD-ROM technology, creativity, writing and graphic design skills, ability to stay abreast of rapidly changing market
Equipment needed:	Top-of-the-line computer with MIDI, video, and CD-ROM hardware and software, printer, copier, scanner, microphone, speakers, fax, phone
Home business potential:	Yes
Staff required:	No
Hidden costs:	Equipment upgrades and new purchases to stay abreast of changing technology

LOWDOWN:

CD-ROMs have revolutionized the computer game industry. Now the market is turning to more practical uses: education, marketing, training, and communications. Business presentations are being enlivened by animation, 3-D effects and sound; some CD-ROM services specialize in free-standing products such as the kiosks found in malls. As a multimedia specialist you will draw first on your project planning skills. What does the client want, and what is the best means of achieving that goal? Writing a multimedia presentation is more challenging than producing simple, linear text. Making full use of the capabilities of this medium will require you to have a lively imagination, graphics skills, and familiarity with multimedia authoring software. If you have the skills and you're up to the challenge, the opportunities that await you are practically unlimited.

STARTUP:

This business requires some "heavy-duty" technology—a computer with MIDI, video, and CD-ROM hardware and software, for starters. Some multimedia specialists work with their clients' equipment, but most opt to acquire a full range of the most up-to-date components available for themselves. Expect to spend around $15,000 for a complete and powerful system that is upgradable; bill out your services at $50–$75 per hour or charge per project depending on size and complexity.

BOTTOM LINE ADVICE:

You're creative on many levels, a "techie" of major proportions. If you can communicate with businesspeople to determine their needs and how your skills can best address them you've got an amazing opportunity here. Marketing and pricing will be your major challenges. Keep in mind, too, that you may have to do a fair amount of education with regard to your services; this is still a relatively new field and many potential clients may not fully grasp the capabilities of multimedia.

NANNY SERVICE

Startup cost:	$15,000–$40,000
Potential earnings:	$40,000–$70,000
Typical fees:	$20–$35 per hour per child, or weekly/monthly rates
Advertising:	Yellow Pages, newspapers, parents' groups, business associations
Qualifications:	Good instincts with regard to job candidates; ability to communicate with parents and nannies; background in child care and/or child development would be helpful
Equipment needed:	Computer, printer, phone, fax, copier
Home business potential:	Yes
Staff required:	Yes (about 20 to 30 nannies, ready and able to work)
Hidden costs:	Liability insurance, personnel costs such as health benefits and workers' compensation

LOWDOWN:

Not just your average babysitter, a nanny provides daily in-home care for children in addition to helping with household chores. For many busy households, having a nanny is, in a sense, like having another mom; some nannies actually live with the family 24/7, others just come in for the day. In this business, you won't actually be a nanny, you'll hire them and match them to the families that are your clients. You'll need to carefully screen your nanny candidates, of course (including a background check with local law enforcement) and match them carefully to prospective households. Likewise, you'll want to screen your client homes, too; interview the parents and have them complete a questionnaire detailing their preferences in child care styles and exactly what kinds of work they expect the nanny to do. The more you know about your client families, the better the nanny match you'll be able to make.

STARTUP:

Your costs to start a nanny service are relatively high for a number of reasons, including liability insurance, office overhead, and employee benefits. Once you factor in your advertising costs (a good-sized ad in the Yellow Pages and fliers or brochures for parents' and professional groups), you've easily spent anywhere from $15,000–$40,000. A nanny service would prosper best in a large metropolitan area since that's where dual-income couples with the money to afford a full-time nanny are most likely to reside.

BOTTOM LINE ADVICE:

Matching the right nannies to each of your clients' households represents a major challenge, but if you ask all the right questions up front, your chances of success will be high. Nannies fill an important void in the lives of working families, one that does not appear to be closing up anytime soon. The number of dual-income households continues to rise, which bodes well for your service. On the downside, are the liability issues. Screen your nanny candidates carefully; the welfare of children is at stake here and you cannot afford to make a mistake.

OCCUPATIONAL HEALTH CARE SERVICES

Startup cost:	$25,000+
Potential earnings:	$30,000–$50,000+
Typical fees:	$35–$50 per hour
Advertising:	Newspapers and periodicals read by businesspeople, networking, referrals, direct mail
Qualifications:	Degree and/or experience in occupational health or related field; experience in health care administration; strong business connections in market area; well-developed knowledge of industrial hygiene issues
Equipment needed:	Computer, business management software, printer, marketing materials, van and medical office equipment for mobile services
Home business potential:	No
Staff required:	Yes
Hidden costs:	Recruiting and equipment costs, ongoing training for staff and management

LOWDOWN:

Occupational health care is a service many companies could use, but especially those in manufacturing or with jobs that require heavy lifting or other physical activity, such as movers, storage companies, and delivery services. Your employees would either staff an on-site occupational health clinic, or visit businesses on a regular, rotating basis to provide occupational health services. Your target market would primarily be small and mid-sized businesses. In today's changing health care climate, creating a profitable business that provides care to employees can be a real challenge. But if you're an innovative thinker and a dedicated marketer, you'll be able to identify openings for your enterprise in almost any business. For maximum profit, be prepared to offer everything from training in injury pre-vention to actual on-site treatment and rehabilitation.

STARTUP:

Startup costs will vary, depending on the levels of service you provide. Your costs will be lowest if you can simply staff an existing facility. Line up personnel for whatever services you might possibly ever need—nursing, physician specialties, employee trainers, etc.— before you launch your marketing campaign. If you decide to go the mobile route—essen-tially offering a clinic on wheels—you will incur some significant expenses, equipping your mobile units with all the necessary diagnostic/treatment instruments and supplies. This won't be a get-rich-quick scheme, but, with careful planning and creative marketing, you should be able to make around $30,000–$50,000 in your first year.

BOTTOM LINE ADVICE:

You may find it effective to target your market with a specific type of service: preventive training to strengthen back muscles and avoid injury, work processes designed to minimize carpal tunnel syndrome, or a quick-response service for on-the-job injuries. Outstanding customer service, high-quality medical care, and excellent business management will be necessary to distinguish you from the other types of providers competing in this market: hospitals, orthopedic physician groups, and clinics.

OFFICE EQUIPMENT LEASING

Startup cost:	$15,000–$40,000
Potential earnings:	$35,000 and up
Typical fees:	Varies, depending on the equipment. For planning purposes, consider a range of $75–$1,000 per month for each rental unit and require a security deposit
Advertising:	Local newspapers, radio spots, Yellow Pages, fliers, direct mail, networking, memberships in business organizations
Qualifications:	Excellent marketing ability, knowledge of office equipment and office needs
Equipment needed:	Inventory of equipment to lease (at least two of everything), computer, Internet access, fax, copier, scanner, cell phone, printer, marketing materials, vehicle if you plan to offer delivery and pickup
Home business potential:	No
Staff required:	Possibly
Hidden costs:	Legal assistance in setting up lease agreements, equipment maintenance and repair, vehicle expenses

LOWDOWN:

Today's changing business climate means great opportunity for you. New businesses are springing up daily, but many simply cannot afford the capital expenditures required to purchase outright the equipment they need. By renting the equipment they need and thereby making it available at a cost they can afford, your leasing service is the perfect solution to this problem. Eventually, as business grows, your clients may be able to purchase equipment outright; in the meantime, they can still get up and running. Leasing in general is growing in popularity. Everything from computers to tractors is now available to rent. There's a lot of competition out there, so your marketing efforts need not educate potential customers about the value of rental vs. purchase; instead, you need to distinguish your business from the rest of the pack.

STARTUP:

To make any kind of splash in the marketplace, you need to have an inventory of goods to rent. You'll need to establish excellent relationships with your suppliers in order to get the best purchase prices. Depending on your inventory and the prices you work out with suppliers, you could earn upwards of $35,000. You could start out by leasing the equipment yourself, then subleasing it to your clients, but for liability reasons, this can be risky. Outright purchase is a better option for you.

BOTTOM LINE ADVICE:

Outstanding organizational skills are what will enable you to pull the pieces of this business together. Your customers will want what they want, when they want it. You must be able to supply the machines they need, and all in excellent condition. Business needs change right along with technology, so you'll need to stay abreast of both in order to have the right machines available at the right time. Are color copiers going to be popular in offices next year? What about laser printers? CD burners and portable disk drives? You'll need to know what's hot in order to survive.

OUTPLACEMENT SERVICES

Startup cost:	$15,000–$20,000
Potential earnings:	$75,000–$150,000
Typical fees:	Retainer fees of $1,000–$3,000 per month (paid by businesses, rather than employees)
Advertising:	Yellow Pages, direct mail to human resource managers, trade shows, promotional items, networking
Qualifications:	A background in human resources; researching abilities (especially online), resume and cover letter writing skills
Equipment needed:	Computer, fax, high-speed Internet access, phone, corporate directories, career counseling/skills assessment materials
Home business potential:	Not typically; you'll probably be meeting with clients at their worksites
Staff required:	Not initially (but you may need extra help, depending on demand)
Hidden costs:	Insurance, phone bills, and time spent with each client (some will want more of your time than is profitable for you)

LOWDOWN:

Needless to say, the last few years haven't been exactly kind to the traditional workforce. Layoffs are coming faster, and with less warning than ever before. There's a whole bunch of folks out there who are suddenly out of work, and with the right mix of marketing and promotion, you can create a profitable business helping individuals displaced from one company find new work elsewhere. Read the business pages daily to keep tabs on local companies. Who's doing well? And more importantly, who's not? Generally speaking, wherever there's a bad quarter, there's a layoff in the making. Your goal is to be the first (and best) to approach these companies—at the time just before they realize they actually need someone like you. That way, your services can be in place before the downsizing is even announced to the employees. That kind of timing is good for you and good for the company because it shows they care—they're not just letting people go, they've got a plan in place to help them get on their feet again.

STARTUP:

Your startup costs are likely to be in the neighborhood of $10,000–$15,000. Most of the money will go into the cost of purchasing the fastest and most powerful computer system you can afford, plus high-speed Internet access for doing online job searches and similar research. You'll be able to find much of the information you need online, but in case you decide to purchase detailed corporate directories to reinforce your efforts, expect to spend as much as $6,000 per set. Once you've established a name for yourself—and have satisfied, formerly downsized employees with new jobs to show for it—you can expect to pull in $75,000–$150,000 per year. This is a business that can be lucrative for those who establish a good reputation. Word of mouth travels fast in industry these days, especially via e-mail, so make sure that the message getting around about you is a positive one.

BOTTOM LINE ADVICE:

Although you'll be working with people who are looking for jobs and possibly even new careers, your primary client is not the displaced employee. Your target market is the businesses who are forced to let employees go due to downturns in the economy or shifts in corporate strategies. The best thing you can do to build your business is to always stay on top of things—keep an ear to the ground (perhaps by networking closely with members of the Society for Human Resource Managers) and always get your materials in front of the vice president of operations or other key decision-makers before your competitors do.

PEST CONTROL SERVICE

Startup cost:	$15,000–$25,000
Potential earnings:	$25,000–$45,000
Typical fees:	$150–$300 per treatment for a medium-sized home or business
Advertising:	Newspapers, classified ads, Yellow Pages, direct mail, fliers
Qualifications:	Knowledge of pesticides, insects, and rodents; some states require licensing
Equipment needed:	Chemicals and applicators, flashlights, pager or cell phone, vehicle
Home business potential:	Yes
Staff required:	Not initially
Hidden costs:	Materials, insurance, phone bills

LOWDOWN:

Almost every structure could use your pest control services; the challenge lies in getting the owner to admit it. Needs vary in different regions, but the termites that gnaw on Louisiana plantations are happy to chew on Idaho log cabins as well, and cockroaches are just plain everywhere. The business of pest control has a bit of an old-fashioned, grungy image, but you can turn that around by turning the buildings you treat into safer, cleaner environments. Environmental awareness and regulation has changed the world of pest control; one of your biggest selling points could well be your controlled use of the least harmful agents to provide this very necessary service. Whatever chemicals you use, make sure your knowledge about them is fairly extensive; you want to be able to address any safety concerns potential clients might have.

STARTUP:

The tools of this trade can be somewhat expensive, with application equipment and chemicals starting at about $15,000. Some pest control specialists manage their businesses in person and ask for payment at the time of application. Should you decide to do the same, there's no need for a fancy computer and printer; you can get by with paper and pen. A pager or cell phone is essential, however, so you are readily accessible to your customers.

BOTTOM LINE ADVICE:

People tend to either love this work or hate it. The advantages are that you are always on the move, not tied to a desk. You're providing a service that people readily understand, and pretty much know they need to have. It can sometimes be dirty and, when facing down a mouse- or cockroach-infested property, downright disgusting, but it isn't terribly difficult once you have the knowledge. Exposure to chemicals could have negative health consequences if you're not careful. Clambering around in one dark, dirty basement after another can get you down, but, if you strive to set up regular accounts, you can generate a steady income. Keep in mind, however, that there's a fair amount of competition out there, so you'll need to be creative about finding your own unique market niche.

ADVICE FROM THE EXPERTS

What sets your business apart from others like it?

"We have a real concern for the environment," says Leslie Wyman, vice president of marketing for EPCON, the Environmental Pest Company, in Akron, Ohio. "We rely less on pesticides and more on structural and behavioral modification."

Things you couldn't do without:

Chemicals, flashlight, stethoscope, BNG spray can, computer, and phone are all Wyman needs to keep her business running.

Marketing tips/advice:

"Get good training and state licensing first. Then, use cold call surveys to ask people what kinds of trouble they're having with pests. After that, it's pretty much: mail-call-mail-call-mail-call." You would do well, says Wyman, to pick a specialty area (such as mice) or an industry niche (such as health care).

If you had to do it all over again . . .

"I would have gotten started in this business much sooner. Also, if you've got a family-run business, you should always give your family a chance—but don't be afraid to go outside of your family network to hire additional staff if you need to."

PET TAXI SERVICE

Startup cost:	$15,000–$25,000
Potential earnings:	$15,000–$30,000+ (with just one vehicle)
Typical fees:	$20–$35 for one-way transportation; fees may vary by distance traveled, pet size, and number of pets per owner
Advertising:	Local/community newspapers, Yellow Pages, networking with veterinarians and dog groomers; donate services to the local Humane Society to build publicity and goodwill
Qualifications:	Love of animals; experience working with animals at a pet store, animal shelter, or veterinarian's office; physical strength, commercial driver's license
Equipment needed:	Travel cages, vehicle large enough to accommodate several animals at once, two-way radio or cell phone
Home business potential:	Yes
Staff required:	Yes
Hidden costs:	Repairs, insurance, maintenance/cleaning

LOWDOWN:

We humans know when to call a cab, but what does Fido do when he needs a ride to the vet's office and his owner can't take time away from work? Pet transportation is a highly specialized service that caters to dual-career families and pet lovers with higher than average incomes. Market yourself in upscale areas and target folks who work or take extended vacations without their animals. For maximum efficiency, you'll likely be carrying several animals at a time, so your vehicle will need to be a van or small delivery-type truck, and you'll probably need to make some adaptations to its interior in order to accommodate shelves and cages of various sizes. In terms of personal qualifications, you, and any drivers you hire, will need general knowledge of pet care and handling—not just dogs and cats, but reptiles, birds, rabbits, and hamsters, too. If you live in a rural area, you'll need to know something about livestock as you may be called upon occasionally to transport small animals like sheep and goats. Anything out of the ordinary routine tends to make animals nervous, and that means "accidents," so make sure that your vehicles are equipped with plenty of clean-up materials. Janitorial cleaning supplies work best to combat pet messes; they generally run about $30–$40 for a three-month supply. To generate enough business to fill a 40-hour work week, you'll initially need to knock on a lot of doors, but once you become established, your phone will start to ring. Referrals from satisfied customers will keep you busy.

STARTUP:

Not surprisingly, your largest startup expense is for the "taxi" itself; you'll need a van or small delivery-type truck that is large enough to accommodate several animals in cages. Start with one vehicle and see how it goes; add a second one as business warrants. Fees typically run $20–$35 one-way per animal, but may vary depending on the distance traveled and size of the animal; if you're transporting more than one animal for a single owner, offer a reduced fare for the second one.

BOTTOM LINE ADVICE:

To some pet owners, your service will seem like little more than a frivolous luxury, but make sure they understand this is no easy task. Some clients may ask you to let yourself in and, as long as you're inside, feed the animal before you go or give it a quick walk around the block when you return. Be careful about taking on too many extra services; it reduces your efficiency and you could actually wind up losing customers. You'll need to schedule carefully so that while you're inside tending to one customer's idiosyncrasies, the animals belonging to others aren't left inside the van for too long. The number one qualification for success in this business is a genuine love of animals. Just treat each one as if it were your own and you'll do fine.

POOL MAINTENANCE

Startup costs:	$15,000–$30,000
Potential earnings:	$30,000–$50,000
Typical fees:	$75–$150 per total cleaning
Advertising:	Fliers at pool sales and supply centers, direct mail coupons, Yellow Pages, local newspapers
Qualifications:	Knowledge of maintaining and repairing in-ground and above-ground pools, willingness to work outdoors
Equipment needed:	Pool cleaning equipment (water vacuum, hose, skimmers, etc.), pool chemicals and cleaning solvents, vehicle
Home business potential:	Yes
Staff required:	No
Hidden costs:	Insurance, phone, vehicle expenses

LOWDOWN:

Many people like the convenience of having a pool in the backyard, but who really likes the maintenance pools require? You do—and you can earn a living providing this necessary service for busy pool owners who have neither the time nor the desire to keep their pools clean and running efficiently themselves. You'll clean, repair, chemically shock, and maintain each client's pool, either on a preseason/postseason basis or, if you live in a warm climate, at regular intervals throughout the year. Simply stated, you're selling convenience and peace of mind to the luxury-minded. They'll tell you how often they need your services, then you'll lock them into a slot on your calendar and just show up to do your thing. Of course, you'll do better at this business if you're located in a part of the country where pools can be operated year-round and just about everybody has one. In cooler climes, you may have to service a wider geographic area and possibly piggyback this warm-weather business with another one, like snow removal, that operates only in the opposing season.

STARTUP:

You'll need a van and the right cleaning equipment and chemical supplies to stock it; expect to spend at least $15,000 on these items up front. However, with a full complement of standing appointments for cleaning at $75–$150 each, you could stand to make a pretty decent living in the pool maintenance business. Advertise with a Yellow Pages listing and selected newspaper placement and spend a few hundred dollars on business cards to leave behind for repeat business and referrals.

BOTTOM LINE ADVICE:

By offering excellent service, you can build a loyal customer base. Strive for regular standing appointments, but if customers won't commit, remember to call them back periodically for repeat business. Follow-up could reap you thousands of more dollars in the long run.

POWER WASH SERVICE

Startup cost:	$15,000–$25,000
Potential earnings:	$35,000–$65,000
Typical fee:	Varies, based on square footage; figure on $300–$500 for a medium-sized building
Advertising:	Business directories, personal contacts with fleet managers, building superintendents, painting contractors
Qualifications:	Willingness to work outdoors and get dirty, physical stamina and strength
Equipment needed:	Pressure-wash system, van
Home business potential:	Yes
Staff required:	Possibly three to four
Hidden costs:	Insurance, vehicle expenses, workers' compensation

LOWDOWN:

Who cleans the graffiti from buildings or the exteriors of airplanes or large trucks? It can be you with some ingenuity and energy, plus the desire to work outdoors. You can start little or buy into a franchise that could supply you with the equipment and van. You'll offer a service that literally "powers" off dirt, grease, even peeling paint using a high-pressure water system, and the best part is, once the surface is clean, you're done. You don't have to repaint the vehicle or building, unless, of course, you want to in order to earn additional income. And as we all know, dirt has a way of coming back, so if you offer a superior service, you'll get repeat business—especially if you call your clients back from time to time. Just think how often you wash your own car. Trucks and airplanes get even dirtier so the opportunity for repeat business is huge.

STARTUP:

To keep your startup costs under control, try leasing your equipment rather than purchasing it in the first year of business. You could get away with as little as $10,000 if you lease; otherwise, expect to spend up to $25,000 getting this business off the ground (more if you decide to employ a team of helpers). Charge by the square foot and add a surcharge if the grime is particularly deep and dirty; figure on about $300–$500 for a medium-sized building.

BOTTOM LINE ADVICE:

Getting a large contract—several buildings or vehicles belonging to a single owner— could keep you in business for a long time. Go after building contractors, trucking or aviation companies, or businesses with fleets of vehicles.

RECORDING STUDIO RENTAL

Startup cost:	$15,000–$25,000
Potential earnings:	$35,000–$50,000+
Typical fees:	$25–$75 per hour
Advertising:	Music stores, industry trades, local paper, fliers, direct mail, musicians' associations, Web site
Qualifications:	Knowledge of audio equipment and mixing processes
Equipment needed:	Microphones, amps, distribution amps, mixing boards, digital audiotape machine, multichannel capabilities, MIDI system
Home business potential:	Yes, if you have the space to build a soundproof room
Staff required:	Not initially
Hidden costs:	Replacing obsolete /damaged equipment, insurance

LOWDOWN:

Local musicians and advertising agencies need to record their music and commercials somewhere, and why not provide them with a place to do so? Running your own recording studio can be pretty straightforward stuff, with sound mixing and engineering being your most critical functions. It can, however, become highly complex once you start adding state-of-the-art features like MIDI systems and computerized music composition equipment. You can produce some great-sounding tracks if you have the absolute best in equipment and know how to use it. And once you establish a reputation for having the best, you'll likely get more business quickly; the music industry thrives on word of mouth. In all likelihood, even the best equipped recording studio won't be booked 52 weeks out of every year. If you have everything you need to record and you're not using it, why let all that expensive equipment go to waste? Rent your studio out to other sound technicians; you'll be bringing in additional income for essentially doing nothing. Market yourself in the music stores musicians are likely to frequent and network with advertising agencies for commercial work.

STARTUP:

Equipment and the cost of building a soundproof room will be your biggest startup expenses. Your fees will depend on your geographic location, the type of equipment you offer, and the length of time your studio space will be needed for a particular project. Recording music takes longer than most people think; a 60-second commercial can take a few days to record, CDs several weeks, even a month or more. If you play your cards right and set your prices accordingly, you may not need very many customers to begin making $50,000 or more annually.

BOTTOM LINE ADVICE:

If you're the kind who doesn't care who uses your studio as long as they're willing to pay for it, you can make a healthy chunk of change renting your facility; just make sure that your insurance policy is up to date. Be careful about your equipment choices; the technology is changing so quickly that some of what you buy today could become obsolete before you have a chance to pay it off. Computers have definitely made an impact on the music industry; an extensive MIDI system is a must.

RENTAL BUSINESS

Startup cost: $15,000–$40,000
Potential earnings: $30,000–$100,000+
Typical fees: Half-day, full-day, and weekly rates, depending on the item; charge extra for delivery and require a security deposit
Advertising: Yellow Pages, newspapers, billboards, local specialty magazines
Qualifications: Good organizational and bookkeeping skills; knowledge of the products you are renting; maintenance and repair skills
Equipment needed: Dolly, moving pads, truck/trailer (size of vehicle depends on rental item), cash register and credit card processing equipment, inventory of items to be rented
Home business potential: No
Staff required: No
Hidden costs: Repairs, insurance

LOWDOWN:

The rental business is solid and recession-proof because people always seem to need tools, equipment, or appliances on a short-term basis. If they need a carpet shampooer or a rotary tiller but would rather not purchase one, they'll need to come to you. Salesmanship and advertising are going to be your best friends. Nail down the parameters of your rental stock, and develop strong product knowledge about everything you carry so you'll be able to advise your customers on proper usage. The more things you have to rent, the busier you'll be, of course. However, in the beginning, you may choose to focus on a particular area—say, home furnishings and electronics (televisions, home entertainment systems, etc.) or tools, such as power mowers, floor sanders, and carpet shampooers. If you offer delivery of furniture and other large items, be capable of setting them up on-site and efficient in your scheduling so you can turn around and make another delivery right away. The ability to keep books and track merchandise as it comes and goes will keep the money rolling in.

STARTUP:

Your startup costs could be a little or a lot depending on what you decide to rent, how many of any one item you keep in stock, and whether you need to purchase a vehicle for delivery of furniture, large appliances, and the like. If you're going to make any kind of splash in this business, you will need to have a storefront and visible location; you simply wouldn't be able to stock enough items to make a go of a rental business operating out of your home. Charge for use of the equipment by the half-day, full-day, or week, and don't forget to ask for a security deposit. You could earn in the range of $30,000–$100,000.

BOTTOM LINE ADVICE:

Let your people skills shine and provide the best possible service for your customers. Most of the do-it-yourself chores that require your rental equipment take place on weekends, so you will have to give up your Saturdays at least. If you plan to offer pickup and delivery services, you will probably need to hire a second person to help with loading and lifting. Still, if you offer quality stock and take care of your customers, word will get around and before you know it, you'll have more business than you know what to do with.

RESIDENCE FOR THE ELDERLY

Startup cost:	$15,000–$100,000
Potential earnings:	$15,000–$40,000
Typical fees:	$450–$1,000 per month, per client depending on geographic location and facilities/services provided
Advertising:	Referrals from community groups, church bulletin boards, word of mouth, networking with senior citizens groups
Qualifications:	Excellent organizational ability, hospitable personality, genuine concern for the welfare of older persons, good reputation in the community
Equipment needed:	One or more easily accessible bedrooms, suitable furniture, bathroom with special handrails, dining space, efficient kitchen; you may use your own home or another property
Home business potential:	Yes
Staff required:	Probably. You will not be able to carry out 100 percent of the tasks required, 100 percent of the time; reliable backup workers will be needed occasionally
Hidden costs:	Insurance, food (may have residents with special dietary requirements), home alterations

LOWDOWN:

In most regions of the United States, there is an enormous need for housing for older people who do not wish to live alone but who do not require the level of care offered by either assisted living facilities or nursing homes. Many independently minded healthy elderly men and women simply cannot find affordable apartments or prefer to live with others but do not have family living nearby. Opening your own home to a few elderly people or transforming a rental property you already own into a residence for the elderly can be a rewarding business. You will rarely have a vacancy if you can "knit" your residents into a cheerful family unit and meet their day-to-day needs for food, shelter, companionship, and amusement. Many families who are caring for one or more of their own parents find that adding another elderly resident provides many benefits, including compatible company and increased family income.

STARTUP:

Equipping your home or another property for older residents may require only a few changes, or you may need to do extensive work. Before you spend any money, however, be sure to check your local zoning regulations and state requirements with regard to housing the elderly; you may discover that your plan is simply not possible and there's no sense getting started on something you cannot finish. You may already own adequate and/or appropriate furniture, or you may allow the residents to bring their own. Your startup costs will depend on the extent of renovation and furnishings required; for planning purposes, figure on between $15,000 and $100,000 to get up and running. You'll be providing meals, of course, which can be a challenge in terms of both budgeting and time. Keep in mind that some elderly residents may have special dietary needs and you will want to take that into account when setting your monthly fees. Depending on your geographic locale and the services/facilities you intend to provide, you can charge $450–$1,000 per month. With an anticipated annual income of $15,000–$40,000 this is not a get-rich venture, but it is a rewarding one.

BOTTOM LINE ADVICE:

Not everyone is aware of the possibilities that providing a residence for the "well" elderly can bring to an energetic, compassionate entrepreneur. Your challenges will come in planning the physical changes needed in your home or other residence to accommodate elderly residents, and in running the business so that it doesn't overwhelm your own life.

SECURITY SYSTEMS DESIGN/ INSTALLATION

Startup cost:	$15,000–$20,000
Potential earnings:	$30,000–$60,000
Typical fees:	$25–$100 per hour, depending on the service (i.e., design costs more than installation); some projects bill on a per-job basis
Advertising:	Yellow Pages, trade journals, referrals, networking, Web site
Qualifications:	Degree and/or experience in drafting or design; extensive knowledge of security products and electronic security systems; ability to analyze situations/sites and to read and/or draft blueprints; proficiency in using CAD software;
Equipment needed:	Top-of-the-line computer with oversized monitor, CAD software, laser printer with 11" X 17" paper capacity, blueprint copier, high-speed Internet access, flat bed scanner, fax, phone
Home business potential:	Yes
Staff required:	No
Hidden costs:	Equipment upgrades, insurance, keeping abreast of changes in technology and security systems

LOWDOWN:

More than ever, businesses are looking for systems that will protect people and property and improve overall peace of mind. As a security systems designer, your job will be to analyze a worksite with regard to its current level of security and offer recommendations for improvement. You'll take into consideration such factors as the nature of the business, entry procedures for personnel and visitors, and the value of equipment and/or inventory stored on-site. Then, using your extensive knowledge of available security systems and protective devices, you will put together a comprehensive security plan incorporating the necessary equipment and procedures for safeguarding the site as well as the people who come and go from it. You'll need to be proficient with computer-aided design software and able to read and/or draft blueprints. And if you decide to carry the business one step further by handling the installation as well as the design, you'll need to know your way around a toolbox and be able to work with highly sophisticated electronic surveillance systems.

STARTUP:

Your design work will require a powerful computer, oversized monitor, and CAD software, plus a laser printer with large-paper capacity and a blueprint copier. Use your high-speed Internet connection to research online and stay abreast of new developments in security technology and equipment. Expect to spend around $10,000 for your computer and peripherals alone. The bulk of your business will come from networking and referrals; however, to broaden your base of potential clients, you'll want to have a professionally developed Web site describing your capabilities.

BOTTOM LINE ADVICE:

Security systems design is a relatively new field, but, just like terrorism and crime, it is growing by leaps and bounds. So is the technology, and you'll need to make a concerted effort to stay on top of new developments so that you can make the best and most timely recommendations to your clients.

SHORT-TERM AUTO RENTAL SERVICE

Startup cost:	$25,000–$40,000
Potential earnings:	$25,000–$60,000
Typical fees:	$30–$40 per day
Advertising:	Radio, newspaper, direct mail, fliers, billboards, referrals from auto repair services and dealers
Qualifications:	Excellent organizational skills, knowledge of car maintenance and repair
Equipment needed:	Rental vehicles, computer, printer, marketing materials, cell phone
Home business potential:	No
Staff required:	Yes
Hidden costs:	Insurance, vehicle maintenance and replacement

LOWDOWN:

In most communities, rental cars are available only at the busy, congested airport sites that serve long-distance travelers. But what about local residents who need to rent a vehicle for a short period (like when their own car is in the shop), but would prefer to avoid the hassle of going to the airport or the high prices the nationally known rental car chains typically charge? They'd surely welcome the opportunity to obtain a vehicle from your convenient, cost-effective service. In addition to individuals looking to rent vehicles on a short-term basis, you could link up with auto dealerships and repair shops to provide the "loaner" cars for their customers. And don't limit your business to renting ordinary cars, either. Offer vans and SUVs, which are almost impossible to rent in many areas, maybe even small pickup trucks and luxury cars, which many people would like to rent for a weekend or just overnight.

STARTUP:

The type of vehicles you offer will define your costs; if you start with just a few gently used vehicles, you could get by for as little as $25,000. Will your focus be rent-a-heap, luxury-for-less, or convenient compacts? Will you buy four-year-old cream puffs or lease several vans? Your choice will ultimately determine your earnings, as much as $25,000 in the first year alone (at a daily rental rate of $30–$40). Keep in mind, too, that you'll need a secure place to park your vehicles; zoning regulations in most locations will prohibit operating this business from your home.

BOTTOM LINE ADVICE:

Your challenge is to distinguish yourself from the national chains. The excellence of your service and the convenience you bring to your customers will set you apart. You'll need to be creative in getting your message to your potential market. And last but not least, excellent management skills will be required to keep track of services, drivers, billing, and costs.

SOFTWARE ENGINEER/COMPUTER PROGRAMMER

Startup cost:	$15,000–$30,000
Potential earnings:	$50,000–$100,000
Typical fees:	$50–$75 per hour
Advertising:	Personal contacts in trade and business associations, referrals from computer stores and professional contacts, opportunities to teach classes on programming to businesspeople, Web site
Qualifications:	Minimum of two to five years of programming experience in several languages and platforms; ability to understand and speak knowledgeably with clients about their business needs, ability to learn quickly and keep up with constantly changing technologies
Equipment needed:	Two or three high-end computers with high-speed Internet access and printer; network system file server; communications, compiler, and miscellaneous software; fax; scanner; and copier,
Home business potential:	Yes
Staff required:	No
Hidden costs:	Errors and omissions insurance, keeping up with rapid changes in technology, vendor training courses

LOWDOWN:

As more and more companies downsize their staffs, programming is increasingly being done by freelancers rather than in-house. Your reputation for effective and efficient programming will make your business as a software engineer a success. You may specialize in adapting off-the-shelf software to meet the specific needs of your client organization, or you may design computer programs customized specifically for one business. The ability to analyze business issues and apply your findings to a particular situation is essential. What does your client's computer system really need to accomplish, and what will be the best way to meet that need? Excellent communication and people skills will be necessary so that you can learn everything you need to know about your client's operations in order to engineer effective software. Writing the program and loading it into your client's computer system, then implementing the program and, perhaps most important of all, debugging it are the major tasks for which you will be responsible in this field. You must be on top of the latest technology, including changes in hardware and software, in order to develop the program that will directly address your clients' needs.

STARTUP:

You'll need some significant computer power and peripherals to set up your programming operation. High-speed Internet access and subscriptions to as many computer publications as you can read are musts in order to stay on top of changes in technology. Your expertise is valuable, so don't be afraid to charge what you're worth ($50–$75 per hour). Some computer programming projects take many months to complete, so you may work with only one or two clients per year; even so, if you are good at what you do and can communicate in terms your client can readily understand, you can easily make $50,000–$100,000 per year.

BOTTOM LINE ADVICE:

It is satisfying to develop a program that makes your client's business work. Knowing what information is needed and writing original code or adapting a commercially available package are high-level activities that can produce a real sense of achievement. If you understand the business language of the field in which you are working, you will be able to build on your successes and keep new projects rolling in. Your expertise will be highly valued and you can choose your own hours. If you're like most people who excel at writing code, you're probably somewhat introverted; marketing yourself will be a real challenge, but you must make the effort if you are to survive in this business. There are plenty of other programmers out there willing to step in if you do not. Programming projects can be lengthy, sometimes stretching out over several weeks or months, so you need to develop a payment policy that keeps funds coming in on a regular basis. Determining the charges for a complex project is not always easy and your work will often be done under pressure. Clients may be both demanding and unappreciative, partly because they don't understand what it is you do. Make an effort to explain what you are up to in the simplest possible terms.

TELEVISION REPAIR

Startup cost:	$15,000–$25,000
Potential earnings:	$20,000–$40,000
Typical fees:	$40–$50 per hour for labor, plus parts
Advertising:	Yellow Pages, local newspapers, direct mail coupons
Qualifications:	Thorough knowledge of and skill in television repair; optional training and certification from various television manufacturers
Equipment needed:	Full array of testing and repair equipment: oscilloscope, meters, solder and soldering irons, special devices for removing microchips, screwdrivers in a variety of sizes
Home business potential:	Yes
Staff required:	No
Hidden costs:	Insurance, phone, vehicle expenses

LOWDOWN:

Your TV's on the blink again . . . and you don't want to miss your favorite soap opera. Or, the best play in yesterday's game was rudely interrupted by an annoying horizontal line stretched across the screen; you don't want it to ruin the playoff game next week. So what do you do? Call a television repair service to take a look at the set . . . if you can find one, that is. Interestingly, despite the increasing number of television sets in American homes these days, there aren't that many technicians around to repair them, so if you can offer these services, your skills are quite valuable. If you're interested in starting this business, look into becoming officially trained and certified by specific manufacturers to repair their sets. This will probably involve a written test and possibly a practical, hands-on exam. Stock a variety of parts; consumers will be impatient about getting their sets back as quickly as possible and they won't want to wait while you order replacements.

STARTUP:

You'll need to spend at least $10,000 or more on parts, benches, tools, and diagnostic equipment to get a good start in this business. In addition, your training certification could cost anywhere from $100–$500 per manufacturer. Charges for your services will vary according to what needs to be done, but as a rule, television repair technicians bill $45 or more per hour for labor, plus parts.

BOTTOM LINE ADVICE:

Don't limit your business just to the general public; contact service centers and retailers who often farm out repairs rather than maintain expensive in-house repair operations. If you offer free pickup and delivery, you're sure to attract even more business from sources like these.

TICKET BROKER

Startup cost:	$15,000–$35,000
Potential earnings:	$25,000–$35,000+
Typical fees:	5 to 40 percent of each sale; it varies depending on whether you're selling nationally, regionally, or locally
Advertising:	Industry trade publications, newspapers, Web site
Qualifications:	Knowledge of state licensing requirements, tenacity and persistence to search for high-demand tickets at the best price
Equipment needed:	Computer with specialized software program/hookup, 800 number phone line
Home business potential:	No
Staff required:	No
Hidden costs:	Unsold tickets

LOWDOWN:

How many times have you wanted to buy tickets for an event or a show, only to find that it's sold out or that the only tickets left are in the last row of the arena's top tier? That's when ticket brokers can help. Ticket brokers offer hard-to-get tickets to a variety of entertainment venues, including rock concerts, stage shows, and sporting events. Consumers typically pay a higher price for tickets purchased from a broker than they would if they waited in line to purchase them directly from the box office; however, they are willing to pay a little more for the convenience of purchasing online or by phone and because they know they stand a good chance of securing better seats through a broker than they could get on their own. Ticket brokering is a competitive business in which organization and responsibility are the keys to success. Your job includes assigning seat locations, providing ticket sales information, making recommendations about ticket pricing according to the area or event, soliciting group sales, and keeping a customer ticket list. You'll need to purchase specialized software that allows you to search online for ticket availability and to accept credit card orders over the phone. To be competitive, you must have a Web site and a toll-free phone number; for credibility, licensing and membership in the National Association of Ticket Brokers (*www.natb.org*) is a good idea. Although there is no specific training program necessary to call yourself a ticket broker, an accounting or bookkeeping background would prove especially helpful; there are a million details that need to be managed on a daily basis to keep this business up and running.

STARTUP:

There's just no way you can possibly run this business without a computer. You have to be able to search online and to hook up to the ticket distribution center. Your fee will depend on the event and place. Typically you get a 5 to 40 percent cut of each sale. The prices you set for your tickets are directly related to market demand; you pay more for tickets that are in high demand and can, in turn, command higher prices from your clients. Beware, however, of overinflating your prices to make a quick buck. That's called "scalping," and many states have strict laws prohibiting the practice.

BOTTOM LINE ADVICE:

Due to some unscrupulous business practices among a small segment of the industry, the ticket brokering business has had some image problems. Consequently, NATB has developed a code of ethics for its members. So, while it's possible to run a brokering business from home with a couple of phone lines and a Web site, a storefront is required for NATB membership. Whether you choose to join the association or not, for the sake of credibility, you may want a more visible location, too; at some point, you'll probably need to move out of your home anyway in order to accommodate your growth and the need for staff. There's a lot of competition in this business and most of the big ticket brokers have been around for a long time. It's a good idea to get to know them; when you can't seem to get your hands on the tickets you need, one of the big brokers may be able to help.

TRANSPORTATION PROVIDER
(LIMOUSINE/VAN)

Startup cost:	$15,000+ for van, $30,000–$90,000 for limo
Potential earnings:	$40,000–$65,000
Typical fees:	$50 per hour
Advertising:	Yellow Pages, local newspapers, brochures at bridal salons/tuxedo shops/hotels
Qualifications:	Vehicle licensing and insurance, commercial driver's license
Equipment needed:	A dependable fleet of vehicles, short-wave radio for regular contact with dispatcher
Home business potential:	Yes
Staff required:	Not at first; you may add a dispatcher later on, however
Hidden costs:	Liability insurance

LOWDOWN:

Business travelers and partygoers alike need dependable transportation services wherever they go. That's why the limousine and van service business has enjoyed a steady increase over the last decade. Also, because more and more people are willing to spend on small indulgences, your investment in a decent fleet could net you giant profits. The mainstay for these types of transportation providers is airport service, but flexibility is key as rentals become more popular and affordable. The average fee is $50 per hour plus tips, and the customers range from wedding and prom parties to well-heeled tourists and locals headed to sporting events and rock concerts. A good way to establish yourself is by contracting to handle the overflow from larger limo companies.

STARTUP:

Typically, newcomers to this business don't have enough money to outright buy several shiny new vehicles, especially when they run anywhere from $32,000–$90,000 each. This is why deciding on one option to fit many needs is important in the beginning; you can always add vehicles as your capital grows. This is not the time to cut corners, however. A new vehicle is important for both image and reliability; buying a used one can mean breakdowns and loss of customers as a result. The only exception to this rule is if you have exceptional mechanical ability and can handle any necessary repairs quickly and personally. Licensing and insurance regulations will vary from state to state; check the regulations that could apply to you before launching this business. Be creative in your advertising; try to offer "extras" (such as a bottle of champagne or wine and cheese/beer and pretzels) as incentives for people to use your service over others.

BOTTOM LINE ADVICE:

Good driving skills and a comfortable ride for passengers are vitally important if you want to stay on top of the competition. A congenial disposition will increase the chances of your customers calling on your services again and referring their friends. As the popularity of limo rentals grows, clientele will come from more varied backgrounds; be prepared to deal with a variety of personalities.

USED BOAT SALES

Startup cost:	$15,000–$40,000
Potential earnings:	$25,000 and up
Typical fees:	Percentage of sale price
Advertising:	Billboards, road signs, Yellow Pages, classifieds in local newspapers, possibly radio spots, referrals from boatyards and marinas, Web site
Qualifications:	Excellent consumer sales skills; wide knowledge of boats, engines, and marine equipment; ability to appraise the value of power and/or sailboats accurately
Equipment needed:	An inventory of used boats and a lot for displaying them; cradles, trailers, and tarpaulins; digital camera for photos to post to your Web site; just enough office equipment/space to be able to keep accurate business records
Home business potential:	Yes
Staff required:	Possibly
Hidden costs:	Security, lot maintenance, boat maintenance and repairs

LOWDOWN:

Selling used boats comes almost naturally to some individuals who have suitable property and an interest in watercraft. This business may be an add-on to a yacht yard or marina, or even to a new boat dealership. To make a financial success in the used boat business, you will need to know everything there is to know about boats and about boat buyers. The purchase of a boat for recreation tends to be emotion-driven, and you need to understand how to best help your customers choose the boat they want. You may also need to be something of an educator, particularly with regard to first-time boat buyers, who may need everything from lessons in how to maneuver a boat back into its slip to tips on safety gear and engine maintenance. Some used boat dealers specialize—in power boats or sailboats, brands, length, or uses (fishing boats, for example). Whether you decide to go the general or specialty route, just be sure you know your boats; your customers are relying on your expertise.

STARTUP:

If you simply want to put people in boats but don't want to keep an inventory, you can launch your used boat business at the kitchen table on a shoestring. But if you want to make any kind of splash in the used boat business, you'll need a small inventory of boats to sell and a place to put them. And since boat buyers are often willing to travel long distances to purchase the boat they have their hearts set on, you'll definitely want to have a Web site. You can use it to display the boats you currently have for sale and to seek additional stock. Annual income should be at least $25,000 to start, depending on the amount of time you put into your business.

BOTTOM LINE ADVICE:

Do not expect used boat sales to be the route to great riches, even if you deal primarily in 60-foot Cigarette boats on Biscayne Bay. Unlike cars, which pretty much everyone has to have no matter what, boats are discretionary purchases. For the top of the market, new yachts will be your toughest competition, and for the rest, it'll be the economy that primarily determines your income; the boat business is not recession-proof. You can't plan too far ahead because you can't really count on a steady income. It's boom or bust. But look at the bright side—you get to work outdoors with the boats you love, enjoy plenty of opportunity to make friends with potential customers—boat lovers like yourself—and, hey, you might even get the chance to rescue a wonderful old piece of marine design and set it afloat once more.

Venture Capitalist

Startup cost:	$15,000–$40,000+
Potential earnings:	$25,000–$100,000+
Typical fees:	Percentage of investment or stock in company
Advertising:	Classifieds in business publications, Web site
Qualifications:	Investment savvy and /or serious experience in a particular industry, ability to evaluate business plans with regard to return on investment, advanced degree (MBA) desirable
Equipment needed:	Computer; printer; word processing, database, and spreadsheet software; high-speed Internet access; copier; scanner; fax; cell phone
Home business potential:	Yes
Staff required:	No
Hidden costs:	Travel time and costs to visit potential investment businesses

LOWDOWN:

There's nothing like seeing a new business grow and prosper; being in on the ground floor as an investor is even more exciting. As a venture capitalist, you are a unique participant in the business process. You've got a bird's-eye view of the possibilities, the energy, the creativity, and the drive of new enterprises that might well become the next Microsofts or Chryslers. But energy, creativity, and drive can only carry them so far. To make it the top, these fledgling businesses desperately need capital, and you can provide it. Your contribution—either singly or in combination with others—is based on a careful assessment of the nature and value of the enterprise. High-technology areas are perhaps the most fertile grounds for investment these days, but many other types of businesses also are searching for the capital to start or expand.

STARTUP:

Even making small businesses your focus, you'll need a hefty wad of cash ($30,000–$50,000) to make your first investment. In all likelihood, you won't take the complete responsibility; you'll assemble a team of other investors to share the risk. You'll need to get the word out with classified ads in business publications and a Web site. You'll want a professional office setup to write reports and model business plans; expect to spend around $5,000 for a computer, printer, business software, copier, scanner, fax, and phone. If you choose your investments wisely and have a solid network of financing sources available, you could make some serious money as a venture capitalist for small businesses.

BOTTOM LINE ADVICE:

Homework pays off. The value you bring to the table is more than dollars and cents; it's knowledge and experience. Don't try to go it alone. Gather a list of sources of available capital, and keep it up to date. The shortage in the venture capital world is not with the borrowers but with the "venturers." The fact that you can find and work with others who share your vision is your primary strength. Often the challenge lies simply in the presentation. Funds may sometimes be accessible only in the presence of a professional business plan that reflects the new enterprise in business-oriented terms.

VIDEOTEXT SERVICE

Startup cost:	$30,000–$50,000
Potential earnings:	$45,000–$75,000
Typical fees:	Can be as low as $500 for a low-budget feature and as high as $5,000 for a commercial motion picture
Advertising:	Trade publications, direct mail, Yellow Pages, word of mouth
Qualifications:	Technical training in videotext equipment; professional certification may be required
Equipment needed:	Videotext equipment and film-editing/dubbing equipment, control panels, TelePrompTer
Home business potential:	No (unless you have a studio in your home)
Staff required:	Possibly
Hidden costs:	Insurance, equipment maintenance and upgrades

LOWDOWN:

When the credits start to roll at the end of a movie or television program, did it ever occur to you that someone had to enter that text? Although we take it for granted as a viewing audience, those words you see printed across the screen in everything from commercials to major motion picture credits have to be input by someone. Launch a videotext business and that's essentially the service you'll be providing. You'll enter whatever information, narration, or credits a producer requests, making sure that everything is spelled correctly and that it appears in a logical order and readable format. You may even go so far as to suggest or actually write the narrative, particularly if you're working with corporate clients who are producing their own in-house videos for training purposes. Essentially, you're serving as a kind of technical typing service for television, film, and video producers. Yours is a small piece of the production pie, but you'll need to have certification or training to provide this highly specialized service.

STARTUP:

To accomplish this kind of work, you'll need the basics of a small studio, minus the recording equipment. Your costs for videotext and film-editing/dubbing equipment, control panels, and a TelePrompTer will likely be in the $30,000–$50,000 range. You could sensibly expect to earn $40,000–$75,000 per year, depending on your geographic location. For instance, a videotext business in southern California or New York City would fare much better than, say, one in the middle of Iowa. You must be located where the work is.

BOTTOM LINE ADVICE:

There will be plenty of ebbs and flows in your workload; try to compensate for the downtime by accepting subcontracting work from fellow videotext services. Network continually, so that when the time comes and your business declines, you'll have regular contacts in place that you can call to pick up the slack.

VOICE-ACTIVATED HOME AUTOMATION

Startup cost:	$15,000–$25,000
Potential earnings:	$50,000–$80,000
Typical fees:	$75–$150 per client per month, depending on extent of system
Advertising:	Yellow Pages, community and metropolitan newspapers, direct mail (especially to builders and contractors)
Qualifications:	Training in installation/use of equipment
Equipment needed:	Home automation system units, van, complete set of tools
Home business potential:	Yes
Staff required:	No
Hidden costs:	Insurance, equipment maintenance/upgrades

LOWDOWN:

Microsoft Corporation's Bill Gates has one; so do many celebrities. Voice-activated home automation systems are the wave of the technological future, especially in the home market. However, even though this is a potentially hot market, it's certainly not for everyone; at $75–$150 or more per month to keep the system running, only the rich and powerful can afford to have systems they can literally "tell" what to turn off and turn on. Still, sales figures from voice-activated home automation franchises indicate a $3 billion market for these systems, so there may be more potential customers out there than you'd realize. Now it's your job to locate them, fire off a dynamite direct mail piece, and follow up to sell them on an installation. Each system can include the following components: security system, appliance and electrical system control, and even sensors that "feel" people entering and leaving a room (and turn on/turn off the lights accordingly). You'll sell, install, and maintain each system, suggesting upgrades when they seem appropriate and making sure each client is getting the maximum use out of every unit you install (recognizing, of course, that your business will largely grow out of a satisfied referral base).

STARTUP:

Your startup fees will likely reflect a franchise or distributor fee of about $15,000 in addition to advertising monies; it wouldn't be unusual to spend as much as $25,000 getting this unique business going. In the plus column are the $50,000–$80,000 per year earnings you are likely to achieve, if you market this service wisely.

BOTTOM LINE ADVICE:

While this seems to be a growing industry, it isn't exactly affordable for everyone. Your own early sales figures may reflect a reluctance on the public's part to buy into what at first seems to be a fad. Concentrate heavily on the security aspect rather than the convenience factor; concern for personal and property security is what will ultimately translate into sales.

WINERY

Startup cost:	$20,000–$50,000
Potential earnings:	Unlimited
Typical fees:	2–5 percent of gross from distribution channels
Advertising:	Newspapers, upscale magazines, restaurants, groceries, gourmet shops
Qualifications:	Extensive knowledge of growing grapes, wine manufacturing, aging, bottling, and marketing of the finished product
Equipment needed:	Depends on the size and scope of your business, but regardless, you will need plants; pruning and watering equipment; production, bottling and labeling equipment; production/storage facilities
Home business potential:	Yes
Staff required:	None at first, except for help at harvest time
Hidden costs:	Insurance, marketing, weather losses

LOWDOWN:

The healthful atmosphere, the beauty of the grapevines, the perfume of the finished product, the joy of producing something that brings pleasure to many people—running a winery certainly has its romantic side. This can be an extremely lucrative business, over time, but it is also a risky one. Creating wine from grapes is a technical process that can be learned pretty readily. Proper care of the vines is essential; so is a good working knowledge of wine growing, production, and marketing. If you start small at first, you'll have a better opportunity to gauge the level of work required and if this is the right business for you. You can start this one at home if you have considerable acreage, but you may need more room to expand later on.

STARTUP:

Startup costs vary dramatically according to how ambitious you are. If you start small, experimenting with a few vines and a few dozen bottles of wine, you will incur minimal expense (and realize only minimal profits, of course). A larger business will be expensive to start and may take a considerable amount of time to become profitable. In addition, if you choose to offer more than one type of wine (as most vintners do), you will need more knowledge, more vines, and more processing and labeling equipment. Legal and zoning regulations can be costly, too.

BOTTOM LINE ADVICE:

For every moment of satisfaction with the beauty of the vines and the success of the finished product, you will have many moments of frustration and hard work. This is a demanding business, and a time-consuming one. It takes years for the vines to grow enough to produce fruit; you will need extensive knowledge to prune and care for them. In addition, these plants are very vulnerable to weather. All wine must be aged—some for months, others for years–before they are ready to market. But of all the agricultural businesses you could launch, a winery may well be the most rewarding because it is truly a labor of love.

STARTUPS OVER $40,000

Aerial Applicator

Startup cost:	$150,000–$1,000,000
Potential earnings:	$40,000–$80,000
Typical fees:	Vary per spray job, depending on the acreage and chemicals applied
Advertising:	Direct mail, advertising in local farm journals and newspapers, Yellow Pages, membership in farmers' organizations, Web site
Qualifications:	Pilot's license, outstanding piloting skills, knowledge of agricultural chemicals, training/experience in aerial application
Equipment needed:	Fixed-wing or helicopter specifically designed for aerial application, application equipment, chemicals
Home business potential:	Yes
Staff required:	No
Hidden costs:	Insurance, plane maintenance, airfield costs, fuel, continuing education

LOWDOWN:

Aerial application—formerly known as crop dusting—is one of the quickest and most efficient ways to deliver insecticides, herbicides, and fertilizer to fruit, vegetable, and grain crops. And it's cost effective too. An airplane can accomplish more in one hour than it would take a full day for ground equipment to complete, and it can effectively treat areas such as wet fields and thick canopies where heavy ground rigs might sink or do serious damage to plants and trees. You'll have your best chance of breaking into this business if you live in a heavily agricultural region. Your challenge will be to develop relationships with farmers whose land holdings are large enough to support your very high overhead and still leave you with a profit. In the agricultural market, two significant factors will directly impact your business from year to year: the weather and the global economy. Sadly, you have control over neither one, but sure as death and taxes, the boll weevils will still zero in on your customers' cotton, and disease-carrying spores still float through the air toward their amber waves of grain, so even in hard times, you may be able to make a living. Aerial application is also being used these days to fight forest and grassland fires, feed fish, melt snow, and control mosquitoes.

STARTUP:

To become an aerial applicator, you must first earn a pilot's license; expect to spend at least $3,000–$5,000 for basic flight training, testing, and FAA certification. Not surprisingly, your largest startup expense will be for the plane, and you can't use just any old kind for this type of work. The planes used for aerial application must be built to withstand multiple landings and takeoffs from rough landing strips, and they must offer both protection and good visibility for the pilot. The "crop dusters" of today aren't anything like the old open-cockpit planes with a chemical drum attached that were used for crop dusting back in the 1920s and '30s. Today's aerial application planes are equipped with sophisticated GPS satellite technology, flow controls, and precisely calibrated spray devices to ensure accurate delivery of the chemicals. And as you might suspect, they don't come cheap. New, these aircraft cost between $100,000 and $1 million; used planes, if you can find them, go for considerably less, of course. Aerial application is an expensive business to launch, but if you market effectively and provide services beyond the agricultural sector and your immediate geographic area, you should be able to begin making a profit within a year or two.

BOTTOM LINE ADVICE:

As you develop your business plan, you will need to factor in the likely ups and downs of agriculture in your area. If, after completing your projections, you find that even the worst-case scenario leaves you with a reasonable expectation of a profitable operation, go ahead—launch the business and start marketing yourself. Careful attention to customer service will help set you apart from the competition. Aside from the vagaries of agricultural profitability, the biggest negative about this business is its danger. If you've ever watched an aerial applicator in action, you know why. Next to piloting a jet fighter, aerial application is the most demanding type of aviation. You have to concentrate on at least three things at once—your instrument panel, the plane's position over the field, and when to start and stop the chemical application—and you must do it all just a few feet above the ground, traveling at approximately 140 miles per hour! Aerial application is not for the careless or the faint of heart.

AIR CHARTER SERVICE

Startup cost:	$1–$5 million+
Potential earnings:	$500,000–$1.5 million
Typical fees:	$150–$1,000 per passenger, per flight
Advertising:	Yellow Pages, newspapers, billboards, word of mouth, Web site
Qualifications:	Pilot's license (twin-engine and instrumental)
Equipment needed:	Fleet of turbo-prop, twin-engine airplanes or a Lear jet
Home business potential:	No
Staff required:	Yes
Hidden costs:	Insurance, workers' compensation, training/testing fees, equipment maintenance

LOWDOWN:

From turbo-prop to Lear jet, you could be soaring with an air charter service if you're in the right location, or if you have the ability to fly special products to the rich and impatient. One air charter service out of Cincinnati, for example, regularly flies delectable ribs from the Montgomery Inn along the Ohio River to Palm Springs, where a well-known celebrity awaits with salivating anticipation. You could offer similar delivery services, catering to the idiosyncrasies of the rich and famous, or you could ferry passengers on demand—corporate executives who need to get from one place to another in a hurry, or vacationers who want more flexible flight schedules than commercial airlines offer. Either way, you should have no trouble booking business and flying regularly if you get the word out successfully from the start. Promote your new business with ads in your local newspapers and business journals, create a Web site, and consider promotional opportunities that let you link up with other businesses to offer giveaways and free trips. Maybe even design your own theme-based mini-vacation packages to out of the way places, such as seaside resorts, gambling casinos, or quaint little history-rich towns. One word of caution, however, before you embark on this opportunity: The air charter business is a high-risk enterprise in more ways than one. A downturn in the economy could quickly leave you grounded, and even the tiniest hint of mismanagement or inattention to safety issues could crash your business altogether.

STARTUP:

Your startup costs for this one will be incredibly high ($1–$5 million), because you'll need to secure a reliable fleet of aircraft and a stable of experienced pilots, in addition to unleashing some heavy-duty advertising. And we haven't even mentioned the insurance; those premiums are astronomical! Unless you're independently wealthy yourself—and few pilots are—you'll need to go shopping for some heavy-duty investors. If you get off to a good start and do things right, however, your income should soar into the six-figure category and beyond in no time.

BOTTOM LINE ADVICE:

While it takes a lot of money to launch and operate an air charter business, the income potential makes this opportunity quite compelling. Once you pay off your investors, you could make a bundle. And you get to fly besides. What's not to like about that?

ARCADE/PARTY RENTALS

Startup cost:	$75,000–$200,000
Potential earnings:	$50,000–$80,000
Typical fees:	Rentals vary according to product and duration, but generally start at $25–$30 per day
Advertising:	Billboards, radio spots, direct mail, Yellow Pages, Web site
Qualifications:	Basic business and marketing skills; ability to repair and maintain equipment
Equipment needed:	Computer, bookkeeping and billing software, printer, marketing materials, party supplies and video games to rent, van or small truck
Home business potential:	No
Staff required:	Yes
Hidden costs:	Equipment maintenance and replacement, storage, vehicle expenses

LOWDOWN:

You have a stock of video games to rent to arcades, and you supplement this with rentals of party equipment such as tables, chairs, and punch bowls. You make a success of your enterprise by marketing vigorously, providing excellent customer service, and managing costs with an eagle eye. Timing is always a challenge: You'll need to have what your customers want, in the quantity they need, and at the time they expect to have it delivered. You'll need to keep on top of the trends too. Video games come and go, and party themes change from one year to the next; You'll need to know what's hot now and into the future so you have on hand what your customers will come looking for. Managing your delivery and repair personnel will be especially important so that you minimize wasted time and maximize the service you can provide.

STARTUP:

This is a capital-intensive business, relatively speaking. Expect to spend at least $75,000 to build a sufficient product base from which your customers may make selections. You will be charging at least $25–$30 (and maybe as much as $100) per day, depending on the product you're leasing out; to protect your investment, be sure to get a security deposit in advance. Your success is directly related to the equipment you carry, so be sure to purchase only what you know will be a sure bet.

BOTTOM LINE ADVICE:

If you do things right, your business will become automatically woven into the fabric of your community. Your "neighbors" will just naturally come to think of your place as the place to find equipment for wedding receptions, Christmas parties, and local arcades. Getting to this position won't necessarily be easy or quick. Your success will depend on the nature of the competition you face and your ability to offer the products and services your specific market wants and needs.

ASSEMBLY WORK

Startup cost:	$40,000–$75,000
Potential earnings:	$60,000–$200,000
Typical fees:	$1,500–$5,000+ per job
Advertising:	Trade/industry publications, direct mail to manufacturers, networking
Qualifications:	Hands-on assembly experience
Equipment needed:	Extensive tool collection, assembly benches and equipment
Home business potential:	No
Staff required:	Yes (one to three assemblers; more for large jobs)
Hidden costs:	Insurance, workers' compensation, attorneys fees for preparing contracts

LOWDOWN:

Many small- to medium-sized manufacturers farm out their smaller assembly work to subcontractors; you can be on their list of regular suppliers if you can demonstrate a thorough understanding of product manufacturing and a hands-on background in assembly. You'll need to circulate in the manufacturing world by attending trade shows, technical conferences, and association events; mix, mingle, and put your business cards in as many hands as possible to make sure your name is out there as someone who can handle their subassembly work. Once you get established, you'll be taking calls from many different types of manufacturers—from small appliance makers to medical product manufacturers—each one asking you to perform a different, yet specific function. You'll need to be well-versed in what constitutes manufacturability, as well as adept at turning around products in a short period of time. Remember, one of the primary reasons they called on you in the first place is because they have a deadline to meet and they're running behind schedule.

STARTUP:

You'll need sufficient capital ($40,000–$75,000) to create a working environment, complete with assembly benches, tools, and assembly equipment. Once you get established, you could earn as much as $200,000 per year.

BOTTOM LINE ADVICE:

Turnaround times will often be quite tight, and it may take 45 to 90 days, or even longer, to receive full payment for your work. That's why it makes smart business sense to draw up a contract that allows you to receive at least a percentage of your fee up front.

AUDIOBOOK PRODUCER/DISTRIBUTOR

Startup cost:	$40,000–$100,000+
Potential earnings:	$50,000–$75,000+
Typical fees:	40 percent commission on selling price
Advertising:	Direct mail to publisher's representatives and retail outlets, cold calls, ads in magazines and travel publications, Web site
Qualifications:	Recording/engineering experience, basic business and marketing skills
Equipment needed:	Extensive recording, dubbing and editing equipment, duplication equipment, CD burners, tapes/CDs and boxes
Home business potential:	Not likely
Staff required:	Not at first; you will need to hire narrators, however
Hidden costs:	Insurance, equipment maintenance and upgrades, excessive promotional costs, fees for securing audio rights to existing materials

LOWDOWN:

Audiobooks are selling like hotcakes these days, and no wonder. It seems we're all locked up in our cars, driving for hours, and listening to our favorite books and bestsellers or other audio programs on cassette or CD just makes good sense. You can produce audiobooks that are readings of printed books (after securing the audio rights, of course) or you can produce your own innovative series of programs. For instance, one entrepreneur sells tapes that tell the local lore of a particular highway on the West Coast—guaranteed to appeal to those traveling along that road. Producing the tapes will require technical and sound engineering expertise; if you don't have that particular skill, you'll have to subcontract for it, which adds to your costs. And unless you have professional narration experience, don't try to read the books yourself; secure narration talent by hiring celebrities (if you can afford them) or by screening local talent through regular casting calls.

STARTUP:

You'll need $40,000–$100,000 or more to launch this business, but it is a remarkably growing field and could bring you a sizable return on investment if you have the right mix of unique and high-quality products. If your tapes and CDs are steady sellers, you could see earnings as high as $75,000 or more.

BOTTOM LINE ADVICE:

You can cash in on this vast consumer market if you can manage to produce audio productions that will entertain, teach, or delight. Securing the rights to existing material can be expensive, so price your products accordingly.

AUTOMOTIVE TESTING EQUIPMENT

Startup cost:	$40,000–$100,000
Potential earnings:	$45,000–$60,000
Typical fees:	Equipment sells for $500–$10,000 or more, depending on its complexity and precision; your cut is usually 30 to 40 percent of sale price
Advertising:	Periodicals aimed at automotive dealers and repair shops, newspapers, Yellow Pages, business publications, direct mail or sales to automotive manufacturers
Qualifications:	Familiarity with automotive testing regulations in your state, knowledge of testing equipment operations, marketing skills
Equipment needed:	Inventory of automotive testing equipment for sale or lease, computer, billing and bookkeeping software, printer fax, phone
Home business potential:	No
Staff required:	Probably
Hidden costs:	Equipment repair and updating, vehicle expenses

LOWDOWN:

As an automotive testing equipment dealer, your focus is on a very narrow market niche. Your customer base will be drawn from garages in a state that has emission testing requirements. You will sell or lease the specialized equipment that assesses the quality and quantity of tailpipe emissions. Your ability to keep the equipment in good repair and working accurately will make your service an extremely valuable one to many testing sites in your area.

STARTUP:

Startup costs are relatively high ($40,000–$100,000) as you must acquire and maintain a reasonable inventory of this expensive equipment in a suitable warehouse. In addition, you'll need a full complement of tools for maintenance, and a vehicle for delivering the equipment to your customers.

BOTTOM LINE ADVICE:

On the plus side, this business provides a critical service that is needed by many customers in a healthy, recession-proof field. The downside is that you'll need to be upgrading your equipment constantly to keep up with industry changes and continually evolving government regulations (such as freon level testing, etc.).

BED & BREAKFAST

Startup cost:	Varies from $10,000–$150,000 per guest room depending on whether you're purchasing a functioning inn or converting a home
Potential earnings:	$35,000–$175,000
Typical fees:	$65–$150+ per room, per night (depending on location, season, and whether bathrooms are shared)
Advertising:	Yellow Pages, B&B directories, direct mail to travel agencies, Web site
Qualifications:	Basic business and marketing skills; outgoing personality; background/experience in the hospitality industry is helpful
Equipment needed:	Beds and bedding, towels, dining tables/chairs, stationery/brochures
Home business potential:	Yes
Staff required:	Probably (could be family members)
Hidden costs:	Utilities, upkeep on rooms and furnishings, licensing

LOWDOWN:

The aroma of fresh-baked blueberry muffins. . . the look of billowy white curtains and fluffy handmade quilts. . . the feel of quiet evenings in comfortable chairs by the fireplace. The sheer romance of owning and operating a B&B can be intoxicating enough to entice you into starting one of your own. Bed & breakfast inns can be profitable enterprises, but they require significant capital to get started and a lot of elbow grease to operate. However, if current travel trends remain on target, more and more city folks will go looking for unusual escapes—and what better place to find one than in a quiet little inn in the middle of nowhere (but within close driving proximity to somewhere)? Not just any old building will do, of course. You'll do best if your house has an interesting history or some unique architectural details, like turrets or gingerbread, or a huge wrap-around porch. You can open a B&B with as few as two guest rooms, but industry studies have shown that you'll need at least six to turn a profit; any more than 12 guest rooms, however, and you're no longer cozy and quaint. In addition to guest rooms, you'll need adequate common space—a parlor or sitting room where guests can relax in the late afternoon or evening, as well as a kitchen for preparing the breakfast, and a dining area for serving it. As innkeeper, you'll not only play the role of the genial host/hostess, you'll be responsible for the cleaning, cooking, and serving. In order to meet state and local regulations, you'll need to be meticulous about your housekeeping and food preparation. And since B&Bs do best in regions/towns where there's something interesting to see and do, you'll need to become an authority on all of the tourist attractions in your immediate area—you'll be surprised how often customers will count on your local expertise to help them devise their plans for the day.

STARTUP:

The easiest—and possibly the costliest—way to get started in this business is to buy an existing B&B and simply take over the business. It shouldn't be too difficult to find one for sale; turnover in this business is relatively high, as many owners burn out after ten years or so of working 24/7. Expect to pay anywhere from $35,000 to $150,000 per guest room.

If, on the other hand, you'd like to convert a house you already own into a fully licensed B&B, you can count on spending about $15,000–$50,000 per guest room depending on your geographic locale and the extent of the renovations you'll need to make. In either case, plan on putting about $10,000 per room toward your initial operating expenses to cover marketing, insurance, utilities, maintenance, linens, and other supplies. If you do an effective job of marketing and, as they say in the hospitality trade, "put heads in beds," you can expect to break even in about three years or so.

BOTTOM LINE ADVICE:

Many a person gets sucked into the idea of living the seemingly idyllic country inn life-style that a B&B appears to promise. But before you launder the sheets and fling open your doors to guests, give a lot of thought to the hard work you're facing; most B&B owners will tell you that this job means long hours of intense work (cooking, cleaning, and assisting guests in all of their needs). If you don't mind having strangers in your house 24/7 or putting in work weeks of 60 hours and more without the promise of grand riches, a bed & breakfast inn can be a great business to own.

BEER BREWERY

Startup cost:	$100,000–$1.5 million
Potential earnings:	$300,000–$2 million
Typical fees:	Varied according to distributor agreements
Advertising:	Direct mail to distributors, ads in newspapers and magazines, articles in beer brewing magazines, participation in beer clubs, event sponsorship, Web site
Qualifications:	An avid interest in beer, knowledge of brewing techniques, basic business and marketing skills
Equipment needed:	Brewing equipment, brewer's yeast, other key ingredients
Home business potential:	Possibly
Staff required:	Yes
Hidden costs:	Insurance, licensing from state liquor boards in every state in which you plan to distribute

LOWDOWN:

Beer brewing, especially microbrewing, is one of today's hottest entrepreneurial trends; virtually all beer aficionados believe they can make the best brew on the planet. There are actually beer clubs where members taste-test beers from all over the country (and sometimes the world), then rate them according to their flavor. Yours could be one of the top-rated if you have the know-how to brew beer properly (and tastefully). Beer conventions are a great place for you to check out all the competition before sinking your investment capital into a brewery of your own; you can see what's out there, then set about.figuring out how to make a product that will truly stand out. You could even open a "brewpub" reminiscent of the English ale house or a restaurant next door to your brewery to give yourself an immediate market for your product. However you choose to produce.and market your beer, you'll need to make sure you set up strong distribution channels from the get-go; in the beverage business, it's where you are—not just the stores you're in, but your place on the shelves—that truly determines how successful you'll be.

STARTUP:

Your startup is high ($100,000–$1.5 million), because you'll need lots of specialty beer brewing equipment and plenty of space to produce your product. You'll also need licensing from the state where you produce your beer as well as every state you plan to sell it in, and, since beer is a product for human consumption, you'll need certification from the health and food safety arenas as well. Even if yours is a microbrew (you produce fewer than 20,000 barrels per year), you can still make a good living if you build a loyal following among beer lovers, for whom there can never be enough of the good stuff.

BOTTOM LINE ADVICE:

Beer brewing is a fiercely competitive business to be in right now, mainly because it looks so easy and because some microbrewers have really cashed in. Recognize up front that a huge amount of work goes into the successful brewing of beer. This is more art than science, and just like fine wines, which take years to perfect, you can't rush a good beer.

BOAT TOURS

Startup cost:	$50,000–$80,000+
Potential earnings:	$45,000–$75,000 (depending on whether your business is seasonal)
Typical fees:	$4–$20 per person, per trip
Advertising:	Yellow Pages, radio spots, billboard, newspapers, magazines, travel guides and directories, networking with convention and visitor bureaus, Web site
Qualifications:	Captain's license, nautical skills, knowledge of the area, outgoing personality
Equipment needed:	Boat with seating, restrooms, snack bar; docking space, parking area, ramp; life jackets and other safety devices
Home business potential:	No
Staff required:	Yes
Hidden costs:	Maintenance and fuel, marine and liability insurance, dry dock/storage fees for winter, if applicable

LOWDOWN:

Boat tours are a family favorite for vacation activities. Almost everyone who can walk can take a boat tour, even if they aren't fit enough for more vigorous water sports. You'll need a dock, or docking rights, in a central location that has available parking. Obviously, the type of tour you offer will depend on your area. City tours on rivers can offer a fascinating glimpse of familiar territory from a different perspective. Harbor tours take people around giant container ships, yachts, and even naval vessels like aircraft carriers. Some tours focus on the magnificent estates lining the shore, as in Newport, Rhode Island. Others focus on whale watching, dolphin spotting, or environmental education. The nature of your tour will dictate the appropriate advertising. You'll need helpers on shore to sell tickets and interact with potential passengers. And you'll need at least one deckhand to help with docking. Sales of snacks can be a big contribution to your bottom line.

STARTUP:

Startup costs are high, and so is ongoing maintenance. You'll shell out $50,000–$80,000 or more for a decent rig, and you'll need to set aside even more for liability insurance. The biggest determinant of your success in this field is whether you live in a place where your business would be seasonal. Obviously, the folks who build their business on Lake Erie won't make as much as those in the Florida Keys.

BOTTOM LINE ADVICE:

Showmanship has to be mixed with seamanship in the boat tour business. Many people just enjoy the opportunity to get out on the water, but your line of patter about the sights alongside and around your vessel will add a lot to the experience. Your business plan must allow for the effects of weather. No one wants to go out on rough seas, and extremely hot or unseasonably cold temperatures can cut down on expected ticket sales, too.

Canoe Livery

Startup cost:	$65,000–$150,000
Potential earnings:	$45,000–$60,000
Typical fees:	$5–$10 per hour, per canoe, or half-day and full-day rates
Advertising:	Entertainment and outdoors magazines, recreation guides, sporting goods shops, referrals, travel guides and directories, Web site
Qualifications:	Experience with all aspects of managing a water-oriented business, canoeing skills
Equipment needed:	Staging area, canoes, paddles, life preservers and vests, van for transporting canoes and paddlers back to the staging area, cell phone
Home business potential:	No
Staff required:	Yes
Hidden costs:	Insurance, maintenance, replacement of canoes and paddles, vehicle expenses

LOWDOWN:

If you have land access to a suitable river, you can translate your love of canoeing and the out-of-doors into a steady, although in some parts of the country fairly seasonal, business. You will need a small staff of experienced, reliable helpers, which may be difficult to procure if you are able to offer only part-time positions. Everyone involved in the business must put safety first. Canoes tip over easily and so, in addition to renting these watercraft, one of your primary jobs will be teaching safe canoeing practices. Your most valuable marketing tool is one you don't have to provide because Mother Nature has done it for you—the beautiful, soothing river with its interesting eddies and graceful trees lining the banks is likely to be your biggest customer draw.

STARTUP:

Equipping your enterprise will be more capital-intensive than for many types of small businesses, but once you have a good supply of canoes and paddles, your continuing costs will not be too great. Like the canoes you rent, your business may be a little tipsy for the first year or two, but long about year number three, you should be paddling steady and making a profit; earnings of up to $60,000 per year are not unreasonable if you're a savvy marketer.

BOTTOM LINE ADVICE:

Many successful canoe liveries are family enterprises. There are times when many willing hands will be needed to do maintenance, cope with several busloads of teenagers arriving at once, and drive the canoes and paddlers back to the staging area at the end of their trips. The attractiveness of your piece of the river will automatically draw groups of people to your business; in addition, marketing to schools and church youth groups may turn out to be a successful approach.

ADVICE FROM THE EXPERTS

What sets your business apart from others like it?

Mel Reinthal, owner of Pleasant Hill Canoe Livery in Perrysville, Ohio, says coming up with a gimmick that works is what ultimately brings in business. "I made up a story about Perrysville being named after Commodore Perry, and made up a whole humorous tale about the good commodore. You'd be surprised how many people ask about that—we even had a Japanese tourist once!"

Things you couldn't do without:

"I couldn't do without eighteen-year-olds with strong backs to carry the canoes, a telephone and, most important, good weather!"

Marketing tips/advice:

"Nothing beats good word of mouth, but we also do direct mail pieces and advertising co-ops through tourist associations. It helps to have access to low-cost advertising through group deals."

If you had to do it all over again . . .

"I would issue a warning about relatives and partners . . . and would encourage others to really do their research first."

CAR WASH

Startup cost:	$140,000–$400,000
Potential earnings:	$75,000–$250,000
Typical fees:	$5–$10 per car
Advertising:	Print media, radio, fliers, discount coupon distribution, location
Qualifications:	Business and financial management knowledge; a technical and/or mechanical background might be helpful with regard to equipment
Equipment needed:	Washing and drying equipment for full-service, hoses and brushes for self-service, water reclamation system, vacuum system
Home business potential:	No
Staff required:	Yes
Hidden costs:	Security and change machines for self-service stalls; insurance coverage for workers and customers; maintenance cost for machinery; water (usage will increase as equipment wears)

LOWDOWN:

Since southern California receives fewer than 20 days of rain each year, it sounds like an ideal place to launch your car wash business! But seriously, operating a successful car wash does not mandate a move to the West Coast; dirty cars are on the road everywhere. Common sense should tell you that car washes do best in places where two-thirds of the year is dry. So, for maximum success, you'll want to consider a geographic location with approximately 250 rain-free days a year. Nationwide, there is less business during the months of June, July, and August; people tend to wash their own cars in warm weather. Surprisingly perhaps, car washes in the North do more business in the winter months as car owners strive to keep their cars free from corrosive road salts. And don't completely rule out those rainy days either. In fact, a few hours or the day after a heavy rain are usually busier than normal times because owners want to rinse off the grime caused by sloppy roadways.

STARTUP:

Excluding the cost of land, you can start a four-bay self-service car wash for approximately $140,000. A full-service car wash, with the kind of machinery that propels the car along a washing course, requires an investment of at least $400,000.

BOTTOM LINE ADVICE:

With the increase in double-income families and the constant struggle to find more hours in every day, who wants to spend time washing their car? Busy professionals would rather enjoy a Saturday afternoon playing a round of golf or just relaxing than soaping up the family vehicle. Car washes—both full- and self-service—are more popular than ever. Your toughest decision won't be whether to own one; it will be whether to build or to buy. In either case, be aware of possible shifts in demographics that could affect your business and large expenditures for replacing major components.

CHILD DEVELOPMENT CENTER

Startup cost:	$40,000–$80,000
Potential earnings:	$35,000–$50,000
Typical fees:	$150–$300 per month per child
Advertising:	Community newspapers; church and school bulletin boards; referrals from pediatricians, teachers, and counselors; direct mail; seminars to community groups; brochures
Qualifications:	Advanced degree in child development, education, or a related field; many years of experience in counseling or teaching children with learning difficulties
Equipment needed:	Facility that meets the codes and requirements for your state, child-sized furniture, appropriate play materials, teaching tools, office equipped with computer, printer, copier, and phone
Home business potential:	Yes
Staff required:	Possibly
Hidden costs:	Insurance, acquisition/replacement of furniture and play materials

LOWDOWN:

The body of knowledge concerning the developmental needs of children continues to expand at a rapid pace. There is an intense focus on the problems that prevent many children, especially boys, from doing well early on in school. Increasingly, parents find that overcrowded public schools alone cannot meet the needs of their children, and they are turning to child development centers for the services that will enable their kids to make better progress. Individuals with the background and ability to assist young people in learning and feeling better about themselves can build a child development center into a successful business.

STARTUP:

Startup costs will be substantial ($40,000–$80,000) because you must have a fully equipped center in place before the first fees even begin to arrive. The process of obtaining the necessary permits and insurance alone can be quite expensive. And then there's the marketing; getting the word out about your new enterprise can cost a pretty penny too. Still, at $150–$300 per month per child, you could earn $35,000–$50,000 and feel good about expanding the minds of children.

BOTTOM LINE ADVICE:

If you are trained in and skilled at helping children with their developmental needs, your services will be in demand in most areas of the United States. As parents and schools become more overburdened, the demand for assistance with children's learning problems is on the rise. It will probably take you a good full year to discover precisely where to focus your services: on children with reading difficulties, attention-deficit disorder, or special gifts and talents that make traditional schools inappropriate, etc. Overseeing your organization, managing your own time and energy, and keeping up with new developments in the field will be among the challenges you can expect to face in this business. Pricing your services to make an adequate profit will also be difficult. But for a gifted teacher or counselor who desires to make a real difference in the lives of the children that desperately need help, this business can offer much more than financial reward.

COIN-OPERATED LAUNDRY

Startup cost:	$50,000–$100,000
Potential earnings:	$30,000–$60,000
Typical fees:	$1.25–$1.75 per self-service washer load, 25 cents for every 10 minutes in the dryer; drop-off wash/dry/fold services can be charged by the pound (usually $2–$4 per)
Advertising:	Yellow Pages, coupon books, location
Qualifications:	Basic business skills, mechanical ability for minor equipment repairs
Equipment needed:	Heavy-duty washers and dryers, laundry detergent dispensing machines, coin changing machines
Home business potential:	No
Staff required:	Yes (two to four people)
Hidden costs:	Insurance and equipment maintenance

LOWDOWN:

Wherever there are apartments, there's a need for coin-operated washers and dryers. Clean laundry is something that never goes out of style, so you can be assured that this is both a recession-proof business, and one that may never be affected by technological advancements. Sure, the equipment may get better, and electronic key cards rather than coins may be used in the laundries of the future, but until dirt-free clothes are invented, people are always going to need access to laundry services. Many innovative entrepreneurs are expanding their coin-operated laundries to include amenities that help customers pass the time while they wait—they're adding bars with big-screen TVs, tanning booths, even video game arcades. You don't have to go quite so high-tech, of course; you could simply offer traditional services, like washing, drying, and folding the clothes for your customers (these services are usually priced by the pound). In all cases, the basics of running a coin-operated laundry are pretty cut and dried, so to speak: You rent or buy space, install 25 to 50 heavy-duty washer/dryer units, and hang up your sign (which, by the way, will be your primary means of advertising). Unless you offer some unusual extras, there's no need to spend precious dollars on newspaper ads; if you're in a visible location, your customers will find you.

STARTUP:

Taking into account the large amounts of space and equipment you'll need, you can expect to spend at least $50,000 launching a coin-operated laundry business. Spend another $1,000 or so on advertising (Yellow Pages and coupon books) during your first six months more if unusual amenities like a big-screen TV or tanning booth warrant newspaper advertising. Check around your area to determine the going rate for self-serve washers/dryers before programming your machines.

BOTTOM LINE ADVICE:

Running a coin-operated laundry puts you in contact with different types of people every day, and to some that's a plus, to others it's a negative. Make sure you have some sort of policy in place against loiterers, or your coin-operated laundry could easily start looking like a flophouse.

COLOR SEPARATION AND FILM ASSEMBLY SERVICES

Startup cost:	$100,000–$200,000
Potential earnings:	$75,000–$250,000 per year
Typical fees:	Varies; could range from $150–$3,500 per project (depending on size and complexity)
Advertising:	Trade journals, networking with ad agencies and others who use four-color work, word of mouth
Qualifications:	Graphic design, photography background
Equipment needed:	Highly specialized camera, darkroom, photo enlarger, processing chemicals
Home business potential:	Yes
Staff required:	No
Hidden costs:	EPA guidelines for disposal of chemicals, cost of materials and equipment updates

LOWDOWN:

The film production business is a technically precise one, so be sure you have had thorough training before embarking on this as a full-time career. If you have an interest in this type of business, you probably have had some experience with it and perhaps even own some of the necessary equipment already. If so, it should be relatively easy to set up your production studio. What will you do all day? Handle a wide variety of projects for an array of clients, ranging from magazine photos to motion picture film. Basically, you'll shoot a picture of a picture that is being prepared for publication; you might even shoot an entire page so that it can be taken to the printer in sheets ready for reproduction. You'll prepare the photos using the standard four-color process. In terms of personal expertise, you should have thorough knowledge of the two primary processes required to do this job: color separation and film developing.

STARTUP:

To be successful in this business, you need to have all of the equipment and chemicals required to do this job, plus the necessary space to work in; expect to spend around $100,000 to get up and running. You'll be working with some pretty powerful chemicals, which, when you're finished with them, can't be tossed out just anywhere. You'll have to be familiar with EPA regulations; compliance can be costly, but there's no getting around them. The good news is, your potential income after initial investment will be high—in the $75,000–$250,000 range.

BOTTOM LINE ADVICE:

A major drawback to this business is that not only is the equipment expensive, it may become obsolete before you even have time to pay it off. Consequently, it might take you quite a while before you reap any sizable profit. Also, people who go into this business tend to make it part of a full-service printing operation; if you go that route, too, you'll need to add a four-color press to your equipment list, in which case you'll also have to expand to a larger space.

COMMODITIES BROKER

Startup cost:	$100,000+
Potential earnings:	$1,000,000+
Typical fees:	The difference between what you pay when you buy and what you get when you sell
Advertising:	None
Qualifications:	Extensive knowledge of commodities prices and everything that affects them, from famine to genetic engineering; knowledge of human psychology
Equipment needed:	State-of-the-art communications equipment (pager/beeper/cell phone), computer and high-speed Internet access, seat on the Chicago Board of Trade and/or other commodities exchanges
Home business potential:	Yes
Staff required:	No
Hidden costs:	Insurance

LOWDOWN:

Being a commodities broker is the ultimate entrepreneurial activity: It's you against the market. Commodity investments are notorious for their high risk. In a heartbeat, you can either lose everything you own, or become enormously wealthy. By their very nature, commodities (agricultural and mining products) are much more volatile than stocks and bonds, even junk bonds and over-the-counter offerings. Commodity prices vary according to such factors as "the market" (popular attitudes), the weather, the effectiveness of farming techniques in a certain season, and government actions (an oil or grain embargo, for example). Successful commodities brokers gather enormous amounts of information, assess its influence on the market for a specific commodity, and buy or sell shares of stock (not the actual product) accordingly. This is a very high-stakes way to make a living.

STARTUP:

The cost of your seat on the commodities exchange and your need for working capital make entering this business a very expensive proposition, to the tune of $100,000 or more. However, if you're good at it, you could become a millionaire many times over.

BOTTOM LINE ADVICE:

Some people thrive on risk. If you are overseeing the commodity trades of others, you need to have people skills as well as financial savvy in order to operate in this dynamic world. Everything is heightened in this fast-paced, risky business: the possibilities, the danger, and the opportunity to balloon your bank account.

CREATIVE ARTS DAY CAMP

Startup cost:	$50,000
Potential earnings:	$20,000–$35,000
Typical fees:	$50–$100 per child for a two-week session
Advertising:	Local newspaper, bulletin boards, fliers at schools, organized groups (i.e., Girl Scouts, Campfire Girls)
Qualifications:	License to run a camp, creativity, background in a wide range of arts and crafts activities; education degree and/or teaching experience would be helpful
Equipment needed:	Campsite/building with running water and restroom facilities, arts and craft supplies, cell phone, vehicle (optional)
Home business potential:	No
Staff required:	Yes
Hidden costs:	Insurance, vehicle expenses, first aid supplies. Be careful about choosing your activities; some arts and crafts materials can be quite costly.

LOWDOWN:

Day camps are extremely popular these days, primarily because dual-income families are looking for ways to keep their children occupied in interesting, healthy hobbies during the summer months. A creative arts day camp is a great way to get kids involved in a worthwhile summertime activity, and it can provide a nice second income for you if it's promoted effectively—aim for ads in community publications that reach families and align yourself with school officials early on so that you can tap into a ready-made market in the easiest, most direct way. Your curriculum can consist of as many as 16 to 20 different activities throughout the week, from basket weaving to ballet. Imagine the fun you'll have teaching the children how to paint landscapes (or even portraits of one another)! You'll probably need a staff of at least two more people to offer a wider range of activities and to improve your adult-to-child ratio; kids can bring sack lunches from home or you can provide the sandwiches; if you choose the latter option, don't forget to build the cost of the food into your program registration fees.

STARTUP:

You'll have to have a place to hold your camp, of course, and acquiring one will likely be your biggest startup cost. Ideally, you'll want to hold your sessions outdoors, but you'll need a backup plan for rainy days. If you plan ahead, you might be able to rent space from your local parks and recreation department; otherwise, you may have to buy a piece of land and erect a shelter, which could boost your startup costs significantly. Keep in mind that you'll need to have bathroom facilities, running water, and, possibly even a kitchen. If the campgrounds are located outside of town, you may need to provide transportation, too. Since you will likely need a staff, consider rounding up people who are interested in educating children too, such as stay-at-home moms or college-age education majors looking for practical experience. It might be a good idea to have a nurse on staff or on call during camp hours; at the very least, you should have certification in first aid and pediatric CPR. Your geographic location and the cost of the supplies for the arts you intend to offer will determine your fees per week. Once you get established in a good area, you could make upwards of $35,000.

BOTTOM LINE ADVICE:

This is a great job to consider if your own kids are sitting around saying, "There's nothing to do, Mom!" The best part is, your program doesn't get stale after the first couple of sessions. Each day can be a different, unique, creative experience. Plan to explore different cultures or time periods by making art or crafts in traditional ways. On the downside, even though this business can be fun, it represents a tremendous commitment of time and energy. Even if you're under the weather, the kids will still get dropped off at your camp and the show must go on. That's why it's a good idea to not go it alone; have a backup staff of people who enjoy working with kids and have unique arts and crafts skills to share.

CUSTOM EMBROIDERY

Startup cost:	$50,000–$150,000
Potential earnings:	$30,000–$250,000
Typical fees:	$5–$150 per item
Advertising:	Local newspaper, bulletin boards, direct mail, municipal parks and recreation departments, YMCAs, school systems, youth sports teams
Qualifications:	Skills needed to run embroidery equipment, basic business and marketing skills
Equipment needed:	Sewing machines with embroidery capabilities, ironing press, threads
Home business potential:	No
Staff required:	Yes
Hidden costs:	Workers' compensation, fluctuating materials costs

LOWDOWN:

Companies everywhere have been purchasing custom embroidery for as long as it's been available—to proudly display their corporate logos or slogans on T-shirts, hats, jackets, and other apparel items. As a custom embroiderer, you will work with customers to select the article of clothing that would be most appropriate for their purposes, determine a color scheme, and then reproduce their logo/slogan on as many items as the customer deems necessary. You'll charge by the piece ($5–$150 per item), and offer special prices for large orders. If you're extremely knowledgeable in and already skilled at the process of custom embroidery, you can start your own independent embroidery business. If you have no experience at this, but think you'd like to try your hand at it, look into buying a franchise. For your investment of $50,000 or more, you'll receive the necessary equipment, training, and marketing support.

STARTUP:

Investing in a franchise means a high startup investment ($50,000 or more), but that may well be worth it considering that your money will go toward equipment, training, and marketing support. Your earnings in a custom embroidery business may range anywhere from $30,000–$250,000, depending on the types and quantities of items you sell and whether you're able to secure a fair amount of repeat business. For maximum impact in the marketplace, align yourself with school systems, YMCAs, youth sports teams, and municipal parks and recreation departments, in addition to local businesses. Put your bid in early for big-ticket items like letterman jackets and jerseys, etc. Your prices will vary widely, from as little as $5 to as much as $150, depending on the complexity of the design, the number of colors required, and how difficult the item is to work with.

BOTTOM LINE ADVICE:

Your standing in the community will spread your good name and help grow your business; work hard at building a strong network of people who can, in turn, help you bring in the customers. With this business, you have the flexibility to be creative; keep in mind, however, that orders have a way of all coming due at one time, so be prepared to work long hours and weekends to fill them.

DAY SPA

Startup cost:	$50,000–$100,000
Potential earnings:	$65,000–$100,000
Typical fees:	$150 per day, plus or including lunch (you decide)
Advertising:	Newspapers, women's magazines, Yellow Pages, coupon books
Qualifications:	Business and marketing skills, strong customer service orientation; creativity; some licensing may be required—i.e., cosmetology, massage therapy
Equipment needed:	Massage tables, sauna/tanning equipment, standard hair salon equipment, supplies for facials and makeovers
Home business potential:	No
Staff required:	Yes
Hidden costs:	Insurance

LOWDOWN:

It's the ultimate working woman's fantasy—a whole day of relaxation and escape at a place where nothing gets in the way of pure pampering. Customers at a day spa can expect to spend their time in a soothing sauna, followed by a relaxing massage, and perhaps a facial and makeover session. Light lunches can be offered as part of the package, as can hotel suites laden with goodies for an overnight stay. To bring the business in, you may want to offer coupons or special packages (i.e., a romantic couples' getaway with free champagne or a working woman's package that includes a motivational speaker as a highlight). You're in the business of pleasure, so you'll need to provide the ultimate in service for your clients. This is your chance to turn fantasies into reality, so think creativity: If you had $150 or more to burn on a full day of pampering, what would you want?

STARTUP:

If you're going to offer a slice of the finer things in life, expect to make a large initial investment in your business, then wait at least a couple of years before you see a profit. Just like any luxury service, a day spa requires a significant capital investment; your equipment and space rental costs will run anywhere from $50,000–$100,000. Make sure you have an airtight business plan to take to bankers or other investors. Fees generally average $150 per day for the works: sauna, massage, facial, hair care, and makeover. You can also set half-day rates or charge by the specific service.

BOTTOM LINE ADVICE:

A lot goes in to creating the perfect day spa, so you'll likely be spending money hand over fist in the beginning stages of your business. But hang tight . . . if you can wait for the return, you could make a small fortune for your patience. As America's stress levels continue to mount, luxurious escape-type businesses are on the rise and turning big profits.

DEMOLITION/WRECKING CONTRACTOR

Startup cost:	$65,000–$100,000
Potential earnings:	$50,000–$70,000
Typical fees:	As high as $10,000–$15,000, depending on the complexity of the job
Advertising:	Yellow Pages, classified ads, trade associations, networking, referrals
Qualifications:	Extensive experience in demolition, knowledge of construction methods, ability to operate and maintain the required heavy machinery, project planning skills, knowledge of explosives and related safety procedures
Equipment needed:	Wrecking ball, radio equipment, bulldozers, and waste receptacles
Home business potential:	No
Staff required:	Yes
Hidden costs:	Licensing, insurance, maintenance, overtime pay for crew, workers' compensation

LOWDOWN:

Demolition isn't just about tearing down buildings any which way; it's an occupation that requires training and skill. If you live in a densely populated area of the country and have previous experience in this field, you'll find many opportunities for subcontracting demolition work. Getting the old out of the way so the new can take its place is a profitable business for many small operators. Your knowledge of up-to-date approaches to environmental issues may give you an edge in the field. You'll also need an ability to organize the wrecking process so that it occurs on time, in coordination with the other activities related to the project. A simple crash-and-smash approach is no longer acceptable in most municipalities. Recycling as many materials as possible and disposing of the rest responsibly have become integral parts of each operation.

STARTUP:

The equipment you will need demands that you make a heavy capital outlay before any revenue can flow back into the business; expect to spend as much as $100,000 up front. If you can raise the capital and get this business off the ground, charge your clients on a per-job basis, or by the hour ($75–$100 per hour is standard).

BOTTOM LINE ADVICE:

There is a man-in-the-street fascination with the process of taking down something as big as a building. Beneath all the rumbling and dust, however, lies a careful plan and many hours of tedious preparation. Once you demonstrate that you can handle the demolition process with precision, you will draw referrals for many new projects. Keeping a capable crew can be difficult. The work can be somewhat sporadic and there is always the possibility of danger in even the best-planned wrecking projects. In many parts of the country, the demolition business is seasonal.

DIAPER SERVICE

Startup cost:	$45,000–$60,000
Potential earnings:	$40,000–$55,000
Typical fees:	$40–$80 per client, per month
Advertising:	Yellow Pages, parent's publications, local newspapers, fliers, direct mail, networking with hospitals and obstetricians
Qualifications:	Basic business and marketing skills; time-management and organizational abilities; some states require licensing and/or adherence to sanitation regulations
Equipment needed:	Heavy-duty washers, dryers, and ironing equipment; baby-safe detergents; delivery vans; plastic diaper pails; diaper inventory
Home business potential:	No
Staff required:	Yes (four to 25 people, depending on the size of your market)
Hidden costs:	Insurance, workers' compensation, cost of lost diapers, utility bills, vehicle expenses

LOWDOWN:

New parents love everything about their little bundles of joy—until they have to contend with dirty diapers. That's where you come in. Your service will help harried parents cope with a task they don't particularly relish in an environmentally conscious way. Although it takes more fuel to clean and sanitize the cloth diapers you provide than to manufacture the disposable kind, at least your parents can take comfort in knowing that they're not filling up landfills with non-biodegradable materials. That's your first selling point. The second is convenience, since you will send a delivery person out to each customer's home on a regular basis to pick up the dirty diapers and drop off clean ones. Your delivery team will drop off pails, liners, and a specific number of clean diapers (based on the average number dirtied per week), then bring back the dirty ones to be washed, dried, sanitized, and ironed by your cleaning team. Buy your initial mailing and phone lists from hospitals (they often let companies like yours know of new births each week or month); then, sell your services by making cold calls or sending direct mailings to each new parent's home. Babies are born no matter what the economic conditions, so you can consider your diaper service pretty much recession-proof.

STARTUP:

You'll need some heavy-duty washers and dryers to start, along with baby-safe detergents, a large ironing press, and a small fleet of delivery vehicles. Add to this your basic office setup (computer with bookkeeping and billing software, fax, phone, copier) and you're looking at a startup of $40,000–$55,000. You will have lots of staff overhead costs, too. But if you're looking for a dependable means of making a living, you could do a lot worse than $35,000–$55,000 per year.

BOTTOM LINE ADVICE:

This is a dirty job, but somebody's got to do it, and it might as well be you. Just make sure that you use strong air-freshening chemicals in your plant, and provide your employees with the proper masks, gloves, and gels to keep the smell of ammonia away from even the most sensitive noses!

DISTRIBUTOR

Startup cost:	$40,000–$60,000+
Potential earnings:	$50,000–$150,000+
Typical fees:	Varied, depending on the product you're representing
Advertising:	Yellow Pages, business-to-business
Qualifications:	Knowledge of retail/wholesale practices; some training will likely be provided if you purchase a distributorship from a licensing agent or corporation
Equipment needed:	Computer, printer, fax, Internet access, possibly a delivery vehicle
Home business potential:	Yes, unless you're required to store inventory
Staff required:	No
Hidden costs:	Insurance, price wars, vehicle expenses

LOWDOWN:

Distributors are the lifeline of any manufacturing business; they provide the vital link between manufacturer and consumer, selling products to the right channels to ensure that the consumer has the best chance of purchasing a particular item. If you decide to purchase a distributorship, choose a product with which you have at least some experience. For instance, if you have a background in electronics, distributing auto parts would be a bit of a leap; selling satellite dishes, on the other hand, would be a better match for your knowledge and skills. Keep in mind, however, that many companies offering distributorships will train you as thoroughly as they train their in-house personnel so that you can be a better representative for their products. They do, after all, have a vested interest in your success. You can shop for a distributorship to purchase in an entrepreneurial publication or online; be sure to thoroughly check out the company you'll be doing business with. Just because they have Web sites or the magazine agrees to run their advertisements does not automatically guarantee that they're above-board.

Once you find a solid company to represent (and preferably a product you can really believe in), you'll set weekly contact goals and monthly sales goals. All the rest of your work will be devoted to selling products (be they satellite dishes, prerecorded videotapes and DVDs, or even specialty petroleum products) and making sure they get to the right selling points.

STARTUP:

You'll need approximately $40,000–$60,000 to purchase a distributorship with a company that has a great reputation; less if it's a startup or unknown business or product (make sure you do your homework!). Somewhere in that figure should be your advertising costs ($3,000 or so) and the basic office setup you'll need to succeed (computer, printer, fax, Internet access, copier, and phone—all under $5,000). If you're good at making the right contacts, you could earn $50,000–$150,000 or more.

BOTTOM LINE ADVICE:

It seems easy enough to pitch a product to sales outlets and individuals, but this work is harder and the hours tend to be much longer than one would think. If you're a hardworking professional with wide-ranging sales experience, you should have no trouble. It's the novices who tend to struggle.

DRUG TESTING SERVICE

Startup cost:	$50,000+
Potential earnings:	$45,000–$75,000
Typical fees:	$125–$300 per test
Advertising:	Yellow Pages, direct mail, ads in specialized trade journals or newsletters
Qualifications:	Laboratory technician background, including phlebotomy training; attention to detail and technical know-how, basic business and marketing skills
Equipment needed:	Disposable needles and blood/urine collection kits; highly sensitive blood and urine testing equipment
Home business potential:	Not likely
Staff required:	Two or three lab technicians and one administrator
Hidden costs:	Retesting at no charge if first-time results are not conclusive

LOWDOWN:
Drugs and alcohol cost U.S. companies millions of dollars each year in accidents and mistakes. Therefore, as a preventive measure, it makes incredibly good sense for companies to require job applicants and current employees to participate in random drug testing. As a drug testing service, you would conduct the tests on-site, then provide corporations with the results they could use to make hiring decisions and prevent costly disasters from occurring. You would travel to the client company site to collect and label blood and urine specimens, then return them to your lab for assessment to determine whether the individuals tested show any traces of drugs or alcohol in their systems.

STARTUP:
Equipment and office space, in addition to personnel overhead, put your startup costs at a minimum of $50,000. You'll also need to promote your services in industry newsletters and business newspapers—so add another $2,000–$3,000 at least to cover six months' worth of advertising.

BOTTOM LINE ADVICE:
A drug testing service can be a great business for someone who is methodical, well-organized, and enjoys working independently without a great deal of supervision. The money's not bad, either. If you like precise, technical work, this is the perfect opportunity to do something you enjoy. On the downside, precise results will always be expected of you, and you simply cannot afford to make mistakes. Jobs and people's reputations—including your own—are on the line. Be prepared to retest at no additional charge if first-time results are inconclusive.

DRY CLEANING SERVICE

Startup cost:	$75,000–$125,000
Potential earnings:	$45,000–$60,000
Typical fees:	Many charge on a per-pound basis ($5 per pound in some areas); otherwise, fees are extremely varied depending on the item being cleaned
Advertising:	Yellow Pages, location, coupon books, community newspapers, billboards
Qualifications:	Training in use and care of dry cleaning equipment, basic business and marketing skills
Equipment needed:	Dry cleaning equipment and supplies
Home business potential:	No
Staff required:	Yes (to cover many shifts)
Hidden costs:	Insurance, equipment maintenance, workers' compensation

LOWDOWN:

Lately, the resurgence of natural fabrics like wool, silk, and linen, combined with increases in the number of women in the workplace, has sparked a boom in the dry cleaning business. Dual-income households don't have the time to care for fine fabrics at home, and certain items, such as bulky draperies and comforters, are just too large for most residential-sized washers and dryers. Your dry cleaning business provides a practical service that nearly anyone in your community can use. The bad news is there's a lot of competition out there, so your challenge is to set yourself apart from the other dry cleaners and laundry services in your immediate area. Think creatively—run regular specials (this is, after all, a price-driven business) and throw in an unusual promotion from time to time (trip giveaways are always good). Running a dry cleaners is not what you'd call a glamorous job. You'll spend your days inside a hot building, getting spots out of other people's dirty clothes, but, if you don't mind the steam and the sweat, you could stand to make a pretty healthy profit in this business.

STARTUP:

Startup costs will be high because you need a lot of equipment just to launch this business; expect to spend $75,000–$125,000 to cover everything from the cash register on the front counter to ironing presses and steamers. Set your advertising budget at around $10,000 for your first year to cover coupon specials, a Yellow Pages listing, and small ads in community newspapers. Expect to earn $45,000–$60,000 per year.

BOTTOM LINE ADVICE:

Dry cleaning is hot, hard work, and the hours are long, especially in the beginning, when you are learning the job and have a limited staff. You have to be organized in this business and you must deliver on your promises; if you tell a customer his suit will be ready by five, then fail to meet your deadline, he'll take his business somewhere else next time around. But if you can stand the heat and the stress of constant deadlines, dry cleaning can be a good business. Keep in mind, however, that you'll need to hold your costs down and promote heavily at all times in order to consistently make a profit.

EARTHQUAKE PRODUCTS/SERVICES

Startup cost:	$75,000–$150,000
Potential earnings:	$45,000–$85,000
Typical fees:	Varied according to product or service; from $500 for a consultation to several thousand for earthquake-sensitive equipment
Advertising:	Yellow Pages, ads in business publications, referrals, offering expert opinions/interviews to the media, Web site
Qualifications:	Degree in seismology or environmental geography
Equipment needed:	Inventory of earthquake sensors and related seismographic products; delivery van equipped with tools/maintenance equipment; basic office setup (computer, printer, fax, high-speed Internet access, and phone system); cell phone for field work
Home business potential:	Possibly (although not typically)
Staff required:	No
Hidden costs:	Equipment upgrade/maintenance, travel expenses for continuing study in seismology (you'll want to travel to earthquake sites, and your clients probably won't cover those expenses)

LOWDOWN:

At any given time, seismic activity is taking place beneath the surface of the earth somewhere in the United States. Although most people associate earthquakes with California, tremors have, in fact, occurred in the Midwest and along the East Coast, which bodes well for this business no matter where you are located. As a supplier of earthquake products and services, you'll be selling extremely sensitive earthquake-detecting instruments and seismographs—but you'll also be offering your expertise in earthquake readiness and protection. You'll evaluate buildings for their ability to withstand major earthquakes, and assign them a rating for insurance or related purposes. In addition, you may be educating consumers on how to prepare for earthquakes and protect themselves and their property in the event that one occurs in their area. Position yourself as an earthquake expert—get your name out in the marketplace and offer your expertise to the media on a regular basis so that they'll call on you when the next tremor happens.

STARTUP:

Since so much of your equipment is highly specialized and of a delicate nature, you'll need to build up a sensible inventory and store it in a secure environment; expect to spend at least $75,000–$150,000 on stock and storage space, along with a delivery/maintenance vehicle and your marketing materials. That sounds like a big chunk of change just to get started in this business, until you consider that you can look forward to an income potential of $45,000–$85,000 or more per year just for positioning yourself as the go-to expert for earthquake equipment and advice.

BOTTOM LINE ADVICE:

You're selling folks on peace of mind, by trying to turn a violent natural event into something somewhat less threatening. Be sensitive to the fact that you're providing products that help people prepare for the worst, which is not always a particularly happy business to be in. Your challenge is to admirably walk the fine line between fear-mongering and sound common sense preparation.

FIBER OPTIC TRANSMISSION SYSTEMS

Startup cost:	$800,000–$1.5 million
Potential earnings:	$100,000–$1 million+
Typical fees:	$1,500–$5,000 per fiber optic network, per month
Advertising:	Direct mail to potential clients (such as long-distance telephone carriers), networking and referrals
Qualifications:	Fiber optics experience and access to cable burial sites
Equipment needed:	Heavy-duty cable, tools, fiber optic technology, computer, printer, fax, Internet access, copier, cell phone
Home business potential:	No
Staff required:	Yes
Hidden costs:	Insurance, workers' compensation, subcontracting fees, related maintenance

LOWDOWN:

Most of the nation's largest long-distance services depend on fiber optics to carry their customers' voices clearly across the country and around the entire world—so why shouldn't this be an area ripe for business opportunity? Keep in mind, however, that because fiber optics is so highly specialized only those with experience in this technology are likely to succeed in this business. That being said, your fiber optics transmission service will provide a near-perfect means for transmittal and receipt of electronic and voice messages for telephone carriers and related communications businesses—primarily by transmitting impulses through extremely sensitive fiber optic cable. Your own background should include telecommunications experience and sales ability; you need a combination of up-to-the-minute technical knowledge and good old-fashioned sales skills to effectively promote your company's services to large players in the communications field. Be prepared to spend a lot of long hours supervising the initial installation of the fiber optics networks you sell; rather than oversee the jobs yourself, you may opt to subcontract much of this work to other specialists in the field.

STARTUP:

Startup costs in this industry run quite high (in the $800,000–$1.5 million range), mainly because the equipment and related accouterments are of an intricate, complex nature, and they need to be placed in the most conducive environments possible (usually under water). You'll pay a pretty penny for your "burial" sites, in addition to the regular maintenance that will be required to keep them operating at optimum levels. Keep in mind, too, that you'll have plenty of staff overhead, particularly if you do not choose to subcontract your installation work. Still, this business could easily make you a millionaire, if you know the ropes in terms of promoting your services over those of your competitors.

BOTTOM LINE ADVICE:

Remember that fiber optic cables are buried beneath the ocean floor—and that sharks and other underwater predators have been known to cut through the cables with their teeth. New and stronger materials are now available to prevent such mishaps, so be sure to investigate all of your options thoroughly. In order to stay profitable, your systems need to remain operational.

FITNESS RENTAL EQUIPMENT

Startup cost:	$50,000–$150,000
Potential earnings:	$20,000–$60,000
Typical fees:	$15–$25 per piece, per month, plus delivery charges and security deposit
Advertising:	Direct mail, Yellow Pages, newspaper ads in the sports section
Qualifications:	Basic business and marketing skills; knowledge of fitness equipment and the ability to teach others how to use it
Equipment needed:	Various exercise equipment (stair steppers, ellipticals, treadmills, weight machines, stationary bikes)
Home business potential:	Yes, but you'll need somewhere to store the equipment that's not out on loan
Staff required:	No
Hidden costs:	Insurance protection against theft or damaged equipment

LOWDOWN:

The fitness craze is on—and you can capitalize on it if you are knowledgeable about the types of equipment that are popular, safe, and produce results. If you know your stair-steppers from your treadmills and ellipticals, and can teach others how to use this equipment, you can not only market your rental business but also tack on lessons for a small additional fee. Depending on what you buy and how much of it you are able to rent, it should take you at least a year to break even on your investment. You need to sell your customers on service and the convenience of using your equipment in the privacy of their own home vs. having to travel to a health club.

STARTUP:

Your initial investment of $50,000–$150,000 might seem high compared to first-year earnings. However, keep in mind that you will need to start your business with at least four to five different types of equipment and have at least two of each type so that you always have something in stock to rent. You will want to purchase the best equipment on the market; yes, it will cost a little more, but it's likely to last longer too. Surf the Web and research different options to find the equipment you need at wholesale prices. Rent your equipment by the week or month; figure on charges of about $15–$25 per piece, per month. Realistically, you probably cannot charge much more because your chief competition, namely health clubs, charge just a few dollars more for monthly membership fees.

BOTTOM LINE ADVICE:

This business might be slow getting off the ground—so be persistent. Emphasize the fact that delivery is included in the rental contract and that customers can exercise at their convenience, in private, without having to leave their homes. Go for long-term contracts, if you can (use the money to acquire more machines), and ask for referrals. The more you get the word out, the more customers you'll have.

FRAMING SERVICE

Startup costs:	$40,000–$60,000
Potential earnings:	$35,000–$50,000
Typical fees:	$15–$25 per hour for custom work plus materials; materials only for frame-it-yourself
Advertising:	Yellow Pages, local newspapers
Qualifications:	Understanding of retail business operations, framing skills, ability to train staff and teach customers
Equipment needed:	Mat and glass cutters, knives, wood for framing, cash register, work area and retail space
Home business potential:	No
Staff required:	Yes
Hidden costs:	Insurance and materials costs

LOWDOWN:

The framing business is a lucrative one because many people buy unframed posters, prints, and other artwork. They either want to frame the pieces themselves, or, if they don't have the time or patience to frame, turn the work over to a custom framer. You can appeal to both market segments—the 60 percent who are frame-it-yourselfers, and the remaining 40 percent who will look to you for custom framing. A framing service can prosper just about anywhere, but you'll do especially well in communities that are home to a thriving colony of artists and/or art enthusiasts. Your customers will be everyone from the artists, photographers, and calligraphers themselves to art collectors, home decorators, needlecrafters, and people simply wanting to hang their diplomas, wedding and baptismal certificates, and professional or personal recognitions. To build visibility, consider offering framing classes through your local community college or adult education program, or sponsor an art contest and frame the winning entries.

STARTUP:

You'll spend at least $40,000 launching a frame shop, primarily because you'll need a shop with a display room, plenty of storage space, and a work area with sufficient lighting. Look for rental space near an art gallery. Your charges will vary according to size and style of frame.

BOTTOM LINE ADVICE:

Be mindful that this is a retail establishment, so take into consideration the size of the shop, location, and rent. Many framing shops sell ready-made frames and mats as well as posters and prints of well-known works of art to supplement the framing business.

FRANCHISEE

Startup cost:	$40,000–$100,000+, depending on the type of business
Potential earnings:	$10,000–$50,000+
Typical fees:	Depends on size and type of business
Advertising:	Newspapers, brochures, direct mail, location
Qualifications:	Ability to produce and/or sell the service or product; basic business and marketing skills
Equipment needed:	Depends on the product or service
Home business potential:	Possibly; some franchises can be started from home
Staff required:	Depends on the product or service
Hidden costs:	Depends on the franchise. Expect to incur some legal costs to examine the contracts. It is important to fully explore the specific opportunity you're considering in order to thoroughly understand your startup expenses and liabilities.

LOWDOWN:

Franchise businesses, especially in the food category, are very popular in the United States. The instant name recognition that comes with a franchise gives your business a powerful boost. You don't have to tell people what you sell, the name says it all; your marketing is off to a good start without so much as a single penny spent on advertising. In the food business especially, you have a wide variety of franchises from which to choose: anything from cookie shops to ice cream parlors to full-service restaurants. Franchisees have an edge over many first-time business-owners because the mistakes have already been made and corrected; a large part of what a franchisee purchases is the experience others have had before him or her. That's not to say that you should jump into a franchise without any preparation. It is very important that you research the company thoroughly before signing on the dotted line. Make sure you understand what, if any, marketing, purchasing, and other assistance you will be entitled to as a franchisee. And make sure that the geographic area you have settled on for your business is one that can support it.

STARTUP:

The cost of becoming a franchisee varies considerably depending on the type of business you choose. Some enterprises have modest startup requirements; others are quite expensive. Marketing and legal fees can run as much as $10,000 or more, depending, again, on the product and the structure of the franchise offer.

BOTTOM LINE ADVICE:

One concern about franchises: the legal ramifications. It can be a tedious job plowing through all the legal issues surrounding your franchise, but you must do your homework; read all documents concerning the business thoroughly—and seek legal counsel before signing anything. If your franchise involves food in any form, you must also consider any applicable health regulations in your area. Owning and operating a franchise business can be wonderful in many ways—the support of the franchise company is invaluable in getting started. But you'll still have to put in the long hours and hard work that are required for starting any new business—and you may at times feel restricted by some of the guidelines/requirements of your franchise.

FREELANCE TV PRODUCER

Startup cost:	$75,000+
Potential earnings:	$50,000–$150,000+
Typical fees:	Vary per project; the bigger your reputation, the bigger the bucks you can command
Advertising:	Industry trade publications, word of mouth; the best advertising is to produce one great TV show
Qualifications:	Degree/experience in television production; ability to write grants, excellent marketing and selling skills, "vision" with regard to what makes great TV
Equipment needed:	Computer, printer, Internet access, fax, phone
Home business potential:	Yes
Staff required:	No
Hidden costs:	Insurance, union fees, travel and entertainment expenses

LOWDOWN:

As a freelance TV producer, you are responsible for every phase of a program's production—including raising the capital to create the program in the first place. Affiliate yourself early on with casting directors, talent agencies, and writers (contact the Screenwriters Guild for the names of script writers). Pass your card along to anyone you meet in the industry, and work hard to build a solid stable of projects instead of focusing on only one. There's a good reason to spread your interests across several projects at a time: Namely, your chances of actually selling something to a studio or network greatly increase with the number of projects you have available at any given time. You'll need to find good scripts, hire everyone from actors to pages, and know what goes on in the actual pre- and postproduction stages. Experience in all phases of the television industry is essential to success in this business; hopefully, you've worked your way up from the ground floor just to get to this position of power and tremendous responsibility. In addition, you'll need good marketing and sales skills.

STARTUP:

If your program strikes the right chord with the powers that be, a studio will back you in your endeavor. If not, brush up on your grantwriting skills, lean on your rich friends, and get ready to empty your savings account. Considering that even modest productions cost between $75,000 and $300,000 to produce, it's going to take every penny you can muster to accumulate the capital you need to get your show off the ground. And even after you've raised your capital, you have to wisely decide how to spend it; of course, you won't forget to factor your own salary into your budget plan, right? Your fee to produce a television show will range from $45,000–$150,000+.

BOTTOM LINE ADVICE:

This profession requires you to assume a tremendous amount of personal responsibility. If the show flops, you flop. If it's a hit, you're the next up-and-coming producer. Freelance TV production is a hard way to make a living, moving from one project to the next and never really knowing which one might hit, but, if you're up to the challenge and don't mind a few disappointments, you stand to make a decent living, maybe even big bucks.

FUNERAL HOME

Startup cost:	$100,000
Potential earnings:	$100,000 or more
Typical fees:	Usually a flat fee of $3,000–$10,000
Advertising:	Billboards, advertisements in program books for fundraising events, newspapers, local magazines
Qualifications:	Mortuary training and experience; licensing
Equipment needed:	Mortuary equipment, fleet of vehicles including a hearse and at least one limousine, "home" with suitably furnished rooms for services and meeting with families, basic business office setup, marketing materials
Home business potential:	No
Staff required:	Yes
Hidden costs:	Utility costs, donations to community charities, upkeep of facilities

LOWDOWN:

Establishing a funeral home is a delicate project. You will need to plan carefully for the market you intend to serve. The contemporary focus on respect, care, and counseling may allow you to create an enterprise that stands apart from the existing funeral homes in your area, some of which may have dubious reputations or have not kept up their premises. In today's fragmented culture, many people live far from family and friends. When a death occurs, they may need more support and guidance than funeral homes have traditionally provided. You can offer planning, grief counseling, and a range of support services that may extend over a period of time well beyond the memorial service and burial in order to ease the inevitable feelings of loss. Finding a way to present your fees and payment plans in a sensitive yet clearly understandable manner will also help set your business apart as different from, and even better than, the competition.

STARTUP:

Startup costs are clearly quite high relative to the expenses of beginning other, more "typical" small businesses; plan on spending no less than $100,000 for a suitable building and furnishings, mortuary equipment, a fleet of vehicles, and a basic office setup. But consider that you are establishing an enterprise which will be woven into the fabric of the community you serve, and, since many funeral homes become family businesses, possibly passed down to future generations. Once your business becomes established, you should be able to make close to $100,000 per year.

BOTTOM LINE ADVICE:

Every community has the need for funeral homes and mortuary services, but you must be prepared to overcome many negative assumptions, fears, and prejudices as you develop your clientele. Community standards will define, to some extent, the way you can express your message about the positive differences you offer. In all cases, your claims must be supported by reality. It's one thing to say, "We care," and quite another to actually show it. Your personal involvement in community organizations, charitable activities, service to the elderly, and/or similar philanthropic actions will go a long way toward building your credibility.

GEOLOGIC DRILLING SERVICE

Startup cost:	$45,000 or more
Potential earnings:	$35,000–$60,000
Typical fees:	Varied according to length of job; $600–$1,000 is an average daily rate
Advertising:	Networking and referrals, partnerships with related businesses, advertising in trade periodicals
Qualifications:	Extensive experience, knowledge of drilling equipment operation, ability to read geological survey maps and interpret field reports
Equipment needed:	Specialized drilling equipment, heavy truck(s)
Home business potential:	No
Staff required:	Yes
Hidden costs:	Insurance, equipment maintenance and replacement, travel costs to distant locations, workers' compensation and salaries

LOWDOWN:

Oil and gas companies are constantly on the lookout for dependable drilling services to help them locate energy sources. They need extensive wells in order to have steady, regular supplies of oil and gas. Once a potential site is located, you will be called in to drill and set up the well. Your experience and skills will enable you to carry out the complex drilling process in a cost-effective and productive manner. Each well is different, and you will need a sophisticated understanding of geologic formations and the environment to make a success of this heavy-equipment enterprise. Typically, you will operate as a subcontractor on a larger project; in addition to the actual drilling, your responsibilities may include site identification and the management of a well's production. Other types of drilling could provide add-on or subspecialty income.

STARTUP:

Drilling for oil and gas requires a lot of up-front capital, and the payoff may be slow in coming; right from the start, you'll need to be vigilant about your cash flow management. Even at a billing rate of $1,000 per day, it will take considerable time for you to earn a sizable return on your investment.

BOTTOM LINE ADVICE:

Forming relationships with businesses that use your drilling services will be vital to your startup and long-term survival. Networking and referrals will be your main marketing avenues. Once you have an established customer base, the word will get around about your services and you will likely receive ongoing business. Clearly, travel will be necessary as it is unlikely that all your well sites will be grouped together in a single area. You'll require a highly skilled crew, so expect to pay them well. Drilling can be hard, dirty work, but it has its satisfactions, too. You'll be in close contact with the earth, and working outdoors for the better half of each business day.

GROUND WATER ASSESSMENT

Startup cost:	$40,000–$65,000
Potential earnings:	$40,000–$60,000
Typical fees:	$350+ per job
Advertising:	Referrals, trade association memberships, networking, business relationships with related services
Qualifications:	Extensive experience in ground water assessment, scientific background in water quality testing, knowledge of heavy equipment operation, report-writing skills
Equipment needed:	Trenching and/or drilling equipment, truck, computer, printer, Internet access, fax, cell phone; laboratory equipment if you do your own testing
Home business potential:	Yes
Staff required:	Possibly
Hidden costs:	Equipment maintenance, lab fees, insurance

LOWDOWN:

Water constantly flows through the "solid" ground under our feet. It's America's most valuable natural resource; we can't live without it. And with a population of more than 260 million people who need water daily, providing an acceptable water quality is no longer simply an option, it's vital to our survival. Pollution is a growing problem all across the United States, and your ground water assessment service can highlight the location of water in addition to the nature of any contamination it may contain. Even if most of the houses in an area are linked to a municipal water treatment facility, tracing the purity of the ground water is essential—especially in areas where new building is a critical facet of the local economy.

STARTUP:

The level of the water table in a given area will define the type of equipment you'll need to reach and sample the ground water. What you'd need to establish your assessment business in Minnesota where the water table is high, for example, would be entirely different from what you'll need in a more arid landscape like New Mexico. In either place, however, you'll need your own lab or the ability to subcontract lab services, and you must have the basic office equipment to generate and finalize a professional-looking report. Expect to spend anywhere from $30,000 on equipment; bill your services at a minimum of $350 per job.

BOTTOM LINE ADVICE:

Ground water assessment is a logical career for the kind of person who'd rather not vegetate behind a desk for the rest of his or her life. If you love the outdoors and have a lively interest in what lies beneath the earth's surface, plus the relevant scientific background, you're a perfect candidate for this business. And considering the necessity of what you'll be up to, you shouldn't have any trouble raising the necessary capital. Keep in mind, however, that your initial cash outlay will be quite high and it may take you several years to establish your name and reputation for accurate, on-time work. Building a customer base will be challenging, and in northern states, you'll be limited by seasonal considerations.

HEALTH CLUB

Startup cost:	$50,000–$100,000+
Potential earnings:	$40,000– $85,000
Typical fees:	$300–$1,000 per membership
Advertising:	Word of mouth, bulletin boards, newspaper/TV ads, coupon books and mailings that offer corporate discounts, location
Qualifications:	Degree and/or background in fitness, recreation management, or related field
Equipment needed:	State-of-the-art exercise equipment, whirlpool/sauna/steam room/ pool (optional), location
Home business potential:	No
Staff required:	Yes
Hidden costs:	Utilities, equipment updates and maintenance; markup on new equipment can be quite high, so shop around for best deals

LOWDOWN:

Today, with services like on-site day care, massage therapy, personal training, and well-ness instruction, health clubs are for every age, interest, and fitness level. Whatever facili-ties and services you decide to offer, you'll face some interesting challenges and plenty of competition. You'll need more than just an interest in fitness; you'll need manage-ment experience, too, in order to direct the growth of your club and hire a competent staff (which can range from 10 to 50 people, depending on the size of your club). The good thing is, you don't have to hire everyone right away. You can open with a small staff of part-timers—college students who can get certified to teach aerobics and other group activities. Ask around to see what kinds of equipment and services people want most in a health club; make sure you meet all municipal and state requirements and that you secure any necessary certificates well before opening day.

STARTUP:

Startup for a health club is expensive, mostly because you need so much space to accom-modate bulky exercise equipment, areas for aerobics instruction, and men's and women's locker rooms, each with plenty of showers. You can count on spending at least$25,000 on equipment alone (and that's with just a few starting pieces—imagine a complete room full of treadmills, stationary bikes, stair steppers, and ellipticals at about $1,000 each. Add another $25,000–$30,000 minimum if you intend to have a whirlpool, steam room, sauna, and/or swimming pool. And don't forget parking; you'll need plenty of space so it's easy in/ easy out for your members, especially during those peak periods immediately before and after work. By the time you add in salaries, advertising/promotional costs, and liability insur-ance, you're looking at an investment of well over $100,000 just to get up and running— but you'll recoup your costs quickly if you price your rates competitively and market well.

BOTTOM LINE ADVICE:

You'll need to come up with innovative ways to set your club apart from the large health club chains—and offer people a real incentive for coming to your facility (discounts, or special services such as on-site day care, etc.).

HOME HEALTH CARE SERVICE

Startup cost:	$40,000–$150,000 (depending on size and location)
Potential earnings:	$50,000–$100,000
Typical fees:	$40–$50 per hour
Advertising:	Newspapers (especially those geared toward seniors), television, networking with hospitals and geriatric services providers, direct mail
Qualifications:	Training and experience in health care administration and/or direct patient care (a nursing degree is desirable); organizational and personnel management skills; basic business and marketing abilities; knowledge of medical billing and insurance claims filing procedures
Equipment needed:	Basic office setup, including computer, billing and bookkeeping software, Internet access, printer, copier, fax, and phone; pagers and/or cell phones
Home business potential:	Yes
Staff required:	Yes (usually 20 to 30 on-call RNs or LPNs, plus two to three administrative assistants to handle insurance claims and billing)
Hidden costs:	Liability insurance

LOWDOWN:

Home health care is one of today's fastest growing business opportunities for three reasons: People don't want to stay in the hospital any longer than they have to, insurance companies don't want to pay to keep them there, and, thanks to recent medical advances, quicker release is possible after most surgeries and illnesses. By caring for patients who can be treated at home with medications and followup, you could offer a caring, human touch to an otherwise impersonal health care industry. In most instances, home health care not only offers more comfort for the patient, it's usually more cost effective too. But aside from the financial benefits, you can offer peace of mind, particularly for many working couples who need the services of a trained professional to care for an elderly parent.

STARTUP:

You'll need to secure an office and maintain a staff of about 20 to 30 on-call nursing professionals who can provide hands-on care for your clients; expect to spend a minimum of $20,000 on these two items alone. You'll also need to advertise in high-profile places (such as large metropolitan newspapers, possibly even local television), so add in another $15,000 for your advertising budget. To help keep your advertising costs under control, try placing the bulk of your ads in the less-pricey weeklies and newsletters aimed specifically at senior citizens. Your biggest expense, however, will be for the liability insurance you must carry. Every state has its required minimum amount of coverage; be sure you check the prices in your location as you put together your business plan for launching a home health care service.

BOTTOM LINE ADVICE:

As our population ages and insurance companies require shorter hospital stays, home health care services represent the wave of the future in medical care. Make sure, in addition to your own background as a health care provider that you also have a clear business sense and the ability to manage several people simultaneously. Personnel management and cost control can easily overwhelm you if you're not paying attention.

INDOOR PLAYSPACE

Startup cost:	$50,000–$150,000
Potential earnings:	$50,000–$75,000
Typical fees:	$8–$10 per person; you can make more money by adding concessions
Advertising:	Newspapers, magazines, Yellow Pages, parents' groups
Qualifications:	Background in recreation management, basic business and marketing skills, certification in first aid and pediatric CPR
Equipment needed:	Indoor playground equipment (i.e., Junglegym, sliding boards, and places to swing and jump); balls, jump ropes, hula hoops, and other active toys
Home business potential:	No
Staff required:	Yes
Hidden costs:	Liability insurance, employee overhead, equipment acquisition and maintenance

LOWDOWN:

Operating an indoor playspace for children can be extremely rewarding, both personally and financially. First, there's the joy of seeing laughing kids chasing each other and just having an all-around great time; second, there's the knowledge that their parents are paying you for the experience. High-profile success stories like the Discovery Zone have got a lot of people thinking that indoor centers for kids aren't just child's play; they can be fun to own and downright profitable, too. To be successful in this venture, you'll need to love kids, first and foremost, but a background in recreation management would be a big help, too.

STARTUP:

Since your initial investment is considerably high ($50,000–$150,000) for adequate space and playground equipment, and because, for the sake of safety and adequate adult-child ratios, you'll need to have a staff of 10 to 20 employees, it may take a while to roll in the profits. However, there is such a critical need for children's recreation facilities that are clean and safe (and possibly even offer extras like birthday party services), your chances of success may be greater than you can imagine. At $8–$10 a head, your earnings could become quite considerable after your company's first few years in business.

BOTTOM LINE ADVICE:

There's nothing cuter than a group of kids having a ball—and several Kodak moments are likely to occur at your facility. However, you're up against a lot of competition, and not just from other indoor playgrounds, but from anything that draws the attentions of young ones—like DVDs and computer games. Your challenge is to come up with inno-vative ways to tear them away from the television and want to play inside with you.

INSTANT SIGNS

Startup cost:	$65,000–$100,000 (depending on whether you buy into a franchise)
Potential earnings:	$25,000–$50,000
Typical fees:	$15–$150 per sign (depending on size and type)
Advertising:	Yellow Pages, coupon books, and signs of your own (including a storefront)
Qualifications:	Basic business and marketing skills, creativity, short-term training on sign-making equipment
Equipment needed:	Computer with specialized software, printer, color foils, specialty paper/sign materials
Home business potential:	Not typically
Staff required:	Not at first
Hidden costs:	Insurance, advertising

LOWDOWN:

From garage sales to small businesses, lots of folks need good (and inexpensively produced) signs that meet their particular needs. Whether it's a spur-of-the-moment mom-and-pop flea market or a permanent car repair service, your customers need to draw in the customers and they'll pay decently for you to help them do just that. One customer might need a magnetized sign for his company vehicle, another wants a banner announcing a special sale or promotion. Whatever the need, you'll provide the sign. You'll have an easier time producing the goods if you have previous experience in this field or a backing franchise operation with training and 24-hour support. If you can get financing from the franchise itself, do it. You can then rest your laurels on that company's corporate history, rather than trying to build a reputation from scratch—and that buys you the kind of credibility you'll need to compete. However, if you don't have the funding necessary to franchise, consider joining the Better Business Bureau, chamber of commerce, or similar organization to get the credibility boost you'll need to get off the ground.

STARTUP:

You'll need to purchase a computer system with specialized software that allows you to produce professional-looking signs; expect to spend at least $65,000 on your hardware and software, retail space, and advertising budget. Your charges will vary greatly ($15–$150) according to the size and type of sign you're creating, but, once you're up and running, you can expect an annual income of $25,000–$50,000.

BOTTOM LINE ADVICE:

The signs all point to profit—if you're reputable and create a high-quality product for your customers. Consider offering packages of signs for various needs (such as garage sales or a special promotion value pack) to price your services more attractively.

KEY CONTROL SYSTEMS
MANUFACTURER/DISTRIBUTOR

Startup cost:	$50,000–$100,000
Potential earnings:	$40,000–$120,000
Typical fees:	Varied according to product; can be as low as $125 for small units and as high as $1,000 for a key control station to serve a large manufacturing facility
Advertising:	Business/trade publications, Yellow Pages, direct mail
Qualifications:	Manufacturing and sales background; basic business and marketing skills
Equipment needed:	Sheet metal, key tags, and small hardware; adequate space for production; computer, printer, phone, fax, copier
Home business potential:	Not typically
Staff required:	Yes (for assembly, unless you subcontract)
Hidden costs:	Insurance, workers' compensation, fluctuating materials costs

LOWDOWN:

How many times have you been locked out of your home or office—and can't remember where you hid that extra key? It happens every day in the work world; from hotels/motels to large manufacturing facilities, people simply misplace keys, or lose them altogether. One of the best ways to handle situations involving lost or misplaced keys is to have a centralized location for the spares. As a key control system manufacturer/distributor, you can provide the items to accomplish just that—from small key hooks that clip onto a door to large key cabinets with several compartments. You develop a professional-looking catalog of your products, then advertise in industry publications to assess your market size and sales potentials within specified territories. You follow up with direct mail or independent sales representatives who stay in tune with your customers' needs. Like many manufacturing businesses, yours is fairly straightforward; you can quickly teach your production staff how to assemble product, or you can save some time by subcontracting the work to a small job shop.

STARTUP:

You'll need at least $50,000—and perhaps even as much as $100,000—to secure a suitable inventory of sheet metal and other raw materials, and put together a basic office setup (computer, printer, and customer tracking, accounting and/or inventory control software). At $125–$1,000 or more for a key control system, you can expect to earn anywhere from $40,000–$120,000 per year. Your potential market is nationwide, so expect at some point to employ or retain outside sales help beyond your immediate geographic area.

BOTTOM LINE ADVICE:

You're providing a much-needed service, and yet, up against the increasingly popular electronic key card systems, you stand the chance of becoming obsolete. Sell your customers on the benefits of using your products because they'll never fail in an electrical outage, or beat the opposition at its own game by adding electronic key cards to your product line.

LEAK-DETECTION SERVICE

Startup cost:	$50,000–$100,000
Potential earnings:	$75,000–$250,000
Typical fees:	$200–$300 for residential inspections; several thousand for industrial sites
Advertising:	Business-to-business advertising, networking, referrals
Qualifications:	Leak detection training, ability to work with and maintain various types of leak detection equipment, self-marketing skills
Equipment needed:	Depends on type of leak; detecting carbon dioxide leaks requires one type of equipment, water seepage another
Home business potential:	Yes
Staff required:	No
Hidden costs:	Insurance, equipment repair and updates

LOWDOWN:

Leak detection is a growing business all across the country. For homeowners, there's nothing more annoying than a leak you know is there, but the source of which you just can't find. Building codes require inspections before a roof is repaired, and the need to keep costs down makes detection of leaks ever more important. Hurricanes and earthquakes have produced a great deal of business for leak detectors, and in many areas the importance of conserving fresh water gives another boost. Gas leaks must be contained before they damage the environment or endanger lives; even swimming pool leaks can cause serious trouble unless they're detected early and repaired. Leak detectors work closely with plumbers, maintenance supervisors, and others to pinpoint the problem; some take the process one step further by carrying out the needed repairs. Certain types of leak detection require strength and skill with various pieces of machinery, including carbon dioxide detection equipment, while others use computers to pinpoint the problem.

STARTUP:

The training and equipment necessary for leak detection can be quite expensive, but once you become proficient you can expect a good return on your investment. You'll need to advertise in the Yellow Pages, so expect to spend at least $1,000 annually on that alone. You can bill at the rate of $200–$300 for residential leak inspections; leak detection at industrial sites, which takes much longer, may run into the thousands of dollars.

BOTTOM LINE ADVICE:

Leak detection is a big, exciting business that could potentially involve you in many major projects. You'll be providing a much-needed service and can expect to see your profits grow as you become established and develop working relationships. The downside can be having to work under constant pressure; leaks don't always happen at the most convenient times and they must usually be repaired immediately. Leaks tend to happen in waves—in the aftermath of a natural disaster, for example—so you may find yourself too busy at times, and not busy enough at others; try to fill the slack times with maintenance work. Leak detection can be a physically demanding job and, depending on what's leaking and where, you could easily find yourself in some hazardous environments.

MACHINERY REBUILDING/REPAIR

Startup cost:	$50,000–$150,000+
Potential earnings:	$100,000+
Typical fees:	Varied according to project; ranging from $500 to several thousand
Advertising:	Business directories, direct mail, Yellow Pages, word of mouth
Qualifications:	Mechanical aptitude and an understanding of manufacturing equipment
Equipment needed:	Repair equipment pertaining to your area of specialty; welding equipment is widely needed
Home business potential:	No
Staff required:	Yes
Hidden costs:	Insurance (accidental damage), long payback periods

LOWDOWN:

Serious downtime, not to mention financial loss, can result when a piece of machinery breaks down in a manufacturing plant. That's why it's so critical for a manufacturer to be tied into a service such as yours; when something goes wrong, you can work on-site or have the equipment moved to your own facility for speedy repair. It's a mistake to try and be a jack-of-all-trades in this business; attempting to repair everything for everybody could wind up costing you your reputation. For best results, choose instead to focus on an area of expertise; for instance, if you know a lot about robotics, make that your specialty. You'll need mechanical ability, a technical mind, and manufacturing experience to be able to talk the same language as your clients and convince them that you're the right one for the job. This is not a fiercely competitive field, so you should have little trouble finding work if you're connected and produce quick results for your clients. Your biggest challenge may be that you're forced to grow too quickly in order to meet the needs of your clients, who experience machinery downtime much more frequently than they like to admit.

STARTUP:

You'll need sufficient capital to buy your own repair equipment; what you buy will depend upon your area of specialty, but expect to spend $50,000–$150,000 or more. Each individual job will bring a different fee, but you could easily make $100,000+ per year; don't forget to tack on additional fees for quick turnaround and emergency calls. Your clients need to get up and running quickly and they need your expertise to do it. Don't be afraid to charge what you're worth.

BOTTOM LINE ADVICE:

You're basically going to be on call 24/7, and you may need to work on the equipment at times when others are not using it (like in the middle of the night). That means you should expect to spend a lot of the wee hours of the morning making repairs; if emergency calls and odd hours don't bother you, you'll find this business a happy and profitable experience.

MAILBOX RENTAL SERVICE

Startup cost:	$50,000–$80,000
Potential earnings:	$35,000–$65,000
Typical fees:	$15 and up per month, depending on the size of the box
Advertising:	Yellow Pages, direct mail to home-based entrepreneurs, newspaper ads, radio spots
Qualifications:	Basic business and marketing skills; knowledge of postal regulations and shipping procedures
Equipment needed:	Mailboxes, scales, parcel packaging equipment, cash register, security system for after-hours; inventory of labels, tape, envelopes, boxes, and other shipping supplies for sale; consider installing a pay-per-copy photocopy machine
Home business potential:	No
Staff required:	Yes (could be part-time, to cover shifts)
Hidden costs:	Insurance, security (vandalism could be costly)

LOWDOWN:

Ours is an age of entrepreneurism and mailboxes are a booming business as a result. Home-based businesses, in particular, benefit from having your service, largely because they need to establish a professional-sounding address. Using your services, they get a street address and suite number (actually their mailbox number) for a monthly fee of as little as $15, depending on geographic location. The mailbox business is straightforward and easy to manage, especially for those who have even a limited retail background. With just some basic training in postal regulations, you can become quite knowledge-able in a short period of time, and downright competitive in four months or less. Your biggest competitor, of course, is the United States Postal Service. But in terms of the price, convenience, and customer service you're able to offer, it's really no contest.

STARTUP:

Your startup investment ($50,000–$80,000) will likely involve buying into an existing franchise, although you can go it alone if you are familiar with shipping and receiving procedures and have the ability to procure your own equipment. If you buy into a fran-chise, you'll get technical and managerial support as well as a procedures/operations manual that could solve most of your early startup problems. It's worth it to at least investigate a few franchises. If you choose an area close to students and home-based entrepreneurs, you'll likely earn $35,000–$65,000 per year.

BOTTOM LINE ADVICE:

You would be especially wise to locate your service in a busy shopping complex where there's plenty of parking and people are likely to come and go for other services; even though the rent will be higher than some other spots, your location can prove to be your most cost-effective means of advertising. You need visibility to succeed in this business and a busy shopping complex will provide it.

MANUFACTURER OF LICENSED PRODUCTS

Startup cost:	$50,000–$150,000 (more if you have extensive manufacturing facilities of your own)
Potential earnings:	$200,000–$500,000+
Typical fees:	25 to 30 percent of gross profit
Advertising:	Direct mail, referrals, Yellow Pages
Qualifications:	Manufacturing and/or sales background
Equipment needed:	Depends on product you're producing; computer, printer, fax, Internet access, phone
Home business potential:	Not likely
Staff required:	Yes (primarily production workers)
Hidden costs:	Workers' compensation, insurance, legal fees

LOWDOWN:

If you make the right connections, this can be an extremely lucrative field—after all, what kid doesn't want a Mickey Mouse sweatshirt or a Big Bird dinner plate? These products are all manufactured by someone, and it might as well be you if you've got the manufacturing and marketing ability to attract the attention of licensing agents. Any character can be incorporated into virtually any type of product, from dinnerware to clothing to food packaging. Your expertise will be to help the customer decide which type of product(s) might sell best, then to go about producing their product lines in the least expensive way possible (i.e., overseas manufacturing). You must recognize, however, that the license to produce products bearing the name or likeness of any character rests solely with the licensing corporation; you can't take it upon yourself to produce and sell any items beyond the number stated in your contract. This is serious business; legal action will result if you get caught exceeding the limits specified in your contracts.

STARTUP:

You'll need $50,000–$150,000 for some no-frills manufacturing equipment (lease, buy it used or, better yet, subcontract production) and basic office setup (computer, printer, fax, Internet access, and phone). You'll need to have a warehouse for receiving and shipping products, so be sure that your startup costs reflect the necessary overhead. If producing in-house, you'll need a production staff (and with it comes more overhead). Sounds like a lot to shell out up front, but since the demand for licensed products is high (many become highly collectible and hence, worth a good deal of money later on), you can expect an income potential of $100,000–$500,000.

BOTTOM LINE ADVICE:

The manufacture of licensed products can be an exceptionally competitive field. Be sure your quality is top-notch. If Disney doesn't like what it sees, the next job will go to one of your competitors, and your name could be mud in this industry. With such high overhead, you can't afford to produce a product on the cheap. You may save money up front, but you'll wind up paying for it later.

MANUFACTURER OF SELF-ADHESIVE PRINTED LABELS

Startup cost:	$40,000–$50,000
Potential earnings:	$25,000–$40,000
Typical fees:	$5–$10 per roll of 1,000 labels
Advertising:	Newspapers, Yellow Pages, direct mail, Web site
Qualifications:	Knowledge of printing, sales and marketing skills
Equipment needed:	High-speed, low-heat printer; adhesives applicator, computer, printer, fax, phone
Home business potential:	No
Staff required:	Possibly
Hidden costs:	Pickup and delivery time

LOWDOWN:

This business appeals to a very narrow market niche. Your marketing will be direct and uncomplicated, although demanding in terms of time and effort. Self-adhesive labels are used widely, and your ability to print them on time for a competitive price will be your major selling point. You will need to really enjoy selling in order to keep up your enthusiasm for the marketing process. Once you're established, you'll probably get a lot of repeat business, but the initial effort to compete with other types of printing companies for those important first sales will require time and dedication.

STARTUP:

This business is not a shoestring startup. The necessary equipment and supplies are not an option; you must make the investment up front, but you may be able to find used equipment in professional publications aimed specifically at your industry. Be prepared to spend at least $40,000 to get started, expect to earn around $25,000 your first year, and more each successive year.

BOTTOM LINE ADVICE:

To hold costs down, at least initially, our best advice is to either lease your equipment or subcontract the actual printing. This way, if your business doesn't take off in this rather competitive field, you'll be liquid enough to get out of it quickly—without losing your shirt on the acquisition of costly equipment you can no longer use.

MANUFACTURER/RETAIL ITEM

Startup cost:	$1 million–$5 million
Potential earnings:	$2–$15 million+
Typical fees:	Varied according to product
Advertising:	Business/trade publications, Web site
Qualifications:	Experience in design, purchasing, manufacturing, distribution, and marketing
Equipment needed:	Various types of machinery pertaining to mass production (specific type depends on the product you're manufacturing)
Home business potential:	No
Staff required:	Yes (possibly two to three shifts)
Hidden costs:	Insurance, workers' compensation, warehousing and costs relating to inventory, production and product design

LOWDOWN:

Whether you're a manufacturer of clothing, shoes, kitchen products, or tools, you'll need to have a solid product design and plenty of space for manufacturing facilities and ware-housing. That's why your startup is so costly—you'll need to produce a high enough volume of product to be able to see the kinds of profit margins you'd like, and all that product has to be made and stored somewhere. While manufacturing and warehous-ing can be accomplished in one location, it is becoming more common to subcontract manufacturing to an overseas facility and to store product in a warehouse here in the United States. Right or wrong, it is cheaper to have products made in countries such as Korea and China, which is why so many manufacturers elect to do so. Still, if your prod-uct line is small enough, and your volume limited at first, you could produce your own products to be offered at retail shops within a limited geographic area. Your market can be as vast as you'd like it to be, provided you have proper distribution channels and the opportunity for high visibility.

STARTUP:

You're going to need quite a bit of capital to get started in retail product manufacturing; figure on $1 to $5 million to cover your capital equipment expenses, employee-related costs, and manufacturing/warehousing facilities. If all goes well, you could make $15 mil-lion or more; if your product dries up before it saturates the market, however, your profits might be closer to $2 million, or even less.

BOTTOM LINE ADVICE:

It's a volatile market out there—you can never be absolutely sure what will sell well and what won't. It's not uncommon for a manufacturer to spend millions on a product line only to see it wind up on the 75 percent off rack a few months down the road. On the positive side, when things go well, they really go well (financially speaking, of course). If you produce a good product, and the market is receptive to it, you could become a multimillionaire.

MAP PUBLISHER/DISTRIBUTOR

Startup cost:	$40,000–$65,000
Potential earnings:	$40,000–$80,000+
Typical fees:	30 to 40 percent of list price
Advertising:	Direct mail/catalogs, sales calls, Web site
Qualifications:	Surveying and/or publishing experience
Equipment needed:	Computer with map making software program (often custom-designed), printer, fax, Internet access, and (sometimes) surveying equipment
Home business potential:	Yes
Staff required:	No (but you'll likely contract with sales representatives)
Hidden costs:	Insurance, costly mistakes

LOWDOWN:

We all use maps on a regular basis, but rarely do we think of the work that goes into producing them. True, a twenty-first-century mapmaker is basically just updating the work of previous mapmakers, but in today's volatile world where countries redefine their boundaries on what seems like an almost annual basis, it's important to be able to respond quickly for those who need to travel. You'll likely use older maps to generate the new ones, but you'll need to have some design software (possibly custom-produced to suit your needs) to change borders and town names where appropriate. This is very detail-oriented work; people are relying on what you produce to make decisions about their travel plans, so you must be accurate. Your income potential will be even greater if you can offer your maps as both hard copy and CD-ROM versions. Consider creating an online version, too, for those who would like to download their own copies for a small fee.

STARTUP:

You'll need at least $40,000 to get started in this business, mainly because you will need to purchase the high-end computer hardware and software necessary to create the kinds of maps that can be reproduced clearly and easily. In addition, if you're creating smaller maps from scratch for private clients, you'll either need your own surveying equipment or a subcontractor who can do the survey work for you. If you set up solid distribution channels, you could earn $40,000–$80,000 or more per year from the production and distribution of your maps.

BOTTOM LINE ADVICE:

The only problem with this type of business is that it is a fairly narrow niche; when there's work to be done, you'll be quite busy—but expect there to be some significant downtimes. Use the quieter moments to plan ahead or produce CD-ROM versions of your product.

MEDICAL PRODUCTS MANUFACTURER

Startup cost:	$40,000 and up
Potential earnings:	$50,000+
Typical fees:	Your products could sell for anywhere from $150–$1,000,000 depending on the technology
Advertising:	Trade publications, direct mail, sales calls to physicians or hospital administrators/operations managers, Web site
Qualifications:	Scientific, technological and manufacturing skills; medical training to determine market needs and products that could meet them; testing and planning abilities; marketing and finance skills; ability to secure investors/venture capital
Equipment needed:	Production equipment; basic office setup, including computer, printer, Internet access, copier, scanner, fax, phone
Home business potential:	No
Staff required:	Yes
Hidden costs:	Planning and development stages can be very long; cost of financing, testing

LOWDOWN:

Medical products continue to be developed, manufactured, and added on a daily basis to the arsenal of tools physicians can use in their practices. As technological advances are made in other fields, they are often being applied to medical products. If you have one foot in each camp—an extensive technology background and a knowledge of the medical needs to which a new product might be applied—you can develop your own product (a new type of shunt, a better suture, a more flexible brace, a more effective laser scalpel, a state-of-the art imaging system, etc.), manufacture it, and make a significant contribution to health care, and, incidentally, to your own wealth. Obviously this type of enterprise requires a number of highly developed skills and abilities, but it is hardly impossible; successful small companies have sprung up in "research valleys" all across the United States, near universities, and in association with technological enterprises of other kinds.

STARTUP:

Startup costs will be significant, and you may not realize a return on your investment for many years. The stakes are high, but so is the opportunity. Your manufacturing costs could run into the millions, particularly if you're involved in laser or magnetic resonance imaging systems. You'll need to spend at least $10,000–$20,000 just on marketing alone; potentially $100,000–$300,000 or more on product development and research.

BOTTOM LINE ADVICE:

Your links to the market—a medical subspecialty like pediatric orthopedics, perhaps, or a group of geriatric care centers—will be vital to the success of your business. You must have a viable idea for a product that is a real addition to what is currently available. You must be able to test and develop it in-service to the patient population it is meant to address. And unless you are independently wealthy and can underwrite the costs of research, development, and manufacturing, you will need to find venture capital sources. Marketing, sales, and financial professionals will be needed by your new enterprise as it moves from the tinkering-at-the-workbench stage to actual production.

MESSENGER SERVICE

Startup cost:	$40,000–$65,000
Potential earnings:	$45,000–$60,000
Typical fees:	$35–$50 per delivery run
Advertising:	Yellow Pages, business publications, promotional items (such as pens, magnets, or notepads)
Qualifications:	Basic business and marketing skills; driver's licenses for motor vehicle operators
Equipment needed:	Fleet of delivery vehicles or bicycles and/or supply of skateboards and inline skates
Home business potential:	Yes
Staff required:	Yes
Hidden costs:	Insurance, workers' compensation, medical bills (this is a high-risk profession, particularly for bicyclists and skaters in large metropolitan areas)

LOWDOWN:

What happens when you have an important message or document that absolutely, positively has to be there ... well, sooner than overnight? You call a messenger service to hand carry it across town to the appropriate local business. Your messenger service might be made up of a small fleet of vehicles, or perhaps you'll hire a bunch of college students to make deliveries using inline skates, skateboards, or bicycles. Couriers on skateboards? Sounds a little crazy, but just think of the publicity you'll garner! However you decide to power your fleet, you'll be wise to invest in safety gear and first-aid training for each of your employees. It's a dangerous world out there, particularly in the big city, and even though it's definitely faster to deliver an envelope via bicycle as opposed to a car or van in a congested city center, there's a greater chance of personal injury. A couple of trips to the emergency room for your couriers could make this business a little more costly to run than you'd anticipated.

STARTUP:

You'll need a reliable fleet and lots of delivery personnel to make this business work profitably. Ideally, you'll have a small, energetic staff that works quickly enough to tackle several runs per hour—making your profit margin higher than most of the larger, better-known delivery services. You'll charge $35–$50 per delivery (add a surcharge for speedier runs), so you can expect an income potential of $45,000–$60,000 per year.

BOTTOM LINE ADVICE:

Make sure your staff is physically fit, able to handle multiple tasks, and just plain quick about it. Consider paying bonuses to the swiftest. And don't forget to stress safety. You'll make lots more money if every member of your staff can manage to get through the streets in one piece on a daily basis.

MINIATURE GOLF COURSE

Startup cost:	$75,000–$150,000
Potential earnings:	$50,000–$75,000
Typical fees:	Admission fees of $5–$10 per person; percentage on concessions
Advertising:	Billboards, local magazines, coupon books, fliers; listings in travel directories and guidebooks
Qualifications:	Design and building skills, creativity, business and marketing savvy
Equipment needed:	Clubs, balls, maintenance equipment
Home business potential:	No
Staff required:	Yes
Hidden costs:	Maintenance, insurance

LOWDOWN:

If you have a piece of land with a reasonable amount of drive-by traffic, you can probably draw customers for a miniature golf course without too much advertising. Creativity in the course layout will help draw in your customers and build return business. Some miniature golf courses have a theme, while others focus on the complicated holes featuring loop-the-loop shots and, of course, the standard windmill. Miniature golf is appealing to almost everyone, from young kids to their grandparents; there's even been talk recently of making it an Olympic sport. By entering this business you're keeping up a wonderful tradition of fun for the whole family, and perhaps even paving the way for a future world-class athlete.

STARTUP:

How much of the construction can you and your family do on your own? Minimizing expenses for labor and materials will make a big difference in your startup costs. If you need to hire professional contractors, expect to spend between $75,000–$150,000 from the get-go. At $5–$10 per admission, it may take you five years or so to earn back your return on investment, but amusement-type businesses do seem to have a recession-proof nature if they're not too trendy, and miniature golf certainly meets that criteria.

BOTTOM LINE ADVICE:

You'll be working when everyone else is off having fun: evenings, weekends, holidays, and just about any other day as long as the weather allows. You may find it hard to get away from your work unless you have reliable assistants to cover for you. The other principal disadvantage is that a miniature golf course is not likely to be the road to untold riches. It's a good, seasonal business, but don't expect to be parking a couple of BMWs inside your garage anytime soon.

MUSICAL INSTRUMENT LEASING

Startup cost:	$50,000–$100,000
Potential earnings:	$50,000–$65,000
Typical fees:	$40–$100 per month, depending on type and quality of instrument
Advertising:	Yellow Pages, referrals from band leaders and music teachers
Qualifications:	Familiarity with all types of instruments, ability to perform basic repairs, good managerial skills, organizational abilities
Equipment needed:	Instruments to lease, display area, basic office setup
Home business potential:	Yes
Staff required:	No
Hidden costs:	Replacement and repair of instruments and cases

LOWDOWN:

Areas with active high school music programs, especially marching bands, will easily support a musical instrument leasing business. When kids are just getting started with a musical instrument, leasing makes more sense than purchase because children grow, change interests, and gradually work their way up to playing more sophisticated instruments. Some companies make an excellent profit on leasing quarter- and half-size violins as children progress through Suzuki programs in the elementary grades. Other enterprises focus on band instruments, some of which are much too big and expensive for purchase by individual students (i.e., bass drum, tuba, etc.). Your connections with band directors and other music teachers in the public and private schools in your area will be essential to your marketing. You'll also want to appeal to parents who are reluctant to purchase an instrument until they're sure their child has a genuine, long-term interest in playing it; for these families, you can offer instruments on a lease-with-option-to-purchase plan.

STARTUP:

Costs for your inventory of instruments will be high, perhaps even in the $50,000–$100,000 range, depending on the types of instruments and how many of each you stock; the quality of product lines you select is another option to consider in your pricing. Your rental fees will range from $40–$100 per month or more (again, depending on whether you're leasing a concert quality violin, for example, or just a plain old fiddle).

BOTTOM LINE ADVICE:

A love of music is a wonderful thing. Your business allows children, young adults, and parents to become proficient musicians using instruments they would otherwise not be able to purchase outright. As the lessons continue, a proportion of the lessees will likely become committed instrumentalists who are interested in a purchase. Checking your instruments in and out and keeping track of their whereabouts at all times will be challenging. Be sure your bookkeeping and other records are always up to date and that you can readily access the information you need. If you lose track of your inventory, profits may dribble away before you're even fully aware of the problem.

900-NUMBER SERVICE

Startup cost:	$50,000–$100,000
Potential earnings:	$60,000–$150,000
Typical fees:	$3 to $5 per minute, per customer
Advertising:	Newspapers, magazines, television
Qualifications:	Basic business and marketing skills
Equipment needed:	Telephone centers or special phone codes or hookups to allow your staff to work from their homes
Home business potential:	Yes
Staff required:	Yes (at least five to ten to manage incoming calls)
Hidden costs:	Insurance, workers' compensation

LOWDOWN:

Believe it or not, there are some 900-number services that don't cater to the sexually depraved—although, admittedly, that's where the biggest money can be made. Singles classifieds and sex-talk lines get the biggest bang for the buck, so to speak, so if you're in this business for straight cash, that's the kind of 900-number service to offer. Once clients get on the line, they have to be encouraged to stay on, and that may require a script of sorts to keep hangers-on from hanging up. Time is definitely money in this business, and the longer you can keep a caller on the line, the greater your own reward. If the "talk-dirty-to-me" approach doesn't appeal to you, there are plenty of other options for 900-number services. Look around for gaps in the marketplace or special interests people might pay money to learn more about—virtually any kind of highly specialized information can be sold over the phone using a 900 number.

STARTUP:

You'll need lots of capital to get your phone system up and running, plus sufficient funds to cover the salaries of the folks who "man" your phones until you start to make a profit; expect to spend $50,000–$100,000 to get your business up and running. Much of that will go to the phone company for use of their lines, including a security deposit of around $20,000. But, your income potential can be as high as $150,000 or more, so it shouldn't be long before you earn back your investment. The key to success in this business is advertising. People won't call your number if they don't know about it, so be prepared to sink a significant chunk of change (about 30 percent of total revenue) into print and television ads.

BOTTOM LINE ADVICE:

While a sex-talk telephone line may not be the kind of business you'll want to tell your parents about over the Thanksgiving dinner table, you can make a small fortune with a well-visited 900-number service. They'll be proud to learn of your success, even if you don't share all the details of how you came by it.

PILOT/FLYING LESSONS

Startup cost:	$45,000–$125,000+
Potential earnings:	$3,000–$5,000 per month
Typical fees:	$3,000–$5,000 per student (includes classroom and in-flight instruction and FAA testing for pilot's license)
Advertising:	Yellow Pages, entertainment sections of local papers, brochures, visitor convention bureaus
Qualifications:	Federal Aviation Administration (FAA) license, 20/20 vision, 1,500–3,000+ hours flying time, certification as a flight instructor
Equipment needed:	Plane and appropriate safety equipment
Home business potential:	No
Staff required:	No
Hidden costs:	Fuel, maintenance, insurance

LOWDOWN:

Flying may look easy from the ground, but there's way more to being a pilot than just climbing into the cockpit. You need to have the ability to work with words and numbers, follow procedures and read the instrument panel, be alert and ready to make decisions, and communicate accurately. If you decide that you'd like to teach others to fly the friendly skies, you must be incredibly thorough and have a great many hours in the air yourself. The more "fly time" or experience you have, the better teacher you will be. Skipping over any details could cost lives, and you certainly don't want that on your conscience. Still, if you have a high degree of knowledge and are able to convey that information in an accurate, concise way, you could make this business soar—particularly if you live in an area where the weather cooperates regularly and you can log a lot of air miles.

STARTUP:

It's the cost of the plane itself that can cause your startup costs to soar. Expect to spend at least $35,000 for a used single-engine plane. Of course, by the time you've logged enough miles to be eligible for instructor status, the chances are good you already own or have unlimited access to a plane. The rest of your overhead will be wrapped up in insurance and advertising. You'll need to set aside adequate funds for fuel and aircraft maintenance, too; flight instruction, with its many takeoffs and landings is particularly hard on planes. Your typical annual earnings will be in the neighborhood of $36,000–$60,000.

BOTTOM LINE ADVICE:

If you love to fly, the great part about this business is that you're up in the sky enjoying the tranquility and breathtaking views. The bad part is you are working in a confined space with a beginning pilot; your instructions must be very accurate and your attention riveted to the task at hand. A mistake in teaching could be life-threatening. You can run a flight school as a solo operation, but you're limited to the number of students you can train at any given time. A better option, and one to consider as you grow, is to bring in additional instructors; hopefully, they'll have their own planes, which will further boost your business capabilities.

PINBALL/ELECTRONIC GAME ARCADE

Startup cost:	$50,000–$75,000
Potential earnings:	$45,000–$60,000
Typical fees:	25 cents to $1 per play
Advertising:	Location
Qualifications:	Basic business and marketing skills, organizational abilities
Equipment needed:	Pinball/electronic games, token or change machine
Home business potential:	No
Staff required:	Yes (one to two to cover shifts; you can't possibly be everywhere your machines are at once)
Hidden costs:	Insurance, maintenance

LOWDOWN:

You don't have to be a "pinball wizard" to make a go of a pinball/electronic game arcade—all you need are the most popular games and a good token or change machine. You don't even necessarily need a storefront of your own, because many shopping malls rent out floor space in their corridors precisely for games like yours. If you're in an accessible, highly trafficked area, you can probably earn a pretty penny while doing minimal work to maintain your machines. If you start out small enough (with one to four games in a mall corridor setting), you can earn a great deal in a short period of time. Obviously, your hours will be the same as the mall's—and when the mall is busy (weekends and holidays in particular), you'll be busy. Just make sure to drop by every few hours to check that your machines are running properly and to collect your money.

STARTUP:

Your startup costs will mostly be in the equipment purchases themselves—and pinball/game equipment doesn't come cheap. You can save money by purchasing used equipment, but then you run the risk of shelling out your cash for potentially obsolete or less-popular games. Invest wisely and sensibly ($50,000–$75,000 for eight to ten units) and count on a payback period of four to five years. That's not too bad, really, because you don't have to work very hard to maintain this business and your overhead will be low as a result.

BOTTOM LINE ADVICE:

This business affords you the freedom and flexibility that many people who start their own business are hoping to find—but your income depends on how many games you have running simultaneously in different places. In this case, the more machines you have, the merrier (and wealthier) you'll be.

PREFAB HOME SALES/CONSTRUCTION

Startup cost:	$75,000–$150,000+
Potential earnings:	$40,000–$80,000+
Typical fee:	$10,000 more than the cost of materials and labor
Advertising:	Yellow Pages, local newspapers, Web site
Qualifications:	Knowledge of construction and building codes, firsthand construction experience, management ability
Equipment needed:	Construction equipment, materials, plans
Home business potential:	No
Staff required:	Yes
Hidden costs:	Insurance, equipment maintenance, workers' compensation

LOWDOWN:

Prefab homes are considered by many to be the housing wave of the future, largely because they are far less expensive than custom-built homes and provide families and singles, who otherwise might forever be relegated to apartment dwelling, the ability to own their own homes at a cost comparable to what they'd pay for monthly rent. As a sales rep for prefab homes, you may be required to purchase the components, then assemble them on your customer's lot. (Note: Many prefab homes are manufactured in Elkhart, Indiana; you may want to surf the Web and check out possibilities before taking the plunge into this business.) While it's possible to sell a prefab home from pictures, you're probably going to want to purchase a large lot where you can assemble several different models for display and also store the components prior to installing a home on a customer's lot. To get a double bang for your buck, you could use one of your model homes as your office.

STARTUP:

Your initial investment will be quite high ($75,000–$150,000), as you'll need to cover such items as materials, supplies, insurance, workers' compensation, and shipping of the pre-fab home components (or rights to the plans if you'll be constructing the components yourself).

BOTTOM LINE ADVICE:

Transporting a prefab home, or its components, is no easy task. They must be transported on wide-load tractor-trailer rigs, and be sure to hire truck drivers with excellent safety records. Instead of hiring the trucks on an as-needed basis, you might consider long-term leases. Keeping a few trucks on-site and drivers on-call could save you money in the long run.

REAL ESTATE INVESTOR

Startup cost:	$40,000 and up
Potential earnings:	$50,000+
Typical fees:	There's no "typical," each deal is different; however, your cut could be as high as 40 percent
Advertising:	Real estate publications and networking through investment clubs, banks and real estate agents
Qualifications:	Better-than-average knowledge of the local real estate market; minor repair/maintenance skills; sufficient capital and/or blemish-free credit record
Equipment needed:	Computer, printer, fax, Internet access, phone
Home business potential:	Yes
Staff required:	No
Hidden costs:	Appraisals, interest, finance fees, eviction costs, downturns in the real estate market

LOWDOWN:

Real estate (both commercial and residential) is a good, solid investment to make in the first place, since it's one of the few places you can put your money where its value consistently tends to increase with time. Imagine your potential to earn two or three times the value of your property by becoming an investor! Your research, knowledge, business sense, and awareness of real estate market trends are the basis for your income. You will focus on land suitable for a strip mall, apartment buildings that can be upgraded and made more profitable, recycled factory buildings, even high-end residential properties that can easily be "flipped." What real estate investors do may look easy from the outside, but serious work and considerable risk-taking are involved. Success requires a dedication to learning, patience, and constant research. There are no "easy pickings" out there; instead, opportunities exist for those investors who can readily recognize and exploit them.

STARTUP:

You'll need sufficient investment capital and excellent credit—not to mention the capability (with money or "sweat equity") to fix up and maintain your properties. You could earn as much as 40 percent off of your investments—or, if primarily renting spaces, your income could easily be between $30,000 and $50,000 annually (depending on what you own and—particularly—where it's located).

BOTTOM LINE ADVICE:

If you know your community like the back of your hand and have a strong sense of the value people put on their places and spaces, give real estate investment serious consideration. If you're good, there are no limits to what you can achieve financially. The flip side of the coin is that maintenance can be very costly if you don't keep up or if you have to contract out for much of it; also, you may run into some situations in which you are forced to evict tenants (and that can get costly, not to mention uncomfortable, too).

REPAIR SHOP

Startup cost:	$40,000–$65,000
Potential earnings:	$35,000–$50,000+
Typical fees:	Varies according to service provided; can be as little as $5 and as much as $150 or more
Advertising:	Yellow Pages, newspaper ads, referrals, coupon books
Qualifications:	Ability to make minor repairs on a variety of items, organizational and time-management abilities, good people skills
Equipment needed:	Sewing/mending equipment, leather repair kits, miscellaneous tools and/or repair equipment specific to specialization
Home business potential:	No
Staff required:	No
Hidden costs:	Insurance, fluctuating materials costs

LOWDOWN:

Even the most reliable products break down once in a while, and that's why repair businesses continue to be such an economic mainstay. After all, in our busy, dual-income society, who has the time, let alone the tools or expertise, to stop and fix anything? You'll be filling a niche, fixing everything from golf clubs to small appliances like blenders and irons to ladies' shoes and purses. You can go one of two ways with this business: Settle on a specialty area to set your repair service apart and not spread yourself too thin, or become a jack-of-all-trades, willing to tackle just about any repair job that comes your way. You'll need to have a small shop or storefront so that your customers can easily drop things off as they circulate in the area; you would do well to invest in a spot near a shopping mall or along some other heavily traveled route so that your sign becomes your main form of advertising. The people who don't have time to do their own repairs will be looking as much for a convenient place to bring their broken "stuff" as for someone who can fix it for them.

STARTUP:

You'll need to start with about $40,000–$65,000, which will cover the cost of your equipment/tools, rent, and advertising (Yellow Pages listing, small newspaper ads, and coupon books). What you'll earn in this business may depend on your area of specialization; repairing golf clubs, for example, is likely to be more lucrative than fixing a broken purse strap. Expect to earn around $35,000–$50,000.

BOTTOM LINE ADVICE:

The hours can get long very quickly, and you'll find that you're competing in a fast-food society in which everyone wants his or her broken item fixed on the spot or overnight. Calm their nerves (and yours) by tacking on a hefty surcharge for speedier service; it works as a deterrent, and your customers may find that it's worth the wait for your good service and attention to detail after all.

RESALE/CONSIGNMENT SHOP

Startup cost:	$40,000–$100,000
Potential earnings:	$35,000–$80,000+
Typical fees:	Varied according to the items you're reselling; you could sell items from 50 cents–$1,000, but don't forget the profit split if you're working with consignment goods
Advertising:	Yellow Pages, community newspapers, coupon books, location
Qualifications:	Basic business and marketing abilities; eye for quality and customer appeal; organizational and people skills; previous retail experience is extremely helpful
Equipment needed:	Cash register and credit care processing equipment; retail clothing racks, shelves, and display cases; computer, printer, fax, phone
Home business potential:	No
Staff required:	Possibly
Hidden costs:	Insurance, cost of sales

LOWDOWN:

Resale shops of all kinds abound in the shopper's market. In a sense, charities like Goodwill Industries and Salvation Army paved the way for this business. Not-for-profit thrift shops did so well that other retailers, looking to make a profit, saw the potential in used goods, and opened up their own resale and consignment shops. If you decide to go into this business, you'll need to get the word out about your shop well before you open the door because you'll need to build a healthy inventory of used "stuff." You can either buy the goods outright or negotiate individual contracts with each supplier to sell said items at an agreeable percentage split (usually 60/40 or 50/50). Unlike a thrift store that serves as the fundraising arm of a charitable organization, you can be choosy about what you accept, agreeing to take only those items you feel will sell well; you may even have a return policy—if an item doesn't sell within a certain preset period of time, it goes back to the owner, so your valuable floor space can be given over to other items your customers will be more likely to buy. And speaking of customers, there's a whole subculture of people out there who frequent resale shops. Some are collectors, looking for specific items like glassware, rare books, or old records. Others are just shopping for nothing in particular, except a bargain; for them, it's the thrill of the hunt that matters. And then there are the really serious customers, the ones who need specific items, like clothing, a radio, or pots and pans, but can't afford to pay full price. Some resale shops specialize, offering just one category of goods, like clothing, books, or furniture (children's consignment shops are particularly successful); others stock the full gamut, everything from shirts and shoes to small appliances. In any case, you'll likely have lots of repeat business, so you need to change your stock on a regular basis. No one wants to see the same navy blue blazer hanging on the same rack six months from now.

STARTUP:

There are franchises available in the resale shop business; if you decide to purchase one, you'll spend at least $50,000 for the buy-in alone (not including your advertising, office equipment, and store location). A better bet might be to go it alone; you'll still have to come up with about $40,000 to start, but you get to call the shots in terms of merchandise, pricing, and consignment arrangements.

BOTTOM LINE ADVICE:

The lure of selling used items has drawn many into the resale business; how many actually last in this business is quite another story. You are likelier to beat the odds if you already have some retailing experience under your belt, have a good eye for what will sell and, more importantly, what won't, and are adept at buying low and selling high. Interestingly, this is one business where locating in close proximity to your competition may actually be an advantage; resale shopping is, for many people, a form of entertainment. They delight in finding a bargain and are willing to spend several hours looking for one. The more shops they can hit in just one stop, the better they like it.

RESTAURANT

Startup cost:	$50,000–$500,000
Potential earnings:	$50,000–$75,000
Typical fees:	3–5 percent of gross sales
Advertising:	Word of mouth, newspaper ads, phone directories, location
Qualifications:	Good business management and marketing skills; knowledge of food and high-volume cooking; organizational and multitasking skills; ability to hire and fire
Equipment needed:	Prime location, kitchen equipment and cooking utensils, furnishings, linens and tableware, cash management system
Home business potential:	No
Staff required:	Yes
Hidden costs:	Liability insurance, legal advice, decorating costs, staffing costs, possible remodeling of facility to meet your needs, rising food prices, equipment replacement and maintenance

LOWDOWN:

With the continuous increase in the number of dual-income households, people have less and less time to cook and more money to spend at restaurants. Providing people with good food and a nice atmosphere in which to consume it can be a satisfying occupation, but don't make the mistake that so many would-be restaurateurs have—don't go into this business simply because you like to cook and are good at it. Running a restaurant takes way more than kitchen savvy; you have to know business basics and marketing too. That said, your restaurant can take any format and offer any kind of cuisine you like, from a cafeteria-style establishment (which won't require as many personnel as a restaurant with table service) to an elegant, haute cuisine bistro. Not surprisingly, your costs will vary widely, depending on the size of your restaurant, the hours you're open, whether it's located in the city or the suburbs, and the type of cuisine you offer.

STARTUP:

Startup costs vary greatly. Consider your own geographic area, where the restaurant will be located (suburb? upscale neighborhood? downtown?), the cost of labor (how many employees will be required?), the type of menu you wish to offer (sandwiches and soup? French cuisine? burgers?), marketing requirements, legal and health requirements, etc. Obviously, you will need cooking equipment and utensils, seating for your patrons, linens, tableware, signage, and lighting, in addition to foodstuffs and beverages. If you plan to serve liquor, even just beer and wine, you'll also need to spring for the cost of obtaining the appropriate license.

BOTTOM LINE ADVICE:

The restaurant business is a volatile one. Restaurant owners face myriad challenges on an everyday basis. Finding and keeping good employees can be difficult; getting people to try your restaurant may take time (word-of-mouth is your greatest marketing tool); zoning and health regulations must be met; the hours are long and typically involve nights, weekends, and holidays. If you enjoy working with people, relish a busy, high-stress working environment, and can handle multiple tasks at once, a restaurant business may suit you.

RESTAURANT EQUIPMENT AND SUPPLIES

Startup cost:	$40,000–$70,000
Potential earnings:	$40,000–$60,000
Typical fees:	$5–$5,000 per item
Advertising:	Trade publications, newspapers, direct mail, Yellow Pages
Qualifications:	Business and marketing skills; sales ability; knowledge of the restaurant business and, in particular its equipment needs
Equipment needed:	Wide-ranging stock of restaurant supplies; display models of the large items you plan to sell—i.e., ovens, dishwashers, mixers, etc.
Home business potential:	No (unless you're selling from a catalog or direct-mail only)
Staff required:	One to five employees
Hidden costs:	Investments in inventory can be costly; prices vary widely so be sure to shop for the best deal and terms

LOWDOWN:

In any given metropolitan area, there are literally hundreds of thriving restaurants, not to mention a constant surge of new ones opening up on a weekly basis, so the opportunity to sell new and/or improved restaurant equipment is practically endless. You'll need to be constantly on the lookout for opportunities, and, if your market is large enough, you may have to hire a sales representative to call on restaurant owners. If you have a background in the restaurant field, use it as a marketing point; if not, stress the benefits of the product lines you carry and perhaps include information regarding the various manufacturers' reputations for quality. There are thousands of products you can stock to sell to your customers, from napkins in bulk to industrial-sized ovens. Be aware, however, that you won't be the only game in town; in some geographic locations, there are almost as many restaurant supply businesses as there are restaurants.

STARTUP:

Your inventory alone can easily run as high as $50,000, while advertising costs could add another $10,000 or more per year. Still, the markup on restaurant equipment is generally quite high, so you could stand to be pretty profitable—especially on big-ticket items, if you price your products competitively. Keep in mind, however, that your inventory has to include the small stuff, too—like bar blenders, soup ladles, carving knives, and the like. When a Mexican restaurant gets low on Margarita glasses, it needs to restock in a hurry and you need to be ready with the supplies.

BOTTOM LINE ADVICE:

While it can be stressful to manage and sell a huge product line in an extremely competitive market, you can generate business if you provide potential customers with satisfactory products when they need them. Use incentives, develop marketing programs that create interest in your company and, most of all, hang in there. It could easily take you a good year or two to start making money in this field.

RETAILER

Startup cost:	$60,000–$200,000
Potential earnings:	$35,000–$200,000
Typical fees:	40 to 100 percent markup on list price
Advertising:	Print, TV/radio ads, newspaper ads, billboards, Web site, location
Qualifications:	Degree and/or background in merchandising; previous retailing experience would be helpful; high interest in/commitment to whatever you're selling
Equipment needed:	Cash registers, scanning equipment (for bar codes), retail equipment/fixtures, credit card processing equipment
Home business potential:	No
Staff required:	Possibly
Hidden costs:	Insurance, employee benefits, workers' compensation, high staffing turnover costs

LOWDOWN:

In retailing, two things count: timing and pricing. You will live on the competitive edge, constantly dreaming up schemes to keep the dollars flowing in. It could be that you're in the clothing retail business, where you'll need to slash prices regularly in order to compete with fellow retailers in your geographic area. Or, you could be in the bookselling business, where added services (such as espresso bars and music-listening areas) are hot. Whatever you choose to sell, you'll need to do it at a fair enough price to bring in a sizable profit and yet not lose your shirt on a regular basis. There will be times when you'll need to sell at cost just to clear inventory and make way for newer, more popular products. Your biggest challenge probably won't be pricing, however; it will be getting your name on the top of every consumer's mind. For that, you'll need to advertise heavily in just about every medium out there; expect to shell out a few thousand dollars on advertising alone.

STARTUP:

You'll need a significant amount of capital (at least $60,000) to launch a small retail business, considerably more if you intend to buy into a franchise. Depending on what you're selling, you'll need to have counters, shelves, display cases, etc., plus a cash register and credit card processing equipment. And then there's the inventory, of course, not to mention advertising and staffing costs. If you're going to go it alone, your best bet is to not try and go head-to-head with the big guys; specialize instead to capture a unique segment of the market. For example, suppose you want to open a toy store. As an independent retailer, you can't possibly compete against a Wal-Mart or Toys Я Us in terms of inventory and prices. So do something different—carry hard-to-find or high-end imported toys, or build a store around just board games and puzzles, kites, miniatures, or stuffed animals. If you market effectively and your store fares well in the stormy retail market, you could make a nice living selling specialty items.

BOTTOM LINE ADVICE:

Retailing is a rough way to make a living, but it can be quite profitable for those who do it well. Choose a well-established retailing name if you're going to buy into a franchise; if you're building your own retail empire, think specialty shop and prepare for an uphill battle of at least five to seven years.

ADVICE FROM THE EXPERTS

What sets your business apart from others like it?

Ingredients standards and an emphasis on organics are what set apart the Mustard Seed Market in Akron, Ohio. Chairman and CEO Margaret Nabors, who co-owns the health food grocery store with her husband, Phil, says: "We don't allow any harmful chemicals to come in contact with our foods, and we sell only cruelty-free products (such as cosmetics)." The Nabors's grocery store is unique in that it also houses a health food restaurant.

Things you couldn't do without:

"Our management staff . . . they're the essence of our business. Also, we need tremendous amounts of refrigeration and restaurant equipment, fixtures."

Marketing tips/advice:

"You should definitely work for someone else for a while, and build a high level of commitment to your beliefs. Owning a health food store is a belief system, not just a business. Phil and I are lucky to be paid for doing something we believe in so deeply."

If you had to do it all over again . . .

"I would have hired my management staff much earlier. Our business manager transformed us from an idea to a viable business—we were just not as focused on that kind of growth as she was."

SATELLITE EQUIPMENT/SYSTEMS
(WHOLESALE)

Startup cost:	$150,000–$500,000
Potential earnings:	$75,000–$100,000
Typical fees:	$3,000–$5,000 per installed system
Advertising:	Yellow Pages, trade publications, direct mail, referrals, Web site
Qualifications:	Electrical contracting experience would be helpful, specialized training in installation and repair of satellite equipment is essential
Equipment needed:	Parts and product stock, van
Home business potential:	No
Staff required:	Yes
Hidden costs:	Insurance, workers' compensation, vehicle expenses, equipment maintenance

LOWDOWN:

With literally hundreds of channels available today, and only one way to truly get all of them, your satellite equipment business should have no problem making money. Actually, it's staying on top of the competition and keeping ahead of demand that will be your biggest challenges. As a systems wholesaler, you'll be selling to distributors and installations professionals who in turn install the systems in hotels/motels, office complexes, and private homes. Therefore, you'll need to provide excellent training and technical support to those who resell your product.

STARTUP:

Your startup costs will be high ($150,000–$500,000), mainly because your product is expensive to produce. Once you're established, however, you can cut costs by working out special deals with your parts suppliers. Look for an annual income between $75,000–$100,000—but remember, too, that you can't go it entirely alone. Budget for at least one additional staffer.

BOTTOM LINE ADVICE:

The hours in this business are long, and your work isn't exactly easy—after all, you need to sell your distributors on the quality of your product and your ability to out-service the competition, neither of which is simply a given in the satellite jungle. Set yourself apart by offering incentives that will encourage people to do business with you instead of someone else.

SEGWAY RENTALS

Startup cost:	$100,000–$250,000
Potential earnings:	$65,000–$100,000
Typical fees:	Varied, from $20–$350 per day, depending on the length of the rental period with one-day rentals being the most costly
Advertising:	Yellow Pages, newspaper ads, networking with local businesses that require a lot of "foot power"; possibly free publicity (the Segway is still new enough to generate some media interest), Web site
Qualifications:	Product knowledge, sales ability, enthusiasm for innovative ideas
Equipment needed:	Fleet of Segway™ Human Transporters and accessories; instruction manual and/or video; computer with printer and software for bookkeeping and desktop publishing (to produce your instruction manual), fax, copier, and phone
Home business potential:	No
Staff required:	Possibly
Hidden costs:	Insurance, legal fees, equipment maintenance and repairs

LOWDOWN:

Get in on the ground floor of what could become this century's favorite form of human transportation by launching a Segway rental business. First introduced to the public in December 2001, the computer-controlled, battery-powered Segway Human Transporter is the brainchild of inventor Dean Kamen who was looking to use balancing technology as a way to improve human transportation. Reaching top speeds of just under 13 miles per hour and with a range of up to 15 miles per charge, these two-wheeled, self-balancing "vehicles" are showing up for duty all across America as replacements for walking and to carry light loads (up to 83 pounds in addition to a 250-pound passenger); some even sport specially-designed mini-billboards called Seg-Signs. There's a cargo version of the Segway too, that is designed to carry a 95-pound load, plus passenger. You would rent the transporters themselves, plus a full range of accessories such as extra battery packs, locks, handlebar bags, etc., by the day, week, or month. Your charges would be based on the length of the rental period—i.e., the longer the rental period, the lower the per-day rate. You'll need to do a fair amount of advertising to get the word out about your products, and because this is still a relatively new mode of transportation, some customer education will be in order. It takes just a few minutes to learn how to handle a Segway, but make sure you allow for that instruction time and that every customer takes home a manual and/or video for backup. Segways are still unique enough that they practically sell themselves, so look for opportunities—community events, trade shows, fairs, flea markets, etc.—where you can set up a display and demonstrate your product. When people see a Segway in action, they're likely to want to try one out.

STARTUP:

The basic Segway retails for around $4,000 brand new. To make a splash in this business, you'll need to keep a fairly large fleet of them on hand—probably at least 25, including a few cargo models and some Seg-Signs—plus plenty of accessories. You'll need a basic office setup, too (computer, printer, fax, and phone), to keep track of your rentals and to put together contracts and instruction materials for your customers. Advertise in local newspapers and Yellow Pages; use a Web site for broader appeal, but don't forget to tack on shipping charges for customers residing beyond your immediate geographic area.

BOTTOM LINE ADVICE:

Make sure every renter understands his or her responsibility with regard to damages and liability. Work with an attorney to create an ironclad contract that spells out your responsibilities and those of the renter so there is no confusion later on. And don't forget to set aside a Segway for your own personal use. You'll be surprised how much attention you draw just zipping down the street to pick up a newspaper or to grab a latte around the corner at your neighborhood coffee shop.

SHIPPING/FREIGHT
FORWARDING SERVICE

Startup cost:	$80,000–$150,000
Potential earnings:	$800,000–$2 million
Typical fees:	Commission percentages from shipper, carrier, insurance company
Advertising:	Yellow Pages, direct mail, referrals, Web site
Qualifications:	Previous background in shipping industry would be helpful; excellent organizational, time-management, and communication skills
Equipment needed:	Computer, printer, tracking software, fax, Internet access, copier, phone system
Home business potential:	Yes
Staff required:	No
Hidden costs:	You may have to carry transit or cargo insurance on commodities

LOWDOWN:

Suppose you're a manufacturer who needs to ship your product to a customer located along some back road in West Virginia, but the load's too small for a large trucking business to care about. What do you do? You call a shipping/freight forwarding service, that's what. You explain the problem and the shipping/freight forwarding service finds a suitable carrier with an already partial load headed in the same direction to carry your product safely and economically to its final destination. If you decide that freight forwarding is the kind of business you'd like to be in, be prepared for logistical challenges on a daily basis; none of your loads is going to be easy to place with a carrier, and it may take several phone calls to find any trucker (independent or affiliated) who's going your way. You'll need to have expert time management, organizational, and communications skills, as you'll be dealing with three different "clients": the company needing your services to ship its product; the carrier you link up with to transport the load; and the insurance company earning money from your referrals.

STARTUP:

You'll need a sizable startup investment ($80,000–$150,000) to cover your own liability insurance, office equipment (computer system with tracking software), and advertising. Your income, which might well reach the seven-figure mark, will come from three different sources: a commission from the shipper of the products, a finder's fee from the carrier, and cash from the insurance companies that benefit from your client's need for their services. No matter how you cut it, you're in a win-win-win situation.

BOTTOM LINE ADVICE:

Your greatest challenge will be finding carriers who are not only willing to transport the goods, but can do so in the allotted time frame so that the delivery arrives on schedule; often, you'll need to work extra hours trying to find the perfect match. Still, the rewards when you do find the right match are worth the extra effort you put in; if you're good at this, you could make a rather sizable fortune in a short period of time.

SPECIALTY PAPER PRODUCER/ DISTRIBUTOR

Startup cost:	$600,000–$1.5 million+
Potential earnings:	$80,000–$2 million
Typical fees:	Varied according to product; usually $16–$20 per 100 sheets
Advertising:	Direct mail (catalogs) to thousands of businesses, Web site
Qualifications:	Experience in printing, sales ability, attention to detail
Equipment needed:	Four-color process printing equipment, computer with desktop publishing software, graphic design tools and supplies
Home business potential:	No (you'll need a warehouse)
Staff required:	Yes (20 to 50 people to run presses, design papers, handle customer service)
Hidden costs:	Maintaining inventory, fluctuating paper prices

LOWDOWN:

Prior to the days of the computer and laser printer, individualized, truly professional-looking letterhead, business cards, and brochures cost a small fortune to produce. Now, using the papers and individualized designs your company provides, a business owner or professional working from home can develop his or her own materials—beautifully, cost-effectively, and in a short period of time. You'll develop an extensive product catalog, complete with photos of each type of paper, typestyle, and design element you offer; you'll also need to develop a sample kit for those who want to actually touch and see the papers up close. This is an increasingly competitive business—one that even photocopying businesses are getting into—so make sure that your designs are unique and attractive to many different types of customers.

STARTUP:

Startup for a preprinted specialty paper business will be incredibly high—at least $600,000—mainly because of the high cost of the paper itself. You'll need to contract with a paper mill for the best prices and availability. Factor into your startup expenses the cost of designing a Web site, as well as creating, printing, and mailing a four-color catalog of your products to thousands of businesses nationwide. If you market aggressively and competitively, you could see earnings as high as $2 million.

BOTTOM LINE ADVICE:

Rising paper costs have made this a tricky industry to excel in; also, you'll really need to keep a handle on your customer service professionals. If you hire only the least expensive employees to greet and serve customers, you'll wind up losing in the long run because there are plenty of competitors who treat their customers with greater respect. Your business is about getting and keeping customers—if you do a good job with the first order, they'll be back for refills and possibly even new designs.

SPORTS EQUIPMENT
SALES/SERVICE

Startup cost:	$40,000–$100,000
Potential earnings:	$80,000–$150,000+
Typical fees:	5 to 15 percent commission on goods sold
Advertising:	Print advertising, direct mail/catalogs, cold calls, sports equipment fairs, networking with coaches and parents
Qualifications:	Sales experience, knowledge of and interest in sports and sporting goods
Equipment needed:	Computer, printer, fax, high-speed Internet connection, phone system, cell phone
Home business potential:	Yes
Staff required:	No
Hidden costs:	Insurance, mileage

LOWDOWN:

Any parent knows how large and profitable the junior and senior high school market is for sports equipment; all they have to do is look at their checkbooks. But parents aren't the only market for sports equipment sales and service: You'll also be selling to the school systems themselves. They'll depend on you to supply quality equipment at a competitive price, and their sports departments will probably seek special deals for purchasing in large quantities. You will likely have worked out a distributorship or sales representative contract with one or many sports equipment manufacturers, and your income will be directly tied into how well you are able to sell each product line. Set realistic goals, research your market, and then get out onto the playing field—literally.

STARTUP:

You may need a large amount of capital to get into this business, especially if you purchase a franchise; expect to spend $40,000–$100,000. Included in these figures is the office equipment you'll need (computer, printer, fax, high-speed Internet connection, copier, and cell phone). If you are able to establish regular customers and constantly increase your sales volume by organizing or participating in sports equipment fairs, you stand a good chance of making anywhere from $40,000–$100,000 or more, depending on your geographic location.

BOTTOM LINE ADVICE:

Sports equipment fairs are becoming increasingly popular; these are excellent venues for you to sell your wares at high-volume, competitive prices—and you don't have too much overhead because the companies you're representing will likely provide complimentary samples of each product, or at the very least let you display them on consignment.

STOCK PHOTO SERVICE

Startup cost:	$50,000–$75,000
Potential earnings:	$45,000–$65,000
Typical fees:	$30–$500 per photo, per use
Advertising:	Direct mail to businesses, publishers, and ad agencies; ads in related trade publications; Web site
Qualifications:	Photography/marketing background, organizational skills, attention to detail
Equipment needed:	Computer with desktop publishing software, printer, fax, high-speed Internet access, and phone with 800 number for customer service/ordering; storage for photographs/slides
Home business potential:	Yes
Staff required:	No
Hidden costs:	Percentages/royalties, Web site management (updates)

LOWDOWN:

As a stock photo service, you'll be serving business professionals and individuals who need photos for a specific purpose, such as a brochure, presentation, or class project. Advertising agencies, for example, often purchase the rights to stock photos for use in brochures or print ads rather than go to the expense of paying a photographer to shoot what they need. You'll have a stable of photographers steadily providing you with black-and-white and color photos that are generic enough to be used by virtually anyone in any industry and for a variety of purposes. Your inventory, for example, might include a complete range of generic shots in many different subject areas, such as sunsets and sunrises, beaches, mountains, forests, country roads, freeways, people eating in restaurants, etc. Or, you can specialize in specific subject categories, such as famous people, food, or travel-themed photographs. You'll charge per photo, per use, and you'll have to be careful to ensure that you don't rent the same photo to competitive businesses; in other words, if the photo one client selects for a magazine ad shows up in another client's ad, you're in trouble. To be profitable at this business, you will have to have a wide selection of photos and be renting them all the time. One of the best ways to do this is to offer discounted prices if customers sign on for a monthly rate. To interest photographers in supplying shots for your service, you'll need to advertise in the professional publications they read (*Photographer's Market*, for example). You'll pay the photographer a percentage or royalty for each photo used (usually, 5 to 10 percent).

STARTUP:

You're going to need to spend a lot of money promoting this business to two unique markets: the photographers you'll be soliciting to supply the photos, and the businesses (i.e., advertising agencies) that would likely rent them. You'll definitely need a Web site to display the photos you have available and possibly a hard-copy catalog too, which will drive your startup costs to $30,000 or so. Add to that your own advertising, direct mail (including both production and postage costs) and follow-up calls, and you'll wind up with a total startup cost of close to $75,000. But, if you market effectively to the right people, you can make $45,000–$65,000 your first year alone.

BOTTOM LINE ADVICE:

Production costs will be your biggest expense—so be cautious and conservative when producing your first catalog. Use your Web site as your primary advertising vehicle and test the market with a smaller version of what you eventually hope to send out. The only downside to embarking on a stock photo service is that you'll need to constantly come up with new images while making sure to keep some of the old stuff—someone will inevitably want that one picture you just discontinued.

ADVICE FROM THE EXPERTS

What sets your business apart from others like it?

Howard Mandelbaum, president of the New York City–based Photofest, says his business is unique because it specializes in the performing arts. "Our customers get better research here because we're all experts in the entertainment industry."

Things you couldn't do without:

"Believe it or not, we don't use a computer. Our most important pieces of equipment are the telephone, fax, and a light box."

Marketing tips/advice:

"Don't look down on what might be considered trashy . . . the fact is, trashy often sells best. Also, try to get as much as you can and worry about aesthetics later."

If you had to do it all over again . . .

"I would've bought more at thrift shops and flea markets, where a lot of celebrity photos are sold for next to nothing. False thrift kept me from doing that, but now I realize that even the smallest things can be surprisingly useful."

STORAGE SERVICE

Startup cost:	$50,000–$150,000 (depending on whether you buy a franchise)
Potential earnings:	$40,000–$60,000
Typical fees:	Varied; rental space typically starts at $25 per month and may run as high as $150 per month
Advertising:	Yellow Pages, community newspapers, bulletin boards
Qualifications:	Basic business and marketing skills; organizational abilities
Equipment needed:	The storage building and property itself; computer, fax, phone, master key box, credit card processing equipment
Home business potential:	No
Staff required:	Yes (at least one to two to cover shifts)
Hidden costs:	Insurance, security systems

LOWDOWN:

Comedian George Carlin is famous for his routine called "A Place for My Stuff"; in it, he talks about how we Americans spend a lot of our time making money so that we can buy stuff . . . and we buy so much stuff that we need to buy larger houses so we can buy more stuff, and so on. Funny as it sounds, Carlin's take on Americans and their stuff definitely rings true. We just don't have enough room for everything we own these days. That's why storage services are becoming so popular. For a relatively small monthly fee, customers can rent a space to store anything from an antique car to those empty computer boxes they can't bear to part with. Your service is primarily one of convenience, and the only inconvenience to you is that you must have a large enough space to accommodate everyone else's stuff. Storage centers are often offered as franchises, and this may be a good way for you to start out, since the franchiser provides everything you need to get this business up and running efficiently, including, in some cases, financial assistance. Whether you decide to go it alone or link up with a franchise, your building should typically accommodate 50 to 100 or more customers, each paying $25 to $150 per month for rental space. They will want to have 24/7 access to their space, so you'll need to make sure you have adequate staff, a security system and insurance against losses due to theft, fire, and any other possible disaster.

STARTUP:

Your startup costs for this business will be fairly high due to the need for a large enough building and property. You should expect to spend at least $50,000 on a building alone, then another $25,000 for overhead. Add in your advertising costs ($1,500–$3,000) and you've got a sizable investment. However, this is a fairly stable, recession-proof business—it's a necessary convenience that never really goes out of style.

BOTTOM LINE ADVICE:

If you're able to get financing to pull this off successfully, go for it! You'll enjoy the ability to make money without doing a lot of legwork. The people may be difficult sometimes—it's their stuff you're storing and they can sometimes be touchy about it. Then, too, there's always the possibility that, unknowingly, you might rent spaces to criminals who want to conceal some stolen loot. Be prepared to work with the police at times.

TANNING SALON

Startup cost:	$50,000–$75,000
Potential earnings:	$45,000–$65,000
Typical fees:	Varied ($25 per half hour is common)
Advertising:	Yellow Pages, newspapers, bulletin boards, coupon books
Qualifications:	Familiarity with health codes/regulations; basic business and marketing skills
Equipment needed:	Tanning beds, heat lamps, sanitizing equipment; sunscreens and after-tanning moisturizers
Home business potential:	No
Staff required:	Possibly
Hidden costs:	Insurance and equipment maintenance

LOWDOWN:

It's a well-known fact that the sun's direct rays are becoming more dangerous than ever due to a reduction in the ozone layer, and that's why more people in search of the perennial tan flock to tanning salons. Of course, there's the convenience factor too. Even if you work all day, you can still look like you've been to the beach by slipping into a tanning bed at a time that's convenient for you. There's a lot of competition in this business, so you'll need to advertise heavily, and you'll have to lay out large amounts of cash for equipment. However, since this field remains a constantly growing one, and since it has the potential for add-on services such as hair and nail care, massage therapy, and even coin-operated laundry services (tan while your clothes dry!), you can convince a banker of your financial worthiness if you've got a solid business plan that shows you're thinking ahead. Once you get the word out about your tanning salon, you can pretty much just sit back and schedule appointments, accept payment, and turn the machines on for those who wish to sun their buns in comfort and style.

STARTUP:

Tanning booth equipment can start at $50,000 or more; investigate the used equipment market first (take a mechanical expert with you to be sure the equipment is functional and safe). Advertising will run $3,000–$5,000, and a staff could cost you thousands more. Check around to see what others in your area are charging, then set your fees according to what the market will bear ($25 per half hour and $40 per hour is pretty standard).

BOTTOM LINE ADVICE:

While some folks see this business as a real opportunity for success, others frown upon it for health reasons. It hasn't been conclusively proven that tanning booths cause skin cancer, but there are ongoing questions about the safety of this business. P.S. You will be inspected regularly by the Board of Health, so be prepared.

TAXI SERVICE

Startup cost:	$50,000–$75,000
Potential earnings:	$35,000–$50,000
Typical fees:	Based on local rates and distance traveled
Advertising:	Local paper, Yellow Pages, magnetic signs for your cars, business cards
Qualifications:	Commercial driver's license
Equipment needed:	Car, two-way radio, cell phone
Home business potential:	Yes
Staff required:	Yes
Hidden costs:	Repairs, insurance, workers' compensation (if you have employees)

LOWDOWN:

To make any money in this business, you need to be on call 24 hours a day, seven days a week (including and especially on holidays, since some folks just can't help but over-indulge and need rides home). You will need to hire a dependable staff to make this business work long-term; most taxi services run in three shifts so that each person has a 40-hour work week. Screen your drivers carefully because to the people who ride in your vehicles, your drivers represent your business; make sure every one of them is polite, well-groomed, knows the area well, and has a clean driving record. You'll need someone at home-base, too, to radio back to your drivers where their next pickup will be, so be sure to set aside the money to pay for at least one dispatcher per shift.

STARTUP:

Prepare to spend about $50,000 to get started with a small fleet of vehicles and some radio equipment. The pay will vary by hours and miles driven. In most cases, taxi drivers keep a percentage of customer fares plus tips. One full-time taxi could bring in $1,500–$3,000 per month. If clients are willing to share a taxi, you can carry up to four people and offer special group fares.

BOTTOM LINE ADVICE:

You will have to constantly deal with all types of people, and heavy traffic can be exhausting. You'll need to have an extremely flexible schedule (including early mornings, evenings, weekends, and holidays). The good news is that this is a growing industry, and with every car you add to your fleet, you can potentially add significant dollars to your income.

Temporary Employment Agency

Startup cost:	$60,000–$150,000
Potential earnings:	$75,000–$200,000
Typical fees:	Vary depending on the placement; usually a percentage of the going salary for the position filled
Advertising:	Yellow Pages, direct mail, newspaper ads, billboards, networking, referrals
Qualifications:	Previous temporary employment agency experience would be helpful; business background, organizational skills, ability to successfully match candidates with positions available
Equipment needed:	Computers (four to six) with printers for testing purposes, office computer with Internet access and scheduling/billing software, copier, scanner, fax, phone system
Home business potential:	No
Staff required:	Yes
Hidden costs:	Workers' compensation, employee benefits packages

LOWDOWN:

It used to be that temporary agencies specialized only in clerical types—but the age of corporate downsizing has led to an increase in professionals entering the "temp" field, from marketing communications professionals to product designers and even attorneys. Temporary help is a $60+-billion-dollar industry, mainly because the large companies that employed thousands a few years ago are now using help only as they need it. Understandably so, because, after all, from their point of view, why pay the huge benefits packages and salaries for work that can be done on a project-by-project basis? From your standpoint, this philosophy makes perfect sense too. You make your money on the fact that both workers and corporations are seeking less permanent commitment, workers are beginning to see the positive side of nonpermanent employment (they can freelance, launch businesses of their own, etc.), and the companies see the obvious benefit of saving money where possible. It's a win-win . . . all you have to do is match the right temp to the right assignment, and make sure that all of your employees are trained and able to work on short notice. You'll do an extensive background check and intake (including typing tests, computer aptitude assessments, etc.) and ensure that each temporary employee has sufficient credentials and/or experience to do the job to which they are assigned. Remember, your reputation depends on how well you match your temporary employees to the needs of your corporate clients.

STARTUP:

You'll need $60,000–$150,000 to buy into a temporary help franchise. You can certainly go it alone in this business, but keep in mind that you'll need a comprehensive benefits plan, several computers, and the placement staff or account executives to manage each account thoroughly and professionally. This is an extremely lucrative field, and you can make as much as $200,000 if you develop the right contacts, service them well, and build a fine reputation.

BOTTOM LINE ADVICE:

You can dig yourself an early grave if you don't spend enough time preparing up front; know that your competitors are out there, that they have just as many good candidates as you do, and that you must find a way to set yourself apart by advertising the uniqueness of your service. Consider the value of establishing your services in a market niche like health care, communications, or technical/engineering. If businesses can associate your company with a specialized category of temporary staffing, they'll automatically know who to call when they have a specific need (i.e., Acme Personnel = engineering specialists).

ADVICE FROM THE EXPERTS

What sets your business apart from others like it?

"We have a personal approach and a high level of applicants to choose from; in that sense, we're a cut above the rest," says Fran Doll, president of Superior Staffing, Inc., in Akron, Ohio, and recognized Ohio Entrepreneur of the Year.

Things you couldn't do without:

Doll says her business thrives on a telephone system, a computer, and fax machine. "If our phones go down, we're dead," she says.

Marketing tips/advice:

"You need to have worked in this industry for a while before embarking on your own. It's not as easy as it looks. Also, be sure you have enough capital or you'll have cash flow problems because you're underfinanced."

If you had to do it all over again . . .

"I would be more careful about the accountants I chose to work with. I had two accountants who really messed me up."

TOW BOAT OPERATOR

Startup cost:	$50,000–$200,000
Potential earnings:	$45,000–$75,000
Typical fees:	Free tow with annual membership; $300 per tow/service call for nonmembers
Advertising:	Marinas, fliers, Yellow Pages
Qualifications:	Captain's license, extensive knowledge of waters in service area
Equipment needed:	Tow boat with radio, answering service and/or pager, cell phone, insurance
Home business potential:	Yes
Staff required:	Yes
Hidden costs:	Maintenance of boat, insurance

LOWDOWN:

Your love of the water will draw you to this specialized (yet, in many parts of the country, seasonal) business, where you'll come to the aid of boaters in distress, towing their boats to deeper water or out of precarious situations. Just like a land-based towing service you have to be on-call 24/7. You must be extremely familiar with the body of water you service (i.e., know the location of every drawbridge, buoy, and sandbar) and if it's large, you may need to hire a crew and have several tow boats on constant call. Be prepared to handle any type of water-related mishap, such as a stalled engine, a capsized vessel, a fire on board, or even a "man overboard" situation. Keep in the good graces of the competition, as you may need to call on each other for help on exceptionally busy days. Getting to know the boating retailers and businesses along the shore will help spread the word about your business. Work with boat sellers to see if they would be willing to pass out your brochures to their customers.

STARTUP:

A tow boat business is costly to run, both in dollars and man-hours. Your best bet is to become a franchisee for a company like Sea Tow, which will provide you with a recognized name, plus training, referrals, and marketing support. However, to even be considered for a franchise you will need to already have your captain's license and a boat with an engine of at least 150 horsepower, plus navigational aids, communications capability, pumps, and towlines. Most of your income will come from up-front prepaid memberships. For an annual fee of around $120 per year, members receive free unlimited towing. Nonmembers would pay upwards of $300 per tow/service call. Sea Tow requires that you be on call 24/7, which means you will need a crew, so be sure to factor the cost of salaries, insurance, and benefits into your business plan.

BOTTOM LINE ADVICE:

If you're in this business by yourself and your own boat breaks down, you're out of operation until the boat is repaired, possibly for good, if your customers lose faith and go elsewhere; that's another good reason to go the franchise route. This is an expensive business to operate on a part-time basis, so you'll probably want to live in a place where you can tow boats year-round. On the upside, if you love being on the water and have a yen for adventure, this could definitely be the job for you.

TRUCKING BROKER

Startup cost:	$50,000–$75,000
Potential earnings:	$70,000–$100,000+
Typical fees:	Commissions of 5 to 10 percent per load
Advertising:	Yellow Pages, referrals, print advertising in business/manufacturing publications
Qualifications:	A background in trucking or shipping would be useful
Equipment needed:	Computer, printer, fax, high-speed Internet access, tracking software, phone
Home business potential:	Yes
Staff required:	No
Hidden costs:	Insurance, phone expenses

LOWDOWN:

A trucking broker is just one small piece of the shipping/freight forwarding business; in this case, you act as a linkup service, matching manufacturers needing product shipped with those freight lines able to transport. You do not handle the insurance aspect of shipping at all, which sets you apart from the freight forwarder. The logistics of matching a shipper to a carrier are your primary day-to-day concerns, and it isn't always easy to find a suitable carrier for each load. Still, if you can manage to keep up with the fast pace of being basically on-call for shippers in need, you can make a profitable living in this liaison-type service.

STARTUP:

You'll need between $50,000 and $70,000 to get started, mainly because your business will require high insurance premiums and some basic office equipment (i.e., computer, printer, and high-speed Internet access) plus tracking software to help maintain information pertaining to carrier whereabouts. Expect to earn $70,000–$100,000 for your efforts.

BOTTOM LINE ADVICE:

Your days will be spent searching for rigs en route to the same destination that your shipping client has targeted, and your nights will likely be spent handling your accounting and other daily chores. If you'd like your nights off, you'll need to hire someone to take care of the paperwork and day-to-day details of running the business.

UNDERWATER ADVENTURES/ SCUBA INSTRUCTION

Startup cost:	$100,000+
Potential earnings:	$55,000–$85,000
Typical fees:	Varied, depending on the length of the dive/level and length of instruction
Advertising:	Ads in diving magazines, free listings in travel guides and directories, Yellow Pages, Web site
Qualifications:	Extensive underwater diving experience; general certification as a diving instructor, plus individual certifications in any specialty diving techniques you intend to teach—i.e., rescue diving, cave diving, etc.; aquatic first aid and CPR; physical strength and stamina; sense of adventure and knowledge of underwater creatures and their environment
Equipment needed:	Boat(s) large enough to carry multiple divers and gear; full complement of diving and snorkeling gear (tanks, weights, snorkels, fins, masks, regulators, etc.) for instruction and underwater trips; basic office setup, including computer, printer, bookkeeping software, Internet access, fax, cell phone
Home business potential:	No
Staff required:	Yes
Hidden costs:	Insurance, equipment maintenance and replacement, fuel costs

LOWDOWN:

Have you been "bitten" by the SCUBA bug? Do you live for the opportunity to strap on your tanks and head out to swim with the fishes, maybe explore an ancient shipwreck? Would you like to turn others on to the thrill of seeing what lies beneath the sea? Here's your chance. Underwater adventures are more popular than ever these days and if you're located in the right place, you can make a pretty penny doing something you already enjoy. You can take this business in many directions—feature half-day and full-day underwater trips for beginning, intermediate, and advanced divers and snorkelers; offer SCUBA instruction/certification and snorkeling lessons at all levels; open a dive shop where you sell and service all the necessary gear.

STARTUP:

This is not the kind of business you can start with pocket change. Before you can instruct others in diving techniques, or even just lead them on a dive, you need to have some serious training yourself, including certification in diving instruction, specialty diving, and aquatic first aid/CPR, plus extensive personal diving experience. Many of your classes can take place in fairly shallow water—basic SCUBA can be taught in a pool, lake, reservoir, or along the ocean's edge. At some point, however, you're going to need to go deeper, and that means a boat. The size pretty much depends on how many divers you intend to carry at any given time (be sure to allow enough room for all their gear). And since you can't leave the boat unattended while you supervise a dive, you'll have to hire an experienced crew for backup. You'll need a healthy stock of diving gear, of course, which you must keep in tip-top shape (not an easy task considering how many people of different skill levels will be using it). Advertise in the local Yellow Pages and in the magazines divers read, link up with travel directories and guidebooks for free listings, and by all means, have a Web site. There's a lot of competition out there, so find a way to set your dive business apart.

BOTTOM LINE ADVICE:

Even though you may have started this business because you love to dive yourself, keep in mind that this is no hobby; you won't be able to spend every day at play. You'll still have the same basic chores every businessperson has, like hiring and firing, bookkeeping, and marketing. Your best chance for success is to locate in an area—like Florida or southern California—where you can offer year-round diving opportunities. Keep in mind, too, that like any adventures-type business, this one is not without risk. Accidents can happen, so make sure you are heavily insured.

UNIFORM SERVICE

Startup cost:	$150,000–$300,000
Potential earnings:	$50,000–$150,000+
Typical fees:	$500–$1,500 per client per month
Advertising:	Yellow Pages, direct mail, cold calls, coupon books, newspaper ads
Qualifications:	Previous dry cleaning/delivery service experience
Equipment needed:	Heavy-duty, industrial-size appliances (washer, dryer, dry cleaning equipment, and sterilization chemicals), pickup and delivery vans, inventory of uniforms
Home business potential:	No
Staff required:	Yes (a staff of 10 to 12 initially, from drivers to dry cleaners)
Hidden costs:	Insurance, workers' compensation, vehicle expenses, equipment maintenance

LOWDOWN:

Businesses as diverse as restaurants, institutions, hospitals, and mechanic's shops all require their employees to wear uniforms, partly to protect the employee's regular clothing from stains associated with the job, and partly to create a unified appearance. Your service provides crisp, clean uniforms for groups of employees as small as 10 and as large as 1,000; you will regularly pick up the soiled uniforms and deliver clean ones in their place. This service usually costs the average medium-sized client in the vicinity of $500–$1,500 per month. Your costs will cover a multitude of laundry and pressing equipment in addition to the cost of the uniforms themselves. Work with your own suppliers to get the best possible prices on uniforms, then pass along the savings to your clients. Because this is a price-driven field, you'll need to try every trick in the book to keep your costs down while providing quality uniforms and personalized service. It's not an easy balancing act, but one you'll need to perfect if you intend to stay competitive in this business.

STARTUP:

You'll need to spend a significant amount of money ($150,000–$300,000) up front, mostly to cover your delivery vehicle and cleaning equipment costs. You can expect to spend around $10,000 of that money on advertising your services, which you will need to be aggressive about since yours is a competitive business that sells on price as well as great service. If you can manage to keep your clients in close proximity to your home base and to one another, you can cut your vehicle expenses and realize a higher-than-average profit. Expect to earn anywhere from $50,000–$150,000 or more, depending on the size of your metropolitan area, and how much of that market you control.

BOTTOM LINE ADVICE:

Finding good help may be your biggest obstacle; your need to contain costs may hold you back from paying the kind of wages that will ensure employee dependability and loyalty, the very qualities your business needs. Consider hiring retirees as delivery personnel; their work ethic is often stronger than that of younger employees.

USED CAR LEASING

Startup cost:	$40,000–$80,000
Potential earnings:	$40,000–$65,000+
Typical fees:	Varied; lease payments are often $100–$300 per month, depending on the size and condition of the vehicle and length of the lease
Advertising:	Yellow Pages, auto clubs, community newspapers, small business publications
Qualifications:	Organization/management skills; it may be helpful to have mechanical ability to do your own repair work and make wise purchases of used vehicles
Equipment needed:	Fleet of decent used cars, minivans, and vans
Home business potential:	No
Staff required:	Not initially, but you may want to add one or two staffers once the phone starts ringing
Hidden costs:	Insurance, advertising, auto maintenance and repairs

LOWDOWN:

With the price of new cars rising steadily, it's easy to see why leasing is becoming a more popular option. But what if you can't afford to lease a brand-new car? You turn to a company specializing in leasing used vehicles. In this business, you will assist individuals in securing dependable transportation—and you may also offer a lease-to-own program for those interested in keeping the vehicles once they've passed their mileage limit or the term of their lease agreement. The biggest challenge you'll face is securing a large enough fleet to service your customer base; you'll have to make a sizable investment in vehicles before you see any significant return. However, if you plan well and are able to secure financing, you should have no problem finding suitable vehicles at auctions and even through short-term car rental agencies; you would select from among the cars that have exceeded a certain mileage limit and are consequently sold off at reasonable prices in order to be replaced with new vehicles. In all likelihood, you should be able to work out pretty good deals on these "retired" rental vehicles.

STARTUP:

Not surprisingly, most of your startup funds will go toward the acquisition of your fleet. Aside from that, you'll also need to consider how to spend your advertising dollars. For planning purposes, set aside approximately $3,000–$5,000 per year, to cover Yellow Pages ads and regular advertising in newspapers. Networking with auto clubs might bring in additional business at very little cost to you. Your leases will bring in anywhere from $100–$300 per month, depending on the size of the vehicle and the length of the lease (usually one to three years).

BOTTOM LINE ADVICE:

Position yourself as an economical alternative to traditional leasing programs and you'll likely generate a regular stream of responses to your advertising. If you're not particularly savvy about used vehicles, take along someone like a certified auto mechanic who is. Take care in purchasing your automobiles; no matter how attractive the price, a bad car could cause you more trouble than it's worth.

VIDEO-ON-DEMAND

Startup cost:	$80,000–$100,000+
Potential earnings:	$75,000–$150,000
Typical fees:	$300–$500 per installation, plus a percentage each time the video is watched
Advertising:	Hotel trades, service conventions, networking
Qualifications:	Knowledge of electrical installation procedures; some states may require an electrical contract permit
Equipment needed:	Tools for electrical installation, cables, jacks, satellite dishes, van(s) for transport
Home business potential:	Yes
Staff required:	Yes
Hidden costs:	Workers' compensation, vehicle expenses

LOWDOWN:

Hotels and motels by the thousands are installing video-on-demand services for their guests. These systems operate through regular television sets, but offer the viewer the chance to pick and choose which movies to watch and when to watch them. Unlike HBO or the Movie Channel, which air movies according to a predetermined schedule, video-on-demand lets the viewer decide when it's convenient to watch a particular movie. You'll work long, hard hours initially to install a system, but the good news is, most jobs will be a one-time shot with minimal follow-up service. Basically, you're simply installing a cable system and a satellite dish, although occasionally you may be asked to come up with a more sophisticated system, so the guests in rooms 315 and 325 can play Nintendo against one another, for example. Be prepared for unusual requests by constantly reading up on your industry and keeping in step with what's new and hot. You'll need good marketing skills for this business, but your service skills must be great, since this is a competitive field and service is where you'll make your mark.

STARTUP:

Your startup fees will be high ($80,000–$100,000 or more) because you need to lease the movies. You can pass that cost on to the hotel you're working with, who may pay you a fee for installation plus a percentage on the movie each time it is watched. Look for your earnings to be between $75,000–$150,000, depending on the size of your market.

BOTTOM LINE ADVICE:

There is a high turnover rate in this field, so screen your people well. In order to keep your business thriving, you'll need to travel extensively, and so will your staff. You'll also need to price your service competitively or offer extra features to stay in the running.

VIDEO PRODUCTION COMPANY

Startup cost:	$40,000–$100,000
Potential earnings:	$45,000–$100,000+
Typical fees:	Varied, from $150–$300 for simple duplication of an existing videotape to several thousand for complete production, from script to finished copies
Advertising:	Yellow Pages, business publications, direct mail, Web site
Qualifications:	Degree and/or experience in video production, organizational skills, ability to hire the necessary talent and freelancers
Equipment needed:	Complete video production studio, including full complement of taping/mixing/dubbing/editing equipment
Home business potential:	Not typically, unless you have space for a studio in your home
Staff required:	No (use freelancers for specialty assignments)
Hidden costs:	Studio construction costs (rent if you can), insurance

LOWDOWN:

Businesses and organizations in and around your community frequently need the services of a small production house, and your video production service can assist them. You may offer everything from scriptwriting to rounding up local talent to assisting with purchase of airtime. You need to decide up front how extensive you'd like to have your services become, and then make sure you have the pool of talent to help you achieve it all. The best thing you can do is build a strong stable of freelancers (from writers to actors to production people) who can work together behind the scenes to produce the videos while you're out front selling to potential clients. Corporate clients will likely be your best bet, because they tend to produce many in-house training videos and sales/promotional productions per year. But don't discount the smaller folks entirely, because they're the ones who will come back again and again with small projects if you treat them well the first time. A final tip: Look for inexpensive talent at universities and community theaters; audition folks even when you don't have specific needs in order to build a talent file; having a stable of talented people already in place can save you precious time when you're ready to film.

STARTUP:

If you decide to make a total investment in this business, you'll need $100,000 or more to build a state-of-the-art studio with all of the necessary taping/mixing/editing/dubbing equipment. You can make $45,000–$100,000 or more, depending on how many corporate clients you manage to snag.

BOTTOM LINE ADVICE:

You'll be able to make a sizable profit if you can manage to keep your overhead low; so often in this field, entrepreneurs go crazy over "image," spending more money than they make in order to impress clients. The only impression you need to make is the one that counts—solid, well-crafted video productions that do the job. To really make the big bucks in this business, keep quality high and pomp low.

WEIGHT LOSS CENTER

Startup cost:	$75,000–$150,000
Potential earnings:	$45,000–$80,000
Typical fees:	$8–$12 per client per week for basic weight loss counseling and services; more if additional services are provided (such as an exercise program)
Advertising:	Yellow Pages, print advertising, radio/TV ads, location
Qualifications:	A degree/background in nutrition or counseling would be helpful; some states require certification; personal experience in losing weight and keeping it off adds credibility
Equipment needed:	Complete diet and exercise regimen (workbooks, videos, food diaries, etc.), exercise equipment, display shelves/cabinets for related sales items, such as food products and supplements)
Home business potential:	No
Staff required:	Yes
Hidden costs:	Insurance, legal fees

LOWDOWN:

Considering that the majority of Americans are tipping the scales these days at weights that are at least 10 percent more than ideal body weight, the market for businesses aimed at helping "trim the fat," so to speak, is hot and getting hotter. Think about all the exercise equipment, health club memberships, diet books, and over-the-counter diet pills that the weight-obsessed buy each year—then think about how your weight loss center can benefit from the trend. Perhaps the best (and most credible) way to get into this business is to purchase a franchise; you'll get all of the operations and management training you'll need, along with expert assistance in learning weight loss methodology. You'll likely have a retail-like storefront, complete with a reception area and private offices plus a classroom and possibly even an exercise space; expect to spend some big bucks ($60,000 or more) on your location and furnishings alone. Still, since your image is just as important as the one your clients are hoping to achieve with a new body, you'll need to shell out more than most small businesses for your business location. The payoff could be worth it, however, since this is (and traditionally has been, in spite of some negative publicity in recent years) a profitable industry.

STARTUP:

You'll likely spend $75,000–$150,000 or more on your location, since your credibility and professional appearance are of utmost importance in bringing in the dollars. If you affiliate with a well-known and respected franchise, you could earn anywhere from $45,000–$80,000 per year helping others lose weight.

BOTTOM LINE ADVICE:

This is a high-risk liability business, which means you'll need to spend some significant money on insurance premiums and possibly legal fees. On the plus side, there will never be a shortage of potential customers; as long as there are fast-food restaurants, folks will need to burn off what they put on.

WHOLESALER

Startup cost:	$50,000–$80,000+
Potential earnings:	$100,000–$150,000+
Typical fees:	Varies according to list price; based on percentage of markup
Advertising:	Yellow Pages, direct mail, cold calls, word of mouth, ads in trade publications
Qualifications:	Degree/background in merchandising; previous retail experience would be helpful
Equipment needed:	Computer, printer, fax, Internet access, copier, phone, delivery vehicle (optional)
Home business potential:	Yes
Staff required:	No
Hidden costs:	Insurance

LOWDOWN:

Wholesalers deliver goods to retail outlets so that they can, in turn, be sold to the consumer; these are the sales professionals who strike the deals between manufacturers and retail outlets. For instance, a wholesaler would be the key negotiator in a retail clothing business, selling the maximum amount of clothing to a store at a competitive bulk rate. Therefore, the wholesaler's income is actually a percentage based on the markup on list price. As a wholesaler, you'll be working in the trenches of the retail market; you'll spend long hours meeting with retailers trying to strike the best and most profitable deals for both of you on items ranging from office equipment to clothing. Expect there to be lots of give and take; this is a business in which bartering plays a pivotal role.

STARTUP:

You'll need some seed money to secure deals with product manufacturers as well as furnish your office with some basic equipment; expect to spend anywhere from $50,000–$80,000 getting this business started. You'll also need some money for advertising, so set aside an additional $5,000 or so for your first year. You could earn $100,000–$150,000 or more if you are shrewd and sales-oriented.

BOTTOM LINE ADVICE:

Wholesalers are starting to open their own shops—offering goods at near-cost prices and raking in even bigger bucks. You'll do well to consider your market for its maximum potential, then pick the option that best suits your financial needs. For many, running a wholesale shop is a profitable way to go.

X-RAY INSPECTION SERVICE

Startup cost:	$40,000 or more
Potential earnings:	$50,000–$75,000
Typical fees:	$50–$80 per X-ray
Advertising:	Trade journals, direct mail, business association meetings, referrals
Qualifications:	Training/experience in radiological technology, knowledge of business issues and shipping operations
Equipment needed:	Mobile X-ray equipment, van, marketing materials
Home business potential:	Yes
Staff required:	No
Hidden costs:	Equipment maintenance, repair, and replacement

LOWDOWN:

For shippers, storage firms, and other businesses that must handle packages of unknown content, an X-ray service provides a "look into the unseen." In this time of almost daily terror threats and greater emphasis on homeland security, the analysis of packages is no longer a luxury, it's a necessity. If you are located in a large urban area or near any major shipping facility/port, you can develop an X-ray inspection service that meets the highly specialized needs of this market. Many of your potential clients are old-fashioned in their modes of operation, and you will show them how your services can improve the safety and efficiency of their operations, at less cost than they may have anticipated or even experienced previously.

STARTUP:

The costs of the equipment and of the startup marketing to develop a loyal client base will be the largest drains on your new-business budget; you'll need a minimum of $40,000 to get started. With an effective marketing effort and perseverance, you could make $50,000 the first year.

BOTTOM LINE ADVICE:

Getting your foot in the door will be the challenge. While your potential clients will likely recognize the value of your inspection service, they may be operating on a thin profit margin and so will be reluctant to fork over the cash. If you can demonstrate that your service meets a real need, one that can be met no other way nor at such a competitive price, you will build a strong client base that will garner referrals and repeat business. Your marketing must focus on the practical advantages of your service as well as its value in terms of both price and peace of mind.

PART THREE

BUSINESS TIPS

BUSINESS BASICS:
WORDS OF ADVICE FOR BUSINESS
OWNERS OF ALL TYPES

"MUST-HAVE" CHECKLIST FOR NEW BUSINESSES
Here are some of the more critical items you'll need for your new business:

- Computer system, high-speed Internet access, and special software packages pertaining to your business and its needs (accounting, desktop publishing, spreadsheet, word processing, etc.)
- Multifunction printer/fax/scanner/copier or individual machines
- Phone system with voice mail capability or answering machine; cell phone
- File cabinets and hanging files/file folders.
- Comfortable, ergonomically designed chair (often a last thought, but incredibly important to your productivity, particularly if you will be spending a lot of time in front of your computer screen)
- Desk with plenty of arm space (so that you can comfortably work on projects without bumping into your computer)
- Guest chairs and a conference table for meeting with employees, clients, and/or suppliers
- Bookshelves to hold your numerous resources and reference books
- Office supplies: stapler/staples, paper clips, pens/pencils, tape, legal pads, date stamp, binders, index cards, clasp envelopes in various sizes, etc.
- Letterhead, envelopes, and business cards
- Storage shelves or cabinet (used to house supplies)
- Waste receptacles (don't forget a separate one for recyclable paper!)
- Background music (if that's important to you or your customers)
- Aesthetically appealing, yet professional-looking décor. Whether traditional, contemporary, or eclectic, your decorative choice sends a solid visual message about your company. If you consider yourself decoratively

challenged, hire a professional to help; perhaps you can work out a trade for services.

- Most important: good lighting. One tiny desk lamp just won't do. You and your staff will work more productively if you invest in proper, adequate lighting.

TYPES OF BUSINESS INSURANCE

- Property damage: Covers fire, storm damage, vandalism, etc., for the replacement costs of the contents of your business. Traditional insurance policies may not cover catastrophic loss; if you live in a hurricane- or earthquake-prone region, make sure that you are adequately covered. Your deductibles for losses due to natural disaster will likely be higher than for more traditional property damages.
- General liability: Provides protection from personal injury and property damage.
- Product liability: Protects from claims for damages or injuries related to defects in the products you make or sell. Regardless of outcome, litigation in these cases is time-consuming and expensive. Judgments often run to multimillion-dollar sums; make sure you have adequate coverage. If someone files a suit against your business, you will incur some costs, even if you eventually win.
- Disability: Provides income replacement should you miss work through injury or illness. This is important for all business owners to have, but especially if you are the major income source for your family.
- Worker's compensation: Covers employees for loss of income and for medical costs arising from a job-related injury or illness. This coverage is required by law in all fifty states. You are legally required to: 1) provide a safe workplace, 2) hire competent employees, 3) provide safe tools, and 4) warn employees of existing dangers. Check the coverage of any contractor you hire.
- Business interruption: Covers extra expenses and loss of income caused by an interruption of normal business due to an unforeseen event, such as fire. Lost income is defined as the difference between normal income and the income earned during the interruption of normal business. This is crucial insurance for businesses located in geographic areas prone to hurricanes and earthquakes.
- Key person: Protects your business in case of the death or disability of an owner, partner, or key employee.
- Health or medical: Protects against the costs of major medical expenses, and it is becoming increasingly expensive. Whereas in the past, many businesses underwrote the full amount of individual premiums as an employee benefit, more and more are passing along a significant share of that cost to the employees themselves.

- Special insurance: Many special types of insurance are available, such as automobile, crime, computer, life, malpractice, and glass insurance. Take a close look at your business to see which of these may be necessary or advisable.
- Financial insurance: Depending on the structure of your business, you may need Sole Proprietor Insurance, Partnership Insurance, or Shareholder Insurance. Fidelity Bonds protect against loss from embezzlement.

WRITING GRANT PROPOSALS AND LOAN APPLICATIONS

Applying for a grant or loan requires the same thinking process you went through in putting together your business plan. The reason is the same: You are presenting the facts and assumptions about your new venture to an outsider for the purpose of tapping into available financial resources.

Depending on the state you live in, a business development grant may be available to you if you are a member of a special group. Subsidized loans may also be a possibility. Women and minority business owners should make special efforts to discover what financial support programs are available specifically to them. Typically, such programs are administered at the state level.

The persistence that has allowed you to develop a business concept and get it off the ground needs to be applied to the process of seeking a grant or loan as well. You will probably have to ask many people before you find the right door to open, the right office to call in your state government, and the right person, the one who is ready and willing to assist you with your search. A professor at a local business college may know the direction in which to point you. A women's business group might offer assistance. So might your state representative; try calling his or her office. And don't forget to consult your library for resource guides.

A loan could be all that's necessary to start you on the road to success, and a grant, which need not be paid back, would be an even bigger boost!

Tips on Filling Out the Proposal or Application

- Make sure your business plan does the best possible job of presenting your concept, marketing approach, and financial projections.
- Follow the loan or grant guidelines to the letter. If possible, obtain a model application and study it carefully.
- Have your business advisors review your completed application for errors and possible additions.
- Include all required elements:

    Credit request (the amount of money needed, its intended use, and, if you're applying for a loan, your plans for paying it back)

    A copy of your business plan

    Federal Income Tax returns for the last three years for all significant members of the management team and the business owners

Your projected income statement, monthly for a year and quarterly for the following three years

Cash flow projected similarly

Specifics on all business debt

Resumes for significant participants in the enterprise

Sources of equity, describing the contribution of each significant business backer

Other requirements as needed depending on the business type (i.e., construction contract for a building business) or loan type (SBA Compensation Agreement, etc.)

LEASE VS. BUY DECISIONS

If your startup venture requires a lot of equipment, instead of purchasing outright consider instead a "lease-with-option-to-buy" arrangement that allows you to pay as you go. Why is this scenario more desirable than an outright purchase? Two reasons:

- First, a lease allows you the flexibility of using the latest equipment without making a long-term commitment to it. If, for some reason, your business goes under, you can usually negotiate your way out of a lease—and you're not faced with the prospect of having to find a buyer for equipment that is now used and yet may not even be fully paid for.
- Second, your cash flow isn't tied up in equipment expenses—freeing you up to put your capital toward other, more pressing needs, such as advertising, staffing, or insurance premiums.

Most leases run thirty-six to sixty months, but you can often negotiate both the length of the lease and the interest rate. Since leasing is a very competitive field, your chances of finding a deal that is both suitable to your needs and compatible with your budget is quite high.

COMPUTER EQUIPMENT "MUSTS"

Keeping in mind that computers and peripherals change at such lightning speed these days that what you buy today will be obsolete next month, here's a checklist for setting up your computer system with the features you will likely need:

- Intel Pentium 4 processor with HT technology
- 512MB DDR2 SDRAM and 160GB hard drive with Microsoft Windows XP
- DVD-ROM drive and CD burner
- Laser printer
- 17" flat panel display monitor
- High-speed DSL or cable Internet connection

- Accounting program (such as Quicken or QuickBooks) to keep accurate records and manipulate data to create reports
- Word-processing software (such as WordPerfect or Microsoft Word); database, spreadsheet, and presentation software, if desired
- Graphics or desktop publishing software (to create your own marketing materials, slides, and graphs)
- Network software if you have two or more computers sharing information
- Internet Service Provider
- Mouse and mousepad, keyboard
- Sound card and speakers

BUSINESSES ON THE SUCCESS TRACK

What are the top opportunities for making money as an entrepreneur in the first decade of the twenty-first century? A quick look at recent issues of *Entrepreneur* magazine reveals they are pretty varied, and some of them may be appealing to you:

- Online auction sales
- Home health care and geriatric services
- Executive temporary services/employee leasing
- Alternative energy installation
- Computer training services/consulting
- Private tutoring
- Virtual assistance
- Fitness training and weight loss programs
- Pet pampering services
- Security consultants
- Business and management consultants
- Adventure tourism
- Personal chefs and specialty foods
- Alternative medicine/wellness programs

And if you're considering a change in careers and looking for some general direction, the U. S. Department of Labor's list of the top fastest growing occupations through 2012 shows some interesting trends. Of the 30 occupations listed, 16 have something to do with health and wellness. The second largest group (7) includes careers related to computers, electronics, and technology. Coming in a distant third are jobs in the field of environmental protection.

LOCATION, LOCATION

Is it really true that location is everything—to every kind of business there is? Well, yes and no.

While it is important to have an actual location of some kind, that doesn't always mean that you need a high-profile storefront or a high-rise corporate office to make your business respected and profitable.

You can get by on a shoestring with a neatly decorated area of your own home, as long as it's separate from the rest of the household activity. An extra bedroom or a den would make a fine office, as would a finished basement or garage. For some home business people, simply sectioning off a part of their living room works just fine.

The fact is, home offices have become increasingly popular; thousands of people meet with clients every day in their homes and experience no lapse in credibility whatsoever. If you're concerned about a professional image, invest in the kind of furniture and high-end equipment you'd see in any corporate office, and don't meet clients at your kitchen table if you can avoid it.

If you are opening a retail establishment or other business that depends on high visibility and being located in close proximity to companion-type businesses (such as a clothing store that would do well next to a tailoring service), you would greatly benefit from renting a small- to medium-sized shop. Strip malls and small shopping plazas offer the best choices, and cost considerably less than large shopping mall space.

Above all else, be sure to check the zoning regulations in your area. A florist once failed to do so, and began running her business out of her house only to be subjected to complaints from neighbors. She was forced to move out of her house and into a small storefront, the cost of which she was sure could severely cut into her profits. But thanks to higher visibility and increased drive-by traffic, her business nearly *quadrupled* in the first two months. The lesson here: Never underestimate the power of the right location. In the right spot, this florist ended up realizing the kind of business she'd only dreamed of.

Know where you are likely to be seen and reached by the most customers. If, on the other hand, your customers are buying your product or service because there is none other like it, you may be successful in getting them to come to you, no matter where you decide to locate.

UNDERSTANDING YOUR CASH BUDGET

For those business owners who are "mathematically challenged," here is a quick breakdown of the items that should appear on your cash flow projection statements. Basically, you need to look at what's coming in and what's going out on a regular basis.

"In" column:
- Cash sales
- Accounts Receivables
- Funds from sales of assets or equipment
- Refunds (such as tax refunds)
- Collections (outstanding accounts)

"Out" column:
- Inventory/stock purchase

- Operating expenses
- Fixed expense payments
- Credit payments on long-term debt
- Tax payments (most often quarterly)
- Shareholder/stock payments

Taking a look at these items and how they change over a period of a year can provide you with a Profit and Loss statement that clearly shows you what your business is earning and spending.

You can use this information to build your following year's budget, by making educated assumptions based on what happened the previous year. For instance, if you have a bad winter quarter because your business is somewhat dependent on good weather, you'll know to build sales up in the fall to cover your winter operating budget and make sure the bills get paid.

DYNAMIC GOAL-SETTING

If you want to succeed in business, you need to start with a good goal-setting program. Seek out professional help in this area if you are not sure how to identify and set your own goals.

Here are just a few tips to get you started:

- Make your goals specific. The only goals that stand a chance of being achieved are the ones that are clear enough to become part of a mind-set and visualization process. The clearer the goal, the easier it will be to accomplish.
- Have a deadline for achievement. You can have a terrific goal, but wander around aimlessly without a drop-dead date for its achievement. Remember these words: A goal is a dream with a deadline.
- Consider and anticipate your obstacles. Know where the pitfalls might occur, and devise a plan to work around any such impediments.

Above all else, make sure there is a personal benefit to achieving the goal you set, or it will not serve to motivate you. You need to reward yourself . . . say, with a vacation if you sell one million dollars' worth of product. If the reward isn't enticing enough, you might not be able to see the benefit of working so hard to achieve the goal.

CUSTOMER SERVICE TIPS

Getting and keeping customers is the challenge for any new business. Are your customers being served as well as they should be?

Here is a checklist of questions you can ask yourself from time to time:

- Are customers being helped in a timely manner? Are phones being answered promptly and cordially?

- Are your customer service representatives knowledgeable enough about your product or service?
- Do problems get resolved quickly and productively?
- Are your reps following up on a regular basis—especially to thank customers for their business?
- Are your customers receiving regular information, discounts, and other special offers from your company?
- Is your customer database being updated and expanded constantly?
- Are your delivery services top-notch?
- Are all requests for materials (brochures, catalogs, etc.) being handled as quickly and professionally as possible?
- Is it easy for customers to order your product or service, or do they have to punch a million numbers into a phone or click several screens on your Web site to do so?
- Have you noticed a significant increase in referral business (a primary indication of excellent customer service)?

Customer service is not a one-shot deal; your business can only grow if you constantly maintain relationships and treat every customer as if he or she is a customer for life.

CREATIVE IDEA-GENERATING

You have a business problem (or opportunity) staring you in the face; now, how do you come up with a suitable solution or answer in a short period of time?

Try one or more of these tactics:

- Mind-mapping. You draw a circle with the ultimate goal in the center, and lines extending outward like a sunburst. On each line, you write down one possible way to achieve your goal.
- Brainstorming. Invite a few business friends (or, better yet, fellow business owners) over for an evening of pizza and brainstorming. Listen to what others have to say. Even if you end up using your own initial ideas after all, their feedback might influence you later.
- Learn from others' mistakes. Read trade journals and business publications—or e-mail other business owners in entrepreneurial or specialty online business forums or chat rooms.
- Go where your customers are (if they're not with you). If you have a resume service, try hanging out in the resume book section of your local bookstore to listen in to what your potential customers are needing and wanting. You might be amazed by what you learn.

The important thing to remember is that there isn't just one possible solution: The value of thinking creatively is that you can explore many different possibilities— and if one doesn't work, you still have others left to choose from.

FRANCHISING

A franchise is a mutually beneficial agreement between a franchiser (parent company) and a franchisee (business operator), which allows the franchisee to sell the franchiser's well-established product or service, while the franchiser collects previously agreed-upon fees from the franchisee. The rules of operation vary from business to business, but generally speaking, the franchiser retains close control of the product in order to ensure uniformity.

A franchise can be an attractive way of becoming your own boss. Remember, however, that you will need a good deal of startup capital to go the franchise route. You may, for instance, be required to own your own premises, which can be expensive considering that in running a franchise business, location is everything. Be aware, too, that as a franchisee, you are not the only boss of your business; the parent company has its stake, too.

Benefits to the Franchiser

The parent company sees the franchise agreement as a cost-effective method of expanding its business. The explosion of franchise industries in recent years can be attributed to the need for companies to expand while remaining lean at the corporate level. The franchiser can expand his or her business without the need for excessive capital and without adding extra layers of management that would not only cost money but could compromise efficiency. The franchiser collects an agreed-upon revenue from each franchisee. This revenue varies, but can be as high as 20 percent.

Benefits to the Franchisee

As a franchisee, you can tap into economies of scale (in purchasing, for instance) that would normally be available only to a large corporation. You also gain by being able to take advantage of the parent company's advertising and promotional support, and from the franchiser's business and industry know-how.

Pitfalls

Most problems in franchising arise from the differing objectives of the franchisee and the franchiser. You, as franchisee, will be watching your bottom line in order to maximize your profit. The franchiser, on the other hand, who calculates his or her fees based on what you sell, will want you to maximize your sales even when, because of discounting, remodeling, etc., this could cut into your profits. If you decide to purchase a franchise, be aware that you are not the only person trying to make money from this enterprise, and that, while you may make a good living out of it, you won't take all of the profits.

KEEPING THE RECORDS YOU NEED

Probably the most important device for managing the paperwork of your business is the circular file. Do not keep any piece of paper unless you are sure that you want it, or need it. Hanging a "Bless This Mess" sign over your desk is no solution. Instead, plan how you will manage your paper and just do it. You want to spend your time on profit-making tasks, not on searching through mountains of unorganized material for that one vital receipt or order slip.

What records are you required to keep? The IRS has issued the following guidelines: "Your permanent books (including inventory records) must show not only your gross income, but also your deductions and credits. In addition, you must keep any other records and data necessary to support the entries in your books and on your tax and information returns." This includes paid bills and canceled checks. The IRS lets you decide how to store this material, as long as you choose an "orderly" approach.

For very small businesses just getting started, the checkbook register can be enough of a financial record, along with one shoe box for receipts and another for invoices. Most organizations move rapidly past this stage, however. Spend some time early on planning for storage, so as to prevent yourself from wasting many hours at year-end to pull figures together for your accountant. Set up a filing system you feel comfortable with, and stick to it during the year. Color-coded file folders in hanging files are appropriate for almost all types of organizations.

There's nothing glamorous about file folders in a box, but this kind of system can expand as you grow. It lets you put your hand quickly on the paper you need and efficiently store the records you must keep. It gets stuff off your desk when you're not working on it, and it lets you bring it back easily whenever you need it.

A popular approach is to devote one color to each major business topic. Marketing, for example, could be blue. Set up a tabbed hanging folder, in blue, for whatever marketing papers you have now. Later, you will probably need to subdivide the hanging folder with individual tabbed blue file folders for your marketing plan, market research, new ideas, special promotion plans, sales forecasts, and so on. And remember that labeling the file folders is just as important as labeling the files you keep on the hard drive of your computer.

Further refinements to your filing system depend on the nature of your business. For sales people, a tickler file system arranged by date may be essential. You need to keep track of which accounts should be called on two weeks from now, then six months down the road. Service businesses may need files of information and concept-oriented material arranged by topic area: employee motivation, training systems, new approaches, etc.

Most businesses keep client files alphabetically. Your clients or customers are the lifeblood of your business, and you need a quick, efficient way of storing and retrieving their information: desires, wants, needs, buying history, future possibilities. A computer spreadsheet or database program works well for tracking this information; however, you will probably also want to have hard copies as backups. The IRS does not particularly care about this aspect of your business, but you should; it's the basis of the ongoing marketing relationship that supports everything you do.

So choose a system, put it together, and put away every piece of paper you have kicking around your company. Keep using the files all year. Then stop thinking about this boring topic and get busy with the action steps that lead you toward your business goals.

MARKETING:
PROMOTING YOUR BUSINESS
EFFECTIVELY AND/OR ECONOMICALLY

MARKETING ON A SHOESTRING

Marketing is a component of every business, no matter how large or small. The people who need your product or service must know what you have to offer and be able to reach you. Make use of every available route to communicate your message to prospective customers. That does not mean you should pour money into untested ad campaigns or produce expensive giveaways. Creativity is much more important than money in marketing a new venture. Your ideas and commitment to the value of your product or service are the keys to your marketing success. The first step to successful marketing is self-analysis. What are you really selling? What are the values of your business? What makes you different from similar companies? What do you offer that your customers can't do without, and can't get anywhere else? It can be difficult to come right out and tell people the answers to these questions, but you—and everyone else in your organization—must learn to say, in one sentence, what your business has to offer.

Advertising is only a small piece of the marketing puzzle, and some businesses thrive without doing any at all. Others use one type of advertising exclusively, but they generally go through a process of discovery first in order to find what works best. What kind of advertising will your business need? Beware of simply settling for the least expensive option. Any cost is too high if it does not result in sales. Experiment with different media, tracking the results of each carefully. Repeat only those methods that work. Otherwise you could go broke fast.

An effective marketing plan is essential. Work with it for a year, then reassess. Do not neglect some of the proven techniques for marketing that cost very little and serve to make your name known in your community.

- *Cooperate with other businesses*—consider a joint promotion (fitness classes and nutrition counseling would be a nice fit, for example).
- *Be an expert*—give speeches before community groups, write articles on topics related to the products and services you offer, etc.
- *Participate in trade shows*—with careful planning, you can build follow-up opportunities, demonstrate your product many times over, and make contacts with prospects.
- *Gain free media exposure*—get publicity at no cost, thereby receiving third-party endorsement for your story.
- *Consider direct mail*—guided by an expert, you can create an effective mailing list to reach your target market.
- *Become involved in your community*—genuine public service on boards and committees enhances your reputation, makes friends for your business, and gets your name out.
- *Publish a newsletter quarterly*—include information of interest to your target market, appealing graphics, and a focus on one of your products or services.

MARKETING TRENDS OF THE FUTURE

How your business will look in the future depends upon your changing consumer base. Here are just a few trends you should be aware of:

- *The age factor.* The number of Americans over 65 continues to grow at an unprecedented rate as more and more baby boomers reach retirement age. Aging bodies have distinct needs in everything from health care to cosmetics, and aging minds may be focused on more than retirement planning; they're searching for continuing education and travel opportunities, nostalgic collectibles, and more.
- *Health and well-being.* Notice this in the increasing popularity of wellness programs and homeopathic therapies, aromatherapy, reflexology, organic foods, etc.), and a desire for the simpler life as reflected in the growth of home-based businesses, a shift of population to smaller towns, and the pursuit of spiritual fulfillment. And don't forget the whole obesity issue—diet and exercise programs are more popular than ever.
- *Cocooning.* 9/11 dealt a serious blow to our sense of security. People are drawing closer to their families these days and claiming control of their immediate environments. This shows itself in greater-than-ever expenditures on items for the home, in increasing gun-ownership (particularly among women), in the rise of homeschooling, and in the explosion of e-commerce. People are no longer eager to leave home to do business; instead of your customers coming to you, you may have to go to them instead.
- *Adventure.* People still want excitement, but they want it with minimal risk and on their own terms. The trend is toward exotic foods, sports, and travel.

- **The informed consumer.** Easy and affordable access to the information superhighway allows a consumer to research your product thoroughly before even speaking to you. Today's consumers are bright and well-informed. Be ready to listen, to get to know your customer, to establish trust.

These are some of the broad trends. Get to know the narrower trends, too, that directly affect your neighborhood and business area.

ADVERTISING EFFECTIVELY—AND ECONOMICALLY

You've started a business and you need to get the word out. The problem is, you simply don't have the kind of budget that General Motors or Microsoft does to advertise your products or services. What can you do?

You could try one or more of these more economical methods:

- **Press releases.** Free press is the best, when you are lucky enough to get it. Try to offer tips that will appeal to a particular group of people, and you'll have a better chance of catching the interest of an editor.
- **Fliers.** Post them everywhere your potential customers are likely to go. If you own a moving or packing service, for example, a flier strategically placed on the bulletin board at a coin-operated laundry or apartment complex might yield some quick results for you.
- **Consider a Web site.** Ten years ago, no one could have predicted the influence the Internet would have on all our lives. Today, it's a major advertising force to be reckoned with. Why? Because it is relatively inexpensive compared to most other media and because it reaches millions of people worldwide. Will a Web site help you get all the business you need? That depends on what you're selling, but all indications are good. And lest you doubt the power of the Web to sell goods and services, just take a good look at what's happened with eBay.
- **Offer coupon deals regularly.** Coupons are ads that come with "souvenirs" for your customers; you get the sale, they walk away with a prize—a lower price or a better deal—just for doing business with you. What could be better than that?
- **Trades for advertising space.** You might have a service that a local newspaper or TV/radio station needs. Consider trading your special products or skills for free space or airtime.
- **Direct mail.** You can spend a small amount of money and reach a large number of potential customers through direct mail. Be sure, however, that what you send is both interesting and captivating. Your clients are deluged with "junk mail," so your piece had better be fairly innovative and attention-getting. Work with a professional (you can possibly trade services here, too) to write and design your direct mail pieces. And hone your mailing list carefully; with the cost of postage these days, you can't afford to waste a dime.

GETTING THE WORD OUT: PUBLICITY

- *Create the hook.* To create your own publicity, you need to develop a "hook" or a compelling reason why someone should listen to your story. Media contacts must feel strongly that your product or service would be of some value to their audience. Take time to build a cohesive "pitch" that really conveys the unique qualities and benefits of your product or service.
- *Make a list.* Make a list of media contacts whom you think would be interested in your product or service. Prioritize the list and decide what you want to tell each contact.
- *Create a "mini" press kit.* It isn't necessary to mail out an elaborate press kit. It is often just as effective to send a personalized "pitch" letter and a press release in a standard business-sized envelope to your media contacts.
- *Follow up with a phone call.* Follow up your mailings with a phone call to each media contact. If you fail to connect the first time or if your media contact is too busy to talk with you, be persistent.
- *Take extensive notes to the interview.* Take additional material relating to your product or service to your media contact meeting. Product samples, testimonials, brochures, and a list of current vendors or customers (with their permission, of course) will assist you in conveying an interesting and powerful story about your company. Create a list of possible questions the media representative might ask you. Be ready with answers!

BOOSTING SALES

One thing you can never have enough of is sales. But how do you drive sales up in the fastest way possible? What methods tend to bring results for small business owners?

Here are just a few things you might try, especially if you've never really considered yourself a salesperson:

- *Listen before you talk.* Ask your potential customers about their needs, and listen. As many sales pros will tell you, there's a reason you have two ears and only one mouth.
- *Find out exactly what your clients' problems are.* Too many novices don't listen well enough to their customers' problems, which are the real keys to selling. If you know what's going wrong at a client's place of business or in his or her home, you stand a much better chance of setting things right. You are in the business of making your customers' businesses and/or lives run better with whatever products or services you can offer.
- *Match your best solutions to each problem.* After you've identified your client's problems, dive into your list of solutions. But don't offer all of them as potentials; spend time highlighting the ones that seem the most viable and compatible with your customers' needs.

- *Offer your services as a continual process.* Your services are not over when you finish the job; you must also convey the idea that you are an expert whose services and advice can be depended on for a time that extends well beyond the initial sale. If you want repeat business, you have to build a long-lasting relationship with your client—one that is based not only on the problem-solution orientation, but also on the human level. Get to know your customer on a personal basis; find out the things he or she enjoys in life and remember to talk about them every time you meet.
- *Remember to always say "thank you."* No sale is ever complete until it is fully acknowledged by some show of appreciation. Two simple words can bring in a lot of residual and repeat business.

Getting and keeping customers is not easy work, and even the pros need to have regular workshops on increasing sales effectiveness. So, if your first few attempts at sales don't go as smoothly as you'd like, don't give up. It takes a while to perfect the "art of the deal"!

MARKETING IN A WEB SITE WORLD

If it seems these days as though just about everyone has a Web site, it's because just about everyone does. In 1998, there were approximately 2.6 million Web sites worldwide. Today, that number is in the billions, and growing, according to one estimate, at a rate that doubles every 50 days.

From a new business owner's perspective, this interesting bit of trivia should tell you two things: 1) if you're going to do business in the twenty-first century, you ought to be at least thinking about a Web site, and 2) you're competing for attention against several billion other Web sites, so the one you come up with had better stand out from the crowd.

Before you head out to the bookstore for a step-by-step guide to creating your own Web site, consider this: Not every business absolutely, positively needs one. If you own a small auto repair shop or petsitting service and your customers are primarily your neighbors, don't waste your marketing money on a Web site; put it into a Yellow Pages listing or newspaper ads instead. If, on the other hand, you're selling a product or providing a service that could potentially be of interest to vast numbers of people all over the country and you're willing to ship your goods, or even yourself, beyond the immediate geographic location of your business, then a Web site is probably a good idea.

Let's suppose you've decided you do need a Web site, but you don't know diddly-squat about the Internet, except how to access your e-mail. What do you do next? Here are a few helpful tips to get you started:

- *Reserve a domain name.* Maybe even two. Or three. A domain name is your Internet address—like lovetoshop.com or headed4rio.net. Ideally, your domain name would be the name of your business . . . unless, of course, that name is already taken, which is why you need to reserve it as quickly as possible. There are many horror stories out there of celebrities who didn't act quickly enough and now someone else is using their name for a Web site over which they have no control. Even if you decide not to have a Web site right away (or never get around to having one at all), you'll still own your business name for Web marketing purposes. You can reserve your domain name from several different sources (surf the Web for possibilities). Domains with the .com appellation are going fast, so are .net names. There's no limit to how many domain names you can purchase, so snap up as many as you think you might need. They go for as little as $5.95 each, per year, and as part of the registration process, you'll find out if the ones you want are still available. Once you reserve your names, be vigilant about renewing your rights to them; if you slip up and let your subscriptions lapse, someone can (and probably will) slip in and buy your names right out from under you, then possibly charge you a bundle to buy them back.

- *Hire a professional.* Yes, you can design your own Web site. There are plenty of how-to guides, not to mention several software packages, on the market today that will take you step-by-step through the process. In the end you will have a Web site—how shall we put this delicately?— that's adequate. If you're serious about your Web site (and you should be), hire a professional—someone who's not only grounded in good graphic design, but who understands how it can best be applied to the Internet. You can find professional designers (surprise!) by surfing the Web. They usually "sign" their work; so when you see a Web site you particularly like, look for the designer's name.

- *Expect to spend some money.* Think of your Web site as an investment in your company's image. Would you cut costs to come up with a logo or letterhead design? Of course not. Nor should you try to design a Web site on the cheap. Hopefully, your business is going to be around for a long time and so is your Web site. Expect to spend a minimum of $2,000 for the design of your Web site, and, if your Web site is particularly active and needs frequent updating, possibly another several hundred dollars per month to manage it. If those figures have you saying, "Hmmm . . . I could do this myself and save a lot of money," try this: Spend some time on the Web comparing actual sites. You'll quickly be able to pick out the ones created by amateurs vs. those designed by professionals. Is that the impression you want to make for your business?

- *Set some goals for your Web site.* Think about why you want to have a Web site in the first place. Is it to increase the sales of a specific product? Or, are you looking for name recognition or a way to highlight your credentials? Do you have important information or tips to share with consumers? Answers to these and other similar questions will help determine your Web site's focus and style.

- *Beware of the flash.* Technology is a wonderful thing, but it can also be deadly to a Web site. You want your Web site to stand out from the crowd, of course, but beware of adding too many bells and whistles. They can end up detracting from your message and may actually make your Web site more difficult for customers and clients to navigate. Do you really need sound or images that move and flash to get your message across? If not, don't waste the money creating them.

- *Keep it current.* Once your Web site is up and running, set aside some money in your marketing budget for regular updates. You can maintain the site yourself, or pay a webmaster to do it for you. Just be sure you do it. There are few things more frustrating for a user than to find that the Web site he or she just pulled up on the screen hasn't been updated in a year or two. No joke—this happens a lot!

GROWTH:
THINKING AHEAD AND
PLANNING FOR SUCCESS

WHEN TO HIRE A CONSULTANT OR SUBCONTRACTOR
Your desk is piling up with unpaid bills, tax forms, and work orders. Your time is eaten up in the all-encompassing aspects of running your business entirely by yourself—and the work just keeps rolling in anyway. What can you do?

You could hire a consultant or subcontractor to pick up the slack, help arrange your office so that it runs neatly and efficiently, or simply offer advice in an area where you are weakest. You can bring in such additional help on a short-term, per-project basis, by calling on a professional for one-time-only or once-per-month assistance.

But how do you find such a person, and how do you know if his or her services are worth the price? If you're looking for an accounting subcontractor, for example, you might start by contacting a local association for accounting professionals (they meet regularly and often have a directory of members that they're willing to share).

You could also ask for referrals or recommendations from the members of your own professional association, as they have likely had the same needs as you and may have used the services of a subcontractor at least once before. These folks will tell you everything you need to know about the pros and cons of hiring outside help, but be prepared to listen and learn. You're likely to hear a lot of horror stories.

GAINING CREDIBILITY
Once you've opened your doors for business, how do you get potential customers to learn your name and trust your company as a reliable source in the community? Ultimately, the way to build credibility is to develop a strong business with a solid reputation for delivering what it promises to the customer. But what can you do in the meantime, until you're a household name? Here are some possibilities:

- Volunteer at local charitable foundations and corporate events. Simply being out there where other influential types are likely to be found (either as sponsors or as participants) will put you face-to-face with people who can help spread the word about your business. It's worth the donated hours on your part, and you'll get to widen your circle of acquaintances.

- Offer yourself as an expert on your topic of interest. Send regular press releases with tips for consumers to local and regional newspapers and magazines. Editors are always looking for filler and by getting your name in front of them, you stand a good chance of being interviewed the next time a story on your area of expertise rolls around. Be sure to keep in regular contact with the media in your area, even if it's just a quick phone call to ask if they need any help with upcoming features.

- Give free speeches at local association dinners. Or lunches. Or breakfasts. Seriously, you should make it a point to be just about anywhere that potential clients gather to learn more about improving their professional (and possibly personal) lives. Association meetings work best because they are always in need of interesting new speakers; so are civic groups and universities.

- Create and mail a regular newsletter with useful tips. Giving some information for free can create positive awareness of your company and what it has to offer. People do tend to read newsletters, and even though they may not need your services today, such publications, if well-done, will keep you in their minds tomorrow.

- Perform to your personal best. Ultimately, it's going to be a reputation based on fair pricing, high quality, and exceptional service that will gain you the credibility you need to bring in new business. Set high standards and work every day toward achieving them, and you will have your credibility sooner than most.

BECOMING A NETWORKING GIANT

Want to move to the networking fast track? Here are some great tips on becoming a top networking professional:

- Develop as many contacts as you can. Add one new person each day, and you'll have met at least twenty new people per month.

- Tell people the one thing you feel you do best. Don't give them a rundown of all that you can do. It confuses, and even annoys, some people when the conversation seems one-sided; be concise about what you do so that the other person may reciprocate.

- Become a host/leader, not a wallflower. Show initiative; introduce yourself. Don't throw your business card at anybody until you've at least established a verbal connection.
- Cultivate your contacts. Don't try to use the situation to get immediate business; instead, ask to meet privately later on. Nobody likes to feel pressured in social situations.
- Extend your own expertise first whenever possible. Be available to those who call on you for help when they need it.
- Keep in touch. Mail or fax articles that might be of interest to your contacts—it shows you were listening when you met them, and, perhaps even more importantly, that you remembered what they said.

10 TIPS ON ATTRACTING INVESTORS

1. **Know what type of capital you can raise:** equity capital (from wealthy individuals or venture capital companies), or debt capital (borrowing against cash flow or your business assets).
2. **Know your investors' needs.** Remember that investors have needs, too, and be sure you approach the kind of people whose needs you can fulfill.
3. **Start with your own money,** from savings, a second mortgage, etc. This demonstrates your commitment to the business. Spend it on preparing a business plan, building a prototype, executing a market study. Then show these to potential investors.
4. **Know what you need.** Plan to grow your business in stages, know how much you need for each stage, and seek only that amount.
5. **Minimize the risk to your investors,** by minimizing your irreversible capital expenditures. For instance, buy off-the-shelf equipment that could, if necessary, be put to alternate uses.
6. **Find a big name investor,** someone with name recognition in your field, who will indicate to other prospects that you show promise. Just imagine if Bill Gates were to invest in your computer business, how many other investors would follow.
7. **Sell yourself as well as your business.** Show that you are reliable, have honored former commitments, and have not abandoned ventures in midstream.
8. **Anticipate objections.** Real or imagined, objections to your proposals must be acknowledged, and you must explain your contingency plans.
9. **Manage the process.** Set a schedule; coordinate finding customers with finding investors; form a team with your lawyers, accountants, etc.; follow up on every approach and every agreement.
10. **Follow through.** Once you have the money, don't wait to get the business off the ground. This is no longer a hobby, and investors are looking for results, now.

KEYS TO BUILDING A PROFITABLE CONSULTING BUSINESS

Experts agree that, regardless of the specialty, there are a few common steps to building a successful consulting business. Of course, before you can embark on your own journey to consulting success, you must first determine your field of expertise.

Once you've identified your niche market, you can focus your energy on the following areas:

- Relationship-building. It's the mantra of the twenty-first-century business professional: build relationships that last beyond the initial sale. Don't expend a lot of energy if it looks like you'll make only one sale; spending too much time on a one-shot deal can blow a whole year's worth of sales with another potential client.
- Clearly stating your objectives and strategies. As a consultant, you'll be expected to solve some problems of a fairly large nature. You need to be as clear as possible in your proposal with regard to what you'll be providing for the price you're asking. How else can a company determine if you're worth it? (P.S. Always remind the client in your proposal of why they called on you in the first place.)
- Present a polished, professional image. Like it or not, you are in the image business; your clients' perceptions of you are what will ultimately make or break the sale. Potential clients need to see you as successful, in demand, and of the highest quality there is—so make sure all of your materials, from business cards to sample videos, reflect the image you want to convey.
- Don't be afraid to offer free, introductory sessions when you need to. Consultants often make the mistake of thinking that every hour should be a billable one. Keep in mind that you need to build awareness of your business before you can sell folks on your services (particularly if you are just starting out); the best way to attract the interest of potential clients is to hold a free informational seminar once every quarter or so.
- Charge by the hour, not by the job. Too many consultants make the mistake of underestimating the number of hours a job will take, and lose a great deal of money charging on a per-project basis rather than by the hour. Make sure that even if you have an hourly rate as high as $100, your estimate reflects every penny of the time you expect the project to take. It's perfectly acceptable to offer a 10 percent discount for timely payment—but never discount the value of your own time.
- Update your client list regularly. At least once per year, weed out those folks who only generate a tiny portion of your annual income. To be profitable, you need to focus on the bigger accounts—and constantly fill your time with more of them.
- Remember to follow up with every client. As a consultant your job is never ending; once you sign on as an expert, you remain one for life (or until you make a mistake). Instead of concentrating solely on news business development, look to your past and present clients for additional work.

KNOWING WHEN TO MOVE

Your files are constantly ending up on the kitchen table . . . and the work seems to follow you into your bedroom. Is it time to move to an office outside of your home?

If you're carrying your work all over the house with you, it probably wouldn't hurt to make a clean break. A new office, outside of your home, could do wonders in helping you achieve a better balance between work and personal life (which we're sure your family will greatly appreciate). Too many entrepreneurs get caught up in their businesses to the extent that the work piles up and creeps into the living room and other places in the home—even though there is a designated office space in the basement or studio.

Are you one of those types who can't stop working, even past 10 o'clock at night? Are you often at the center of family arguments about when to work and when not to? Or, are you overwhelmed by customers constantly invading your living space with their demands and needs?

If you answered yes to any of these questions, it would probably be a good idea to start looking for an office space, preferably close to your house but definitely outside of it.

If your business thrives on a homey atmosphere, there are plenty of homelike spaces available. You may be able to rent space in one of the many older homes now being converted into office campuses for much less than the $5 per square foot that many corporate-looking spaces charge.

The type of space you choose really depends on your business and the image you wish to convey; for many, there is nothing like the sound of a professional, high-profile business address (like 1 Corporate Center, or the Landing at Prospect Place). You would do well to look into the possibility of renting space from a business incubator-type office complex, where you pay a flat monthly rent and share secretarial, copy center, and other services with fellow budding entrepreneurs.

Ultimately, the need to move is determined by two primary factors: 1) Have you outgrown your current space?, and 2) Can this growth support a regular rent payment? If you can substantiate the reason for moving, and can find a suitable space that allows for even more growth at an affordable price, you can continue building your empire in a classy space that could make you more productive—and consequently more profitable—than your cushy little space at home.

Sure, it's convenient to have a home office, but the price you pay in productivity may not be worth it in the long haul after all.

TAKING YOUR COMPANY PUBLIC

When your small business becomes successful and is experiencing rapid growth, you might want to look into offering the general public shares of your business in exchange for more working capital.

Going public essentially means finding new owners who will participate with you in the ups and downs of your business. They will add their dollars to yours in order to permit the new, larger enterprise to expand.

You could sell shares in the company yourself and pocket the profits, but that may not be wise. Taking a company public is a serious and complicated business and you should find an attorney experienced in the process to work with you. Even if it costs you a fair amount in legal fees, you'll be money ahead if you do.

As a public company, you will need to be open and forthcoming with regard to your financial statements, but in exchange, you get the opportunity to become wealthier—particularly as your stock prices rise.

Should I Go Public?

That's a tough question to answer, and, before you do, you should have the advice of lawyers, accountants, and other business professionals. Some factors you'll need to consider are:

Advantages
- Access to a large amount of capital for the future. Keep in mind that even if you go public, you may still be able to raise capital through private debt or equity.
- Greatly increased liquidity for your firm's securities.
- Wealth creation: Taking your company public will establish its value, and, through a secondary offering of stocks, allow your founders and backers to sell some of their interests in the firm.
- Prestige: Enhanced image with your customers, suppliers, and employees, as well as a boost to your own sense of personal achievement.

Disadvantages
- Cost: Going public is expensive both at the outset and in ongoing costs. An attorney familiar with the process will be able to make you aware of cost-saving procedures available from the SEC, such as Form SB-2.
- Public scrutiny: A public company must make financial and other information public, even when you as owner would prefer not to.
- Change of focus: Top management at a public company has to concern itself with pleasing Wall Street; a private firm does not.
- Loss of autonomy: In a public company, the owners and managers are not the same people and they may have differing priorities. Then too there is always the possibility of a hostile takeover.

Choosing an Underwriter

Underwriters (investment bankers) are required to guide you through the process of making a public offering, and to sell your securities in exchange for some portion of the proceeds. Talk to several underwriters, and take these factors into account in your final selection:

- Reputation: The underwriter's reputation will affect its ability to sell your stock.
- Distribution: Be sure that your underwriter can get you the right mix of institutional and individual investors.
- Ongoing support: Look for an underwriter who can give you continuing support and advice after the initial public offering.

Deciding Your Stock Price

Negotiation on stock price may take considerable time, from your opening discussions with your underwriter continuing, perhaps, right up to the night before the offering. **Be aware of how your underwriter's interests differ from yours.** You want the best price you can get; the underwriter needs to be able to sell those shares, and offer its customers a good price. You will incur many expenses during the course of registration; at some point, your underwriter may try to bring down your stock price by threatening to back out of the deal, thus leaving you holding the proverbial bag in terms of all the expenses. Try to have the underwriter bear some of its own expenses (such as legal fees). An underwriter that has something to lose, too, may be less likely to back out of a deal.

Other Decisions

- Where to list: Before choosing an exchange, make sure you know what its requirements are
- Amount of primary offering: Know how much your firm wants to raise.
- Amount of secondary offering: Decide how much of their stake, if anything, your founders and backers are to sell. Remember, this will be their money, not your company's.

10 WAYS TO EXPAND YOUR BUSINESS FOR LITTLE CASH

1. **Get on the Internet.** Once your Web site is up and running, for a minimal investment per month, you can market your services worldwide. It's tough to beat that with any other advertising medium.
2. **Trade services with a franchisee prospect.** You could work a deal whereby a potential franchisee's buy-in fee would be cut if he or she helps produce the operations manual; this way, you use one franchisee to get more franchisees. The payoff comes later.
3. **Hire commission-only sales reps.** You pay them only what they actually earn.
4. **Hire interns from colleges and universities.** They generally work for free, or next-to-nothing, in exchange for college credits and valuable firsthand experience.
5. **Participate in business organizations** where you can network for free.
6. **Find inexpensive ways to advertise your company** on a regular basis (such as asking all family members with a car to sport your company logo).

7. **Join forces with a compatible business.** For instance, if you own a resume service, you could easily merge with a word-processing or secretarial service.
8. **Put on seminars,** charging a fee for teaching others your own skills.
9. **Sponsor trade shows** or other events.
10. **Develop a program** or system for your business that can be marketed and sold to others. You could write a book or develop a CD-ROM program for mass production.

MORE NETWORKING TIPS

- The best time to make new contacts is when you don't need them. It's best to call on others in happy times so that your business image is positive, and new contacts will come to respect you before you need help.
- Don't forget to follow up. Most of all, never forget to say "thank you."
- Set up a good filing or business card management system. Choose one that will actually work for you, not one that merely sounds good.
- Weed out nonproductive relationships every six months. But don't throw away every card! You never know when you might need that person in the future.
- MOST IMPORTANT, ALWAYS BE YOURSELF. We all have different styles of networking, and there are no real hard-and-fast rules when it comes to the joy of meeting new people—and making new friends.

MANAGEMENT:
LEADING YOUR EMPLOYEES
TO GREATER PRODUCTIVITY

FIVE STEPS TO BETTER TIME MANAGEMENT

1. **Know your company's goals** and set your own priorities accordingly. Give your tasks priority according to what must be done today, and what can be done tomorrow, next week, or even next month.
2. **Delegate wherever possible.** Invest adequate time at the outset to explain the task, the result you expect, and the deadline. You'll begin noticing the benefits of effective delegation in no time.
3. **Clear your desk each day,** at a time when you can prevent interruptions, or, better yet, before they begin. You can manage interruptions by using voice mail to screen calls and by focusing on completing tasks by the end of each day.
4. **Make "wasted" time productive.** This may call for investment in a cell phone or a laptop, but, with these tools and a little preparation, much of the time you spend waiting for planes or sitting in lobbies can become productive.
5. **Give yourself creative time.** Spend it alone with your ideas, or over coffee with an employee, but be sure to log some brainstorming time into your schedule.

HIRING SMART

Even though there are, generally speaking, more workers available than ever before, you need to be choosy when sifting through the resumes of potential employees. Here are five things you should look for in an outstanding candidate.

- A willingness to learn new things. So often, as you embark on your entre-preneurial venture, you'll develop job descriptions that are subject to change. Hiring someone who is flexible and willing to try a new assignment could be the smartest move you make.

- Experience in the area you need to cover most. If you're looking for an accounting or bookkeeping professional, you'll need to be certain that the candidate's primary area of expertise is in those fields. Even though you may be looking for flexibility, you need to be sure you can adequately cover your areas of primary need first and foremost.
- Demonstrated results. It's one thing for a candidate to say that his or her responsibilities included X, Y, and Z; it's quite another to see what kind of impact that employee had on the rest of the organization. Look for key phrases that document some kind of end result, such as "increased profit share by 110 percent" or "boosted credibility and public awareness of product."
- Creativity. In a fledgling business, you need to surround yourself with staffers who understand your business and are constantly on the lookout for improvements. These are the people who know that your success will have an impact on their success, and vice versa. You'll appreciate creative solutions to problems because they will likely save your company money and increase productivity at the same time.
- Self-direction. Let's face it, you're totally consumed by your business; in fact, that's probably why you need help in the first place. Recognize that for everything to work smoothly, you need to give up a piece of your business to someone else who is more focused on that particular area. You'll need to trust that person to take control so that you are freed up to concentrate on growing the business. So make sure new hires can work independently, yet are not afraid to ask questions.

Finally, be sure to check with federal, state, and municipal employment bureaus to make certain you're in compliance with all regulations. There's more involved in hiring than you might at first imagine; in today's litigious society, it pays for you to familiarize yourself with all components of employment law.

10 STEPS TO MANAGING AND MOTIVATING YOUR EMPLOYEES WITHOUT EXTRA CASH

1. **Be approachable:** Use employees' names; say "Hi! How are you?"; shake hands and smile.
2. **Know your employees:** Ask some of them to join you for coffee; inquire about your workers' families; recognize important events in your employees' lives.
3. **Be an active listener:** Make a note of others' ideas, and take those ideas seriously; accept differences of opinion, and say when you agree; express your feelings and recognize the feelings of others.
4. **Ask for help:** Seek out problem-solving ideas.

5. **Create an affirming environment:** Workers who are treated as though they are competent are more likely to act competently.

6. **Set helpful goals:** See that your goals are quantifiable, realistic, and easily understood; have the worker help set them.

7. **Give goals meaning:** Show employees where they fit into the broader company objectives.

8. **Evaluate:** Measure employee productivity constantly.

9. **Reinforce productive behaviors:** Even expected performance must be positively reinforced.

10. **Inform:** Let your employees know how your company is doing.

TWO SIDES TO SUCCESSFUL LEADERSHIP

Communicate:

- Your company's vision. Create a mission statement. Show how your employees are contributing to the vision, and how that influences your decisions.
- By example. Remember, you set the standard in integrity, dependability, and commitment.
- Your expectation of success, at every level of your business. Be ready to redefine success as your goals change.
- Where the company is. Be prepared to share with your employees information about what goals have been met, what problems have arisen, and what opportunities exist.

Listen:

- In a way that establishes trust. Let your employees speak to you openly, without fear of retribution. Encourage informal conversations and casual e-mail messages.
- Before you make any decision. The decision will remain yours, but you will make it more constructively by listening to employees, customers, vendors, etc.
- To diverse ideas. Acknowledge when you use an employee's idea, even if not in the form in which it was given to you.
- As you prepare for the future. All the information you can gather from your market, your vendors, your employees, and your business network will help you to be ready for tomorrow's challenges.

PERSONAL CONCERNS:
STRIKING THE RIGHT BALANCE
BETWEEN BUSINESS AND HOME

JUGGLING FAMILY AND WORK

Raising a family and growing a business are both full-time jobs. So, how can you give 100 percent to each and still maintain your sanity?

Start by setting aside a special time each day or week that is designated "family time." During this period, you will accept no phone calls, set no appointments, and not even think about your business. You probably won't even want to stay near your office. Here's a suggestion: Take your family out to dinner once a week and have each one, you included, share the three best things that happened during the past seven days.

Or, if you feel it's appropriate, incorporate your family into some aspect of your business. It might help them better understand your needs and constraints. It's one thing for your spouse or children to see you arrive home exhausted and stressed out; it's quite another for them to be in your office when that high-volume order comes in on short notice and you kick into high gear. Demonstrating your strong work ethic is a great idea, especially for children.

All children, girls and boys alike, need positive workplace role models—and who better to provide them than Mom or Dad? History shows that children who are raised by entrepreneurs tend to become entrepreneurs themselves.

What should you do in the event that a client or customer wants to meet during one of your special family times? You can handle it in one of two ways. You could rearrange your family time to accommodate your client, but the better solution might be to simply say, "I have a meeting scheduled at that time ... is there another time that works for you?" Others will respect your attention to commitments, and you never have to offer an explanation for whom you're meeting with, or why.

However you decide to work your children into your business, or your business into your family life, one thing is for sure: There will never be a time without challenges and disruptions.

As an entrepreneur, you will need to develop the skill to work around any obstacle or challenge; following an effective time-management program can help you strike the right balance between work and home life. Scheduling time for all aspects of your life is one way to make sure that everything gets done. The other is to recognize that it is possible to have two loves: your business and your family.

HOW TO STAY POSITIVE

What's the best thing about owning your own business? It's your own business. And the worst thing? It is your own business. When things are going great, it's easy to be positive, but how can you stay on top of the world and your game when the slow times come, as they inevitably will? Here are a few ideas:

- Take inventory of all the good things that have happened to you in the last month. Write them down, and take some time to really appreciate them.
- Put a "plus" sign over your desk, at eye level, so you remember to try and remain positive at all times (especially when you're on the phone with customers).
- Concentrate on the opportunities you still have. So often, we expend all of our energy on negative thinking. Focusing on the future will keep you from ignoring potentially great opportunities that you might have missed while wallowing in your sorrow and self-pity.
- Surround yourself with positive people. If you've got friends in business, try to support one another in times of despair. Offer positive advice and encouragement—but, most of all, learn to accept the same when it's given to you.
- See, then be. Picture yourself succeeding again, and your chances of success will nearly double. Never underestimate the power of creative visualization.
- Don't give up. Even the most successful entrepreneurs have experienced setbacks, so you're not the only one. Have the courage to go on.

CHECKLIST FOR SUCCESS: CAN YOU BE A SUCCESSFUL ENTREPRENEUR?

Here are some questions you might ask yourself before embarking on a new business:

- Are you unhappy with your current situation—and ready for a change?
- Are you completely self-directed; that is, able to come up with and complete your own job requirements?
- Are you able to meet with and sell to many different types of people?

- Are you an expert planner—someone who can see not only the big picture, but every tiny line that created it?
- Can you set and keep deadlines?
- Are you a clock-watcher, or someone who quickly loses track of time?
- Can you commit to projects and follow them through to completion every time?
- Are you adaptable and open to learning new ways of doing things?
- Do you have the mental and physical stamina you need to run your business?
- Are you afraid of risk?
- Do you have adequate savings to cover your first year's salary?
- Are you a positive person?

HOME ALONE: HOW TO FEEL "CONNECTED" WHEN YOU'RE HOME-BASED

You work anywhere from thirty to sixty hours per week in your cozy little home office, where you curl up with a cup of coffee every morning and enjoy the solitude of working alone. No office politics, no petty disagreements, no feeling of corporate pressure.

But too much solitude can be a bad thing. When the sound of silence gets to you, where can you go for some human interaction? Here are a few places you can start:

- Check out a home-based business forum or chat room available through an Internet Service Provider such as America Online, Earthlink, or Yahoo!
- Find a professional organization made up of business professionals like yourself (check with your chamber of commerce for listings of such groups).
- Toastmasters International—this organization offers you the chance to improve your speaking/presentation skills as well as meet with several others in your community (and from all walks of life).
- Volunteer at your local hospital, community organization, or even professional associations.
- Work one day per week at your local library.
- Take yourself out for a latte or lunch; you can bring along an assignment and make it a "working break."
- Spend at least one half-day per week networking at a function or event.
- Form a "business buddy" system with another home-based worker, sharing trials and tribulations.
- Form a success team with a dozen or so other home-based business professionals, then meet once a week to discuss your business problems and offer solutions to one another.
- Stop feeling alone—there are literally thousands of self-employed, home-based workers in the United States today.

PART FOUR

APPENDICES

LISTING OF BUSINESSES BY CATEGORY

AGRICULTURAL SERVICES

Aerial Applicator
Agricultural Marketing
Farmer of Fruits or Vegetables
Farmsitting

Feed Consultant/Broker
Herb/Flowers Farming
Irrigation Services
Winery

ARTS AND CRAFTS

Airbrush Artist
Art Gallery
Art/Photo Representative
Art Restoration Services
Arts Festival Promoter
Boudoir Photography
Calligrapher
Candlemaker
Caning Specialist
Cartoonist
Collectibles/Memorabilia
Creative Arts Day Camp
Custom Carpentry/Furniture Maker
Custom Embroidery

Custom Sewing/Alterations
Doll Repair Service
Floral Shop
Gift Basket Business
Ice Sculpting
Jewelry Designer
Knitting/Crocheting Lessons
Patient Gift Packager
Personalized Children's Books
Rubber Stamp Business
Scrapbooker
Silk Flower Arranger
Stenciling

AUTOMOTIVE

Auto Maintenance
Automobile Window Stickers
Automotive Loan Broker
Automotive Marketing and Training Services
Automotive Parts Rebuilder
Automotive Testing Equipment
Auto Paint Touchup Professional

Auto Swap Meet Promotion
Car Wash
Mobile Automotive Detailing
Mobile Car Inspection/Repair
Motor Vehicle Transportation
Short-Term Auto Rental Service
Used Car Leasing

BUILDING AND MANUFACTURING

Assembly Work
Construction Management Services
Construction Services
Consulting Engineer
Demolition/Wrecking Contractor
Factory Site Location Consultant
Liquidator

Machinery Rebuilding/Repair
Manufacturer of Licensed Products
Manufacturer/Retail Item
Manufacturer's Representative
Medical Products Manufacturer
Used Industrial Equipment Sales

BUSINESS SERVICES

Abstracting Service
Art Broker/Corporate Art Consultant
Association Management Services
Audio Recording for Trade Shows and Seminars
Barter Systems
Business Broker
Business Consulting
Business Form Sales and Service
Business Plan Writer/Packager
Buyer's Information Service
Color Consultant
Consumer Researcher
Coupon Distributor
Cost Reduction Consultant
Direct Marketing/Sales
Efficiency Expert
Errand/Messenger Service
Franchisee
Franchise Idea Center

Greeting Card Sender
Home-Based Business Consultant
Importing/Exporting
Incentive Programs/Promotional Material
Incorporation Service for Businesses
Information Consultant
International Business Consultant
Invention Consultant/Broker
Inventory Control
Liquidator
Management Consultant
Manufacturer of Self-Adhesive Printed Labels
Map Publisher/Distributor
Marketing Consultant
Market Mapping Service
Meeting Planner
Middleman
Mobile Notary Public

Mobile Paper-Shredding Service
Multilevel Marketing
New Product Researcher
Office Equipment Leasing
Online Internet Researcher
Packaging Consultant
Payroll Administrative Services
Personnel Safety Consultant
Product Developer
Secretarial and Office Support Services
Shipping/Customs Consultant
Sign Painting
Small Business Consultant
Specialty Paper Producer/Distributor

Security Systems Consultant
Security Systems Design/Installation
Stenography Service
Telemarketing Service
Time-Management Specialist
Trademark Agent
Translation Services
Trucking Broker
Uniform Service
Virtual Assistant
Word-Processing Service
Workers' Compensation
   Consultant
X-Ray Inspection Service

CHILDREN

Child Care Referral Service
Child Development Center
Child ID Products
Children's Party Planner
Creative Arts Day Camp
Day Care Service (Children)
Diaper Service

Indoor Playspace
Magician
Nanny Service
Parenting Specialist
Personalized Children's Books
Storyteller

COMMUNICATION

Advertising Agency
Advertising Sales Representative
Audiobook Producer/Distributor
Bookbinder
Book Indexer
Book Packager
Broadcast Sales/Advertising Broker
Classified Advertising Newspaper
Clipping Service
Commercial Photographer
Desktop Publisher
Desktop Video
E-Zine Publisher
Fiber Optic Transmission Systems
Freelance Illustrator/Artist
Freelance TV Producer

Freelance Writer/Editor
Graphic Designer
Handbill Distribution
In-Home Mail Service
Instant Signs
Mailing List Service
Message Retrieval Service
   (Answering Service)
Messenger Service
Multimedia Service
Newsletter Publisher
Newspaper Delivery Service
Newspaper Features Syndicate
900-Number Service
Photocopying Service
Printing Broker

COMMUNICATION *continued*

Public Relations
Public Speaking Consultant
Satellite Equipment/Systems (Wholesale)
Seminar (Speakers) Service
Speechwriter
Stock Photo Service
Technical Writer (Documentation and Onscreen Text)

Telecommunications Consultant
Translation Services
Video/DVD Transfer Service
Video-on-Demand
Video Production Company
Videotext Service

COMPUTERS

Computer-Aided Design (CAD) Service
Computer Composer
Computer Consultant
Computerized Special Effects Designer
Computer Repair and Maintenance
Computer Software Sales
Computer Trainer
Database Consultant
Data Retrieval Service
Digital Imaging Service

Online Auction Sales
Online Internet Researcher
Online Job Search
Software Conversion Service
Software Development/CD-ROM Packaging
Software Engineer/Computer Programmer
Systems Integrator
Technical Writer (Documentation and Onscreen Text)
Webmaster
Web Site Designer

EDUCATION

College Application Consultant
College Internship Placement
Educational Product Development
Homeschooling Consultant

Private Tutor
Standardized Test Preparatory Services

EMPLOYMENT SERVICES

Career Counselor
Corporate Trainer
Disability Consultant
Drug Testing Service

Economic Development Consultant
Employee Benefits Consultant
Employee Harmony Consultant
Employee Leasing

Executive Recruiter
Human Resources Services
Interim Executive
Interviewer
Labor Relations Consultant
Motivational Speaker
Networking Services
Online Job Search

Outplacement Services
Relocation Consultant
Resume Service
Sales Trainer
Secretarial and Office-Support Services
Temporary Employment Agency
Workers' Compensation Consultant

ENTERTAINMENT/ARTS

Acoustical Services
Arcade/Party Rentals
Arts Festival Promoter
Band Manager
Bridal Show Promotions
Calendar Service
Casting Director
Comedy Writer
Commercial Actor
Concert Promoter
Costume Design and Construction
Dance Instructor
Entertainment Directory Publisher
Fan Club Management
Home Entertainment System
    Installation and Service

Literary Agent
Magician
Mobile Disc Jockey Service
Motion Picture Research Consultant
Movie Site Scout
Murder Mystery Producer
Musical Instrument Leasing
Novelty Messenger Service
Pinball/Electronic Game Arcade
Portrait Artist/Photographer
Recording Studio Rental
Storyteller
Talent Agency
Television Program Distributor
Theatrical Lighting Service
Ticket Broker

ENVIRONMENT AND LANDSCAPING

Aerial Applicator
Earthquake Products/Services
Environmental Consultant/Contractor
Fish Restocking
Flowerscaping
Gardening Consultant
Geologic Drilling Service
Graffiti Removal
Ground Water Assessment
Herb/Flowers Farming
Hurricane Products/Services
Invisible Fencing Sales/Installation
Irrigation Services

Landscape Designer
Lawn Care Service
Leak-Detection Service
Noise Control Consultant
Oil and Gas Field Services
Pest Control Service
Recycling
Snow Plow Service
Traffic Control Consultant
Tree Service
Water Pump Repair Service
Water Quality Analysis

FINANCIAL SERVICES

Accountant
Auditing Specialist
Bookkeeping Service
Collection Agency
Commodities Broker
Corporate Insurance Broker
Credit Consultant
Financial Aid Consultant
Financial Planner

Insurance Agent
Investment Club Organizer
Money Broker
Mortgage Loan Broker
Profit Sharing Plan Consultant
Retirement Planner
Tax Preparation Service
Venture Capitalist

FOOD AND BEVERAGE

Banquet Facility
Bartending Services
Beer Brewery
Cake Decorator
Caterer
Coffee Bar/Tea Salon
Commercial Fisherman
Cooking Class Instructor
Food Delivery Service
Food Manufacturing Consultant

Herbal Products Distributor
Personal Chef
Personal Menu Service
Restaurant
Restaurant Equipment and Supplies
Retail Bakery/Specialty Desserts
Specialty Food Production
Taste Tester for Food Companies
Winery

HEALTH AND WELLNESS

Ambulatory Services
Biofeedback Therapist
Childbirth Instructor
Counselor/Psychologist
Day Spa
Doula/Midwife
Feng Shui Consultant
First Aid/CPR Instructor
Fitness Rental Equipment
Health Club
Health/Fitness Centers for
    Corporations
Health Insurance Consultant
Home Health Care Service
Lactation Consultant
Medical Billing Service
Medical Claims Assistance Professional

Medical Coding
Medical Practice Management Consul-
    tant
Medical Products Manufacturer
Medical Transcriptionist
Nutrition Consultant
Occupational Health Care Services
Personal Instructor/Fitness Trainer
Personal Weight Loss Management
    Consultant
Pharmaceutical Returns Consulting
Reflexologist
Respiratory Equipment Repair
Stress Management Counselor
Weight Loss Center
Wellness Instructor
Wilderness-Based Therapeutic Programs

HOME IMPROVEMENT AND DÉCOR

Carpet Installation
Carpet/Upholstery Cleaning
Chimney Sweep
Construction Services
Damage Restoration Service
Decks/Outdoor Furniture
Electrical Contractor/Electrician
Exterior (House) Painting
Fabric Wallcoverings
Feng Shui Consultant
Framing Service
Furniture Refinisher
Handyman Network
Hardwood Floor Refinisher
Hauling Service

Home Inspector
Interior Designer
Invisible Fencing Sales/Installation
Mini-Blind Cleaning Service
Pest Control Service
Pool Maintenance
Power Wash Service
Restoration Services
Upholsterer
Vacuum Cleaner Repair
Voice-Activated Home Automation
Wallpapering/Interior Painting
Window Treatment Specialist
Window Washing Service

MISCELLANEOUS

Archaeological Services
Bounty Hunter
Coin-Operated Laundry
Color Separation and Film
    Assembly Services
Funeral Home

Graphologist
Key Control Systems Manufacturer/ Distributor
Mailbox Rental Service
Reunion Organizer

PERSONAL SERVICES

Blade-Sharpening Service
Custom Sewing/Alterations
Dating Service
Dry Cleaning Service
Etiquette Advisor
Facialist
Firewood Service
Genealogical Service (Family History
    Writer)
Home Entertainment System Installation
    and Service
Housesitter/Caretaker
Identity Theft Recovery Specialist
Image Consultant

Jewelry/Clock/Watch Repair
Laundry/Ironing Service
Lock Box Service
Locksmith
Maid Service
Makeup Artist
Manicurist/Pedicurist
Massage Therapist
Mobile Hair Salon
Mobile Notary Public
Modeling School/Agency
Monogramming Service
Mover
Packing/Unpacking Service

PERSONAL SERVICES *continued*

Party Planner
Personal Chef
Personal Coach
Personal Instructor/Fitness Trainer
Personality Analysis/Testing Service
Personal Menu Service
Personal Shopper
Personal Weight Loss Management
   Consultant
Plant Maintenance Service

Professional Organizer
Referral Service
Reminder Service
Roommate Referral Service
Storage Service
Tanning Salon
Television Repair
Trophy/Engraving Service
Wedding Planner
Welcoming Service

PETS AND ANIMALS

Animal Broker/Dealer
Aquarium Maintenance and Setup
Dog Trainer
Horse/Cargo Trailer Service
Horse Trainer
Invisible Fencing Sales/Installation

Pet Breeder
Pet Grooming/Care
Petsitter
Pet Taxi Service
Taxidermist

PUBLIC SERVICE/LEGAL

Accident Reconstruction Service
Adoption Search Service
Arbitration Service
Expert Witness
Forensic Consultant
Fundraiser
Government Contract Consulting
Grants/Proposal Writer
Lawyer
Legal Cost Control/Litigation
   Management Services

Licensing Agent
Lobbyist
Mediator
Paralegal
Political Campaign Management
Political Marketing Consultant
Pollster
Private Detective/Intelligence
   Specialist
Professional Rescue and Recovery
   Diver

REAL ESTATE

Apartment Preparation Service
Architect
Boardinghouse Operator
Building Maintenance Service
City Planner
Draftsman/Blueprinting Service
Home Inspector

Prefab Home Sales/Construction
Property Management Service
Real Estate Agent/Home Researcher
Real Estate Appraiser
Real Estate Investor
Residence for the Elderly
Surveyor

RECREATION AND SPORTS

Athletic Recruiter/Scout
Bicycle Rental
Boat Maintenance/Cleaning Service
Boat Operation Instructor
Bungee Jumping Instructor
Canoe Livery
Hot Air Balloon Rides
Indoor Playspace
Miniature Golf Course

Outdoor Adventures
Recreation Activities Consultant
Recreational Coupon Distributor
Sports Equipment Sales/Service
Underwater Adventures/SCUBA Instruction
Used Boat Sales
Wilderness-Based Therapeutic
   Programs

SENIOR SERVICES

Day Care Service (Elder Adults)
Gerontology Consultant
Home Health Care Service

Residence for the Elderly
Retirement Planner

TRANSPORTATION

Air Charter Service
Boat Maintenance/Cleaning Service
Boat Operation Instructor
Boat Tours
Canoe Livery
Mobile Book/Magazine Distributor
Motor Vehicle Transportation
Pilot/Flying Lessons
Segway Rentals

Shipping/Freight Forwarding Service
Short-Term Auto Rental Service
Taxi Service
Tow Boat Operator
Transportation Provider
   (Limousine/Van)
Trucking Broker
Used Boat Sales
Used Car Leasing

TRAVEL AND HOSPITALITY

Bed & Breakfast
Boat Tours
Hospitality Service
Sightseeing Excursions

Travel Agent
Travel Consultant
Vacation Rentals Broker

WHOLESALE/RETAIL SALES

Antiques Dealer
Auctioneer
Bridal Show Promotions
Catalog Retailer
Designer/Retail Items
Distributor
Flea Market Organizer
Floral Shop
Garage Sale Coordinator
Importing/Exporting
Mall Promotion
Manufacturer of Licensed Products
Manufacturer/Retail Item
Manufacturer's Representative

Merchandise Demonstrator
Middleman
Mystery Shopper
Online Auction Sales
Rare Book Dealer/Search Service
Rental Business
Repair Shop
Resale/Consignment Shop
Retailer
Sales of Novelty and Promotional
    Products
Textile Broker
Vending Machine Owner
Wholesaler

Alphabetical Index